HOMOSEXUALITY & CIVILIZATION

HOMOSEXUALITY
&
CIVILIZATION

Louis Crompton

THE BELKNAP PRESS OF HARVARD UNIVERSITY PRESS
CAMBRIDGE, MASSACHUSETTS, AND LONDON, ENGLAND

Printed in the United States of America

First Harvard University Press paperback edition, 2006

Library of Congress Cataloging-in-Publication Data

Crompton, Louis, 1925–
Homosexuality and civilization / Louis Crompton.
p. cm.
Includes bibliographical references and index.
ISBN-13: 978-0-674-01197-7 (cloth)
ISBN-10: 0-674-01197-X (cloth)
ISBN-13: 978-0-674-02233-1 (pbk.)
ISBN-10: 0-674-02233-5 (pbk.)
1. Homosexuality—History. 2. Gender identity—History.
3. Homophobia—History. I. Title.

HQ76.25.C76 2003
306.76′6′09—dc21 2003245327

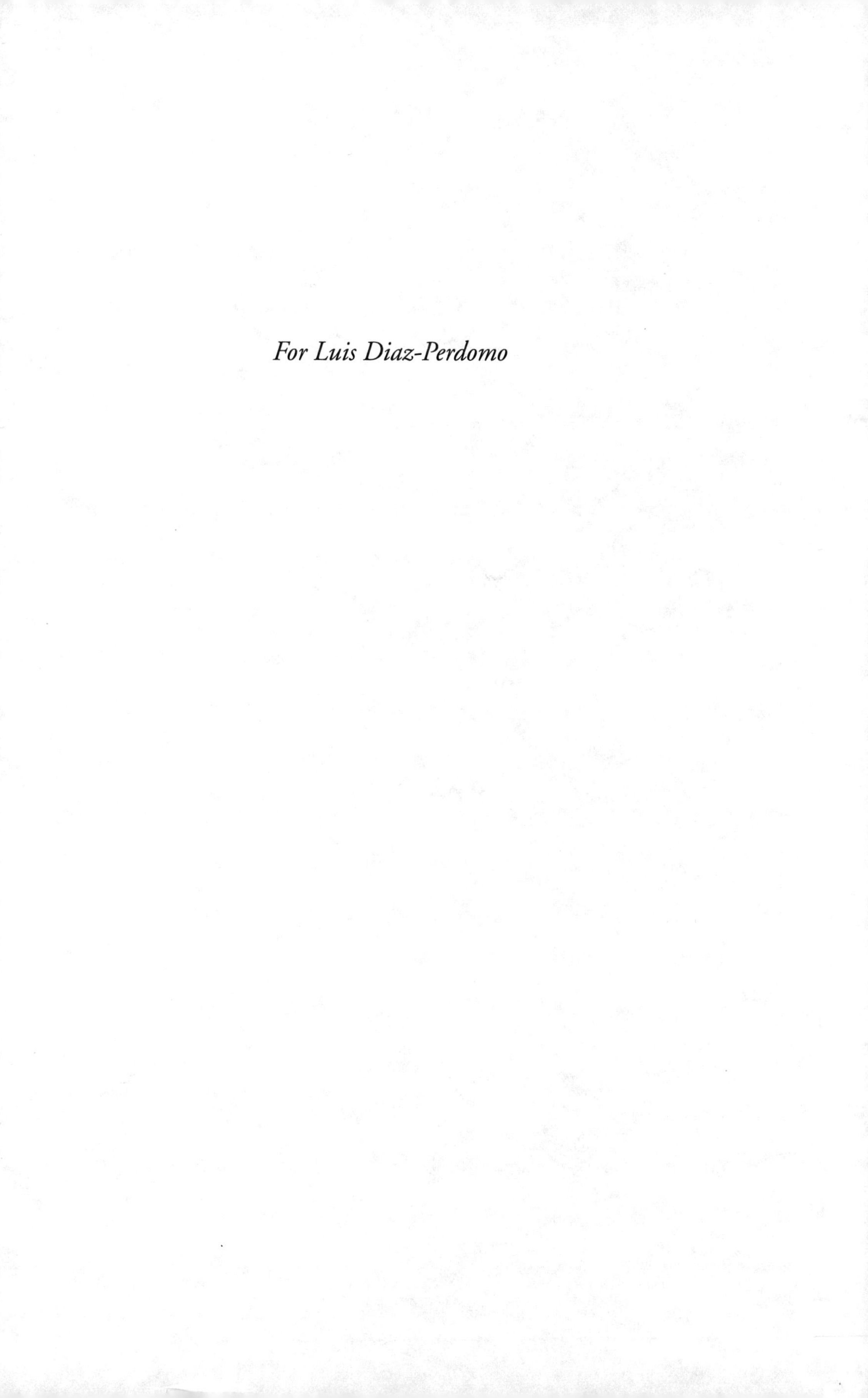

For Luis Diaz-Perdomo

Contents

PREFACE

1 · EARLY GREECE 776–480 BCE

2 · JUDEA 900 BCE–600 CE

3 · CLASSICAL GREECE 480–323 BCE

4 · ROME AND GREECE 323 BCE–138 CE

5 · CHRISTIANS AND PAGANS 1–565 CE

6 · DARKNESS DESCENDS 476–1049

7 · THE MEDIEVAL WORLD 1050–1321

8 • IMPERIAL CHINA 500 BCE–1849

9 • ITALY IN THE RENAISSANCE 1321–1609

10 • SPAIN AND THE INQUISITION 1497–1700

11 • FRANCE FROM CALVIN TO LOUIS XIV 1517–1715

12 · ENGLAND FROM THE REFORMATION TO WILLIAM III 1533–1702

13 · PRE-MEIJI JAPAN 800–1868

14 · PATTERNS OF PERSECUTION 1700–1730

15 · SAPPHIC LOVERS 1700–1793

16 · THE ENLIGHTENMENT 1730–1810

CONCLUSION 536

Preface

The idea for this book was spurred by the fate of a pioneering course on homosexuality I helped organize as long ago as 1970. The undertaking served as a reminder that homosexuality was indeed the *peccatum mutum*—the silent sin—for it prompted a legislator to draft a law banning such academic efforts. The legislative bill, which would have forbidden discussion of the subject at state institutions other than the state medical school, failed to pass, but the course was not repeated. Though it had focused on civil disabilities and then-popular psychiatric theories, the opposition it aroused convinced me that historical research was needed to understand the strength of the taboo homosexuality had inspired.

My original plan was to trace the religious beliefs that shaped European opinion in the Middle Ages and their punitive consequences. But first it seemed appropriate to begin with Greece and Rome, if only to demonstrate that such negative views were not the universal judgments of mankind. It came as a surprise to find how much literature on homosexuality had survived in the form of Greek poetry, biography, history, and philosophical debate. This plenitude made Kenneth Dover's ground-breaking study (1978), valuable though it was, seem narrow in its focus on archaic vases and such classical authors as Plato and Aristophanes. The material soon filled two chapters and spilled over into two more—on Rome and early Christianity—since Greek documents, far from being limited to the classical age, turned out to be abundant well into the Common Era.

Beert Verstraete's work on homosexuality and slavery in Rome provided a valuable clue to that culture, but John Boswell's reading of early Christian attitudes appeared open to question. Boswell's thesis, briefly stated, was that the Christian church did not develop markedly hostile views of same-sex relations until the twelfth century. But a candid examination of the evidence soon indicated that, from the very birth of Christianity, a hatred existed fully comparable to the hatred directed at pagans and Jews in the first millennium and at heretics, Jews, and witches in the first seven centuries of the second. Certainly, the resulting deaths were in this case fewer, but the rhetorical condemnations were violent in the extreme and chillingly insistent on the need for the death penalty. Boswell's book, with its impressive scholarship, did good service in legitimizing gay history, and his work with the Roman Catholic group Dignity was admirably courageous, but his relentless discounting of evidence that went counter to his thesis, though an intellectual tour de force, failed ultimately to convince.

David Greenberg's wide-ranging sociological analysis extends from archaic civilizations to the age of AIDS. But Greenberg, though not sharing Boswell's views on early Christianity, also chose not to deal with persecutions. The result has been a hiatus in the historical consciousness of our times. The modern world is aware of the wrongs committed in the name of Christianity by crusaders and inquisitors, of the horrific effects, in times past and present, of clerical anti-Semitism, and of the atrocities committed by Catholics and Protestants alike in the wars of religion. But campaigns against homosexuals, which, though sporadic, could also be ferocious, have received little notice. Invisibility and silence may have provided some protection, but inevitably they have left a void in the record. To take a modern example: the relegation of thousands of homosexuals to Nazi death camps went all but unpublicized in the English-speaking world until some thirty years after the fall of Hitler. Today, the Roman Catholic Church, to its credit, seeks "reconciliation" with groups who have in the past suffered under "those who have borne or bear the name of Christians" and has called upon historians to uncover the truth as a necessary first step.[1] This book attempts, among other things, to provide documentation of how religious organizations have, in the past, treated men and women accused of homosexual behavior.

In the Middle Ages fierce laws were passed, at clerical prompting, that led to the burning, beheading, drowning, hanging, and castration of male "sodomites" who, through the broadest possible interpretation of the Sodom story and other biblical texts, were blamed for such disasters as plagues, earthquakes, floods, famines, and even defeat in battle. Lesbian acts, too, were condemned, and women were executed. It is a relief to turn from these atrocities and the intense fear and hatred that bred them to the contemporaneous civilizations of China and Japan, which demonstrate that, beyond the domain of the three Abrahamic religions, same-sex relations could be recognized and on occasion honored in the post-classical world.

In Europe the unity of the Middle Ages gave way to the national variety of the Renaissance, but prejudice remained strong. In Catholic states, executions now reached their peak. In Italy, cities like Venice and Florence inaugurated "sodomy police" to hunt down victims; in Spain, the Inquisitions of Aragon, Catalonia, and Valencia energetically aided the civic authorities; and in France, men and women who did not enjoy aristocratic privileges were routinely burned or hanged. Nevertheless, despite its legal and ecclesiastical reign of terror, in this age we are able, for the first time since antiquity, to trace in some detail the intimate emotional life of individuals who loved their own sex—in Italy, of artists who left letters and notebooks or attracted biographers, and in France of prominent noblemen, clergy, and military leaders whose amours were described with scandalous relish in a plethora of diaries and memoirs. This new possibility of observing these relationships exists especially for reigning royalty, whose every word and act might be noted, and whose most personal correspondence might be preserved as state papers.

Some of these men and women—Leonardo, Michelangelo, Christopher Marlowe, Francis Bacon, Queen Christina, William III, Thomas Gray, Frederick the Great—were individuals whose achievements were remarkable by any standards. For others, such as Edward II and Henry III, their positions at the center of national affairs brought fates that were ultimately tragic. Some, like Louis XIII and Queen Anne, were mediocrities whom history would have ignored had they not worn crowns. But modern research now makes us able to understand in some detail the role homosexuality played in their varied destinies and, when they were rulers, in the politics of their reigns. At last we can move beyond silence and obfuscation.

Anyone who attempts to tell the story of homosexuality faces a frustrating reality, however. Apart from Sappho and some brief references in Lucian and Martial, lesbians hardly appear in the literature of the classical world. Though they become objects of theological opprobrium in the Middle Ages, only in the seventeenth century are full-length portraits possible, as in the case of Queen Christina, and not until the end of the eighteenth century do social groups come into view. Indeed, only in the last three decades have lesbians occupied the stage in numbers approximating those of their male counterparts. Though their relative invisibility before 1800 has relegated them to a minor space in this history, it seemed to me they should not be excluded, if only to show that they suffered the same religious abuse, harsh laws, and social ostracism as homosexual males.

The history of civilization reveals, above all, how differently homosexuality has been perceived and judged at different times in different cultures. In classical Greece male love carried associations very much at odds with those in republican Rome. Among the Greeks it was associated with courage in battle, philosophical mentorship, and the defense of democracy; among the Romans, with handsome slave boys and the disgraceful loss of manhood. In Arab Spain and medieval France perceptions diverged just as radically. In the former, love between men was a romantic possibility constrained by a strict religious code; in the latter, sodomy was a filthy and unmentionable vice punishable at the stake. In China, the "southern fashion" called to mind the loves of emperors, Fujian "marriages," and Mandarin scholars paired with opera stars; in Japan, *nanshoku* (male love) was associated with Buddhist saints, samurai warriors, and the kabuki theater. To the English in Tudor and early Stuart times, "devilish" sodomy was a Catholic sin unknown to Protestant lands. In eighteenth-century France it was *le beau vice, le vice ultramontain,* or *le vice philosophique,* that is, it was associated with the fashionable world, with Italy, and with Greek philosophers and modern skeptics. In the Netherlands, in the same age, it was a threat to national survival, to be extirpated by a national pogrom.

Yet behind these varied and conflicting views was a commonalty. Whatever the vocabulary, two elements are present—the sexual fact and the possibility of human love and devotion. For many centuries in Europe, homosexuality was conceived principally as certain sexual acts. This was because it was viewed theologically and in the light of the legal system this theology spawned—that is, as a sin and a capital crime. But we must not be complicit in this dehumanization. These "sodomites" were human beings with whom the modern gay man may claim brotherhood and the modern lesbian recognize as sisters. To divide history in two in 1869 at the moment when the word "homosexual" was coined is to deny this bond. To adopt Michel Foucault's view that the homosexual did not exist "as a person" until this time is to reject a rich and terrible past.

Nor does this theory of a "cognitive rupture" make sense historiographically. In the secular world of the late nineteenth century, theology gave way to psychiatry, the priest to the doctor. But flesh and blood homosexuals did not spring magically into being as at the wave of a wand; they were only perceived differently. Karl Heinrich Ulrichs, in a dozen books published between 1864 and 1879 under the title *Researches into the Mystery of the Love between Men,* developed the idea of sexual orientation not only through introspection and contact with others of his "kind" but also by drawing on his knowledge of the classical and post-classical past. Contemporaries like John Addington Symonds and Edward Carpenter had a similarly keen historical and cross-cultural awareness which we are challenged to reclaim.

But even the idea of a sexual identity is not uniquely modern. Aristophanes expressed it plainly enough in the *Symposium,* and the Romans used it, in a limited sense, in their concept of the *cinaedus* ("faggot"), who was certainly a distinct sort of person. In Plutarch's philosophical debate, half the speakers share an identity as lovers of youths and the other half as heterosexuals, though they lacked the term, and the same dichotomy appears in a brilliant dialogue from seventeenth-century Japan. Even in medieval times, when the view of same-sex relations as sins and crimes predominated, a French poet could make his heroine speak of "men of that sort" *(de ce métier),* that is, of a certain kind of individual.

Whether we may properly speak of homosexual subcultures before modern times has been another point of controversy. In England a subculture, much maligned, becomes visible and an object of attack at the start of the eighteenth century. Michael Rocke in his richly documented study of Renaissance Florence argues that the term is not generally applicable to that milieu. But Guido Ruggiero, writing of Venice during the same period, Rafael Carrasco, analyzing the social life of sodomites in early modern Valencia, and Luiz Mott, tracing the voluminous records of the Inquisition in Lisbon, all perceive bonds between men that seem to them to justify the label. Details in the *Compendium* of Don Pedro León, who recorded the experiences of sodomites condemned to death in Seville between 1578 and 1616, suggest the same interpretation.

In attempting to catch the distinctive tones of different times and cultures and avoid homogenization, I have tried to quote rather than to paraphrase texts and to keep as close as possible to the language of the historian, poet, biographer, or theologian cited. Since, however, the vast majority of quotations are translations from foreign languages, a certain amount of modernization has been necessary. Until we are all polyglots commanding the historical vocabularies of a dozen languages, this seems unavoidable.

Any work which aspires, however inadequately, to the mode of universal history must necessarily depend on the efforts of predecessors who have researched specialized subjects in various periods. While gratefully acknowledging these debts, I have tried, wherever feasible, to go back to primary sources, not just to give immediacy but also to reassess earlier interpretations. Many gaps in our knowledge remain. Some I have tried to fill with research of my own, an effort that inevitably made for slow progress. In a field of study still in its infancy, many current judgments will be open to revision. This is especially true in the case of non-Western cultures, as well as some Western fields, such as papal history and the literature of the Italian Renaissance.

On one issue, however, research now presents an inescapable conclusion—the dire consequences of officially sanctioned prejudice. To illuminate this record, I have added a Conclusion that summarizes acts of cruelty and oppression that the most powerful and pervasive civilization known to history has committed under the banner of morality and religion.

CHAPTER ONE

EARLY GREECE

776–480 BCE

• A Millennium of Greek Love •

In all history, no society has aroused the same enthusiasm as ancient Greece. This is a truism, yet the fact remains incontestable. Greek achievements in literature, art, and architecture set norms for the Western world for two thousand years. When we think, we still employ the intellectual categories its philosophers and scientists devised. By resisting Persian might, Greece made Europe possible. In politics, democracy was a Greek invention. Though women and slaves failed to share the benefits of freedom and equality, it was these ideals that ultimately called into question their own exclusions. Above all, the Greeks charm us by their sociability, their lively openness to ideas, and their liberality of spirit. Civilization, already millennia old in Egypt, Sumer, India, and China, took a vast leap forward under the stimulus of the Greek experiment.

Yet there was one aspect of Greek life that students of antiquity long chose to consign to the category of the "unmentionable." In E. M. Forster's novel *Maurice,* the Cambridge translation class is routinely cautioned, "Omit: a reference to the unspeakable vice of the Greeks."[1] The novel is set in 1910, but four decades later a scholar of repute could still remark, "This aspect of Greek morals is an extraordinary one, into which, for the sake of our equanimity, it is unprofitable to pry too closely."[2] And indeed, despite the importance of the subject, no book on Greek homosexuality was circulated openly in English until 1978. Christian Europe, from the fourth century onward, regarded same-sex relations as anathema, and its nations competed in devising punishments for "unnatural" crimes. Homosexuality became the *peccatum non nominandum inter Christianos,* "the sin not even to be mentioned among Christians." Such references as did appear were mainly confined to legal treatises, where penalties were spelled out, or to works of moral theology, where it was necessary for completeness' sake to list the worst human vices.

In Greek history and literature, on the other hand, the abundance of accounts of homosexual love overwhelms the investigator. Homer's intentions in the *Iliad* (c. 800 BCE) have been the subject of much debate. There is ample evidence, however, that by the beginning of the classical era (480 BCE) his archaic heroes Achilles and Patroclus had become exemplars of male love. Greek lyric poets sing of male love from almost the earliest fragments down to the end of classical times. Five brilliant philosophical dialogues debate its ethics with a wealth of illustrations, from Plato and Xenophon to Plutarch and the pseudo-Lucian of the third century CE. In the public arena of the theater we know that tragedies on this theme were popular, and Aristophanes' bawdy humor is quite as likely to be inspired by sex between males as by intercourse between men and women. Vase-painters portray scores of homoerotic scenes, hundreds of inscriptions celebrate the love of boys, and such affairs enter into the lives of a long catalogue of famous Greek statesmen, warriors, artists, and authors. Though it has often been assumed that the love of males was a fashion confined to a small intellectual elite during the age of Plato, in fact it was pervasive throughout all levels of Greek society and held a honored place in Greek culture for more than a thousand years, that is, from before 600 BCE to about 400 CE.

Greek religion, too, testifies to the hold pederasty had upon the Greek imagination. Mythology provides more than fifty examples of youths beloved of deities.[3] Poetry and popular traditions ascribe such affairs to Zeus, Poseidon, Apollo, Hercules, Dionysus, Hermes, and Pan—that is, to nearly all the principal male gods of the Olympian pantheon. Only the war god Ares is (surprisingly) missing. Among the poets, Sappho, Alcaeus, Ibycus, Anacreon, Theognis, Pindar, and a host of contributors to the Greek Anthology sang of same-sex love. Aeschylus, Sophocles, and Euripides produced important plays, now lost, on the subject. The lives of Greek political leaders in a host of cities record episodes, crucial or trivial, of homoerotic passion. These include Solon, Peisistratus, Hippias, Hipparchus, Themistocles, Aristides, Critias, Demosthenes, and Aeschines in sophisticated Athens; Pausanias, Lysander, and Agesilaus in militaristic Sparta; Polycrates in his cultivated court on Samos; Hieron and Agathocles in Sicilian Syracuse; Epaminondas and Pelopidas in bucolic Thebes; and Archelaus, Philip II, and Alexander in semi-barbarous Macedon. Socrates spoke, and Plato and Xenophon wrote, of the inspirational powers of love between men, though they decried its physical expression. After Plato's death the presidency of his Academy passed from lover to lover. Among the Stoics, Zeno, Cleanthes, and Chrysippus extolled the love of boys. We know much less of the lives of Greek artists, but Phidias's love for Pantarces was memorialized in marble. In the later Hellenistic age (332 BCE–400 CE) Plutarch, Athenaeus, and Aelian recorded the history of Greek love from its earliest times, while poets from Theocritus to Nonnus celebrated pederastic affairs in idylls, epigrams, and epics. This is an astounding record, including as it does most of the greatest names of ancient Greece during the greatest period of Greek culture.

Throughout these accounts, male attachments are presented in an honorific light, though there were always some skeptics. But for many biographers, for a man not to have had a male lover seems to have bespoken a lack of character or a deficiency in sensibility. It is this enthusiastic note, marked by a kind of spirited élan, that so clearly distinguishes the Greek view of homosexuality. We hear it sounded clearly and strongly in what is probably the most notable defense of male love in Greek literature, the speech that Plato puts in the mouth of Phaedrus at the beginning of the *Symposium.* Here is how the idealistic Athenian praises the male eros:

> For I know not any greater blessing to a young man who is beginning life than a virtuous lover, or to a lover than a beloved youth. For the principle that ought to be the guide of men who would nobly live—that principle, I say, neither kindred, nor honor, nor wealth, nor any other motive is able to implant so well as love. Of what am I speaking? Of the sense of honor and dishonor, without which neither states nor individuals ever do any good or great work . . . And if there were only some way of contriving that a state or an army should be made up of lovers and their loves, they would be the very best governors of their own city, abstaining from all dishonor and emulating one another in honor; and it is scarcely an exaggeration to say that when fighting at each other's side, although a mere handful, they would overcome the world.[4]

Phaedrus believes that no man would run away in battle if his lover's eyes were upon him: this would be too ignominious to imagine. We shall consider Plato's reservations more generally in a later chapter. But Phaedrus is giving voice to what was probably the typical view of an educated Greek of his time. Nor was this view restricted to intellectual circles. Its peculiar note of exaltation echoes repeatedly through all levels of Greek society. Like the rest of humanity, the ancient Greek was susceptible to various erotic moods—heroic, tender, frivolous, ribald, even, on occasion, brutal. But the notion of the potential ennobling effect of such love remained common currency from almost the earliest days of recorded Greek history down to the triumph of Christianity. It cast over the idea of *paiderastia* a strong aura of glamor. On public occasions it might be respectfully saluted before an audience made up of all classes, as in the case of Aeschines' speech to the jurors of Athens. Belief in its edifying possibilities was one of the pieties of the tribe, not just for an elite but for the average citizen.

• Homer's *Iliad* •

The ancient Greeks had no word that corresponded to our word "homosexual." *Paiderastia,* the closest they came to it, meant literally "boy love," that is, a relation between an older male and someone younger, usually a youth between the ages of fourteen and twenty. The older man was called the *erastes* or lover. Ideally, it was his duty to be the boy's teacher and protector and serve as a model of courage, virtue, and wisdom to his beloved, or *eromenos,* whose attraction lay in his beauty, his youth, and his promise of future moral, intellectual, and physical excellence. In the *Symposium,* Phaedrus and the other speakers are always careful to use one term or the other as the occasion requires.

This is especially striking in Phaedrus' discussion of the *Iliad.* Here he finds his ideal lovers, for Achilles determines to revenge the death of his comrade-in-arms Patroclus, even though he has been warned by the gods that this will cost him his life. But Phaedrus is puzzled as to which role to assign to which man. He notes that Aeschylus, in one of his most famous tragedies, the *Myrmidons,* had made Achilles the protector, the *erastes.* But Phaedrus thinks this is at odds with Homer, since the *Iliad* emphasizes the remarkable beauty of Achilles, which in Phaedrus' view, qualifies him rather for the role of the *eromenos.*

Plato wrote the *Symposium* about 385 BCE. By that time a well-established Greek tradition saw Achilles and Patroclus not just as comrades in battle but as lovers in the full physical sense. But did Homer himself mean us to perceive Achilles and Patroclus as lovers? At least since Plato's day, the question has been a matter of debate. Aeschylus, writing a century earlier, clearly regarded their relation as sexual. We know his *Myrmidons* was an extremely popular tragedy, though only fragments have come down to us. These fragments, however, make the erotic nature of their love quite explicit. In them Achilles reproaches his dead friend for letting himself be killed, and in the agony of his grief speaks over Patroclus' naked corpse—in language whose directness must have startled even the Athenians—of the "devout union of the thighs."[5] Aeschylus' sexual reading of the relation was shared by many (though, as we shall see, not all) Greeks at the zenith of the classical period.

We find evidence for this interpretation in a speech made by the Athenian politician Aeschines at his trial in 345. Aeschines, who is seeking to emphasize the importance of *paiderastia* to Greek culture, argues that though Homer does not clearly state that Achilles and Patroclus are lovers, sophisticated Greeks will read between the lines: "Although [Homer] speaks in many places of Patroclus and Achilles, he hides their love and avoids giving a name to their friendship, thinking that the exceeding greatness of their affection is manifest to such of his hearers as are educated men."[6] Other ancient writers follow this tradition, which seems to have been the predominant one.

The question is of historical as well as literary importance. Homer's two epics, generally supposed to have been composed between 800 and 700 BCE, are by far the most important source we have for the state of Greek manners and morals in archaic times. They are of unique significance for the period before Greek literary texts began to be abundant, that is, before 600. Thus it is noteworthy that Homer in depicting male companionship in the *Iliad* does not use the classical terms *erastes* and *eromenos* and gives us no clear in-

1. Achilles binds the wounds of Patroclus. Painted pottery, fifth century BCE.

stance of the typical Greek love relationships so often depicted in later poetry, philosophy, and biography. Apparently, in Homer's Ionian culture, homosexuality had not taken on the form it was later to assume throughout the Greek world. Some scholars, like Bernard Sergent, have argued that it had, though it was not reflected in Homer.[7] But Sergent's view that ritualized man-boy relations were widely diffused through Greece and Europe from prehistoric times is a theory for which the evidence is slim.

It is impossible to fit the roles Achilles and Patroclus play in the *Iliad* into the classical Greek pattern. Achilles is clearly the dominant member of the pair. Among the Greeks assembled on the plain of Troy, he has the greatest prestige as a warrior and athlete: he gives the orders and takes the lead. Patroclus performs some domestic chores, such as cooking and nursing the wounded, as a squire might. This could be seen as fitting him for the *eromenos* role, but Homer tells us Patroclus is older than Achilles and, as Phaedrus notes, pointedly stresses Achilles' youth and beauty. And both engage in relations with the opposite sex: on one occasion, the two men retire to opposite sides of their tent to enjoy the favors of captured slave women.

Nevertheless, the emotion Achilles and Patroclus feel for each other is intense and absorbing. Achilles treats Patroclus with an indulgent tenderness strikingly different from the arrogance and egotism he routinely exhibits. Usually Greek warriors fought for their own personal glory or for their clan or city. But in Book 16 Achilles indulges in a romantic fantasy that exalts their personal relationship over all else. He wishes that the other Greeks might all perish so that he and Patroclus might face the foe alone together and win the honor of conquering Troy.[8] When Patroclus is slain fighting in Achilles' armor, Achilles goes wild with grief. He caresses and embraces the body of his dead friend, smears his own head with ashes, and refuses to eat and drink. Finally, the desire to kill Hector, who had killed Patroclus, moves him from the sullen refusal to fight he has shown till then, even though he knows this will mean his own death.

Serious attempts to edit Homer's text in a scholarly fashion were made in Alexandria in the second century BCE. Aristarchus of Samothrace, who has been called "the founder of scientific scholarship," believed Homer did not intend to present Achilles and Patroclus as lovers. Since, however, he thought the "we-two alone" passage did imply a love relation, he argued that it must be a later interpolation.[9] But most modern editors have accepted the lines, and other passages show emotions that at least approximate them. Aristarchus' view, of course, is paradoxical: even a Greek who wanted to rule out an amorous interpretation of the men's relationship thought these lines argued against such a view. Clearly, if modern scholarship is perplexed by this question, so were the Greeks. On balance it seems reasonable to trust the received text, conceding that it suggests (as even Aristarchus was forced to admit) a lover-like relation and yet provides no indication that this love took on an explicitly sexual form, as it did in Aeschylus.

• Crete, Sparta, Chalcis •

Whatever view we take, we are left with an intriguing problem. Since *paiderastia* does not appear in Homer as the important institution it later became, we must ask when did the change occur and what brought it about? The most celebrated answer is the so-called Dorian hypothesis first put forth by K. O. Müller early in the nineteenth century and more fully developed in a controversial essay published by Erich Bethe in 1907.[10] According to this theory, *paiderastia* was part of the culture of the warlike Dorian tribes who swept down from northwestern Greece in the twelfth and eleventh centuries BCE, conquering most of the Peloponnesus and such islands as Crete, Thera, and Rhodes. They drove the original inhabitants—the Ionian Greeks—eastward to the shores of Asia Minor (modern Turkey) but left important Ionian settlements in Athens and on Euboea, the long narrow island that hugs the east coast of the Greek peninsula.

Without question, man-boy relations played a significant part in the social organization of such Dorian communities as Crete and Sparta. Plato singles out both cultures in the *Laws* disapprovingly, because of the license he thought they provided for the physical expression of same-sex love. Aristotle also claimed that the Cretans encouraged homosexuality, specifically as a check to population. The Cretan "lawgiver," he tells us, devoted much ingenuity to "segregating the women and instituting sexual relations among the males so that the women would not have children."[11] But by far the most detailed account we have of the way Cretans ritualized homosexuality and incorporated it into their culture appears in Strabo's *Geography.* Strabo, who lived at the time of Augustus, drew on Ephorus of Cyme, who wrote about 380 BCE. The passage is of such anthropological interest that it is worth quoting at length:

> [The Cretans] have a peculiar custom in regard to love affairs, for they win the objects with their love, not by persuasion, but by abduction; the lover tells the friends of the boy three or four days beforehand that he is going to make the abduction; but for the friends to conceal the boy, or not to let him go forth by the appointed road, is indeed a most disgraceful thing, a confession, as it were, that the boy is unworthy to obtain such a lover; and when they meet, if the abductor is the boy's equal or superior in rank or other respects, the friends pursue him and lay hold of him, though only in a very gentle way, thus satisfying the custom; and after that they cheerfully turn the boy over to him to lead away; if, however, the abductor is unworthy, they take the boy away from him.

It is the boy's character—his "manliness"—not his beauty that recommends him to a lover. The boy then retires with his lover to a country retreat, where he is given a military outfit, an ox (to sacrifice to Zeus), and a drinking cup—three costly gifts. Moreover,

> it is disgraceful for those who are handsome in appearance or descendants of illustrious ancestors to fail to obtain lovers, the presumption being that their character is responsible for such a fate. But the *parastathentes* [who "stand by" their older lovers in battle] receive honors; for in both the dances and the races they have the positions of highest honor, and are allowed to dress in better clothes than the rest, that is, in the habit given them by their lovers; and not then only, but even after they have grown to manhood, they wear a distinctive dress, which is intended to make known the fact that each wearer has become *kleinos,* for they call the loved one *kleinos* [distinguished] and the lover *philetor.*[12]

It seems likely the Spartans developed their own form of institutionalized man-boy love under Cretan influence.[13] In Sparta the boy in such a pairing was called the "hearer" *(aites),* while his mentor was called the "inspirer" *(eispnelos).* Plutarch tells the story of a man who was punished because his pupil cried out in pain in battle.[14] This pattern of mentorship was supposed to have been inaugurated by Sparta's legendary lawgiver, Lycurgus, who had visited Crete. Xenophon, in his account of Spartan customs, says Lycurgus explicitly forbade sexual contact and that the Spartans maintained that such pairings were chaste. But, he adds, "I am not surprised, however, that people refuse to believe this. For in many states the laws are not opposed to the indulgence of these appetites."[15] The Athenians shared Xenophon's skepticism. In Attic speech, to "laconize" meant to sodomize, by implication ascribing this practice to the Laconians, that is, the Spartans.[16]

Since Bethe, the theory of the Dorian origin of Greek *paiderastia* has often been called into question. Kenneth Dover, in his classic study, points out that Plato's *Symposium* names not Crete and Sparta but Elis and Boeotia, two non-Dorian communities, as those whose laws most unqualifiedly endorsed boy love.[17] Elis, a few miles northwest of Olympia, was the city responsible for the administration of the Olympic games. As for Boeotia, proverbially rustic and uncouth in Athenian eyes, its capital was Thebes, where the famous Sacred Band of male lovers was later organized. At any rate, it seems to have been the Ionians (whose dialect Homer employed) who were exceptional in lacking the practice.

More recently, William Percy, in an excellent study, has argued that its first institutionalization occurred not in the Dorian north but in Crete itself and not until the seventh century.[18] Percy marshals impressive evidence to show that most Greeks perceived Crete as the preeminent source of pederastic traditions. He also argues that mainland cities had ample reason, because of their own exploding populations, to follow the Cretans' example. Yet there is one episode, recounted in Plutarch's "Dialogue on Love" (c. 120 CE), which suggests that at least some cities may have been influenced by northern cultures at a fairly early date. The event took place at Chalcis, an important Ionian city on Euboea. The unique element in the story is that it actually purports to explain how one community changed its negative view of boy love to a positive one. It concerns an engagement in the so-called Lelantine War, which, it is conjectured, began before 700 and did not end until about 650.[19] Here is Plutarch's account:

> You know, of course, the story of Cleomachus of Pharsalia [in Thessaly] and the reason for his death in battle . . . Cleomachus came to help the Chalcidians when the Lelantine War against the Eretrians was at its height . . . His allies requested Cleomachus, a man of splendid courage, to be the first to charge the horse. His beloved *[eromenos]* was there and Cleomachus asked him if he was going to witness the battle. The youth said that he was, embraced Cleomachus tenderly, and put on his helmet for him. Filled with ardor, Cleomachus assembled the bravest of the Thessalians about himself, made a fine charge, and fell upon the enemy with such vigour that their

2. Zeus and Ganymede. Painted terracotta, c. 470 BCE.

cavalry was thrown into confusion and was thoroughly routed [so that] the Chalcidians had a decisive victory. It was however, Cleomachus' bad fortune to be killed in the battle. The Chalcidians point out his tomb in the marketplace with the great pillar standing on it to this day. Formerly they had frowned on pederasty, but now they accepted it and honored it more than others did.[20]

The story of Cleomachus has a romantic ring—Plutarch loved a good tale. Aristotle gave a somewhat different version of the episode and cited a popular poem expressive of communal feeling

> Ye lads of grace and sprung from worthy stock,
> Grudge not to brave men converse with your beauty:
> In cities of Chalcis, love, looser of limbs,
> Thrives side by side with courage.

The preeminence of Chalcis among Greek cities that honored *paiderastia* is also attested by another authority. Athenaeus' *The Sophists at Dinner* is a rambling discourse, written in Egypt about 200 CE, a generation or two after Plutarch, which covers an enormous range of topics, serious and trivial. Love is one of its important themes, and Athenaeus tells us that the Chalcidians ranked next after the Cretans in their public glorification of boy love, and even claimed that Zeus carried off Ganymede not from Mount Ida near Troy but from a myrtle grove in Chalcis which they called, after this event, the Harpagion.[21] The Athenians saluted this tradition by adding the verb "to chalcidize" to their erotic vocabulary.[22] Though we cannot be sure exactly where or when institutionalized pederasty first originated in archaic Greece, we may conclude that it was particularly associated with Crete and Sparta and reached such Ionian settlements as Calchis and Athens at a later date.

• Athletics and the Cult of Beauty •

Besides its presumed incentive to valor, three other aspects of Greek culture also favored male love. These were the Greeks' passion for athletics, their acceptance of male nudity, and their cult of male beauty. From early times the Greeks had exalted athletics, first as useful training for the warrior, then for their own sake. Athletic contests are prominent in the *Iliad,* which has elaborate descriptions of the games held at the funeral of Patroclus. The Greeks dated other events in their history from the first recorded Olympic games, assumed to have begun in 776 BCE. Sparta, especially, encouraged athletics as part of its military regimen.

As for nudity, one doubtful tradition held that it began at the Olympics as early as 720, when a runner from Megara was supposed to have shed—or lost—his loincloth.[23] Thucydides, however, calls the innovation of nudity a recent one. Eventually not only athletics but also communal celebrations were so distinguished: the sixteen-year-old Sophocles, his naked body gleaming with oil, led the victory parade in Athens after the battle of Marathon.

The municipal schools for exercise took their name from this custom—our "gymnasium" derives from the Greek word *gymnos,* naked. These schools served both for physical training and as social centers where men and youths might meet, talk politics, philosophize, and on occasion find lovers. The

3. Greek wrestlers. Attic red-figure vase, c. 525 BCE.

palaestras or wrestling schools for youths served a similar function. Some of these buildings were adorned with statues of Eros, as if to suggest that a beautiful physique might inspire a passionate relationship. Several of Plato's dialogues take place in wrestling schools. *Lysis* is set at the palaestra of Miccus; in the *Charmides,* Socrates, who has a keen appreciation of handsome youths, asks Critias who is the outstanding beauty of a palaestra where they have met. When Charmides arrives, the men and boys fall into awed silence and are so entranced that some are inadvertently shoved off their benches as others make room for him. In the modern world one might find a similar fascination with a female movie star at an isolated military base. It would be unthinkable to imagine such a demonstration of enthusiasm for male good looks.

As we have noted, Elis was the community most closely connected with the Olympic games. Plato, Xenophon, and Plutarch all mention Elis as a city whose code of laws encouraged male love affairs. Among its civic festivals was a male beauty contest whose first prize, Theophrastus informs us, was a set of weapons. The occasion had religious as well as aesthetic significance: a solemn procession accompanied the winner to the altar of Athena, where the arms were dedicated to the goddess.[24] A like contest was held at Megara, a Dorian city near Corinth. Once again, celebrations of beauty, love, and valor were combined. The festival, called the Diocleia, commemorated an Athenian warrior named Diocles who had died protecting his Megarian lover in battle. Theocritus describes it charmingly in his twelfth Idyll:

> Men of Megarian Nisaea, skilled with the oar,
> May your lives prosper, for beyond all others you
> Honored your Attic guest, Diocles, who gave his life for his love.
> Around his tomb ever at the beginning of springtime
> Crowds of boys gather and vie for the kissing award,
> And he who more sweetly presses lip against lip
> Goes home to his mother proudly laden with garlands.[25]

The beauty of youths was also commemorated in Greek art. Archaic and early classical sculpture found its principal inspiration in young male athletes, gods, or warriors. So did much painting on vases. Decorated vases were often inscribed with a dedication that consisted of a young man's name and the adjective *kalos*—beautiful. Over five hundred of these have come down to us.[26] Scholars have counted over two hundred different names, all male, except for about thirty which designate Athenian *hetairai,* or courtesans. Respectable women, who were secluded within the women's quarters of their houses, could not have been celebrated in this way: such publicity would have insulted and compromised them. But beautiful boys of high social standing were a different matter, and many of the most famous vase painters inscribed their work with the names of boys of rank and repute. Among the

4. Boy kissing man. Red-figure cup, c. 480 BCE.

names that appear are Miltiades and Alcibiades, Theognis the poet, and Agathon the dramatist. Robinson and Fluck have identified several members of the Socratic circle, a score of generals, and a significant number of Athenian orators and statesmen. The name most often found—it appears over forty times—is Leagros, an Athenian general who died in 465 commanding a fleet in Thrace. Whether depicted as a young man, in middle age, or in old age, he always inspires the epithet *kalos.*[27]

We must inevitably wonder: did these relations remain "platonic," or did they take on a specifically sexual form? Literary evidence is relatively scarce in the pre-classical period, but again ceramics provide clues. In the late archaic age—from about 570 to 470—painters frequently decorated vases with erotic scenes. Many show heterosexual intercourse, that is, men disporting with courtesans, some of whom submit to vaginal and anal penetration and fellate their partners. But a significant number of scenes are homoerotic. These are less explicitly sexual. Men court boys with love gifts, usually a gar-

5. Erastes courting an ephebe. Attic black-figure cup, c. 520 BCE.

6. Banquet scene. Fresco from the Tomb of the Diver, Paestum, Italy, fifth century BCE.

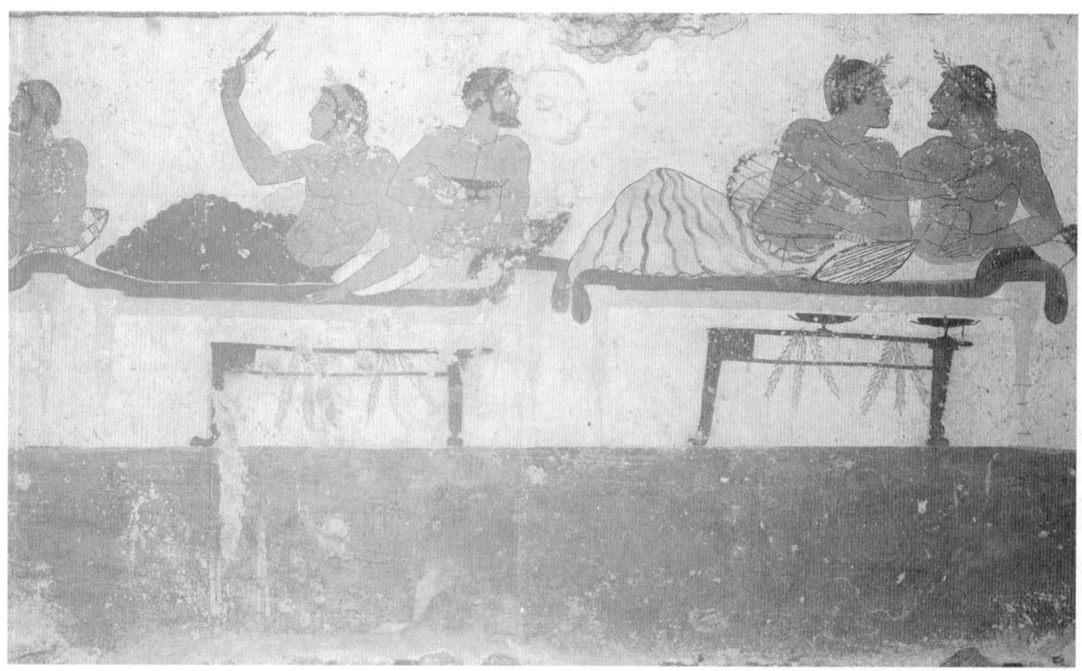

land or a rabbit or a cockerel. Sometimes the boy is absent—on one vase a middle-aged man lies on a couch and sings the words (inscribed on the cup)—"O most beautiful boy" (the beginning of a poem by Theognis), while a gift rabbit crouches beneath.[28] Sometimes the approach is more direct; one man places his hand firmly on the shoulder of a boy who is walking before him in a religious procession.[29] On another vase, a boy raises his head to receive a kiss from a handsomely coifed youth, presumably of the aristocratic warrior caste. A stereotyped motif shows a man reaching to touch a boy's penis with one hand while with the other he caresses his chin in supplication.[30] Occasionally the boy extends his arm to discourage the advance.[31] Other boys respond eagerly: some leap up to kiss taller men.[32] One striking design shows a seated naked man, with a powerful physique and an erection, titillating the genitals of an athlete who stands between his thighs and throws his arm around his neck. In most cases the artist portrays an older and a younger male. Suitors are not always bearded adults, however. Courtship scenes may also depict adolescent boys with younger ones. A famous vase shows several couples: on one side youths court maidens decorously, on the other three male pairs embrace in poses unmistakably sexual.

Fired ceramics may survive in pristine condition for centuries. Wall paintings are much less durable as colors fade or darken and plaster flakes off. The impressive masterpieces Greek critics extolled have been lost to us, and very few murals of any sort have survived. It was therefore of great interest when, in 1968, a tomb with well-preserved paintings dating from about 470 was discovered at Paestum, an ancient Greek city near Naples. The wall of this Tomb of the Diver, so-called from the design on its under-lid, is decorated with scenes of a festive drinking party. Men recline in pairs on couches in the traditional Greek fashion. Some wave their empty cups at the wine-bearer. But one stares with amusement at the couple who share the couch on the right. They are engaged in a lively flirtation: a handsome bearded young man smiles, fascinated, into the eyes of the youth who lies beside him, pulling him closer for a kiss, which the young man resists. The life-like casualness of the scene suggests how common such behavior must have been at Greek banquets once a little wine had flowed and suggests the matter-of-fact way Greek society looked on this kind of love-play.

• Sappho •

No reputable Athenian woman of this period would ever have appeared at a social gathering where men were present, even in their own homes. To have done so would have been prima facie evidence she was a prostitute. Married at fifteen or sixteen to men twice their age and confined to the house except for religious festivals or visits to relatives, women were so deprived of education and knowledge of the world that there was little they could talk about

7. Sappho and Alcaeus. Attic vase, c. 480 BCE.

with their husbands. On this account some commentators, like Shelley, have speculated that the low intellectual status of women in classical Athens may have encouraged male homosexuality.[33]

Women appear to have had been less constrained in Homeric times than they were later. The impressive heroines of Athenian tragedy are drawn from this earlier heroic age. This greater freedom for women seems to have lingered in one culture especially, the Aeolian culture of Lesbos, which produced Sappho. In the beauty contests of Mytilene, it was young women, not boys, who competed for the prizes. Sappho's contemporary, the poet Alcaeus, described an annual public festival "where Lesbian girls in trailing robes go up and down, being judged for their beauty, and about them rings the marvelous holy cry of women in every year."[34] Apparently some religious cult was associated with this festival.

For Lesbos' most famous citizen, the worship of beauty was the center of her existence. Our knowledge of Sappho's life remains fragmentary and problematic. But of this we can be certain: Sappho sings of the beauty of flowers, of gold and sunshine, of shady temple gardens, and, above all, of the beauty of women. Born about 610 into an aristocratic family, she grew up in the city of Mytilene, married, and bore a daughter. Though a revolution exiled her temporarily to Sicily, she soon returned to become the leader of a coterie of women and girls who shared her artistic and erotic tastes. Her lyrics tell of the powerful feelings these women aroused in her:

> He seems as fortunate as the gods to me,
> The man who sits opposite you
> And listens nearby to your sweet voice and lovely laughter.
> Truly that sets my heart trembling in my breast.
> For when I look at you for a moment,
> Then it is no longer possible for me to speak:
> My tongue has snapped,
> At once a subtle fire has stolen beneath my flesh,
> I see nothing with my eyes, my ears hum, sweat pours from me,
> A trembling seizes me all over,
> I am greener than grass,
> and it seems to me that I am little short of dying.[35]

Repeatedly, Sappho strikes her characteristic note of intense feeling. "Love shook my heart like a wind falling on oaks on a mountain," "Once again limb-loosening Love make me tremble, the bitter-sweet irresistible creature," "You came and I was longing for you; you cooled my heart which was burning with desire."[36] It is not surprising that Sappho's favorite goddess was Aphrodite, whom she invokes in a passionate prayer, here translated in an approximation to the so-called "Sapphic" meter she made famous:

> Throned in bright colors, deathless Aphrodite,
> Zeus' most subtle daughter, now I pray you,
> Do not violate my soul with sorrow,
> And pain, O Goddess!
>
> Come to me now as once you came, down swooping,
> Hearing my voice from far, heeding my prayers.
> For once you stepped down from your father's palace,
> All bright and golden.

Your chariot you harnessed; fair and swiftly
Down to the dark earth then your sparrows bore you,
Their wings spinning from heaven through the ether,
Through the sky's centre.

Suddenly they were here. And you, O blessed,
A smile upon your deathless face, asked gently
The reason for my sorrow, and the reason
Why I had called you.

You asked me then what most of all I wanted
In my wild heart, and said: "Whom shall I conquer?
What pretty girl must I now lead to love you?
Sappho, who harms you?"

"For though she shuns you, soon she will pursue you;
Though she rejects your gifts, she'll soon be giving;
Though now she loves you not, she soon will love you,
Though first unwilling."

Come to me now as then you did! Release me
From all my sorrows, speedily fulfilling
My heart's desire! Fulfill it! You yourself
Fight in my battle![37]

As a poet, Sappho stood next to Homer in the esteem of many Greeks—the greatest lyric poet as he was the greatest writer of epics. Plato called her "the tenth Muse." Her profile appeared on the coinage of her native Mytilene and other cities; statues and paintings honored her throughout the Mediterranean world. All this occurred despite her avowals of love for women in her poems, avowals that have made the word "lesbian" a synonym for female homosexuality. One ancient commentator, Maximus of Tyre, writing in the second century CE, compared her love for her disciples to the love of Socrates for his, but few readers of her poems can have shared this view, which implied a restraint hardly to be found in her verses.[38] To her own contemporaries their erotic tenor must have been clear: how then, we may wonder, did her contemporaries in the Greek world react to this knowledge?

We have abundant documentation on male affairs in ancient Greece but nothing comparable for lesbian love, perhaps because we have such slight knowledge of the personal lives of women. Later, in Christian times, prejudice reduced Sappho's nine books of poems to the two poems quoted and a handful of fragments. There is evidence, however, that in some states in sixth-century Greece love between women was openly countenanced. Plutarch, after speaking of Spartan boy love, remarks that "this sort of love was so approved among them that even the maidens found lovers in good and noble women."[39]

But any tolerance was lost in classical and late antiquity.[40] The hard-boiled lesbians in Lucian's *Dialogues of the Courtesans* (c. 160 CE) are stereotypically masculine and presented from an unsympathetic point of view. A speaker in a pseudo-Lucianic dialogue dating from a century or so later refers to "tribadism" (lesbianism) as "that word seldom heard, which I am ashamed even to utter."[41] A fragmentary biography of Sappho written about 200 CE on an Egyptian papyrus seems to reflect this negative judgement: "She has been accused by some of being irregular in her ways and a woman-lover."[42] One of our chief sources for Greek biography, the so-called *Suidas* or *Suda,* a Byzantine lexicon compiled about 980, is equally condemnatory and at odds with Maximus: "She had three companions and friends, Atthis, Telesippa and Megara, and she got a bad name from her impure friendship with them."[43] But the *Suidas* often reveals a Byzantine Christian animus.

Sappho's contemporaries did not seem to share this deprecating view. Indeed, one can hardly imagine a writer expressing herself with such direct candor if she thought her poems would bring her obloquy. For two thousand years after her death, social conventions (not to speak of religious sentiment) in the Western tradition made it impossible for women openly to avow passionate love for each other. But Sappho speaks confidently, almost arrogantly, of the fame that will be hers, with no hint that she desires to *épater les bourgeois.*

These paradoxes have sparked a war among commentators. A century ago the famous German scholar Wilamowitz thought Sappho could not possibly have been "lesbian" in the modern sense because she was commissioned to train girls of good families in song and dance for religious festivals and weddings. Denys Page has ridiculed this Victorian de-eroticizing of Sappho and has scoffed at the notion of her being anything so proper as a schoolmistress. But both scholars seem to have missed the point by creating a false dichotomy. Even the *Suidas,* for all its bias, lists her "pupils"—"Anagora of Miletus, Gongyla of Colophon, and Eunica of Salamis," women who must either have gained fame in their own right or, more likely, through being named in her poems. Sappho's reputation as a mentor must have been great to attract girls not only from the Ionian mainland but from as far away as Salamis on the other side of the Aegean. Many of her fragments are loving farewells, such as a doting teacher might have written to young women leaving to return home to be married. An undated papyrus fragment speaks of her teaching the "noblest" girls of Lesbos and Ionia and declares unequivocally that she was "highly esteemed among the citizens" of Mytilene.[44] In our age the discovery of a teacher's lesbianism might still be cause for alarm in a conservative community. But this does not seem to have been the case in Sappho's culture.

In hostile Western societies, Sappho has, through the ages, been a beacon for women writers who have identified themselves as lesbians in the modern sense. Today, little of her work remains, but these remnants have been enough to inspire women like Natalie Barney and Renée Vivien, Americans who at the beginning of the twentieth century lived openly lesbian lives in Paris, translated Sappho, wrote poems and plays about her, and attempted to live out a Sapphic idyll in a villa on Lesbos. Hilda Doolittle ("H.D.") incorporated her phrases into her own poetry, and Amy Lowell used her images to celebrate her lifelong companion, Ada Russell.[45] In 1895 the novelist Willa Cather published a bold tribute in a Nebraska newspaper:

> There is one woman poet whom all the world calls great, though of her work there remains now only a few disconnected fragments and that one wonderful hymn to Aphrodite . . . If of all the lost richness we could have one master restored to us, one of all the philosophers and poets, the choice of the world would be for the lost nine books of Sappho. Those broken fragments have burned themselves into the consciousness of the world like fire . . . Twenty centuries have not cooled the passion in them.[46]

• Alcaeus, Ibycus, Anacreon •

Sappho's lines are the first we have that tell of the love of one woman for another. By a coincidence of literary history it was a fellow Mytilenean who composed the earliest known lyrics expressing love for a boy. Alcaeus knew Sappho and reputedly addressed love poems to her; to one solicitation, Aristotle tells us, she made a tart reply. The fragments of Alcaeus that have survived excoriate tyrants who seized power in Lesbos, especially Pittacus, who was the enemy of Sappho's family. But Cicero, who admired Alcaeus' courage but disapproved of his erotic verse, complained that he was extravagant in writing of the "the love of youths."[47] Horace is more explicit and identifies one of his favorites by name. He praised Alcaeus, "Who, though brave in war, / Still amid the fighting or when he had moored his storm-tossed ship on a wet shore, / Sang of Dionysius and the Muses and Venus . . . / And of Lycus with his dark eyes and hair of ebony."[48]

Alcaeus was a man embittered by political reverses. But not all poets who sang of male love lived dour lives. Ibycus and Anacreon, contemporaries in the latter half of the sixth century, were revelers who extolled the pleasures of wine and love. Ibycus, who was born at Rhegium, the modern Reggio di Calabria, wandered through mainland Greece, then settled at the luxurious court of the tyrant Polycrates on the island of Samos off the coast of Asia Minor. In antiquity Ibycus won fame for his seven books of poetry and his amorous nature. Cicero, who had the texts we know now only from sparse fragments, described Ibycus as even more erotic than Alcaeus and Anacreon. An epitaph for his grave at Rhegium has come down to us in the Greek Anthology: it calls him a "lover of the lyre" and a "lover of lads."[49] Only a few lines remain of the poems that led Alexandrian critics to rank him as one of the

Nine Lyric Poets of Greece. In one excerpt he laments that, though spring has come, love still shakes his heart like a blustering, winter tempest. In another he trembles at the approach of love, like an old racehorse forced to compete once again. A third celebrates a boy whom he loved—"Euryalus, scion of the delicious Graces . . . darling of the lovely-tressèd Muses . . . the nursling of Cypris [Aphrodite] and tender-eyed Persuasion."[50]

Polycrates established a small empire in the Aegean centered on beautiful Samos with its splendid temples and made it a center of learning and the arts. Besides Ibycus, he also entertained Anacreon, a native of Teos on the Ionian coast. In later days Anacreon's fame eclipsed the older poet's, and he became for classical Greece and Renaissance Europe the archetypal celebrant of wine, women, and song—and, since he was Greek, of boys. (Few patriotic Americans, negotiating the demanding cadences of "The Star-Spangled Banner," realize that the music derives from an old English drinking tune, "To Anacreon in Heaven.") Like Sappho and Ibycus, he invokes a powerful image to describe the force of love: love is a smith who has beaten him with a hammer and plunged him in cold water like tempered steel. His fragments speak of women he has yearned for, but more often of boys. A complimentary poem in the Palatine Anthology addressed him as a *philopaides.* Maximus of Tyre names three of his loves: Smerdies, Bathyllus, and Cleobolus, the first two also favorites of Polycrates, who had a statue of Bathyllus set up in the great temple of Hera at Samos. Anacreon's attachment to Smerdies seems to have run deeper than his usual flirtations. Aelian says he loved him "for his soul, not his body."[51] Jealous, Polycrates cut off Smerdies' hair. Anacreon rebuked Smerdies in verse, as if the boy had done the deed himself. For this he has been praised for his tact and damned for his cowardice. To a boy whose name we do not know he wrote lines that parallel Plato's conceit of the charioteer in the *Phaedrus:*

> O boy with maiden eyes,
> I seek you and you do not listen,
> Little knowing that you hold the reins to my soul.[52]

Eventually Polycrates was lured into a trap set by the Persians who captured and crucified him. Anacreon's good fortune, however, did not desert him. This was an age of brilliant tyrants, and Anacreon immediately found a congenial home in Athens with Hippias and Hipparchus, sons of Peisistratus. Hippias inherited his father's political power in 527, but his younger brother Hipparchus was devoted less to politics than to love and the arts, and in his role as minister of culture sent a fifty-oared galley to Samos to conduct Anacreon to Athens. There the poet lived in the house of his *eromenos,* Critias, who reversed the prescribed roles by writing poems in praise of the older man. The Athenians, in later democratic times, raised a statue to Anacreon, wine cup in hand, next to one of Pericles.

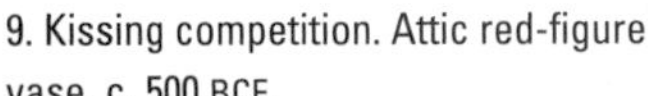

8. Man and young athlete. Red-figure drinking cup, c. 480 BCE.

9. Kissing competition. Attic red-figure vase, c. 500 BCE.

• Theognis of Megara •

The most substantial writing on homosexual love to survive from the sixth century was not, however, of Athenian origin. These poems, of uncertain authorship, have been traditionally ascribed to Theognis, a citizen either of Megara in Boeotia or of its colony in Sicily. (Possibly he was born in the one city and spent his exile in the other.) A Dorian settlement, Sicilian Megara, like so many Greek communities of this age, was wracked by class strife. The staunchly conservative Theognis sided with the nobility, who were overthrown in a revolution that made Theognis an embittered wanderer dependent on others. Yet, despite their pessimism, the *Elegies* collected under his name were admired for their moral teachings and exemplary wisdom. Popular pedagogic texts, they were forceful in expression and conservative in sentiment: "Keep away from rascals"; "It's better to be poor and good than rich and crooked"; "All real gentlemen obey the rules."[53]

Theognis' dates have been much disputed, but ancient authorities thought he wrote about 540 BCE. His poems have come down to us in two books, the shorter second book consisting of forty-six brief poems, nearly all on the love of boys. Some lines addressed to his favorite Kurnos foreshadow Shakespeare's promise of immortality in his sonnets two thousand years later:

> I give you wings. You'll soon be lifted up
> Across the land, across the boundless crests
> Of ocean where men dine and pass the cup,
> You'll light there, on the lips of all the guests . . .
> At length, my boy, you'll enter Hades' dwelling,
> That black hole where departed spirits moan,
> But even there your glory shall not cease,
> Your well-loved name will stay alive, unworn . . .
> As long as light exists and earth endures.[54]

But all did not go smoothly in this affair, and the sudden turn in feeling at the end of this eulogy is also Shakespearean:

> I give you this, for what? to be reviled,—
> To be betrayed and lied to, like a child.

The poems of Book II alternate between admonition, complaints (you are fickle and ungrateful), pleas (don't torture me, someday you'll want a boy to favor you), and a small ration of praise (you are lovable and handsome). Some poems express placid content: "Happy the lover who exercises, then / Goes home to sleep all day with a handsome boy."[55] But others are anguished. At one moment boys are commended as more loyal than women, at another derided as faithless and cruel. Finally, the poet decides the fascination lies in the contradictions:

> The love of boys is fine to have, and fine
> To leave—it is much easier to find
> Than satisfy. Ten thousand evils come
> From it also ten thousand benefits
> But even this gives it a certain charm.[56]

These songs were composed to be sung at symposia, or drinking parties, in aristocratic circles. They give us not a philosophy of life but the stuff of a thousand arias and a hundred thousand popular songs, the joyous outpourings and the concomitant "blues" of Greece's ancient homoerotic culture.

• Athens' Rulers •

Sappho and Alcaeus belonged to the same generation that produced Solon, who was born about 640. But where they won renown as poets, Solon's fame was a statesman's. For the skill he showed in governing the Greeks he was ranked among the Seven Sages of antiquity. A successful merchant with an aristocratic background, he assumed power when the city was on the verge of a civil war between rich and poor, a disaster he averted by softening Draco's harsh penal laws, canceling the debts of the poor, and laying the groundwork for Athens' democratic constitution.

But in his younger days Solon also wrote poems. One verse speaks of a youth loving a boy, "desiring his thighs and his delicious mouth."[57] His most significant pronouncement on the love of males, however, appears among the gnomic verses that became a standard part of an Athenian literary education and found their way into the collection known as the *Theognidea:* "He's lucky who has boyfriends and smooth-hoovèd / Horses and hunting dogs and foreign friends."[58] Male love was not simply a source of pleasure. According to Plutarch's biography of Solon, it played an important role in Athens' political life:

> Solon's mother . . . was a cousin of the mother of [the tyrant] Peisistratus. And the two men were at first great friends, largely because of their kinship and the youthful beauty of Peisistratus, with whom, as some say, Solon was passionately in love. And this may be the reason why, in later years, when they were at variance about matters of state, their enmity did not bring with it any harsh or savage feelings, but the former amenities lingered in their spirits . . . And that Solon was not proof against beauty in a youth, and made not so bold with Love as "to confront him like a boxer, hand to hand," may be inferred from his poems. He also wrote a law forbidding a slave to practise [nude] gymnastics or have a boy lover, thus putting the matter in the category of honorable and dignified practices, and in a way inciting the worthy to that which he forbade the unworthy. And it is said that Peisistratus also had a boy lover, Charmus, and that he dedicated the

statue of Love in the Academy, where the runners in the sacred torch race light their torches.[59]

Aristotle, in his *Constitution of Athens,* had argued that Solon and Peisistratus could hardly have been lovers, since Solon was the elder by thirty-five or forty years.[60] Whatever the nature of their relationship, Plutarch and his contemporary Aelian chose to ignore Aristotle's skepticism.[61] Perhaps they simply liked a reasonable amount of romance in their history. But as a Greek, Plutarch would also have felt that an amorous affiliation was the right apprenticeship for politics in ancient Athens. Even if those relations did not exist, Greek historians thought they should have.

Plutarch, indeed, added a further link in a kind of erotic genealogy. He makes Peisistratus the *erastes* of Charmus, who endowed the Athenian cult of love with an emblem in the shape of a statue of Eros. Elsewhere we learn that Charmus became the lover of another ruler of Athens, Peisistratus' son Hippias, whose brother was to be fatefully enamoured of Harmodius. In fifth-century Athens the roster of *erastoi* included Themistocles (who led the Athenian navy to victory at Salamis), Aristides (his rival in politics and for the love of Stesilaus, "in beauty of person the most brilliant of youths"), Critias (one of the Thirty Tyrants imposed on Athens by the Spartans), and Pericles' stepson Callias.[62]

Pausanias, who wrote a comprehensive guide to Greece in the second century CE, took note of Charmus' Eros, then still standing. He also gives the history of another monument of unspecified date but with a striking provenance. This was the altar of Anteros, or "love avenged." So great was the prestige of love in the city that even resident aliens, who had no rights as citizens and whose status was often precarious, did not fear to build a cenotaph to heartlessness, though it implied a reproach to their hosts. According to Pausanias: "The Athenian Meles, spurning the love of Timagoras, a resident alien, bade him ascend to the highest point of the [Acropolis] and cast himself down. Now Timagoras took no account of his life, and was ready to gratify the youth in any of his requests, so he went and cast himself down. When Meles saw that Timagoras was dead, he suffered such pangs of remorse that he threw himself from the same rock and so died. From this time the resident aliens worshiped as Anteros the avenging spirit of Timagoras."[63] In Athens at the end of the sixth century, another drama of love and vengeance would end the Peisistratid tyranny and provide the city with its most renowned couple, the tyrannicides Aristogeiton and Harmodius.

• The Tyrannicides •

The crucial events took place in 514. Harmodius, "being then in the flower of his youthful beauty," was beloved by Aristogeiton.[64] When Hipparchus tried to seduce Harmodius, Aristogeiton, fearing that he might try to achieve his ends by force, organized a conspiracy to overthrow him and his brother, the tyrant Hippias. A new provocation came when Harmodius rejected Hipparchus a second time and Hipparchus retaliated by insulting Harmodius' sister at a public ceremony. Incensed by pride and jealousy, the two men plotted to act at the Great Panathenaea—the festival immortalized on the Parthenon frieze, the one occasion when citizens were allowed to carry arms. But when the day arrived, they were alarmed to see one of their co-conspirators talking familiarly to Hippias. Fearing that they had been betrayed, they rushed to the agora and killed Hipparchus, who was organizing the procession. Harmodius himself was immediately struck down by Hipparchus' followers. Aristogeiton died after prolonged torture, ended only when his repeated taunts goaded Hippias into dispatching him. (Aristotle, in his *Athenian Constitution* [18:1–6], gives a slightly different version of these events, making Thetallus, Hipparchus's half-brother, the wooer and insulter of Harmodius.)

The tyranny of Peisistratus and his sons had not hitherto been harsh. Indeed, the city had made its first great cultural advance under their rule. Peisistratus had built the city's first great public buildings, had the Homeric epics written down, and inaugurated the performance of tragedies at the festival of Dionysus. But after his brother's assassination, Hippius' rule turned harsher; so many were killed or exiled that the city turned against him. Four years later he was overthrown, democracy was restored, and Athens entered on the days of her glory.

Aristogeiton and Harmodius were hailed as the sponsors of this new freedom. The cult of the "heroes," as they came to be called, evolved into a pervasive feature of Athens' political and social life. Before this, the city had honored only the gods, not men, with statues. Now a dramatic representation of the lovers about to strike Hipparchus was erected in the agora not far from the spot where the drama had been acted out in real life. These bronze figures became the main secular emblem of Athens, as closely associated with the city as the Statue of Liberty is with New York. The image was endlessly reproduced on coins, in paintings, and finally in marble copies in Athenian residences and Roman villas. For many years the statue's position in the center of the marketplace was so sacrosanct that no other statues could be raised nearby. An annual festival commemorated the deaths of the lovers, and an edict of Pericles decreed that their eldest descendants should be supported at public expense at the prytaneum, Athens' ancient city hall.

The tyrannicides were celebrated not only by public monuments and ceremonies but also at private gatherings in citizens' homes. A popular *skolion,* or drinking-song, praised their achievement. Aristophanes mentions it in the *Wasps* and *Lysistrata,* and Athenaeus's savants recited its simple verses at their dinner-party in the Greek city of Naucratis in Egypt seven hundred years after the deed it honored took place:

> In a myrtle branch I will carry my sword,
> As did Harmodius and Aristogeiton
> When at the Feast of Athena
> They slew the tyrant Hipparchus.
> Ever shall your fame live in the earth
> Dearest Harmodius and Aristogeiton,
> For that you slew the tyrant
> And made Athens a city of equal rights.[65]

The song so strongly influenced the popular imagination that historians protested that it was a gross simplification of Athenian history. Herodotus was at pains to explain that the assassination had not, in fact, freed Athens and that it was the exiled Alcmeonid clan who through their manipulation of the Delphic oracle finally persuaded a Spartan army to attack the city and depose Hippias some four years later.[66] And Thucydides, to whom we are indebted for the details of the love affair and Hipparchus' ill-advised interference, corrected two points the popular song misrepresented, noting that Hippias, not Hipparchus, was the principal tyrant-ruler of Athens and that the primary motive for the assassination was personal and not political.[67]

But the facts of history faded before a myth with such potent appeal, and the cult of the lovers continued to flourish as an essential part of the Athenian civic consciousness. Miltiades, to spur on his troops, saluted the lovers before the battle of Marathon as Athens' greatest heroes.[68] Despite Aristotle's own detachment from the popular enthusiasm that beglamored the tyrannicides, his nephew Callisthenes, when asked who were the men most honored by the Athenians, unhesitatingly replied: "Harmodius and Aristogeiton, because they slew one of the two tyrants and destroyed the tyranny."[69] Demosthenes, in his oration *On the False Legation,* called them "the men to whom, in requital of their glorious deed, you have allotted by statute a share of your libations and drink-offerings in every temple and at every public service, whom in hymns and in worship, you treat as the equal of gods and demi-gods."[70]

As a symbol of democracy, their statues, commemorating courage, martyrdom, and devoted love, had an attraction hardly to be matched by any portrayal of intriguing exiles, a corrupt oracle, or a Spartan general. Indeed, these civic tokens shared the fortunes of the city in a dramatic way. The Roman historian Pliny tells us that the first monument, cast in bronze by Antenor, was set up in 509, a year after Hippias fell, though this date is uncertain.[71] But in 480, when Xerxes' Persian troops sacked and burned Athens, they carried off the statues to the Persian capital, Susa, as trophies of war.

10. Aristogeiton and Harmodius. Roman marble, after bronze by Kritios and Nesiotes, 477 BCE.

There Alexander found them when, one hundred and fifty years later, he conquered the Persians. The statues were then returned. But the Athenians had, in the meantime, commissioned two other famous sculptors, Kritios and Nesiotes, to cast a new pair of figures, which were set in place in 477. It was this work that was copied on coins and in paintings over the centuries. On their retrieval, Antenor's originals were re-erected side by side with the new statues, and they stood together until the destruction of the city by the barbarian Heruli in 267 CE.

Their modern recovery took place in slow stages. During the Renaissance, mutilated copies of the Aristogeiton figure stood unidentified in the loggias of wealthy connoisseurs in Rome. Then, in 1859, the German scholar Karl Friedrichs realized that two marble figures of athletes in the Naples Museum labeled simply "gladiators" in fact belonged together and were copies of the tyrannicides. The head of Harmodius had, however, been replaced by a Hellenistic head far different in style from the late archaic body. Finally, in 1922 a head hidden away in the Vatican collection was found to fit, and a replica provided for the Naples pair. Using vase paintings, it has been possible to correct the arm positions that the Naples Museum had misrestored. The reconstructed pair now shows Harmodius striding forward with his sword raised to strike, while Aristogeiton holds his cloak over one arm to protect his young lover.[72] For the first time since antiquity it has been possible to realize one of the best known images of ancient Greece, familiar to Athenians and visitors to their city for seven centuries.

Male love had been held in high regard in Athens before the demise of the tyranny. Now its esteem increased still more, as the cult of the heroes took root. In the eyes of the Athenians, *paiderastia* assumed an added meaning. In Crete, Sparta, and Megara, boy love had been the means by which a military aristocracy initiated young males into its traditions; now it was seen as a bulwark of popular liberty against tyranny. In Plato's *Symposium* Pausanius' panegyric on love emphasized its political importance:

> In Ionia [then, in 385, under Persian domination] and other places, and generally in countries which are subject to the barbarians, [male love] is held to be dishonorable; because of their despotic governments, loves of youths share the evil repute in which philosophy and gymnastics are held, because they are inimical to tyranny; for the interest of rulers require, I suppose, that their subjects should be poor in spirit and that there should be no strong bond of friendship or society among them, which love, above all other motives, is likely to inspire, as our Athenian tyrants learned by experience . . . And, therefore, the ill-repute into which these attachments have fallen [in Ionia] is ascribed to . . . the self-seeking of the governors and the cowardice of the governed.[73]

Polycrates the tyrant of Samos did indeed close the gymnasia, seeing them as places where dissent might germinate.

The idea that love between men was a threat to tyrants persisted as a rhetorical commonplace for centuries. In the dialogue on love that Plutarch wrote in Roman imperial times, he speaks admiringly of the Athenian tyrannicides and two other couples. "You know the tales of Aristogeiton of Athens and Antileon of Metapontum and Melanippus of Agrigentum: they had at first no quarrels with their tyrants, though they saw that these were acting like drunkards and disfiguring the state; but when the tyrants tried to seduce their beloveds, they spared not even their own lives in defending their loves, holy as it were and inviolable shrines."[74]

If the story of Aristogeiton and Harmodius rests on well-attested facts, the stories of Antileon and Melanippus may be in part romantic fables. But popular inventions are perhaps even more significant than facts in revealing underlying cultural attitudes. For if facts pertain to real events, fables—whether amorous or heroic—are reflections of what a people wishes to believe. They tell us what kinds of behavior appeal to its imagination and stir its heart. From this point of view it is worth looking at the details of Plutarch's two examples.

The story of Melanippus is told by Heracleides of Pontus, a pupil of Plato's, who wrote a lost book, *On Love Affairs.* Melanippus lived in Agrigentum in Sicily, whose tyrant Phalaris (r. 570–554) was notorious for his cruelty. Among his enormities was a bull of brass in which he roasted victims so that their cries imitated the bellowing of the animal. Appalled by these atrocities, Melanippus plotted with his lover Chariton to overthrow the dictator. The attempt failed, but Phalaris was reputedly so moved by the lovers' bravery under torture that he freed them with praise. As a result, so the legend goes, Apollo postponed Phalaris' death, and his oracle at Delphi praised the lovers with a couplet "Happy were Chariton and Melanippus, / Guides for mortals in divine loving."[75]

Antileon's story was recorded by Phanias of Eresus, a pupil of Aristotle's, less than a century after the events purportedly took place. According to Phanias, Antileon was scorned by a handsome young nobleman, Hipparinos, until he performed a seemingly impossible task: he stole the alarm bell from the fortress of the tyrant at Herculea Lucania, a small Greek colony in southern Italy near Metapontum. When the tyrant himself became enamoured of Hipparinos, Antileon killed his rival, only to be captured when he was entangled in a flock of sheep. After its liberation, the town, we are told, imitated Athens by setting up statues to the lovers—and made it illegal to tie sheep together.[76]

It is worth noting that the heroes of these anecdotes are by no means all men of noble birth. Romantic love, reborn in southern France in the eleventh century, was to be preeminently a cult of aristocrats, not merchants or peasants; but in the wide expanse of the Greek world, men of any class were deemed capable of heroic self-sacrifice. Thucydides identifies Aristogeiton as a citizen of middle rank, that is, a businessman or artisan. Xenophon in his *Anabasis* tells of a common soldier who offered his life to save a boy from Chalcidian Olynthus.[77] Athenaeus, in his plenitude, gives an account of a formidable leader of a slave revolt on the Greek island of Chios off the coast of Asia Minor who, grown old, begged his young lover to kill him so he could pay for his education: "I have loved you more than anyone else in the world; you are my favorite, my son, everything that I have. But I have lived long enough, whereas you are young and in the flower of life. What, then, remains? You must become a good and noble man. Since now the Chian state offers a large sum to the man who kills me, and promises him freedom, you must cut off my head and carry it to Chios."[78] If this story is true, it demonstrates tellingly how every level of Greek society was inspired by the ideal of *paiderastia;* if it is an invention, as the skeptical reader may suspect, it shows how the Greeks could imagine even a desperado harboring exalted sentiments and acting heroically under the influence of male love.

What must strike the dispassionate observer is the extent to which the post-classical West moved in the opposite direction of vilification, associating homosexuality with sin, crime, and sickness and, in the political sphere, with weakness and treason. In the modern world the expression "homosexual hero" would strike most people as an oxymoron. Far from being an honorable relation, love between men or between women became a secret to be hidden at all costs. What brought about this reversal? To understand the change we must leave the clarity and ample records of the classical world to examine a society in which the facts bearing on the subject are definitive but few and the social environment obscure.

CHAPTER TWO

JUDEA

900 BCE–600 CE

• The Judgment of Leviticus •

It is an irony of history that the two cultures which have done most to shape Western civilization should have adopted antithetical views on homosexuality at almost the same time. In the sixth century before Christ, Greece produced the homoerotic poetry of Solon, Theognis, Ibycus, and Anacreon; and at its close in 514, Athens witnessed the martyrdom of the tyrannicides, who became emblems of heroic male love. But in the same century, a few hundred miles away in ancient Palestine, a law was incorporated into the Hebrew scriptures which was ultimately to have far greater influence and, indeed, to affect the fate of homosexuals in half the world down to our own day. We do not know precisely when the authors of the book of Leviticus promulgated this legislation. As with the dating of most books of the Hebrew Bible, controversy abounds, but the date most widely accepted by modern scholarship for the so-called Holiness Code in Leviticus is about 550 BCE, during the captivity of the Jews in Babylon.

As one of the five books of the Torah or Law, Leviticus is a compendium of legislation purportedly decreed by Moses. But Moses is assumed to have lived about 1300 BCE, and it is now generally agreed among biblical scholars that the five books (Genesis, Exodus, Leviticus, Numbers, Deuteronomy) traditionally ascribed to him by Jewish tradition and the medieval Christian church took their present form at a much later date. Moses, for instance, can hardly have written the account of his own death that concludes Deuteronomy, and, more tellingly, the books of the Torah speak as though the Jews had been long settled in Palestine, an experience Moses was denied. We may assume then that, though some of the laws may be ancient and even Mosaic, many originated in later times in response to later conditions.

The opening chapters of Leviticus prescribe rites for burnt offerings, priestly consecrations, and the treatment of leprosy and give dietary rules for distinguishing clean from unclean animals. Among Christians and among

Jews not strictly orthodox, these statutes are regarded as archaic and nonbinding in today's world. Chapter 18, however, condemns certain sexual acts, including incest and male homosexuality. The Jews are warned that "these abominations" were common among the Canaanites who ruled Palestine before the Israelite conquest and that the Jews, like their predecessors, will be dispossessed—"spewed out"—if they commit them. "Defile not ye yourselves with any of these things: for in all these the nations are defiled which I cast out before you: And the Land is defiled: therefore I do visit the iniquity thereof upon it, and the land vomiteth out her inhabitants" (Lev. 18:24). In their conquest of the New World we shall see Spanish Conquistadors employing similar arguments to justify a transfer of territories.

Chapter 20 adds to the general condemnation of chapter 18 a specific penalty for sexual relations between males. In framing this enactment, the authors of Leviticus wrote two dozen words which sealed the fate of men who loved men in the Western world for more than fourteen centuries. As rendered by the translators of the King James Bible, they were:

> If a man also lie with mankind, as he lieth with a woman, both of them have committed an abomination: they shall surely be put to death; their blood shall be upon them. (Lev. 20:13)

Unlike the legislation on ritual, this law was also taken to apply to non-Jews living under Jewish jurisdiction. John Boswell is mistaken in arguing that it was akin to enactments on ritual and not binding on gentiles.[1] Leviticus 18:26 specifically extends the prohibition to "any stranger that sojourneth among you." Such a law was one of the so-called Noachid precepts, binding on all the descendants of Noah—that is, on all humanity.

The ethic of the Hebrew Bible contains much that is humane. Its prophets and lawgivers show a sensitive concern for the oppressed and the weak. Perhaps their position as underdogs in Egypt and in the struggles with formidable empires that so often ended their independence bred in the Jews a special compassion. The Hebrew scriptures reveal sympathy for the "stranger" or alien, for the poor, for the deaf and blind, for orphans and widows, even for hungry animals whom the law protects. The same Levitical code that ordered the extermination of male homosexuals commanded men and women to love their neighbors as themselves. But for the priestly authors of Leviticus, a man who engaged in same-sex relations was not a neighbor. He was instead a deadly danger to be extirpated.

If Judaism had remained merely the religion of a tiny tribe in the eastern Mediterranean, such fierce bigotry, though deplorable, would have had relatively small effect. A man would simply have had to walk for a few days to escape its jurisdiction. But Judaism became the parent of a powerful world religion, Christianity; and though Christianity discarded Jewish rules on diet and grooming, on sowing mixed crops or wearing garments of mixed fabrics, it retained many Old Testament laws about sexuality. The Levitical statute thus became the model for laws decreeing capital punishment for homosexuality in Europe and in as much of the world as came under Europe's sway, down to the end of the eighteenth century. Indeed, the moral authority of Leviticus has been determinative even in this day; American courts routinely cited it as an argument for retaining state sodomy laws.[2] In 1986 the chief justice of the United States Supreme Court appealed to "millennia of moral teaching" as a reason for denying homosexuals any constitutional "right of privacy."[3] This moral teaching, as Chief Justice Warren Burger made clear, is in fact essentially Christian teaching with its roots in ancient biblical beliefs.

When the Roman Empire became Christian in the fourth century, the Old Testament death penalty for male homosexual behavior was incorporated into Roman law. Later, this same precedent was cited when death for homosexual behavior was prescribed by criminal codes in France, Spain, England, the Holy Roman Empire, the Italian states, Scandinavia, and every land settled by European colonists who professed Christianity. In all of these jurisdictions, so-called sodomites feared for their lives. William Blackstone, writing his *Commentaries on the Laws of England* (1765–1779), argued that the death penalty was a "universal" law of God and "not merely a provincial [that is, Jewish] precept."[4] Lesbians also, after the thirteenth century, suffered death in such countries as France, Spain, Italy, Switzerland, and Germany. Nor was this the whole story. Those men and women who did not directly feel the weight of the law still lived under its cloud. They faced intimidation, humiliation, and that kind of extra-legal violence that the moral authority of the law seemed to condone.

When a legislative tradition has caused unnecessary suffering for millions through more than a dozen centuries, we naturally wonder about its source. The question is especially acute when this harshness is so much at odds with other major cultures throughout world history—for example, Confucian China, Buddhist Japan, or Hindu India. But the answer is not easy to find, since our sources are few and obscure and we must often rely on speculation when certainty proves elusive. Laws proclaimed as divine decrees, like those of Leviticus, do not have explanatory preambles or rationales, and there is a paucity of records to which we may look for clues.

• The Threat to Population •

Most writers who have tried to understand the fierce homophobia of ancient Judea have sought an explanation, understandably enough, in its political and military situation. The Israelites, according to the Bible, were originally a nomadic people desperately seeking land on which to settle. Their ideological justification for their claim to Palestine lay in their belief that Yahweh had given them the territory of the Canaanites in return for loyalty to the cult his priests had evolved. Because of constant external threats, tribal solidarity—which came in time to mean religious solidarity—seemed crucial. This desperate need helps to explain the difference between the cultural history of the Jews and the Greeks. The Greeks triumphed over the Persians; the Jews were a much conquered people. Compared with Judaism, Greek religion seems lacking in heart, soul, and compassion for the unfortunate. Compared with Hellenism, Judaism in biblical times seems given to fanaticism and hysterical fears.

As a small tribe facing mighty and hostile powers—Egypt, Assyria, Babylonia, Persia—the Jews naturally strove to increase their numbers: military security demanded this. The concern for procreation has been the most commonly suggested rationale for the anti-homosexual legislation of Leviticus. Jewish popular tradition put great emphasis on marriage and large families. In Talmudic times unmarried men were censured and, on occasion, could be forced to wed. The ancient Jews frowned on celibacy and, the presumption is, on exclusive homosexuality. Yet it seems difficult to believe that this, in itself, would lead to so draconian a measure as the death penalty. Societies that have sought to discourage bachelorhood and childlessness have most often, as in the case of ancient Rome, laid civil disabilities on unmarried men, taxed them, or offered positive incentives to procreation.

An exception would be Nazi Germany, where Heinrich Himmler, chief architect of the Holocaust, was fanatically determined to increase the number of Nordic Aryans. To this end he favored the extermination of German homosexuals. "We must exterminate these people root and branch," he wrote. "Just think how many children will never be born because of this, and how a people can be broken in nerve and spirit when such a plague gets hold of it."[5] In the end Himmler and the Nazis sent thousands of homosexuals to death camps. Yet, though Philo and medieval theologians repeatedly raise the bugaboo of depopulation, no such idea is raised in the Hebrew scriptures or the Talmud. Rather, the motive for the prohibition and death penalty seems to have been religious and cultic, namely, anxiety over "defilements" that might incur the wrath of Yahweh.

A related explanation for the Levitical taboo has been anxieties about the waste of seed.[6] Yet the Hebrew Bible is, in fact, silent on the subject of masturbation. In Genesis 38, when Judah's son Onan is commanded by God to marry his brother's widow and father children by her, Onan deliberately "spills his seed" on the ground during intercourse. As punishment, he is struck dead. Though masturbation later came to be called "onanism" after this episode, for the authors of Genesis Onan's sin lay in his failure to fulfill the obligations of so-called Levirate marriage. The one law on wasted semen requires only that "if any man's seed of copulation go out from him, then he shall wash all his flesh in water and be unclean until the even" (Lev. 15:16).

In other words, the loss could be expiated by a simple act of ritual ablution. Despite the heated rhetoric of some Talmudists and medieval theologians who equated loss of sperm through masturbation with homicide, no society has ever been willing to legislate on this principle.

• Sodom's Gold •

William Blackstone argued that the death penalty for male homosexual relations was more than a merely Jewish law on the grounds that "the destruction of two cities by fire from heaven" took place long before Moses lived. But did the story of Sodom and Gomorrah in fact influence the authors of Leviticus? It is almost universally assumed that it did, and early Christian writers routinely invoked the fiery end of Sodom as proof of God's anger against the men who came to be known as "sodomites." But was this the meaning the tale actually bore in Old Testament times? A careful reading of the text, of early commentaries, and of the popular traditions preserved in the Talmud suggests that it was not.

The story of Sodom and Gomorrah belongs to the "J" narrative. This thread of Genesis, so called because in it God is referred to as Yahweh (German *J*ahweh), is regarded as the oldest of the various documents interwoven to make up the book of Genesis. It is generally thought to have been completed before 850 BCE, though J. A. Loader in his impressive study of the Sodom story in early Jewish tradition argues that the last part of Genesis 18 was not added until the eighth century.[7] The destruction of Sodom forms part of the Abraham saga, which, if we try to place it in historical context, would have to be dated about 2000 BCE. But how old the Sodom narrative is in its present form, or what details may have characterized earlier versions, we do not know.

The catastrophe that engulfs Sodom appears to embody the folk memory of some volcanic disaster, though no such event is known to have taken place near the Dead Sea in historical times. Like the story of Noah and the flood, the story has the style of a moral fable meant to emphasize God's power. This literary stylization is especially apparent in Abraham's repeated appeals to God in Genesis 18 to save the city if it has fifty, forty-five, thirty, twenty, or even ten righteous citizens. But despite the traditional interpretation of the Sodom story, no reference to homosexuality appears until the angelic messengers arrive in the next chapter. Before that we are merely told that "the men of Sodom were wicked and sinners before the Lord exceedingly" (Gen. 13:13). Sodom is to be destroyed for its generic wickedness. The threatened rape comes after the decision to annihilate the city has already been made. Nowhere has there been any statement as to what in particular had earlier roused God's wrath.

Genesis 19, by contrast, is full of specific details. When the angels warn

Abraham's nephew Lot to flee the city, he offers them shelter and is horrified when the men of Sodom—"young and old, all the people from every quarter"—demand that he surrender the visitors so they may "know" them. Shocked by this breach of the laws of hospitality, Lot offers instead his virgin daughters, "who have never known men," but the offer is rejected. The Sodomites attack but are blinded by God, and Lot and the angels escape. The city is then consumed by fire from heaven; along with the guilty men, women as well as children perish.

What are we to make of this drama? Some scholars, like Derrick Sherwin Bailey, have argued that to "know" in this context means simply to "identify" the angels, who are seen as suspicious strangers, but the offer of the daughters to assuage the men's lust would appear to support the traditional sexual interpretation.[8] Nevertheless, the subsequent use of the Sodom legend for anti-homosexual rhetoric and as a justification for harsh penalties for consensual relations is clearly wide of the mark. What is at issue here is not a consensual act but mass rape—sexual violence against two heavenly emissaries by an entire community.

Eventually the "sin of Sodom" was identified by the fathers of the church as male homosexuality in any context, regardless of consent. But not only is this interpretation not implied by the original story, the "sin of Sodom" does not seem to have been perceived as homosexuality by any of the Hebrew prophets who refer to it. As Bailey and Loader have aptly noted, the prophets often name Sodom as a wicked city but nowhere do they mention homosexuality. Isaiah, Jeremiah, Amos, and Zephaniah speak only in generalities. Jeremiah denounces the false prophets of Jerusalem as liars who commit adultery and abet evildoers, adding, "They are all unto me as Sodom" (23:14). This might seem to imply that one of the sins of Sodom was adultery, but this is by no means clear.

Only one prophet is specific as to the nature of Sodom's offense. Ezekiel, a contemporary of Sappho and Solon, grew up in Judea during the ministry of Jeremiah, was carried off captive to Babylon in 597 BCE, and began his preaching a few years later. He provides a unique list of Sodom's vices: "Behold, this was the iniquity of your sister [city] Sodom: she . . . had pride of wealth and food in plenty, comfort and ease, and yet she never helped the poor and wretched" (Ezek. 16:49, New English Bible). It is notable that Ezekiel names no sexual offenses, only sins against charity. Sodom is a city of men whose wealth makes them proud, luxurious, and idle and who remain indifferent to the plight of the poor.

We may ask if Ezekiel's view is idiosyncratic or whether it represents a significant interpretive tradition. Here the so-called *haggadoth,* or folkloric tales, of the Babylonian Talmud prove helpful. William Orbach has called these stories a window into "the collective psyche and ideas of the Jewish people."[9] When we examine them, we find that a tradition supporting

Ezekiel's view did indeed exist. The Babylonian Talmud, compiled between c. 370 and 500 CE, provides a series of stories about Sodom that are surprising both in content and tone. Instead of the usual solemn portentousness, we find touches of ironic humor. Sodom is presented as a city of great wealth, which it does not wish to share: "They said: since there cometh forth bread out of our earth and it hath the dust of gold [in it], why should we suffer wayfarers, who come to us only to deplete our wealth. Come, let us abolish the practice of traveling in our land."[10] One commentator in the Midrash described the city as so rich that gold dust fell from the roots of vegetables when they were dug from the ground.[11]

In these *haggadoth* the Sodomites go to great lengths to discourage immigrants, and a spate of anecdotes paints the extravagant injustice of their law courts. We are told that if someone cut off the ear of his neighbor's ass, a judge would order, "Give it to him till it grows again." A man who has injured another man's wife and caused a miscarriage is ordered by another whimsical magistrate to make her pregnant again. When another man accuses a Sodomite of wounding him, the judge makes the victim pay a fee for the "bleeding." Only Abraham's clever servant Eliezer outwits this unjust justice. Ordered to pay a fee for being assaulted, Eliezer smites the judge and asks that his own fee be transferred.[12] In this Kafkaesque world, victims are routinely found guilty, and impoverished aliens are treated with hypocritical charity, as in this succinct fable: "If a poor man happened to come there, every resident gave him a *denar* [a brick of gold], but no bread was given him. When he died, each came back and took his."[13]

Occasionally the Talmud glances at sex, as when the Sanhedrin calls the Sodomites "immoral in their bodies," but we are given no more details. Throughout, by far the commonest rebuke is for lack of charity. One third-century rabbi undertook to describe the precise act that provoked God to annihilate the city. In Genesis 18 the Lord tells Abraham that the "cry [complaint] of Sodom and Gomorrah" has reached him. Rabbi Judah's grim tale gives specificity to the "cry": "A certain maiden gave some bread to a poor man [hiding it] in a pitcher. On the matter becoming known, they daubed her with honey and placed her on the parapet of the wall and the bees came and consumed her. Thus it is written, *And the Lord said, The cry of Sodom and Gomorrah . . . is great.* Whereon Rab Judah commented . . . On account of the maiden."[14]

From these *haggadoth* we can understand why the expression "in the manner of Sodom" came to refer not to sexual conduct but to someone who refused to help, even though it would cost him nothing to do so—what we would call a "dog in the manger."[15] But how, then, does the dramatic detail of the threatened rape of the angels fit into this view of Sodom's guilt as social oppression? In the Midrash on Genesis—a commentary written about

700 CE—robbery and male rape are said to be means the Sodomites use to discourage strangers.[16] Such assaults are seen not as illicit pleasure but as a violent means of warding off intruders—just as Roman gardens sported phallic statues of the god Priapus inscribed with threats of rape to ward off thieves and trespassers.

The book of Ezekiel, which made Sodom a city heartless toward the needy, is generally dated about 590 BCE. But not until the writings of Philo is homosexuality unequivocally represented as intrinsic to Sodom's lifestyle and its preeminent sin—the view adopted by the fathers of the early church. What we may call the "Sodom of selfish wealth" considerably antedates the later Philonic-Patristic conception of the "homosexual Sodom." In the Gospels, Jesus, who was Philo's contemporary, refers often to Sodom but always as an inhospitable city, never as a homosexual one.[17]

• Who Were the *Kedeshim?* •

If the population hypothesis is dubious and the Sodom story scarcely relevant, we are left with the question, what was the motive for the draconian law in Leviticus? We may find a hint in the King James Bible, where the translators saw fit to introduce the word "sodomites" some half dozen times. It is used to translate the Hebrew word *kadesh* (plural *kedeshim*), which means literally "consecrated one" or "holy man." But who were these holy men and how did they come to be associated with homosexuality? The question has led to much debate and disagreement among commentators. This is not surprising, since the evidence is sparse and enigmatic. Yet it may in fact hold the most plausible clue to the Bible's homophobia.

The earliest mention of the *kedeshim* occurs in the first book of Kings during the reign of Solomon's son Rehoboam (c. 922–915 BCE). Rehoboam, whose tyrannical rule led the ten northern tribes to rebel and secede from Jerusalem, was the son of an Ammonite woman with pagan leanings. The author of the book of Kings accuses him of several heretical acts, including the building of "high places" for the worship of foreign images, especially images of the love-goddess Asherah. Then we are told in the King James rendering: "And there were also sodomites in the land: and they did according to all the abominations of the nations which the Lord cast out before the children of Israel" (1 Kings 14:24).

By way of contrast, Asa, Rehoboam's grandson, is described as doing "right in the eyes of the Lord," since he "removed all the idols which his fathers had made" and "took away the sodomites out of the land" (15:11–12). Nevertheless, the cult of the *kedeshim* proved tenacious, for we later learn that Jehoshaphat (c. 873–849) "took out of the land the remnant of the sodomites which remained in the days of his father, Asa" (22:46). Indeed, they are mentioned as late as the reign of King Josiah (c. 621), who is described as breaking down the "houses of the sodomites that were by the house of the Lord," that is, in a privileged position on the Temple Mount (2 Kings 23:7).

In Josiah's reign, a return to orthodoxy had taken place. The priest Hilkiah is represented as finding in the temple a scroll he identifies as a book of laws purportedly written by Moses some six hundred years earlier. When the book is read aloud, the young king tears his garments and laments that the Israelites had strayed so far from its teachings. The book found by Hilkiah was first identified as some portion of the book of Deuteronomy by the German scholar M. L. A. De Wette in 1805, an identification which has since won general acceptance. Deuteronomy has, moreover, proved the key to understanding much of biblical history. Modern scholarship regards the two books of Kings as strongly influenced by it, since rulers are praised or excoriated to the degree that their religious practices conform to those of the Deuteronomic reformers. In Deuteronomy we find the following prohibition: "There shall be no whore *[kadeshah]* of the daughters of Israel, nor a sodomite *[kadesh]* of the sons of Israel. Thou shall not bring the hire of a whore *[zonah]*, or the price of a dog *[kelebh]*, into the house of the Lord for any vow: for even both these are abominations unto the Lord thy God" (23:17–18). (At a Phoenician temple near Kition in Cyprus a tablet was found in the late nineteenth century listing "dogs" *[kelabhim]* as temple personnel to whom payments were made. The tablets, however, give no hint as to their function.)[18]

The modern reader is startled to find the Hebrew term *kadeshah* (the feminine of *kadesh*), which literally means "holy woman," translated by the blunt English word "whore." But concerning the role of the *kadeshah* we can be relatively certain. Female prostitution in religious cults was a phenomenon quite familiar in the ancient Near East.[19] Herodotus observed it at Babylon.[20] Temples of Astarte or Aphrodite housed sacred prostitutes in Phoenicia, Cyprus, and Sicily. The famous temple of Aphrodite at Corinth had one thousand sacred prostitutes in classical times. The custom of sexual service in honor of a deity engaged thousands of women in Indian temples well into the twentieth century. The ancient Hebrews were very familiar with such rites, which were repeatedly denounced by the prophets. Indeed, as the passage above makes clear, the word *kadeshah* or "holy woman" became synonymous with *zonah*, which meant simply a streetwalker. The Revised Standard Version of the Bible translates *kadeshah* with more exactness as "female cult prostitute."

But what of her male counterpart, the *kadesh?* Here is much confusion. The passage in Deuteronomy might be taken to suggest that he was also engaged in prostitution in a religious context. Was homosexuality in fact associated with religious cults in the ancient Near East? Writing about the time of Christ, Strabo, in his *Geography*, identifies the hierodules or temple servants in Corinth in Greece and at Eryx in Sicily as female prostitutes. But in describing the cult of the love-goddess Anaitis in Armenia, he mentions both female *and* male hierodules in a context which suggests that these "dedicated" men, like their female counterparts, performed the functions of sacred courtesans.[21] Such evidence is, however, rare. We learn much more, in fact, about male transvestites who served as priests or holy men. These were often eunuchs or self-castrates who lived the lives of pseudo-women, adopting feminine dress, ornaments, hair styles, and mannerisms.

Ancient Assyrian texts speak of religious functionaries called *assinnu* whom the goddess Innana (or Ishtar) had "changed from men to women in order to show the people piety," that is, to impress them with her supernatural power.[22] Transvestite priests or shamans have been described by anthropologists in India, in Dahomey, and in present-day African cults in Brazil.[23] Among the Eskimos of Siberia and Alaska, men who underwent a symbolic change in gender role were revered as shamans with potent magic. In many Native American tribes in the Great Plains and southwest, the so-called berdache—men who took on a "third-sex" role and on occasion "married" other males—were supposed to have special supernatural powers. A change in gender identity seemed so unusual that it was thought to signal a divine force at work.[24]

In classical times men of this sort were most in evidence as priests of the goddess whom the Mediterranean world knew as the Great Mother or Cybele. Her cult was ceremoniously introduced into Rome during the Punic War in 204 BCE when Rome's leaders sought to boost national morale in the struggle against Hannibal by transferring the holy stone of the goddess from Phrygia to the Palatine Hill.[25] Lucretius and Ovid depict in vivid detail the wild music, singing, and dancing of Cybele's priests during their processions in Rome, and Lucian describes similar phenomena at the shrine of the Syrian goddess at Hierapolis.[26] At the climax of the cult's frenzied rites, initiates castrated themselves and received women's garments.

Literary descriptions tend to emphasize these men's flamboyant theatricality and exaggerated femininity. Passive homosexuality, however, seems to have been imputed to them rather than openly acknowledged as part of their ritual. Augustine hints at it in *The City of God,* where they appear as religious beggars "with oily hair and whitened faces and soft limbs, passing with feminine gait through the squares and streets of Carthage, demanding [like] hucksters the means to continue their shameful life."[27] Apuleius makes them incontestably homosexual in *The Golden Ass,* and indeed *gallus,* the Latin term for Cybele's priests, became all but synonymous with *cinaedus,* a passive male.[28] These men were clearly assumed to play women's roles in private sexual encounters as well as in public ceremonies.

But did the *kedeshim* in fact have sexual relations in a religious context? The Revised Standard Version translates the term as "male cult prostitutes," which implies they did. The suggestion that they served women (made by Bailey and taken up by Boswell and Orbach) seems unlikely. If we call them "prostitutes" we must face the fact that historically male prostitution has overwhelmingly implied a homosexual context. Bailey argues that homosexual relations could have no part in "fertility cults."[29] But the term "fertility cult" begs the question. The sailors who resorted to the temple of Aphrodite in Corinth did not have reproduction in mind. Such cults simply celebrated the power of sex as a force of nature. Orbach, as a conservative Jew, is happy to adopt Bailey's view, since it removes any homosexual taint from earlier Judaism.[30] Boswell, on the other hand, simply says, "There is no reason to assume such prostitutes serviced persons of their own sex."[31]

We must look at the texts and weigh their implications carefully, however. The most important document used to decipher the language of the Hebrew scriptures has been the Septuagint, a Greek translation made in Alexandria sometime between 285 and 150 BCE, when Hebrew had ceased to be widely understood and the original text was unintelligible to many Egyptian Jews. But the Septuagint varies widely in accuracy from book to book, as can be seen from comparisons with the oldest Hebrew manuscripts. The Greek-speaking Jews of Alexandria clearly were often puzzled as to the meaning of the original Hebrew. When the translators tried to render *kedeshim* into Greek, they faced special problems. They may have been uncertain what the word meant, they may have known the meaning but were unable to find a Greek equivalent, or they may have wished to be evasive about a scandalous past. The prohibition in Deuteronomy 23:17 banning *kadesh* from "among the sons of Israel" they translated as "There shall be no prostituting *[porneuon]* of the sons of Israel." The Rehoboam passage "There were *kedeshim* in the land" becomes simply "There was coitus *[syndesmos]* in the land." In the case of Asa's purge, the word *kedeshim* becomes *teletas* ("initiation ceremonies"), turning the persons into a religious rite. With Josiah's reforms the Septuagint gives up and merely represents the Hebrew word by its Greek phonetic equivalent. So some of the words chosen suggest a sexual context, others a religious context, since Greek lacked a word for a male temple servant that united both connotations.[32]

The most interesting word choice, however, occurs in the Jehoshaphat episode, where the Septuagint translates the term *kadesh* as *endiellagmenos,* literally, one who was changed. Though the Greek translations that associate the *kedeshim* with sexual and religious functions might be merely a deduction from Deuteronomy 23:26–27 (verses which parallel them with their female counterparts), the conception of the *kedeshim* as those who were "changed" can hardly be derived in this fashion: its very oddity and specificity suggest that the translator was aware of some historical tradition not explicit in the text. One is inevitably struck by the parallel with the Assyrian *assinnu* who had been "changed" by the goddess into women and other cases of gender nonconformity in a religious setting, such as the *galli.*

One clear indication that later Jewish scholars interpreted *kadesh* in a homosexual sense appears in the Sanhedrin, that part of the Talmud which deals with legal procedures. Rabbi ben Elsiha, who taught in the first half of the second century CE, read the prohibition against the *kadesh* in Deuteronomy as a general condemnation of passive sodomy.[33] The influential commentary of Rashi (1040–1105) also gave *kadesh* a homosexual interpretation.[34] Saint Jerome adopted the same view in his Latin translation of the Hebrew Bible in 390–405. Jerome translates *kadesh* as *scortator* (fornicator) in Deuteronomy 23 but everywhere else uses the word *effeminatus,* which suggests a male who engages in passive relations. This is the tradition the King James translators presumably drew on.

Anxieties about population hardly seem to account for the death penalty in Leviticus, but concern for religious and tribal solidarity may well explain its adoption. In this regard, the ferocity of the law fits a clear and common biblical pattern. Certainly the book of Kings associated homosexuality with aboriginal Canaanite religions, and men who engaged in it would have been suspect as apostates. In ancient Judea, apostasy was regarded as a capital offense, as in medieval Christianity and in some modern Islamic states. The terrible words of Deuteronomy 13:6–10 leave no doubt about the orthodox view:

> If thy brother, the son of thy mother, or thy son, or thy daughter, or the wife of thy bosom, or thy friend, which is as thine own soul, entice thee secretly, saying, Let us go and serve other gods, which thou hast not known, thou, nor thy fathers, namely, the gods of the people which are round about you, nigh unto thee, or far off from thee, from the one end of the earth even unto the other end of the earth . . . thou shalt surely kill him, thy hand shall be first upon him to put him to death, and afterwards the hand of all the people. And thou shalt stone him with stones that he die.

The *kedeshim,* as devotees of a heretical religion, would presumably have been liable to similar punishment.

• Philo of Alexandria •

Few Jewish authors in antiquity refer even briefly to homosexuality, and only one treats the subject in any detail. This was Philo of Alexandria, a theologian and mystic who sought to reconcile Mosaic law with Platonic philosophy. Since his life span encompassed the lives of both Jesus and Paul, Philo's writings are of special interest; they give us vivid insight into the mind of an orthodox Jew at the moment of the birth of Christianity. Widely read by early Christian theologians, Philo has been called the father of the fathers of the church, though he remained a faithful Jew all his life. What gave him preeminence was his thorough familiarity with both Judaic and Greek traditions. Equally steeped in Plato and the Bible, he took as his mission the defense of Jewish religion and law before Greek and Roman readers. This was a project that interested early Christian apologists greatly, since they were also trying to bridge the two worlds of Jew and Hellene.

In *The Special Laws,* written about 30 or 40 CE, Philo defends the Levitical penalty for homosexuality, attempting to rationalize a purportedly divine command so at odds with Greco-Roman customs. He first makes a case against the kind of homosexual the gentiles in his audience would be most inclined to despise, the effeminate passive male. Philo's comments are unique in their detailed specificity:

> Much graver than [adultery] is another evil, which has ramped its way into the cities, namely pederasty. In former days the very mention of it was a great disgrace, but now it is a matter of boasting not only to the active but to the passive partners, who habituate themselves to endure the disease of effemination, let both body and soul run to waste, and leave no ember of their male sex-nature to smolder. Mark how conspicuously they braid and adorn the hair of their heads, and how they scrub and paint their faces with cosmetics and pigments and the like, and smother themselves with fragrant unguents . . . In fact the transformation of the male nature to the female is practised by them as an art and does not raise a blush. These persons are rightly judged worthy of death by those who obey the law [of Moses], which ordains that the man-woman who debases the sterling coin of nature should perish unavenged, suffered not to live for a day or even an hour, as a disgrace to himself, his house, his native land and the whole human race.[35]

Since, in traditional fashion, Philo sees women as inferior to men, androgyny is threatening to him: any man who willfully adopts female characteristics has irredeemably degraded himself in his eyes.

The Greeks and Romans also ridiculed men who compromised their masculinity by wearing women's clothes. But cross-dressing on ritual or festive occasions was often acceptable. Hercules and Achilles, archetypal male heroes, were both supposed to have worn women's dress. The priests of Hercules regularly cross-dressed, though women were banned from his temples. In Sparta a bride cut her hair short and wore male attire when she first received her husband; at Argos she wore a false beard. On the island of Cos the pattern was reversed, and the bridegroom dressed as a girl to meet his new wife. In the cult of the hermaphroditic Aphroditos, each sex assumed the dress of the other.[36] But Hebrew law forbade the wearing of garments of the opposite sex as "an abomination unto the Lord" (Deut. 22:5), no doubt because such exchanges were associated with other religions.

But what is most startling is Philo's violence—he thinks effeminate men should not be allowed to live "for a day or even an hour" and in effect urges his co-religionists in Alexandria to attack and kill them on sight. Whereas a Greek or Roman might have scorned or satirized male effeminacy, Philo is roused to homicidal fury by this subversion of gender roles. His willingness to dispense with traditional procedures and allow individuals to act extralegally is especially shocking when we recall that Philo was a jurist of some renown. He was a highly respected member of Alexandria's Jewish community, chosen as its representative in a famous embassy to Rome to plead against a law of the Emperor Caligula, an occasion on which he displayed great courage.

Philo's intolerance of sodomites was of a piece with his intolerance of apostates from Judaism. These, he wrote, should be taken "to no court" but should be summarily punished by mob action. Such a mob, he wrote, should "regard themselves for the time being as everything, as counselors, as judges, Roman magistrates, members of the legislative assembly, accusers, witnesses, laws, and the public itself so that unhindered and unafraid they may dauntlessly carry out the fight for holiness." As Erwin Goodenough has remarked, "It would be difficult to find the lynching spirit better [expressed] in any literature."[37] Street violence against homosexuals today is most often the expression of young men seeking to assert their masculinity and only rarely "a fight for holiness," though murders have been justified on this ground. But this tradition of violence obviously has deep historical roots in religious prejudice.

Of especial anthropological interest is Philo's brilliant picture of effeminate priests marching in proud splendor among the crowds of first-century Alexandria. From a Greek point of view, the prestige of male homosexuality sprang, first of all, from its association with heroic warriors. In Philo's hostile eyes, it derived from the prominent role effeminate homosexuals played in certain religious cults. The popularity of such abominations, he thinks, can best be explained by

> the prizes awarded in many nations to licentiousness and effeminacy. Certainly you may see these hybrids of man and woman continually strutting about through the thick of the market, heading the processions at the feasts, appointed to serve as unholy ministers of holy things, leading the mysteries and initiations and celebrating the rites of Demeter. Those of them who . . . have desired to be completely changed into women and gone on to mutilate their genital organs are clad in purple like signal benefactors of their native lands, and march in front escorted by a bodyguard,

> attracting the attention of those who meet them. But if such indignation as our lawgiver [Moses] felt was directed against those who do not shrink from such conduct, if they were cut off without condonation as public enemies, each of them a curse and a pollution of his country, many others would be found to take the warning.[38]

Demeter, a mother goddess, did not have transvestite priests. Philo is probably identifying her with Cybele, who was more often identified with Saturn's wife Rhea, the Mother of the Gods.

Philo wants to begin his pogrom with the killing of transvestite priests as the most heinous manifestation of homosexuality. But Leviticus 20:13 required that *both* men in a homosexual relationship be put to death. Thus Philo must still give reasons for killing the active partner. In a much calmer mood, he invokes the threat to population: the active homosexual male, he claims, "renders cities desolate and uninhabited by destroying the means of procreation."[39] But Philo is now obviously trying to think up reasons instead of giving vent to violent feelings. When he prescribes the death penalty for the active role, his arguments have an after-the-fact perfunctoriness and indeed, as we shall see, rather closely echo the arguments and language of Plato's *Laws.*

• The Talmud •

The Hebrew scriptures make no mention of lesbianism. Unlike male homosexuality, it does not seem to have been regarded as a crime. The Talmud records that Rabbi Huna (d. 296 CE) ruled that "women who practise lewdness with one another are disqualified from marrying a priest." (Jewish law required that a priest's wife be a virgin.) But even this mild sanction is rejected by the Talmud, which accepts instead the view of Rabbi Eleazar (c. 150 CE), who saw lesbianism as no bar to priestly marriage, since "the action is regarded as a mere obscenity."[40]

Many centuries later, in medieval Europe, female and male homosexuality were placed on a par by the law in Christian states, and women were executed.[41] How then are we to account for Jewish leniency? Obviously lesbianism, like male relations, might have also been considered a threat to population. One theory is that less concern was shown because no seed was wasted, or that men did not care what women did among themselves (though this view hardly applied to witchcraft). If the legislation against males derived from the prejudice against *kedeshim,* however, this would explain the discrepancy. No prejudice against lesbianism would have derived from the religious practices of the *kadeshah,* which were heterosexual in nature.

In the fourth and fifth centuries of the Common Era Jewish scribes labored at writing down the immense compilation of oral law and interpretive opinions that came to make up the Talmud. In the Sanhedrin, the tractate dealing with legal procedure in criminal cases, the rabbis followed Leviticus in making male relations a capital crime. But here, as elsewhere, they were not rhetorical in the style of Philo or Paul or the fathers of the church. The legend of Sodom was not used to rouse hysterical fears, as it was in contemporary Christian literature. Homosexuality was always condemned but rarely singled out for special emphasis. Rabbi Huna quaintly held that "the Generation of the Flood were only blotted out of the world on account of their having written hymenean songs for sodomy."[42] Another rabbi thought sodomy had caused an eclipse, but so had the death of a judge who had not been properly mourned.[43] Homosexuality is presented less as a sensual temptation—Jews in Talmudic times were not even to be suspected of sodomy—than as an indignity a Jew might suffer, like the threatened assault on the angels at Sodom.[44] Male Jewish captives should be ransomed before Jewish captive women because their defilement would be the greater outrage.[45] One story, not otherwise known to history, told how three shiploads of Jewish men, condemned to the brothels of Rome by Vespasian, had committed suicide by plunging overboard.[46]

The Talmud is not without tenderness and compassion, even in its treatment of criminal law. On some occasions, lynching was condoned, as Philo had proposed, but some rabbis thought it a shame to apply the death penalty once in seven years, or in seventy.[47] Elaborate rules of evidence must at times have made convictions difficult. Still, the Talmud is consistent in its view that relations between healthy adult males were to be regarded as capital offenses. Indeed, the execution was to be accomplished by the most severe method—stoning. The Talmud lays down the procedure in gruesome detail:

> The place of stoning was twice a man's height. One of the witnesses pushed him by the hips, [so that] he was overturned on his heart. He was then turned on his back. If that caused his death, [the witness] had fulfilled [his duty] but if not, the second witness took the stone and threw it on his chest. If he died thereby [the witness] had done [his duty] but if not, [the criminal] was stoned by all Israel. For it is written: the hand of the witnesses shall be first upon him to put him to death, and afterwards the hand of all the people.[48]

The stone that was dropped from the height was so heavy that two men were needed to lift it. As with most crimes designated as capital in the Bible, we have no record of the death penalty's actually being carried out. It may have been, and homosexuals may have been beaten to death in Alexandria and other Jewish settlements. But after 70 CE the Romans deprived the court at Jerusalem of its legal powers, and we do not know how homosexuals were treated in the Jewish communities of the Diaspora.

In modern times, history's first homosexual liberation movement began in

Germany in the last decade of the nineteenth century. It was led by Magnus Hirschfeld, a Jewish sexologist and reformer. In the 1920s he was beaten and left for dead by Nazi thugs; when Hitler came to power, Hirschfeld's research institute was destroyed and the movement he founded suppressed.[49] In conservative anti-Semitic Vienna, Sigmund Freud spoke out bravely for homosexual law reform. In the United States, Reform Judaism has proved more liberal than most Christian churches. Its national organization, the American Union of Hebrew Congregations, has granted official recognition to a number of gay synagogues. On the other hand, Orthodox Judaism in America has strongly opposed homosexual civil rights, citing Leviticus' genocidal verse at public hearings. The article on homosexuality in the compendious *Encyclopaedia Judaica* (written by the Grand Rabbi of the British Commonwealth) is strongly hostile to modern "liberal" views. But contemporary developments in Israel have nevertheless moved in a liberal direction. In 1988 the Israeli parliament decriminalized sodomy, negating the prohibition in the land where Western laws had their ancient birth. And in January 1992 the Knesset approved a measure "safeguarding equal opportunities in jobs, stating that employers shall not discriminate between employees or applicants for jobs because of their sexual preference."[50] In 2002, Jews and Arabs marched together in Jerusalem's first gay pride parade.

Taking the world as a whole, Judaism in itself has had very little direct influence on the fate of homosexuals. Indirectly, however, through the prejudices it passed on to Christianity, its influence has been enormous. As with other religious teachings that have fostered persecutions and bloody wars, the burning of witches, the silencing and subjection of women, and the practice of slavery, the noble and generous side of the Hebrew scriptures has been too often overshadowed by darker forces. Above all, it was one of the tragedies of world history that the Jewish convert to Christianity who did most to shape the theology and sexual ethics of the new religion—Saint Paul—was to approach the subject with Philo's vehemence rather than in the spirit of his new faith's founder.

CHAPTER THREE

CLASSICAL GREECE

480–323 BCE

• Pindar's Odes •

The classical age in ancient Greece is usually conceived as extending from the battle of Marathon in 490 to the defeat of the Greek allies by Philip of Macedon at Chaeronea in 338. Among its finest achievements are to be reckoned the establishment of democracy at Athens, the Athenian tragic drama, the comedies of Aristophanes, the sculpting of the Olympian Zeus by Phidias, the philosophical dialogues of Plato in the fourth century, and—if we extend the period by a generation or two—the teachings of the Stoics. After 400 the political leadership of Greece passed from Athens to Sparta and then to Thebes. The Macedonian phalanxes extinguished Greek liberty at Chaeronea but spread Greek culture to undreamt-of distant realms through the campaigns of Alexander. In all of these culminating developments in literature, art, philosophy, and war, male love in some form or other was to play a part.

The herald of this cultural efflorescence was the poet Pindar, who was thirty when the Athenians triumphed over the Persians at Marathon. Born in a Boeotian village near Thebes, he ranked after Sappho as Hellas' greatest lyric poet. Like Alcaeus and Theognis before him, Pindar was an aristocrat with ties to many noble families. Consequently his poetic eulogies of young men pay much heed to birth and breeding. But unlike his predecessors, he was not soured by political strife. Pindar saw his art as a noble calling in which inspiration and a superbly polished technique served one high purpose. His odes are stately, dignified, and sublime, his elevated style contrasting with the unbuttoned casualness of Ibycus and Anacreon in much the same way that Milton's solemnity in seventeenth-century England would differ from the witty colloquialism of Donne and the cavalier poets. But if Pindar differed from his predecessors in style, he shared one characteristic: Athenaeus classed him with Ibycus and Anacreon as a notably, even "immoderately," erotic poet. After citing some of Pindar's most impassioned praise of youthful athletes, he observed, "Altogether, many persons prefer liaisons with males to those with females."[1]

A cliché of traditional classical scholarship claims that "the homosexual ethos seemed limited to an elite subculture."[2] But Pindar's odes—which were very much public poetry, sung formally at ceremonies in halls or temples or in front of a victor's house—unselfconsciously treat of homoerotic desire. In his first Olympian ode Pindar rewrites Greek mythology. According to the received legend, Tantalus had chopped up his son Pelops and served him to the gods at dinner to test their omniscience. Pindar rejects this story as degrading to the gods' dignity. Pelops temporarily disappears in Pindar's ode, not because he is boiled in a cauldron but because Poseidon has abducted him for amorous purposes, thus setting a precedent for Zeus's later rape of Ganymede. Pindar's remodeling of the story was meant as a compliment to Pelops, whose history, told in marble, adorned a famous temple at Olympia, and to Elis, the nearby city that claimed Pelops as its legendary founder.

Though he challenged Ganymede's precedence, Pindar used the myth in other odes. In the tenth Olympian, he describes the young boxer Hagesidamus as "fair to look upon" and "graced with that bloom which, in olden days, by the blessing of Aphrodite, warded off from Ganymede a ruthless fate"—that is, the mortality Zeus's love spared him.[3] But it is not only handsome faces and muscled bodies that appeal to Pindar; in the Sixth Pythian he also compliments Thrasybulus on his modesty, his literary talent, and the amiability of his temper, which outdoes the sweetness of the "honey-bee."

Though Pindar preached moderation in love and cautiously limited it to its "due season," his emotions did not always accord with his maxims. In his old age he fell in love with Theoxenus of Tenodos, who revived all his youthful ardor:

> Right it were, my heart,
> To cull the flowers of love in due season, in life's prime.
> But whosoever, once he has seen the rays
> Flashing from the eyes of Theoxenus,
> Is not tossed on the waves of desire
> Has a black heart forged, in cold flame, of adamant or of iron,
> Having no honor from Aphrodite of the quick glance . . .
> But I to grace the goddess, like wax of the sacred bees
> When smitten by the sun,
> Am melted when I look at the young limbs of boys.[4]

One account of Pindar's death tells how, aged eighty, he died in the theater of Argos leaning upon the shoulder of Theoxenus.[5]

• Greek Tragedy •

We may assume that some Greek lyric poetry, like some modern verse, was written for a specialized audience. But Athenian drama, to justify the expense of public performances, must necessarily have had a wide appeal. Were homoerotic themes popular in the classical Athenian theater? Here is Athenaeus' testimony on the point: "So active was the pursuit of love-affairs, since no one regarded erotic persons as vulgar, that even a great poet like Aeschylus, and Sophocles, introduced in the theater love themes in their tragedies—the first that of Achilles and Patroclus, the second that of the boys in *Niobe:* hence some call the tragedy *Paederastria* [sic] and the audience gladly accepted such stories."[6] Here Athenaeus not only reveals the existence of a class of dramas now lost to us but vouches for their breadth of appeal.

It is assumed that Aeschylus' lost play *The Myrmidons* showed Patroclus donning the armor of Achilles to fight at Troy and Achilles' grief when his friend was killed. We know it now only from fragments, but its outline is fairly clear.[7] Its emotional climax was Achilles' speech over his lover's corpse. Finding Patroclus' body stripped naked on the battlefield by the Trojans, Achilles reproached the dead man in two lines that underlined the sexual side of their passion: "Had you no reverence for the unsullied holiness of your thighs / Ungrateful for the many kisses I gave you?"[8] Sophocles struck a similarly erotic note in another lost play, *The Colchian Women,* where he described Ganymede as "setting Zeus's majesty aflame with his thighs."[9]

That Sophocles' *Niobe* should have been renowned as a play about male love may seem especially strange. In the legend, Niobe boasts that she had borne more children than Leto, the mother of Apollo and Artemis. For this hubris the divine pair shoot dead her seven sons and seven daughters. It is difficult to imagine how an erotic interest can have been paramount in this devastating maternal tragedy. Plutarch, however, gives a detail that confirms Athenaeus: "When the children of Niobe, in Sophocles, are being pierced and dying, one of them cries out, appealing to no other rescuer or ally than his lover."[10] The moment cannot have been merely incidental: the re-titling of the play as the *Paederastria* shows that the theme must somehow have been fully developed in the drama.

Though we know little of Aeschylus' love affairs, a plethora of tales have come down to us about his fellow dramatists. We learn that, in bisexual Athens, Sophocles, a strikingly handsome youth himself, was chiefly attracted to young men. Athenaeus calls him "as fond of young lads as Euripides was fond of women."[11] Plutarch, in his life of Pericles, records an episode during a naval expedition: when the poet praised a beautiful boy, presumably a young recruit, Pericles warned him that a general must keep not only his hands clean but even his eyes.[12] Yet, as was customary, Sophocles married and had children; one son, Iophon, also wrote tragedies.

Matthew Arnold hailed Sophocles as a serene sage who saw "life steadily and saw it whole." But this Victorian dignity is hardly projected by Plutarch or Plato or by other anecdotes that have come down to us. One story tells how, on a visit to Chios, Sophocles tricked a handsome wine-bearer into bringing his lips near his cup so he could steal a kiss. In his defense Sophocles declared: "I am practicing strategy, gentlemen, since Pericles told me that though I could write poetry I didn't know how to be a general."[13] The gossipy Hieronymos of Rhodes recounts another anecdote: when Sophocles was sixty-five he lost his cape to a boy who made off with it after they had consorted in a field outside Athens. Euripides teased him by boasting that he had enjoyed the youth "without paying any bonus."[14]

Euripides, the last of the three great tragedians, also wrote at least one play on a pederastic theme, his lost *Chrysippus,* which told of the boy's rape by Oedipus' father Laius, king of Thebes. Euripides' fascination with women did not preclude an interest in his own sex. In 408, at odds with the Athenians who disapproved of his religious skepticism, he accepted an invitation to the court of King Archelaus of Macedon. Archelaus, an enthusiastic patron of Athenian culture, was already host to Euripides' fellow dramatist Agathon, who ranked next after the three immortals as a writer of tragedies. Agathon was both beautiful and effeminate—a side of his personality satirized by Aristophanes in the *Thesmophoriazusae.* In Plato's *Symposium,* supposedly set in 416 BCE on the occasion of Agathon's winning the prize for tragedy, Aristophanes classifies Pausanias and Agathon as males who are attracted to other men, hinting that they are lovers, and Socrates makes the same assumption when he encounters them together in the *Protagoras.*[15] When Euripides (at age seventy) arrived in Macedon, he fell in love with the younger playwright, who was then about forty. As a couple they became the proverbial instance of love between older men. Plutarch concludes: "Euripides . . . observed upon embracing and kissing Agathon, though the latter's beard had already grown, that even the autumn of the fair is fair."[16]

· Phidias ·

As Aeschylus, Sophocles, and Euripides were supreme in drama, so Phidias ranked first in sculpture. His Olympian Zeus was perhaps the most admired work of art in classical antiquity. To Dio Chrysostom it was "the guardian of Hellas when she is of one mind and not distraught with faction": "When you stand before this statue, you forget every misfortune of our earthly life, even though you have been broken by adversities and grief . . . so great is the splendor and beauty of the artist's creation."[17] Pliny called it the statue "which nobody has ever rivaled."[18] Quintilian declared that "its beauty can be said to have added something to traditional religion, so adequate to the divine nature is the majesty of his work."[19] Eventually it was counted among the Seven Wonders of the World. Unfortunately, all of Phidias' masterpieces have perished: his manner can now best be judged from the Parthenon frieze, which he designed and supervised.

Two of Phidias' *eromenoi* are known to us. One was Agoracritus of Paros, his pupil and disciple, who modeled a colossal Nemesis at Rhamnus in Attica.[20] So close was this statue in style to Phidias that it was rumored Phidias crafted the work for his lover and allowed him to palm it off as his own. Pantarces of Elis was even more closely associated with the sculptor. A statue at Olympia commemorated his victory in the games, and another at Elis honored him for making peace with the Achaeans and effecting the release of prisoners of war.[21] Pausanias reports a tradition that Phidias memorialized their love by representing Pantarces as an athlete in the frieze that decorated the base of his Zeus at Olympia, where the young man was shown binding his head with a ribbon.[22] Phidias also paid amorous homage by inscribing on the finger of the god the words *Pantarces kalos* ("Pantarces is beautiful"), much to the scandal of one Christian critic, Clement of Alexandria, who found united in this one detail two of his prime aversions, homosexuality and paganism.[23]

• The Comedies of Aristophanes •

Greek tragedies on male love have vanished, leaving only comments and occasional lines. But there is no dearth of references to homosexuality in the comedies of Aristophanes, the first of which was performed in 427, a few years after Phidias' death. In the *Thesmophoriazusae* ("The Women at the Thesmorphoria," a festival of the mother-goddess Demeter, from which men were excluded), Agathon appears dressed as a woman, his excuse being that he is writing a tragedy and must imagine himself in the role of its heroine. Another favorite target is the contemptible Cleisthenes (not the restorer of democracy but a professional informer of ill repute), who is mocked in the *Acharnians* as an effeminate eunuch and in the *Lysistrata* as a resource for sex-starved husbands whose wives are on strike.

This ridicule shows that not all forms of consensual homosexual behavior were approved by the Greeks. In particular, it demonstrates how the Greeks saw effeminacy in the male as degrading. The masculine status of the adult Athenian male was not jeopardized by sexual acts with other men or boys so long as he took the dominant, active role. Literary and anthropological evidence shows this bias to be widespread. It is reflected in Greek comedy and in the satirical epigrams of the Greek Anthology; in Roman poetry in the attacks on effeminate men in Catullus, Juvenal, and Martial, all of whom favor boy love but violently excoriate the passive adult; and in the "macho" ethic of the modern Mediterranean world and Latin America, where the maintenance of the male role is the crucial concern. In imperial Rome, as Christianity took hold, this cultural trait was to have deadly consequences in Roman law.

This being the case, *katapygnos* (having broad buttocks) and *euryproctos* (having a wide anus) were common abusive epithets in Attic Greek. Aristophanes uses them freely. Sometimes they mean merely "contemptible" or "trashy," but some sexual coloring remains. What is surprising is how frequently Aristophanes applies them to his fellow citizens. Politicians, lawyers, and generals are all berated as *euryproctoi,* that is, men who will stoop to anything to succeed. In *The Clouds,* Aristophanes' spokesman, Right Logic, includes the audience generally in the charge. There is, undoubtedly, something unpleasant in this phenomenon—the closest Aristophanes comes to gay-baiting. It must have elicited forced and uneasy laughter by playing on the audience's fear of demasculinization and reinforcing prejudices against men who did not conform to the Athenian male stereotype. Philo's homicidal fury lay ahead.

But Aristophanes is no puritan. Casual sexual encounters of all sorts seem as desirable to Aristophanes' plebeian heroes as they seemed abhorrent to Socrates, Plato, and their circle. As usual in Greek society, bisexuality is taken for granted. When Dionysos in *The Frogs* admits to an urge, Heracles unselfconsciously asks whether it is for a woman, a boy—or a man? (Only the latter would have provoked a snicker: Dionysos is the only Greek deity represented in myth as playing a passive role.)[24] The boisterous Athenian workmen who are Aristophanes' protagonists are randy for any kind of sex that does not compromise their maleness. Philocleon in the *Wasps* enjoys examining naked boys as part of his jury duty. In the *Acharnians,* Dicaepolis hails the phallic god he worships as an "adulterer" and *paiderastes.*[25] At the conclusion of the *Knights,* its hero is awarded both a boy and a troop of girls as prizes.[26] In the *Birds,* Peisetairos fantasizes a utopia "where the father of a good-looking boy will meet me and go on at me as if I've done him a wrong: 'That was a nice way to treat my son, Stilbonides! You met him when he'd had a bath, leaving the gymnasium, and you didn't kiss him, you didn't say a word to him, you didn't pull him close to you, you didn't tickle his balls—and you an old friend of the family!'"[27]

No side of human life is idealized in Aristophanes. Gods, statesmen, poets, military commanders, wives—everyone in these comedies is venal, coarse, lecherous, gluttonous. Even Dionysus, the patron of the festival at which the plays were presented, is portrayed as a coward and buffoon. It is not surprising, therefore, that male love is treated without glamour or sentiment. Perhaps the character who comes closest to recognizing an ideal side to pederasty is Karion in *Wealth,* who laments that boys no longer yield to men from love but only for gifts or money.[28]

• Plato's *Symposium* •

So far, our picture of male amours in ancient Greece has been drawn from poetry, drama, art, and historical anecdotes. With the dawn of the fourth century, new and more complex perspectives appear. The philosophical discourses of Plato and Xenophon offer a cornucopia of opinions and insights, with vivid glimpses of the intimate side of Greek social life. In the place of fragmentary comments we have elaborate debates, with a wealth of sociological detail and, in the case of Plato, subtle characterizations and touches of irony. Undoubtedly the most brilliant and instructive of these works is Plato's *Symposium.* But its very richness presents special challenges. Its seven speakers were well-known Athenians who express significantly different views on the male eros. This raises important questions. Do the words Plato puts in their mouths, so often at odds with his own, represent views widely held in Athens, or were they simply idiosyncratic? And to what extent was Plato's own position, conveyed through his mouthpiece Socrates, accepted by Greek society? Was it typical, or was it rather the view of a utopian dreamer, like his proposals regarding marriage and property in the *Republic?*

Plato's outlook was colored by his heredity. He was born into a wealthy aristocratic family claiming descent from Solon and Athens' ancient kings. In 404, at the end of the Peloponnesian War, relatives and friends of Plato participated in the oligarchic terror that convulsed Athens under the Council of Thirty; the restored democracy, in revenge, executed Socrates in 399. Plato's detestation of popular government must have been powerfully reinforced by this judicial murder. His own social philosophy combined the Cynics' devotion to the simple life (rejecting both luxury and familial comforts) with an aristocratic ideal of service which sank individualism in Spartan communalism. Like most Greeks, he was passionately devoted to intellectual debate. He was also Greek in his ardent belief in love—that is, male love. But he abhorred pleasure as much as he did democratic politicians, and sexual pleasure was for him especially threatening. Plato's ideal lovers remain palpitatingly desirous of each other but unremittingly chaste.

His own susceptibility to young men—to judge from his poignant descriptions of such feelings in the *Charmides* and *Phaedrus*—must have been intense. Diogenes Laertius in a biographical sketch quotes five poems ascribed to Plato as evidence of his "passionate affection" for males. (There are also three, less certainly Plato's, addressed to women.) Agathon's kisses, Plato declares, draw his soul fluttering to his lips. Of Aster, his pupil in astronomy, he wrote, punning on his name: "Star-gazing Aster, would I were the skies, / To gaze upon thee with a thousand eyes."[29] In another poem he hesitates to praise Alexis' beauty: he lost Phaedrus through such praise. Plato's authorship of these lines has occasionally been challenged, but most scholars regard them as authentic.

Plato's best-documented attachment, in which love, politics, and philosophy mingled, was for Dion of Syracuse. Dion was the nephew of the tyrant Dionysos, who ruled Sicily and southern Italy. Enamored of Plato's wisdom, Dion brought him to Syracuse in 387 hoping to win his uncle over to a less harsh and arbitrary form of government. The visit was a notable failure, but Plato returned twenty years later, again at Dion's request, to act as mentor to the tyrant's heir. But the second Dionysos proved no more tractable than the first: Dion was exiled and Plato with him. After throwing himself enthusiastically into the founding of the Academy at Athens, the conscientious but arrogant and self-righteous Dion invaded Sicily and overthrew Dionysos, only to be himself assassinated after a brief, turbulent reign. The depth of Plato's feeling for him is clear in the epitaph he composed: "[Now] in your wide-wayed city, honored at last, you rest, / O Dion, whose love once maddened the heart within this breast."[30]

Plato wrote the *Symposium* about 385, shortly after his first journey to Syracuse. The dialogue, set thirty years earlier at Agathon's house where friends have met to celebrate his victory as a dramatist, provides an engaging picture of casual Greek manners. The men recline in pairs on couches, a custom which invited some amorous teasing, and compete in composing panegyrics on love—what modern stag party would choose such a theme? Though statements by the various speakers are often carelessly cited as "according to Plato," they represent, in fact, quite various attitudes, and it is necessary, if we are to understand what the dialogue has to tell us about Athenian views on homosexuality, to differentiate them carefully.

Some assumptions are shared. All assume that serious love will usually mean love between men, generally love of an older for a younger male. Phaedrus strikes the keynote: love is an exalted experience, to be fostered and cherished. His argument is first of all, as we have seen, the traditional military one. The crucial test is the lovers' willingness to face death, a more likely test of men than of women. Phaedrus does, however, recognize one notable exception—Alcestis, who died to prolong the life of her husband, Admetus. But Achilles, who sacrificed himself to avenge his beloved Patroclus, ranks as the archetype of hero-lovers.

Phaedrus' speech is naive, enthusiastic, uncritical. It is no doubt meant to represent the first notions that might come into the mind of a literate Athenian of an idealistic turn. In his pro-amorist zeal he goes so far as to conjure up an "army of lovers" who, fighting side by side, might conquer the world. More startling still is his novel claim that a city of lovers would be, of all communities, the "best governed"—another speaker will take up this theme. But throughout we are left in the dark on one point: is the love he is extolling "platonic" in the common sense of the word, or does it allow for a sexual element?

Pausanias, the next speaker, takes up this point. The Greeks worshiped gods under different aspects in different places: Aphrodite bore, among others, the epithets Pandemos ("of all the people" or "of the streets") and Urania (daughter of Uranus or Heaven). From these two designations Pausanias derives his distinction between two kinds of love, a lower (or common) love and a higher (or heavenly) love, both associated with the goddess. This distinction is so much a commonplace of Western ethics that one is startled to realize that this is its first appearance. The lower love is purely carnal, the higher adds spirit to flesh. (It is important to realize that Pausanias' "heavenly love"—unlike later versions—does not exclude the physical.) They are further differentiated by the objects of their desire. The common love is such as the "meaner sort of men" feel for women as well as youths. The other, higher love is the love of youths whose beards have started to sprout, that is, of "intelligent beings whose reason is beginning to be developed."[31]

Pausanias thus gives a rationale for Athenians who are attracted to post-adolescent males. In this he challenges the traditional norm: most Greeks considered beardless boys the more appropriate objects of desire. To argue that his is no merely eccentric taste, Pausanias appeals to two other Greek values: pleasure in intellectual converse (which only older youths are capable of) and enduring fidelity. The love of boys is fleeting, but devotees of the Uranian Aphrodite who choose young men, he claims, "are ready to be faithful to their companions, and pass their whole life with them, not to take them in their inexperience and . . . then run away to others."[32] We know that many Greeks had relations with both women and boys. But Pausanias clearly identifies another class of man—a *class* who are exclusively devoted to their own sex, approximating the modern conception of the "homosexual." This idea of a homosexual "orientation," though by no means central to Greek thinking as it is to ours, was certainly understood by Plato and his contemporaries.

Sentiment in ancient Greece overwhelmingly approved male love, but on the question as to whether such love should be physical, opinion was divided. Pausanias takes a middle ground: boys may grant their favors to men but only under certain conditions. In Elis and Boeotia male relations are fully accepted by the law, and sexual contact is taken for granted. The suppression of male love in Ionia he explains as a policy of tyrannical rulers. Pausanias rejects both traditions, the first as libertine, the second as repressive, arguing instead that an honorable young man should yield his favors only to an older man who will be his mentor in the pursuit of wisdom and virtue.

Eryximachus, who speaks next, is pompous and prudential. Aristophanes, who follows him, is as fantastic and imaginative as Eryximachus is prosaic and sets forth an engaging myth. Originally, he speculates, all human beings were double creatures with two faces, four arms, and four legs, and of three kinds—double males, double females, and doubles formed from both sexes.

But when these quadrupeds rebelled against him, Zeus split each in two, whereupon the severed halves desperately tried to reunite by embracing. Aristophanes, of course, lacks our modern vocabulary, but his taxonomy, in effect, distinguishes what we would today call heterosexual and homosexual orientations. But his prejudice against heterosexuals is marked, even outrageous, and homosexuals get all the praise:

> Men who are a section of that double nature which was once called androgynous [made up of a man and a woman] are lovers of women, adulterers are generally of this breed, and also adulterous women who lust after men. The women who are a section of the woman do not care for men, but have female attachments: the female companions [that is, lesbians] are of this sort. But they who are a section of the male follow the male, and while they are young, being slices of the original man, they have affection for men and embrace them [the Greek verb implies a sexual sense], and these are the best of boys and youths, because they have the most manly nature.[33]

In this passage male chauvinism passes into gay chauvinism, so far did Greek conservatism invert modern conservatism. The coupling of men and women provided, Aristophanes tells us, for the continuation of the race; in the case of male pairs, their intercourse made it possible that, "if man came to man, they might be satisfied, and rest, and go their ways to the business of life."[34] Like Pausanias, he also speaks of pairs of males who "pass their whole lives together."

Aristophanes' myth also stakes out a moral position. Aristophanes admits that some Greeks call such lovers "shameless," but this criticism merely stimulates him to a more emphatic defense.[35] Not only do male halves make the *best* politicians, *only* they, he claims, have distinguished themselves in public life—an obvious exaggeration, as the case of a Pericles indicates. Since Aristophanes so often attacks politicians in his comedies, Kenneth Dover has speculated that he must be speaking here with dead-pan "sarcasm."[36] But Phaedrus has already made a similar claim that male lovers make the "best governors" of cities. And, as we have seen, this association of statesmanship with male love affairs would have seemed not a paradox but a truism to Athenians familiar with the history of their city.

In Aristophanes' romantic peroration we sense that the spirit of Plato has made him his medium:

> When they [halves of the double male] reach manhood they are lovers of youth, and are not naturally inclined to marry or beget children—if at all, they do so only in obedience to custom; but they are satisfied if they may be allowed to live with one another unwedded . . . And when one of them meets with his other half . . . the pair are lost in an amazement of love and friendship and intimacy, and one will not be out of the other's sight, as I

> may say, even for a moment: these are the people who pass their whole lives together; and yet they could not explain what they desire of one another. For the intense yearning which each of them has towards the other does not appear to be the desire of lover's intercourse, but of something else which the soul . . . has only a dark and doubtful presentiment . . . And the reason is that human nature was originally one and we were a whole, and the desire and pursuit of the whole is called love.[37]

But can couples who formed such life-long bonds be identified in a culture where the norm was more often pederastic? The answer would appear to be yes, in the Platonic Academy. After the death of Plato, headship of the school passed to his nephew Speusippus. Then, with the accession of Xenocrates, it devolved for a century (from 339 to 240) from lover to lover. Diogenes Laertius (who wrote his *Lives and Opinions of the Eminent Philosophers* about 220 CE) tells us that the young Polemo, on a dare, burst into Xenocrates' class quite drunk, wearing a garland on his head. Xenocrates, unfazed, continued his lecture on temperance. Polemo, enchanted, stayed, became first Xenocrates' pupil, then his *eromenos,* and in the end a teacher famed for his austere dignity. Polemo in turn took as his lover Crates, to whom he became so attached that they lived together and "not only shared the same pursuits in life but grew more alike to their latest breath, and dying, shared the same tomb." Laertius gives their epitaph: "Passing stranger, say that in this tomb rest godlike Crates and Polemo, men magnanimous in concord, from whose inspired lips flowed sacred speech, and whose pure life of wisdom, in accordance with unswerving tenets, decked them for a bright immortality."[38] Polemo and Crates took their meals together with another pair of co-habiting philosophers, Crantor and the brilliant young Arcesilaus, whose critically probing mind was to revitalize the Academy.

At the conclusion of the *Symposium* Plato uses the persona of Socrates to communicate what we may assume to be his own doctrine of love, a view that tacitly rejects the "mixed" love defended by Pausanias. When a temperate man finds beauty in a youth and tries to educate him, such an intellectual marriage, Socrates declares, is more intimate than the union of man and wife. But Socrates thinks men should ideally turn their attention from the beauty of individual boys to a beauty that is abstract and general. They should turn from intense love of one person to a love of all beautiful forms and finally to an abstract love for the beauty of political institutions. So, step by step, the love of fair boys and youths leads ultimately to a love of divine beauty purged of the alluring beguilements of the material world. By such stages the pederast becomes a contemplative sage and social philosopher.

For all its clever charm Socrates' argument seems, in the end, more than a little strained. Looking back at its beginning, one wonders how an admiration for a civil code or a constitution can bear any intelligible likeness to those feelings Socrates entertained, say, for Charmides. To clinch his argument and establish his point that sexual temptation can be overcome by a wise and temperate man, Plato ends on a dramatic note: a newcomer to the party, the young and handsome Alcibiades, his tongue loosened by wine, tells how Socrates resisted his attempt at seduction, much to the amazement of the youth, who thought his charms irresistible.

• The *Phaedrus* and the *Laws* •

In a second dialogue, the *Phaedrus,* Plato's Socrates elaborates on his doctrine of love to provide what was only briefly sketched in the *Symposium,* an erotic psychology. In these pages devoted to a vivid analysis of homoerotic arousal, Greek prose reaches its greatest poetic heights. Once again, Phaedrus is the naive enthusiast, commending a speech by Lysias which argues that a boy should prefer a non-lover to a lover as a sex partner, since the non-lover will be less jealous and more likely to remain a friend when their affair is over. Phaedrus is delighted with Lysias's paradoxes, but Socrates ironically praises the speech, then revises its logic, and finally condemns it as blasphemy against the holy ideal of love.

For Socrates, love is a god, and the feelings love inspires are not common madness (as Lysias had claimed) but a divine madness to be cherished. Other ideas such as justice and temperance exist without shape or color; only beauty among the eternal realities possesses an immediately seductive visibility.[39] While corrupt men will feel only desire for beauty, the true initiate will be enraptured by its godlike image. Content merely to gaze upon the youth who embodies it, he will overcome lustful impulses and strive to lead his beloved to wisdom and dignity. So Socrates appropriates Pausanias' pedagogic eros but outlaws physical contact.

Plato's ideal is wholly asexual; a Spartan at heart, he worships discipline, not liberty and spontaneity. For Plato, pleasure, and especially sexual pleasure, is the great evil to be resisted. To experience an orgasm is for him the ultimate humiliation, for at such a moment reason is out of control and passion supreme. To make his point, Plato, in the voice of Socrates, introduces the famous myth of the soul as a charioteer guiding a white and a black horse. The black horse, symbolizing sexuality, is ugly and deformed; the charioteer must struggle at all costs to subdue him by jerking the bit and covering "his abusive tongue and jaws with blood."[40]

Socrates advises the *eromenos* to respond positively to the lover who treats him with reverence, since "the good will of the lover" is "worth all other friends or kinsmen."[41] Reciprocating, the boy will yearn to be yearned for. Like the lover, though less strongly, he desires "to see him, touch him, kiss, embrace [lie down by] him, and probably not long afterwards his desire is accomplished."[42] But for Plato every expression of affection is permissible short of this sexual release. Yet at the end of the *Phaedrus,* Socrates does not wholly despair even of those men who enjoy "that desire of their hearts which to the many is bliss."[43] The wings that will ultimately carry the lovers to heaven will sprout less quickly, but the boon of love-madness will assure that, as they grow more chaste, they too will at last escape the darkness of earthly existence.

Contemplating this remarkable flow of eloquence, we may concede that few writers have written so enthusiastically of love between males or traced the ebb and flow of erotic stimuli so brilliantly. Fewer still have labored so hard to make frustration seductive. The fathers of the church, who frequently looked askance at Plato because of his homoerotic sensibility, could at least appreciate this last achievement.

Plato died in 348 at the age of eighty while working on his final treatise, the *Laws.* The *Republic* had depicted an ideal communist utopia ruled by philosopher-kings. In the *Laws,* an Athenian, a Spartan, and a Cretan discuss a city the Cretan proposes to found, less utopian but more realizable. It is, in fact, a blueprint for a narrowly repressive commonwealth on the Spartan plan, marked by a harsh puritanism. There will be no freedom of thought or opinion, and strict censorship is to control literature, art, and science. Since humans are by nature anarchic, Plato wants to adopt some religion to provide a supernatural sanction for morals and inculcate strict obedience to the state. Forgetting, or disregarding, the fate of Socrates, he proposes that any who question this faith shall be imprisoned and, if recalcitrant, killed. It is not surprising that a critic has called the *Laws* "these prolegomena to all future Inquisitions."[44]

Nowhere is this growing intolerance more evident than in Plato's treatment of homosexuality. In the *Laws* Plato attacks all non-procreative sexual behavior. He praises Sparta and Crete because their Dorian communal life subordinates the individual to the order and obedience he admires, but he complains that both fail in one particular—their toleration of sexual relations between males.[45] The Athenian (who is usually taken to be Plato's spokesman) attacks Sparta's laws as encouragingly permissive and accuses the Cretans of inventing the tale of Ganymede to justify their own practices.[46] In his new city, Plato wishes to abolish such acts entirely.

Plato defends this severity on the grounds that relations between men are "unnatural."[47] We may justly ask what, exactly, he means in this context by this slippery and ambiguous word. Obviously, he does not think this behavior rare or uncommon among human beings. Indeed, he admits that it is not. Usually moralists who condemn certain kinds of sexual activity as unnatural (as, for instance, masturbation, coitus interruptus, or the use of contraceptives) base their condemnation on a teleological assumption, that is, that sexual activity has a unique purpose, namely procreation. Plato does in fact object that same-sex relations are infertile, tacitly ruling out other possible ends, such as intimacy, bonding, or pleasure.

Plato gives a second argument that might seem to justify the term: he maintains that homosexuality does not exist in the animal world. This is a view we now know to be false.[48] Finally, Plato attacks the widely held Greek belief that same-sex bonds promote military courage, complaining that the passive partner demasculinizes himself by adopting a female role inappropriate for a warrior, while the active partner fails to show a proper disdain for pleasure. Courageous men, in his eyes, should be steeled to pain and indifferent to pleasure. In failing to show contempt for pleasure, the dominant partner has succumbed to what Plato calls an "effeminate" or cowardly temptation.[49]

Plato's Athenian candidly admits how drastically his new law will go against popular Greek opinion. Virile young men will scoff and call his effort to ban pederasty absurd and unfeasible. But, Plato argues, some famous athletes have been known to abstain from boys and women during their training for the Olympic games. If these vigorous and healthy but uneducated men are capable of this feat, he thinks the average Greek should be.[50] Nevertheless, Plato freely acknowledges the difficulty in getting the Greeks to adopt a law forbidding male relations. How can Greek society be persuaded to perform a *volte face* and repudiate so strong a tradition? Plato's solution is a radical one, uncannily prophetic of the course Christian Europe was later to follow. To suppress homosexuality, lawmakers must invent a new religious taboo, a taboo that will inspire in the average man a horror akin to the horror he feels toward incest. The act must be labeled (like incest) "unholy" and "hated of God."[51] Only such an extreme measure will terrify him into chastity and make him willing to support the new legislation.[52]

Few readers have warmed to the *Laws.* The discipline Plato advocates would subject all citizens to the minute supervision usually found only in military barracks. Liberals have perceived in his ideal state not just a foretaste of medieval Europe but of twentieth-century fascism. Nor have modern conservatives been drawn to his utopia; it drops the communism of goods and wives advocated in the *Republic,* but it is a closed society that bans foreign trade and foreign travel, forbids its citizens to engage in business, strictly limits wealth, and condemns all money-making as hostile to civic and personal virtue. Totally remote from the modern world, his inward-looking state, severed from the rest of humanity and decrying commerce, has indeed more in common with medieval Japan, where samurai warriors led Spartan lives, sealed themselves off from outside influences, and looked with contempt on trade and business. But, by an irony of history as we shall see, this unique society, otherwise so similar to that envisaged by Plato, failed to embrace his sexual puritanism.

✦ Xenophon ✦

Another disciple of Socrates, Xenophon, also wrote a *Symposium*, less well known than Plato's and less scintillating but illuminating as to Socrates' views on love. Xenophon was not a professional philosopher but first a soldier and later a country gentleman. At thirty he joined the expedition of Cyrus, who was trying to overthrow his brother, the Persian king. His *Anabasis* tells how he helped lead ten thousand Greeks back to safety through many hardships after Cyrus' defeat and death. Later, his Spartan sympathies and service with the Spartan king Agesilaus led to his exile from Athens and twenty years of retirement on a Spartan estate. There, he wrote on practical subjects like horsemanship and estate management and set down his recollections of Socrates in his *Memorabilia*.

Xenophon's *Symposium* imitates Plato's in its setting. Friends have gathered at a celebration arranged by Callias for the handsome Autolycus, who has just won a victory in the Panathenaic games. Once again we witness the power of male beauty to inspire love:

> A person who took note of the course of events [at the feast] would have come at once to the conclusion that beauty is in its essence something regal, especially when, as in the present case of Autolycus, its possessor joins with it modesty and sobriety. For in the first place, just as the sudden glow of a light at night draws all eyes to itself, so now the beauty of Autolycus compelled everyone to look at him. And again, there was not one of the onlookers who did not feel his soul strangely stirred by the boy; some of them grew quieter than before, others even assumed some kind of a pose . . . Those who are inspired by chaste Love [Eros] have a more tender look, subdue their voices to more gentle tones, and assume a supremely noble bearing. Such was the demeanor of Callias at this time under the influence of Love.[53]

Socrates declares that all the men present are lovers. One, he notes with catholic tolerance, is even in love with a woman—his wife! Finally, he sets forth at length his own views, arguing for the superiority of a purely spiritual love, which, since it is not based on physical bloom, will last until old age and, since it respects the honor of the beloved, will more likely be reciprocated by him. In contrast, carnal love turns the boy into a possession and must be clandestine so as not to offend the boy's relations. Moreover, the boy will not, he thinks, share in the pleasure of intercourse as a woman does and must consequently look with chilly contempt on his partner's ecstasies.

Aware of the sanctions Greek tradition provided, Socrates employs all his rhetorical skill to de-eroticize homoerotic myths and legends. He argues that Zeus was attracted to Ganymede solely for his mental attributes and that Homer portrayed Patroclus not as an object of Achilles' passion but as his comrade. Harkening back to Plato's *Symposium,* Socrates also counters Phaedrus' argument that homosexuality promotes military morale. He admits that the Eleans and Thebans may encourage such practices but denies the Athenians do and claims that in Sparta male love between warriors exists without the least spark of concupiscence. (We note the disagreement here with the *Laws.*) In every way, spiritual and mental qualities are supreme; the body and its desires are to be sternly repressed.

The dialogue ends curiously. Excited by a boy and girl who mime the love of Dionysus for Ariadne, the eager guests say farewell to their lovers and take horse for home and their wives. With this conclusion, Xenophon anticipates Shakespeare's Sonnet 20. There, enraptured by his young friend's beauty, Shakespeare proposes the same schizophrenic solution and also divides his love between the sexes:

> But since she [Nature] prick'd thee out for women's pleasure,
> Mine be thy love, and thy love's use their treasure."

Xenophon's own attitudes toward love do not seem to have been quite so puritanical as Socrates', as Clifford Hindley has recently demonstrated. In the *Anabasis,* where Xenophon speaks of himself in the third person, he recounts a romantic tale whose hero is a common soldier:

> There was a certain Episthenes of Olynthus [a Chalcidian settlement in northern Greece] who was a lover of boys, and upon seeing a handsome boy, just in the bloom of youth and carrying a light shield, on the point of being put to death, he ran up to Xenophon and besought him to come to the rescue of a handsome lad. So Xenophon went to Seuthes [a Thracian prince] and begged him not to kill the boy, telling him of Episthenes' turn of mind, how he had once assembled a battalion with an eye to nothing else save the question whether a man was handsome, and that with this battalion he proved himself a brave man. And Seuthes asked: "Would you even be willing, Episthenes, to die for this boy's sake?" Then Episthenes stretched out his neck and said, "Strike, if the lad bids you and will be grateful." Seuthes asked the boy whether he should strike Episthenes in his stead. The boy forbade it, and besought him not to slay either. Thereupon Episthenes threw his arms around the boy and said: "It is time, Seuthes, for you to fight it out with me for this boy; for I shall not give him up." And Seuthes laughed and let the matter go.[54]

Episthenes' histrionic gesture—it is almost Shakespearean—might tempt us to dismiss the episode as a literary invention if it were not vouched for by an eyewitness in a sober historical work.

In his *Economist* Xenophon gives another example of the effect that Greek love might have on men who do not belong to the cultured elite. There, he speaks of the kind of steward a wise owner will avoid employing on his farm, warning against three particular sorts: those who are too fond of wine, or of sleep, or of "amorous affection." The latter, we are told, will be too sentimentally obsessed with his *eromenoi* to attend properly to business. It would be, he comments, "no light task . . . to discover any hope or occupation sweeter to him that than which now employs him, his care for his beloved . . . [or] to invent worse punishment than that he now endures in separation from the object of his passion."[55] Since Xenophon is giving hard-headed practical advice on estate management, we may assume that some men of the slave class did in fact behave this way and that the intractability of lovesick stewards could be a serious problem for their masters.

· Aristotle's Dicta ·

Aristotle was Plato's pupil and studied with him for two decades at the Academy. Their temperaments, however, contrasted. Plato was the poetic utopian, Aristotle the down-to-earth scientist and social observer. Hailed in the Middle Ages as "the master of those who know," Aristotle produced treatises on physics, biology, politics, metaphysics, and ethics and is known to have written, in addition, a dialogue *On Love* and *Theses on Love.*[56] Unfortunately, these latter works have both been lost, and we are left to guess his opinions by piecing together miscellaneous remarks. These suggest a skeptic who cautiously distances himself from the popular Hellenic enthusiasm.

What does he say? In the *Politics* Aristotle takes note of the Cretans' effort to curb population through pederasty but fails to give us his opinion (after promising to do so) on the morality of such relations.[57] He lists tyrants who have been assassinated for sexual misbehavior, including some who met death at the hands of *eromenoi*—for instance, Periander of Ambracia, who was killed "because, when drinking with his boy lover, he asked if he was yet pregnant by him."[58] Nowhere does Aristotle strike the idealizing note of Plato and Plutarch. On the other hand, his comments on the passive adult in the *Nicomachean Ethics* are neither contemptuous in the popular style of Aristophanes nor moralizing in the style of Plato. Rather, they smack of the clinician who seeks a scientific explanation for human behavior. He thinks that male sexual passivity may sometimes be classified with plucking out the hair or nail-biting as "morbid propensities . . . acquired by habit," as in the case of those "who have been abused from childhood." Other cases appear to result from "natural disposition." We should not blame men of this sort, since they suffer from a morbid disposition which, however, does not "fall within the limits of Vice."[59] In the *Problems,* a work traditionally ascribed to Aristotle but in fact compiled much later, we encounter a physiological explanation for sexual passivity. In such cases, the unknown author conjectures, semen is diverted to the anal region, causing congestion which seeks relief.[60]

In one instance, Aristotle's misogyny inclines him to see a certain advantage in male relations. He complains in the *Politics* that women in warlike states have too much power, since they often rule cities while their husbands are on campaigns, an arrangement he thought had proved especially disastrous in Sparta. Such a danger, he notes, does not arise among "the Celts and any others who have manifestly honored sexual intercourse among males." Rejecting as unrealistic Plato's ideal of the chaste soldier, Aristotle finds the myth of Ares consorting with Aphrodite suggestive, "since all warring types are conspicuously obsessed by sexual relations either with men or women."[61]

• Zeno and the Stoics •

At the end of the classical age in Greece the most influential school was not the Platonic Academy or Aristotle's Lyceum but the Stoa, or "porch," founded by Zeno, a Cypriot businessman converted to philosophy who began to teach in Athens about 301. Stoicism is often perceived as an ascetic philosophy that subordinated feeling to duty and held pleasure in contempt—the opposite of what is popularly conceived as Epicureanism. It is, consequently, often assumed that the Stoics held a negative view of sex. But this was not true. There was a major divergence between Stoicism's original Greek and later Roman exponents, who did indeed reject same-sex relations. This was because the first Stoics derived their ethical teachings from Diogenes and his fellow Cynics. Diogenes, like Socrates, favored simple living, without luxuries, and tried to reduce life to its bare necessities. He lived in a clay tub, ate raw meat, and shocked the Athenians by breakfasting (against custom) in the agora. To make the point that one should satisfy one's needs as simply as possible, he masturbated in public, remarking only that he wished he could assuage his hunger as easily by rubbing his belly.[62]

Zeno of Citium was a pupil first of Polemo in the Academy, then of Crates the Cynic, Diogenes' disciple. Central to his teaching was the doctrine that the law of morality was the same as the law of nature. But this rule meant something different to the Stoics than to Plato. In its early phase, Stoicism was, like Cynicism, a back-to-nature movement, with a contempt for artificial conventions and taboos. Their philosophical detachment *(apatheia)* extended not just to pain and sickness, good or ill fortune, life or death but also to what they saw as popular superstitions. Sometimes they interpreted this doctrine in a way that startled their contemporaries. Why condemn incest, Zeno asked, when Oedipus had given Jocasta fine children?[63] Where Plato toyed with the idea of introducing new prohibitions, the Stoics sought to demystify sex by challenging custom and placing consensual behavior in the category of things indifferent.

Zeno held that sexual relations were neither good nor bad in themselves:

men, he declared, should "have carnal knowledge no less and no more of a favorite [*paidika,* beloved boy] than of a non-favorite, nor of a female than of a male."[64] Despite his radical theorizing, Zeno, we are told, was abstemious about sex. But he was not unsusceptible. Once, "being enamoured of Chremonides, as he and Cleanthes were sitting beside the youth, he got up and upon Cleanthes expressing surprise, 'Good physicians tell us,' said he, 'that the best cure of inflammation is repose.'"[65] One biographer, Antigonus of Carystus, faulted Zeno for not holding to his professed policy of nondiscrimination, complaining that he "never resorted to a woman, but always to boy-favorites."[66] Cleanthes, Zeno's successor as head of the Stoa, and Chrysippus, whose voluminous writings defined orthodox Stoic doctrine for subsequent generations, also held relations with boys to be morally neutral.[67]

But if the Stoics regarded sexual activity as itself indifferent, they nevertheless placed a high value on love that involved more than desire. Like Socrates and Plato, they perceived its educational possibilities. Zeno and his followers held that "the wise man will feel affection for the youths who by their countenance show a natural endowment for virtue," that is, not for beautiful boys but imperfect specimens who nevertheless show some promise of improvement.[68] Cicero noted the high esteem the Stoics showed for love in his *Tusculan Disputations*—in a somewhat dyspeptic fashion, since he did not share this enthusiasm.[69] Their interest in the subject is attested by the number of treatises they wrote: we have records of books on love not only by Zeno, Cleanthes, and Chrysippus but also by later Stoic writers such as Persaeus of Citium, Aristion of Chios, and Sphaerus.[70] This partial catalogue reminds us what a vast literature in Greek on this theme has been lost; what remains are a few stars from a galaxy.

Later adherents to Stoicism, embarrassed by what came to be seen as the somewhat scandalous views of its founders, tried to expurgate Zeno's writings. Yet in spite of his heterodox teachings, Zeno himself was regarded as living an exemplary personal life. "More temperate than Zeno" became a proverb in Greece. When he died at ninety, having taught in the city for some forty years, Athens, more generous to Zeno than to Socrates, voted him a golden crown as someone who had "exhorted all the young men who sought his company to the practice of temperance" and made his own life "a model of the greatest excellence."[71]

• Aeschines' *Against Timarchus* •

Philosophers' ideals may differ widely from popular standards. Drama of the sort that flourished in Athens under civic sponsorship is a better index of public opinion. Better still are speeches addressed to political bodies or juries; on such occasions the orator must above all else take into account common prejudices and common enthusiasms. Fortunately history has preserved for us an oration—Aeschines' *Against Timarchus*—which makes judgments of homosexual conduct its central theme. Dover is surely right in identifying it as a key document in assessing Athenian popular morality as it bore on male love.

Aeschines had every incentive to consider carefully the sentiments of his audience when he spoke in Athens in 345, since his life was at stake. During Philip of Macedon's military and diplomatic struggle to dominate Greece, Aeschines had supported a treaty that turned out badly for Athens, and Demosthenes had accused him of accepting bribes. Allied with Demosthenes in his attack was a young politician named Timarchus. Aeschines' defense was to charge that Timarchus was legally incompetent to address the jury because of his immoral life.

Aeschines, in his long and impassioned indictment, cites Athenian laws that prohibited any citizen who has prostituted himself from serving as a civic magistrate, priest, or herald. They also forbade such men to plead cases before public bodies "for the man who has made traffic of the shame of his own body . . . would be ready to sell the common interests of the city also."[72] Aeschines charges that Timarchus has notoriously led the life of a male courtesan, passing from one wealthy patron to another in order to indulge his extravagant tastes after he had exhausted his patrimony. Sometimes jealousy among his clients had led to brawls in the street. All this, Aeschines claims, is public knowledge.

What is most interesting about Aeschines' attack, however, is the stance he adopts toward homosexuality generally. His position is roughly that of an American politician indicting a football player of note. He is at pains, so to speak, to make it clear he does not disapprove of football. Indeed, Aeschines tries to anticipate the defense Timarchus' party will make. Some Athenian general, he predicts, "a graduate of the wrestling schools" and "a student of philosophy," will try to make it appear that Aeschines' attack is a "first step in a dangerous decline in the culture of our youth," invoking the names of Achilles and Patroclus and Aristogeiton and Harmodius.[73] Aeschines' strategy is to anticipate this by casting himself in the role of a defender of the chaste and honorable love "that is the experience of a kind-hearted and generous soul."[74] We have already noted Aeschines' argument that Homer in the *Iliad* meant Achilles and Patroclus to be perceived as lovers.[75] Aeschines quotes lengthy passages from the *Iliad* to support this view. Obviously, this was the popular line to take, and Aeschines expects his hearers to approve an exegesis that made the heroes lovers.

Aeschines also names with approval a number of handsome young men then living in Athens well known for having attracted lovers. This, he implies, is entirely acceptable, but he contrasts them pointedly with Timarchus, who has disgraced himself by selling his favors. He even makes a personal confession: "I do not deny that I myself have been a lover and am a lover to this day [he was about 45], nor do I deny that the jealousies and quarrels that commonly arise from the practice have happened in my case."[76] He frankly admits to having made a nuisance of himself in the gymnasia in his pursuit of young men and to composing erotic poems, which he predicts the opposition will read aloud to embarrass him.

Though Aeschines skirts the delicate question whether the "honorable" loves he describes were Platonic or "mixed," his description of his own affairs suggests sexual possession. Taken as a whole, his speech is potent testimony that ardent attachments to young men were acceptable to the average Athenian who might serve on a municipal jury. Aeschines won his case.

• The Sacred Band of Thebes •

In classical Greece, not only Athens but cities with every kind of constitution took notice of the fact of male love. Aristocracies where the privileged few held sway recognized its power to forge bonds between promising youths and conservative mentors. Democracies saw it as insurance against tyranny. Tyrants sometimes forbade it or, more often, tasted its pleasures, suffered the revenge of rivals or alienated lovers, and lamented that their very omnipotence made it impossible ever to be sure they enjoyed disinterested affection. But the major source of its prestige remained (despite Plato) its contribution to military morale. In the fourth century this heroic tradition found its most famous embodiment in the so-called *hieros lochos,* the Sacred Band of Thebes. This force, created by the Theban general Gorgidas, was made up of pairs of lovers who at first fought interspersed throughout other regiments. Then, under his successor, Pelopidas, it fought as a separate contingent of shock troops. Its success was to make Thebes for a generation the most powerful state in Greece, and its fate was in the end the fate of Greece itself.

Theban tradition easily sanctioned such an institution. Thebes and Elis are repeatedly cited as the two states of the Greek mainland which most unqualifiedly encouraged male relations. Xenophon, in his *Constitution of Sparta,* observed that such relations were transitory at Elis but that at Thebes men and boys lived together "like married people"; perhaps this reflected Cretan patterns.[77] The cult of Heracles was especially strong in Boeotia. Aristotle, in a lost work, described a "tomb of Iolaus" dedicated to the hero's lover and companion-in-arms, where Theban lovers in his day still plighted mutual devotion. Plutarch thought the "Sacred" Band derived its name from this rite.[78]

In 404 the Peloponnesian War had come to an end with Sparta's total defeat of Athens. But the victors misused their power. Sparta wielded its new hegemony harshly, imposing oligarchic rulers favorable to their interests on states that formerly had democratic regimes. Among these was Thebes, where in 382 a Spartan commander treacherously seized its citadel and installed new pro-Spartan leaders. Three years later democratic Theban exiles returned and recaptured the fortress, the Cadmeia, in a daring coup that drove the Spartans out. Conflict with the most formidable military regime in Greece now seemed inevitable. At this crucial juncture Gorgidas, in 378, organized the Sacred Band, which realized—within a few years of the writing of the *Symposium*—Phaedrus' fantasy of an "army of lovers."

Plutarch was born (c. 46 CE) in the tiny village of Chaeronea some twenty miles west of Thebes and lived there all his life. Particularly interested in Boeotian traditions, he gives us, in his life of Pelopidas, the only substantial account we have of the Sacred Band. In tracing its origins, Plutarch shows himself unhappy with the legend that Oedipus' father, Laius, had been the first to introduce pederasty to Thebes. Instead, he ascribes its institution to judicious civic authorities "who first made this form of love customary among the Thebans." Finding Theban youth unruly, they sought to "relax and mollify their strong and impetuous natures in earliest boyhood." To this harmonious end, Plutarch tells us, they trained them in the music of the flute and "gave love a conspicuous place in the life of the *palaestra,* thus tempering the dispositions of the young men."[79]

Apparently Gorgidas was killed in some skirmish shortly after he founded the band, for the next year its leadership passed to Pelopidas, the young Theban who had led the exiles in their rebellion. Under siege by the Spartans, the Thebans at first hesitated to challenge their redoubtable enemies in a formal battle. But having unexpectedly come upon a Spartan force while reconnoitering at Tegyrae, Pelopidas daringly attacked. Though the Spartans outnumbered them two or three to one, his spirited leadership won the day. Plutarch thought the occasion remarkable: "For in all their wars with the Greeks and Barbarians, as it would seem, never before had Lacedaemonians in superior numbers been overpowered by an inferior force, nor indeed in a pitched battle where the forces were evenly matched. Hence they were of an irresistible courage, and when they came to close quarters their reputation sufficed to terrify their opponents, who also, on their part, thought themselves no match for Spartans with an equal force."[80]

Plutarch called the undefeated Pelopidas "valiant, laborious, passionate, and magnanimous."[81] But his fame was eventually overshadowed by his friend Epaminondas, whose life in several points contrasted with his own. Pelopidas was rich but modest in his style of living; Epaminondas, despite his renown, remained poor until the day of his death. Pelopidas married and had children; Epaminondas died unwed. At the time the Cadmeia was seized, Epaminondas was looked upon as a scholarly recluse. A devoted disciple of the Pythagorean sage Lysis of Tarentum, who had settled in Thebes, he divided his time between exercises in the gymnasium, lectures, and philosophy. Though he declined to participate in the assassination of the Spartanizing

Thebans, once the revolt began he joined Pelopidas in re-establishing democracy. Early in their careers he bravely risked his life to save his wounded friend. Though they competed for glory on the same narrow stage, they were never rivals—an unusual circumstance among jealous Greeks. Epaminondas now developed into an orator and statesman as well as a soldier. Indeed, it was he who, at a peace conference in 371, challenged Sparta's overlordship of the Peloponnesus. In retaliation the Spartan king Agesilaus angrily excluded Thebes from the peace treaty. Thebes hastily prepared for full-scale war.

The battle that tried the issue between Sparta and Thebes was, according to Pausanias, "the most famous [victory] ever won by Greeks over Greeks."[82] At Leuctra in 371, Epaminondas devised a new maneuver. He strengthened his left wing and, holding his right wing back, attacked the Spartans obliquely, throwing them into confusion. Then Pelopidas led the Sacred Band to the charge and smashed the squadron commanded by the Spartan co-king, Cleombrotus, who was killed on the field. Epaminondas' lover Asopichus also won fame in the battle. He put up so formidable a fight that his shield, decorated with a representation of the trophy that the Thebans had erected at Leuctra, hung as a conspicuous offering at Delphi.[83]

Their defeat at Leuctra destroyed at a blow the military supremacy the Spartans had enjoyed for centuries. In the wake of his victory, Epaminondas invaded the Peloponnesus, freed the provinces of Messenia and Arcadia from the Spartan yoke, and carried the war into the suburbs of the city; this was the first siege the Spartans had suffered during the six hundred years that the Dorians had occupied the Peloponnesus. Thebes was now the leading power in Greece.

The victorious Epaminondas acted with a magnanimity that contrasted with Spartan tyranny. He reestablished Messene as Messenia's provincial capital and built a new city, Megalopolis, as a center of defense for the long-subjugated Arcadians. Though the hegemony of Greece now fell to Thebes, he declined to subject other cities to Theban domination and pillage, as the Spartans and Athenians had done earlier when they wielded power. No doubt he had the intelligence to realize that the economic and military resources of Thebes would not have sustained this enterprise. As a result he won a unique fame as a liberator rather than an exploiter.

Classical and modern historians alike have joined to salute Epaminondas as Greece's greatest warrior-statesman. Diodorus Siculus, who wrote in the age of Julius Caesar, thought he "excelled . . . all Greeks in valor and shrewdness in the art of war."[84] Diodorus ranked him above Solon, Themistocles, Miltiades, Cimon, Pericles, and Agesilaus in generalship and reputation. "For in each of the others you would discover but one particular superiority as a claim to fame; in him, however, all qualities combined. For in strength of body and eloquence of speech, furthermore in elevation of mind, contempt of lucre, fairness, and, most of all, in courage and shrewdness in

11. Epaminondas. J. Chapman, engraving, 1807.

the art of war, he far surpassed them all."[85] Diodorus was a Sicilian Greek and perhaps partial, but his Latin contemporary, Cornelius Nepos, a man of a markedly different tradition, was if anything even more eulogistic. In his *Book of the Great Commanders* Nepos expresses concern that his readers will look askance at Epaminondas' reputation as a musician and dancer but begs them to remember the Greeks esteemed such frivolities. He praises without reservation Epaminondas' intellectual and athletic prowess and finds he meets Roman standards of temperance, prudence, and seriousness: he was "practised in war, of great personal courage and high spirit" and "such a lover of truth that he never lied even in jest." One part of his character was quite unclassical (if we except Caesar): "He was self-controlled, kindly and forbearing to a surprising degree."[86] Nepos acclaims him as one of the few successful Greek military leaders whose integrity was equal to his talent. His contemporary Cicero agreed. Discussing the influence of culture and philosophy on such leaders as Peisistratus, Pericles, Timotheus, and Agesilaus in his *De Oratore,* Cicero hailed Epaminondas as "perhaps the most outstanding figure in Greek history."[87]

Theban pre-eminence lasted only as long as Epaminondas lived. Pelopidas, leading a force north to free the people of Thessaly from the vicious Alexander of Pheras, was killed in 364 in a rash attempt to engage the tyrant in single combat. The Thessalians mourned and granted their would-be liberator heroic honors.[88] Alexander was subsequently dispatched by his wife: one of her grievances was that the tyrant had made her younger brother his bedmate.[89] In the meantime, the weakening of Sparta left the Peloponnesus in turmoil. Rival factions in Arcadia summoned Thebes and Sparta to their aid, and Epaminondas once more found himself face to face with his old foes at Mantinea in 362. His brilliant strategy again routed the Spartans but at a fatal cost. Diodorus records the story of his death. Pierced by a spear, he was told he would die when the point was withdrawn from his chest. After conversing with his friends, he said, "It is time to die," and ordered them to withdraw the spear.[90]

Another lover of Epaminondas, Caphisodorus, also died at Mantinea; Plutarch tells us they were buried together on the battlefield.[91] Pausanias, visiting Thebes in the second century after Christ, found these verses inscribed on a statue raised in Epaminondas' honor:

> By my counsel was Sparta shorn of her glory,
> And holy Messene received at last her children:
> By the arms of Thebes was Megalopolis encircled with walls,
> And all Greece won independence and freedom.[92]

A few years before Pausanias' visit, the Emperor Hadrian had inscribed his own tribute on another monument to the Theban which stood on the site of his death.[93]

The Theban Sacred Band met its nemesis in Philip of Macedonia. In 367 when Philip was about fifteen, he had been sent as a hostage to Thebes and remained there for three years while Thebes was at the height of its prestige. Philip must have been stirred by the victories of Epaminondas and Pelopidas and fascinated by their new fighting methods, since we later find him revolutionizing military practice by adapting them to his own purposes. Dio Chrysostom credits Philip's later diplomatic sagacity to the education he received from Epaminondas and makes him the *eromenos* of Pelopidas.[94] Perhaps he was, or perhaps this is an honorific assumption in accordance with the Hellenic motto, "Cherchez l'amant," for Plutarch says Philip lived not with Pelopidas but in the house of Pammenes, the general who was to assume leadership after the death of Epaminondas.[95] As a military leader, Pammenes was an enthusiastic advocate of the discipline that formed the Sacred Band. Plutarch quotes (several times) Pammenes' criticism of Homer's Nestor for organizing regiments on tribal lines. "For tribesmen and clansmen make little account of tribesmen and clansmen in times of danger; whereas, a band that is held together by the friendship between lovers is indissoluble and not to be broken, since the lovers are ashamed to play the coward before their beloved, and the beloved before their lovers, and both stand firm to protect each other."[96]

On his return to Macedon, Philip put to use what he had learned at Thebes. When he came to the throne, he organized a strong professional army and, having secured his position in the north, managed by a series of adroit diplomatic maneuvers to extend his power into southern Greece with the intention of unifying the entire country under his command. When Thebes and Athens belatedly formed an alliance to oppose him, the crucial battle took place in 338 at Plutarch's Chaeronea. The Sacred Band, still intact and undefeated, remained the prime troops of the Greek army, but this was their *Götterdämmerung*. True to their traditions, they stood their ground and were killed to the last man, so that the bodies of the three hundred lay strewn on the field. In the triumph of victory Philip came upon the remains of the regiment he had known in Thebes as an adolescent thirty years before. Plutarch describes his response: "And when, after the battle, Philip was surveying the dead, and stopped at the place where the three hundred were lying, all where they had faced the long spears of his phalanx, with their armour, and mingled one with another, he was amazed, and on learning that this was the band of lovers and beloved, burst into tears and said: 'Perish miserably they who think that these men did or suffered aught disgraceful.'"[97]

When the geographer Pausanias visited the site four hundred years later, he saw their memorial. In the empty fields, overlooking the common grave of the Thebans, before a row of cypress, stood a gigantic marble lion.[98] It stands there still. Its present restoration was undertaken in 1902 by an organization called the Order of Chaeronea. (This was in fact a secret, quasi-Masonic society of English homosexuals, founded and led by the reformer George Cecil Ives.)[99] Modern excavations of the battleground have recovered the remains of 254 men, almost the whole complement of the Sacred Band, laid out in seven rows.[100]

• Philip and Alexander •

Philip had used Theban lessons to smash Thebes. He did not long outlive his victory. Successful in his effort to unite Greece, Philip stood poised to invade

12. Memorial to the Sacred Band at Chaeronea. 338 BCE.

Persia when, two years later in 336, he was assassinated at his daughter's wedding under sensational circumstances. Most accounts of the deed speculate on the possible complicity of his wife, the fierce Olympias, and his half-estranged son, Alexander. The full story is less well known, but it is given in circumstantial detail by Diodorus Siculus and confirmed by Aristotle.[101] The polygamous Philip, who "waged war by marrying," had several wives and numerous mistresses, but he also had male favorites. One of these, Pausanias ("beloved by him for his beauty"), had been succeeded in his affections by another young man who bore the same name. The elder Pausanias denounced his rival as a whore who did not love the king: "Unable to endure such an insult, the other kept silent for the time, but, after confiding to Attalus, one of his friends, what he proposed to do, he brought about his death voluntarily and in a spectacular fashion. For a few days after this, as Philip was engaged in battle with Pleurias, king of the Illyrians, Pausanias stepped in front of him and, receiving on his body all the blows directed at the king, so met his death."[102]

Appalled at this suicide, Attalus, who was one of Philip's chief generals, invited the elder Pausanias to a feast, made him drunk with wine, and had him raped by his muleteers. When Pausanias demanded vengeance from Philip, the king was sympathetic, but since Attalus was one of his most valued commanders and the uncle of Philip's newest wife, he did not punish him. Pausanias bided his time; then when Philip was walking in his royal robes unguarded at his daughter's wedding, he stabbed him to death before the assembled guests. Such violence, occasioned by an offense given to a lover, was not new in Macedon. Sixty years earlier, in 399, Archelaus, the patron of Euripides and Agathon, had been killed by two former lovers bent on revenge for what they regarded as slights at the hands of the king.[103]

The ranks of the Sacred Band had been broken at Chaeronea by a cavalry charge led by the eighteen-year-old Alexander. With Philip dead, Alexander now began the astonishing career that would make him master of Greece, Asia Minor, Egypt, Persia, and northwestern India. In one respect, however, he differed strikingly from his father—he was not a womanizer. Plutarch conjectures that he had known only one woman before his marriage, a remarkable record for a Macedonian ruler. He was also restrained toward male slaves: when a commander offered to procure him two beautiful boys, he indignantly declined.[104] When Alexander praised the *eromenos* of Charon of Chalcis, Charon told the boy to kiss him, but Alexander demurred: "That will not delight me so much as it will pain you."[105]

Later in his career he relaxed this abstemiousness. Male favorites were popular among the Persians whom Alexander conquered. (Herodotus had taken note of this a century earlier and ascribed it to Greek influence.[106] Here is a unique case of a culture claiming precedence with a new form of sexual activity.) According to Quintus Curtius, a Persian general who had served the defeated Darius presented Alexander with a peace offering at Hyrcania, namely, a Persian boy named Bagoas, "a eunuch of remarkable beauty and in the very flower of boyhood, who had been loved by Darius, and was afterwards to be loved by Alexander."[107] Later, Alexander met and married the Bactrian princess Roxana, but he seems to have kept Bagoas with him during his Indian campaign and even during the terrible march across the desert of

13. Alexander at the Battle of Issus. Mosaic from Pompeii, second century BCE.

Gedrosia. Plutarch recounts an incident that took place at the end of this adventure. To celebrate his arrival at the Gedrosian capital, Alexander held athletic and musical contests. "His favorite, Bagoas, won the prize for song and dance, and then, in all his festal array, passed through the theatre and took his seat by Alexander's side; at sight of which the Macedonians clapped their hands and loudly bade the king kiss the victor, until at last he threw his arms around him and kissed him tenderly."[108]

Athenaeus, at his gossipy dinner party, cites Alexander's contemporary, Dicaearchus, for a slightly different version of the incident which makes the conqueror less shy: "He was so overcome with love for the eunuch Bagoas that, in full view of the entire theatre, he, bending over, caressed Bagoas fondly, and when the audience clapped and shouted in applause, he nothing loath, again bent over and kissed him."[109] If this account is true, it suggests that Alexander publicly acknowledged the role Bagoas played in his life. Even more striking is the enthusiasm with which the Macedonians applauded the Persian, considering the distaste his troops showed for Alexander's adoption of Persian dress and customs. Perhaps the fact that Bagoas had shared their hardships in the desert had made him acceptable.

Alexander's closest and most enduring emotional tie was not with his Persian favorite, however, but with his boyhood friend Hephaestion, who had studied with him under Aristotle in Macedon, commanded armies during the march to the East, founded cities at his friend's bidding, and become his grand vizier in Persia. One important inspiration for Alexander's ambition was Homer. He slept with the *Iliad* under his pillow and consciously took Achilles as his model. In this romantic dream, Hephaestion was cast for the part of Patroclus. On a visit to the site of ancient Troy, Alexander deliberately dramatized these identifications: he himself sacrificed to the hero Achilles, Hephaestion at the shrine of Achilles' companion. They assumed the same oneness. When the aged queen mother of Persia, brought captive to Alexander's tent, bowed by mistake to Hephaestion, who was taller and handsomer, Alexander eased her embarrassment with the remark: "Never mind, Mother. For he too is Alexander."[110]

When Hephaestion died of a fever in Ecbatana in 324, Alexander's grief surpassed even Achilles'. He hanged the doctor who had attended the sick man, refused to eat or drink, cut his hair and the manes and tails of his horses, dismantled the battlements of cities, and sent to the oracle at Siwah to ask divine honors for his friend. Hephaestion's enormous funeral pyre was a Babylonian ziggurat, an eighth of a mile square at the base and two hundred feet high, tier after tier decorated with magnificently ornate wooden statues. His cremation, which cost ten thousand talents, was arguably the most spectacular funeral in history. Yet, here in the fourth century, we are left with the same ambiguity we found in Homer. The same cloud of uncertainty surrounding the love of Achilles and Patroclus envelops the Macedonians. Despite the intensity of Alexander's feelings, we cannot be sure that they were lovers, though they may have been in their early years. Even Plutarch, the indefatigable chronicler of amours, who seems to have read very widely in now-vanished sources for his biographical sketch, fails to make that claim.

With Alexander, the classical age of Greece comes to an end. From now on Greek culture would recognize not one but two intellectual capitals: Athens and Alexandria, the splendid new metropolis Alexander had established in Egypt. Even more than in the archaic age, male homoeroticism had played a visible and important part on the major stages of the Greek world. To understand Greek culture at its zenith, we must take this into account. Whether expressed as heroic devotion, playful amorousness, or brutal violence, male love was often a crucial element in war or politics. In art and literature it had left its mark abundantly, while inspiring the subtlest and most daring philosophical speculations. Wherever the spotlight of history shines in this brilliant world, we find the love of male for male.

CHAPTER FOUR

ROME AND GREECE

323 BCE–138 CE

• Sexuality and Empire •

What the followers of Alexander failed to achieve, the Romans accomplished during the next three centuries—the consolidation by force of arms of a far-flung and stable empire. After their bitter struggle with Carthage for control of Sicily and the western Mediterranean, they were able to extend their rule first to Spain, north Africa, Macedonia and Asia Minor, and then to Gaul, Egypt, and Britain. Impelling the Romans to these victories was what Nietzsche was to call, admiringly, "the will to power," an overwhelming need to dominate. The Pax Romana brought peace, order, and prosperity to Rome's new provinces, but it also brought subjugation and an enormous proliferation of slavery. This development was to have a significant influence on the way Romans viewed sexuality, and homosexuality in particular.

The conquest of Hellenistic Greece was fraught with ironies. Rome's supreme achievements were in civic administration, law, and engineering. But in 180 BCE Greece far surpassed Rome in philosophy, science, and the arts. The relatively crude and unpolished Romans were soon forced to recognize the cultural superiority of a people they had defeated in the field. Their admiration, however, was selective. Greek culture had enormous influence on Roman literature and art and colored the expression of erotic feeling; but some venerable Greek institutions—such as civic gymnasia—never took root in Rome at all.

Inevitably, when the Romans encountered Greek civilization they encountered Greek homosexuality. Here, in particular, the two cultures diverged. The Greeks were able to conceive of love between an older and a younger male as a protective and affectionate mentorship, while the Romans, generally speaking, did not accord this privileged status to male relationships. There was no taboo of silence such as developed under Christianity—the Romans were quite willing to acknowledge the prevalence of same-sex desire. Indeed, the earliest Latin literature treats it quite openly. The swaggering hero of Plautus's comedy *The Braggart Soldier* (c. 200 BCE) has an eye for handsome young men as well as women, and numerous casual references to male homosexuality appear in Plautus' other plays.[1] But male love was not, as with the Greeks, a theme for philosophical or forensic panegyrics. It did not have the same high cultural import and was not regarded as the root of deep, inspiring personal devotion.

On the contrary, homosexual relations were perceived primarily as a form of dominance, an extension of the will to power. We see this in early Roman comedy, where the same-sex intrigues are not between men and freeborn youths but exclusively between masters and slaves.[2] The Greeks deprecated such servile liaisons as ungentlemanly, but these relationships were the only ones that Roman society accepted unreservedly. Since the slave population of Italy increased dramatically in the late third and second centuries BCE—some authorities calculate that slaves made up as much as 40 percent of the population—opportunities were ample for Roman masters. By 200 BCE Cato the censor was to complain that a good-looking slave boy cost as much as a farm.[3] The spread of slavery had a paradoxical effect, preventing any general prohibition against male homosexuality per se from taking root but casting a special stigma on the passive partner and preventing Romans from idealizing male passion as the Greeks had.

For the Romans, homosexual relations were not in themselves good or bad. But to submit to penetration was to be feminized and humiliated. Such an experience, if it became public knowledge, invited reproach and ridicule from a man's enemies. The analogy between military and sexual defeat was strongly felt. A striking instance was the teasing of Rome's greatest general at his triumph, when Caesar's soldiers sang mockingly of his youthful affair with the king of Bithynia: "Caesar conquered the Gauls, but Nicomedes conquered Caesar."[4]

In Greece, to be the beloved protégé of a respected ruler was an honor. In Rome, it was an embarrassment and an occasion for ribald humor. The amorous-sexual vocabularies of the two languages reveal the distinction. In the line just quoted, the same verb, *subigere,* "to subjugate," signifies both the public and the private "conquest." Greek usage incorporated some form of the root *eros* (love) into such words as *paiderastia, erastes, eromenos.* Roman men did not embrace lovers *(amantes)* but rather *pathici, cinaedi, exoleti*—terms suggestive of passivity, degradation, and abuse. No cultural heroes exemplified male love in Rome, as Achilles did in Greece, the Yellow Emperor in China, and an exalted bodhisattva in Japan. What homoerotic myths the Romans knew were borrowed from Greece.

Indeed, if we look for the first records of homosexuality in Roman history, we find them not in legends but in Valerius Maximus's *Memorable Facts and Sayings,* a handbook compiled about 30 CE for rhetoricians and orators.

Book VI recounts a dozen notorious offenses against "chastity," half of them homosexual and involving military or civil officials who abused their rank to coerce subordinates. Family honor might also be at stake: Fabius Maximus Servilianus (126 BCE) is said to have killed his son for his complacence to men and then voluntarily exiled himself for shame at this dishonor.[5] The earliest anecdote, dating from 326 BCE, is perhaps the most revealing. Livy tells the story at length as an important development in Roman jurisprudence. A freeborn boy enslaved for debt had been beaten by his master when he rejected his advances. The populace, hearing his cries and seeing his lacerated back, objected to these indignities. What is significant, however, was the Senate's response. They did not pass a law to protect slaves from assault; instead, it was decreed that freeborn Romans could no longer be enslaved for debt.[6] Faced with a choice between limiting sexual access to slaves or limiting slavery, the Romans chose to limit slavery.

Valerius Maximus' cases were handled by administrative or paternal action with no reference to any specific law against homosexuality. Such a measure has been assumed to exist in the so-called *Lex Scantinia.*[7] Our knowledge of this statute is, however, fragmentary and uncertain; its date, scope, and relevance have all been called into doubt. It has been suggested that it was enacted in 226 BCE, when a Roman tribune, C. Scantinius Capitolinus, was convicted of soliciting another aristocrat's son.[8] But Roman laws were named not after offenders but after the men who proposed them. The first known mention of the Scantinian Law appears in 50 BCE in two letters to Cicero, but the context provides no hint of what it dealt with.[9] The Emperor Domitian (81–96 CE) invoked it in a campaign to enforce sexual morality, but again exactly what it punished is not clear.[10] The only text in the pre-Christian period to connect the law definitely with homosexual behavior is Juvenal's second satire, c. 100 CE, where it seems to be understood as penalizing *cinaedi,* that is, passive males.[11] Writing shortly before this, Quintilian, in his *Institutes,* tells us that a fine of 10,000 sesterces ($2,000?) was the penalty for seducing a freeborn boy.[12] Most authorities think he is referring to the Scantinian Law, but the matter remains unclear.

Nevertheless, sex with freeborn boys was certainly frowned on in Roman society, along with adultery and the seduction of virgin daughters, all of which violated the honor of the *paterfamilias.* An orator named Haterius, pleading in the courts in the Augustan age, put the matter succinctly: "Losing one's virtue is a disgrace *[crimen]* for a freeborn boy, a necessity in a slave, and a duty [owed to his emanicipator] for the freedman."[13] (In Rome emancipation was a civil and religious procedure by which the freed slave might still be required to render certain services, including, on occasion, sexual ones, to his former master.) But though sex with freeborn boys was disapproved, it was not seen as degrading. The "conqueror" was regarded with the ambivalent mixture of censure and envy successful Don Juans have met with in most societies.

• Cicero and Roman Politics •

The Senate under the Republic was Rome's most respected institution, arguably one of the world's greatest deliberative bodies, and Cicero was its most admired orator. But the dignity of the assembly imposed no reticence when it came to sexuality. Accusations of adultery, incest, and homosexuality were common. Such indiscriminate smears were one of the least attractive sides of Roman public life. Whether they had any serious effect is a question. So much mud was thrown that its consequences must have been slight. Julius Caesar and others withstood attacks of this sort repeatedly, apparently not much damaged. Such scandal was the spice of political debate, not a determining element. If allegations of homosexuality had ended careers in ancient Rome—as they would have, certainly, in eighteenth- or nineteenth-century England—the Roman political stage during the turbulent last century of the Republic would have been bereft of Sulla, Pompey, Catiline, Caesar, Clodius, Mark Antony, and Octavius; in short, it would have lacked most of its principal players.[14]

Cicero's surviving speeches amply demonstrate how politicians used such insinuations. In 60 BCE Cicero prosecuted Verres, the governor of Sicily, for financial corruption and accused him of using violence against married women and freeborn youths. Still worse, he was not only "a man among women" but "a degraded contemptible woman among men."[15] A decade later Cicero delivered his celebrated attack against Cataline, who had plotted with discontented radicals and debt-ridden aristocrats to overthrow the Republic, depicting his followers as effeminates, ready "to love" and (more damagingly) "to be loved."[16] Publius Clodius Pulcher, the patrician who had deserted his class to become a leader of street mobs and who had instigated Cicero's exile in 58 BCE, was accused of numerous affairs with women, including his sister. To these charges Cicero added another, alleging that as a boy he had been the "debauched favorite of wealthy rakes."[17]

After Caesar's assassination, Cicero launched his most famous political campaign—against Mark Antony. In the series of bitter denunciations we know as the Philippics, he repeatedly impugned Antony's morals and manhood. To the modern imagination, fed on Shakespeare and Hollywood, Antony is the Roman heterosexual lover par excellence; to his contemporaries, he was also known as an ardent pursuer of youths. (The Jewish historian Josephus mentions the unwillingness of King Herod to entrust his wife's handsome sixteen-year-old brother to him.)[18] Cicero was able to attest to an especially damaging episode. Alleging that Antony in his youth had sold himself to older men, Cicero, in the second Philippic, gives an unusually intimate picture of a turbulent Roman love affair, purportedly at first hand:

> You assumed a man's gown [at 17], and at once turned it into a harlot's. At first you were a common prostitute, the fee for your infamies was fixed, and that not small; but Curio quickly turned up, who withdrew you from your meretricious traffic, and, as if he had given you a matron's robe, established you in an enduring and stable wedlock. No boy ever bought for libidinous purposes was ever so much in the power of his master as you were in Curio's. How often did his father eject you from his house, how often did he set watchmen that you might not cross the threshold! while you nevertheless, with night as your abettor, at the bidding of lust, and the compulsion of your pay, were let down through the tiles.[19]

Antony's lover, Gaius Scribonius Curio, Cicero claimed, had begged him to defend him if his father should sue to recover the six million sesterces ($120,000?) he had given Antony to pay his debts.

But the crux of Cicero's speech is the dramatic moment when Antony publicly offered Caesar a crown. Accusing Antony of asking "slavery" for the Roman people, Cicero harks back to his affair with Curio. "You should have asked for it for yourself alone, whose life from boyhood showed you would submit to anything, [and] would lightly be a slave."[20] In the thirteenth Philippic Cicero repeated the incriminating analogy: "For if his boyhood had suffered the lusts of those who were tyrants over him, was he also to set up over our children a master and a tyrant?"[21]

In his philosophical writings, Cicero appeals not to Plato or the Stoics but to Epicurus, who thought the ideal life was one of unruffled calm and considered love a threat to this equanimity. Epicurus' chief Latin disciple was Lucretius, who, in Book IV of *On the Nature of Things,* paints a vivid but alarming picture of sexual passion, reducing love, in his materialist view, to a physiological phenomenon. Just as blood from a wound in battle spurts toward the foe who has dealt the blow, so the man smitten by the shafts of Venus, Lucretius tells us, is drawn toward his tormentor, whether it be "a lad with womanish limbs, or a woman radiating love from her whole body."[22] For Lucretius, love is not a divine madness, as in the *Phaedrus,* but madness in a pathological sense. Wounded men should not turn away from sex but should cure love's wounds by promiscuous affairs. "Do not think that by avoiding grand passions you are missing the delights of Venus," he assures his readers. "Rest assured that this pleasure is enjoyed in a purer form by the healthy than by the love-sick."[23]

The view of love in the philosophical debates Cicero sets in his villa at Tusculum is equally sour. It is astonishing to realize that, compared to the voluminous writings of the Greeks, the four or five pages in Book IV of the

Tusculan Disputations are the most extensive treatment of love in extant Latin prose. Appearing in an account of "undesirable perturbations" of the soul, they parallel Lucretius. Quoting the Latin comic poet Caecilius to the effect that love may be wise or senseless, insane or desirable, Cicero can accept only the negative judgments. Medea's destructive passion for Jason is, for him, love's prototype.[24] Plato and Zeno were wrong in valuing love: Epicurus was right.

The cult of love, Cicero thinks, originated in that scandalous institution, the Greek gymnasium.[25] Even if such a thing as chaste love could exist, it would be wise to avoid it, since it can bring only trouble and anxiety. Cicero's recommended treatment parallels Lucretius': the lover must be shown how contemptible the object of his affections is and distracted by a change of scene or new interests, though Cicero stops short of endorsing promiscuity.

• Greek Love in the *Aeneid* •

Given the hostility toward homosexuality of Rome's native traditions and of Roman philosophy, it may seem surprising that any Latin writer would make a serious effort to naturalize Greek love. Yet one poet attempted the feat. In most respects the *Aeneid* is a conservative poem, telling the story of Aeneas, who after the fall of Troy founded a colony in Italy from which Romans claimed descent. Taking the *Iliad* as a model, Virgil made his poem a propaganda piece for Roman imperialism. In line with Augustus' policy, he sought to revive the *mos maiorum,* the "customs of our ancestors," in a nation where they were fast vanishing. The theme of the poem is *pietas* (devotion)—to fathers, to the gods, to national ideals. Its message is that Romans must sacrifice their individual desires to destiny and the state. With such an ethos, we would expect duty to triumph over love—and it usually does. Dido, the queen of Carthage, is a sympathetic figure, but Aeneas, at the gods' command, must leave her to fulfill his fate in Italy. Virgil seems to be saying, "Make war, not love." So it is surprising to find one grand passion in the *Aeneid* not just condoned but presented for emulation, and that a love affair *more Graeco,* "in the Greek fashion," as the Romans put it.

We first meet Nisus and Euryalus in Book V, when Aeneas pauses in Sicily to celebrate funeral games in memory of his father. Eager men line up for the footrace—"Nisus and Euryalus in the lead— / Euryalus exceptional for beauty / And bloom of youth, whom Nisus dearly loved."[26] In Book IX the Trojans land in Italy and are besieged by the Rutulians while Aeneas is on a diplomatic mission. The lovers reappear, this time sharing military duty:

> Nisus guarded a gate—a man-at-arms
> With a fighting heart . . .

Euryalus was his comrade, handsomer
Than any other soldier of Aeneas
Wearing the Trojan gear: a boy whose cheek
Bore though unshaven manhood's early down.
One love united them, and side by side
They entered combat, as that night they held
The gate on the same watch.[27]

Nisus conceives a daring plan: he intends to slip through the besiegers' lines under cover of night with a message for Aeneas, who does not know the danger his troops are facing. When Euryalus begs to go with him, Nisus is at first unwilling, but the boy prevails and the two set out, wreaking much butchery on the sleeping enemy. Then, separated from his comrade in the darkness of a thick wood, Euryalus is surrounded by enraged soldiers, whom Nisus tries to distract with shouts and taunts but to no avail—Euryalus is cut down.[28] Nisus, mad with grief, charges Euryalus' attackers and is himself slain; he falls dead on the boy's body.

Clearly, Virgil is trying to incorporate into a Latin poem a love that would parallel the devotion of Achilles to Patroclus in the *Iliad.* He is challenging both Roman tradition and the cynicism of Cicero and Lucretius. Why does he do this? The Romans' anxieties about sexual submission had inhibited their acceptance of the Greek ideal, but Virgil is not plagued by these fears—he values a personal tie that is protective, self-sacrificing, and heroic for its own sake, quite apart from its military utility.

Moreover, the Greek view seems to have appealed to something in his own personality. The authorship of the earliest biography of Virgil is in doubt—it may be by Suetonius or Donatus. But the sketch characterizes the poet's desires as directed especially to boys ("libidinis in pueros pronioris").[29] Since it is unusual for a biographer to assign a specific sexual orientation to a Roman, we may assume that this side of Virgil's personality struck his contemporaries. This was because Virgil seems to have adopted toward his favored boys something like the protective, nurturing role of the Greek *erastes,* taking responsibility for their education and upbringing. As his biographer puts it, "He was especially given to passions for boys, and his special favorites were Cebes and Alexander, whom he calls Alexis in the second book of his 'Bucolics.' This boy was given to him by Asinius Pollio, and both his favorites had some education, while Cebes was even a poet."[30]

When Nisus falls in Book IX of the *Aeneid,* Virgil addresses the dead lovers and makes a prophecy:

Fortunate both! If in the least my songs
Avail, no future date shall ever take you
Out of the record of remembered Time,
While children of Aeneas make their home

Around the Capitol's unshaken rock,
And still the Roman Father governs all.[31]

But Virgil failed. Nisus and Euryalus never became exemplars of love and valor for the Romans, as Achilles and Patroclus and the tyrannicides were for the Greeks.

• Meleager and Callimachus •

Despite this, Latin erotic poetry was strongly influenced by Greek poets of the sixth and fifth century and their successors in the Greek Anthology. The anthology, a collection of some 3,700 epigrams by over three hundred poets, was edited by the Byzantine scholar Constantinus Cephalas about 917 CE. It devotes two books to love poetry. Book V contains some 309 short poems on the love of women. But Book XII rivals it with 258 poems on the love of boys composed over a period of more than a thousand years, from 600 BCE to the sixth century CE.

It is assumed that the nucleus for Book XII was the so-called *Garland* of Meleager, a collection of poems that appeared about 60 BCE. Meleager, a Syrian who lived in Gadara (one of the ten Greek cities that formed the so-called Decapolis in Palestine), is passionate, with an Oriental exuberance, and playfully histrionic. His poems, forty of them addressed to boys and another forty to women, are full of pretty conceits that he is not averse to repeating. If a certain boy had wings and arrows, he declares, he could pass as Eros himself. (So he describes Praxiteles in epigram 56, Zoilus in 75, and Antiochus in 78.) Quick, he begs his friends in mock alarm, pour cold water on me, I've dared to look on Dionysius—a boy, not the god (81). He is driven to the verge of ecstasy and despair by Andragathus, Diodorus, Charidemus, and Cleobolus and is at least mildly attracted to Heraclitus, Dion, Uliades, Philocles, Diophantus, Aristagoras, Theocles, and Sopolis. (There is a matching list of enticing women.) No wonder he exclaims "the heavy gale of Desire drives me storm-tossed; for now I swim in a [varied] sea of boys."[32] He does name a few special favorites whose charms have (temporarily) blinded him to all else. He is philosophical about Charidemus; if Zeus bears him away as a second Ganymede, all he asks is a "sweet, melting glance" and a kiss at parting (68). But he will fight the god himself for Myiscus. Zeus has promised not to take him, but Meleager is nervous if he so much as hears a fly buzz—it might be Zeus's eagle (70). At times he professes a preference for women, but in this as in all else he is inconstant: "It is Cypris [Aphrodite], a woman, who casts at us the fire of passion for women, but Love [Eros] himself rules over desire for males. Whither shall I incline, to the boy or to his mother? I will tell you for sure that even Cypris herself will say, 'The bold brat wins.'"[33]

Homoerotic poetry in this vein appears in Latin poetry at least as early as

Meleager. Light on this subject comes from Aulus Gellius, a litterateur who wrote in Athens two and a half centuries later. His *Attic Nights*—conversations between Greeks and Latins who compare their literary cultures—provide much information about lost authors. A Latin-speaking guest at one symposium shows some embarrassment when the Greeks complain that Latin poetry is *anaphrodisias,* that is, without (the charms of) Aphrodite. To this end he recites four early Latin poems, two of which are addressed to males. One is by Valerius Aedituus, who in the age of Marius and Sulla was already imitating Greek erotic epigrams:

> O Phileros, why a torch that we need not?
> Just as we are we'll go, our hearts aflame.
> That flame no wild wind's blast can ever quench,
> Or rain that falls torrential from the skies;
> Venus herself alone can quell her fire,
> No other force there is that has such power.[34]

The second homoerotic poem is by Valerius' contemporary Quintus Catulus, who was consul in 102 BCE with Marius. Catulus was a member of the Scipionic circle, an aristocratic intellectual with a distinguished career as a soldier, politician, and poet. He has no hesitation, however, about revealing that he has fallen passionately in love with another male, one Theotimus.[35]

Latin literature entered upon its golden age in the first century BCE and showed a marked dependence on Greek models. The chief influence on lyrical poetry was the Alexandrian school, which had flourished in Hellenistic Egypt some two centuries earlier. The Alexandrians strove above all else for elegance, polish, and sophistication, and they prized erudition. Their leader, Callimachus, who wrote in the early third century BCE and held an important post at the famous library, was no Walt Whitman: "I loathe all common things," he wrote in an epigram. Like Ezra Pound and T. S. Eliot, he consciously forged a new style and was content to limit his audience to the learned few. But though Callimachus was an innovator in style, he was an erotic traditionalist: a dozen of his epigrams appear in Book XII of the Greek Anthology. As fastidious in love as in art, he would have disapproved of Meleager: "I hate the cyclic [epic] poem, nor do I take pleasure in the road that carries many to and fro. I abhor, too, the roaming lover, and I drink not from every well."[36] He apologizes for having once let his feelings run away with him. Love and wine were to blame: he appeared at a boy's door at night, but, he protests, he did not make a disturbance by calling out his name—he only kissed the doorpost.[37]

• Catullus and Tibullus •

Catullus, Rome's first major love poet, whose short life ran from c. 84 to 54 BCE, admired Callimachus and translated him. His arrival on the scene dramatizes as nothing else does how deeply divided Roman views were on love and sex. Livy had pictured an austere, puritanical early Rome, a society of hardworking farmers who did not know luxury or dissipation. Catullus, who did not share this ideal, inaugurated an age in which poets defied tradition and mounted a veritable erotic revolt. Famous as the lover of "Lesbia" (whom he begins by praising rapturously and ends by cursing obscenely), he admonishes his mistress, "Let us live and love, and value at one farthing all the talk of crabbed old men."[38] In the same poem he begs her for some thousands of kisses. As if to confirm his bisexual impartiality, he later addresses a boy named Juventius, on whom he bestows even more:

> If I should be allowed to go so far as kissing
> Your sweet eyes, Juventius,
> I would go on kissing them three hundred thousand times;
> Nor would it ever seem I had had enough,
> Not if I harvested
> Kisses as numerous as the ears of standing corn.[39]

It has usually been assumed that Latin poems to boys must be addressed to slaves. Catullus appears to have broken the taboo by writing to a freeborn boy and, moreover, using his real name, for he calls his favorite "the flower of the Juventii" (24), implying that Juventius was the scion of a distinguished family. The love affair did not run smoothly, however. Catullus steals a kiss but is devastated when the boy wipes it away as if it was from a "dirty whore" (99). Yet Catullus himself hardly cuts an amiable figure. The most unlovable of love poets, he can be meanly snobbish about his rivals: how, he asks, can Juventius tolerate Furius, who is poor, or another suitor who is sickly (24, 81)? When he fears that someone may seduce his boy, he becomes violent, threatening him with the punishment of an adulterer—a radish in his rectum (15). His hypermasculinity finds vent in insults hurled at anyone suspected of taking the passive role. His favorite term of abuse, employed in poem after poem, is *cinaedus* ("faggot"). He calls Caesar a *pathicus* and makes the same charge against his lieutenant Mamurra (57). (He later apologized and was forgiven.) When his own manhood is called into doubt by acquaintances who snicker over his "thousand kisses," he begins an untranslatable poem (16) with a threat of rape: "Pedicabo ego vos et irrumabo, / Aureli pathice et cinaede Furi" ["I'll sodomize you anally *(pedicabo)* and orally *(irrumabo),* Aurelius, you queer, and Furius, you faggot"]. Few Latin writers have dramatized their anxieties about masculinity so vehemently.

Tibullus, the first of the Latin elegists, was of a gentler mold. Tibullus had served with Augustus' generals in Gaul; but, like young Americans of the Vietnam generation, he favored love above war, which he saw as mere plunder. "Down with bugles and flags!" he writes. "Wounds and wealth to the greedy!"[40] He prefers the modest comfort of his farm, where he wields a

14. The Warren cup. Roman, silver, first century CE.

15. The Warren cup, reverse.

pitchfork and carries home stray lambs. The pleasures of rural life include the delightful Delia, but she proves fickle. He veers in another direction—his fourth elegy is a homosexual counterpart to Ovid's *Art of Love,* for which, indeed, it may have provided a model.

The poem opens with Tibullus' plea to the god Priapus to tell him how boys may be wooed. Priapus, whose phallic image guarded fields and crops, was generally associated with rough sexual humor. But here, in a different vein, the god instructs Tibullus with sympathetic tenderness:

> "Trust to no gentle band of boys," he told me.
> "They give you too much reason to grow fond—
> one by his skill in reading will attract you;
> one, swimming strongly in a quiet pond;
> one by his young and touching self-assurance,
> and one, perhaps, still shy enough to blush."[41]

Like the Cretans, Tibullus places personality above beauty. It is the boy's intellectual promise, or his boldness or vulnerability, which attracts him. Priapus' speech gives a unique picture of a man and boy sharing pastimes in the Italian countryside:

> "Whatever it may be your lad asks of you,
> do not refuse. Love gains by what love yields.
> Go where he goes—a thousand miles or farther,
> under the August sun that burns the fields
> or under skies grown dark and heavy-clouded,
> marked with the colored bow that threatens rain."[42]

In the end, Tibullus makes a painful confession: he has set himself up as a guide to lovers, but his Marathus has scorned him. Was this boy a slave? Commentators have thought so, but can the elaborate courtships Tibullus describes be directed at slaves? Possibly they were: sensitive Romans must have renounced the rights of sexual access the law theoretically gave them and declined to force themselves on unwilling boys. Whatever the case, elegy nine of Book I is a litany of reproaches: Marathus has been seduced by money and gifts. Tibullus hopes Marathus' new lover's wife will cuckold him in turn. The passion and recriminations fall into the same pattern as the Delia poems: they are the common coin of the Latin love elegy.

· Theocritus and Corydon ·

Theocritus, who wrote about 270 BCE, shared with Callimachus the leadership of the Alexandrian school. Indeed, one of Callimachus' love poems is addressed to a young man named Theocritus whom authorities identify with the poet. Here, two hundred years after Euripides and Agathon, is another example in Greek literary history of the two leading poets of the age appearing as lovers.[43]

Theocritus is a typical Alexandrian in his elegance, grace, and internationalism. The setting of his poems spans the ancient Greek world—Syracuse (where he was born), southern Italy, the Aegean island of Cos, Alexandria itself. Literary scholarship knows him best as the fountainhead of the so-called pastoral, whose conventions two thousand years of poets imitated, from Virgil to Spenser, Milton, and Arnold, by affecting to don the garb of simple shepherds. His so-called idylls, or "short pieces," run typically from two to ten pages. Those in the pastoral mode vary considerably in tone and style. "The Harvest Festival" (Idyll 7) is artificial and subtle, while "Goatherd and Shepherd" (Idyll 5) is an impolite exchange between two unlettered countrymen.

The shepherds in "The Harvest Festival" are sophisticated poets in disguise. One of them, Lycidas, laments the departure of his (male) lover for Mytilene, while his comrade loves the girl Myrto but devotes his song to the plight of his friend Aratos, who "yearns deep in his heart for a boy."[44] Both rustics speak with elaborate courtesy. By contrast, Comatas and Lacon in "Goatherd and Shepherd" counter boast with boast and insult with insult. Comatas brags of the girls who favor him, Lacon of the boys he enjoys. With peasant malice, Comatas reminds Lacon of an earlier encounter: "But don't you remember that screwing I gave you, when you grinned / And wagged your tail briskly and held tight to the oak tree?"[45]

Most poignant of the tales is Theocritus' account of Heracles' tragic love for Hylas (Idyll 13). The hero, seeking the golden fleece, had set sail with the Argonauts and the curly-haired Hylas, whom he loved. Heracles, we are told, taught the boy "as a father would his dear son, / All that had made him a good man and famous."[46] (No Roman would have written in this style!) But when the ship docks near the Hellespont, the boy is lost. Sent for water, he fascinates the nymphs of a pool, who seize him so that he drowns in their embrace. The distraught Heracles searches long and far, plaintively calling the boy's name and refusing to return to the ship. Finally, his exasperated comrades depart and leave him to his grief.

Not all of Theocritus' poems are dramatic vignettes. In Idyll 12 he speaks his own voice:

> You have come, darling boy! At last after two nights and days
> You have come! But those anxious with longing grow old in a day.
> As much sweeter spring is than winter, as apple than beach plum . . .
> So great is my joy at your coming, and to you I run
> Like a wayfarer parched by the sun to the shade of the oak.
> O that the Loves might breathe alike on us both,
> That we two might become a legend for all men hereafter!

> "Divine were they among those who lived in earlier times,
> The one the inspirer," as a man of Amyclae [Sparta] might put it,
> "The other a mirror," as a Thessalian might say,
> "And under an equal yoke did they love one another,
> Then there were golden men, when the beloved reflected the love of
> the lover."[47]

He hopes that two hundred generations hence someone will bring him word in Hades that their love is still known among men. In Idyll 29 he promises a fickle boy the same devotion Achilles showed to Patroclus; in Idyll 30 he complains that he is still the victim of love, though the hair on his temples is white. Reading these poems, we are struck by how much of the classical tradition of Greek love is still alive in the Alexandrian age.

This rich tradition runs much thinner in Latin. We have seen how Virgil, with small success, tried to habituate the idea of heroic love in the *Aeneid.* Yet his second eclogue became the most celebrated expression of male love in the Latin language. The poem, Theocritean in style and setting, is a lament by Corydon, the head shepherd on an estate in Sicily, who is distraught at the indifference of Alexis, his master's spoiled darling. Despite its dramatic form, Latin commentators regularly read the poem as a personal statement. Virgil's Latin biographer, we have seen, assumed he was in love with "Alexis" and identified the boy with a slave Virgil's patron had given him.[48] Later writers have added to the poem's notoriety. Byron shocked regency England by citing it in the opening canto of *Don Juan,* and André Gide gave the title *Corydon* to the controversial defense of homosexuality he published in 1924.

Virgil depicts Corydon's passion with psychological realism and a touch of wry irony. Corydon describes himself as *rusticus* and bemoans Alexis' disdain for the simple pleasures of rural life. (Virgil's biographer noted his own rustic appearance.) The shepherd tries desperately to recommend himself, but we smile at the self-deception of the besotted lover. This is the Epicurean view of love as a futile madness, softened by a touch of sympathetic humor. Do something practical, the shepherd counsels himself at last in frustration, prune your vines, weave a basket—you'll find another Alexis.

• Horace's Odes •

Horace was a close friend of Virgil and shared with him the munificence of Augustus' wealthy confidant, Maecenas. Though he wrote no epic to rival the *Aeneid,* he was recognized as Virgil's successor and Rome's new laureate. Horace had more firsthand knowledge of Greek life than his friend Virgil, having spent two years in Athens as a student, and his poetry often imitated recondite Greek meters while remaining quintessentially Roman in its sentiments. Amiable (when not irritated), modest (when not praising his own talents), pointedly uninterested in politics (when not singing the glories of Augustus' Rome), Horace took a relaxed attitude to love and sex that demonstrates all too well how a Roman slaveowner might disregard the sensitivities of the human beings he controlled:

> If you're dying of thirst, do you ask if the goblets are golden?
> Or if you're famished and starving, refuse every food in the world save
> Peacock and turbot? Then why, if your groin is distended, and right at
> Hand is a slave girl or slave lad of yours that you crave in the moment's
> Urgency, why should you choose to endure the discomfort of passion?
> *I* wouldn't. I'm for a love that's accessible, easy to come by.[49]

Horace's love poems, as we might expect, lack the idealism of Virgil's tale of Nisus and Euryalus and the passion of Catullus. A multitude of Lalages, Glyceras, Pyrras, and Chloes flit dimly through his pages. He informs us that his solicitous father chaperoned him to school to prevent any hint of scandal, but this does not seem to have inhibited Horace in his own pursuit of youths. In one satire he makes a Stoic philosopher chide him for his "crushes on thousands of girls" and "thousands of boys."[50] In Epode 11 he claims to have spent three summers enamoured of Inachia; now he loves Lyciscus, whose tenderness surpasses any woman's—only a new passion for a girl or boy will free him. He comes closest to real feeling in the opening of his last book of odes, which he published in 13 BCE when he was fifty. He has been heart-free for eight years; now, he asks

> Must it be war again
> After so long a truce? Venus, be kind, refrain
> . . . I take no joy
> In the naive hope of mutual love with woman or boy . . .
> Why then, my Ligurinus, why
> Should the reluctant-flowing tears surprise these dry
> Cheeks, and my fluent tongue
> Stumble in unbecoming silences among
> Syllables? In dreams at night
> I hold you in my arms, or toil behind your flight
> Across the Martian field,
> Or chase through yielding waves the boy who will not yield.[51]

Such verse was acclaimed, but was it respectable, that is, could it hurt a political career? It is a paradox that Roman law and Roman oratory decried male liaisons, while Roman poets felt free to avow their love of boys quite unselfconsciously. What are we to make of this cultural schizophrenia?

First, we must note that, if there was a law, prosecutions were all but unheard of. Nor did the possibility that youthful male affairs might be raked up in politics seem to deter upper-class boys from indulging in them. As for moral attitudes generally, these varied widely, from conservatives who lamented the passing of the *mos maiorum* to others who, like Ovid, rejoiced that the "good old days" were past. Some later Stoic philosophers, such as Musonius Rufus and his pupil Epictetus (60–140), deplored all sexual relations with slaves, but the typical Roman's view was more lax.[52] Sexual behavior was not proscribed on religious grounds; the concern was rather that a male should not violate another man's property—that is, his wife, daughter, or son—or take a passive role. This, and not the gender of a man's partner, was the operative principle in Roman morals.

Cicero himself provides a piquant example of these contradictions. He had attacked male liaisons in his speeches and denounced Greek love in his *Disputations,* but he was not above writing love poetry himself on occasion. The poems have been lost, but evidence of their tenor comes from the letters of Pliny the Younger, who comments on them. Cicero's example gave Pliny the courage to imitate him: "I have discovered the wanton *jeu d'esprit* of Cicero [in which] he complains that, with malice prepense, Tiro had deceived his lover [Cicero] and cheated him at night of a few kisses that had been promised him after dinner. After reading this, I said to myself: why conceal my loves and timidly avoid publishing them? Why not admit that I too know the tricks of a Tiro, and a Tiro's flirtatious charms and the deceits that add fuel to the fires?"[53] Tiro was a slave of Cicero's, but an unusual one. The twice-divorced Cicero made him his secretary and later, having freed him, his literary executor. After Cicero's death Tiro wrote his biography and had a distinguished literary career of his own. This was almost Greek love.

• Ovid's Myths •

With Ovid there were no contradictions or hesitations: from the start his sympathies were with the poets of the moral revolt. Inevitably this put him at odds with Augustus, whose new official policy encouraged marriage and large families to provide officers for Rome's armies and administrators for her colonies. Finally, the outraged emperor expressed his anger by exiling Ovid, alleging the subversive influence of his *Art of Love,* a manual of stratagems for seducing women.

Ovid can confidently be identified as a tolerant heterosexual. At the outset of the *Loves*—poems dramatizing an affair with a woman that did not run smoothly—Ovid makes the typical Roman assumption that love is genderless when he asks, "What can I do in light verse? I have no boy I can sing of, / No nice long-haired girl making a theme for my lays."[54] In the same vein, Ovid's most famous poem, the *Metamorphoses,* treats the bisexuality of Greek myth without prejudice. What was for the fathers of the Christian

16. Zephyrus and Hyacinthus.
Red-figure cup, c. 490 CE.

church an indelible blot on Greek religion is for Ovid a source of poetic inspiration. He is limited only by his theme, which is supernatural transformations. The homoerotic tales in the *Metamorphoses* center on the figure of Orpheus in Book X, where he tells the story of Orpheus' loss of Eurydice and then recounts the legend that Orpheus' interest later turned to boys. In addition, he makes Orpheus sing at length "the love of boys," a device which allows Ovid to describe Jupiter's metamorphosis into an eagle for the love of Ganymede and the transformation of Cyparissus, beloved of Apollo, who, after his pathetic death is changed into a tree.

17. The Bacchantes attack Orpheus. Fresco, Casa dei Vettii, Pompeii, 1st century BCE.

Among these tales Ovid lavishes most art on the story of Hyacinth. Apollo, setting aside his divinity, leaves Delphi for love of the young man, but once again an accident deprives him of the boy: Apollo throws a discus that inadvertently kills his beloved. (In some versions of the myth, the jealous wind god, Zephyrus, himself enamoured of Hyacinth, directs the fatal missile.) Ovid's depiction of Hyacinth's death echoes Virgil's lines on the death of Euryalus:

The wound was past all cure. So in a garden,
If one breaks off a violet or poppy
Or lilies, bristling with their yellow stamens,
And they droop over, and cannot raise their heads,
But look on earth, so sank the dying features.[55]

Apollo assures him that he will be reborn as a flower that will commemorate his grief.

When Orpheus finishes his song, a fierce band of Thracian Maenads set upon him. Infuriated that he has deserted women for the love of boys and taught this "art" to other Thracians, they beat him to death with clubs and stones. For this deed, Bacchus turns the women into a grove of oaks. This brutal murder, which is presented as a crime by Ovid, seemed just to medieval moralists, who damned Orpheus as the malign inventor of pederasty.

• Lesbianism •

Quite different in mood is the tale of Iphis and Ianthe in Book IX. As a lesbian love story, it is all but unique in classical literature. When Iphis' mother becomes pregnant, her husband decrees that the child must die if it is a girl. She bears a girl, conceals her sex, and gives her a name of ambiguous gender: Iphis. When this "son" is thirteen, the father chooses the golden-haired Ianthe as "his" bride. Ovid treats the love of the two girls sympathetically:

They were of equal age, they both were lovely,
Had learned their ABC's from the same teachers,
And so love came to both of them together
In simple innocence, and filled their hearts
With equal longing.[56]

But as the marriage with its inevitable disclosure draws near, Iphis recoils in horror, calls her love "monstrous and unheard of," and bemoans her cruel fate. The goddess Isis resolves the impasse by turning her into a boy. Iphis' self-loathing may serve as an instance of what we might now call internalized homophobia. But what, we may ask, is Ovid's own attitude toward lesbian love? Perhaps he wants us to see Iphis' self-rejection as the naiveté of youth—she is, after all, only thirteen. More likely, however, Ovid is reflecting the prejudice of the classical world, which did not extend to lesbianism the same tolerance it granted pederasty.

References to love between women are sparse and rare. An epigram in the Greek Anthology by a third-century poet, Asclepiades, blames two women of Samos for taking the wrong path to love: he asks Aphrodite to hate them (Book 5, epigram 207). Phaedrus, the Roman fabulist, writing about 50 CE,

18. Female athletes. Mosaic, Villa Romana del Casale, Piazza Armerina, Sicily, 3rd–4th century.

explained lesbianism by a poetic allegory: Prometheus coming home drunk from a party had mistakenly interchanged the genitals of some women and some men. It is revealing that Phaedrus parallels female homosexuality not with male homosexuality generally but only with the passive form, as something akin to it in perversity. As a result of Prometheus' error, he comments, "Lust now enjoys perverted pleasure."[57]

Seneca the elder, discussing a legal case, mentions a husband who killed his wife and her female lover and implies that their crime was worse than ordinary adultery.[58] A few decades later, Martial, with his typical blunt crudity, satirized a woman he calls Philaenis, an athlete who plays ball in a bikini, wrestles in the mud, vomits wine before dinner, gorges herself, and drinks again (Book 7, epigram 67). Stereotyping lesbians as hypermasculine, Martial introduces the curious theory that lesbians had unusually long clitorises that allowed them to penetrate other women sexually. More oddly still, Philaenis sodomizes boys to prove her masculinity.

Male homosexuality appears occasionally in the extant prose Greek romances, but lesbianism is far less common. In the *Babyloniaca* of Iamblichus

(c. 150 CE), we hear of an Egyptian princess, Berenice, who loves and marries another woman. The novelist, however, denounces such love as "wild and lawless."[59] Lucian's fifth "Dialogue of the Courtesans" (c. 180) parallels Martial a century later by again presenting a masculine stereotype: Megilla calls herself Megillus and wears a wig to cover her shaved head. She is "married" to Demonassa of Corinth but is herself from Lesbos. Her new friend Leaena comments: "They say there are women like that in Lesbos, with faces like men, and unwilling to consort with men, but only with women, as though they themselves were men."[60] Megilla seduces Leaena who, however, thinks the experience too disgusting to describe. Obviously we are far from the sophisticated aestheticism of Sappho's circle, where women cultivated beauty and the arts.

In another dialogue, also ascribed to Lucian but in fact written some time after his death, two men debate which is better, male love or heterosexuality. One speaker protests that legitimizing male affairs would logically lead to the condoning of lesbianism—which would be unthinkable. His rhetoric gives a glimpse of how a hostile Greek male of about 270 CE conceived of women who loved women:

> But if males find intercourse with males acceptable, henceforth let women too love each other. Come now, epoch of the future, legislator of strange pleasures, devise fresh paths for male lusts, but bestow the same privilege upon women, and let them have intercourse with each other just as men do. Let them strap to themselves cunningly contrived instruments of lechery, those mysterious monstrosities devoid of seed, and let women lie with women as does a man. Let wanton Lesbianism ["tribadism"]—that word seldom heard, which I feel ashamed even to utter—freely parade itself, and let our women's chambers imitate Philaenis, disgracing themselves with [androgynous] amours.[61]

One clue to the speaker's disgust may lie in the reference to Philaenis. Martial, as we have seen, had used the name as generic for what we would now call a lesbian. The historic Philaenis purportedly wrote a sex manual in the fourth or third centuries BCE describing lesbian sexual practices in a fashion that was regarded as outrageously obscene. Philaenis' work may have colored ancient views of love between women adversely. But the speech indicates another reason lesbianism appeared so offensive in Hellenic eyes. The crime (as in the case of male passivity) lay in its violation of prescribed gender roles.

• Petronius' *Satyricon* •

To turn from Ovid to Petronius is to leave poetic myth for street-corner realism, sentiment for satire. It is generally assumed the author of the *Satyricon* was Nero's "arbiter of elegance," a man who was said to have "made luxury a fine art" and who probably composed his story as entertainment at the imperial court. Called the first novel, the *Satyricon* may also claim to be the first gay fiction, for the characters' embroilment in homosexual affairs forms the center of the rambling plot. The book is a merciless picture of low life in first-century southern Italy, unedifying but funny, mixing many styles from the rhetorically pompous to the racy and illiterate.

The chief figure is Encolpius ("the crotch"), who is consumed with passion for Giton, an effeminate sixteen-year-old who is also courted by Ascyltos, the third member of this trio of thieves. Ascyltos' adventures take him to the dinner table of Trimalchio, heavy with the most extravagant meal ever served. Trimalchio, the freed slave, is a boastful vulgarian, enormously rich—he would like to buy Sicily—but quite candid as to how he got his start in life: "For fourteen years I was my master's pet. But what's the shame in doing what you're told to do? But all the same, if you know what I mean, I managed to do my mistress a favor or two."[62] Petronius' contemporary, Seneca the philosopher, inveighed against the "troops of catamites *[exoleti]*" with smooth skin and down on their cheeks who met with shameful treatment at the end of Roman banquets.[63] In the *Satyricon,* Trimalchio and a friend infuriate their wives by fondling their own favorite slave boys at the dinner table.

Eventually Giton elects to leave Encolpius after a night with Ascyltos. Encolpius berates the errant couple in this Ciceronian fashion:

> Was it for this that I fled from justice, that I deserted the [gladiatorial] ring and murdered my host? Is this the reward of my courage and my crimes—to be abandoned, an outcast, a beggar, in a cheap inn in a Greek town [that is, in southern Italy]? And who is the author of my loneliness? A young man [Ascyltos] polluted with every perversion and vice; a man who by his own admission deserves to be banished; who paid for his freedom with his debauchery and for his debauchery with his freedom; whose body is bought as one buys a ticket; who was treated like a woman even by those who knew him to be a man! And what of his partner in crime? A little boy [Giton] who gave up his trousers for skirts; whose mother persuaded him never to be a man![64]

As in senatorial politics, it is the lovers' participation in the female role that is the point of Encolpius' scurrility.

The one moment of tenderness in the novel comes when Encolpius, reunited at last with Giton, faces shipwreck with him:

> I, meanwhile, was clinging to Giton with all my strength, sobbing with terror and tragic despair. "O gods in heaven," I cried in bitterness of heart, "is this your justice, that two lovers should be united only at the moment of death? Alas, not even that: for the Fates are cruel and soon the seas will overturn the ship and the wild waves sunder even two lovers' last embrace

> . . . Quickly stripping off his clothes, Giton snuggled underneath my tunic and lifted his face to be kissed. Then, to keep the jealous sea from breaking our embrace, he bound his belt about us both and buckled it tight. "One last solace at least remains, Encolpius," he cried. "Whatever may happen now, at least we shall lie united in love upon the heaving swell a while, and if perchance some kinder current than the rest should cast us on the shore, some passerby, by simple human kindness moved, may build us both a single grave."[65]

The rogues, of course, survive. The sentimental rhetoric of this passage looks forward to the Greek romances of following centuries, in which, however, homosexuality plays only a subordinate role.

• Suetonius and the Emperors •

The *Satyricon* is a unique document whose witty pages condemn offenses against taste but hardly against morals. In this it reflects the libertine side of imperial Rome. If the erotic poets are conscious rebels who live to love, and Petronius wholly amoral, Roman historians of the period continue to reflect the censoriousness of the republican age, so that male affairs are used to denigrate the politically powerful much as they had been in Cicero's day. Indeed, the amount of personal scandal in political biographies gives the impression that such amours were all but ubiquitous at the highest levels of Roman society. So Edward Gibbon, learned in the Latin sources, added an acerbic footnote to his pages on Hadrian in his *Decline and Fall:* "Of the first fifteen emperors Claudius was the only one whose taste in love was entirely correct."[66]

Much of our information about the sex lives of the Roman emperors comes from Suetonius' *Lives of the Twelve Caesars.* These much-browsed biographies appeared a few years after Plutarch's *Parallel Lives,* and yet their treatment of male relations could hardly be more different. But to what extent is Suetonius merely retelling scandalous gossip? Are his accounts colored by political bias? Suetonius' sketches are on the whole dry, factual, and unrhetorical. He has sometimes been read as hostile to the institution of the empire, as in his biography of Julius Caesar, where, after praising Caesar as a general and statesman, he criticizes him for usurping authority. Such overt judgments, however, are rare. Nevertheless, Suetonius seems unwilling to let slip any detail that might reflect negatively on an emperor's character.

Suetonius wrote about 120 CE but, like Cicero, mentions male relations only in a hostile context. His first chapter, on Julius Caesar, sets the pattern:

> There was no stain on [Caesar's] reputation for chastity except his intimacy with King Nicomedes, but that was a deep and lasting reproach, which laid him open to insults from every quarter. I say nothing of the notorious lines of Licinius Calvus: "Whate'er Bithynia had, and Caesar's

> paramour [*pedicator,* active partner]." I pass over, too, the invectives of Dollabella and the elder Curio in which Dollabella calls him "the queen's rival, the inner partner of the royal couch," and Curio, "the brothel of Nicomedes and the stew of Bithynia." I take no account of the edicts of Bibulus, in which he posted his colleague as the "queen of Bithynia," saying that "of yore he was enamoured of a king, but now of a king's estate" . . . But Gaius Memmius makes the direct charge that he acted as cup-bearer to Nicomedes with the rest of his wantons *[exoleti]* at a large dinner-party, and that among the guests were some merchants from Rome, whose names Memmius gives. Cicero, indeed, [has] written in sundry letters that Caesar was led by the king's attendants to the royal apartments, that he lay on a golden couch arrayed in purple, and that the virginity of this son of Venus was lost in Bithynia.[67]

Suetonius then records Mark Antony's charge that Augustus had earned adoption by Caesar through sexual favors but discounts this story as a political slander.[68]

Suetonius explores the sexual histories of the tyrannical emperors Tiberius, Caligula, and Nero with particular relish. We may feel that in some cases he is simply repeating stories uncritically without trying to assess his sources. This is especially true of Tiberius, whom Suetonius accuses of staging sex shows in the privacy of his retreat at Capri and systematically abusing children.[69] With Caligula and Nero he is more circumstantial. Of Caligula he reports that a young aristocrat named Valerius Catullus "publicly proclaimed that he had violated the emperor and worn himself out in commerce with him."[70] Nero's profligate nature is illustrated by his castration of the young Sporus, their mock marriage, and his treating him publicly as his empress. Suetonius then claims that Nero married his freedman Doryphorus in the same fashion as Sporus had married him, "going so far as to imitate the cries and lamentations of a maiden being deflowered."[71] Even the short sketches of the three men who held the throne for brief intervals after the death of Nero are rich in sexological detail. We are told that the elderly Galba, whose parsimoniousness with his troops cost him his throne, preferred "full-grown, strong men" to boys, that the spendthrift Otho "according to some" was Nero's bedmate, and that the gluttonous Vitellius had got his start in life as a performer in Tiberius' erotic entertainments so that he bore the nickname "Spintria" (sphincter).[72]

Suetonius would have had a vivid recollection of Domitian's reign of terror, which he had lived through as a young man. The first two Flavian emperors, Domitian's father and brother, are treated favorably. He admires the modest and amiable Vespasian and hails his son Titus enthusiastically as the "delight and darling of the human race." Though Suetonius describes the young Titus as maintaining "troops of catamites *[exoleti]* and eunuchs" before ascending the throne, he treats this as a piece of youthful folly that Titus put behind him before his short but exemplary reign.[73]

Suetonius wastes no time, however, in damning Titus' younger brother Domitian, the last emperor whose reign he records. His opening paragraph charges that Domitian, as an impoverished young man, had sold himself to the consul Claudius Pollio, and he cites a letter in which the emperor-to-be promised the older man an assignation.[74] He says nothing, however, about Domitian's well-known attachment to the handsome eunuch Earinus, to whom both Statius and Martial addressed complimentary verses. Presumably this is because sexual relations with a slave carried no stigma. But even if we discount some of Suetonius' allegations, we are left with a remarkably high incidence of homosexuality among Rome's rulers in the first century of the empire. Indeed, same-sex liaisons seem to have been as common in the world of high politics as they were among the poets of love.

• Statius, Martial, Juvenal •

Contrasting with the gritty realism of the *Satyricon* and the succulent scandals of Suetonius is a poem Statius wrote for his lawyer friend Flavius Ursus on the death of a beloved youth named Philetus. Statius, who lived in the second half of the first century, was much admired in his own day and by Dante and Chaucer in the high Middle Ages, when he was (inexplicably) thought to be a Christian. The sixth poem in the second book of his *Silvae* is a rarity in Roman literature, lines which treat a male love affair from a point of view essentially Greek.

Philetus, whose name means "beloved," is described as loyal and affectionate. Most favored slave boys were curled darlings with girlish features. But Statius insists that this fifteen-year-old was manly, modest, and mature in judgment and bore himself proudly, "like a young Spartan" or an athlete in the Olympic games. His appearance recalled not Ganymede but heroes like Theseus and Achilles. Statius compares his devotion to Ursus with Patroclus' love for Achilles and calls it "Cecropian," that is, Athenian. So exorbitant is Statius' praise that we suspect he was half in love with the boy himself. In the end he feels compelled to remind us that the youth was, after all, only a slave.

Martial and Statius were contemporaries who shared the same friends and patrons, but neither mentions the other. Perhaps this silence is significant, since few poets can have been so antipathetic. Statius is learned, idealistic, and literary; Martial is cynical and, in matters of sex, unblushingly explicit. His fourteen books of epigrams describe erotic behavior with the thoroughness of a first-century Kinsey. He is more revealing than any other Latin writer as to his own preferences and quite as willing to let us know what he disapproves. He does not, however, assume the dignity of a moral philosopher. His brief, witty poems end not with sermons but with malicious innuendoes. He is the tabloid reporter who reflects not high principles but the visceral reactions of the man on the street.

Martial's hierarchy of sexual prejudices is clear. He has no aversion to what we know invidiously as the "missionary" position, but anal intercourse with women is quite as acceptable; so is pederasty. Playing the role of a pathic or *cinaedus* will, he assumes, bring any man into contempt (2.51, 3.71, 9.47). But worst of all is the fellator or cunnilinguist (2.28, 2.50, 3.81, 6.26). Such men or women, whether they perform heterosexually (1.77, 4.84) or homosexually (7.67, 9.27), are beyond the pale. He admits he enjoys having women fellate him, but to reciprocate would be unthinkably degrading (9.40, 9.67).

Martial is avowedly, even aggressively, bisexual. He cites Virgil's Corydon eclogue (8.55) and, like Catullus, whom he resembles in many respects, writes "kissing poems" to boys (3.65, 6.34, 10.42, 11.6, 11.26). He straightforwardly portrays the frustration his thwarted lust brings and its manual relief (11.73). He confesses that effeminate boys hold a special attraction for him (12.75). But he is not prejudiced against boyish masculinity; one fantasy paints his ideal boy as an exotic blond Egyptian with unbraided hair who is a "man" to all others but a "boy" to him (4.42). He sycophantically flatters Domitian's favorite, the beautiful Earinus, in a whole series of poems (9.11, 12, 16, 17, 36), but this was no more than Statius had done before him. He allows himself a single moment of sentiment in an ocean of filth, writing tenderly of two young men whose romance ended in death (6.68). More typically, he reports, with a scandalmonger's relish, the marriage of "bearded Callistratus" to "rugged Afer" in a ceremony that included a bridal veil and a dowry (12.42).

Like Martial, Juvenal is a satirist, but where Martial is content with short squibs whose point of view does not differ from a street boy's, Juvenal writes powerful verse and wears the frown of an angry preacher. He inveighs fiercely against effeminate men and masculine women, upstart plebeians, and foreigners—especially dark-skinned men from the East. His sixth and longest satire is directed against women generally, whom he denounces as shrews, spendthrifts, nymphomaniacs, and murderers. Here is the most vitriolic misogyny in the ancient world. Juvenal's second satire, attacking effeminate males, is only one third as long, but its one hundred and seventy scornful hexameters still make this diatribe the most extensive piece of writing on homosexuality in classical Latin.

Juvenal begins by singling out a class of moralists who offend him—men with bristly arms and "hair shorter than their eyebrows" who profess austere masculine virtue but are in fact *cinaedi* who allow themselves to be penetrated by other males. ("Sleek are your buttocks when the grinning doctor cuts into the swollen piles"—that is, the doctor interprets the man's depilation as a sign of passivity.)[75] Juvenal protests that he finds it easier to forgive openly effeminate men who do not hide their tastes. But he belies this professed tolerance by attacking a lawyer who sports a transparent robe in the courts, men who wear necklaces and ribbons and take part in the worship of the Bona Dea (a women's cult), and men who are concerned about their complexions—like the Emperor Otho, whom he denounces as a pathic who carried a mirror into battle.

Juvenal is especially shocked when such practices appear in patrician families. The Gracchi clan was uniquely associated with Rome's masculine power—they traditionally carried the heavy shield of Mars in state processions. Juvenal is incensed by a Gracchus who appeared as a bride in a same-sex wedding in Rome. Will such affairs, he asks, eventually be announced in the news of the day? (He did not foresee the twenty-first century.) Given his xenophobia, one might expect Juvenal to blame these alarming new tendencies on foreign influences, but he finds the source of the "plague" in Rome itself. Rome, he thinks, will infect the barbarians.

Modern readers may be puzzled by Juvenal's sixth satire. Juvenal paints women as such undesirables that no man in his right senses would think of marrying one and counsels a friend to prefer suicide. Then he makes a startling proposal: wouldn't it be better, he suggests, "to take some boy-bedfellow, who would never wrangle with you at night, never ask presents of you when in bed?"[76] But of course from the Roman point of view there was no contradiction: pederasty did not compromise a man's male status. Verses by Juvenal's friend Martial throw further revealing light on Juvenal's own preferences. Extolling the pleasures of his Spanish farm, which he invites Juvenal to visit, Martial commends one of his new servants, a young huntsman "that you would like to have with you in a secret grove."[77] Perhaps men who were attracted to other men felt most strongly the need to denounce *cinaedi.*

Hadrian and Antinous

The first century after Christ saw an unusual number of bizarre and tyrannical personalities assume supreme power in Rome, most notably Nero, Caligula, and Domitian. But in 96 Domitian was succeeded by the elderly Nerva, the first of the "good emperors" of the Antonine line. His short reign inaugurated what Gibbon—taking a Eurocentric view—called "the period in the history of the world during which the condition of the human race was most happy and prosperous."[78]

This zenith was first attained under Trajan and Hadrian, both of whom seem to have been predominantly homosexual. The Spanish Trajan was a robust and simple soldier, unassuming and accessible, without guile or harshness, so that, Dio Cassius tells us, he was "loved by all and dreaded by none save the enemy."[79] Extending the empire by his conquest of Dacia (modern Romania), Mesopotamia, and Assyria, he was the only emperor to rival Alexander in reaching the Persian Gulf. He made the laws more humane and built a forum in Rome that was one of the architectural marvels of antiquity, where his triumphal column and arch still stand. A grateful Senate bestowed upon him the title Optimus, recognizing him as the best of emperors. Dio Cassius commented on his love of wine and boys but thought he remained within the bounds of Roman decency: "I know, of course, that he was devoted to boys and to wine, but if he had ever committed or endured any base or wicked deed as a result of this, he would have incurred censure; as it was, however, he drank all the wine he wanted yet remained sober, and in his relation with boys he harmed no one."[80]

Trajan was succeeded by his protégé Hadrian, a fellow Spaniard and second cousin. As energetic as his predecessor, Hadrian was a much more complex man. His imperial policy was not as aggressive as Trajan's: keeping the army well equipped and its morale high, he withdrew to more defensible borders along the Danube and the Euphrates. But where Trajan was not well educated, Hadrian was an ardent philhellene who spoke better Greek than Latin. Arguably the most brilliant of Rome's rulers, he was an expert in mathematics and military affairs, a musician, a painter, and a poet who was fond of erudite debate. Like Trajan, he built lavishly: we still marvel at the Pantheon and at the architectural synopsis of the empire he designed for his villa at Tivoli. Usually just, generous, and kind, he could be moody and harsh and did not enjoy Trajan's universal popularity. He was perhaps the best administrator among the emperors and an adroit statesman in all but his handling of the Jews, who cursed him as a persecutor. He shared Trajan's attachment to boys, wrote poetry on this theme, and was rumored to have had affairs with some of his predecessor's favorites.[81] In the end, death was to blazon one such passion before the world.

19. Antinous. Delphi, c. 130 CE.

A tireless traveler, Hadrian made it a policy to visit every part of the empire, from Gaul and Britain (where he built his famous wall) to Egypt and the East. In Athens in the winter of 128–129 he acted as archon or chief magistrate, was initiated into the Eleusinian mysteries, and raised the city to a new height of splendor, endowing it with an extensive new suburb, a magnificent library, and imposing temples to promote his romantic Panhellenism. Somewhere during these peregrinations he met and fell in love with Antinous, a handsome youth from Bithynia, who became part of his entourage. Perhaps he came upon him during an earlier visit to that province, perhaps he met him as a student in Athens. All we know for certain is that Antinous accompanied Hadrian on a tour of Egypt and that he drowned in the Nile at the age of eighteen or nineteen.

The portraits of Antinous show him as a young man of astonishing beauty. The face is princely, brooding, melancholic, with full features crowned by luxuriantly curling hair. Sometimes the expression is boyishly naive, sometimes sophisticated and sensual. His physique combines the athleticism of a Greek ephebe with a hint of oriental voluptuousness, as if the artist had studied both Praxiteles and Hindu sculpture. But if a thousand statues, coins, and gems reveal what Antinous looked like, we have only limited knowledge of his life with Hadrian.

A circular relief set into the Arch of Constantine in Rome shows him on a boar hunt with the emperor in Asia Minor. Another relief, which depicts Hadrian standing on the mane of a slain lion, illustrates a better-documented episode. On his arrival in Egypt in 130 Hadrian heard of a ferocious lion that was ravaging Libya. Always an enthusiastic hunter, he set out with a party to rid the desert of this menace. An account of the hunt, and Antinous' part in it, appears in a commemorative poem by the Alexandrian poet Pancrates. The details may have been provided by the emperor: "Antinous sat in wait for the man-slaying lion, holding in his left hand the bridle-rein, and in his right a spear tipped with adamant. Hadrian was the first to hurl his brass-fitted spear; he wounded the beast but did not kill it, for he intended to miss the mark, wishing to test to the full the sureness of aim of the beautiful Antinous."[82] But the lion charged before Antinous could act, and Hadrian was forced to make the kill.

Within a few weeks the boy whose life the emperor had saved was dead. Hadrian's grief was overwhelming: we are told "he wept like a woman."[83] Yet the circumstances remain a mystery. Was Antinous' death an accident, or did he drown himself deliberately? Dio Cassius' *History,* written a century later, gives the earliest and fullest account. Dio had consulted Hadrian's autobiography (now lost) but offered his own speculations:

> [Antinous] died in Egypt, either by falling into the Nile, as Hadrian writes, or, as the truth is, by being offered in sacrifice. For Hadrian, as I have stated, was always very curious and employed divinations and incantations of all kinds. Accordingly, he honored Antinous, either because of his love

> for him or because the youth had voluntarily undertaken to die (it being necessary that a life should be surrendered freely for the accomplishment of the ends Hadrian had in view) by building a city on the spot where he had suffered this fate and naming it after him; and he also set up statues—or rather sacred images of him—over almost all the world.[84]

In all likelihood the death was an accident. But perhaps some prophecy had been made by Egyptian priests, whose religion keenly interested the emperor. Later legend assimilated the presumed immolation to the Alcestis myth. Thus, Aurelius Victor wrote in 360: "Others maintain that this sacrifice of Antinous was both pious and religious; for when Hadrian was wishing to prolong his life, and the magicians required a voluntary vicarious victim, they say that, upon the refusal of all others, Antinous offered himself."[85]

Fifteen centuries later a grieving Mogul emperor memorialized his beloved wife in the majestic Taj Mahal. Hadrian worked on a grander scale, raising a whole new city, Antinoopolis, on the banks of the Nile where his lover had died. The founding edict, issued on October 30, 130, ordained that it should be a monument to the dead boy, a religious shrine, and a new Greek settlement and administrative center. Hadrian's dream was amply realized. Sumptuous with temples, marble colonnades, and statuary, the new town grew and flourished for centuries, surviving Christianity and the Arab conquest of Egypt. In 1798, when Edme-François Jomard surveyed the site at the behest of Napoleon, he was overwhelmed by the vast ruins. Two majestic avenues were flanked by hundreds of columns. Topping these, and elsewhere in the city, Jomard counted 1,344 statues and busts of Antinous. Fortunately, Jomard oversaw the publication of a giant folio with handsome illustrations recording the scene.[86] For when another French Egyptologist arrived in 1863, the magnificent ruins had disappeared. The city had fed a cement works that relentlessly ground up its centuries-old columns, temples, and statues.[87] Enterprise had turned into dusty lime the greatest monument ever built by love.

Antinoopolis was above all else the city of a new god. Hitherto, Roman emperors and their relatives had been deified by the Senate, but for a commoner to be divinized was unheard of. But Hadrian, in the extravagance of his devotion, had Antinous proclaimed an immortal. Such an idea seems strange to us today, but Roman, Greek, and Egyptian tradition provided ample precedents. An obelisk inscribed with hieroglyphs honoring Antinous, now on the Pincian Hill in Rome, hails him as "companion to the gods of Egypt" and identifies him with Osiris, the god of death and rebirth. Among the Greeks, too, a mortal might become divine: the Spartans had dedicated a temple to Apollo's *eromenos* and celebrated his festival annually at the Hyacintheia. The new worship of Antinous had a surprisingly wide popular appeal. Archaeologists have found half a million jars that held offerings to his shrine at Antinoopolis. In his cult the mystery religions of Eleusis and

20. View of Antinoopolis, c. 1800. From *Description d'Égypte.*

the East blended with the Greek ideal of the heroic lover. It fitted the religious mood of an age that exalted oriental belief in salvation, sacrifice, and resurrection.

Inevitably, parallels were drawn with Christianity. The pagan apologist Celsus, hostile to both new faiths, protested that the honors paid to Jesus were "no different from those paid to Hadrian's boy-favorite," a comparison that must have galled the church fathers.[88] None of the cult images of Antinous hints at any relation with Hadrian. It was left for hostile Christians to emphasize Antinous' sexuality. The Spanish poet Prudentius imagined the new god lying in Hadrian's bosom, "robbed of his manhood." Athanasius, the embattled defender of orthodoxy, writing in Alexandria (c. 350), accused the cultists of "worshiping a sordid and loathsome instrument of his master's lust."[89]

Hadrian himself conceived of Antinous' godhead in a highly mystical fashion. It has been plausibly argued that the inscription on the Pincian obelisk is a translation into hieroglyphics of a Greek text by Hadrian. It hails the new god as "Osiris-Antinous the Just" who has been "raised again to life" and "grants the requests of those who call upon him."[90] Despite opposition, devotion to Antinous was widely diffused, as a detailed survey by Royston Lambert has shown. Images of Antinous have been found scattered throughout the length and breadth of the Roman Empire. More than thirty cities in Asia Minor, Greece, and Egypt depicted Antinous on their coinage as a god or hero, and children who had known the apostle Paul might have prayed for salvation in the new god's temple at Tarsus.[91] Since Bithynia was an Arcadian colony, Hadrian made the Arcadian city of Mantinea the center of his cult in Greece.[92] Athens also had two congregations of devotees, and excavations at Delphi, Olympia, Corinth, Argo, Eleusis, and Epidaurus attest to local homage.[93] Even in Italy, where his veneration might have been suspect as a foreign importation, seven temples have been found. Antinous' cult was not only widespread, it was also lasting. We might expect it to flourish only as long as Hadrian reigned. But it survived the emperor's death by several centuries. Annual commemorative games were still being held at Athens in 266 and at Argos a century later. Attacks by Christian polemicists—Tertullian, Clement, Jerome, and others—attest to the cult's persistence until the definitive triumph of Christianity under Gratian and Theodosius in the late fourth century.[94]

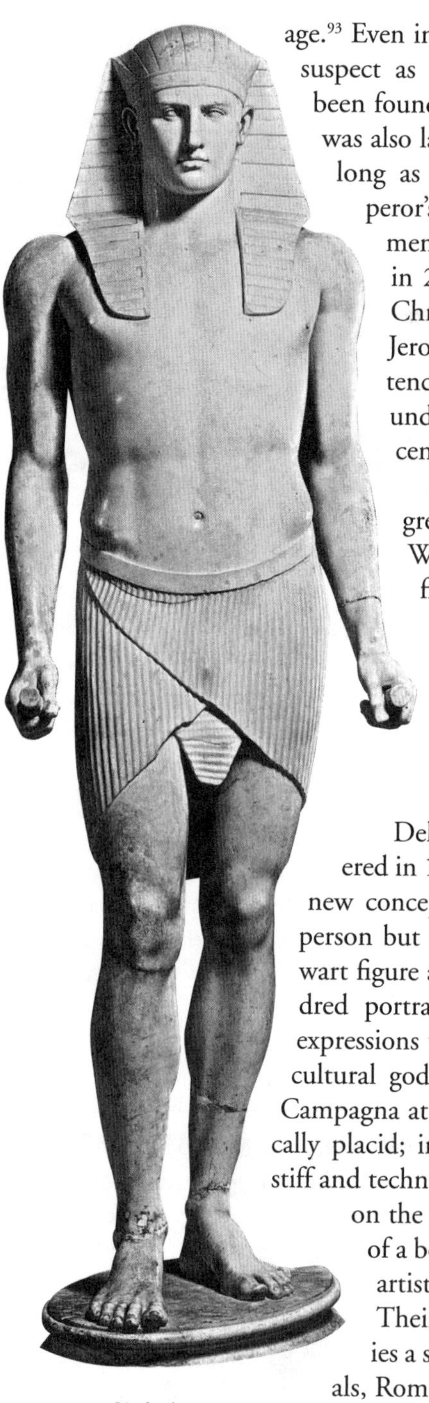

Representations of Antinous rank among the greatest masterpieces of late classical art. Winckelmann called the noble and superbly finished Mondragone head, disinterred at Frascati in 1760, "one of the finest things in the world" and the relief from the Villa Albani "the crown and glory of sculpture in this age."[95] The most majestic statue is the powerful Antinous-Dionysos of the Vatican Sala Rotunda; the finest is the ephebe of Delphi, the so-called Antinous-Apollo, discovered in 1893. In all of them there appears a strikingly new conception of beauty, inspired by a single living person but multifaceted. The unique face and the stalwart figure are unmistakable in the more than two hundred portraits that have come down to us, but the expressions vary. The bas relief of Antinous as the agricultural god Sylvanus, dug up by vine-workers in the Campagna at the beginning of the last century, is bucolically placid; in contrast, the statue from Eleusis, though stiff and technically awkward, looks with painful sympathy on the sufferings of humanity. Into these likenesses of a boy loved and deified by an emperor, different artists have poured a multitude of aspirations. Their homage to divine beauty and grace embodies a synthesis of Greek religious and aesthetic ideals, Roman power, and oriental mysticism.

21. Antinous as an Egyptian god. Marble, c. 130 CE.

CHAPTER FIVE

CHRISTIANS AND PAGANS

1–565 CE

The Gospels

Christianity was born when Rome stood at the peak of its power and Greek culture still dominated the Mediterranean world. But Christianity was the child of Judaism and inherited much from the earlier faith. Its founder, Jesus, endorsed the Deuteronomic command to love one's neighbor and shared the prophets' passionate concern for the poor and downtrodden. In sexual matters, he mixed conservatism with compassion, condemning divorce but intervening to save an adulteress from stoning, the Mosaic penalty.[1] It has been suggested that the mysterious word *raca* in Matthew 5:22 may be an abusive term for an effeminate passive male: in the Sermon on the Mount Jesus warns his hearers not to use it.[2] But otherwise, on homosexuality Jesus, in the Gospels, is oddly silent. This is surprising, since male love must have been relatively common in the Greek communities of Palestine where he often preached. The Gospel of Mark, for instance, tells of his visit to the "country of the Gadarenes."[3] Gadara belonged to the Decapolis (the ten Greek cities that dated from the age of Alexander) and was the birthplace of the exuberantly erotic Meleager. We are told that many of Jesus' followers came from Decapolitan Palestine.[4]

Could this silence have been influenced, some have wondered, by Jesus' own temperament? The notion that Jesus might have been attracted to men rests on Saint John's reference (four times repeated) to the disciple "whom Jesus loved."[5] Several writers—Christopher Marlowe, James I, Denis Diderot, and Jeremy Bentham among them—have seen Jesus and John as lovers. Bentham, moreover, thought the naked youth in a "linen cloth" who alone stood by Jesus when he was seized at Gethsemane (Mark 14:51) was a boy prostitute and that his devotion was a consequence of Jesus' sympathy for his outcast status.[6] But these are only speculations; so, as with David and Jonathan, we must suspend judgment. Since few men are uninfluenced by their culture and times, it is likely Jesus shared the traditional prejudices of his fellow Jews. As a sensitive man, he may have chosen silence so as not to provoke popular violence of the sort Philo encouraged. When he speaks of Sodom and Gomorrah, Jesus, like the Talmud generally, refers not to sexual sin but to inhospitality, as when he tells his disciples "it shall be more tolerable for the land of Sodom and Gomorrah in the day of judgment" than for any city that refuses them welcome.[7]

• Intertestamental Judaism and Paul •

We have seen with what ferocity Philo preached the extermination of homosexuals in the *The Special Laws.* References by Jewish writers of the intertestamental period are regularly as hostile, if not so violent.[8] Most appear in the curious body of writings scholars have dubbed the Pseudepigrapha—various narratives, poems, and prophecies, usually in Greek, which, to gain authority, misrepresent themselves as the work of earlier teachers or prophets. To this class belongs the *Letter of Aristeas,* an account of the origin of the Septuagint, claiming contemporaneity but probably written at least a century after the translation was completed. Its Jewish author accuses the rest of mankind of intercourse with males, while boasting that Jews have been preserved from such behavior by the laws of Moses.[9] An odder invention is the "Sentences of Pseudo-Phocylides," gnomic verses in Greek hexameters but of Jewish provenance, supposedly by an Ionian poet who lived at the time of Theognis. Compiled about the time of Christ, the bogus "Sentences" include anachronistic warnings against the "intercourse of male with male."[10]

Another series of pious forgeries, the so-called Sibylline Oracles, imitated the "official" Sibylline prophecies preserved as sacred books at Rome but are of Jewish origin. Much quoted by the church fathers, some of these prophecies have Christian interpolations. It is in their honor that Michelangelo placed majestic female sibyls beside his bearded prophets on the Sistine ceiling. The third oracle, composed shortly before 30 BCE, contrasts Jewish abstention from pederasty with the mores of the Phoenicians, Egyptians, Romans, Greeks, Persians, Galatians, "and all Asia."[11] Jewish hostility at this point in history was a tiny island in a sea of relative tolerance.

Historically, members of one faith have routinely accused others of moral iniquities. Jews and Christians, like their pagan opponents, freely indulged in this unamiable practice and sometimes included charges of homosexuality. The so-called *Wisdom of Solomon,* written in Greek by an orthodox Jew about 100 BCE and included in the Apocrypha of the Roman Catholic Vulgate, ascribes a host of atrocities to Jewish apostates in Alexandria:

> For either performing ritual murders of children or secret mysteries or frenzied revels connected with strange laws, they keep neither their lives nor marriages pure, but one either slays his neighbor insidiously or pains him by adultery. All is confusion—bloody murder, deceitful theft, corruption,

22. Christ and Saint John. German, painted and gilded wood, c. 1320.

> treachery, tumult, perjury, agitation of decent men, ingratitude, soul defilement, interchange of sex roles *[geneseos enallage]* irregular marriages, adultery and debauchery. For the worship of the unspeakable idols is the beginning, cause, and end of every evil.[12]

The Greek phrase *geneseos enallage,* literally "change of kind," has generally been taken to refer to homosexuality, and the context seems to support this interpretation. The Jerusalem Bible translates it as "sins against nature."

From this prejudicial legacy derives the most influential of all Christian denunciations of homosexuality, Paul's Epistle to the Romans. Paul's assault is not the terse condemnation we find in most earlier Jewish writings: in its expansive vehemence it is more akin to Philo. The context is significant: it comes at the end of the first chapter of the epistle, in which Paul excoriates all religious belief which is not Jewish or Christian. These "idolaters" are, in Paul's eyes, capable of every enormity. With fierce disdain he accuses them of a whole catalogue of moral delinquencies, beginning with lesbianism and male homosexuality: "For this cause [their idolatry] God gave them up unto vile affections: for even their women did change the natural use into that which is against nature: and likewise also the men, leaving the natural use of the woman, burned in their lust one toward another; men with men working that which is unseemly" (Romans 1:26–27).

There has been some doubt whether Paul, in speaking of women who have changed the "natural use," meant lesbians or women who engaged in "unnatural" heterosexual relations. Commentators who have argued for the latter interpretation have, however, been a distinct minority, and the passage has most often been read as the Bible's one unequivocal condemnation of lesbian love. When, in the Middle Ages, Christian jurists extended the Old Testament death penalty for male homosexuality to lesbianism, they regularly invoked Romans 1:26. Courts of law, when challenged, routinely supported this reading of Paul's words.

Another controversy centers on Paul's reference to "changing" or leaving the "natural use" of women. Some interpreters, seeking to mitigate Paul's harshness, have read the passage as condemning not homosexuals generally but only heterosexual men and women who experimented with homosexuality.[13] According to this interpretation, Paul's words were not directed at "bona fide" homosexuals in committed relationships. But such a reading, however well-intentioned, seems strained and unhistorical. Nowhere does Paul or any other Jewish writer of this period imply the least acceptance of same-sex relations under any circumstances. The idea that homosexuals might be redeemed by mutual devotion would have been wholly foreign to Paul or any other Jew or early Christian.

Paul assumes that at some earlier time all men and women collectively possessed one true faith and morality, that is, a belief in the Hebraic creator God and a universal morality identical with that of the Hebrew scriptures. (Historically, of course, this is hardly a tenable theory.) Thus, anyone not a Christian or a Jew must have perversely abandoned ("changed") this faith for idol worship. In Romans 1:32 Paul turns on such apostates in a fury reckless of grammar and logic. After accusing them of homosexuality, he continues:

> And even as they did not like to retain God in their knowledge, God gave them over to a reprobate mind, to do those things which are not convenient; being filled with all unrighteousness, fornication, wickedness, covet-

> ousness, maliciousness; full of envy, murder, debate, deceit, malignity; whisperers, backbiters, haters of God, despiteful, proud, boasters, inventors of evil things, disobedient to parents, without understanding, covenant-breakers, without natural affection, implacable, unmerciful: who, knowing the judgment of God, that they that commit such things are worthy of death, not only do the same, but have pleasure in them that do them.

But what deeds does Paul here regard as "worthy of death"? Many of the sins Paul lists are so minor that it would be absurd to single them out for the death penalty. Nevertheless, the reference to those who not only "do such things" but approve them suggests that he is referring to Greek love. This is brought out more fully by the translators of the New English Bible: "They know well enough the just decree of God, that those who behave like this deserve to die, and yet they do it; not only so, they actually applaud such practices." His words, confused as they are, may well be intended to endorse the death penalty for homosexuality as prescribed in the Mosaic code. They were so understood by the Council of Paris in 825.

But whatever Paul's meaning, the rhetorical force of the passage is undeniable. About religious beliefs Paul was fiercely certain. Before his conversion, he had taken the lead, as a devout Pharisee, in persecuting Jewish Christians and had participated in the stoning of Stephen, Christianity's first martyr, whom he condemned as an apostate. At the moment of his conversion, Paul was on his way to arrest Christians in Damascus and bring them to Jerusalem in chains. Paul was not a wholly unamiable man; his first letter to the Corinthians includes perhaps the most eloquent praise of love ever written. But conversion to Christianity did not soften his hatred of those who did not believe as he did, as the Epistle to the Romans, with its rhetorical vehemence, demonstrates.

Romans was Paul's most influential epistle—it has been called "the most important theological book ever written."[14] More, it is said, has been written on it than on any other piece of prose. In the early church, Origen, Pelagius, Ambrose, and Augustine all wrote commentaries on it. Not only did it remain central to Catholic teaching but Reformation theologians found its doctrine of salvation by faith especially to their liking. Melanchthon and Marin Bucer both published treatises on Romans; so did Luther, who thought it was the key to the scriptures. For homosexuals, this preeminence has been tragic, for it has enshrined an intemperate diatribe at the very heart, if not of Christianity, then at least of Christian theology.

• Moses and the Early Church •

Paul's culture was Jewish, but his message was directed to a wider world. In the century following his death, Christianity spread swiftly among gentile

23. Saint Paul. Mosaic, Baptistery of the Arians, Ravenna, sixth century.

converts, many of Greek heritage. What did these Hellenic believers make of the Mosaic and Pauline condemnations of same-sex relations? In fact, intolerance everywhere triumphed, as we can see in the writings of the convert who in this age had the most to say on the subject. This was Clement of Alexandria, an Athenian deeply read in the Greek classics who at the end of the second century headed the catechetical school at Alexandria.

It was Clement who formulated the "Alexandrian rule" of sexual conduct, which held that "pleasure sought for its own sake, even within the marriage bonds, is a sin and contrary both to law and to reason."[15] Here we see the triumph of Plato's anti-hedonism. To indulge in intercourse without the intent to produce children, Clement thought, was to "outrage nature."[16] Given this stance, Clement's view of homosexuality is hardly surprising. His attack on paganism in his *Exhortation to the Greeks* incorporates a lengthy list of Greek gods who had male lovers as a way of discrediting Greek religion. Suppressing half the truth, he describes Plato as "excoriating" all male love in the *Phaedrus* and repeats Socrates' description of men who have surrendered to pleasure as "taking the bit in their own mouths like brutish beasts."[17] Then Clement quotes in full Romans 1:26–27.

But Greco-Roman law in Alexandria, he complains, permitted such things and even recognized them as obligations.[18] In his *Pedagogus* he achieves the marriage of asceticism and religious taboo Plato had hoped for in the *Laws.* At the same time, Clement reveals a keen anxiety about sex roles, deploring bright clothes, perfumes, and beardlessness as dangerous symptoms of effeminacy in men. Any well-groomed man is either a bisexual seeking to attract both sexes or an out and out *cinaedus* who will "prove himself a woman at night."[19] Beards are de rigueur. Shaving is an unnatural act: the human male, like the male lion and the male boar, should be shaggy and bristly.[20]

Clement was not the only early Christian apologist who looked to the Hebrew scriptures for guidance in sexual matters. Though it broke with Judaism over circumcision and rejected Mosaic law on diet, dress, and cleanliness, Christianity emphatically endorsed much of its sexual ethos. Clement's contemporary Tertullian, the most influential of the early Latin church fathers, declared that "God's ordinance . . . punishes with death . . . the portentous madness of lust against male persons."[21] The eminent church historian Eusebius, bishop of Caesarea, in his *Preparation for the Gospel* (c. 320), quoted at length from the *Phaedrus* on the inspirational power of love between men, but then demurred: "Thus spoke Plato, but not Moses, who decreed expressly the contrary, proclaiming with a loud voice the penalty for pederasty: 'If a man lies with another man as one lies with a woman, both have committed an abomination: they shall be put to death: their blood shall be upon them.'"[22]

The *Apostolical Constitutions,* a work purportedly deriving from Saint Peter and the apostles but in fact composed in Syria three centuries later, has been called "a valuable witness to the religious practices and beliefs of its period."[23] The *Constitutions* incorporate many Jewish taboos on sex into Christianity and endorse the death penalty, by appealing to Leviticus: "For the sin of Sodom is contrary to nature, as is also that with brute beasts . . . All these things are forbidden by the laws; for thus say the oracles: 'Thou shalt not lie with mankind as with womankind . . . For such a one is accursed, and ye shall stone them with stones: they have wrought abomination.'"[24] Christian apologists, from the beginning, provided a warrant for the deadly persecutions that were to take place under Justinian and then, later, throughout Europe from the Middle Ages until the early days of the nineteenth century.

• Greek Love in Late Antiquity •

Three centuries were to elapse between the birth of Christianity and its triumph as the dominant religion of the Roman Empire. What, we may ask, were the attitudes toward homosexuality among non-Christians in this time of transition, especially in the Greek homeland and those parts of the empire predominantly Greek in culture? Some historians have seen Greek asceticism as sharpening Christian erotophobia.[25] But the reality was more complex: many Greeks reaffirmed ancient values, ignoring the anathemas of the new religion, if indeed, they were even aware of them. If we read Plutarch (c. 110) or Pausanias (c. 180) or Athenaeus and Aelian (both c. 200) or the Lucianic dialogue on love written about 270, or the later Greek romances, we are struck by the persistence of attitudes close to those of the sixth and fifth century BCE. When these writers speak of *paederastia,* we might well imagine ourselves back in the Athens of Pericles.

This is notably so with the poems contributed to Book XII of the Greek Anthology by Strato of Sardis in the age of Hadrian. Strato's one hundred light-hearted epigrams are in fact the largest contribution of any poet to Book XII, substantial enough that when the Greek Anthology assumed its definitive form in the tenth century, the book was subtitled "Strato's Boyish Muse." Taking a cue from Meleager, Strato tosses off playful lyrics in the style of Alcaeus and Anacreon more than half a millennium after those poets' favorites had moldered into dust. Nor were they the last. As late as the sixth century, two officials at the court of Justinian—Rufinus and Paul the Silentiary—provided more poems in praise of boys.[26]

As for historical scholarship, our knowledge of Greek love in earlier ages comes mainly from the Hellenic revival of the second century CE, a time "dominated by the vision of a glorious Greek past."[27] Without its antiquarian research, most of our information about male love from Solon to the Sacred Band would simply be lacking. Moreover, the way in which Plutarch, Pausanius, Athenaeus, and Aelian treat this past is revealing: they celebrate the homoeroticism of earlier Greek culture, citing its rich literature and memorializing famous love affairs, usually in a sympathetic way. Some new elements enter the picture—Plutarch's praise of marriage would be an example. But Plutarch still retains a keen awareness of the Hellenic bias in favor of male love, a bias that had by no means disappeared, though it had now become debatable in a way it was not in Plato's day.

The Hellenic revival of the second century was marked by a passion for scholarship. Among its feats was the *Deipnosophists* or *Savants at Dinner* of Athenaeus, a conversational marathon which fills seven volumes in its Loeb Classical Library translation. Athenaeus wrote about 200 CE in Naucratis, a Greek trading post in the Nile delta that had been the chief cultural link between Greece and Egypt before the founding of Alexandria. The guests at his monstrous symposium quote more than 1,200 ancient authors, name a thousand Greek plays, and discourse on a multitude of subjects: philosophy, poetry, law, medicine, cooking—and love. Despite its title, Book XIII ("Concerning Women") shows a surviving catholicity: "Altogether," we are told, "many persons prefer liaisons with males to those with females. For they maintain that this practice is zealously pursued in those cities throughout Hellas which, as compared with others, are ruled by good laws. The Cretans, for example . . . and the people of Chalcis in Euboea, have a marvelous passion for such liaisons."[28]

Athenaeus repeats, with variations, Plutarch's catalogue of brave lovers who defied tyrants. Some tyrants, we learn, "even went so far as to set fire to the wrestling-schools, regarding them as counter-walls to their own citadels, and so demolished them: this was done by Polycrates, the tyrant of Samos."[29] He quotes from the homosexual dramas of Aeschylus and Sophocles, provides saucy anecdotes about Sophocles and Euripides, and mentions comedies by Cratinus, Aristophanes' rival, and by Diphilus, a contemporary of Menander.[30] Besides the Cretans and Chalcidians, we are told that the Medes, the Tuscans, the Celts, and the citizens of Massilia (modern Marseilles) were enthusiastically given to same-sex amours.[31] There is much more, chaotically assembled, but amounting, in sum, to a major contribution to the history of the subject.

Athenaeus' Latin contemporary, the sophist Claudius Aelianus, commonly known as Aelian, often borrows from him. A citizen of Praeneste, some twenty miles east of Rome, and a "pontifex" of a local cult, Aelian, like most educated Romans of his time, wrote in Greek. His *Historical Miscellany* is liberally sprinkled with homosexual anecdotes from Spartan, Theban, and Athenian history, from Ptolemaic Egypt and the royal circles of Persia and Macedonia. While Athenaeus is attracted to stories of clever intrigues, Aelian is more interested in the refinements of erotic psychology. When the Persian monarch Artaxerxes mourned for the eunuch Tiridates, "the most handsome and attractive man in Asia," his mistress could only console him, Aelian tells us, when she dressed in the dead man's clothes.[32] At the court of the Macedonian king Archelaus, we learn, Agathon kept Pausanias' love alive by staging quarrels for the sweetness of reconciliation.[33] We note that Aelian, writing of male love for an educated Roman audience in this cosmopolitan age, adopts an essentially Greek point of view.

In the Hellenic revival that took place under the Antonines, Greek and Roman culture converged. In Greece, we see this phenomenon in Plutarch's *Parallel Lives;* in Rome, it manifested itself in the philhellenism of such emperors as Hadrian and Marcus Aurelius. Plato had at last routed Cato, as we may observe in the *Apology* of Apuleius. Apuleius, best known as the author of *The Golden Ass,* was involved in a lawsuit in North Africa in which his opponent cited his love poems to boys as throwing suspicion on his character. He replied by appealing to the *Symposium:*

> I say nothing of those lofty and divine Platonic doctrines that . . . teach that Venus is not one goddess but two . . . The one is the goddess of the common herd, who is fired by base and vulgar passion and commands not only the hearts of men, but cattle and wild beasts also, to give themselves over to the gratification of their desires: she strikes down these creatures with fierce intolerable force and fetters their servile bodies in the embraces of lust. The other is a celestial power endued with lofty and generous passion: she cares for nothing but men, and of them but few . . . Her love is neither wanton nor voluptuous, but serious and unadorned, and wins her lovers to the pursuit of virtue by revealing to them how fair a thing is nobility of soul.[34]

Apuleius' high-flown sentiments may have been mere oratorical flourishes, but they demonstrate what could pass as acceptable coin in public discourse in a colonial Roman town in the Antonine age.

• Plutarch's Dialogue on Love •

For our theme, the major document of the second century is undoubtedly Plutarch's *Eroticus.* This "Talk about Love" is arguably the fullest and most instructive treatment of love and sex to come down to us from antiquity. It has received far less attention than it merits—no doubt because Greek scholars have inevitably focused on the classical era. Kenneth Dover, for instance, makes only incidental reference to it. But the dialogue is of prime importance, first, because it tells us so much about Greek love in the archaic and classical periods we not would otherwise know and, second, because it shows how these early attitudes survived through five hundred years, even though they faced new challenges.

Like the symposiums of Plato and Xenophon, the *Eroticus* has a *mise en scène.* Plutarch and his friends, mainly fellow Boeotians, have gathered to celebrate the festival of Eros in the town of Thespiae. The mother of Bacchon, a handsome young man with many admirers, has asked a wealthy young widow to find him a bride. Impressed "by the throng of noble lovers who courted him," Ismenadora thinks Bacchon so desirable a catch that she decides to marry him herself. Her coup precipitates a quarrel between those who support the marriage and Bacchon's "lovers" who oppose it. Their disagreement is so heated that, in another culture, we might expect a brawl. But since the parties are Greeks, we have instead a philosophical debate—gays versus straights, so to speak, on their rival lifestyles.

It is hard to imagine anyone better placed to register Greek opinion on the issues than Plutarch. Born into a well-to-do provincial family, Plutarch had studied in Athens, traveled widely in Greece and Asia Minor, visited Rome repeatedly, and given lectures and acted as an ambassador there. Eventually he retired to his native Chaeronea, devoted himself to the education of the young, and served as a priest at Apollo's shrine at Delphi, a highly honorific post, though the cult was in decline. His modern counterpart might be the head of a liberal arts college in a small midwestern town. A major speaker in his own dialogue, Plutarch had married young and had several sons and daughters. The debate is imagined as taking place shortly after his marriage, though the *Eroticus* was likely written near the end of his long life, perhaps around 110 C.E.

Bacchon, the ephebe whose bachelorhood hangs in the balance, leaves the decision whether he should marry to Daphnaeus, who advocates wedlock, and Protogenes, a lover of youths from Paul's native city of Tarsus. Daphnaeus at once accuses Protogenes of opposing "true [that is, female] love" because it differs from his own preferences—didn't he come all the way to Athens "to look over the handsome lads and make the rounds with them?"[35] When Daphnaeus defends marriage as a "sacred" fellowship, Protogenes replies testily:

> Why, of course, since it's necessary for producing children, there's no harm in legislators talking it up and singing its praises to the masses. But genuine Love has no connexion whatsoever with the women's quarters. I deny that it is love you have felt for women and girls—any more than flies feel love for milk or bees for honey . . . there is only one genuine Love, the love of boys. It is not "flashing with desire," as Anacreon says of the love of maidens, or "drenched with unguents, shining bright." No, its aspect is simple and unspoiled. You will see it in the schools of philosophy, or perhaps in the gymnasia or palaestrae, searching for young men whom it cheers on with a clear and noble cry to the pursuit of virtue when they are found worthy of its attention.[36]

The pursuit of pleasure, Protogenes holds, is "base and unworthy of a free man"; hence, it is "not gentlemanly or urbane to make love to slave boys: such a love is mere copulation, like the love of women."[37] Not surprisingly, this intemperate outburst provokes a counterblast from Daphnaeus, who quotes suggestive lines by Solon and Aeschylus on the fascination of youths' thighs.[38] Relations with males, he claims, betray "weakness and effeminacy" and are "contrary to nature."[39] The love of boys is a "bastard love" introduced "only yesterday, or the day before [!]" after men had begun to practice a tantalizing nudity in the gymnasia. For good measure, Daphnaeus calls boy-lovers hypocrites who pretend to philosophy but in fact seek pleasure—"when night comes and all is quiet, 'Sweet is the harvest when the guard's away.'"[40] Inevitably, when we look at these polemics we are struck by a certain symmetry. Each argues that the other seeks physical gratification, and each presents his rival's preference as the more "feminine." Daphnaeus complains that boys are forced to play a female role; Protogenes, on the other hand, links the love of women with a luxurious boudoirs, enervating and effeminating milieus inferior to the athletic field or philosopher's study.

At this point a messenger brings startling news. Ismenadora and some male friends have kidnapped Bacchon, donned festive garments, and borne him off to her house to be married. The whole town is in an uproar, and a mob at Ismenadora's door is as hotly divided as Plutarch's company. Complaining that both sides have, in the heat of argument, traduced the high ideal of love, Plutarch himself now embarks on a lengthy speech in praise of Eros, akin to the panegyrics in Plato's *Symposium* but far richer in its historical references.

Plutarch has from the first presented himself as a defender of conjugal love. But his panegyric is in fact a paradox. Since he chooses to draw on episodes from traditional Greek history and myth and the commonplaces of popular opinion, the vast majority of his examples are inevitably homosexual. Whereas the first part of the *Eroticus* accorded equal time to two differing points of view, and though Plutarch will later defend matrimony, heterosexuality assumes a distinctly minor role in the panegyric. So strong was Greek tradition that to reconstruct the idea of love on a primarily heterosexual basis would have been extremely difficult, even at the end of antiquity, and Plutarch does not try. Nothing could be more revealing of the prestige male love still held in late Hellenic culture.

Plutarch's panegyric is a response to the skepticism of Pemptides, a bemused Theban who derides the idea that Eros is a god and love "a divine blessing."[41] But if gods preside over such activities as war, hunting, agriculture, and even childbirth, should there not be a god, Plutarch asks, for boys and youths "when they are at the ripening and flowering season and are being shaped and educated"?[42] Love reveals its divine power, Plutarch contends (echoing Pausanias in the *Symposium*), by inspiring lovers to resist tyrants. Forgetting for a moment that he is defending matrimony, Plutarch declares that men seeking favor "have shared their pleasure" with powerful rulers, even their mistresses and wives. "On the other hand, of all the throngs of lovers past and present, do you know a single one who sold the favors of his beloved even to gain the favors of Zeus himself?"[43] Eros is strong even "in Ares' sphere," that is, on the battlefield. Plutarch reminds his hearers of Cleomachus and the Chalcidians, and the Theban Sacred Band whose leader, Pammenes, "changed the order of battle-line for the hoplites," placing lovers together, "for he considered that Love is the only invincible general."[44] "It is a fact," Plutarch maintains,

> that men desert their fellow tribesmen and relatives and even (God knows) their parents and children; but lover and beloved, when their god is present, no enemy has ever encountered and forced his way through. In some cases, even when there is no need for it, they are moved to exhibit their love for danger, their disregard for mere life. This was what prompted Theron of Thessaly to place his left hand on the wall, draw his sword, and cut off his thumb, challenging his rival to do the same. [We shall encounter such theatrics again in Tokugawa Japan.] When another man had fallen in battle on his face and an enemy was about to kill him, he begged the latter to wait for a moment in order that his beloved might not see him wounded from behind.[45]

Plutarch also reminds Pemptides that the shrine of the Heracles' beloved still stands in Thebes, where "to this very day lovers worship and honour Iolaüs, exchanging vows and pledges with their beloved at his tomb."[46] Plutarch does indeed cite one instance of heroic conjugal love—Alcestis was willing to sacrifice her life for her husband. Thus, though "women have no part at all in Ares, if Love possesses them it leads them to acts of courage beyond the bounds of nature, even to die."[47] Yet Plutarch follows Socrates by presenting these first "mortal reflections of the divine" as deriving from "young men radiant in the prime of their beauty."[48]

Plutarch's speech is not complete in the single manuscript that has come down to us and breaks off abruptly at this point. When he resumes, he appears to be answering another speaker who has rejected married love from a materialistic Lucretian point of view. So this second speech, which takes up the final quarter of the dialogue, is an enthusiastic defense of marriage. Plutarch protests that even from an Epicurean perspective there is no reason why "visual shapes emanating from boys can, but the same from woman cannot, enter into the body of the lover."[49] But Plutarch the Platonist rejects Epicurus' physiological model: love is not caused by a chance concatenation of atoms; it is, rather, a recollection of the divine beauty of another world. And why, he asks, should such recollections "not spring from maidens and women, as well as from boys and striplings, whenever a pure and disciplined character shines through from within a beautiful and charming outward shape . . . or whenever the clearcut traces of a shining soul stored up in beautiful forms and pure bodies are perceived undistorted, without a flaw, by those capable of such perceptions"?[50]

To those who hold women to be morally inferior to men, Plutarch replies with what may be the most winning feminist speech in ancient literature:

> It is ridiculous to maintain that women have no participation in virtue. What need is there to discuss their prudence and intelligence, or their loyalty and justice, when many women have exhibited a daring and a great-hearted courage which is truly masculine? And to declare that their nature is noble in all other relationships and then to censure them as being unsuitable for friendship alone—that is surely a strange procedure. They are, in fact, fond of their children and their husbands; their affections are like a rich soil ready to receive the germ of friendship; and beneath it all is a layer of seductive grace.[51]

Marriage may at first entail painful adjustments, but it can lead to lasting friendship. The love of boys, he contends, is usually brief, though he thinks it "unjust to bring these charges against true and genuine lovers" of males, like the mature Euripides, who "observed upon embracing and kissing Agathon, though the latter's beard had already grown, that even the autumn of the fair is fair."[52] But examples of lasting unions with women, he thinks, are much more common. Then, as Plutarch is paying tribute to a woman who defended her husband before an emperor even to the death, a messenger arrives with news that brings the dialogue to an end. All is now peace and joy in Thespiae: Bacchon's lovers have at last accepted his marriage to Ismenadora.

Plutarch's *Eroticus* is a work of serious intent and great charm, which cannot easily be summed up in a single formula. It has been hailed as signalizing a turn in Greek thought away from the love of youths toward marriage as an ideal, though Plutarch's pro-marital stance is hardly to be found in other Greek writers.[53] But the *Eroticus* also amply reveals the honor that was still accorded male love in Roman Greece. Indeed, it might be said that Plutarch's point is simply that conjugal love can rise to the level of male love.

• The Lucianic "Affairs of the Heart" •

Plutarch was not the only Greek to compare the love of boys with the love of women. A century or so later, a second dialogue on this theme appeared, one in which Plutarch's verdict is reversed. Traditionally ascribed to the satirist Lucian, it is now believed to postdate that Greek Voltaire. Historically, it has been known as the *Amores,* literally "The Loves." (The Loeb editor translates the title as "Affairs of the Heart"; in the quaint style of classical scholarship, its author is often referred to as the "pseudo-Lucian.") It would be helpful if we knew the date of this work, since it is the last formal defense of male love in the Greek world. Scholars have placed it as early as the reign of Septimius Severus (193–211) or as late as Constantine (312–337). A reasonable guess might assign it to the mid third century, about 150 years after Plutarch.[54]

The *Amores* reads in many respects like a response to Plutarch's dialogue, though there is no specific reference to the earlier work. Once more we encounter a narrative frame: in a holiday mood the philosopher Lycinus is celebrating the feast of Heracles with his friend Theomnestus in an unnamed city in Asia Minor—possibly Tarsus, which had such a festival.[55] Theomnestus has been entertaining Lycinus with accounts of his amours with women and boys and justifying himself by the hero-god's example. As to which kind of love is better, Theomnestus declares he is balanced on a knife edge. He begs Lycinus to give his opinion; instead, Lycinus avoids a direct response by repeating a debate between two friends, Charicles and Callicratidas, each resolutely unisexual.

Charicles' household is made up of attractive women, Callicratidas' of handsome boy slaves. Charicles, a native of heterosexual Corinth, wears cosmetics—to attract women. Callicratidas is an athletic misogynist from Athens. Together they sail to Cnidus to view Praxiteles' Aphrodite, the most celebrated image of feminine beauty in the ancient world, which Charicles rhapsodizes over.[56] But the men's opinions clash so violently that Lycinus begs them to compose coherent speeches. (Like Plutarch, the author of the *Amores* invites us to smile at the antagonists' impassioned fervor.)

Charicles calls upon Aphrodite to "plead the cause of womankind, and of your grace allow men to remain male, as they were born to be."[57] As this invocation hints, his oration is more an assault on male love than a defense of heterosexuality and is much concerned with traditional sex roles. Mankind, he argues, was once entirely heterosexual; homosexuality is a late development that violates the laws of nature, since it is barren and sterile. This, of course, echoes Plato's *Laws.* Charicles' other arguments are no more novel: animals, birds, and fishes know nothing of same-sex matings; if they were universal, the human race would come to an end; those Platonists who affect a love for the soul are suspiciously insensitive to the virtues of older men, while "beauty in boys excites [in them] the most ardent fires of passion."[58] But Charicles does offer one new argument: if society condones male love, it should also tolerate lesbianism, a form of sexuality he regards as unspeakably obscene. Better, however, "that a woman should invade the provinces of male wantonness than that the nobility of the male sex should become effeminate and play the part of a woman."[59] Despite its engaging liveliness (and real historical interest), the *Amores* lacks the complexity, richness, and depth of Plutarch's dialogue. Nowhere is this deficiency more noticeable than in its treatment of women. Plutarch had tried to give women new dignity by praising them as selfless and devoted companions. Charicles can only recommend them as remaining attractive longer than boys, offering two options for enjoyment, and experiencing reciprocal pleasure in bed.[60]

In his rebuttal, Callicratidas attacks even this limited view of women as dangerously pro-feminist. He is more concerned, however, to answer Charicles' charge that pederasty was a late and perverse development. He turns the argument on its head—in early days the struggle for subsistence was so dire that men did yet know "the proper way to live."[61] Eventually, however, agriculture superseded the gathering of acorns, and marble mansions replaced rustic cottages. The love of males is another sign of the advance of civilization, the creation of divine philosophy. And why, he asks, make animals our models? "Lions do not have such a love, because they are not philosophers either. Bears have no such love, because they are ignorant of the beauty that comes from friendship."[62]

Callicratidas then makes the well-worn distinction between Heavenly and Common Love, relegating the love of women to the latter. With the extravagance typical of all the debaters in the *Eroticus* and the *Amores,* he denounces women whole-heartedly. "Let women be ciphers," he declares, retained merely for child-bearing.[63] He deplores the spurious beauty of their dyed hair, their cosmetic artifice, and their luxurious jewelry. Against this he sets the sober simplicity of the male adolescent's disciplined athletics, martial exercises, and studious efforts to learn "what hero was brave, who is cited for wisdom, or what men cherished justice and temperance."[64]

Mature lovers, Callicratidas thinks, will share an egalitarian relationship. "For, when the honorable love inbred in us from childhood matures to the manly age that is now capable of reason, the object of our longstanding affection gives love in return and it's difficult to detect which is the lover of which, since the image of the lover's tenderness has been reflected from the loved one as through a mirror."[65] Callicratidas presents male love not as an "exotic indulgence of our times" but as the essence of things Greek, citing Solon, Socrates, and Callimachus as its revered exponents. He takes a Platonic view of pederasty: one must "love youths as Alcibiades was loved by Socrates who slept like a father with him under the same cloak" and be constant in one's affections from boyhood to old age.[66]

Lycinus, embarrassed to choose a winner in the debate, praises both men. But finally he delivers a verdict in favor of boy love: "Marriage is a boon and a blessing to men when it meets with good fortune, while the love of boys, that pays court to the hallowed dues of friendship, I consider to be the privilege only of philosophy. Therefore all men should marry, but let only the wise be permitted to love boys, for perfect virtue grows least of all among women. And you must not be angry, Charicles, if Corinth yields to Athens."[67]

This tactful pronouncement makes a polite bow to marriage, though Charicles, recommending women as sex partners, had had nothing to say for matrimony. Perhaps Lycinus means this as a concession to Plutarch's point of view, though there is nothing else in the dialogue to suggest this, and his verdict explicitly denies women the moral qualities Plutarch had granted them. Theomnestus does not quarrel with the verdict but demurs at Callicratidas' puritanism: "I must say I admired the solemnity of the very high-brow speeches evoked by the love of boys, except that I didn't think it very agreeable to spend all day with a youth suffering the punishment of Tantalus, and, though the waters of beauty are, as it were, almost lapping against my eyes, to endure thirst when one can help oneself to water."[68] He emphatically denies that Socrates' love for Alcibiades was chaste and quotes the notorious lines in which Aeschylus portrayed the physical side of Achilles' love for Patroclus. In an age which historians have described as increasingly ascetic, his position is resolutely libertine. Lycinus does not argue with him. Ever the diplomat, he merely warns Theomnestus that if he says more they will miss the climax of the festival that evening.

Obviously Plutarch did not have the last word in this lively debate. Not everyone was willing to concede the superiority of heterosexual marriage. Indeed, the tactful Lycinus compliments Charicles for his "able defense of the more awkward cause," that is, the love of women, suggesting that, though defenders of pederasty might find themselves sharply challenged, the consensus among non-Christian Greeks of late antiquity still favored the classical tradition.[69] Plutarch's generous defense of women finds no place here. We can only be astonished at this cultural conservatism and marvel that so little had changed in six or seven hundred years—a span that in our time would stretch back to Chaucer.

• Two Romances and an Epic •

But if philosophical debaters may defend male love, we find that the love interest in popular fiction is predominantly heterosexual. This pattern had been set in the theater by Menander and the New Comedy. (Indeed, Plutarch took particular notice that no man ever fell in love with a boy in Menander.)[70] Subsequently, Menander's boy-meets-girl formula dominated a new genre that flourished in the second and third centuries, the Greek romantic novel. In these facile tales, hero and heroine meet, fall in love, and after a multitude of vicissitudes are reunited at the end of fifty or one hundred improbable pages.

Though these stories featured heterosexual pairings, classical Greek love was sympathetically treated in their subplots. Thus the love of the extravagantly beautiful Habracomes and Anthia is the basis of the plot of the *Ephesian Tale* by Xenophon of Ephesus. Captured by pirates, she attracts one ruffian, he another. After his escape, Habrocomes encounters the leader of a robber band, Hippothoos, who, weeping, tells the story of his own love. He had first seen Hyperanthes in the gymnasium in their native city, a town near Byzantium, where the pair shared "kisses and fondlings."[71] But the boy's unscrupulous father sells him to a rich Byzantine rhetorician on the pretext of providing an education. Together they kill the man and flee, but Hyperanthes is drowned near Lesbos in a shipwreck. In the end, Habrocomes and Anthia are reunited in the eternal bliss of prose romance. But Hippothoos joins them at the final curtain. For, "after raising a great tomb" for Hyperanthes in Lesbos, he settles with the couple in Ephesus along with a young Silician, "the handsome Clisthenes," whom he adopts.[72] Here is fiction that takes diversity for granted.

The plot of Achilles Tatius' *Leucippe and Clitophon,* variously dated from 150 to 300, also fits the standard boy-loves-girl formula. (Perhaps Greek novelists found marriage as convenient a closure in romance as death in tragedy.) A dubious tradition made Achilles Tatius a bishop of the church, but his treatment of male love in the novel's subplot shows nothing of Christian influence. Here once again, sentimental pathos is the keynote in the treatment of male love. Clitophon's cousin Clinias loves a youth named Charicles, whose father orders him to marry an unprepossessing heiress. Distraught, Charicles goes riding on a horse Clinias has given him. It bolts, he is dragged to his death, and his father and lover compete in their lamentations.[73]

Later in the novel we meet Menelaus, an Egyptian visitor who has suffered a like bereavement: Menelaus had accidently killed a boy he loved with a javelin aimed at a boar that attacked him. Clinias is reminded of his own painful loss, and Clitophon, the novel's hero, encourages the two men to embark "upon a discussion which would divert the mind by a love-interest."[74] Provocatively, he wonders why "this affection for youths is now so fashionable." This stirs Menelaus to defend the love of youths, and we have a miniature debate between them of the sort we find in the *Eroticus* and the *Amores,* though now there is no vehement antagonism. The speakers are content to wonder which sex Zeus favored, whether the fleeting beauty of boys is too short or all the more tantalizing for its brevity, and which sex's kisses are the more enticing.

One substantial work remains from a later time, well after the triumph of Christianity—a sprawling epic in forty-five books by a poet who wrote in the Greek city of Panopolis in Egypt. Nonnus lived sometime in the fifth century—we do not know his dates or indeed any biographical details at all. His poem celebrates the triumphs of the god Dionysos, who, like Alexander, set out from Greece and, according to an ancient myth, conquered India. (We may assume that sometime after its composition Nonnus transferred his allegiance from Bacchus to Christ, since he also wrote a verse paraphrase of the Gospel of Saint John.)

The *Dionysiaca,* as it is called, is a huge baroque repository of late Hellenic legends which provides a final glimmer, in the twilight of classical literature, of the pederastic tradition. Nonnus devotes the greater part of three books to the story of Dionysos' love for Ampelos, whom the god meets on the banks of the Pactolus in Lydia. He is immediately smitten with his boyish beauty: "What father begat you?" he asks. "What immortal womb brought you forth? / Which of the Graces gave you birth? What handsome Apollo made you?" and so on, through a mythological litany.[75] The flattered youth is proud of the attention the god lavishes on him. Dionysos, for his part, pines when the boy is absent, listens eagerly to his talk, admires his flute-playing even when he blows wrong notes, and is jealous when he dances with the attendant satyrs, with whom he shares an anatomical detail. He is worried that an enamored Zephyrus may slay him as he accidentally slew Hyacinth, or that Zeus or Poseidon may steal him for Olympus. He is desperately infatuated:

> He had a sweet dream on his dream-breeding bed,
> Beheld the shadowy phantom of a counterfeit shape
> And whispered loving words to the mocking vision of the boy.
> If his passionate gaze saw any blemish, this appeared lovely to
> lovesick Dionysos,
> Even more dear to him than the whole young body;
> If the end of the tail which grew on him hung slack by his loins,
> This was sweeter than honey to Bacchos.
> Matted hair on an unkempt head even so gave more pleasure to his
> impassioned gaze.[76]

When Ampelos rides the panthers, bears, and tigers that draw the god's chariot, Dionysos warns him of the danger, but the headstrong youth mounts a wild bull, is thrown, and is impaled.

The god grieves long and melodiously and is comforted by Eros, who recites to him the tale of Calamus and Carpos. Calamus, the son of the god of the river Meander, loves Carpos, a boy of his own age. When Carpos drowns, Calamus dies of grief and is turned into a reed. (Could Whitman, who made the calamus reed symbolize his "love of comrades" in the *Leaves of Grass,* have known this arcane legend?) Ampelos, like Hyacinth and Cyparissus before him, undergoes a vegetative metamorphosis and becomes a vine, source of the wine the Greeks associated with Dionysos. With this archetypal fantasy the bisexual mythology of the classical tradition reaches its bittersweet conclusion.

• Roman Law before Constantine •

After the third century, with the waning of paganism, the climate changes. In 313 Constantine promulgated the Edict of Milan, a dramatic turnabout in imperial policy which established toleration for Christianity, though fewer than one third of the citizens of the empire were as yet converts. From now on, except for the brief reign of the Emperor Julian, Christianity enjoyed imperial favor, becoming in time the official state religion. The consequence was a drastic shift in the moral climate. Love between men had been a significant element of Greek civilization—in civic and military life, in education, art, and literature—at least since the time of Solon. From now on, Christianity, which first dominated and then suppressed paganism, would assert its anti-homosexual bias through imperial laws and in time reshape popular morality.

Male love, which had been memorialized, celebrated, and occasionally decried, was now redefined as something diabolical, forbidden, and unmentionable—"the love that dare not speak its name." The transformation was, above all, the consequence of the triumph of Christianity. John Boswell has suggested that the new morality sprang from the ruralization of the Roman Empire that took place during its decline.[77] But this argument rests upon the premise that rural societies are inherently "conservative" in nature. At this time, however, what would have been "conserved" were the old—that is, pagan—beliefs and practices. Indeed, the word *paganus* signified a countryman and emphasized the tendency for older faiths, rites, and morals to linger in rural parts. As we shall see, the severe new laws would originate in urban centers like Milan and Constantinople, the latter Europe's largest city, where the first savage persecutions took place.

Nor can we lay the blame for the waning of tolerance on the political and economic decay of Greco-Roman society. It has been an unexamined cliché that this decay fostered an ascetic spirit, as though people with little would naturally opt for less. What gave asceticism its weight and force in this era was not any intrinsic appeal it held in a world of diminishing expectations. Divorced from religious beliefs, asceticism has rarely been a social force. But linked to the conviction that the renunciation of pleasure—and especially sexual pleasure—was necessary for personal salvation, it exerted a wide and powerful influence. In an age in which the traditional rewards of industry and ambition were vanishing, the new religion promised eternal enjoyment in heaven and an escape from hell. These were potent incentives promoting an ascetic ethos.

We cannot exonerate the early church of blame for subsequent persecutions merely because some general social forces were at work. Though nationalism was a potent force in Europe before the rise of Hitler, its prevalence does not absolve the Nazis of blame for the deadly form it took at their hands. The tragedy is that, unlike Nazism, which throve especially on hatred and oppression, Christianity preached brotherly love and compassion and was historically, on balance, an influence for good in the world. Both, however, promoted homophobia. But whereas Himmler's desire to annihilate homosexuals fit a typical Nazi pattern, one does not feel it was inevitable that Christianity would embrace the fanatical prejudice of early Judaism. Despite Paul, the spirit of the Gospels does not move in this direction.

This said, we may note that there were developments in Roman law regarding homosexuality before Constantine, some of which set the stage for later punitiveness. Under the pagan Emperor Alexander Severus (222–235), the jurist Julius Paulus issued several pronouncements on the subject in his *Sentences,* formal judgments in criminal cases that were given the force of law in 426 under Theodosius II. Paulus ruled that the seduction of a freeborn boy under the age of seventeen was a "capital" crime, and an attempt at his seduction (as indicated, for instance, by the bribing of his attendants) could be punished by exile to an island.[78] Some commentators have assumed that "capital" meant the death penalty.[79] But in Roman law, "capital" punishment might also include such lesser sanctions as imprisonment, banishment, or loss of citizenship.[80]

Other judgments by Paulus and his colleague Ulpian appear more ominous in the light of later legislation. As for adult passives, Ulpian held that they could be legally designated as "infamous."[81] This was a finding of disreputability of the sort gladiators, actors, and other public performers were subject to, limiting civil rights such as the right to vote or hold office.[82] Paulus' *Sentences,* in addition, denied passive men the right to practice as attorneys in courts of law, deprived them of half their patrimony, and prohibited them from bequeathing more than half of what remained.[83]

• The Edicts of 342 and 390 •

With the coming to power of Christianity, legislation of a much harsher nature was to follow. Even before these new laws appeared, however, we can find evidence of persecution. Under Constantine and his successors, campaigns against non-Christian religions and against homosexuality went hand in hand. Thus the church historian Eusebius in his biography of Constantine praises the emperor for suppressing effeminate pagan priests whose homosexuality was taken for granted. Eusebius describes a temple at Aphaca in Phoenicia, on the remote summit of Mount Libanus, "dedicated to the foul demon known by the name of Venus . . . where men unworthy of the name forgot the dignity of their sex and propitiated the demon by their effeminate conduct." (Here "Venus" is a generic term for eastern love goddesses such as Ishtar or Astarte.) We are told that Constantine took a personal interest in the matter and "gave orders that this building with its offerings should be utterly destroyed" by military force.[84] Did Constantine go beyond the destruction of buildings and votive offerings and act against persons? It would seem that in Egypt he did, for Eusebius tells us that "inasmuch as the Egyptians, especially those of Alexandria, had been accustomed to honor their river through a priesthood composed of effeminate men, a further law was passed commanding the extermination of the whole class as vicious, that no one might thenceforward be found tainted with the like impurity."[85] We may recall that Philo had earlier wanted similar effeminate priests put to death. But

Philo had lived at a time when the civic authorities were unwilling to act on his Levitical prejudices. Now, three centuries later, imperial power was willing to back them.

Under Constantine's sons, the co-emperors Constantius and Constans, the dual campaign against homosexuality and paganism continued. We find this correlation clearly marked in such polemics as Firmicus Maternus' *The Error of the Pagan Religions,* written about 346. Firmicus was a Roman senator, who, after his own baptism, urged the brother emperors to enforce conversions and stamp out paganism by armed force, justifying this policy by citing the ferocious decrees of Deuteronomy 13.[86] Indeed, *The Errors of the Pagan Religions* has been called a "handbook of intolerance."[87] Firmicus repeatedly associates pagan cults with sexual immorality and especially with homosexuality.[88] But as with Eusebius, his chief ire is directed toward effeminate priests or holy men, as in his lurid description of the Carthaginian cult of the Punic love goddess Tanit, whose priests, he charges,

> can minister to [her] only when they have feminized their faces, rubbed smooth their skin, and disgraced their manly sex by donning women's regalia. In their very temples one may see scandalous performances, accompanied by the moaning of the throng: men letting themselves be handled as women, and flaunting with boastful ostentatiousness this ignominy of their impure and unchaste bodies. They parade their misdeeds in the public eye, acknowledging with superlative relish in filthiness the dishonor of their polluted bodies . . . Next, being thus divorced from masculinity, they get intoxicated with the music of flutes and invoke the goddess with an unholy spirit so they can ostensibly predict the future to fools.[89]

Here Firmicus makes an unequivocal claim that homosexual acts were an integral part of a pagan cult. Given the extremely hostile nature of the source, however, it is perhaps wise to regard the charge with some skepticism. In the inflamed rhetoric of the time, sensational charges were made by both sides. Pagan attacks on Christianity included the accusation that Christians worshiped their priests' genitals.[90] What is not in doubt is Firmicus' intense animus, which parallels Philo's in *The Special Laws.*

Firmicus Maternus, writing during the reign of Constantine's sons, mentions with satisfaction a recently passed law that punished homosexuality.[91] It has been assumed he is referring to a curiously worded law issued by Constantius and Constans in 342:

> When a man "marries" *[cum vir nubit]* as a woman who offers herself to men, what does he wish, when sex has lost its significance; when the crime is one which it is not profitable to know; when Venus is changed into another form; when love is sought and not found? We order the statutes to arise, the laws to be armed with an avenging sword, that those infamous

persons who are now, or who hereafter may be, guilty may be subjected to exquisite punishment.[92]

John Boswell has argued that "marries" *(nubit)* here refers to the kind of gay marriages described by Juvenal and Martial.[93] But the consensus is that the term is merely a euphemism for sexual relations. ("Venus" here means simply "sexual intercourse," a sense it bears in poets like Virgil and Ovid.) "Exquisite punishment" probably implies the death penalty, though the reference to the sword may be metaphorical.

What must strike anyone familiar with later English, American, or European laws is that this drastic measure punishes only the passive partner in the relationship but leaves the active male unscathed. Apparently the authors of this decree hesitated to break too suddenly with Roman tradition by punishing the "masculine" partner and felt that public opinion would more readily support strong measures against the despised adult passives.

Despite its obscure wording, the statute of Constantius and Constans was not ignored as a bizarre anomaly, for it played a crucial part in European legal history. In 438 it was incorporated into the Theodosian Code and later into the still more influential code of the Emperor Justinian. When these codes were revived in Italian law schools in the early Middle Ages, the law of 342, cited in traditional legal style by its two opening words as the *Lex cum vir,* was the statute regularly invoked in legal texts to justify the death penalty for both partners in male relations.

Was the law enforced in the years immediately after its passage? We do not know. Possibly, despite its vehemence, it was not. We know that statutes forbidding pagan worship and ordering temples closed were not regularly implemented: pagans were still a majority. But fifty years later, under Theodosius I, the situation was quite different. Where earlier emperors had hesitated to enforce laws against pagans, Theodosius, an ardent Christian and a formidable personality, took strong measures. In 381 an edict against sacrifices led to "an orgy of destruction and spoliation."[94] Though Theodosius did not specifically decree the destruction of pagan temples, bands of monks and fanatics, encouraged by his new laws, roamed the countryside demolishing buildings in a way that has been compared to the Red Guards of China's Cultural Revolution. The temple of Serapis in Alexandria, reputedly the most beautiful building in the world, was destroyed. The fire tended by the Vestal Virgins, which had burned for centuries as one of Rome's most venerable cults, was extinguished, and the statue of Victory was removed from the Senate. Even the Olympic games, celebrated for more than eleven hundred years, were abolished in the last decade of the fourth century because of their association with pagan worship. It has been fittingly said that classical paganism died during the reign of Theodosius.

In 390 Theodosius also issued a vengeful edict condemning homosexuality. (The names of the co-emperors Valentinian II and Arcadius are joined with Theodosius in the proclamation, but since Valentinian was a youth of nineteen and Arcadius only thirteen, we may safely ascribe the initiative to the older man.) Though the language is less obscurely literary than the edict of 342, the rhetoric is similar in its masculinist passion. Now, however, it formulates a specific political concern: effeminacy will weaken the state and is an affront to Roman tradition.

The edict has survived in two forms. The earlier and much fuller version is the text preserved in a treatise entitled *Mosaicarum et Romanarum Legum Collatio (A Comparison of Mosaic and Roman Laws),* which may have been intended to teach Roman law to the Christian clergy. Its format would instruct anyone who wanted to enforce biblical codes how to use Roman law to this end. Title five, "Of Debauchers" ("De Stupratoribus") begins by quoting, in Latin, Leviticus 20:13—"Moses says: If anyone hath intercourse with a male as with a woman, it is an abomination. Let them both die: they are guilty."[95] After citing Paulus' sentences making the rape of a free man a capital crime and condemning passives to the loss of half their property, the writer comments: "This is indeed the law [of Rome]. But a constitution of the Emperor Theodosius followed to the full the spirit of the Mosaic Law." Since, however, the edict of 390 does not have anything to say about the active partners in homosexual relations, we must take "to the full" as meaning the *full* force of the death penalty as applied to passives.

Since translations of the *Collatio* have differed markedly, it may be best if we offer a more or less literal, if awkward, rendering of its contorted Latin: "The Emperors Valentinian, Theodosius and Arcadius to Orientius, Vicar [Viceregent] of the city of Rome. We will not suffer, dearest and most beloved Orientius, that the city of Rome, the mother of all the virtues, should be polluted any longer by the poison of shameful effeminacy, and that the rustic strength of our ancient Founders now enfeebled by a people weakened by such effeminacy should cast a reproach both on the age of those Founders and the present Empire."[96] Where the Greeks thought love between men would inspire military courage, the Romans saw the presumed "feminization" of the passive partner as a hazard to the nation's manhood. After this preamble, a directive followed:

> Therefore your praiseworthy skill will punish all those whose criminal practice it is to condemn the male body to the submissiveness appropriate to the opposite sex (being in nothing different from women), and having seized them—as the enormity of their crime demands—and dragged them forth from the (shameful to say) male brothels, will purge them with avenging flames in the sight of the people, so that they will understand that the lodging of the male soul must be sacrosanct nor without incurring the severest penalty shall they shamefully renounce their own sex.

This turgid pronouncement is at least more explicit than its predecessor. Nevertheless, we may wonder who was exactly liable to its penalty of death by fire. We note that the rhetoric ignores the commercial side of prostitution but is entirely directed toward condemning passivity. Orientius is specifically ordered to seize male prostitutes, but whether he is to limit his arrests to this class or is merely to seize them first as the most easily identifiable criminals is unclear.

While it is uncertain if the law of 342 was enforced, it seems much more likely that Theodosius' edict was, since by 390 the imperial government was acting vigorously against violations of Christian norms. Men in brothels would be much easier to apprehend than men involved in private, noncommercial acts. Some of these wretches may indeed have been burned at the stake for the edification of a newly Christianized public. Since they would have come from the lowest and most scorned ranks of society, they could expect little sympathy.

If we accept 390 as a critical year in the history of Western legal attitudes toward same-sex relations—the moment after which classical tolerance can no longer be counted on in civic life—we may naturally ask, what did the pagan majority make of the new policy of persecution? One famous episode suggests a lack of willingness to go along with the new standards: the rebellion that took place in 390 in the city of Thessalonica in northern Greece. Gibbon gives a vivid account in his *Decline and Fall:*

> The sedition of Thessalonica is ascribed to a more shameful cause, and was productive of much more dreadful consequences . . . Botheric, the general of [Theodosius'] troops . . . had among his slaves a beautiful boy, who excited the impure desires of one of the charioteers of the Circus. The insolent and brutal lover was thrown into prison by the order of Botheric; and he sternly rejected the importunate clamors of the multitude, who on the day of the public games lamented the absence of their favorite, and considered the skill of a charioteer as an object of more importance than his virtue . . . Botheric and several of his principal officers were inhumanly murdered; their mangled bodies were dragged about the streets; and the emperor, who then resided at Milan, was surprised by the intelligence of the audacious and wanton cruelty of the people of Thessalonica.[97]

Gibbon makes it clear that the people of Thessalonica did not condemn the charioteer's conduct as seriously as Theodosius' governor did. But Theodosius took a terrible revenge for Botheric's murder. He invited the Thessalonicans to games in the circus, then surrounded it with soldiers who massacred the spectators, citizens and casual visitors alike. By one account the dead numbered 7,000, according to others 15,000.[98] For ordering this deed, which shocked the empire, Theodosius did penance before Saint Ambrose in the Cathedral of Milan.

Along with the statute of Constantius and Constans, Theodosius' law found its way into the so-called Theodosian Code. This important code appeared in 438 in the reign of Theodosius' grandson, Theodosius II, from whom it derived its name. But there the law of 390 appears in an interesting revision. The compilers quoted only part of Theodosius' decree, keeping about a third, changing the grammar, and adding a phrase. Here is how their version appears in the standard modern English translation of the code: "All persons who have the shameful custom of condemning a man's body, acting the part of a woman's, to the sufferance of an alien sex (for they appear not to be different from women) shall expiate the crime of this kind in avenging flames in the sight of the people."[99] The revised version, omitting any reference to prostitution, now clearly and unambiguously condemned all passive males to death by burning.

• Sodom Transformed •

The fear of homosexuality was immensely increased in the early Christian period by a new development in biblical exegesis: a reinterpretation of the Sodom story. Ezekiel, Jesus, and the Talmudists had laid stress on the sins of inhospitality, arrogance born of wealth, and Sodom's mistreatment of aliens and the poor. Despite the threatened rape of the angels in Genesis 19, the doomed city was not generally associated in early Jewish tradition with sexual license or with homosexuality. This was now to change.

Sherwin Bailey has made a careful study of Sodom in Jewish religious writings later than the Hebrew Bible.[100] In books of the Apocrypha (intertestamental Greek texts included in the Catholic bible) such as the Wisdom of Solomon and Ecclesiasticus, Sodom's sins are still pride and the abuse of foreigners. In the Pseudepigrapha (Greek texts of the same period purportedly by Old Testament worthies but in fact illicit forgeries), Sodom is occasionally associated with sexual misconduct in a vague fashion that hints only remotely, if at all, at homosexuality. The first work Bailey identifies in which Sodom is a city in which homosexual behavior flourished widely is Philo's *On Abraham.*

Like his predecessors, Philo makes wealth the root of Sodom's iniquity. But where they see the city's chief sin as the hoarding of its riches and neglect of the poor, the ascetic Philo deplores chiefly the luxurious enjoyment of food and sex. His commentary, much enlivened by a vivid imagination, must be quoted at length:

> The land of the Sodomites . . . was brimful of innumerable iniquities, particularly such as arise from gluttony and lewdness . . . The inhabitants owed this extreme license to [their] wealth, for, deep-soiled and well-watered as it was, the land had every year a prolific harvest of all manners

> of fruits, and the chief beginning of evils, as one has aptly said, is goods in excess. Incapable of bearing such satiety . . . they threw off from their necks the law of nature and applied themselves to deep drinking of strong liquor and dainty feeding and forbidden forms of intercourse. Not only in their mad lust for women did they violate the marriages of their neighbors, but also men mounted men without regard for the sex nature which the active partner shares with the passive.[101]

It was this last emphasis which was taken up by Christian exegetes. Increasingly as the centuries passed, Christian moralists came to identify homosexuality as *the* sin of Sodom. Eventually "sodomy" was to mean, primarily, same-sex relations, and someone who engaged in homosexual behavior became, simply and generically, a "sodomite." This new interpretation had a fateful effect. For eventually homosexuality became the unique cause of Sodom's destruction and hence a dire threat to any community that condoned it. To the homophobia of the Hebrew scriptures Christian superstition added a hysterical fear that was to justify much cruelty.

This development took place step by step in the new Christian era. Clement of Alexandria, at the beginning of the third century, followed Philo in characterizing the Sodomites as luxurious, adulterous, and driven by "frenzied passion for the objects of their lust."[102] More important, however, were the views of the two most influential fathers of the Latin and Greek churches respectively, Saint Augustine, bishop of Hippo in North Africa, and Saint John Chrysostom, who was to become the patriarch of the Eastern Church at Constantinople.

In *The City of God* (c. 412) Augustine follows Philo in making Sodom a place "where sexual intercourse between males had become so commonplace that it received the license usually extended by the law to other practices."[103] Augustine's crucial role in determining Western Christian attitudes toward sexuality has been widely recognized. Of the Latin fathers, Augustine speaks most directly and fully about sexuality, first in a personal way in the *Confessions* and then philosophically in *The City of God.* For him, concupiscence—that is, Adam's lust for Eve—was the primal sin that made humanity liable to eternal damnation. But if the middle-aged Augustine, after he had committed himself to Christianity, condemned sex, Augustine the adolescent had participated enthusiastically. His sex drive was strong from puberty and involved him in much casual experimentation with lower-class prostitutes. Born in the North African town of Thagaste, he pursued his education in nearby Carthage, where, as he put it in his *Confessions,* "all around me hissed a cauldron of illicit loves."[104]

At least one of these loves, which had a strong emotional side to it, seems to have been homosexual, though Augustine only indirectly reveals the sex of his lover. So, in Book 3 of the *Confessions* he tells us: "To me it was sweet to

24. The destruction of Sodom. Mosaic, duomo of Monreale, Sicily, twelfth century.

love and be loved, the more so if I could also enjoy the body of the beloved. I therefore polluted the spring water of friendship with the filth of concupiscence. I muddied its clear stream by the hell of lust, and yet, though foul and immoral, in my excessive vanity, I used to carry on in the manner of an elegant man about town. I rushed headlong into love, by which I was longing to be captured . . . My love was returned and in secret I attained the joy that enchains."[105] Augustine's reference to "friendship" tells us the lover was a male; in his society, friendship between a teenage boy and a teenage girl would have unthinkable. In chapter four of Book 4 of the *Confessions* we hear the end of this romantic affair. The boy, he tells us, died after their friendship "had scarcely completed a year. It had been sweet to me beyond all the sweetness of life that I had experienced."[106] Augustine gives a moving account of his loss: "My home town became a torture to me; my father's house a strange world of unhappiness; all that I had shared with him was transformed into a cruel torment."[107]

Augustine's experience of this love affair did not, however, inspire him with any sympathy for male love after his conversion. Though he was willing to concede that some deeds of some biblical patriarchs might be moral or immoral depending on the time or place, he held that same-sex relations were universally to be punished. "Even if all peoples should do [such acts], they would be liable to the same condemnation by divine law, for it has not made men to use one another in this way. Indeed, the social bond which should exist between God and us is violated when the nature of which he is the author is polluted by a perversion of sexual desire."[108] Here is an early statement of the medieval notion that homosexuality is a direct affront to God the creator, a kind of lèse majesty against divinity.

Saint John Chrysostom

Augustine was a theologian and moral philosopher who speculated about free will and original sin. His contemporary, John Chrysostom, was before all else a preacher who aimed to rouse and terrify. (His epithet "Chrysostom" meant "golden-mouthed.") Born in Antioch, he lived as a hermit in the desert before he returned as a priest to his native city in 386. Called to be patriarch at Constantinople, he spoke with such fire and eloquence that the congregation frequently interrupted with applause. As late as the eighteenth century, Peter the Great, no model of piety himself, ordered that all Orthodox priests must possess and read his works. He ranks as the most influential of the Greek Fathers, second only to Augustine in his influence on Christendom as a whole.

Chrysostom was a courageous man whose outspoken criticism of the empress eventually led to his exile and death in the desert. But the rancor of his oratory was not reserved for the rich and powerful. Others also felt the scourge of his pulpit wrath, most notably the Jews, for whom he bore a special hatred. Indeed, his sermons mark an epoch in the history of anti-Semitism. In the eight sermons against Judaizing Christians which he delivered in Antioch in 387, Chrysostom denounced the Jews as "sensual, slippery, voluptuous, avaricious, possessed by demons, drunkards, harlots, and breakers of the Law" and condemned them as murderers of "the prophets, Christ, and God."[109] "Saint John Chrysostom," writes a modern commentator, "up to his time stands without peer or parallel in the entire literature *Adversus Judaeos.* The virulence of his attack is surprising even in an age in which rhetorical denunciation was often indulged with complete abandon."[110] The effects of his preaching, we are told, "wielded a baleful influence not only on the clergy and populace of his time but on those of centuries thereafter."[111] Another Catholic scholar, looking at Chrysostom's discourses from the point of view of the modern Church, has concluded that they could not have been deliv-

25. Saint John Chrysostom. Mosaic, Hagia Sophia, Istanbul, tenth century.

ered after Vatican II's "Declaration on the Church's Attitude toward Non-Christian Religions." "For these objectively unchristian acts he cannot be excused, even if he is the product of his times."[112]

But Jews and Judaizing Christians were not unique as objects of Chrysostom's wrath during the dozen years he preached in Antioch. If he gave a special impetus to anti-Semitism, he can also be said to have contributed uniquely to the development of homophobia. With far more to say on the subject than any other church father, he labored unrelentingly to create fear and prejudice. In a homily on the Epistle to Titus, he damned the pagan world before Christ for its indulgence in murder, adultery, and "the love of boys," attacking not only the gods of the Greeks but also their lawgivers and philosophers, from Solon on.[113] In his discourse *Against the Greeks* he does not spare Socrates and Plato, accusing them of making pederasty "respectable and a part of philosophy."[114]

In an early essay, *Against the Opponents of the Monastic Life,* Chrysostom had urged parents to immure their sons in monasteries to preserve them from this evil. In so doing he gives a picture of civic life which suggests that in fourth-century Antioch, at the moment when Christianity was enjoying its final triumph over paganism, there was widespread dissent from the new values:

> A new [!] and lawless lust has invaded our life, a terrible and incurable disease has fallen upon us, a plague more terrible than all plagues has struck . . . Fornication now seems like a minor offense against forms of unchastity . . . and womankind is in danger of being superfluous when young men take their place in every activity. Even this is not as terrible as the fact that such a great abomination is performed with great fearlessness and lawlessness has become the law. No one is afraid, no one trembles. No one is ashamed, no one blushes . . . No benefit comes from law courts.[115]

These words, written about 380, taken along with the riot that erupted in Thessalonica a decade later, suggest some popular resistance to the church's efforts to impose a new morality. (In later centuries, ironically, monasteries would be portrayed as schools of homosexual lust by Protestant polemicists and anti-clerical satirists like Voltaire.)

Chrysostom made homosexuality not just Sodom's preeminent but its unique sin. "If any one disbelieves hell, let him consider Sodom, let him reflect upon Gomorrah, the vengeance that has been inflicted . . . Would you wish also to know the cause for which these things were then done? It was one sin, a grievous one, yet but one. The men of that time had a passion for boys, and on that account they suffered this punishment."[116]

During his tenure in Antioch, Chrysostom preached a series of sermons on the Epistle to the Romans, including one entirely devoted to Romans 1:26. This sermon is, consequently, the fullest and most detailed ecclesiastical pronouncement on homosexuality in the first thousand years of church history. Liberal in his use of epithets, Chrysostom denounces male love as "monstrous," "Satanical," "detestable," "execrable," and "pitiable." Those who speak in defense of Greek love he calls "even worse than murderers . . . For there is not, there surely is not, a more grievous sin than this insolent dealing."[117] He also attacks lesbianism and reads Paul's ambiguous language about women "changing the natural order" as an explicit reference to "women who abused women."[118] Moreover, he assures his hearers that "natural" intercourse is more pleasurable than sodomy; we are bemused to see this devout ascetic speak so knowledgeably.

Chrysostom also addresses the question of punishment. He follows Roman law in denouncing homosexuality chiefly as a contravention of ordained sex roles but prescribes the Jewish option of death by stoning: "For I should say not only that you have become a woman, but that you have lost your manhood, and have neither changed into that nature nor kept that which you had. You have been a traitor to both of them at once, deserving . . . to be driven out and stoned, as having wronged either sex."[119] Finally, he makes his favorite point that Sodom was a type of hell, drawing on popular travelers' tales that fires still raged in that region of Palestine.[120] Above all, in these sermons homosexuality is no longer merely a detail in the story of the Cities of the Plain but the prime cause of their destruction. One more step remained: to convert this theological terror into legal terrorism. This step was taken by Justinian.

• The Persecutions of Justinian •

Justinian, who became Byzantine emperor in 527, was an ambitious and energetic ruler, passionately devoted to the study of theology and ruthless in suppressing opposition. His great achievement was the compilation of Roman law known as the Corpus Juris Civilis or the Code of Justinian. The new emperor commissioned the work in 528, and a final authoritative version was issued in 534. The *Digest,* a summary of the opinions of earlier jurists, and the *Institutes,* an official handbook for students, had appeared a year earlier.

Superseding all previous legislation, the Code of Justinian remained the law in the eastern empire until Constantinople fell to the Turks nine hundred years later. When Roman law was resurrected at the University of Bologna in the twelfth century with the encouragement of medieval rulers, who felt it would strengthen their power, it became the foremost influence on Western European law. As a result, it shaped legal traditions in the Holy Roman Empire and in such states as Italy, Spain, Portugal, and France—and eventually even in Calvinist Scotland. It remained a force until the Napoleonic age and was of prime importance in determining the status of Europe's homosexuals throughout the Middle Ages, the Renaissance, and the eighteenth century.

Justinian's code, like the Theodosian Code of 438, incorporated the *Lex cum vir* which Constantius and Constans had promulgated in 342. However, it omitted Theodosius' statute of 390, no doubt because it was now regarded as redundant, for the *Institutes* arbitrarily increased the scope of the *Lex Julia,* a law on adultery passed in the reign of Augustus, to include the death penalty for *stuprum cum masculis*—illicit sex with males.[121] But now, under this

26. Justinian. Mosaic, San Vitale, Ravenna, c. 547.

revision, the *Institutes* effected a major change by following Mosaic law and penalizing the active as well as the passive partner.

Was this new development prompted by Justinian personally? It may well have been, for we have evidence that Justinian acted aggressively to persecute men for homosexual offenses from the very beginning of his reign. Though Theodosius may have executed passive males as early as 390, Justinian's reign provides the first incontestable evidence for the use of lethal punishments in the newly Christianized Greek world. A contemporary witness, the Byzantine historian John Malalas (c. 491–578), gives a brief but chilling account of an extensive persecution that took place a year after Justinian's succession, when the most notable victims were prominent churchmen:

> At this time, bishops of divers provinces were prosecuted for the lustful act of sleeping with males. Among them were the bishops Isaiah of Rhodes, formerly the Nycteparchus of Constantinople, and Alexander of Diospolis

> in Thrace. After they were brought to Constantinople by an edict of the Emperor they were examined by the prefect of the city, stripped of their rank and punished. After he had suffered severe torture, Isaiah was sent into exile. Alexander, on the other hand, had his male organ cut off, and was placed in a litter and exposed as a spectacle to the people. Shortly after, the emperor passed a law that the crime of sex with males should be punished by castration. And at that time many homosexuals [*androkoitai*, men who slept with men] were seized and their genitals were cut off. And a great fear ensued among those who suffered from the evil desire for males.[122]

Justinian's reign of terror has received surprisingly little attention from students of the history of homosexuality. Canon Bailey minimized it in his *Homosexuality and the Western Christian Tradition* in 1955; indeed, he conjured it away. David Greenberg, in the *Social Construction of Homosexuality*, dismissed the subject of persecutions as one already well explored, though in fact research can scarcely be said to have begun. John Boswell's approach to Justinian is somewhat different. He quotes Malalas but argues that the emperor's pogrom could not have had the approval of contemporary "Christian" opinion. That "the emperor expressed his opposition to homosexuality in religious terms" is discounted on the grounds that "Byzantine emperors justified most of their enactments—and their very authority—with Christian rhetoric."[123] Boswell's argument is in accord with the central thesis of his book: that early Christianity was not "really" hostile to homosexuality, a view it is difficult to accept. But Justinian, however devious he might be as a politician, was devoutly pious, dwelt in his palace as a fasting ascetic, and was so engrossed with religious doctrine that he may be said to have lived and breathed theology. If Justinian is not an example of a statesman acting under Christian influence, it would be hard to name one.

This neglect of Justinian's persecutions by twentieth-century scholars well disposed toward homosexuals has led to a paradox: we must turn to the eighteenth-century historian Edward Gibbon (who did not hesitate to denounce homosexuality as a "moral pestilence") for what is still the fullest modern account:

> [Justinian] declared himself the implacable enemy of unmanly lust, and the cruelty of his persecution can scarcely be excused by the purity of his motives. In defiance of every principle of justice, he stretched to past as well as future offences the operations of his edicts, with the previous allowance of a short respite for confession and pardon. A painful death was inflicted by the amputation of the sinful instrument, or the insertion of sharp reeds into the pores and tubes of most exquisite sensibility; and Justinian defended the propriety of the execution, since the criminals would have lost their hands had they been convicted of sacrilege. In this state of disgrace and agony two bishops, Isaiah of Rhodes and Alexander of Diospolis, were

> dragged through the streets of Constantinople . . . Perhaps these prelates were innocent. A sentence of death and infamy was often founded on the slight and suspicious evidence of a child or a servant: the guilt of the green faction, of the rich, and of the enemies of Theodora, was presumed by the judges, and paederasty became the crime of those to whom no crime could be imputed.[124]

The Greens and Blues were political parties named after the colors they wore at sporting events in Constantinople: the green faction opposed the emperor. In this sweeping indictment Gibbon drew on the Byzantine historians Theophanes, Cedrenus, and Zonaras for his details. He was apparently unaware of Malalas's account, which he does not mention.

When did the persecution take place? The *Chronography* of Theophanes, a Byzantine chronicler who wrote about 800, gives the date in the margin as 521; but since the event is placed in the second year of Justinian's reign, we may assume that this is a mistake for 528: "In that year the bishops Isaiah of Rhodes and Alexander of Diospolis in Thrace were deposed from office, as having been discovered to be lovers of boys, and were punished frightfully by the emperor, having their male organs cut off and being paraded through the streets with a public crier shouting: 'Bishops, do not insult your honorable station.' And the emperor instituted harsh laws against the licentious and many were punished. And great fear and caution arose."[125] (We note that Theophanes fails to differentiate the fates of the two bishops, and Gibbon follows him in this slip.)

Georgius Cedrenus, who wrote about 1060, gives a slightly fuller version of events, with some further details that Gibbon seized upon: "In the following year [after Justinian's accession] bishops Isaiah of Rhodes and Alexander of Thracian Diospolis and many others were arrested as corruptors of men. [The emperor] ordered some of them to have their male organs cut off, and others to have sharp reeds inserted in the opening of their genitals, and they were exposed to view naked in the forum. Many citizens and senators and not a few of the high clergy were [found] guilty, were castrated and exposed naked in the forum and died miserably."[126]

We learn more from Procopius' *Secret History.* Procopius, Justinian's court historian, had lavished praise on the emperor and his wife in his official writings. But he also composed a more intimate account in which he painted both rulers in the blackest colors and gave vent to his personal animosity. It was these *Anecdota* ("things not given out") which revealed to Gibbon Justinian's dubious procedures as Cedrenus and Theophanes had documented his savage punishments. According to Procopius:

> Afterwards [Justinian] also prohibited sodomy *[paiderastein]* by law, not examining closely into offences committed subsequently to the law but concerning himself only with those persons who long before had been

> caught by this malady. And the prosecution of these cases was carried out in reckless fashion, since the penalty was exacted without an accuser, for the word of a single man or boy, and even if it so happened, of a slave compelled against his will to give evidence against his owner, was considered definite proof. Those who were thus convicted had their privates removed and were paraded through the streets. Not in all cases, however, was this punishment inflicted in the beginning, but only upon those reputed to be Greens or to be possessed of great wealth or those who in some other way chanced to have offended the rulers.[127]

Later, in medieval Europe, impecunious monarchs were to use religious prejudice to extract money from wealthy Jews. Procopius tells us that Justinian used accusations of sodomy to the same end against citizens in sixth-century Byzantium.

We do not know exactly what law Justinian acted under. No text of the edict Malalas refers to has come down to us. We should note, however, that Cedrenus assumes that a sentence of castration was a sentence of death and that Gibbon makes the same assumption. This is attested not only by the historians we have cited but also by the preamble of a law prohibiting the making of eunuchs, which stated that "out of the great number upon whom this operation [castration] is performed only a very few survive, so that certain of them have stated in Our presence that of ninety who have been castrated, hardly three have escaped with their lives."[128] We may find this rate incredibly high. But if there was so great a mortality in commercial operations where it was important to preserve lives, what can have been the result when they were performed as punishment?

Justinian's work as a legislator did not end with his compilation of Roman law. Over the years new laws, or *Novellae,* were issued to the Byzantines not in the traditional Latin but in native Greek. Two of them deal explicitly with male homosexuality and demonstrate the ultimate wedding of imperial law and Christian theology, as colored by the myth of Sodom. The first law, Novella 77, appeared in 538 and was addressed to the people of Constantinople. It warned that homosexual acts would "incur the just anger of God, and bring about the destruction of cities along with their inhabitants."[129] The death penalty endorsed by Leviticus, Tertullian, Eusebius, and Chrysostom is here defended on the theory that homosexuality can cause the destruction of entire populations in various ways: "Therefore We order all men to avoid such offences, to have the fear of God in their hearts, and to imitate the example of those who live in piety; for as crimes of this description cause famine, earthquake, and pestilence, it is on this account, and in order that men may not lose their souls, that We admonish them to abstain from the perpetration of the illegal acts above mentioned."[130]

It has been plausibly argued by Sherwin Bailey that a frightening series of natural catastrophes in Justinian's time prompted this legislation. A violent earthquake had shaken Constantinople in 525. A year later thousands died in another quake that leveled Antioch. These calamities would have fed popular terror and provided a background of hysteria for the pogrom of 528. Before the rise of geological science, such phenomena were regularly interpreted as signs of divine wrath. Modern research has revealed that modern Turkey—occupying the site of the ancient Byzantine Empire—lies at the confluence of three tectonic plates, making it especially prone to shocks. What could be more natural than that the Byzantines, lacking any scientific explanation for these catastrophes, should have sought a scriptural explanation and found it in the tale of a city destroyed by God (as they had come to believe) for "unnatural" crimes? Today, we find it difficult to project ourselves back into the mentality of such a world. But these supernatural fears were to play a crucial role in the homophobia of the Middle Ages and still aroused anxieties in the eighteen and nineteenth centuries. They are not unknown today.

Novella 77 was not Justinian's last word on the subject. Twenty years later a further law seems to have been provoked by more natural disasters. In December 557 the earth shook in Constantinople, so that, according to one Byzantine historian, "many people and almost all the upper classes perished"—presumably their houses had heavier ceilings.[131] Once again the Byzantines read the deaths as God's work, and the churches of the city reverberated with supplications. But it was in vain. A terrible plague broke out a few months later and claimed more victims.[132] Who then was to blame for these new horrors? "Men-corruptors" were once again singled out as scapegoats in Novella 141, dated March 15, 559.

If Novella 77 was theologically inspired, this new legislation reads more like a pastoral letter than a criminal statute, demonstrating how closely church and state were allied in the eastern empire. Adopting a tone of paternal benevolence but threatening ferocious punishments, Justinian's jurists see no contradiction in calling their punitive deity kind, tolerant, and patient. The preamble reads:

> As we are always in need of the benevolence and kindness of God, and above all, at this time, when we have provoked Him to anger in many ways, on account of the multitude of our sins, and although He threatens us with the penalties we deserve, He, nevertheless, manifests his clemency to us, and has deferred the exercise of his wrath to some future time . . . Wherefore it would not be just for us to treat with contempt His abounding kindness, His tolerance, and His infinite patience, lest, avoiding repentance, our hearts may become hardened, and we may accumulate His anger upon our heads, on the day of His vengeance. But . . . there are persons who are guilty of abominable offences, which are deservedly detested by

God. We have reference to the corruption of males, a crime which some persons have the sacrilegious audacity to perpetrate.[133]

In later centuries, pious language of this sort routinely added a gloss of humaneness to the declarations of the Inquisition against heretics and Judaizers, in which the mercifulness of God and the persecutors was always insisted on. Moreover, Novella 141 provided that church and imperial prefect should work hand in glove. Failure to identify oneself to the patriarch of Constantinople as a sodomite was considered an aggravation of the crime. Men who did not confess their guilt were warned that they would face a "terrible chastisement."[134]

Procopius's *Secret History* reveals another side to these persecutions; though breathing piety, officials used them for the venial purpose of extorting money. Justinian had exhausted his ample treasury by waging costly wars and building magnificent churches and palaces. But accusations of sodomy, paganism, and heresy could be used to mulct the wealthy: "No sooner had he thus disposed of the public wealth," Procopius tells us, "than he turned his eyes towards his subjects, and he straightway robbed great numbers of them of their estates . . . charging some with belief in polytheism, others with adherence to some perverse sect among the Christians, or with sodomy *[paiderastias].*"[135] This routine of extortion was institutionalized through the appointment of two new city magistrates. One dealt with thieves; to the other, called the "quaesitor" (or inquisitor) Justinian "assigned the province of punishing those who were habitually practicing sodomy *[paiderastountas],* and those who had such intercourse with women as was prohibited by law, and any who did not worship the Deity in the orthodox way."[136]

According to Procopius, the quaesitor not only delivered up suspects to the emperor, but his underlings extracted money from others by threatening to charge them: "For the subordinates of [the quaesitor] would neither bring forward accusers nor submit witnesses of what had been done, but throughout the whole period the unfortunates who fell in their way continued, without having been accused or convicted, and with the greatest secrecy, to be murdered as well as robbed of their money."[137]

So men suspected of homosexual acts were the victims not just of the courts and magistrates but of a corrupt police, who used Justinian's brutal statues to enrich themselves as well as the emperor. A millennium later, the Inquisition in Spain under Torquemada was to be marked by the same sordidness, so that an indignant Sixtus IV would reprove its officers for acting from "avarice and lust for gain" as much as religious zeal.[138]

One last belated glimmer of classical civilization disappeared under Justinian. In 529 the emperor forbade non-Christians to teach and closed the ancient schools of Athens. Plato's Academy, which had existed since 385 BCE, was abolished and its teachers offered positions by the more liberal shah of

Persia. An impressive work of legal scholarship, Justinian's famous code was marred by a similar intolerance. A modern historian has concluded that "it differs most from earlier codes in its rigid orthodoxy, its deeper obscurantism, its vengeful severity. An educated Roman would have found life more civilized under the Antonines than under Justinian."[139] Nowhere was the code harsher than in its treatment of homosexuals. With the laws of Justinian, the medieval world was inaugurated.

CHAPTER SIX

DARKNESS DESCENDS

476–1049

• The Fall of Rome •

Rome fell in 476 when the Teutonic chieftain Odoacer deposed the last feeble emperor, Romulus Augustulus. Did the prevalence of homosexuality contribute to this collapse? The idea is, of course, a cliché endlessly repeated in speeches, proclamations, and letters to the editor, usually with the conclusion that our own society will perish "like Greece or Rome" if homosexuality is tolerated. So serious and commonplace an allegation—that homosexuality was responsible for the demise of two of the ancient world's greatest civilizations—is surely worth some critical consideration, if only to demonstrate how completely the evidence fails to support it.

We must first ask: exactly what are we speaking of? If the Roman Empire formally ceased to exist in the late fifth century, it is far less clear what is meant by "the fall of Greece." Admirers of the classical age might place this fall in 338 BCE when the Athenians lost their liberty to the Macedonians. But the defeat of southern Greece by its northern neighbor can hardly be attributed to differing views of same-sex attachments. If the most potent force on the Greek side at Chaeronea was the Theban Sacred Band, Philip, and Alexander, the Macedonian leaders who triumphed over them were themselves bisexual leaders of a bisexual society. With the establishment of the Byzantine Empire, later Greek civilization, now emphatically Christian, received a thousand-year lease on life, to be finally extinguished in 1453 when Muhammad II captured Constantinople. Here the circumstances are more ironic, for the strongly homophobic culture of Orthodox Byzantium fell before the more indulgent Ottoman Turks.

But what of Rome? We must first note that it was not the pagan Rome of Caligula and Nero—the Rome that looms so large in the imagination of Hollywood and evangelical moralists—that fell. Rome survived the worst of the Julio-Claudian emperors and flourished a century later under the Antonines. It was Christian, not pagan, Rome which fell—a Rome that had been ruled by Christian emperors for more than one hundred and fifty years after the conversion of Constantine. They had, as we have seen, passed harsh legislation intended to impose new Christian norms of sexual conduct, not least in the case of homosexuality. Nor are the pictures of Roman society we find in writers of the late empire particularly lurid. The morality of the fifth-century has been compared by social historians to George III's England, that is, to an age neither notably licentious nor notably prudish. References to homosexuality in any form are rare. Only Salvian, writing of Roman Carthage about 400 CE, makes a special point of the matter. Identifying some transvestite street prostitutes, he is outraged that the civic authorities have not repressed this open display of vice.[1] All in all, we may say that Rome at its fall, far from being a city of orgiastic revels, was a relatively sober community where homophobia had long been the official policy of the state.

Rome's decay has been ascribed to many causes: military, political, economic, epidemiological, demographic, or ecological. The most famous analysis, in Edward Gibbon's *Decline and Fall of the Roman Empire,* made Christianity a major cause of the catastrophe.[2] Gibbon thought that its Christian rulers alienated Rome's sizable pagan minority (who saw their sacrifices forbidden and temples destroyed) and that Christian otherworldliness turned men from their social and military duties. Certainly the severity of Theodosius' legislation must have threatened citizens whose sexual lifestyles were nonconforming. With Rome's new Christian laws threatening public burning, it must have seemed that her barbarian enemies could hardly do worse. Considering these facts, one might perhaps argue with more plausibility that homophobia contributed to the fall of the empire.

Visigothic Spain

When the Roman Empire disintegrated, its parts fell under the rule of barbarian tribes, mainly Germanic. It would be of interest to know what views these non-Roman peoples held of homosexuality, but the evidence from their largely preliterate societies is fragmentary and confusing. The Germanic tribes, originally occupying the land between the Rhine and the Danube, were widely dispersed through migrations—as far as Russia and Asia Minor in the east, the Baltic in the north, and, ultimately, North Africa in the south. Over this wide territory it is not surprising to find widely different cultural patterns. Tacitus, in a famous essay, reported that among the Germans, "cowards," "poor fighters," and men who were *corpore infames* (passive partners) were "plunged in the mud of marshes with a hurdle on their heads."[3] But Ammianus Marcellinus, writing about 380, speaks of the Gothic Taifali, settled in what is today Romania, whose native traditions paralleled Sparta and Thebes: among the Taifali, boys had adult lovers until they killed their first wild boar or bear.[4]

Other writers were also at variance. Salvian described the Vandals as less prone to homosexuality than the North African Christians they conquered, but Quintilian in an imaginary speech has a German soldier named Marianus declare that male love was honorable among his people.[5] Among the northern Teutonic tribes, to call a man *ragr* (effeminate, or given to passivity) was a crime that carried the penalty of outlawry.[6] Yet in some Swedish cults men assumed female roles to perform a kind of shamanistic magic known as *seidr* which was both feared and despised. One ruler, hearing that his son had taken part in these rites, sent another son to kill him "together with eighty *seidmenn,* and this action was much praised."[7]

Early Germanic legal codes lack prohibitions against male relations. These codes, which derived from pre-Christian customary law, exact fines for adultery and rape (seen as infringing on the property rights of a woman's male relatives) but say nothing of sex between men. The oldest Anglo-Saxon code, dating from seventh-century Kent, follows this pattern, and the laws of Alfred the Great (r. 871–899), which do incorporate biblical sources, punish bestiality but not homosexuality. The ninth-century laws of the Bavarians, Burgundians, Alemmani, Saxons, Thuringians, and those Teutons who had crossed the Alps to settle in Lombardy are likewise silent.[8]

The exception was the Visigothic kingdom of Spain, which survived from the fall of Rome to the Arab conquest of 711. By 500 the Visigoths' domain reached from the Loire to the Strait of Gibraltar, and was the largest and most powerful state in western Europe. The Visigoths were Arian Christians who converted to orthodox Catholicism in 589. Henceforth, church and king were closely connected so that bishops helped administer the state. In 642 a seventy-nine-year old noble named Kindasvinth seized the throne through a conspiracy. Fearing further revolts, we are told, he "demolished the Goths" by ordering the death of seven hundred officials and exiling others.[9] In about 650 he also issued the first known Germanic law against homosexuality, which ordered that "those who lie with males, or consent to participate passively in such acts, ought to be smitten by the sentence of this law—namely, that as soon as such an offence has been admitted and the judge has publicly investigated it, he should forthwith take steps to have offenders of both kinds castrated."[10] Kindasvinth's law also provided that the convict's son might seize his property and his wife might remarry.

Forty years later another king, Egica, took further action. Quite as brutal as Kindasvinth, Egica was described by the chronicler of his reign as having "persecuted the Goths with bitter death."[11] Accusing the Jews of conspiring against the state, he issued a decree depriving them of their property and enslaving them.[12] In 693, in his speech to the bishops at the sixteenth council of Toledo, Egica urged the council to take action against sodomites. "Among other matters," he ordered, "see that you determine to extirpate that obscene crime committed by those who lie with males, whose fearful conduct defiles the charm of honest living and provokes from heaven the wrath of the supreme Judge."[13] The council obligingly passed a canon degrading any guilty bishop, priest, or deacon and inflicting the punishment "concerning such offences," that is, castration. Thereafter, the mutilated clergy were to be "excluded from all communion with Christians, . . . punished with one hundred stripes of the lash, shorn of their hair as a mark of disgrace, and banished in perpetual exile."[14]

Egica also revised the secular statute on sodomy, adding a theological rationale:

> We are compelled by the teaching of the orthodox faith to impose the censure of the law upon indecent practices, and to restrain with the bridle of continence those who have been involved in lapses of the flesh . . . Certainly we strive to abolish the detestable outrage of that lust by the filthy uncleanness of which men do not fear to defile other men in the unlawful act of sodomy *[stuprum]* . . . an offence against both divine religion and chastity. Although indeed both the authority of Holy Scripture and the decree of the secular law prohibit absolutely this kind of delinquency, nevertheless it is necessary to repeal that statute [presumably the law of Kindasvinth] by a new enactment lest . . . worse vices are seen to spring up.[15]

But Egica's new law did not "repeal" Kindasvinth's statute; it augmented it by adding to castration the penalties of the ecclesiastical canon of the sixteenth council of Toledo—lashings, shearing, and exile.

The parallels with Justinian's legislation, in penalty and style, are striking. Once again savage brutality was touted as "clemency and piety." But the harshly tyrannical rule of the Visigothic kings alienated their subjects and was their own undoing. In 711, nine years after Egica's death, a Muslim general named Tarik landed at the rock that still bears his name and began the Islamic conquest of the peninsula.

• Church Councils and the Penitentials •

The stance of the early Christian Church toward same-sex relations was defined not just by the Bible and patristic teachings but also by the decrees of ecclesiastical councils, which later became the basis for canon law. The oldest collection of "canons" to come down to us are from the Council of Elvira, held by the Spanish clergy at Granada sometime between 306 and 309.[16] Since the council met immediately following the last great persecution of Diocletian (303–304) and on the eve of the church's triumph under Constantine, we might have expected the bishops' concerns at such a moment to be political: instead, we find them preoccupied with questions of sexuality.

Almost half the eighty-one canons of the Council of Elvira deal with sex, far more than with any other topic, the church choosing to define its identity principally through a strict sexual code that even bade bishops and other married clerics to abstain from their wives. Other canons dealt with premarital relations, divorce, abortion, adultery, and marriage with Jews and heretics. Canon 50 forbade Christians to eat with Jews, and Canon 67 declared: "It is forbidden for a woman, whether baptized or a catechumen, to have anything to do with long-haired men or hairdressers."[17] A hundred years earlier Clement of Alexandria had condemned beardless men with long hair as dangerously effeminate. In a chapter entitled "On the Companions We Should Associate With" he also inveighed against "women who delight in the company of perverts [and] are surrounded by loose-tongued catamites."[18] Christian legislation usually fixed on sexual acts rather than classes of persons. But the first known ecclesiastical pronouncement on homosexuality forbade Christian women to befriend certain men because of their suspect lifestyles.

A more influential pronouncement came a few years later. The Council of Ancyra (modern Ankara) met in 314, a year after the passing of the Edict of Milan. The council was mainly concerned with prescribing penalties for Christians who had apostatized during earlier persecutions. But it also issued two canons—numbers 16 and 17—against certain persons called *alogeusamenoi,* literally, "those who are guilty of irrational behavior." This language of the canons is vague, but the offenses were apparently sexual in nature: "If they have sinned while under twenty years of age, [let them] be prostrators fifteen years [at the church door] . . . And if any who have passed this age and have wives have fallen into this sin, let them be prostrators twenty-five years, and then communicate in prayers; and after they have been five years in the communion of prayers, let them share the oblation [Eucharist]. And if any married men of more than fifty years have so sinned, let them be admitted to communion only at the point of death."[19] Under Canon 17, those who had infected others with the "leprosy" of like sins were excluded from the church and "compelled to remain outside with penitents of the lowest class."[20]

But who were the *alogeusamenoi?* Modern scholarship regards them as men who had intercourse with animals. Nevertheless, the early Latin translations of the Greek text interpreted the canons as referring to homosexuality as well as bestiality. Though the Council of Ancyra was, strictly speaking, a local synod rather than an ecumenical council, its canons were regarded by later councils as ecumenical. As a result, in Western Europe at least, these very harsh penances came to be taken as definitive for same-sex behavior and were cited for many centuries.[21]

Very few parish clergy in this period would have had access to such documents. What did circulate widely for the use of priests who heard confessions were the popular handbooks known as penitentials. These unofficial guides first appeared in Ireland in the late sixth century and reflect the influence of certain canons issued in Wales a century earlier. Canon 8 of the Synod of the Grove of Victory, for example, requires that "he who commits the male crime as the Sodomists *[ut Sodomite]* shall do penance for four years. But he who [has relations] between the thighs, [three] years. However, if by one's own hand or the hand of another, two years."[22] The *Book of David,* dubiously ascribed to Wales's patron saint (d. 588?), required that "those who commit fornication with a woman who has become vowed to Christ or to a husband, or with a beast, or with a male, for the remainder [of their lives] dead to the world shall live unto God," that is, in monastic seclusion.[23]

These works, which first appeared in the British Isles shortly after the fall of Rome, are among the most curious in ecclesiastical history, not least for their sexual specificity. The three most important Irish penitentials—the *Penitential of Finnian* (before 590), the *Penitential of Columban* (c. 600), and the *Penitential of Cummean* (c. 650)—all list detailed penalties for homosexual acts. The *Penitential of Finnian* decreed that "those practicing homosexuality *[in terga fornicantes],* if they are boys [shall do] penance two years, if men three; if, however, it has become a habit, seven." It also makes specific mention of fellation: "Those who satisfy their desires with their lips, three years. If it has become a habit, seven years."[24] Columban provided that a monk who "has committed the sin of murder or sodomy, [should] do penance for ten years."[25] Cummean assigns seven years' penance for sodomy, four to seven years for fellation.[26] There is a variety of penalties for boys: six to ten special fasts for kissing, depending on whether the kisses are "simple" or licentious or cause pollution; twenty to forty days for mutual masturbation; for femoral intercourse one hundred days, on repetition one year. "A small boy misused by an older one, if he is ten years of age, shall fast for a week; if he consents, for twenty days."[27] It is notable that lack of consent on the part of the boy mitigated but did not erase his imputed sin.

The later penitentials derive from Anglo-Saxon England. These include the penitential of Theodore of Tarsus, who became archbishop of Canterbury in 668, and the penitentials of the Venerable Bede (d. 735) and of Egbert, archbishop of York (d. 766). All penance male homosexual acts. Theodore is unusual in making a special reference to lesbianism: "If a women practices vice with a woman she shall do penance for three years."[28] In the eighth century the use of penitentials spread from the British Isles to the continent, where numerous new compilations appeared. A diligent modern scholar has identified thirty-one, dating from the sixth to the eleventh century, that punish male homosexuality and fourteen that punish lesbianism.

We may draw two conclusions from the wide use of these manuals. First, we may assume that the sexual behavior they describe was indeed regularly confessed. The codes were not mere fantasies of a prurient clergy, as some shocked Protestant historians, writing before the age of Kinsey, imagined. Second, they show that homosexual relations ranked among the worst of sexual sins, and indeed of all sins, in the eyes of Christians. John Boswell, who was inclined to discount any evidence for homophobia on the part of the church before 1200, held that the penitentials "hardly constitute an index of medieval morality."[29] But Pierre Payer, who has made the most thorough study of the penitentials to date, thinks that Boswell erred in this assumption.[30] It was through their prescriptions that priests informed parishioners of their all-but-universal sexual sinfulness, instilling guilt and fear of divine retribution for such deeds. By defining morality in this way, the church gained immense power over its adherents and, in time, immense wealth, as affluent sinners, having savored the pleasures of this life, sought to ease the pains of the next through deathbed bequests to the church. Men who loved men and women who loved women must have felt especially threatened.

• The Carolingian Panic •

The penitentials belong to the period from 500 to 1000 when Europe's political life, economy, and culture plummeted, along with the collapse of Roman sovereignty. During the reign of Charlemagne (768–814), however, Western civilization made a partial recovery. Beginning as king of the Franks, Charles created a potent new order, the Holy Roman Empire, which brought Europe a period of peace and stability it had not known for centuries. In addition, he facilitated a revival of education led by monks imported from Ireland and England, lands that had not suffered as severely as the Continent from barbarian depredations. But this rebirth of civilization rested on strict Christian orthodoxy. Anxious to impose unity on his new dominions, Charlemagne entered into a close partnership with the bishops and other clergy. The results were not always humane. When he finally conquered the recalcitrant and pagan Saxons, the defeated tribesmen were given a choice between baptism and death. Charles also supported the church by enforcing Christian sexual morality, which until now had hardly influenced northern Europe, through the "capitularies" he issued in large numbers. Charlemagne's puritanism stopped short at the gates of the palace, however. Within its walls, five mistresses supplemented his four successive wives and bore a due proportion of his eighteen children.

Under Charles's reign, church councils and synods issued at least seven ordinances condemning homosexuality.[31] In 789, in a "General Admonition" to his subjects, he specifically endorsed the heavier sanctions authorized at Ancyra "for those who sin against nature with animals or with men."[32] (By equating love between men with bestiality, this edict, like many before and after, quite literally "de-humanized" it.) In this age also, the penitentials that had been in use for centuries were denounced by church councils for failing

27. Charlemagne's victory over the Saracens, c. 780. Manuscript illustration, *Grandes Chroniques de France,* fourteenth century.

to cite scriptural, patristic, and conciliar authorities and for their leniency, especially with regard to homosexuality. In 813 the Council of Châlons prohibited their use and ordered them destroyed.[33]

The anathemas of Charlemagne and his clergy served to keep homophobic prejudices and fears alive in people's consciousness. As a result, homosexuals became scapegoats in Charlemagne's empire, as they had been in Justinian's. Thus, the Council of Paris, held in 829 some fifteen years after Charlemagne's death, multiplied the disasters that might be blamed on God's wrath against sodomites. Here is a literal translation of its Canon 34, which has been little noted or studied:

> Though human wretchedness often provokes the incomparable mercy of its Creator to severity by the manifold excesses of its weaknesses, it transgresses more seriously and more wickedly against Him when it sins against nature. For, indeed, we read that the Lord . . . has fearfully revenged this sin in three ways.
>
> Among all the other sins which the human race fatally committed at the beginning of creation, it is believed that, provoked to wrath especially by this sin (as certain teachers have maintained), [God] said: "I repent making

> man on the earth" [Gen. 6:6]. Therefore on this account, he utterly destroyed by a cataclysm [the Flood] the whole human race except for eight souls. Furthermore, because of this crime five cities were swallowed up by raging fire from heaven and by the gaping mouth of hell, and forty or more thousand of the race of Benjamin were struck down by the sword's edge in fraternal war [Judges 20]. Thus these manifest proofs show beyond a doubt how detestable and execrable this vice is to divine majesty.[34]

What inspired this canon, which was calculated to raise fear and hatred of homosexuals to new heights by implying they were responsible not only for natural disasters like fires and floods but also for defeat in battle? Undoubtedly, it was prompted by the military and political crises that faced Charles's domain during the reign of his son Louis the Pious. "Saracens" raided the coasts of Italy and Provence, Bulgarian hordes poured into the eastern provinces of the empire, and pagan Vikings and Danes pillaged northern Europe. These dangers created widespread hysteria, and Louis ordered public prayers and fasts in 827. The situation was familiar. Churchmen feared that defeats by pagan or Islamic forces might weaken Christianity's claim to be the one true religion. But by representing defeats as acts of divine chastisement, they became not signs of Christianity's weakness but manifestations of God's wrath. The mood was one of terror, a terror focused on a special class of sinners.

In just such a penitential mood, Bishop Wala, the leading churchman of the Frankish kingdom, convened the Council at Paris in order to "make diligent inquiry into the way in which the rulers and the faithful were observing the law of God."[35] Going beyond Elvira and Ancyra, the council explicitly endorsed the death penalty for sodomy. Moreover, Canon 34 not only endorsed Leviticus but also interpreted Paul's Epistle to the Romans as advocating capital punishment: "Moreover, the Lord in his law commands that any who commit this infamous crime be punished with death [Lev. 20:13], and the Apostle adds that they are "worthy of death [Rom. 1:32]." We may recall that at the end of the first chapter of Romans, Paul accuses non-believers of a long list of sins, in which homosexuality is given a special prominence. Then he adds that the "judgment of God" makes such sinners "worthy of death."

Justinian's jurists had made male love responsible for the "destruction of cities." But Canon 34 went further and made it the reason for Noah's Flood—and the near extinction of humanity. How did it arrive at this conclusion? Genesis 6 says only that "God saw the wickedness of man was great on the earth, and every imagination of the thoughts of his heart was evil continually." Canon 34 mentions "certain teachers" who taught that the Flood was, in particular, a punishment for sodomy. In all likelihood this is a reference to the eighth-century Latin version of *The Revelations of Saint Methodius.* Methodius was a Libyan bishop martyred by Diocletian in 311;

the *Revelations* ascribed to him were in fact an invention of the seventh century. The Syriac original makes no reference to antediluvian homosexuality, but the Latin translation introduces the idea, which seems to have derived from an obscure passage in the Talmud.[36]

The use by the council of a strange and bloody tale from Judges 19 and 20 is less recherché, though quite as questionable. The Book of Judges tells of a Levite offered hospitality by an old man in the Benjaminite town of Gibeah. Certain men surround the house and in language parallel to the Sodom story demand that the host "bring forth the man that we may know him." Again echoing Genesis 19, the old man offers his virgin daughter as a rape substitute. Instead, the Levite's concubine is sent out, is abused "all the night," and in the morning is discovered dead on the doorstep. The Levite dismembers her body and sends a part to each of the tribes of Israel. The outrage provokes a war against the Benjaminites which results in the carnage referred to in Canon 34.

Clearly, the slaughter of the Benjaminites was the result of a heterosexual rape and murder and only indirectly connected with homosexuality. But the council was preoccupied with the great anxiety of the times—the fear of Islam. By interpreting Judges 19 as it did, the council suggested that sodomy might provoke God to give victory to the enemies of Christianity. The sin might be punished in three different ways, the council noted: by "water or blood or fire." Here we see how, once a prejudice has been established, imagined dangers to society posed by a scapegoated class quickly multiply. Thus, in our own century ingenious Nazi propagandists ascribed innumerable undesirable characteristics to Jews and other "lesser races." In defining these new dangers, the council also damned the penitentials and endorsed the more severe canons of Ancyra: "For indeed the holy fathers, inspired by the divine spirit, have justly decreed in the sacred canons that this sin be judged more severely than others, since they plainly understood that while it reigns the state of the Church of Christ is weakened and the kingdom placed in danger." "The kingdom placed in danger": we must project ourselves back to a superstitious age haunted by the fear of conquest to understand how ominously those words would have sounded in the ears of Wala's compatriots.

Though no authentic edict prescribing the death penalty for sodomy was issued by Charlemagne himself, a capital law was invented and foisted on the emperor.[37] Fabricated about 857, it was spuriously assigned to the year 779 by a clerical forger of whom little is known except his name—Benedict Levita, or Benedict "the deacon." That Benedict's *Collection of Capitularies,* an elaborate document of over 1,700 chapters, should have appeared at this moment is perhaps not surprising; the ninth century was remarkable for the number and extent of its ecclesiastical forgeries. To this era belong the notorious "Donations of Constantine," perhaps the most famous forgery in Western history, and the "False Decretals" (manufactured papal letters), a collection ascribed to Saint Isidore of Seville, who had in fact died in 636. (The "Donations," which gave secular authority over central Italy to the popes, went unchallenged until 1440, when the humanist Lorenzo Valla showed that the text's biblical quotations came from Jerome's Latin translation—that is, they were post-Constantinian by a half century.)

In order to strengthen ecclesiastical over secular power, Benedict ascribed to Charlemagne many laws that were not his. To this end he drew on the Theodosian Code, the Novellas of Justinian, papal decretals, the church fathers, and the Bible. Benedict pretended that his work was a continuation of the (authentic) compilations by the Abbot Ansegisus. Since unique copies of imperial laws were often in the hands of the clergy, his work was made easy.

In Capitulary 21 of its *Second Supplement* ("Of Various Shameful Deeds of Evil Men") Benedict incorporates verbatim that portion of Canon 34 of the Council of Paris that makes homosexuality responsible for the Flood and the slaughter of the Benjaminites.[38] The language is presented as Charlemagne's, not the council's, and another forged chapter pronounces sentence of death in the emperor's name.[39]

If we consider such ordinances together with Paul's vehemence in Romans, Clement's fulminations, Augustine's view of sodomy as a kind of treason against the Creator, and the endorsement of the death penalty by such fathers of the church as Tertullian, Eusebius, and John Chrysostom, together with the theologically inspired codes of Justinian and the Visigoths, it is difficult—in fact, impossible—to accept the view set forth by John Boswell that "the peculiar horror which has been associated with male homosexuality in Western culture and the correspondingly violent condemnation of it were products of the twelfth century."[40] Here, long before the twelfth century, the most important body of law promulgated in Europe in the early medieval period allowed for the ultimate penalty to be visited on homosexuals. This, over the forged name of a famous ruler. From a practical point of view it made no difference that the law was a deception: Benedict's "False Capitularies" were widely disseminated, much used, and accepted as authentic until a German scholar questioned their genuineness in an article published in Latin in 1836.[41]

In his *Fourth Supplement* Benedict returns to the subject at length, adding much rhetoric and drawing on Roman law to justify burning.[42] The chapter names "the nations of Spain and Provence and Burgundy" as especially guilty of sodomy and ends with a warning: "It is better for us to shun such things, than through them to come to ruin, so that the nation is annihilated by the heathen or captured by them."[43] Once more Benedict explains defeats in battle as due not to military incompetence or the superior power of the enemy or the treachery of allies but to sexual sin. Commenting on his rhetoric, Gisela Beibtreu-Ehrenberg justly remarks: "Benedict Levita shows himself to be the legitimate father of the misguided jurisprudence of the high middle ages, which later, within the framework of the Inquisition, banished logic and justice from the law courts for centuries."[44]

· Love in Arab Spain ·

What were, we may ask, the attitudes toward homosexuality in those Muslim lands so feared in the Christian West? One index may be found in their literature, which abounds in homoerotic love poetry, most notably in Arab Spain. Its efflorescence here was not unique but paralleled the Islamic world generally. Similar lyrical outpourings also graced the courts of Iraq and Syria, the gardens of Persia, the mountains of Afghanistan, the plains of Mogul India, the empire of the Ottoman Turks, and the North African states of Egypt, Tunis, and Morocco. Medieval Islamic anthologies, whether compiled in Baghdad, Damascus, Isfahan, Kabul, Delhi, Istanbul, Cairo, Kairouan, or Fez, reveal, with astonishing consistency for over a millennium, the same strain of homoerotic passion we find in love poems from Córdoba, Seville, and Granada.

The civilization ruled by the Umayyad caliphs of Córdoba from 756 to 1031 surpassed any in Catholic Europe. Córdoba's only rival among European cities was Constantinople at the other end of the continent. Indeed, the caliphs may have exceeded the contemporary Byzantine emperors in culture and probably maintained a higher level of public administration. Many of their Christian subjects (and certainly Spain's Jews) preferred these infidel rulers to the Visigoths. Moorish architecture produced, in the course of centuries, such masterpieces as the great mosque of Córdoba, the Alcázar and Giralda in Seville, and the Alhambra in Granada. Literature in the form of poetry was enthusiastically cultivated, as in all Arab countries. Native Spaniards studied Arabic eagerly to perfect an elegant and expressive style, and scholars from Christian Europe came to Seville, Toledo, and Córdoba to study medicine, astronomy, and mathematics. The scholarly Sylvester II, Rome's pope in the year 1000, had been a student in Córdoba.

To moralists beyond the Pyrenees, Islamic culture seemed a luxurious paradise tantalizingly endowed with harems, pretty slave girls, and suspiciously handsome sakis. But in sexual matters, Islam maintained a paradoxical ambivalence, not least with respect to homosexuality, for the severity and intolerance that characterized traditional Judaism and Christianity reappear in the laws of this third Abrahamic religion, under the influence ultimately of the Hebrew scriptures.

The Koran shows both Jewish and Christian influence in its interpretation of the Sodom story. Though Muhammad does not mention Sodom by name, he was well acquainted with the tale of Lot and uses the episode several times. He presents Lot as a prophet of God (like himself) and interprets the fire from above as proof of God's willingness to chastise those who ignore his messengers. Muhammad calls the men of Sodom simply "the people of Lot," that is, Lot's neighbors. Through this curious association, the common Arabic word for sodomy, *liwat,* derives from Lot's name, as does the word for homosexual, *luti,* literally a "Lot-ite." In the Koran, Muhammad makes Lot scold "his people" for lusting after men, a taste he condemns as an "abomination," and represents God as smiting them with tablets of baked clay rained from heaven.[45]

When assigning punishment, however, the Koran stops short of the ferocity of Leviticus. After confining adulteresses to their homes, Muhammad adds: "And as for the two of you [men] who are guilty thereof, punish them both. And if they repent and improve, let them be. Lo! Allah is Relenting, Merciful."[46] But the Koran was not the only source of authority among orthodox Muslims. There were also the *hadith,* collected sayings attributed to Muhammad which appeared in five enormous collections in the ninth century. They include a decree that both active and passive partners should be stoned, a view which had a definitive influence on Islamic law.

The theologian Malik of Medina (d. 795), whose school of jurisprudence eventually became the dominant one in Spain and North Africa, endorsed the death penalty. So did the leader of another important school, the literalist Ibn Hanbal (d. 855).[47] Others more lenient reduced the punishment to flogging, usually one hundred strokes. Barbaric sentences were in fact meted out by Muhammad's immediate successors. Abu Bakr, an intimate of the Prophet and the first Muslim caliph (632–634), prescribed burning as a penalty and had one convicted man buried under the debris of a wall. (In modern Afghanistan this punishment was revived by its Taliban rulers in an updated form: the walls were pushed over by bulldozers.) Muhammad's son-in-law Ali, the fourth caliph (later regarded as infallible and semidivine by Shiite Muslims), had a guilty man thrown headlong from the top of a minaret; others were stoned.[48] Thus, through early judicial theory and practice, Old Testament severity came, at least in theory, to dominate the legal side of Islam.

Elsewhere in Islamic culture, however, the evidence is strikingly contradictory. Popular attitudes were more accepting than in Christendom, and European visitors were repeatedly shocked by the relaxed tolerance of Arabs, Turks, and Persians, who seemed to find nothing unnatural in love between men and boys.[49] Behind this important cultural difference lies a vein of romanticism that runs deep through medieval Arab treatises on love. For Islamic writers, emotional intoxication might spring not just from the love of women, as with the troubadours, but also from the love of males.

Arab enthusiasts held that romantic love was a meaningful and valuable experience for its own sake. But how were they to reconcile such a view with their faith? This they did by appealing to another *hadith* ascribed to the

Prophet: "He who loves and remains chaste and conceals his secret and dies, dies a martyr."[50] Nor was this love limited by gender. The Iraqi litterateur Jahiz, who wrote extensively on the subject of love, had laid down the rule that *ishq,* or passionate love, could exist only between a man and a woman. But Ibn Daud, who was born the year Jahiz died (868), recognized the possibility of love between males in his *Book of the Flower (Kitab az-Zahra),* and this view prevailed in later Arab culture.[51] Ibn Daud was a learned jurisprudent as well as a literary man; but according to an account repeatedly cited, his passion for Muhammad ibn Jami (to whom his book was dedicated) made him a "martyr of love." Another friend told their story:

> I went to see [Ibn Daud] during the illness in which he died and I said to him, "How do you feel?" He said to me, "Love of you-know-who has brought upon me what you see!" So I said to him, "What prevents you from enjoying him, as long as you have the power to do so?" He said, "Enjoyment has two aspects: One of them is the permitted gaze and the other is the forbidden pleasure. As for the permitted gaze, it has brought upon me the condition that you see, and as for the forbidden pleasure, something my father told me has kept me from it." He said . . . "the Prophet said 'He who loves passionately and conceals his secret and remains chaste and patient, God will forgive him and make him enter Paradise'" . . . and he died that very night or perhaps it was the next day.[52]

Both these traditions, the punitive and the romantic, figure in the literature of Arab Spain, and especially in the writings of its foremost theorist of love, Ibn Hazm. Ibn Hazm was born in Córdoba in 994 during the last days of the Umayyad dynasty. His father had held political office but was forced to flee when the Umayyads were overthrown in 1013. Later in life Ibn Hazm became famous—and controversial—as a theologian and the author of a notable essay on comparative religion. But about 1022 or 1027 he wrote a treatise on love called, in the poetic style favored by Arab writers, *The Dove's Neck-Ring about Love and Lovers.* He died in 1064, seven years before the birth of William IX of Aquitaine, the first of the troubadours.

Ibn Hazm begins his book with a conventional Muslim prayer and makes haste to justify his undertaking on religious grounds: "Love is neither disapproved by Religion, nor prohibited by the Law; for every heart is in God's hands," that is, love is an inborn disposition "which men cannot control."[53] Later, he elaborates on this defense: "It is sufficient for a good Muslim to abstain from those things which Allah has forbidden, and which, if he choose to do, he will find charged to his account on the Day of Resurrection. But to admire beauty, and to be mastered by love—that is a natural thing, and comes not within the range of Divine commandment and prohibition."[54] Ibn Hazm assures us that "of the saints and learned doctors of the faith who lived in past ages and times long ago, some there are whose love lyrics are sufficient testimony to their passion, so that they require no further notice."[55] By way of proof he mentions several famous imams and jurists of Medina.

Ibn Hazm, unlike the Greeks, does not exalt love because it leads to courage, virtue, and wisdom. It may, but it may also produce simple derangement.[56] Here is Epicurus' diagnosis without his condemnation. Indeed, this Arab psychologist calls love a "delightful malady, a most desirable sickness. Whoever is free of it likes not to be immune, and whoever is struck down by it yearns not to recover."[57] Ibn Hazm emphasizes, and seems almost to relish, a masochist element: a suffering friend rebuked him when he expressed a hope he might be freed from his misery, and a man of rank he knew rejoiced when a page-boy took notice of his infatuation by slapping him.[58]

What does Ibn Hazm's treatise tell us about Hispano-Arabic attitudes toward homosexuality? *The Dove's Neck-Ring* is a mixture of theoretical generalizations and anecdotes, most of them based on the writer's personal observations. Perhaps nine tenths of the anecdotes concern the love of men for women, especially for lovely slave girls. Yet Ibn Hazm repeatedly intermingles stories of men falling in love with other males and assumes that homosexual love is, psychologically, no different from heterosexual love. Aristotle, Plutarch, and the author of the *Amores* had sharply distinguished the two kinds of love. But Ibn Hazm moves from a story of a man's infatuation for a slave girl to a story of male love with no suggestion that one experience differs from the other.

Consider, by way of contrast, a Christian writer like Andreas Capellanus, who wrote his famous essay on courtly love a century and a half later at the court of William IX's granddaughter, Marie de Champagne. In his second chapter Andreas states categorically the assumptions of medieval Christian Europe: "The main point to be noted about love is that it can exist only between persons of different sex. Between two males or two females it can claim no place, for two persons of the same sex are in no way fitted to reciprocate each other's love or to practice its natural acts. Love blushes to embrace what nature denies."[59] Later writers on love north of the Pyrenees would overwhelmingly have agreed. What we may call Ibn Hazm's romantic bisexuality would have been incomprehensible to them.

We may glean some insight as to how Ibn Hazm and his fellow religionists viewed love between men indirectly from his anecdotes and poems. Arab delicacy and discretion is amply illustrated by Ibn Hazm's tales of men who kept silent about their love. It was not regarded as proper in Arab society for two men to avow their love publicly—in contrast, say, with ancient Greece or Tokugawa Japan—though it was perceived as highly romantic to harbor such feelings without naming the beloved. Here is a Platonism that out-Platos Plato. In a chapter on "martyrs of love" Ibn Hazm mentions six lovers who died, or nearly died—two women who loved men, two men who loved women, and two men who loved men. The tales are intermixed and not grouped by gender. One story tells of a friend, Ibn al-Tubni, whom he praises highly for his learning, personal qualities, and his beauty: "It might have been said that beauty itself was created in his likeness, or fashioned out of the sighs of those who looked upon him."[60] They were separated when Berber troops overran Córdoba. In exile in Valencia, Ibn Hazm was saddened by the news that Ibn al-Tubni was dead. When an acquaintance had asked Ibn al-Tubni what made him so emaciated, he had replied:

> "Yes, I will tell you. I was standing at the door of my house in Ghadir Ibn al-Shammas at the time that Ali ibn Hammud entered Córdoba, and his armies were pouring into the city from all directions. I saw among them a youth of such striking appearance, that I could never have believed until that moment that beauty could be so embodied in a living form. He mastered my reason, and my mind was wholly enraptured with him. I enquired after him and was told that he was So-and-so, the son of So-and-so, and that he inhabited such and such a district—a province far distant from Córdoba, and virtually inaccessible. I despaired of ever seeing him again; and by my life . . . I shall never give up loving him, until I am laid in the tomb." And so indeed it was.[61]

Both Ibn Hazm's anecdotes and his poems, from which he quotes unabashedly in *The Dove's Neck-Ring,* reveal something of his own erotic sensibility. His grand passion seems be have been one he experienced at age sixteen for a slave girl. But several poems tell of his feelings for other men. Though Ibn Hazm's poetry rarely rises above mediocrity, his very banalities are instructive:

> If he should speak, among those who sit in my company, I listen only
> to the words of that marvelous charmer.
> Even if the Prince of the Faithful should be with me, I would not
> turn aside from [my love] for the former.
> If I am compelled to leave him, I look back constantly, and walk [like
> an animal] wounded in the hoof.
> My eyes remain fixed firmly upon him though my body has departed,
> as the drowning man looks at the shore from the fathomless sea.[62]

Vouching for his own purity, Ibn Hazm assures us, with naive candor, "I am completely guiltless, entirely sound, without reproach . . . and I do swear to God by the most solemn oath that I have *never* taken off my underwear to have illicit sexual intercourse."[63] Yet he admits to being tempted by the beauty of men: to avoid sin, he had shunned a party where he would meet a handsome man he was attracted to.[64]

In his final chapters Ibn Hazm analyzes the moral, religious, and legal sides of love, which in Muslim culture were of course one. Several of the transgressions he describes in "The Vileness of Sinning" are homosexual. A distinguished religious scholar, he tells us, lost his reputation because of his open liaison with a boy. Another scholar, the former head of the an important Muslim sect, fell so madly in love with a Christian boy that he committed the ultimate enormity—he composed a treatise in favor of the Trinity.[65] But not all Arabs were as censorious as Ibn Hazm. At the house of a wealthy businessman, two guests withdrew repeatedly to a private chamber. When Ibn Hazm showed his disapproval—characteristically by reciting a poem—the host ignored him.

This chapter also contains Ibn Hazm's sole reference to lesbianism. "I once saw a woman," he tells us, "who had bestowed her affections in ways not pleasing to Almighty God." But her love changed to an "enmity the like of which is not engendered by hatred, or revenge, or the murder of a father, or the carrying of a mother into captivity. Such is Allah's wont with all those who practice abomination."[66] But Islamic references to lesbianism were apparently not always this condemnatory. At least a dozen love romances in which the lovers were women are mentioned in *The Book of Hind,* who was herself a lesbian. The ninth century produced a lost *Treatise on Lesbianism (Kitab al-Sahhakat),* and later Arab erotic works contained chapters on the subject.[67] Here lies a challenge for research.

In Islam, questions of morality were inevitably also questions of law. So Ibn Hazm's chapter on sexual sins also sets forth the various penalties prescribed by religious tradition. He recounts a story of Abu Bakr's burning a man alive for playing the passive role.[68] The first caliph, we are told, struck and killed a man "who had [merely] pressed himself against a youth until he had the orgasm."[69] The jurist Malik, he notes, praised an emir who beat a young man to death for allowing another man to embrace him similarly. But for Ihn Hazm this was excessive; he thinks ten lashes might have sufficed, though he admits this is heterodoxy.[70] As for the completed act of sodomy, he cites only Malik's opinion that both parties should be stoned, but he fails to say whether he agrees or not.

In this atmosphere of harsh religious laws and overcharged romanticism, men loved, expressed their feelings openly in fervent verse, and loudly protested their chastity. Perhaps some of the poetic fervor was merely literary. Perhaps some of the protestations were sincere. Occasionally, these affairs involved famous rulers. Caliph Abd ar-Rahman III, who ruled Córdoba at its political and cultural zenith (929–961), was attracted to a young Christian hostage, was rejected, and had him barbarously executed. The boy, canonized as Saint Pelagius, became the martyr-hero of a narrative poem by the German nun Hrosvitha (a contemporary), who condemned Arab lust and glorified Christian chastity.[71]

Architecture, belles lettres, and scholarship flourished in Córdoba under Abd ar-Rahman's son al-Hakam II, who was their eager and discriminating patron. In his youth his loves seem to have been entirely homosexual. This exclusivity was a problem, since it was incumbent upon the new caliph to produce an heir. The impasse, we are told, was resolved by his taking a concubine who dressed in boy's clothes and was given the masculine name of Jafar.[72]

The love of al-Mutamid, emir of Seville and the outstanding Andalusian poet of his day, for another poet, Ibn Ammar, ended violently after a long friendship. Al-Mutamid was a passionate lover of women but also loved males. Of a cupbearer he wrote, "They named him Sword; two other swords: his eyes! / . . . now we *both* are masters, *both* slaves!"[73] His love for Ibn Ammar is the most famous, and most tragic, romance in the history of al-Andalus. In 1053 al-Mutamid, aged thirteen, was appointed titular governor at Silves by his father, who made Ibn Ammar, nine years his senior, his vizier. A story tells how after an evening of wine and poetry his fondness led him to declare to Ibn Ammar, "Tonight you will sleep with me on the same pillow!"[74] In a poem he sent to al-Mutamid's father, Ibn Ammar declared:

During the night of union there was wafted
To me, in his caresses, the perfume of its dawns,
My tears streamed out over the beautiful garden
Of his cheeks to moisten its myrtles and lilies.[75]

Apparently the prince's father came to disapprove of the relation with the commoner, for he exiled the poet in order to separate them.[76] On his succession, al-Mutamid granted Ibn Ammar great political and military power. A famous tale, which we are not required to believe, tells how, when they were sleeping together in one bed, the poet dreamed that his lover would kill him and fled the scene; he was wooed back by the king, who assured him that this could never happen.[77] But later the two men quarreled bitterly. Finally, when Ibn Ammar fell into his hands, the ordinarily humane and generous al-Mutamid first pardoned him and then, when Ibn Ammar boasted too triumphantly of his reprieve, fell into a rage and hacked him to death with his own hands. "Afterwards he wept, as long ago Alexander had wept for Hephestion, and gave him a sumptuous funeral."[78]

Almost any collection of Hispano-Arabic poetry yields a plethora of love poems by men to or about other males. Erotic poetry first flourished in Andalusia at Córdoba under Abd ar-Rahman II (822–852). His grandson, Abdallah (888–912), penned amorous verses to a "dark-eyed fawn."[79] Ibn Abd Rabbihi, a freedman poet at Aballah's court, wrote of another young man in a typical mood of subjection. "I gave him what he asked for, made him my master . . . / Love has put fetters on my heart / As a herdsman puts fetters on a camel."[80] Al-Ramadi, the foremost poet in Córdoba in the tenth century, fell in love with a black slave. Again we see the conscious reversal of roles: "I looked into his eyes, and became drunken . . . / I am his slave, he is the lord."[81] Latin poets in Augustan Rome had likewise addressed love poems to slave boys but never in this style; the self-abasement of these Andalusians more closely prefigures the romantic chivalry of medieval France.

After the fall of the Umayyads at Córdoba, Arab Spain—fatally weakened—disintegrated into a score of petty states. But despite this political disarray, the eleventh century was a golden age of Arabic poetry in the Iberian peninsula. Love songs continued to pour forth under the Almoravid rulers (1090–1145) and the Almohads (1145–1223), homoerotic verse with the rest. The most acclaimed lyricist of this brilliant era, Ibn Quzman (c. 1080–1160), has been called one of the greatest of medieval poets. An irreverent bohemian in the mold of François Villon, he composed racy, colloquial *zajals,* far removed in style from the canons of classical Arabic verse. Tall, blond, and blue-eyed, Ibn Quzman led a licentious life resembling that of Harun al-Rashid's boon companion in Baghdad, the poet Abu Nuwas, who was also unabashedly open about his homosexuality. In short, terse lines and elliptical stanzas that are almost untranslatable, he celebrates "wine, adultery and sodomy."[82] Like the troubadours of Provence, he complains of the hauteur and disdain of his lovers, who are often male, but laughs at the scruples of ideal love: "What do you say about a beloved, when he and you, without anyone else, are alone, and the house door is locked?"[83] Poverty-stricken, he ended his days as an imam teaching in a mosque.

The philosopher Ibn Bajja, better known to Latin Europe as Avempace, was in every regard a more respectable figure. It was he who introduced Aristotelianism to Spain and paved the way for Averroes. Ibn Bajja, we are told by an anthologist, wrote memorial verses on the death of "a black slave with whom he was infatuated and who . . . died at Barcelona, much to his grief."[84] Several Andalusian anthologies appeared in the twelfth and thirteenth centuries, the most important being Ibn Said's *Pennants of the Champions* (1243). A selection of these poems has been translated by the poet-scholar A. J. Arberry. The cautious Briton seems to have eschewed verses whose sexual details were explicit, but his selection still reveals a broad range of male-love poems intermixed with other lyrics.[85] Ibn Said, who was born at Alcalá la Real near Granada, arranged his anthology according to the poets' birthplaces and occupations. Verse in praise of boys appears from Seville, Lisbon, Córdoba, Toledo, Granada, Alcalá, Murcia, Valencia, and Saragossa, authored by kings, ministers of state, scholars, men of letters, and civil servants, as well as professional poets. The translation of this sophisticated poetry presents a formidable challenge. Marked by elaborate word play, compact allusions with subtle connotations accumulated over centuries, complex rhymes, and much alliteration, these poems—to the Western mind—border on the fantastic, even the surreal. One saki's delicate cheek is as intoxicating as the wine he serves, another's fingers are stained with golden wine as the ox's lips are by the pollen of the narcissus it browses. A mole on Ahmad's cheek is like an Abyssinian gardener in a bed of roses. One boy is praised because no trace of moss eclipses the sun of his countenance.[86] Another is thanked for his beard, since it is a sheath that protects the poet from the "saber of his smile."[87] A poet in thirteenth-century Córdoba turns the accouterments of a boy's trade into knightly symbols:

His work stool (as if it were a horse)
  carries him proudly (as if he were a hero).
But this hero of mine is armed only with a needle,
  long like his eyelashes and like them shining.
Watching it stitch up the seams of a cloak
  I think of a falling star trailed by a silken thread of light.
He twists the thread and the thread twists about my heart.
  O that my heart could follow him, close like the thread behind the needle![88]

One surprising consequence of this profusion of Andalusian love poetry was its imitation by Jewish poets writing in classical Hebrew. Hebrew as a spoken language had died out many centuries earlier, but in Muslim Spain the literary language was revived and a renaissance of Jewish poetry followed. Though medieval Jewish religious poetry has been widely studied, far less attention has been paid until recently to secular verse, which shows a strong Arab influence in its imagery and themes.[89] It now appears that these poets enthusiastically emulated Arabic poems to boys and youths, despite Judaism's religious taboos. This unexpected revelation has agitated some conservative Jewish scholars, but the evidence of a substantial body of Hispano-Hebrew male-love poetry now seems incontrovertible.

The most distinguished Hebrew poets of the Arab period were Solomon Ibn Gabriol (c. 1021–1057), Moses Ibn Ezra (1055–1140), and Judah Halevi (1075–1141), all of whom earn admiring articles in the *Encyclopaedia Judaica.* Moses Ibn Ezra is often considered the greatest of the Spanish Hebrew religious poets. All three imitate the subjects, meters, and images of their Arab contemporaries and, steeped in the Hebrew Bible, use erotic conceits from the Song of Songs in poems they write to boys.[90] Arab poets occasionally wrote love poems to Jewish youths; the Hebrew poets reciprocate by professing their love for handsome young Muslims, though they speak only of kisses and embraces and stop short of Arab directness in sexual matters. Like their Arab counterparts, they picture boys as fawns or lovely gazelles who crush hearts with their shining faces and dark hair, yield sleepless nights, and betray their admirers treacherously. One example must serve for a score:

Gazelle desired in Spain, wondrously formed,
Given rule and dominion over every living thing;
Lovely of form like the moon, with beautiful stature:

Curls of purple upon shining temple,
Like Joseph his form, like Adionah [Absolom] his hair.
Lovely of eyes like David, he has slain me like Uriah.
He has enflamed my passions and consumed my heart with fire.[91]

We must not imagine that Jewish theologians condoned such affairs. The greatest of all medieval Jewish scholars, Moses ben Maimon, known to us as Maimonides, was born at Córdoba in 1135 but fled with his family to North Africa at the age of twenty-four to escape Berber fanatics. Maimonides startled the orthodox by explaining scriptural miracles naturalistically and arguing that faith should not contradict reason. But as a moralist he was severely orthodox, interpreting the Pentateuch as teaching that "we ought to limit intercourse altogether, hold it in contempt, and only desire it very rarely. The prohibition of pederasty [Lev. 18:22] and carnal intercourse with beasts [ibid. 23] is very clear. If in the natural way the act is too base to be performed except when needed, how much more is it if performed in an unnatural manner, and only for the sake of pleasure."[92] The fifth book of Maimonides' huge commentary on Jewish law, famous as the *Mishneh Torah* or *Code of Maimonides,* teaches that Jewish law requires that both the active and passive partners in homosexual relations be stoned to death.[93]

From the thirteenth century on, Arab power ebbed in Spain, until it surrendered its last outpost at Granada in 1492. To the end, its poets hymned the love of boys, as in the case of Yusuf III, who reigned in the Alhambra from 1408 to 1417 and composed these lines:

O you who have aimed at my heart with the dart of a piercing glance:
Meet one who's dying, whose eye is shedding fast-flowing tears!
Who will claim justice from an alluring fawn
Slender of body as is the fresh, green bough,
Who has insisted on distance and shunning? . . .
He has seduced me with the spell of his eyelids.
Had it been allowed—yet he shuns me ever—
I'd have won my desires by undoing his sash.[94]

How are we to explain this legal-lyrical schizophrenia, where a potent religion and a flourishing secular culture seem so at odds? Arabs claimed to be the descendants of Abraham's son Ishmael and so regarded the Hebrew Bible as a sacred book, though superseded by the Koran. This racial-religious affiliation assured that Islam would share many of the prejudices of Judaism and Christianity. Homosexuality seems to have been comparatively little in evidence among the Bedouins of Arabia in pre-Islamic times. It has been suggested that Arab attitudes toward sex underwent a change as they conquered more advanced and sophisticated empires, especially Sassanian Persia. Cul-

28. Shah Abbas I with a page. Muhammad Qasim Mussarvir, tempera and gilt, 1627.

turally, the conquest of Persia did for the Arabs what the conquest of Greece did for Rome—it introduced a rather primitive society to a markedly more advanced and luxurious one. Unfortunately, though we know boy love flourished spectacularly in Islamic Persia, inspiring a very substantial literature, we know little about Persian mores before the Arab conquest, and what we know is contradictory. The Zend Avesta (c. 550), the sacred book of the Zoroastrians, forbade it and even decreed the death penalty, but a hundred years later Herodotus reported that the Persians had adopted Greek views in this matter.[95]

One thing the conquest did indubitably achieve, however: it provided an ample supply of young male slaves. A crucially important difference between Islam and Christianity was their relation to slavery. Christianity forbade sexual relations with slaves. Unlike Christianity, which for its first three hundred years lacked political power, Islam from the start had enormous military success, conquering nation after nation. In this triumphal atmosphere, few moralists were prepared to challenge the victors' prerogatives, which included sexual rights to women, married or unmarried, who belonged to men defeated in battle. To these all-powerful rulers, riding the crest of a wave of good fortune, it must have seemed eminently reasonable that attractive young male captives who were not Muslims should also be regarded as legitimate bedmates. Some authorities seem to have sanctioned such intercourse.[96]

The parallel with Rome is clear. But this is not the whole story, for though numerous love affairs with male slaves are recorded and poetry on this theme abounds, we note that in the circles of Ibn Daud and Ibn Hazm and in royal courts men repeatedly fall in love with friends, acquaintances, and sometimes strangers of equal rank. Here we have a pattern akin to the ancient Greeks. The emphasis in such affairs, however, is not on mentorship, as in Sparta and Athens, but on the emotional experience itself, which was allowable under the guise of a quasi-religious Platonism.

Above all, it was the love-martyr *hadith* that conferred an exalted status on love in Islam, providing religious sanction for an extravagant romanticism that later crossed the Pyrenees and found its way into medieval Provence. The startling thing, from a Christian point of view, was that this glorification of love was gender-blind. Linked with a theoretically perfect chastity, it could escape moral condemnation. In the literature of Sufi mysticism, rapturous poetry addressed to male lovers might even symbolize union with the divine. So Muslim religion paradoxically forbade, allowed, and exalted homoerotic desire. It provided striking similarities with Judaism and Christianity in the sphere of law but fostered a radically different literary, social, and affective atmosphere that was much more tolerant. Sexual contact was forbidden, but the man who admitted to love for another male might still be respected and admired. He was not, in Islamic culture, a moral monster, a traitor to his maker, or a pariah who might expose a nation to destruction at the hands of a wrathful deity.

• The Growth of Canon Law •

In the chaotic tenth century the authority of the church in Christian Europe had sunk to its nadir and few councils were held. Nevertheless, the age pro-

29. Two lovers. Riza 'Abbasi, gouache and gold leaf, 1630.

duced a new kind of document, more scholarly and authoritative than the penitentials, that allows us to trace the evolving ecclesiastical consensus on sexuality. These were ambitious compendiums of church teachings bringing together in an organized fashion patristic opinion, conciliar edicts, penitential rules, and papal decrees. The first significant effort was made in 906 by Regino, a German Benedictine from Prüm, a town near Trier, whose archbishop asked him to draw up a collection as a guide for church synods and bishops making diocesan visits. Regino's *Of Synodical Cases and Ecclesiastical Discipline* cites the harsh canons of the Council of Ancyra on homosexuality and then, as a hint that church authority should not be flouted, invokes the Theodosian law of 390 that provided for burning.[97] The *Decretum* of Bishop Burchard of Worms (1012) drew on Regino but was much more systematic and more influential; its most notable feature is the minute detail with which it treats every kind of same-sex relation: interfemoral, masturbatory, oral, and anal, as well as sex between women and between boys. Burchard, too, endorses the lifetime penances prescribed at Ancyra and quotes Augustine and Ambrose on the especial wickedness of the sin of Sodom.[98] Bishop Ivo (or Yves) of Chartres (d. 1116) appealed to these same now-standardized authorities in his own *Decretum,* which followed Burchard closely.[99] We shall hear from him again.

This medieval effort to provide an authoritative guide to church law culminated in the *Decretum* of Gratian (1140), a vast compilation culled from "Roman law, canons of the church council, papal and royal ordinances; Biblical, liturgical, patristic, and penitential texts; and contemporary theological discussion," which its author entitled (with boastful optimism) *Concordia discordantium canonum*—The Concordance of Discordant Canons.[100] Gratian was a Camaldolese monk from Bologna, by now the chief center for the revival of Roman law. Acclaimed as the "Father of the Science of Canon Law," he later found a place in Dante's *Paradise* among the doctors of the Church. His work became the standard text and was eventually incorporated into the *Corpus Juris Canonici,* the church's official collection of canon law, authoritative from the fifteenth century until 1917.

In one important respect Gratian moved beyond his predecessors. He now lists sexual sins in order of increasing heinousness: these are fornication, adultery, incest, and, worst of all, "sins against nature."[101] This moral ordering was to become a basic tenet of scholastic theology. Aquinas, as we shall see, gave it his definitive sanction in his *Summa,* adding some refinements of his own. Where earlier penitentials had wavered in their assessment of homosexuality, Gratian put it unequivocally among the most serious sins, and the sodomite among the most thoroughly damned of sinners.

When reading these dry condemnations of hot-blooded acts, it is easy to forget that their effects were visited on persons in very concrete ways in the form of punishment, contempt, and scorn. Michel Foucault and his followers have argued that the "homosexual" is a modern invention, a mental construct of the last hundred years. This is, of course, true, of homosexuality as a "scientific" or psychiatric category. But it is a mistake to presume that earlier ages thought merely of sexual acts and not of persons. Medieval literature speaks not only of sodomy but also of "sodomites," individuals who were a substantial, clear, and ominous presence. The fact that such beings were perceived from a theological rather than a psychological point of view did not make them any less real, or less threatening.

The classical Greek ideal of the *pederastes* as the heroic lover, protector, and mentor was long forgotten in the West. Now the lover of males appeared in a demonic metamorphosis. As time passed, blame for whatever new disaster vexed society might be placed on his head. When a plague broke out in sixteenth-century Valencia, a fanatical monk incited a mob to kill sodomites.[102] Sometimes the hypotheses achieved a fascinating absurdity: a hundred years later a leading German jurist found sodomites responsible for plagues of "fat, voracious field mice."[103] In the eighteenth century a Dutch crew left a shipmate to die of thirst on a barren island in the south Atlantic, convinced that the sodomite's presence put their lives in jeopardy.[104] If Christianity was concerned primarily with sinful acts, we must remember that it was sentient human beings who suffered, and acknowledge their flesh and blood reality. The killing, maiming, or torture of homosexuals ranks among humanity's innumerable "hate crimes," crimes encouraged in this instance by the Christian clergy. We must deduct such actions, as we deduct the persecution of heretics, witches, and Jews, from the enormous debt our civilization owes to the religion preached in Jesus' name.

• The *Book of Gomorrah* •

Medieval canon law provided a logical structure for moral theology and implied a strong disapproval. But to understand how the eleventh century *felt* about homosexuality, we must turn to polemicists and poets. Preeminence in the first category belongs to a monk born shortly after the millennium, Saint Peter Damian (c. 1007–1072). Damian's *Book of Gomorrah* was not only the most elaborate attack on homosexuality from the pen of a churchman in this age but was to remain the single "book" the Middle Ages produced on the subject. (In translation it runs to about fifty pages.) An ascetic who lived a hermit's life at Fonte Avella in the Apennines, Damian's antisocial lifestyle did not keep him from becoming the foremost Italian man of letters of his time and, ultimately, a cardinal of the church. In his fervent hatred of every form of sex, as in his general asperity of temperament, he reminded his contemporaries of Saint Jerome. His career as a moral crusader links him to the so-called Gregorian reforms which aimed to suppress clerical marriage and concubinage and end the purchase of ecclesiastical offices.

The *Book of Gomorrah* is, however, addressed to an earlier pontiff, Leo IX (1048–1054), who set in motion many of the reforms his successor achieved. Since these efforts where directed specifically at the clergy, the emphasis in Damian's tract is upon homosexuality among priests. Its tone may be savored in its preface:

> A certain abominable and terribly shameful vice has grown up in our region. Unless the hand of severe punishment resists as soon as possible, there is certainly the danger that the sword of divine anger will be used savagely against it to the ruin of many. Alas! it is shameful to speak of, shameful to suggest such foul disgrace to sacred ears! But if the doctor shrinks in horror from infected wounds, who will take the trouble to apply the cauter? If the one who is to heal becomes nauseated, who will lead sick hearts back to health? Vice against nature creeps in like a cancer and even touches the order of consecrated men. Sometimes it rages like a bloodthirsty beast in the midst of the sheepfold of Christ.[105]

This is the spirit of John Chrysostom reborn in the medieval Latin world.

Damian is particularly concerned with a question of canon law: when should clergy be deposed from their offices for unnatural sexual acts? After distinguishing four kinds of reprehensible behavior—solitary masturbation, masturbation performed with other men, interfemoral fornication, and "the complete act against nature"—he argues that, while present practice mandates deposition in the last case only, committing any one of these acts should be sufficient to remove a priest from office. All are "worse than all other crimes": Sodom and Gomorrah were obliterated for them, Onan was struck dead by God for spilling his seed, and guilty men are condemned to death in Leviticus. "Sodomists" share with "demoniacs" (the insane) a common trait—they are under diabolical influence.[106]

Damian was especially concerned with priests who seduced young males in their charge and with sodomitical priests who might assign each other light penances. He cites with approbation the ceremony of degradation for sodomitical monks ascribed to Saint Basil (c. 370): "A cleric or monk who seduces youths or young boys or is found kissing or in any other impure situations is to be publicly flogged and lose his tonsure. When his hair has been shaved his face is to be foully besmeared with spit and he is to be bound in iron chains."[107] Then he speaks again in his own voice:

> Truly this vice is never to be compared with any other vice because it surpasses the enormity of all vices. Indeed this vice is the death of bodies, the destruction of souls. It pollutes the flesh; it extinguished the light of the mind. It evicts the Holy Spirit from the temple of the human heart; it introduces the devil who incites to lust. It casts into error; it completely removes the truth from the mind that has been deceived. It prepares snares

> for those entering; it shuts up those who fall into the pit so they cannot get out. It opens hell; it closes the door of heaven . . . This vice tries to overturn the walls of the heavenly homeland and is busy repairing the renewed bulwarks of Sodom. For it is this which violates sobriety, kills modesty, strangles chastity, and butchers irreparable virginity with the dagger of unclean contagion.[108]

This may strike the modern reader as extreme, but Damian affects to believe that public sentiment is on his side. "Sodomists," he adds, using the noun *Sodomitas* to stigmatize not just the deed but the persons, are "despised among men" and must "bear the disgrace of human derision."[109]

The second half of the *Book of Gomorrah* is addressed not to the pope but directly to sodomite priests. Damian tries every rhetorical device at his disposal to overwhelm such men with guilt and fear and to deprive them of any sense of self-respect. He accuses them of "wallow[ing] voluptuously in the pigsty of foul obscenity."[110] Having defiled their holy office, they must await "the judgment of divine severity." It is clear that Damian himself suffers from an extreme degree of erotophobia linked with the fear of hell fire. In chapter 21 he recounts, with naive simplicity, the story of a hermit who was persuaded by the devil that "whenever he was aroused by lust, he should release semen by rubbing his genitals, just as he blows mucus from his nose."[111] When the gullible monk died, Damian assures us, he was instantly carried off by demons. How can a man, he asks, risk thousands of years of "atrocious, flaming fires" for "the fleeting pleasure caused by a momentary emission of semen."[112]

Pope Leo's reply to Damian's book has survived in the shape of a letter that has sometimes been regarded as a rebuke to the saint's harshness but might more properly be called a moderately conservative response. Leo agrees that men who commit anal intercourse or other acts over a long period should be deposed. But he draws back from Damian's extreme position that those who perform a single act of solitary masturbation or interfemoral intercourse should lose their office. The language of his letter, while not so violently vituperation as Damian's essay, is still abusive in the medieval mode. Pope Leo calls love between men "obscene," "filthy," and "an execrable vice."[113] Later references to Damian's book are, however, rare. We may assume that theologians were unwilling to call attention to a work that exposed clerical scandals so pungently.

CHAPTER SEVEN

THE MEDIEVAL WORLD

1050–1321

• The Fortunes of Ganymede •

For three centuries Europe lagged behind the Islamic world in wealth and learning. Then, after the year 1000, Christian civilization revived. Trade and agriculture recovered, cities grew in number, and a new sense of power was signaled by the climactic event of the eleventh century: the capture of Jerusalem by the First Crusade in 1099. Simultaneously, a cultural renaissance took place. The heritage of Greece had been largely lost in the West, but the study of classical Latin was eagerly pursued, most notably in the cathedral schools of northern France—at Chartres, Sens, Angers, and Paris. There, in a wholly Christian environment, an unlikely development took place. In the neo-Latin poetry of these schools a bisexual eros found expression; poets celebrated youthful male beauty as in contemporary Spain, though their inspiration derived not from Córdoba but from Augustan Rome. But this afterglow of antiquity flared only briefly and seems to have been limited to the Anglo-Norman culture that flourished in the era of England's Norman kings (1066–1154).

The neo-Latin poets of the eleventh and twelfth centuries surprise us by writing poems in which classical Roman eroticism and medieval Christianity clash. This conflict, most notable in the poetry of Marbod of Rennes, Baudri of Bourgueil, and Hildebert of Lavardin, is always resolved in favor of Christian morality. This is not surprising, since these poets were themselves churchmen. What is surprising is the way they express homoerotic desires frankly in dramatic situations, yielding poems that are unique amalgams of antithetical traditions.

Marbod, Baudri, and Hildebert were the most famous Latin poets of their age; in due course all three became bishops. Marbod's long life (c. 1035–1123) encompassed the zenith of Arabic literary production in Andalusia and the rise of troubadour poetry in southern France. Born at Angers on the Loire, he became master of its cathedral school and, then, at the safe age of sixty-four, bishop of Rennes in Brittany. Of the three poets, Marbod writes the most arresting poems of homoerotic desire. One begins with an explicit classical reference: "Horace composed an ode about a certain boy / Who could easily enough have been a pretty girl."[1] The speaker addresses a boy of like beauty who has attracted him and sounds the *carpe diem* theme in a markedly sensual way:

A handsome face demands a good mind, and a yielding one . . .
This flesh is now so smooth, so milky, so unblemished,
So good, so handsome, so slippery, so tender.
Yet the time will come when it will become ugly and rough,
When this flesh, dear boyish flesh, will become worthless.
Therefore, while you flower . . . be not slow to yield to an eager lover.

However, Marbod was careful to distance himself from the poem's unorthodoxy and took pains to present it as a dramatic monologue by adding the title, "Satire on a Young Boy's Lover in an Assumed Voice." This seems disingenuous: without the title, no one would identify the poem as satirical.

In another poem Marbod describes—this time in his own voice—the beguiling charms of a passionate woman who is pursuing him. What, he asks, keeps him from responding to this Venus with his wonted ardor? The answer is direct and shocking: he is "on fire" for the beauty of a boy she scorns. At this point we might be in the world of Catullus or Tibullus, faced with an ironically frustrating triangle. But Marbod shows himself a man of the medieval world when he draws the moral. He rejoices in the paradox that "the vice which usually makes hard men soft" keeps him chaste, that is, his lust for the boy makes him reject a very desirable woman. This discord in "the kingdom of Satan" he welcomes as his salvation: one sin has expelled another. Such a twist allows Marbod to give the poem an exemplary title. He calls it "An Argument against Sexual Love," thus neatly bringing his erotic drama within the bounds of Christian morality.[2]

Another poem, "Against Copulation between People of One Sex," might pass for an episcopal sermon:

There are a hundred thousand sins invented by the devil,
And with them he drags this world to punishment's abyss
Where those who are imprisoned die by being unable to die—
Indeed, they would rather die because no death could equal their pain.
There that wretch rages, roasted by eternal flames.[3]

Along with such general condemnations Marbod also writes a poem expressing personal remorse. His "Repentance for Lecherous Love" repents affairs with *both* sexes and disavows past sinful loves, now presented as real instead of fictional. But ambiguities remain. In the opening lines of the "Repentance," Marbod appears to reject love after the fashion of the church fathers: "Caught in birdlime, now I am ashamed—I have come to my senses . . . / O good Savior! how a lover is deceived!"[4] But having appealed to

Christ, he now drops the moralist's stance and addresses Venus (Cytherea) like any classical poet, protesting that love is simply too painful because of the vagaries of lovers—of either gender. We are left wondering whether Marbod's sensibility is more Augustinian or Augustan:

> Why do those dearer to me than my eyes, either he or she *[ille vel illa]*,
> Scarcely want to talk as long as they feel they are loved?
> If a lover's heart weren't so tortured in so many ways,
> This disdain would be enough to make me live chastely.
> Therefore, stay away, winged boy, author of love;
> There is no room for you, Cytherea, in my house,
> The embraces of both sexes now displease me.

Baudri of Bourgueil was a pupil of Marbod's at Angers whose career paralleled his master's. In 1089, at the age of forty-three, he headed the Benedictine abbey at Bourgueil; eighteen years later he was made archbishop of Dol near Mont St. Michel in Brittany. Many of Baudri's poems celebrate romantic friendships with other men, especially other monks. Deprived of marriage and intimacy with women, men in monasteries often sought emotional closeness with other monks. As early as the age of Charlemagne, loving attachments between monks are celebrated in poems by Alcuin and Walafrid Strabo; in the eleventh century they feature in the letters of moralists like Saint Anselm. Subsequently, the church came to frown on such "particular" friendships in a monastic setting. But for a time, even at the height of the monastic reform movement of the eleventh and twelfth centuries, they were cultivated by a few monastic leaders. One Englishman, Saint Aelred of Rievaulx, went so far as to claim, in his *Spiritual Friendship* (c. 1150), that the Song of Songs, the love of David for Jonathan, and the love of Jesus for John sanctioned friendships between clerics.[5] As the head of the monastery at Rievaulx in Yorkshire, he let monks hold hands as a way of expressing affection. Other abbots, a contemporary reported, frowned on such demonstrations: "If a monk takes a brother's hand in his own [they] demand his cowl, strip and expel him."[6]

Baudri wrote many poems of affectionate friendship. But, like Marbod, he also addressed erotic verse to both girls and boys and, like his mentor, had to square these literary sentiments with his churchly profession. In lines to his friend, the scholar Godfrey of Reims, he tells us that his youthful poems had brought criticism:

> They reproached me too: why did I, speaking in the way of young men,
> Write to maidens and no less to boys?
> For I wrote certain things which treat of love,
> And both sexes are pleased with my songs.[7]

But Baudri was an abbot as well as a poet, and it is the monk's cowl he assumes when he writes to his friend Gerard of Laden to induce him to enter the monastery at Bourgueil. He decries the love of women in a dozen lines but devotes three times as many to the love of boys, as if this were the greater temptation: "Perhaps you attach yourself to unnatural love," he suggests. "Nowadays Ganymede scampers through many chambers, / And many lecherous men now want to be Jupiter."[8] But, he warns, such sin will be punished by the pains of hell, with its foul stench and everlasting flames. Baudri, like Ovid and Martial, excused his erotic poems by claiming they did not reflect his life. At the same time, like Paul and Augustine, he painted himself as black as possible. Thus, in his "Penitential Confession" he lays claim to a remarkable spectrum of sins, including active and passive sodomy:

> The sins which have dominion over me exceed all measure . . .
> I am a thief, sacrilegious, a perjuror, a rogue, a murderer,
> In so far as I could, nor will I speak falsely, a deicide,
> A liar, pompous, a sodomite *[sodomita]*, a *cinedus,* an adulterer.
> A lover of drunkenness, a hater of sobriety.[9]

Granted that this public self-flagellation is more than a little theatrical and is qualified by the implication that some of these sins were only sins in intention, it is still startling to find a bishop making such avowals.

In Marbod and Baudri two contrary currents mingle, the classical with its casual acceptance of bisexuality and the Christian with its utter rejection of same-sex love. These two strands also combine in the poetry of a younger contemporary. Hildebert of Lavardin (c. 1055–1133) was acclaimed as the best Latin poet in France, and during his last eight years he served as archbishop of Tours. But Hildebert's homoerotic poems are more decorous, with no apparent hint of personal feeling. Several retell or comment on tales from Ovid: Apollo's lament for Hyacinth, Jupiter's rape of Ganymede, and the story of the metamorphosis of Iphis into a boy.[10] The moral attitude, however, is distinctly negative. In "The Wickedness of the Age" Hildebert deplores greed, fraud, perjury, corrupt judges, and self-seeking clergy, but the poem's harshest denunciation is reserved for sodomites:

> More common than any other lewdness is the plague of sodomy.
> Men pay what they owe their spouses to other men.
> Countless Ganymedes tend countless hearths,
> And Juno grieves to have lost the duty she used to claim . . .
> Shouldn't you remember the lesson of Sodom's example—
> To beware this sin and shun it lest you perish in brimstone?[11]

Among twelfth-century homoerotic poets, only one personality stands out: Hilary "the Englishman." Of Hilary we know only that he was a cleric and a pupil of Abelard about 1125. He writes in Latin, not in the classical meters favored by Marbod, Baudri, and Hildebert but in the rhymed quatrains of the new vernacular poetry. All his poems show a direct and ardent passion. "To a Boy of Angers" is a lovesick plea to a handsome youth to abandon his chastity. "To William of Anfonia" (presumably English despite the puzzling place name) makes William even more beautiful than extravagant Rumor had foretold; Hilary's suffering is proportional. In another poem Hilary borrows a pope's pun, declaring that a boy he admires should be called not *anglicus* (English) but *angelicus.*[12] The imagery and sentiments, though conventional, nevertheless suggest a genuine passion. But the frankly libertine poetry of Hilary stands almost alone in an age in which hostile references predominate.

Two poems from the end of the twelfth century are of unique interest—counterparts, in fact, to the Greek dialogues of Plutarch and "Lucian" in comparing heterosexual and homosexual love. In "A Debate between Ganymede and Hebe" Juno's daughter complains to the assembled gods that the handsome young Trojan has usurped her place as Jove's cupbearer by day and her mother's as Jove's bedmate by night. When Ganymede appears, Atlas, Apollo, Mars, and Venus are all smitten. The boy proclaims that homosexual anal and oral intercourse have become popular in heaven and that women are at a discount. There is no judgment by the gods. At the end of the poem Ganymede is left unchallenged on the field.[13]

The "Debate between Ganymede and Helen" is a more considerable work, far better known in the Middle Ages, to judge from the number of surviving manuscripts. Three times as long, it presents a genuine debate. In a springtime meadow, the most beautiful woman of antiquity tries to seduce the most beautiful boy. Deducing his preferences from his indifference, she curses him and they quarrel as to whether women or boys are more desirable. When Helen calls Ganymede's love sterile, he replies that pleasure is enough. Sounding a Shakespearean motif, she warns him his beauty will die with him if he has no child; he says he is content to be unique. When she claims that beasts and birds pair only heterosexually, Ganymede asks why men should imitate animals. Helen thinks affection is natural between the sexes; he is less sure: "Opposites always disagree; the right way is like with like."[14] When she calls male love unnatural, he answers that many great men have preferred it.

Finally, the debate degenerates into insults, with references to stained sheets and pungent vaginas. When Helen protests that wasted semen is wasted life, Ganymede falls silent. Reason, asked to judge, does not hesitate to decide against the boy. In the end, Jupiter and Apollo repent their past sins, and Ganymede asks to marry Helen. The poet who has dreamed all this wakes and has the last word in a conclusion that is resolutely medieval, that is, theological:

This vision came to me with God's approval.
Let Sodom blush and Gomorrah weep;
Let anyone guilty of this sin be converted.
O God, if ever I do this, may you forget me.[15]

One may freely admit the fascination of these early medieval love poems. Whatever their literary limitations, their tortured complexities make them more interesting than their simpler Roman models. Yet it is an exaggeration to claim, as John Boswell has, that they are evidence of an "extraordinary efflorescence of gay subculture."[16] Presumably such a culture would at least imply a tolerance for same-sex love. Yet very few of the poets—Hilary would be an exception—show this. It is intriguing to see Augustan themes revived in Marbod's neo-Horatian lines and more equivocally in Baudri. But compared with the genuine explosion of vernacular same-sex love poetry that appeared in Arab Spain, this thin trickle of neo-Latin verse could have reached only a tiny educated audience. Ultimately, the spirit of Augustine and Chrysostom wins out over Horace and Ovid. Ganymede does not "triumph" here; he goes down to defeat in a society that, in the twelfth century, grew more and more rejecting.

• Scandal in High Places •

The literature of the eleventh and twelfth centuries reveals few "sodomitical" writers willing to defend their preferences publicly. Nevertheless, the records of the age suggest that homosexuality was not entirely invisible, especially in the cities and schools of northern France, where anonymous Latin epigrams complain of its prevalence: "Now Chartres and Paris make themselves filthy continually / With Sodom's vice, and in Sens Paris becomes Io." (That is, Helen's lover becomes Jove's mistress.) "The men of Orléans are best, if you like / The customs of men who sleep with boys."[17] These attacks are directed at students and clerics, that is, those who gave these cities their preeminence as centers of learning. There are also reports of homosexuality among the upper nobility of France and Norman England, two closely related cultures. We must not expect to find sympathetic accounts, but these *chroniques scandaleuses,* if hardly edifying, may perhaps tempt a smile from a modern reader.

Consider, for example the election of a new bishop at Orléans in 1097. A short time before, the archbishop of Tours, whose name was Ralph, had prevailed upon Hugh, the archbishop of Lyons, to remove a man from this office who appeared to be unsuitable. Hugh complied, but Ralph's nominee for the now-vacant post was an alarmingly young man named John, widely recognized as his lover. (John's soubriquet was Flora, a common name for a courtesan.) The situation was complicated by the fact that Philip I of France and the papacy were at odds, since Philip had put aside his queen, replacing her with the wife of a subject, without any formalities of annulment or divorce. As a consequence, Hugh, who was the papal legate in France, had formally excommunicated him. To shore up his position, Philip then persuaded Ralph to crown him in a ceremony at Christmas. The reward for Ralph's acquiescence in this charade was the bishopric for John.

This, at least, is the interpretation of the situation that Ivo of Chartres set forth in two indignant letters of complaint, one to Hugh and one to Pope Urban II. Ivo adds that John's morals were notorious, that other adolescents of "his sort" had composed ribald rhymes about him that were sung in the diocese, and that John was not above singing these himself. He sent Hugh a copy of one song he claimed to have snatched from the hands of a performer. In his letter to Urban, Ivo protested, moreover, that John was not only Ralph's lover but had also been the bedmate of Ralph's brother, who was himself a bishop. Ivo's letter to Hugh adds another detail: when Ivo had complained to the king of John's behavior, Philip had been much amused and told Ivo ("not in secret," Ivo adds, "but in public") that he had slept with John himself. The versatile John, it appears, like Ganymede in Baudri's satire, did indeed "scamper through many chambers." Though Urban II was a vigorous pope—he had launched the First Crusade the year before and was much concerned with the morals of the clergy—it seems he failed to act on Ivo's complaints.[18] Ralph held onto his archdiocese, and John occupied his see at Orléans for at least three decades without further ado.

In Norman England, clerical animadversions did not fix on quite so succulent a scandal. The charges were more general, but in this case a king was their principal target. William II, the son of William the Conqueror, commonly called William Rufus for his red beard, ruled from 1087 to 1100 as the only adult English king who never married. A rough and brutal soldier in the Norman style, William was often in conflict with the church; we are not surprised that the three monks who chronicled his reign, Eadmer and William of Malmesbury, who were English, and Ordericus Vitalis, a Norman, are consistently adverse witnesses.

All link William and his court with hints of sodomy. Eadmer was chaplain to Saint Anselm who, as archbishop of Canterbury, was William's chief clerical antagonist. His history describes a meeting in which Anselm saw fit to "rebuke the king for those things which were reported about him . . . for almost everyone in the whole kingdom daily talked about him . . . saying such things as by no means befitted the dignity of a king."[19] Eadmer leaves the accusations vague, but a marked change had taken place in the Anglo-Norman court, which William of Malmesbury describes: "All military discipline [was] relaxed . . . Then the model for young men was to rival women in delicacy of person, to mince their gait, to walk with loose gesture, and half naked. Enervated and effeminate, they unwillingly remained what nature had made them—the assailers of others' chastity, prodigal of their own. Troops of pathics, and droves of harlots, followed the court."[20] Ordericus Vitalis blamed the new fashions on "foul catamites" who "shamelessly gave themselves up to the filth of sodomy."[21] William's own temperament was aggressively masculine, but the prevalence of what contemporaries perceived as stereotypical sodomites in his entourage has led to the theory that he was bisexual.[22] This seems a reasonable supposition, though the chroniclers make no direct accusations and name no favorites.

William was not enthusiastic when Anslem proposed calling a church council and asked him "mockingly" what he would speak about. Anselm replied: "That most shameful crime of sodomy . . . but lately spread abroad in this land, has already borne fruit too abundantly and has with its abomination defiled many . . . I beseech you, let us two make a united effort, you with your power as King, I with my authority as archbishop, to establish some decree against it such that, when it is published up and down the land, even the hearing of it will make everyone that is addicted to such practices tremble and be dismayed."[23] Eadmer, who gives this account of the episode, remarks, "These things found no home in the heart of the King," who cut short the audience brusquely with a "say no more about it."

William's death soon cleared the way. His brother Henry I approved of the plan, and Anselm had the satisfaction of seeing the Council of London pass a canon against sodomy in 1102. The new canon was to be read in every church on Sundays, presumably so that no one would be "ignorant of the censure passed by the leaders of Church and State on the vices of the last reign."[24]

Anselm's avowals of friendship in his own letters to other clerics are sometimes extravagantly romantic in style.[25] A respectful recent biographer is willing to entertain the hypothesis that Anselm himself had homosexual tendencies, and his decision to delay the promulgation of the council's anti-sodomy decree has been taken as indicating some degree of leniency.[26] At any rate, he recommended discretion in applying the new rules. "It must be remembered," he wrote, "that this sin has been publicly committed to such an extent that it scarcely makes anyone blush, and that many have fallen into it in ignorance of its gravity."[27] Yet Anselm's campaign apparently failed: did other officials refuse to cooperate? In 1105 a cleric wrote that "the sodomites, whom Anselm had excommunicated in his great council, and the long-haired men, whom the following Easter, clad in pontificals, he had publicly barred from entering the church, were now unmolested, for there was no one in the kingdom who dared act on Anselm's behalf."[28] All this suggests that under William II and afterward, homosexuality was to some degree open in Norman England. Two decades later, in 1120, the drowning of Henry I's sons and others of the gilded aristocracy in the famous "White Ship" at

Barfleur was read by at least one chronicler as a sign of divine displeasure with sodomy in courtly circles.[29] Not until the 1970s would homosexuality again be so visible in England.

• The Theological Assault •

In that same year, 1120, a joint council of church and state held in the Near East was an ominous harbinger of the future. Crusading Norman and French knights had carved out a kingdom in the Holy Land after their capture of Jerusalem in 1099, but their position there was hardly secure. Gormund, the Latin patriarch of Jerusalem, lamented that beleaguered Christians dared not go even a mile outside the towns they occupied.[30] In 1119 forces under Roger of Antioch had suffered an especially devastating defeat on the so-called Field of Blood, a reversal that seems to have kindled the same kind of siege mentality that had infected Carolingian society three centuries earlier.

Church and state now cooperated in a council that met at Nablus, a historic town thirty miles north of Jerusalem, with a mixed population of Franks, Samaritans, and Muslims. Though the meeting ranked formally as a church council, it was in fact a quasi-political assembly of ecclesiastical and secular officeholders, presided over jointly by King Baldwin II and Gormund. As at the Council of Paris, military anxieties led to harsh morals legislation and several statutes on homosexuality. Active and passive partners were both to be burned. Male rape victims were spared only if they had "cried out loudly," but they still had to perform a religious penance; if a man was raped twice, he might be burned as a consenting sodomite. Self-confessed sodomites were to do penance for the first offense and to be exiled after a second confession.[31] It has been conjectured that concerns about same-sex relations in the Holy Land sprang from several sources: their well-publicized prevalence among the Normans, the fear that crusaders would adopt the freer mores of the Islamic East, and the scarcity of Christian women.[32]

A council held in far-off Palestine would, of course, be remote from the centers of European affairs. But the Third Lateran Council, which met in Rome in 1179, also raised the issue of homosexuality. Convened by Alexander III to deal with his conflict with Emperor Frederick Barbarossa, it was the grandest council the Latin church had yet seen.[33] It addressed the growing threat of heresy, made new rules for papal elections, decreed that no one might (like John of Orléans) be made a bishop before the age of thirty, and issued decrees on sodomy. Canon 11 declared that married clergy should lose their benefices and that priests "involved in that incontinence which is against nature" should be deposed from clerical office and relegated to a monastery to do penance.[34]

By this decree errant priests were hidden from public view and spared secular punishment. Laymen faced a much more severe fate, since the same canon provided that they should be "excommunicated and completely isolated from contact with believers." In the medieval world, excommunication could have dire consequences. In Denmark, Aragon, and the German empire, for instance, it could mean a sentence of death if the secular authorities chose to act.[35]

Far more important, however, than such canons in definitively fixing the church's stance on homosexuality was a magisterial work, completed in 1267–1273, which sought to reconcile faith and reason by wedding Catholic theology with Aristotle. This was the *Summa Theologiae* of Saint Thomas Aquinas. Though he had earlier been suspected of heresy, Thomas was finally canonized in the fourteenth century, and in 1879 his writings were recognized by Leo XIII as the official philosophy of the Catholic Church. There is, however, nothing innovative about Aquinas's judgment of homosexuality; here the *Summa* systematizes and rationalizes long-held opinions.

The distinguishing feature of the *Summa* is its attempt to justify traditional Christian morality by an appeal to natural law. Thus, Aquinas both embraces Old Testament standards and develops a philosophical point of view he thinks has validity quite apart from scripture. Accordingly, he classifies "unnatural" sex acts into four categories according to their seriousness. First is "solitary sin" or masturbation; second, heterosexual intercourse in the "wrong vessel" (that is, anal or oral intercourse) or in the wrong position; third, "sodomy," that is, relations with the wrong sex; and finally, most sinful of all, bestiality.[36]

Aquinas's condemnation of homosexuality as unnatural rests on two principles of natural law, both as ancient as Plato's *Laws*. The first was the theory that animals do not engage in same-sex behavior, and the second was the fact that it is non-procreative. The doctrine of natural law had been enshrined in Roman law by the third-century jurist Ulpian, who in a passage incorporated into Justinian's *Digest* had defined natural law as "what nature has taught all animals." "This law," Ulpian declares, "is not unique to the human race but common to all animals born on land or sea and to birds as well. From it comes the union of male and female which we call marriage, as well as the procreation of children and their proper rearing. We see in fact that all other animals, even wild beasts, are regulated by understanding of this law."[37] Though Ulpian speaks only of heterosexual pairings, Aquinas, in the *Summa,* turns his definition into an implicit condemnation of homosexuality, declaring that some "special sins are against nature, as, for instance, those that run counter to the intercourse of male and female natural to animals, and so are peculiarly qualified as unnatural vices."[38]

All this points to a broader question, again as old as the Greeks: is it really appropriate to take animals as our models? Animal behavior may be admirable or horrifying. Whatever our concern for other species, most people would regard most human achievements as something distinct from animal behavior. Charles Curran, commenting on the use of the Ulpianic-Thomistic conception of natural law in Pope Paul VI's 1968 encyclical on contraception, has suggested that "a proper understanding of the human should start with that which is proper to humans . . . Ulpian's concept of natural law logically falsifies the understanding of the human."[39] Obviously, an appeal to animal behavior as a guide to morals under the rubric of natural law is open to a multitude of reservations.

Today, modern biological science has raised another objection. Extensive research has shown that same-sex behavior is quite common in the animal world. Zoologists publishing in scientific journals have documented same-sex activity among more than 450 species "in every major geographical region and in every major animal group."[40] These include groups as diverse as gorillas, elephants, lions, dolphins, antelope, kangaroos, llamas, warthogs, gulls, and turtles. Indeed, the "natural" world seems deliberately designed to confound natural-law moralists, for not only do hundreds of species engage in every kind of same-sex eroticism but more than one third form male or female couples, bond as devoted pairs, and on occasion feed, protect, and rear young.[41]

The other route by which Aquinas arrives at his category of "unnatural sins" is philosophical rather than zoological. It derives from Aristotle's doctrine of "final causes," that is, those ends or purposes for the sake of which things or activities exist. According to this view, as food exists for the preservation of the individual, so sex exists for the preservation of the race. Thus, sex must always serve its proper "natural" end, and all non-procreative sexual acts are "unnatural."[42]

Aquinas, in addition, endorses Augustine's opinion that homosexuality is the "worst" of sexual sins.[43] To make his point perfectly clear, Aquinas poses a question: are not rape and adultery worse than unnatural acts, since they harm other persons, while consensual sins against nature do not?[44] The answer is unequivocal: the four non-procreative forms of sex are worse, since—though not harmful to others—they are sins directly against God himself as the creator of nature. According to this logic, rape, which may at least lead to pregnancy, becomes a less serious sin than masturbation. And what of contraception? Would marital intercourse using artificial birth control be an unnatural act? Aquinas does not raise the question in the *Summa,* but earlier he so classified it in his commentary on the *Sentences* of Peter Lombard.[45] By this reasoning, conjugal sex with contraception must be ranked as an unnatural sin only one degree less serious than homosexual behavior.

Moreover, as Curran has pointed out, natural-law theory is not "a monolithic philosophical system with an agreed upon body of ethical content existing from the beginning of time."[46] The concept of natural law is exceedingly ambiguous and has been given radically different interpretations at different times by different thinkers. Behaviors as diverse as shaving the beard, using anesthesia in childbirth, and flying have on occasion been labeled unnatural. To take one example: in the seventh circle of his "Inferno" Dante dramatizes the punishment of men guilty of "violence against nature," or, as he alternatively puts, the "sins of Sodom and Cahors."[47] Readers familiar with Sodom's lurid reputation may well wonder what took place in the Provençal city of Cahors. The fact is that Cahors was a financial center, and its unnatural sin was usury.

Dante's judgment rested on a well-established medieval doctrine. Aristotle had called usury unnatural, since money should not breed money.[48] Drawing on the Levitical prohibition (25:36–37) against interest, the fathers of the church and medieval theologians fiercely condemned usury (that is, *any* charging of interest) as a mortal sin, employing the same rhetoric used against homosexuality. Thus, a fifteenth-century canonist could write: "Whenever humans sin against nature, whether in sexual intercourse, worshiping idols, or any other unnatural act the church may always exercise its jurisdiction. [So some have held] that the church could prosecute usurers and not thieves and robbers, because usurers violate nature by making money grow which would not increase naturally."[49] Catholic theologians did not seriously challenge the church's traditional view of usury until the eighteenth century; and the canon law making the charging of interest a mortal sin was not dropped until 1917.[50] Throughout history moralists have branded a multitude of behaviors as "unnatural." This has sometimes meant no more than that they disliked them on whatever grounds, serious or trivial. Far from being an immutable, unchanging, and eternal standard, natural-law philosophy has accommodated itself to the prejudices of particular ages, often lending them a factitious air of philosophical respectability.

The Inquisition and Its Allies

In the early thirteenth century the church undertook a religious crusade against the Albigensians of southern France. The sect was annihilated, but heresy was still regarded as a threat. Accordingly, in 1233 Pope Gregory IX set up the formal machinery of the Papal Inquisition. Hitherto, heresy had been dealt with by individual bishops, but Gregory thought bishops too lax in hunting down heretics and wanted a tribunal immune to local sympathies. To this end, he enlisted the services of the new preaching orders, the Dominican Friars (who specialized in theology) and the Franciscans. Thus was born the most powerful and the most feared organ for the enforcement of religious conformity Europe and its dependencies were ever to know. The main task of the Inquisition was, of course, to stamp out heresy, but on occasion it also undertook to enforce Christian sexual morality. Thus, the Spanish Inquisition, three hundred years later, would seek out homosexuals, and, as we shall see, at certain times and in certain jurisdictions more sodomites than heretics would be sent to the stake. But was the Inquisition, in its original thirteenth-century "papal" form, involved in such persecutions from its beginning? It appears that it was.

In this era heresy and sodomy came to be closely associated in the popular mind. So much so, indeed, that the same terms covered both. In France and England, *bougre* or "bugger" might signify either, so that in some thirteenth-century French laws we are left guessing which sense is meant. In Germany the same ambiguity attended the word *Ketzer* (from "Cathar"); one could speak of *Ketzerei* (heresy) of the spirit or *Ketzerei* of the flesh. The epithet "bugger" derived from Bulgari, a reference to the Balkan origin of a heresy whose followers, when they appeared in northern Italy and Provence, were also known as Albigensians or Cathars. As dualists who believed that the material world had been created by Satan, the Cathars repudiated many Catholic tenets, including baptism, the Eucharist, and allegiance to the priesthood. And because procreation imprisoned souls in material bodies, they objected to marriage and pregnancy. Since this meant the rejection of the one sexual outlet traditionally sanctioned by the church, it was popularly supposed that they must be indulging in non-procreative forms of sexual release, including homosexuality.

Men and women came to the attention of the Inquisition by various routes: through self-accusation (to avoid harsher penalties), through local gossip about suspicious speech or behavior, through denunciations by secret enemies or intimidated friends or relatives. Of course, under ordinary circumstances consenting partners in sexual affairs were not likely to be exposed unless determined efforts were made to seek them out. Were such efforts made? Michael Goodich has found evidence that they were. Confraternities of pious laymen associated with the Dominicans were organized in Italy early in the thirteenth century. One of these, the Society of the Blessed Mary, made a special attempt to hunt down not just heretics but sodomites as well. In 1255 Humbert of Romans, the head of the Dominican order, urged its members in Bologna to be diligent in its pursuit both of heretics and sodomites, and similar letters were dispatched to other Italian cities. In the 1260s the laws of Bologna made the society officially responsible for such duties. How well-organized such man-hunts were in Italy is indicated by the 1242 statutes of the city of Perugia, which appointed forty men (eight from each of the city's five districts) to seek out sodomites. Since a branch of the Society of the Blessed Mary had existed in the city since 1233, we may assume that its members worked together with the civic investigators. "Essentially," Goodich has concluded, "the officials of the confraternity were the local agents of the Inquisition."[51]

It may be instructive at this point to remind ourselves what falling into the hands of the Inquisition meant. For the accused, it was a terrifying fate from which any chance of escape was slight. The inquisitor was both prosecutor and judge, and the prisoner was presumed guilty simply because he had been accused. Frightened witnesses were easily induced to testify in such a way as to confirm the judges' suspicions. The trial was conducted in secret, without a defense attorney, and prisoners were not told the names of their accusers; hence, they could not confront or cross-examine them. Harassed with threats and tempted by offers of more lenient treatment, they might be cajoled or tricked into betraying their friends. If a sodomite had been fortunate enough, in the unfavorable circumstances of the age, to find support among others of his kind, he was expected to name and testify against them. Refusal to do this met with dire threats of reprisal.

Sentence was pronounced in public before the assembled dignitaries of state and church. The Inquisition maintained the pretense that it was not itself condemning men or women to death by formally "relaxing" them "to the secular arm." But as the judges well knew, "relaxation" usually meant execution, often burning alive. Lesser punishments included life imprisonment or wearing the "cross of infamy" publicly. Any sodomite condemned in this way would, of course, be marked for life. To associate with a former lover or friend would have seriously endangered that person's life. For men or women so stigmatized to band together for practical assistance would have been all but unthinkable. Not surprisingly, the thin stream of literary works on the theme of male love now disappears. The crime which the fathers of the church had denounced as unmentionable now became truly so through palpable danger. In literature, sodomites had to be shown as hellbound or, as in Dante's "Inferno," already among the flames.

The danger of conviction by the Inquisition was much increased by the use of torture. If someone accused of heresy or sodomy was unwilling to admit to the crime, severe pain might be inflicted to prompt a confession. Except for the Visigoths, torture had been unknown to the barbarians who founded the nations of modern Europe. Gratian's *Decretum* had forbidden it and denied it any place in canon law. But in 1252 Innocent IV in his bull *Ad extirpandum* allowed it in inquisitorial trials, though he forbade clerics to apply it themselves and required them to call in secular agents for the job. Then, in 1256, Alexander IV allowed inquisitors freely to absolve each other if they had tortured prisoners. This dispensation removed the barriers so that priests and monks dedicated to a life of Christian holiness could now turn the screws on the rack, burn prisoners' feet, or suspend them on the strappado with the tacit permission of their superiors. The merciful provision that torture could only be applied once was obviated by the pretense that sessions were not ended but merely suspended. Under such circumstances almost anyone could be induced to confess to almost anything.

According to contemporary law, heretics and sodomites, if convicted, lost their property to their judges and accusers. Here, as under Justinian, the temptation to press for convictions was strengthened by the lure of financial gain. "The multiplication of trials for the sake of the spoils was occasionally denounced by popes," we are told. "But since they took no measures to cut the evil tree at its roots it continued to flourish and grow."[52] Large sums were pocketed by friars vowed to monastic poverty. "It was this," says Henry Charles Lea, in his monumental history of the Inquisition, "which supplied the fuel to keep up the fires of zeal, and when it was lacking the business of defending the faith languished lamentably . . . There is an intimate connection between the activity of persecuting zeal and the material results to be derived from it."[53]

• The Fate of the Templars •

Generally speaking, we know little of the fate of men or women accused of sodomy by the Inquisition. The early records are obscure and incomplete, and the facts still lie shrouded in obscurity. It was otherwise, however, with the Order of the Knights of the Temple of Solomon, whose downfall shook all of Christian Europe. The brotherhood, founded in Palestine in 1119, was a novelty—a monastic order not of contemplative recluses but of armed men pledged to protect pilgrims and secure the newly won Holy Land. Exempted from all but papal authority, the order flourished for two centuries, winning fame for its initial military successes and growing extremely wealthy through bequests and financial dealings. With its far-flung outposts in Europe and the East, the Templars served as international bankers, and their headquarters in Paris made that city the financial capital of Europe. But when the Crusaders lost Jerusalem and had finally to give up Acre, their last outpost in Palestine, in 1291, the order's prestige was badly damaged. Its fall followed a series of sensational trials for heresy and sodomy, inspired by a king who coveted its riches.

Philip IV of France, commonly known as Philip the Fair, was in desperate need of money for his wars in Flanders and Gascony. In 1306 he arrested the Jews in France, seized their property, and expelled them. But he still owed a large sum to the Templars, whose wealth he coveted. The next year, sensing that they were now vulnerable, Philip acted. On September 14, with great secrecy, he sent sealed orders that all Templars in France were to be arrested. A month later the knights were imprisoned and confessions obtained in the first act of a chilling drama that was to last seven years and bring total ruin to the order. Grotesque to us today, the charges against the Templars were well adapted to the popular fantasies of the age. Since their induction rituals had always been a mysterious secret, Philip exploited absurd rumors: new recruits, it was charged, were required to deny Christ and spit on the cross, to worship an idol in the form of a cat, and to exchange obscene kisses.

30. Templar kissing cleric. Manuscript illustration, Jacques de Longuyon, *Les Voeux du Paon*, c. 1350.

The articles of interrogation also implied that the knights condoned and even enjoined sodomy within the brotherhood. The formal accusations included these charges: "Item, that in the reception of the brothers of the said Order or at about that time, sometimes the receptor and sometimes the received were kissed on the mouth, on the navel, or on the bare stomach, and on the buttocks or the base of the spine . . . Item, [that they were kissed] sometimes on the penis . . . Item, that they told the brothers whom they received that they could have carnal relations together . . . [and] that they did this, or many of them did."[54]

Once the Templars were in his power, Philip reported their confessions to the Inquisition in Paris, which questioned them again. Over a hundred confessed to indecent kissing and stated that sodomy was condoned.[55] Most important of all, the Inquisition extracted a confession of apostasy from the grand master of the order, Jacques de Molay, which Philip exploited to the full for propaganda purposes.

Much debate has centered on the guilt of the Templars. Some scholars have speculated that they might have been guilty of apostasy, but the consensus is that the charges were concocted to serve the penurious king.[56] That an order pledged to risk their lives in combating Muslims should have routinely apostatized from Christianity in a rite with homoerotic overtones is hardly credible: in 1307 few responsible persons in Europe not directly under Philip's influence or control believed this. But why then were there so many confessions? They were almost universal among the hundreds of Templars in France. And why were the bizarre charges of homosexual conduct included?

Clearly the accusations were calculated for their psychological effect on the public and accused. Philip and his advisers—masters of political theater—stage-managed the public rituals. The charge of apostasy, with the inflammatory details of desecration, was intended to undermine the knights' prestige as heroic defenders of Christendom. The sexual insinuations would have sounded plausible: occasional homosexual behavior by warriors in armed camps who had taken a vow to shun women might be expected, and suspicions that they sinned in this way would have been bolstered by the Templars' close contacts with Muslim culture.

That so many confessions should have been obtained is not surprising. Templars were threatened with death if they persisted in denying the allegations. Questioned by the chief inquisitor of France, William of Paris, "with few exceptions, [Templars] made the required concessions. It is assumed that the inquisitor used torture, or the threat of torture, against these men, as he was empowered to do when dealing with the obdurate."[57] In hearings in bishops' courts, men were stretched on the rack or "hauled up to the ceiling and allowed to fall with a violent jerk, stopping within a few inches of the ground. Sometimes weights were attached to a victim's feet to add to the shock of the fall." A fifty-year-old knight named Gérard de Pasagio testified that the royal judge in Mâcon tortured him "by the hanging of weights on his genitals and other members."[58] In 1310 Jacques de Soci claimed that twenty-five Templars had died "on account of tortures and suffering."[59] Jean de Furnes, "a serving brother who had been tortured for three months," told a papal commission he had "falsely confessed to the sin of sodomy because of his fear of this torture being repeated."[60] Proceedings against the Templars instituted in England or Germany, where torture was not used systematically, produced few confessions.

Philip effectively controlled the French Inquisition, as Ferdinand II was later to control the Inquisition in Spain. But for his plan to succeed he needed the support or at least the acquiescence of the pope, since the Templars were responsible only to him. When the king first informed Clement V of the charges, the pope was incredulous and replied indignantly. But Philip had means to enforce the pope's compliance. Clement, who was French, owed his elevation to the papacy to Philip, but Philip's brutal treatment of Boniface VIII, Clement's predecessor, had so angered the Roman populace that Clement felt it wise to remove the papal court to Avignon on the French border. In addition, Philip held over Clement's head as blackmail the threat of a posthumous trial of Boniface for murder, heresy, and sodomy. Persuaded to cooperate, Clement instructed bishops and inquisitors throughout Europe to interrogate the order, declaring, somewhat feebly, that from the time he became pope in 1305 he had "heard secretly" that the Templars had lapsed into apostasy, idolatry, and "the execrable act of the Sodomites."[61]

Given the pope's cooperation, Philip expected the trials to proceed smoothly. But on December 24th he met with a reverse. Transferred from the royal prison to papal jurisdiction, Grand Master Jacques de Molay plucked up courage and revoked his earlier confession that he had "denied Christ," saying that it had been made under fear of torture. Eventually more than five hundred other brothers announced they were ready to make similar retractions. His whole scheme now in jeopardy, Philip reacted swiftly. At the king's direction, the archbishop of Sens had fifty-four Templars conveyed in carts to a field outside Paris and burned forthwith, a highly irregular proceeding since it was customary to burn lapsed heretics but not men who declared they had made false confessions under duress. A contemporary account tells that "all of them, with no exception, finally acknowledged none of the crimes imputed to them, but constantly persisted in the general denial, saying always that they were put to death without cause and unjustly."[62]

But Philip was less concerned with the fate of individual knights than with suppressing the order, since only this could give him legal access to their wealth. Insisting on his papal prerogative, Clement reserved the issue for the Council of Vienne, which met in 1312. The issue was decided, however, when Philip arrived and stationed his troops outside the city. The pope forbade debate and declared the order dissolved on account of "many horrible things," including "the sin of wicked apostasy against the Lord Jesus Christ himself, the crime of detestable idolatry, [and] the execrable outrage of the Sodomites."[63]

There was one more stroke to the drama. Throughout the various trials the statements of de Molay, who was elderly, feeble, and frightened, had been embarrassingly weak and confused. Two of his servants testified that they had shared his bed, but de Molay never admitted to sexual relations at any point during his wavering testimony.[64] On August 20, 1308, however, he

31. Templars burned at the stake. Illustration, anonymous chronicle, "From the Creation of the World until 1384."

repeated his original confession of apostasy. On March 18, 1314, he was finally sentenced by a papal court to life imprisonment. He then astonished his judges by retracting his second confession as also false. He and another Templar leader asserted that they were guiltless of heresy and other sins. "The Order," they declared, "was pure and holy. They had basely betrayed the Order to save their own lives."[65] Without waiting for the startled court to respond, Philip consigned the aged grand master to the flames the same evening.

The fate of the Templars shows how effective an instrument the fear of sodomy and heresy, so frequently linked, could be in the hands of a Machiavellian ruler. Philip, however, lived to enjoy his gains only a few months. Dante, at work on the composition of his "Purgatorio" during the Templars' persecution, denounced Philip (in Canto 20) as a new "Pontius Pilate" whose "cruelty and avarice" had despoiled the Temple.

• Secular Laws: The Sowing •

We have explored the stand of the church vis à vis sodomites in the age of Innocent III and Aquinas. But how was their status in secular society affected by religious beliefs? As we might expect, local and national laws routinely reveal their origin in theological convictions. We shall begin our survey in northern Europe, far from the world of Theodosius, Justinian, and Egica, in lands where biblical and Roman laws were making their first notable impact. Consider the law of the West Frisians, who lived on the northeast coast of what is now the Netherlands and spoke a language closely related to English. The Frisian code, called the *Sendrecht*, dating from the eleventh century, provided that a man "guilty of breaking the law of Octavianus and Moses and the whole world" should be given the choice of three punishments—being burned, being buried alive, or self-castration.[66] Here we have a typical appeal to Leviticus and late Roman law. (The reference to Octavianus refers to the *Lex Julia* of Augustus, interpreted by Christian jurists in the *Digest* as criminalizing male relations.)

In Scandinavia, royal and priestly interests coalesced in the Old Norwegian code called the *Gulathingslog*, which decreed: "And if two men enjoy the pleasures of the flesh and are accused and convicted of it, they shall both suffer permanent outlawry."[67] This new statute was adopted in 1164 by King Magnus at the prompting of Archbishop Esteinn, a forceful cleric who energetically sought to strengthen and enrich his see. When challenged by Magnus's father, who asked whether the new law did not go beyond the traditional laws of Saint Olaf, the adroit churchman answered: "There is nothing in his laws that forbids increasing the rights of God," the rights of God here meaning, presumably, the filling of the archbishop's coffers. To this his canny interrogator replied that a deal might be struck: "If you wish to increase your rights, you will wish to help us increase the king's rights as much."[68] A compromise was struck, and it was agreed that the possessions of the guilty should be equally divided—one half to the bishop and one half to the king. In Sweden, Bishop Brynjulf's statute of 1280 also provided for episcopal remuneration: "Whoever sins against nature," it declared, "shall pay nine marks to the bishop."[69]

In France, laws on sodomy routinely invoked the edict of 342 of Constantius and Constans (regularly cited as *cum vir,* from its two opening words) and Leviticus. Over the centuries, from the Middle Ages to the Revolution, the punitive tradition in France was to prove remarkably conservative. Here is how Muyart de Vouglans, a French jurist of the eighteenth century, expounded the law in his *Institutes au droit criminel* of 1757:

> This crime, which takes its name from that abominable city which is mentioned in Sacred History, is committed by a man with a man or by a woman with a woman. It is committed also by a man with his wife when they do not use the ordinary way of generation. The penalty for so great a crime cannot be less than death. The terrible vengeance which Divine Justice took on the impious cities where this crime was common is enough to show that one cannot punish it with penalties too harsh, and above all

> when it is committed by two persons of the same sex. This penalty is set forth expressly by chapter 20 of Leviticus . . .
>
> The law *cum vir* 31 in the Code *de Adult.* requires that those who fall into this crime be punished by being burned alive. This penalty, which has been adopted by our jurisprudence, applies equally to women as to men.[70]

Muyart laments that—"to the shame of our century"—such acts still took place in France. Two men, he tells us, had recently been burned in Paris.

We may note that Muyart's commentary makes no specific reference to any national statute, only to scripture and Christian Roman law. Indeed, France remained for centuries a patchwork of legal traditions. Southern France followed Roman law, but north of Lyons "customary" laws based not on legislation but on local usage held sway and were first collected in the thirteenth century. The most important were the so-called *Établissements de Saint Louis,* compiled about 1272. Despite its regal title, these are based not on ordinances of Louis IX but on local customary laws. One law (book 1, ch. 90) sported an obscurity that was to puzzle French jurists for centuries: "If anyone is suspected of *bougrerie* [sic] the magistrate shall apprehend him and send him to the bishop; and if it is proved he shall be burned; and all his goods shall go to the baron. And in the same fashion one must deal with the heretic *[d'ome herite]* if he is convicted, and his goods shall go to the baron or the prince."[71] The puzzle was: what, in this context, did *bougrerie* mean? Some argued that since the second crime was heresy, the first must mean something else, namely, sodomy.[72] Others pointed out that this was an anachronism, since the word *bougre* at this date would have meant not a sodomite but a Cathar. Voltaire endorsed this view in his *Philosophical Dictionary,* complaining, with typical wit, that a gentleman had been recently burned in Paris on the basis of *une équivoque.*[73] From a historical and philological point of view, Voltaire was undoubtedly right, though his argument would hardly have saved the victim: there was no dearth of other lethal texts.

In fact, this particular section of the *Établissements* derived from a customary law of Touraine-Anjou dating from 1246.[74] Other customary collections were less ambiguous. The *Livres de jostice et de plet,* c. 1260), based on the customary law of Orléans, first prescribed death for heretics (here called *bogres* and *bogresses*) and then explicitly condemned sodomites in a separate statute: "Whoever is proved to be a sodomite *[sodomite]* shall lose his testicles. And if he does it a second time, he shall lose his member. And if he does it a third time he shall be burned."[75]

Another such collection dating from 1283 by Philip de Remi, lord of Beaumanoir (a judge of Clermont who served in the administrations of Philip III and Philip IV), sets forth the customary law of Beauvais, a region north of Paris. These *Coutumes de Beauvaisis* combine in one statute the punishment for heresy and homosexuality in a way that made the misreading of the *Établissements* plausible: "833. A person departing from the faith by disbelief so that he will not come back to the way of truth, or who commits sodomy *[sodomiterie]*, must be burned and he forfeits all his possessions in the manner described above."[76] This statement of the law waives the brutal surgical penalties of the *Livres,* which were, however, adopted verbatim in a legal *summa* or encyclopedia called the *Somme rural, ou le Grand Coustumier général* compiled by Jean Bouteiller of Tournay, who died in 1395.[77] This was a popular work, in use as late as the seventeenth century. History—or the fragmentary research that goes by that name—has not recorded the infliction of such mutilations in France, though we do have accounts of burnings and hangings. An eighteenth-century dictionary of criminal cases did, however, ascribe a peculiarly sadistic ferocity to the law in neighboring Switzerland: "The Swiss exercise against men guilty [of such] crimes an extraordinary rigor. They dismember them limb by limb over the course of several days, at one time an arm, at another a leg; when the body is only a lifeless trunk they throw it into the fire."[78]

English law, though severe, was not quite this horrendous. The earliest notices of sodomy appear in three treatises all written about 1290 and all of uncertain authorship. The legal compilation called *Britton* probably derives its name from an earlier manuscript by Henry de Bracton (d. 1268) on which it draws heavily. Bracton has been called the most important writer on English law before Blackstone, and *Britton* is generally regarded as a good authority. It specifies fire as the penalty for sodomy, which it calls a "mixed" crime, that is, one which could be tried by either state or church. A note in an early fourteenth-century copy of *Britton* spells out this dual option: "The inquirers of Holy Church shall make their inquests of sorcerers, sodomites, renegates, and misbelievers; and if they find any such, they shall deliver him to the king's court to be put to death. Nevertheless, if the king by inquest find any persons guilty of such horrible sin, he may put them to death as a good marshall of Christendom."[79]

Fleta, a treatise so-called because its unknown author lived in London's Fleet Street, gives a different penalty, namely, interment after the fashion of German and Frisian law: "Those who have connexion with Jews and Jewesses or are guilty of bestiality or sodomy shall be buried alive in the ground, provided they be taken in the act and convicted by lawful and open testimony."[80] Perhaps *Fleta*'s concern with open procedures implies they were not always followed in sodomy cases. The *Mirror of Justices,* which dates from the same period, is a fantastic and enigmatic book full of historical inventions, but its anonymous author's comment suggests formal trials were not always held: "Because of the scandal of sodomy our ancient fathers would not suffer that there should be any actions, accusations, indictments, or audience of any kind concerning so abominable a sin, but ordained that those notoriously guilty should be judged without respite and the judgments executed, and in cases that were not notorious every tongue should hold its peace."[81]

Unlike England, which achieved national unity early, Christian Spain in medieval times was fragmented into many distinct political and legal jurisdictions. The harsh edicts of Kindasvinth and Egica on homosexuality were incorporated into an important Visigothic code called the *Fuero Juzgo* (or *Fuero de los Jueces*), which reached its final form less than two decades before the Arab invasion of 711. Despite the collapse of the Visigoths' power, some of their laws were to have a long and far-flung influence, extending even to the New World. The *Fuero Juzgo* was nominally in force in the Spanish kingdoms of Asturias, Leon, Aragon, and Catalonia, though a plethora of new regional laws supplanted many parts of it. In the thirteenth century a reaction in favor of unity took place, and Ferdinand III of Castile imposed the *Fuero Juzgo* on cities newly liberated from the Moors—Cordoba (1241), Cartagena (1243), Seville (1248). His son Alfonso X (the Wise) continued this pattern and took a further step toward uniformity by compiling a new royal code for Castile, the *Fuero Real.*

Alfonso was a poet, a historian, a distinguished scientist, and a translator of Arabic treatises. The law on sodomy set forth in the *Fuero Real* in 1255 did not, however, reflect the humane side of his character. Indeed, it surpassed the ferocity of the *Fuero Juzgo* by adding an additional punishment: "Although it offends us to speak about a thing which it is very undesirable to talk about . . . [nevertheless] because this evil sin sometimes comes about when a man lusts after another to sin with him against nature, we order that whoever commits such a sin shall both of them, as soon as it has been discovered, be castrated before all the people, and after three days, shall be suspended by the legs until they die, and shall never be taken down."[82]

In contrast to the discreet executions described in the *Mirror of Justice,* this law attempted to increase the public horrors. The final order for a "gibbeting" would have exposed the bodies as food for scavenger birds. The provision that three days should lapse between castration and suspension is more puzzling. Many castrated men would have died of blood loss, infection, or inability to urinate. Perhaps the custom had grown up of suspending those survivors who were so disobliging as not to die quickly. Hanging upside down would have rapidly induced heart failure.

The *Fuero Real* was not Alfonso's only attempt to create a code for his kingdom. About 1265 he issued a still more famous work, *Las Siete Partidas*—a legal encyclopedia "in seven parts," the last treating of criminal law. The *Partidas* are more didactic than the *Fuero Real.* Their preamble to the law on sodomy appeals to the Sodom legend as a warrant for the death penalty: "for our Lord God sends upon the land where they do [such things], famine, pestilence, storms(?), and many other ills that cannot be counted."[83] Through Spain's conquests in the New World, these medieval laws were later imported to the Americas, since Castilian law incorporated the *Fuero Juzgo,* the *Fuero Real,* and *Las Siete Partidas.* These codes were cited by jurists as late as the nineteenth century not only in Spain but also in Mexico and South America.[84] They extended the moral influence of medieval Spain over a vast territory, shaping Hispanic attitudes toward homosexuality in the New World which endured long after their specific sanctions had been superseded.[85]

· The Harvest Begins ·

But were these draconian laws put to use? Were the horrific fates they threatened inflicted in medieval times? The facts are still unclear. The documenting of such theological "crimes" as heresy and witchcraft has long been an academic industry. But trials and punishments for homosexual offenses have, until recently, been either ignored or relegated to brief and embarrassed asides. So little was known about them in 1955 that Canon Derrick Bailey, in his pioneering study *Homosexuality and the Western Christian Tradition* did not record a single execution.[86]

Even today no comprehensive account of executions in earlier periods has been made, though articles on specialized topics have begun to appear. Records hardly exist before the thirteenth century, however, and for centuries afterward are scarce and incomplete. Undoubtedly, many men and women suffered whose fates are forever lost to history. The earliest known death appears in a Swiss document. The annals of the city of Basel record, in one terse sentence, that in the year 1277 "King Rudolph burned Lord Haspisperch for the vice of sodomy."[87] King Rudolph was in fact Rudolph I, founder of the Hapsburg dynasty; the count was an obscure member of the German-Swiss aristocracy. We do not know if there was a political motive for the execution. But men at all levels of society were vulnerable. In 1292, we are told, Jan de Wettre, a humble "maker of small knives," was burned "at the pillory next to St. Peter's in Ghent in Flanders."[88]

In some jurisdictions the victims' religion seems to have made them suspect. The *Archivo General* of the small kingdom of Navarre in northeast Spain records the burning of an unnamed Moor at Arguedas in 1290 "for lying with others."[89] Again, in 1345, two Jews, Juce Abolfaça and Simuel Nahamán, were burned at Olite, a town near Pamplona, "because they had committed the sodomitical sin with each other." It is rare that early records vouchsafe more than the bare mention of such deaths. But since the Navarrese archives list payments to the men who officiated, we are able to visualize the scene. The men were tortured to obtain confessions, then accompanied to the stake by a cortege of twenty men while a musician played the *añafil,* a long Moorish trumpet of lugubrious tone. The trumpet-player received one sueldo for his performance, the man who chained the couple to the tree and "administered the fire" by piling bundles of vines at its the foot earned a fee of ten sueldos.[90] A year later another man, Pascoal de Rojas, was burned in the nearby city of Tudela for the crime of "heresy with his body."[91] In 1373 a servant was burned, again at Olite, for committing sodomy with another servant. Records have not yet come to light for the rest of Spain in the fourteenth century.

Burnings also took place in France: at Laon in 1317, at Dorche in the Savoy region in 1344, at Reims in 1372.[92] In the 1370s two men, Willem Case and Jan van Aersdone, were executed in Antwerp.[93] In 1409 a man was burned in Augsburg and four ecclesiastics were hung in a wooden cage, bound hand and foot, to starve to death.[94] Some of the early cases involved men who had committed acts of violence, including a priest who was castrated in Basel in the 1290s for raping a boy. But in 1357 the Venetian courts sentenced a boatman, Nicoleto Marmagna, and Giovanni Braganza, who had been his lover for three or four years, to be burned alive.[95] In 1406 fifteen or sixteen youths of the nobility were tried in the city along with eighteen commoners.[96] This, as we shall see, was the beginning of a more systematic civic repression in fifteenth-century Venice.

These convictions all involved males. One may legitimately ask: were the same severe sanctions applied to lesbians? So little was known about this point that in 1955 Derrick Bailey could state categorically that lesbianism was "ignored both by medieval and modern law," a rashly optimistic conjecture.[97] In fact, there was a significant evolution in medieval law. We may recall that neither the Hebrew scriptures nor the rabbis of the Talmud treated lesbian acts as crimes.[98] The first known legislation that addresses the question is the Orléans code of circa 1260, *Li Livres de jostice et de plet.* This law, which required that a man should lose his testicles for a first offense, his "member" for a second, and for a third offense should be burned, was extended to women in a way that is curious, to say the least: "A woman that does this shall lose her member each time and on the third must be burned. *[Feme qui le fet doit à chescune foiz perdre membre, et la tierce doit estre arsse.]* And all their goods shall go to the king."[99] This must certainly rank as one of the most bizarre attempts to adapt a law to women. Though exactly what genital mutilations were contemplated must remain a mystery, the intention (however grotesque) to establish punitive parity between the sexes is all too clear.

Nevertheless, the view of lesbianism as a capital crime had certainly taken root in the popular imagination, for in one early fourteenth-century French romance two women are threatened with burning. The episode occurs in the tale of Princess Ide, an extension of the *Huon of Bordeaux* legend. Because of her prowess in battle, Princess Ide, who has been disguised as a man, is commanded by the emperor to marry his daughter. Though the women, in the words of the sixteenth-century English translator Lord Berners, pass their time in nothing more culpable than "clyppynge [embracing] and kyssynge," the emperor, on discovering Ide's true sex, declares that he "wold not suffre suche boggery to be used" and orders that "bothe you and my doughter shall be brent." Ide and her lover are saved from the flames only by a miracle of the Virgin, who answers Ide's prayers by transforming her into a man.[100] (Clearly, the author has been inspired by the metamorphosis in Ovid's story of Iphis and Ianthe.) The distance between Augustan Rome and the medieval world can be measured by the sentence pronounced in the tale.

What inspired the Middle Ages to make this threat, unknown to Judaism in the age of the Talmud or even to Theodosius and Justinian? The most important influence is undoubtedly Paul's Epistle to the Romans, where lesbianism and male homosexuality are equally condemned. Aquinas, following a long tradition among Pauline commentators, had enshrined this moral equivalence in his *Summa,* where he includes, among the forms of "unnatural vice," intercourse "with a person of the same sex, male with male and female with female, to which the Apostle refers."[101] But if the ethical equation was clear, there was still the problem of reconciling the death penalty with ancient Roman law. The two crucial statutes on homosexuality, Constantius and Constans's edict of 342 and Theodosius' of 390, referred only to men, and Justinian's Novella 141 spoke only of "the defilement of males" *(de stupro masculorum).* In the light of this silence, how could Roman law be made to accommodate medieval Christian prejudice?

The solution was ingenious. The crucial step appears to have been taken by Cino da Pistoia, a poet and friend of Dante, who in 1314 published a *Commentary* on the code of Justinian. Cino reached back to an obscure law of the emperors Diocletian and Maximianus dating from 287 CE, that is, from a time before Rome was officially Christian. The law—called, after its opening word, the *Lex foedissimam*—read as follows: "The laws punish the most foul wickedness *[foedissimam nequitiam]* of women who surrender their honor to the lusts of others, although not the blameless will of those who are defiled by violence, since it was properly decreed that they should be of inviolate reputation and that marriage to them should not be forbidden to others."[102] Under Roman law, unchaste women (prostitutes, for example) could not marry Romans of the upper classes. In order to preserve this prohibition while exempting rape victims, the new law began with a general condemnation of female sexual impropriety. But it is patently clear that it was not intended to create any new offense.

Cino's gloss, however, unambiguously interpreted the vague and general language of the law as condemning lesbians: "This law can be understood in two ways: first, when a woman suffers defilement by surrendering to a male; the other way is when a woman suffers defilement in surrendering to another women. For there are certain women, inclined to foul wickedness, who exercise their lust on other women and pursue them like men."[103] Since Cino cites no prior authorities, he himself may have initiated this interpretation of the *Lex foedissimam.* If so, he stands at the start of an important legal tradition. Later, in 1400, Bartholemeo de Saliceto refers to a gloss on the *Lex foedissimam* (which may well be Cino's) condemning lesbian relations. He goes a step further, however, by prescribing the death penalty, which he justifies by appealing to the law of 342 which made male acts capital offenses.[104] Saliceto's *Lectures* remained a standard reference until the eighteenth century.

Since, according to Roman tradition, the opinions of eminent jurists had the force of law, it would have been possible, by using these dicta, to argue for the death penalty for lesbianism even in those parts of the continent with no national or local legislation. In Italy, the influence of Roman law was all-pervasive; in Spain, the *Partidas* were largely based on it; French kings fostered its revival, since it bolstered royal prerogatives; and even in Germany after 1500 and in Calvinist Scotland after 1600 it enjoyed remarkable, if belated, triumphs. Thus, throughout continental Europe lawyers trained in Roman law and imbued with Pauline principles were encouraged to write provisions for the execution of lesbians into civic, regional, and imperial codes in the later medieval period and the Renaissance. Eventually, women in France, Spain, Italy, Germany, and Switzerland were to suffer beheading, hanging, drowning, and burning as the price of their love for other women.

• Poets for the Prosecution •

Throughout history poets have traditionally praised love, while theologians, moralists, and jurists have not infrequently sought to ban it. One group has thrown stones, the other garlands. Against the animadversions of ascetic philosophers, reforming emperors, and testy imams we may set the poets of the Greek Anthology, the rebels of the Augustan age, and a thousand Muslim versifiers, all of whom celebrated the love of men for women and for boys. But by the end of the twelfth century, though troubadours sighing for aristocratic ladies might ignore Augustine, poets as well as priests had grown hostile to same-sex love, reflecting the prejudices of the times and its punitive practices. Poetry and *belles lettres* cease to show any of the tolerance of classical or Islamic writers and take for granted the burning of men and women attracted to their own sex. Occasionally, literature echoes the politics of the day. In the *Roman de Fauvel,* an allegorical poem of the fourteenth century, "Holy Church" condemns the Knights Templars as "heretics / And sinners against nature."[105]

This growing abhorrence appears also in the so-called romances of antiquity of the period 1150–1170. Though these French epics—the *Romance of Thebes,* the *Romance of Troy,* and the *Romance of Aeneas*—are set in classical times, they show little awareness of Hellenic mores. Indeed, they portray the "sodomite" as a new social type—a man hated and feared by women as a mortal enemy. Homoeroticism is no longer perceived as part of a bisexual continuum but as pointedly excluding women. The sodomite's preferences are regarded as a deadly insult not only to those women whose charms he has scorned but also to heterosexual men whose tastes he has failed to appreciate and share.

In the *Romance of Aeneas,* a medieval retelling of Virgil's epic, the hero is mistaken for a sodomite. When Aeneas arrives in Italy from Troy to attack King Turnus, the king's betrothed, Lavinia, finds herself attracted to the newcomer, much to the horror of her mother, who warns her that all Trojans are averse to women. Her diatribe reveals how a hostile Frenchwoman of the twelfth century might typify a male sodomite: "What have you said, crazy fool? Do you know to whom you've given yourself? That wretch is of such a nature *[de tel nature]* that he has no care for women . . . He would value more embraces from a boy than from you . . . Haven't you heard how he treated Dido badly? Never has a woman been well-treated by him, nor will you, I believe, by the traitor and the sodomite."[106] "That wretch is of such a nature that he has no care for women": here the "sodomite" is conceived as a special category of man whose nature is determined and predictable. Lavinia, convinced of Aeneas's depravity, complains that "it would soon be the end of this world if all the men everywhere in it were like this" and joins her mother in expressing scorn: "May a man of such a nature who cares not for women be now accursed."[107] But Lavinia eventually overcomes her suspicions and, as in Virgil, ends by marrying the hero.

A similar false charge is made in the *Lai de Lanval* by Marie de France, who, despite her name, wrote in England at the court of Henry II (1154–1189) and may have been that king's illegitimate half-sister. Her lays, or brief romances, are typical of the age in their Arthurian setting, chivalric manners, and use of courtly love conventions. In the *Lai de Lanval* the hero falls in love with a fairy; she tells him he must keep his love secret, and he vows to do so. But when he spurns Queen Guinevere, she angrily accuses him of not caring "for such pleasure": "People have often told me that you have no interest in women. You have fine-looking boys with whom you enjoy yourself."[108] Lanval is so devastated by the accusation that he breaks his vow of silence, the implication being that nothing less could have made him do so. A century earlier Marbod and Baudri had written Latin poems based on the classical Augustan assumption of male bisexuality. Now, however, a "sodomite" is a man with no interest in women, a man with a peculiar, and deplorable, psychology of his own, a special sort of being.

It was not only vernacular verse that damned the sodomite. Philosophical poetry was quite as condemnatory. Alain de Lille was a much-read theologian and philosopher, hailed in his own time as another Virgil. His *Complaint of Nature,* composed about 1160 in an ornate and convoluted Latin, had an enormous influence on literature in succeeding centuries. Inveighing against the abuse of Nature, its opening lines are a diatribe against homosexuals, specifically characterized as men who perversely reject women:

> I change laughter to tears, joy to sorrow, applause to lament, mirth to grief, when I behold the decrees of Nature in abeyance; when society is ruined and destroyed by the monster of sensual love: when Venus, fighting against Venus, makes men women: when with her magic art she unmans men . . . The very hammer deforms its own anvil. The spirit of the womb imprints no seal on matter, but rather the plowshare plows along a sterile beach . . . Why do so many kisses lie untouched on maiden lips, and no one wish to gain profit from them?[109]

A century later, Alain's animus and his metaphors found an echo in another famous medieval poem, the *Romance of the Rose.* This fantastic allegory was "for nearly three hundred years after its composition in the thirteenth century, one of the most widely read works in the French language" and was "nearly as important in England as in France."[110] The first 4,000 lines were penned by Guillaume de Lorris about 1235; the continuation—a staggering 17,000 lines in a very different, much more satirical style—was added by Jean de Meun some forty years later. In this enormous coda, allegorical personages (Reason, Genius, and so on) hold forth on love. Genius, who is introduced as Nature's priestly confessor, launches a polemic against sodomites which closely parallels Alain's exuberant rhetoric. Praising procreation, Genius castigates those "who do not write with their styluses [penises] . . . on the beautiful precious tablets" Nature has prepared for them. These men, Genius complains, follow the bad example of Orpheus, who "did not know how to plow or write or forge in the true forge—may he be hanged by the throat!" (Jean has in mind, of course, the conclusion of the Orpheus legend as Ovid presents it in the *Metamorphoses.*) Genius wishes such men may, "in addition to the excommunication that sends them all to damnation, suffer, before their death, the loss of their purse [scrotum] and testicles, the signs that they are male! May they lose the pendants on which the purse hangs! May they have the hammers that are attached within torn out! . . . May they have their bones broken without their ever being mended! . . . May their dirty, horrible sin be sorrowful and painful to them; may it cause them to be beaten with sticks everywhere."[111] We note that the mutilations Genius advocates parallel those set forth in the *Livres de jostice et de plet,* which also condemned sodomites to lose their testicles and penises. This particular code, which derived from Jean's native province of Orléans, was compiled about a decade earlier than his portion of the *Romance,* which dates from about 1275.

Jean's archetypal figure for the sodomite is Ovid's Orpheus. It is a paradox of medieval culture that the favorite Latin author of the twelfth and thir-

32. The death of Orpheus. Albrecht Dürer, pen drawing, 1494.

teenth centuries was the rakish Ovid. He was much studied and imitated, both among the profane Goliards and in the cathedral schools. (James I of Aragon even opened a convocation of bishops and nobles with a quotation from the *Art of Love* under the impression he was citing scripture.)[112] Ovid was read in Latin and in translations, one of which, the *Ovid molarisé,* is an enormously inflated French version of the *Metamorphosis* that mixes in much medieval sentiment. The anonymous author retells the story of Orpheus and makes him the malign inventor of a perverse lifestyle: "But never after [the death of Eurydice] did he desire feminine love. He seduced by his bad doctrine fools, who were the first to sin mortally against nature and against law. And to compound his crime . . . he told [stories] of bad loves . . . Thus he bears witness in his teaching that masculine love *[l'amour masculine]* is better than women's love."[113] Once again "masculine love" (homosexuality) is seen not as complementary to the love of women but as incompatible with it. The tradition of the sodomitical Orpheus was not only a medieval conceit. It also appears in the Renaissance, as in Albrecht Dürer's 1484 pen drawing of the bacchantes attacking the cringing poet. A banderole above his head reads, "Orpheus, der erst Puseran"—"Orpheus, the first homosexual." (*Puseran* was a German corruption of the Italian term *bougeron.*)

• Dante's Admirable Sinners •

When Guillaume de Lorris began the *Romance of the Rose,* Italian literature in the vernacular could scarcely have been said to exist. By the beginning of the next century, Dante had raised it to the level of genius in the *Divine Comedy.* Dante's treatment of homosexuality in his great poem, however, has proved puzzling to editors. Cantos 15 and 16 of the "Inferno" assign sodomites to the seventh of Hell's nine circles, the circle of the "violent," far below the heterosexual lovers of history and romance, who are punished in the first, or uppermost, circle. Dante is orthodox in his moral theology and in the "Inferno" concurs with Aquinas in making "violence against nature" a worse sin than violence against one's neighbor. Consequently he places his sodomites below the murderers who share this circle.

But not all of Dante's commentators have identified the sinners who run in the circle of fire as sodomites. Some have gone to considerable lengths to challenge this view.[114] Two curious facts have sparked the controversy: first, none of the eight men Dante mentions by name is associated with homosexuality in any other source; second, nothing we hear of them (with one possible exception) connects them with anything erotic, and certainly not with any medieval stereotype of the sodomite. Yet scholarly opinion generally agrees these men are sodomites in the common medieval sense of the term. Two other facts support this view. Virgil, when he explains the topography of Hell in Canto 11, brands these men with the mark of "Sodom and Cahors." In addition, Virgil accuses them of scorning Nature's gifts, "her beauty and bounty"—possibly an echo of Alain de Lille and Jeun de Meun.[115]

What is most unconventional about Cantos 15 and 16, however, is the respect and affection Dante shows the sinners he meets there. Earlier he had hailed two (Aldobrandi and Rusticucci) as "men whose high deeds might begem the crown of kings," and he seems to make a point of emphasizing that their lifestyle implies no general depravity of character.[116] Brunetto Latini (or

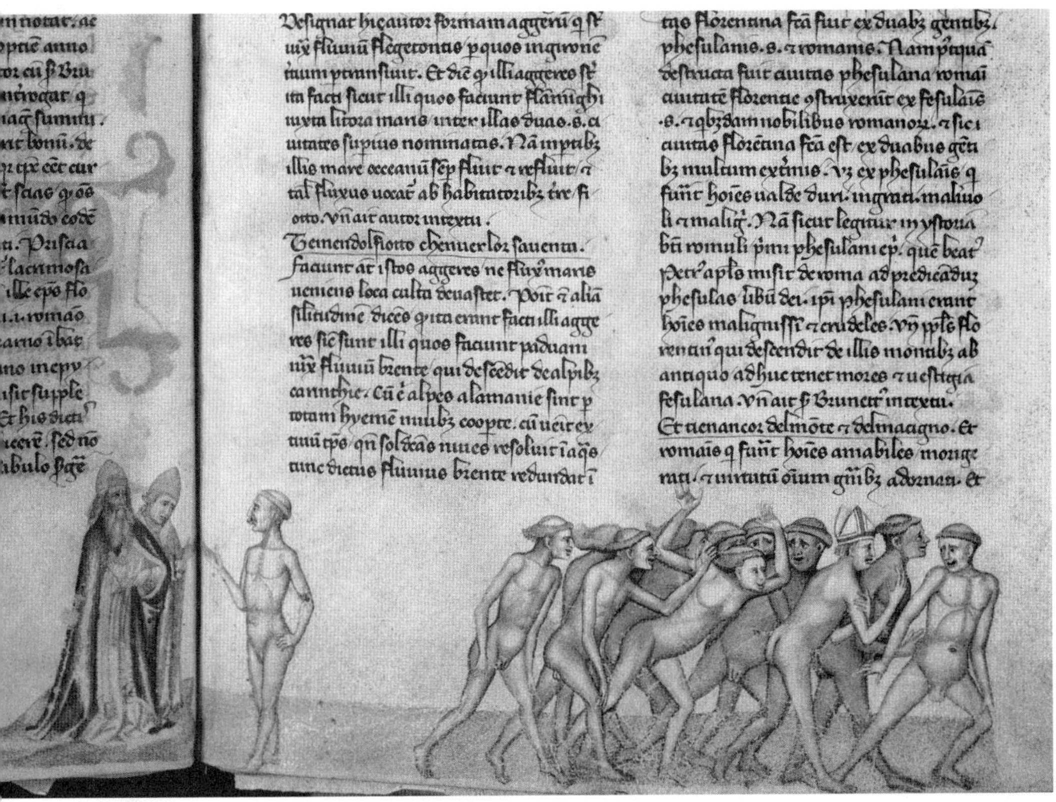

33. Dante and Virgil meet the sodomites. Manuscript illustration, Guido da Pisa, *Commentary on Dante,* c. 1345.

Latino), a famous poet much admired as a political leader in Florence, he greets warmly as a revered teacher and old friend. Dante's treatment of the man is commendatory beyond almost any other figure in the "Inferno." He calls the poet a "radiance among men" and speaks with gratitude of "that sweet image, gentle and paternal, / you were to me in the world when hour by hour / you taught me how man makes himself eternal."[117] Brunetto, in reply, identifies the sinners he runs with as "great men of letters, scholars of renown."[118] He names two—Priscian, a Latin grammarian of the sixth century, and Francesco d'Accorso, a distinguished professor of law at Bologna and Oxford who, like himself, had died shortly before Dante began his masterpiece.

The association of homosexuality with intellectuals and teachers was common in Dante's day. In 1271 Roger Bacon reported that "many theologians at Paris, and men who lectured in theology, were banished from that city and from the realm of France for the vile sins of sodomy."[119] Pedagogues were often equated with pederasts. Perhaps Priscian's name is to be taken as generic for a schoolmaster, since nothing we know of the historical figure implicates him. Brunetto identifies one other man, though not directly by name—Andrea de'Mozzi, bishop of Florence, the only sodomite treated with scorn. (Brunetto refers enigmatically to the bishop's *mal protesi nervi*—a phrase Boccaccio interpreted as signifying his erect male organ, an uncertain but unbettered guess and the only detail in these cantos that hints at sexuality.)[120]

In Canto 16 Dante meets a second group of sodomites—Guido Guerra, Tegghiaio Aldobrandi, and Jacopo Rusticucci, three noble Florentines who were highly esteemed as soldiers and statesmen. Virgil calls them "souls to whom respect is due," and Dante almost risks leaping down onto the fiery plain to embrace them. He protests that he feels not "contempt" but only "compassion" for them and has always "heard with affection and rehearsed with honor / your name and the good deeds of your happier days."[121] Nothing in medieval stereotypes prepares us for this scene. Its image of the lover of males as an honored statesman or warrior is closer to Plato's *Symposium* (which Dante could not have known) or Plutarch. We are thus faced with a paradox. Dante takes for granted the traditional theological condemnation of homosexuality but treats the sodomites with more respect than any other inhabitants of Hell.

Undoubtedly, Dante stands in sharp contrast to other Italians of the early and later Middle Ages, who are unremittingly intolerant. We may recall the censorious remarks of Peter Damian two centuries earlier. Nor did San Bernardino of Siena, who preached in Florence a century after Dante, treat sodomites with respect, attacking them in sermon after sermon with exuberant hate. In 1424, in a Lenten sermon preached in Santa Croce, Florence's Westminster Abbey, he admonished his hearers: "Whenever you hear sodomy mentioned, each and every one of you spit on the ground and clean your mouth out well. If they don't want to change their ways by any other means, maybe they will change when they're made fools of. Spit hard! Maybe the water of your spit will extinguish their fire. Like this, everyone spit hard!"[122] We are told the crowd spat on the church pavement with a sound "like thunder."

It is not surprising that Dante's early commentators were amazed to find sodomites treated so sympathetically by so great a poet, for as a modern Italian scholar has put it, "Sodomy was a sin of such gravity that it was inconceivable for them to treat with respect men seared with such infamy."[123] One anonymous fourteenth-century commentator went so far as to accuse Dante of complicity. "Here our author shows the love and affection he had for [these men]; and by this some understand that the author himself was stained with this vice, for . . . whenever he found sinners punished for a vice which he had experienced himself he grieved and had compassion, thinking he would be punished in the same way for it."[124]

Another writer, also anonymous, developed a novel theory to explain

Dante's unaccountable judgment by making a distinction: "Two kinds of people are [guilty] of this wicked sin. One kind are clerks [*religiosi,* scholars in holy orders] skilled in the sciences who show themselves to be decent people *[gente honeste];* they discover this evil practice out of shame because they cannot look for a wife or other woman and make do with it. The other kind of people are wicked and unbridled and follow their appetites and do not care for anything else. And in this present canto [15] the decent sort of person is tormented."[125] This was a most unusual remark for its time, though the theory hardly fits the warriors of Canto 16, who were not pledged to celibacy.

But many felt the poet had, without adequate proof, outrageously libeled his fellow Florentines, a view originally held by a major fourteenth-century commentator, Benvenuto da Imola. But Benvenuto changed his mind about these "outings" and came to approve them, though hardly in Dante's spirit. His explanation etches a fascinating, if chilling, vignette of medieval academic life:

> Certainly, when I first saw these words of Dante, I was very indignant [at his identifying famous scholars as sodomites]; but afterwards I learned by experience that our most wise poet hath here done excellently. For in 1375, when I was at Bologna and lectured upon this book, I found certain vermin bred of the cinders of Sodom who infected the whole of that University; and . . . I disclosed the matter, not without grievous peril to myself, to the Cardinal of Bourges, who was the [Papal] Legate at Bologna. He, as a man of great virtue and learning, who detested such abominable crimes, commanded an enquiry for the principal offenders, some of whom were caught while others fled in terror. And, but for the hindrances wrought by a certain traitorous priest to whom the commission had been entrusted and who was infected with that same disease, many would have been given over to the flames of fire.[126]

Though Benvenuto appears to commend the poet, his rancor contrasts strongly with Dante's sympathetic respect.

We find another curious twist in the "Purgatorio," the second part of Dante's poem. In the "Inferno" famous lovers are punished in the highest circle of sinners, that which imputed the least blame, and sodomites far below. In the "Purgatorio" Dante adopts a different classification based on the seven deadly sins. Generally the results are consonant with the Thomistic system of the "Inferno." Sins of the flesh are punished on the uppermost terrace of the Mount of Purgatory, while sinners guilty of wrathful violence circulate at the base. But Dante comes upon two distinct groups of sinners on the upper terrace, and the distinction between them is not immediately clear. A sinner from the first group declares "nostro peccato fu ermafrodito": "our sin was hermaphrodite." This has led to misapprehensions, since hermaphrodites and homosexuals were sometimes confused in the Middle Ages. (Some modern scholars of note have been misled as well, among them John Boswell.)[127] But in fact the term ermafrodito is equivalent to "heterosexual," that is, involving both sexes. The other group is less ambiguous: they cry out "Sodom and Gomorrah," and we are told that they have committed the sin which won Caesar the epithet "Regina." But what is notable is that these sinners are not assigned a lower status, as in the "Inferno." Instead, they move on the same level as other men and women who are being purged of lust.

Dante does not identify any of the sodomites by name. The two groups, homosexual and heterosexual, move in different directions around the mountain, but when they meet they kiss. Dante describes their greeting by the odd image of a tribe of ants nuzzling as they greet each other. This salutation, symbolic of respect and reconciliation, suggests that Dante is repudiating the campaign of vehement vilification waged in his day by church and state.

Perhaps Dante's rejection of medieval homophobia was influenced by contemporary events. It is generally assumed that Dante wrote the opening lines of the "Inferno" about 1307, the year Philip the Fair began his persecution of the Templars. In Italy Philip's accusations aroused skepticism and indignation. Dante's contemporary Giovanni Villani, in his famous history of Florence, accuses Philip of manufacturing false charges of heresy and sodomy out of a "desire for gain." Those knights who were burned at the stake are seen as martyrs to the king's lust for gold.[128] In Canto 20 of the "Purgatorio"—the terrace of the avaricious—Dante introduces Hugh Capet, the ancestor of France's kings, who denounces his descendants for this vice. Dante especially singles out Philip as a new Pilate who treated Boniface VIII brutally and, not satisfied with this outrage, carried his "greedy sails" into the Temple, that is, he pillaged the Templars.[129] Presumably Dante, like other Italians, did not credit the charges Philip brought against the order; moreover he seems not to have shared the popular animus that Philip had exploited to gain his ends.

CHAPTER EIGHT

IMPERIAL CHINA

500 BCE–1849

• A Peach, a Fish, and a Sleeve •

So far we have traced changing attitudes toward homosexuality in the Western world from classical times to the high Middle Ages, from Sappho to Dante. But what of other civilizations? Do they show the same development? Were the scorn, contempt, and dire punishment meted out to "sodomites" in Europe after the triumph of Christianity an aberration in world history or typical? In our survey of Arab Spain we have noted one anomaly: Islamic poets might pen ardent love poems to same-sex youths despite religious teachings and severe laws. As for the vast subcontinent of India, the daunting complexities of Hindu teachings on sex still remain largely unexplored. (The influential Laws of Manu, compiled about the first century CE, required only that a "twice-born" man who had relations with a female in an ox-cart, in water, in the daytime, or "with a male," should perform a ritual purification, that is, bathe dressed in his clothes.)[1] Fortunately, modern scholarship has, in recent years, illuminated the homosexual traditions of two other major non-European societies, China and Japan. We shall look first at the older culture.

Three things have ensured a rich abundance of documents on male love in China. From the earliest times the Chinese have shown a passion for detailed, meticulous historical records. Moreover, early biographers felt free to treat sexuality, including love affairs between men, with an openness unheard of in Christian Europe. And finally, this freedom was extended to poets, playwrights, and writers of fiction in the classical Chinese modes. Unfortunately for the student who is not a Sinologist, only a small proportion of these works have been translated, and until very recently writings on China by Western scholars by no means accurately reflected the historical picture. In China itself, especially since the establishment of the People's Republic in 1949, the tolerance of love between men that prevailed in the "Middle Kingdom" and the literature on this theme that flourished for more than two millennia have been all but lost sight of.

Legendary Chinese history provides a list of rulers stretching back almost five thousand years. To this mythical dawn belong several cultural heroes—the inventors of civilization. One of these, the fabled Yellow Emperor, a central figure in Taoist religion, was traditionally credited with inventing the magnet and the wheel, as well as the study of history and astronomy—all this in a mere century (2697?–2597? BCE). He also set a precedent for Chinese sexual behavior that was hardly puritanical: tradition assigned to him a Solomonic quota of wives and concubines. The eminent bibliographer Ji Yun, in his popular *Notes from the "Yue-wei" Hermitage* (1800), provides us with another intriguing detail: the Yellow Emperor was also the first, he tells us, to take male bedmates.[2]

Chinese history before the eighth century BCE, though copious, is largely unverifiable. Only in the period of the *Spring and Autumn Annals* (722–481 BCE) and the subsequent age of the Warring States (403–221 BCE) do we touch solid ground with consistently trustworthy sources. With the Han dynasty (206 BCE–220 CE) these become full and precise, historiographers being by then honored professionals appointed and salaried by the state. To each of these eras belongs a famous anecdote concerning the male lover of a ruler. Eventually, these stories became so well known as touchstones for male romance in a courtly setting that they may be called the three canonical anecdotes. These were respectively the stories of the shared peach, of Long Yang and the fish, and of the cut sleeve.

The first anecdote concerns the infatuation of the ruler of the north-central state of Wei, a contemporary of Confucius and the Athenian tyrannicides, who reigned from 534 to 493 BCE. Duke Ling loved a court official, Mizi Xia, who one day gave him half of a delicious peach he had tasted. "How sincere is your love for me!" Duke Ling exclaimed. "You forget your own appetite and think only of giving me good things to eat!" When Mizi Xia borrowed the ruler's carriage to visit his sick mother, the duke praised him for his filial piety, though such *lèse majesté* would ordinarily have cost a subject his feet.[3]

The second anecdote tells of another ruler of Wei, this time a king of the third century BCE, whose lover, the Lord Long Yang, burst into tears while the two men were fishing. The king asked the reason for his distress. Long Yang explained that he had been impressed by the first fish he caught, but when he caught a bigger one he wanted to throw it back: so, he feared, might the king prefer someone else to him. To reassure him the king issued an edict: "Whoever shall dare to speak of beauties in my presence will have his whole clan extirpated."[4]

The third and most famous story involved not a duke or a king but an emperor, the young Emperor Ai of the Han dynasty who ruled from 6 BCE to 1 CE. According to the Han historian Ban Gu, the emperor once sought to rise when his lover Dong Xian had fallen asleep on the sleeve of his robe. Rather than disturb him, he cut off his sleeve and appeared in public in this mutilated state. Thereafter, reputedly, his courtiers adopted similar abbreviations of clothing to celebrate the love affair.[5]

These three stories are repeatedly invoked in Chinese literary and historical works. Indeed, they became proverbial, so that for two thousand years homosexual love was regularly referred to as the "love of shared peach" or the "cut sleeve," and a favored lover as a "Long Yang." An important anthology of stories and anecdotes published in late imperial days was titled simply *Duan xiu pian (Records of the Cut Sleeve).*[6]

Clearly, these normative tales, if we may so call them, show an unselfconscious acceptance of same-sex relations, an acceptance that was to persist in China for twenty-four centuries. They contrast strikingly with the myth that dominated the imagination of Western Christendom—the story of Sodom with its supernatural terrors. But they are also quite distinct from the traditions of ancient Greece. Instead of legends of heroic self-sacrifice in a warrior society, we have piquant tales of delicate consideration and tenderness. Love for the Chinese was rarely the inspiration it was for the Greeks, the Arabs, and the troubadours. Rather than being ennobling experiences, male love affairs in ancient China were elegant diversions, suffused with poetic sentiment.

This was in keeping with Chinese cultural biases. Unlike the classical and feudal West and medieval Japan, China exalted not the warrior but the scholar—the man of letters, refinement, and taste. It was the literati who, under the Confucian ethos and the imperial examination system, held positions of authority. In this society, moderation and good manners counted for much. In another revealing anecdote from the *Spring and Autumn Annals,* Duke Jing of Qi, a fiefdom in northeastern China, was outraged to discover that an attendant was in love with him and ordered him killed. But an adviser warned him that to rebuff a lover rudely, even one of low degree, was uncouth and inauspicious. The duke, persuaded, elected to promote the man instead of punishing him.[7] Homoerotic desire was perceived as something to be regulated by thoughtful discretion, not force or indignation.

It is of some interest that these stories do not come down to us in books on love or in prose or verse romances but in collections of political writings full of hard-headed advice about the governing of states. The Chinese were acutely aware that romance plays a fleeting role in human affairs. Han Fei Zi, who wrote about 240 BCE, recorded the shared peach episode in an acerbic treatise that has been compared to Machiavelli's *The Prince.* The moral of the story is not the power of love but the fickleness of the mighty, and the advisability of rulers' acts being determined by laws and not by personal attachments. When Mizi Xia grew older and lost his beauty, Han Fei Zi tells us,

34. Scholars of the Northern Qi dynasty. Silk handscroll, eleventh century.

the duke of Wei turned against him. The duke must have been a bit of a humorist, for he excused himself with the cynical remark: "After all, he once stole my carriage, and another time he gave me a half-eaten peach to eat!"[8]

The traditional commentary on the story of Long Yang unromantically doubts the efficacy of the king's edict banning rival beauties.[9] As for the love of the Emperor Ai for Dong Xian, the latter's fate was more tragic still. Though the emperor was faithful to his lover to the end, the court was scandalized by his proposal to alienate the succession in his favor. When the sickly Ai died at an early age, Dong Xian was forced to commit suicide. But the fate of court favorites in imperial China was often dismal. Subject both to the whim of the ruler and to envious intrigues, favorites who survived their protectors, were all too likely to be deprived of their fortunes or their lives by hostile relatives or officials.

This had nothing to do with homosexuality. Wives, concubines, and ministers were subject to the same mischances. Happy endings to romances were more common at a humbler level of society. For instance, a story dating from the era of the Warring States tells of Pan Zhang, a scholar famous for the beauty of his countenance. Attracted by the reports of this unusual comeliness, Wang Zhongxian came to study with him. The two fell in love at first sight, labored together, and slept in conjugal bliss "like man and wife," so that when they died they were buried in one tomb. Then, so the tale goes, a tree sprang out of their common grave. Since its branches intertwined intimately, it was called the "shared pillow tree."[10]

But accounts of the amours of commoners are rare in this period. More typical are books crammed with pithy fables about social policy, like the *Zhanguo ce (Intrigues of the Warring States),* which are nevertheless revealing as to sexual attitudes since they tacitly assume bisexuality as the human norm. Of uncertain date, this substantial collection was first edited from fragmentary manuscripts at the beginning of the first century CE. It tells how Duke Xian of Jin conquered Guo by sending its ruler a beautiful concubine to nullify the influence of a wise advisor, and adds this revealing sequel about a boy who performed the same service: "Next Duke Xian wished to attack Yu but feared the presence of Gong Zhiqi. Xun Xi said, 'The *Book of Zhou* says, "A beautiful lad can ruin an older head." Send the king a comely lad whom you have instructed to ruin Gong Zhiqi. The latter's admonitions will go unheeded and he will flee.' Having done this, Duke Xian attacked Yu and took it."[11]

Han Fei Zi also showed himself aware of such dangers in his advice to potentates. He was no ascetic: "In dealing with those who share his bed," he writes "the enlightened ruler may enjoy their beauty."[12] Yet he lists "making use of bedfellows" to influence a ruler as one of the "eight villainies" without prejudice to gender. "The ruler," he warns, "is easily beguiled by lovely women and charming boys, by all those who can fawn and play at love."[13] But if policy was threatened by love, love at a royal court had itself to be politic. The *Intrigues of the Warring States* recounts a famous incident at the court of a king of Chu who ruled in central China from 369 to 340 BCE. The beautiful An Ling was warned that the king's regard for him was superficial and that he must make his position more secure. He bided his time and then, at the appropriate moment, proposed to be buried with his master as "a shield against the ants." The gambit succeeded: the king, touched, conferred a nobleman's estate on the young man.[14]

• The Han Emperors •

The disunity of the Warring States ended in 221 BCE with the conquests of the formidable First Emperor, whose eastern kingdom of Qin (Chin) provided the West with a name for the newly united country. A brilliant administrator who created the fundamental institutions of the Chinese state and built the Great Wall, the emperor was also a harsh tyrant. The Qin dynasty lasted only a few years and was succeeded by the more humane Han emperors, who mitigated the laws, redistributed land, and revived traditional learning, finding the doctrines of Confucius to be especially to their purpose. Under the Han, whose rule coincided almost exactly with the zenith of the Roman Empire, China expanded its borders and influence so that later patriots came to see it as a kind of golden age. It is also an age particularly rich in accounts of bisexual rulers. Indeed, the first ten Han emperors had male lovers whose careers are well documented by contemporary historians.[15]

We find the most vivid picture of life at the early Han court in the *Records* of Sima Qian. Known to the Chinese as the Grand Historian, Sima Qian has been compared to Tacitus, whose work he anticipated by two centuries, though he lacks the Roman's concentrated scorn. Sima's celebrated history mixes annals and biographies, including the lives of emperors, statesmen, noble families, Confucian scholars, famous generals, and wandering knights. It is significant that along with these luminaries he allots space also to "Biographies of the Emperor's Male Favorites," that is, their lovers. Sima introduces his sketches with this revealing summary: "Those who served the ruler and succeeded in delighting his ears and eyes, those who caught their lord's fancy and won his favor and intimacy, did so not only through the power of lust and love; each had certain abilities in which he excelled. Thus I made 'The Biographies of the Emperor's Male Favorites.'"[16]

After this preamble we might expect a panegyric on male love in the Greek style. But Sima's account is free from romance and cynicism alike, a cool reckoning of these men as individuals and their influence on imperial affairs. Sketching the careers of a dozen lovers of the Han emperors up to the time of the powerful Emperor Wu (r. 140–87 BCE) at whose court he served, Sima tells of famous generals (who elsewhere merit chapters of their own), distinguished musicians or astrologers, and men who were simply "worthy and affectionate" companions to royalty. Others, he admits, were nonentities who owed their positions of power merely to their good looks or some whimsical chance, as in the case of the Emperor Wen (r. 179–159), who made a palace boatman his intimate and an enormously wealthy man because of a fantastic dream. But the tone of his chapter and the unspoken premise on which it rests are instructive. The Grand Historian does not, like Suetonius, treat these affairs as damaging gossip that reflects negatively on the characters of his subjects, nor does he, in the style of Plutarch, treat them as honorific. They are simply natural phenomena. "It is not women alone," he writes, "who can use their looks to attract the eyes of the ruler; courtiers and eunuchs can play at that game as well. Many were the men of ancient times who gained favor in this way."[17] There is no intimation that such affairs are either good or bad: the men are to be judged simply on their merits.

Sima Qian died in 90 BCE. His history is accordingly limited to the first five Han emperors. The founding emperor, Gaozu, the son of a peasant, had led a revolt and established the regime which mitigated the severities of the Qin period. He was, however, blunt and coarse in his manners and had on one occasion seized the cap of a scholar and urinated in it to show his contempt for learning. Gaozu had a trusted personal servant, Jiru, whom he called his "pillow" companion, who had more access to him than his frustrated officials. Despite his crudities, Sima tells us, Gaozu had been won over by the charms of this elegant young man. His son and successor, the Emperor Hui, had a similar youthful favorite named Hong Yu. To gain the attention of the emperors, the courtiers all imitated the young men's colorful dress and make-up, "transforming themselves," as Sima puts it, "into a veritable host of Jirus and Hongs."[18]

The Emperor Wu ascended the throne as a young boy, but he soon imposed his powerful will by extending the bounds of his empire and increasing the magnificence of his capital. His reign of fifty-three years brought China to the peak of its powers, so that it reached the eastern borders of the Parthian kingdom in ancient Persia just as the Romans reached its western edge. But like Louis XIV, to whom he has often been compared, Wu brought economic ruin through his military and architectural extravagance. The emperor was also a great lover of women whose love affairs are celebrated in popular Chinese drama. But despite these amours and his sizable harem of wives and concubines, his attachments to other men seem to have been even stronger than his predecessors'.

Three loves are especially notable. He had grown up with Han Yan, a spirited young man and an accomplished warrior who was raised to high rank after he defeated the Huns. His eminence, however, aroused the envy of the emperor's younger brother, who complained to their mother, the dowager empress. When this strong-minded woman learned that Yan was engaged in an intrigue with an imperial concubine, she sent a message ordering him to commit suicide. Such was the power of filial piety in ancient China that, though the emperor tried to intercede for his lover, he had ultimately to accede to her will. Yan was forced to kill himself.[19]

The emperor's next lover was of much humbler origins. Li Yannian had been castrated for some minor crime and made a kennel keeper at the palace. The emperor had first been attracted to his sister, whom he installed in the women's quarters in the palace, but then found the brother even more to his liking. Li was elevated to the position of court musician and composer of ceremonial hymns, a position in which he distinguished himself. For a long time he was at the emperor's side day and night, as Han Yan had been. Later, the arrogant behavior of a younger brother caused Li to fall out of favor and both men were executed.

The emperor's last great male love affair ended more fortunately. Wei Zifu and her brother Wei Qing were slaves in the household of the emperor's sister. The emperor first became enamoured of the singing of Wei Zifu, whom he married and made his empress. In a bizarre repetition of his former affair, he then fell in love with her handsome brother, whom he made a general. So successful, indeed, were Wei Qing and his nephew against northern invaders that they became known as the Great Generals. When Wu's sister's husband died, he married her to Wei, making the two men brothers-in-law twice over. They remained close throughout the rest of their lives and by the emperor's orders were buried together.[20]

The next four Han emperors also had male lovers, but it was their successor, the Emperor Ai, who represents the culmination of this tradition. The idea of a homosexual identity was rare in China, where marriage was a sacred duty. Indeed, Chinese lacked any term for homosexuality as a condition. In early histories the male bedmates of rulers were described merely as men who received *chong* or favor (which might equally be bestowed on women) or, in Han texts, as *ning xing,* those who obtained love or favor *(xing)* through artful flattery *(ning).*[21] Ai, however, was characterized by Ban Gu (d. 92 CE) in his *History of the Former Han Dynasty* as one who "by nature . . . did not care for women."[22] The lover for whom he sacrificed a sleeve was a married man with children. Raised to the highest honors at twenty-two, the affable Dong Xian was regarded by Ai's ministers as quite unfit to rule. Consequently Ai's plan to make him his heir misfired, and after Dong's forced suicide a usurper seized power.[23]

Taoism, Confucianism, Buddhism

In the West, opposition to homosexuality has most often come from religion. In China, religious attitudes toward sexuality in general and homosexuality in particular have been markedly different. For Taoism, the oldest of China's faiths, asceticism was not an ideal. Taoism found its classical expression in the *Tao-Te-Ching,* the *Book of the Way and Virtue,* ascribed to Lao-tse. Preaching a life of simplicity free from striving after power and wealth, it developed a metaphysical cosmology whose theories had a marked sexual aspect. For Taoists, the universe was pervaded by two complementary vital forces: *yang,* associated with the heavens, heat, fire, activity, and masculinity; and *yin,* associated with the earth, cold, water, passivity, and femininity. The fundamental sexual problem was to keep these two elements in proper balance. A man had to avoid losing too much of his *yang* essence in sexual intercourse while absorbing *yin* from the woman, who was supposed to possess this in an inexhaustible abundance.

A male adept could improve his health and longevity by practicing *coitus reservatus,* that is, bringing women to orgasm without losing his own semen, which was conceived as then strengthening his own vital centers. Self-indulgence with loss of sperm was highly dangerous; so was celibacy, which was disapproved. On the other hand, the Yellow Emperor, whose conduct in sexual matters was regarded as exemplary, was supposed to have attained immortality by having intercourse in the correct style with 1,200 women. For the devout Chinese, sexuality was not an activity hedged about by taboos or divine prohibitions but a challenge to achieve well-being by a proper management of what we might call physiological economy. In this scheme, male homosexuality, as elsewhere in Chinese culture, occupied a neutral position. Van Gulik has suggested that when two men engaged in such behavior they were seen merely as exchanging yang essence; hence, nothing was lost or gained.[24] Lesbianism, in turn, was looked on indulgently as a sexual outlet for women who might be favored only infrequently by the male heads of large households; on occasion, as we shall see, it could be the subject of romance.

In the course of time, it was not Taoism but Confucianism that came to prevail as the official public morality of the Chinese state. Unlike Taoism, which counseled withdrawal from society with its strife and competition, Confucianism encouraged the performance of social duties, decried superstition, and sought to promote domestic and political harmony through the force of moral examples, kindness, and consideration. But in some ways it was more conservative than Taoism. Since Confucianism placed strong emphasis on subordination, showing respect for parents, teachers, and superiors in the social hierarchy was of crucial importance. Where Taoism had granted some status to women and allowed them a degree of freedom, Confucianism favored seclusion and strict submission to husbands. Confucius, like Pericles, thought the best woman was the invisible woman.

Though Confucianism was not antisexual—Confucius had declared that sex was as natural as eating—it promoted public reticence and outward propriety. Because order and reverence for authority were central to Confucian thought, it is not surprising that the emperors employed Confucian scholars in administrative posts and founded schools to train men for the examinations in the classics which were the entree to high office. But we are perhaps not surprised to learn that in their private lives they sought immortality as devout Taoists.

Confucianism seems to have been little concerned with sexual relationship between men. Though it promoted marriage, its insistence on the seclusion of women and their inferiority, the high value it placed on male friendship, and the closeness of the master-disciple bond it fostered may have subtly facilitated homosexuality. Detailed discussion of sexual matters in Confucian works is rare, however. One of the few literary documents that does touch on it directly is a "Table of Merits and Demerits" which Van Gulik thinks is of Confucian origin, though it appears in a collection of Taoist writings. One gains some idea of Confucian values by noting the acts it proscribes and their gradations. Offending one's parents or ancestors, murder, and rape earn a thousand demerits, slandering a virtuous woman or showing preference for one wife over another earns five hundred, and "sporting with a concubine or catamite," fifty.[25]

Buddhism did not spread widely in China until the first century of the

Common Era. It reached its greatest influence some seven hundred years later in Tang imperial circles and was then for a time officially discouraged. Confucian intellectuals deemed it superstitious, demoralizingly pessimistic, and too concerned with personal salvation instead of social duties. In addition, the celibacy of Buddhist monks and nuns was frowned on by the family-oriented Chinese, who thought regular intercourse was desirable for health and sanity and regarded pretensions to abstinence as hypocritical. In popular stories Buddhist nuns were often secret seductresses or lesbians. As with Confucianism, modern scholars have found few references to homosexuality in Buddhist texts. Wolfram Eberhard, in his *Guilt and Sin in Traditional China,* has identified a sixth-century text of Indian origin in which homosexuality is punished in the third hell, adultery in the fifth, and incest in the seventh. A nineteenth-century work, the *Yu-li,* of uncertain authorship and provenance, makes it a more serious sin, consigning it to the eighth of nine hells.[26] These religious handbooks seem to have been popular with the uneducated but were scorned and ignored by the literati.

• Poets and Lovers •

After the death of the last Han ruler in 220, China fell into disunity and was ruled by a confusing welter of minor dynasties until the Tang period (618–907). The political chaos resembled Europe's after the fall of Rome, with the important difference that cultural life flourished without interruption. As Confucian influence waned, the pursuit of pleasure and beauty engaged men's attention. Fantastic styles of dress appeared, mixing male and female fashions. Women wore men's clothes; men affected cosmetics and apparel that was feminine or frankly transvestite: some men are reported to have appeared in their wives' clothes, to public applause.[27] In the West, by contrast, the Bible forbade cross-dressing (Deut. 22:5), penitentials made it a sin, and the Code of Justinian declared it a crime.[28]

Shortly after the fall of the Han, a group of bohemian tipplers and talkers formed a club called the Seven Sages of the Bamboo Grove, famous in Chinese literary history as a symbol of a nonconforming freedom, a kind of third-century hippie community. They met on the country estate of one of their most celebrated members, Xi Kang (223–262), a rebellious and outspoken poet and musician who enjoyed intellectual debate. Another member was Ruan Ji (210–263), perhaps the greatest poet of his day and a free-living Taoist mystic who had a reputation for drink and eccentric behavior. Chinese history is replete with accounts of fervent literary friendships. How many were homosexual it is difficult to say, but in the case of Xi Kang and Ruan Ji (whose friendship was described as "stronger than metal and fragrant as orchids") a curious story attests to the fact: we are told that the wife of another "sage," overcome with curiosity, spied on their intimacy and was impressed by their sexual prowess.[29] One of Ruan Ji's "Poems from My Heart" celebrates male love with characteristic imagery, anachronistically pairing An Ling (of the tomb anecdote) and Long Yang (of the fishing expedition) as lovers, though in fact a century separated their lives.[30]

Ruan Ji's poem was anthologized in a collection of love poems called *New Songs from a Jade Terrace,* presumed to have been compiled by the court poet Xu Ling about 545. This anthology mixed poems in the elegant and ornate new court style of the Liang dynasty (502–556) with simpler folk songs from earlier centuries. One anonymous poem, "The Song of the Yue Boatman," on the theme of a peasant's love for his lord, dates back to Han times:

Tonight, what sort of night?
  I tug my boat midstream.
Today, what sort of day?
  I share my boat with my lord.
Though ashamed, I am loved.
  Don't think of slander or disgrace! . . .
My heart delights in my lord, though he will never know.[31]

Xu Ling's patron was a distinguished poet in his own right, the second Liang emperor Jianwen, who died in 551 after a short reign. His dynasty perished soon after but not for lack of heirs: history, somewhat hazy in its enumeration, gives him "at least" thirty-one children. Among the poems by the emperor in the anthology is a sophisticated poem in the allusive courtly style on a favored boy:

Charming boy—You look so handsome!
You surpass Dong Xian and Mizi Xia.
Our feather curtains are filled with morning fragrance,
Our curtained bed is inlaid with ivory . . .
Your face is more beautiful than rosy red dawn clouds . . .
You're enough to make the girls of Yan envious,
And cause even Zheng women to sigh.[32]

The Buddhist emperor's poem appeared in Xu's anthology just a few years after Justinian's "earthquake" novella of 538 condemned homosexuals to castration and death.

• From Tang to Song •

With the emergence of the Tang dynasty in 618 China regained its unity and grew in wealth and power. The Tang capital, Xian (Chang'an), was the world's most splendid city, outshining its European rivals, Constantinople and Córdoba. Poetry reached new heights in the work of Li Po, Tu Fu, and Po Chu (now known in pinyin as Li Bo, Du Fu, and Bo Juyi). Sculpture and ceramics flourished, later to fill the West's museums with willowy ladies and majestic horses. But official biographies of the Tang emperors are more reticent on the subject of male favorites than those of earlier dynasties, perhaps because the new meritocratic bureaucracy reduced their political importance.

One unique document has, however, come down to us from the Tang age. Chinese science was as much concerned with sex as Chinese history and biography. The official *History of the Former Han Dynasty* (206 BCE–1 CE) lists half a dozen sexological titles in its medical bibliography, under the heading "The Art of the Bedchamber." We know them only by quotations in a Japanese medical text of the tenth century.[33] These fragments make no mention of homosexuality, but a single treatise in this genre, which has survived in the original Chinese, does touch on the subject. This is the *Da-le-fu* by Bo Xingjian (775–826), the younger brother of the poet Bo Juyi and himself an important dignitary in the imperial office of foreign affairs.

The title, in its complete form, can be translated as *Poetical Essay on the Supreme Joy of the Sexual Union of Yin and Yang and Heaven and Earth.* The term "poetical" in the title may surprise a Westerner, used to sexological treatises whose diction is antiseptically scientific, but the Chinese delighted in elegant euphemisms for erotic details. The penis, for instance, is regularly the "jade stalk," the vulva the "precious gateway," the clitoris the "jewel terrace," and so on. Dozens of sexual techniques have similar imaginative designations. Ordinary intercourse is most commonly the "play of the clouds and the rain." Adding humor to their poetry, the Chinese denominated male unions as "upside-down clouds." Bo Xingjian devotes a whole chapter (14) to this topic in a book that circulated freely among Chinese intellectuals, discussing the psychology of homoeroticism and recounting celebrated love affairs, especially those of the Han emperors.[34] Folktales and short stories of the Tang period also occasionally touch on the theme.[35]

The account of male favorites in the official history of the Song dynasty (960–1279) is much abbreviated and, indeed, the last of its kind. Though harassed by foreign armies and weak militarily, the Song made impressive material and cultural advances. The government promoted art, and Song landscapes rank as the zenith of Chinese painting. Moreover, China was at this time technologically more advanced than Europe. Commerce developed, printing reduced illiteracy, paper currency was introduced, and the invention of the compass helped trade abroad. Cities grew in size, and with this new urbanization prostitution began to flourish. Tao Gu noted in his *Records of the Extraordinary:* "Everywhere people single out Nanhai for its 'Misty Moon Workshops,' a term referring to the custom of esteeming lewdness. Nowadays in the capital those who sell themselves number more than ten thousand. As to the men who offer their own bodies for sale, they enter and leave places shamelessly."[36] In reaction to this proliferation of commercialized sex, a law was enacted during the Zhenghe reign (1111–1118) which punished male prostitutes with "one hundred strokes of a bamboo rod and a fine of fifty thousand cash." It seems to have soon fallen into disuse, however, for a century and a half later it was not enforced even in the most flagrant cases.[37]

• Ming China: The West Reacts •

The Ming dynasty came to power in 1368 when a Chinese general of peasant stock overthrew the Mongols whose rule, beginning auspiciously with the brilliant Kublai Khan, had lasted less than a century. The first Ming emperor was a capable and energetic leader, but he was also tyrannical and paranoid, and early Ming China enjoyed less freedom than under the Song. Eventually the dynasty decayed, as palace eunuchs replaced Confucian scholars as the major power at court. But art, ceramics, architecture, literature, and philosophy flourished spectacularly, as if to match the Renaissance then in full flood in Europe. One of the best informed commentators on Ming manners was a contemporary of Shakespeare, Xie Zhaozhe (1567–1624), a widely traveled scholar, official, and judge who described the customs of various regions in his encyclopedia, the *Wu za zu* or *Fivefold Miscellany.* "In today's Peking," he wrote "there are young boy singers who go to all the gentry's wine parties, and no matter how many official prohibitions there are, everyone uses them . . . As soon as one man had them, then the custom spread, and now every single gentleman uses all his energies to obtain them, it's as if the whole country had gone crazy. This has really come to be absurd."[38] Whereas homosexuality had earlier been regarded as especially common in southeast China, this was no longer the case. Half the male prostitutes in Peking, Xie informs us, now come from the more northerly coastal province of Shandong.

Court and commoners were both involved. After Song times, dynastic histories commissioned by the state no longer described the emperors' male love affairs, but unofficial records of the lives of the Ming rulers were quite explicit. The Emperor Wuzong came to the throne at thirteen and died in 1521 at twenty-nine. A revealing account of his male love affairs is given by the historian Mao Qiling (1623–1716). Appointed by the Manchus to write the official history of the emperor's reign, Mao, like Procopius, supplemented it with a second, more candid biography, the *Wuzong wai-ji.*

An energetic and restless young man who delighted more in archery, riding, hunting, and performing music than in state business, Wuzong devoted his time to travel and entertainment. According to court etiquette, the emperor distributed his favors among his numerous wives and concubines by an elaborate rotational system based on rank and precedence. But Wuzong spent only a few nights a month in the royal seraglio and retired the official whose duty it was to record dates and names on these occasions.[39] Instead, he passed his time in the all-male society of his new Leopard House, which accommodated his generals and other military men—against precedent, sleeping and even dying there. Among his early favorites was a Muslim eunuch, Sayyid Husain, who slept with him and controlled access. When General Jiang Bin gained fame by suppressing a rebellion, he bribed Sayyid to introduce him to the emperor. Wuzong, who had a passion for military uniforms and maneuvers, was impressed by Jiang's courage and powerful physique. At military reviews they wore identical dress and looked more like twins than emperor and subject. According to Ming records, the men *tong wo-qi* (slept and rose together).[40] Like many earlier favorites, Jiang used his privileged position to enrich himself. A few days after Wuzong died, his successor's ministers had Jiang executed and his treasure confiscated.[41]

The sixteenth Ming emperor, Xizong, who died at twenty-one in 1627, was more orthodox and divided his attentions between two separate palaces, one for his male, one for his female lovers. As deaf to Confucian lectures as Wuzong, he was a man of simple tastes who devoted himself to making fine furniture in his workshop, where he "forgot cold or heat, hunger or thirst."[42] In this case there seems to have been some rivalry between his male and female bedmates. When a concubine warned an influential male favorite that Mizi Xia (of the shared peach) had contributed to the downfall of the kingdom of Wei, the favorite cited the fate of an emperor led to ruin by a female lover.[43]

But homosexuality was not limited to emperors, generals, and courtiers. According to one Ming commentator, such relations were sometimes incorporated into the traditional Confucian family order. Shen Defu (1578–1642) tells how, in the southern province of Fujian, male couples often lived together in a type of same-sex marriage:

> The Fujianese men are extremely fond of male beauty. No matter how rich or poor, handsome or ugly, they all find a companion of their own status. Between the two the older is called the "bond [adoptive] elder brother" *(qixiong),* the younger "bond younger brother" *(qidi).* When this elder bother goes to the house of the younger brother, the parents of the latter take care of him and love him like a son-in-law. And the younger brother's expenses, including those of his marriage are all covered by the elder brother. They love each other and at the age of thirty are still sleeping in the same bed together like husband and wife.[44]

Though such unions sometimes lasted for twenty years, it was still necessary for the men to marry, fulfill their Confucian familial duties, and maintain the cult of ancestor worship. "In all history," a man asks another in one tale of male love, "has there ever been a precedent for two men to live out their lives together?"[45] Nevertheless, Shen Defu was impressed by the devotion such couples often showed. "Such passion can be so deep that it is not un-

35. The destruction of Sodom. Chinese woodcut illustration commissioned by Matteo Ricci for *The Ink Garden of Mr. Cheng,* 1609.

common that two lovers, finding it impossible to continue their relationship, tie themselves up together and drown themselves."[46] These Fujianese pairings were often called *nanfeng* (the southern custom), punning on the word *nan,* which could mean either "male" or "south."

Under the Ming dynasty China developed its first important contacts with the West, and two proud civilizations learned about each other with amazement, admiration, and disgust. In 1557 Portuguese traders established a settlement at Macao, and Western missionaries made their first systematic efforts to proselytize China. These Catholic missionaries, chiefly Spanish, Italian, and Portuguese Jesuits and Dominicans, came from countries where sodomites were still routinely burned at the stake. Chinese tolerance left them profoundly shocked. To these devout priests, the fires of the Inquisition seemed infinitely preferable to the fires of lust, or even to love or affection in so heterodox a form.

Together with the new science of the Renaissance, European visitors brought European superstitions: the Dominican Gaspar da Cruz, in a book published in 1569, ascribed the earthquakes that had shaken China twelve years earlier to Chinese indifference to sodomy.[47] The most famous scientific missionary to China, the distinguished Jesuit astronomer and mathematician Matteo Ricci, shared his compatriots' concern for such derelictions almost to the point of obsession. A few weeks after his arrival in 1583 he wrote to his superior lamenting "the horrible sin to which everyone here is much given, and about which there seems to be no shame or impediment."[48] When he translated the Ten Commandments into Chinese a year later, Ricci had no compunction about revising Exodus. "Thou shall not commit adultery" became "Thou shalt not do depraved, unnatural, or filthy things."[49] On being asked in 1606 to contribute samples of Western art to a Chinese book on calligraphy, he chose three works illustrating the life of Christ, but the fourth depicted the destruction of Sodom, with Ricci's comment: "Depraved sensuality and vileness bring on themselves the heavenly fire."[50] Shortly before his death in 1610 he lamented once more that unnatural lust was "neither forbidden by law, nor thought to be illicit, nor even a cause of shame. It is spoken of in public, and practiced everywhere, without there being anyone to prevent it."[51]

When East and West met in lands under Spanish dominion, the results could be tragic. In 1598 an attorney-general in Manila wrote to Philip II that sodomy was rife among Chinese traders in the Philippines: "An investigation was carried out. Fourteen or fifteen culprits were caught. The Chinese, however, defended themselves by saying the practice was quite common among men in China. Despite their excuses two of them were condemned to die at the stake, the others were flogged and condemned to the galleys. Notices in Chinese were put up in the Chinese quarters warning against this great offence under pain of capital punishment and confiscation of property."[52] In 1617 the Ming geographer Zhang Xie took note of these burnings "on a pile of firewood" in his *Study of the Eastern and Western Oceans.*[53] To the Chinese, such drastic measures must have seemed a sign of Western barbarism.

• Feng Menglong's *Anatomy of Love* •

If one wished to contrast Chinese with European attitudes toward homosexuality in Ming times, one could do no better than to turn to a book that is both an anthology and a treatise—the *Qing shi* or *Anatomy of Love,* probably compiled during the years 1629 to 1632. This is a collection, mainly in classical Chinese, of more than 850 tales and anecdotes on the theme of love reaching back to the earliest times. We must note that the term *qing* in this context means more than "love," having a broader sense of "emotion" or "feeling," and even takes on a cosmological connotation, as in the idealistic preface to the book by Feng Menglong.

Feng Menglong (1574–1646) was the most celebrated writer and editor of fiction of his time. Opposed to mere belletrism, he held that literature must instruct readers by appealing to their emotions. Feng combined a romantic nature with a devotion to social responsibilities; the poet or tale-teller was not an isolated individual defying society but a man committed to public duties. Later in life he served as a model magistrate in rural Fujian, promoting education, repairing temples, and improving medical facilities. He had, he tells us, long planned to collect the best stories of *qing,* ancient and modern, "so that I might make known to men the abiding nature of *qing,* and thereby turn the unfeeling into men of sensitivity, and transform private feeling into public concern . . . The myriad things are like scattered coins: *qing* is the string that binds them together."[54]

The compendium's view of male love is revealed in its structure. Its twenty-four chapters treat love between men and women under such headings as "Chastity," "Conjugal Destiny," "Clandestine Love," "Passion," and so on. Chapter 22 is headed "Qing wai" (the "Other Love") and contains forty anecdotes and stories about the love of males. Eight are pre-Han, another eight from Han times, nine from the age of disunity, one from the Tang dynasty, two from the Five Dynasties (907–960), and, after a 500-year gap, there are a dozen tales from the Ming era. These male love affairs are treated (like those between men and women) as neither good nor bad in themselves but admirable or deplorable, happy or unlucky, as the case may be. Here is the same impartiality we found in the writings of the Grand Historian, Sima Qian, seventeen hundred years earlier.

The chapter on male love, as we would expect, makes room for the canonical stories of Mizi Xia, Long Yang, An Ling, Dong Xian of the cut sleeve, and other court favorites. Some depict loyal devotion, others violence and betrayal. When the king of Liang, a small principality on the border of the Ming Empire, died in war, we are told his lover mourned him, shaved his own head, and became a monk. Another man vowed faith past death to a lover he nursed selflessly through his last illness; when he broke his vow, the spirit of the dead man claimed him and bore him off to the nether regions. In the Ming tales we are struck by the range of social classes involved: students and school inspectors, merchants, a porter, and a common soldier. In one a young scholar named Wan falls in love with a boy he meets at a theater. They are separated, and the boy loses his good looks. Despite this, when they meet again Wan is even more drawn to him, and they become lovers. The rest of the story is quintessentially Chinese:

> The couple remained together several years this way, until Zheng at last reached adulthood. Now Wan was by no means a rich scholar, but Zheng

36. Man and boy attended by ghosts and a pipe-bearer. Painting on fan, eighteenth century.

> was even poorer. So Wan at last decided to arrange a marriage for Zheng. He also partitioned off one-third of his house and assigned it to Zheng, inviting Zheng's parents to come live with them. Whenever Wan went out Zheng would follow him, like a devoted younger brother. Should Wan have to travel afar, Zheng would stay home and manage the household affairs, like a capable servant. If Wan was sick, Zheng would attend him, preparing his medicine, as if he were Wan's own filial son. In Wan's studio was a separate bed, and Zheng would sleep there five nights out of every ten. Neither family found all of this unacceptable, and nobody showed any surprise, the members of the two families knocking at each others gates and ascending to each others' halls, completely forgetting that they were two families.[55]

Some other stories are lurid tragedies. When a tramp murders a boy, his lover, a soldier, takes the blame; but when his friend fails to bring him food in prison, he reveals the truth, and the tramp is executed. Out of remorse, the soldier commits suicide.[56]

In the commentaries on these stories we find a distrust of affairs based on ephemeral beauty, concern that a ruler's favorites may have a bad political influence, and an admiration for relationships that are firmly grounded and withstand adversity. So Feng Menglong, commenting on "The Story of the Young Man Wan," asks, "When it comes to *qing,* are there any, anywhere, like Wan and Zheng? Some say that Zheng was an ordinary person, endowed with no gifts such as Anling and Long Yang" but if he had "been favored only for his beauty . . . how in that case could we speak of *qing*?"[57]

• Fiction and Drama •

The age which saw the first regular European missions was also the age in which vernacular Chinese fiction developed from folktales into sophisticated short stories and novels. Putting a premium upon individualism, spontaneity, and inventiveness, this new literature reflected new philosophical trends which challenged traditional Confucianism. Wang Yangming (1498–1583) had formulated a theory of "innate knowledge" which made morality a matter of the individual conscience, independent of artificial rules. His disciple He Xinyin (1517–1579) argued that desire was an integral part of life and could not be eliminated without suppressing life itself. This new subjectivism led writers of the last decades of the Ming dynasty to treat aspects of Chinese life not incorporated into "official history." Some defied convention by dwelling explicitly on erotic themes. In two classics of this new pornographic genre, *The Golden Lotus* (*Jin ping mei,* c. 1610) and *The Prayer Mat of Flesh (Rou putuan),* both by Li Yu (1611–1680), the protagonists are ardent womanizers, but they are also both involved with eager or complacent male servants in affairs quite as scandalous as their exuberant heterosexual escapades.[58]

Celebrated in his own time, Li Yu has been rediscovered and belatedly recognized as imperial China's most remarkable writer of short stories. He did not lead a conventional life: he lived luxuriously (on modest means) with a large entourage, including a troupe of female actresses and professed, in the troubled days of the Manchu conquest, a philosophy of Epicureanism. His tales, like those of Voltaire, mix irony, farce, bizarre improbabilities, and the mordant exposure of social injustice. Three works by Li Yu on homosexual themes are typically idiosyncratic.

One story, appearing in a collection entitled *Silent Operas* (*Wusheng xi,* c. 1657), bears a title that reads oddly in translation: *A Male Mother Meng Raises Her Son Properly by Moving House Three Times.* (Mother Meng was the mother of the philosopher Mencius and a model of maternal devotion.) Paradoxically, the story is an exemplary same-sex romance which nevertheless condemns such affairs. The "southern mode," Li complains, defies Heaven's design which made the anatomies of men and women complementary. It is sterile and is devoid of mutual pleasure. It might be excused in the case of men too poor to marry, or handsome boys facing starvation, but today "there are family men who are addicted to this mode as well as affluent young fellows who revel in it—and that is impossible to justify."[59] After this warning we might expect a cautionary tale. Instead, we get a romantic tragedy of mutual devotion and self-sacrifice in which we are invited to sympathize with both lovers.

Jifang, a handsome young scholar and misogynist committed "by nature" to the "southern mode," marries out of filial duty, only to have his wife

37. Woman spying on male lovers. Silk painting, Qing dynasty.

die bearing a son. At a temple festival he falls in love with an attractive thirteen-year-old named Ruilang, who returns his love. When he approaches Ruilang's father, Jifang finds that in Fujian the "bride-price" for boys is high: to meet it he must sell his land. The sacrifices Jifang makes for him deepens Ruilang's love "until it reached the very marrow of his bones." When Jifang worries that the boy may eventually leave him for a woman, Ruilang makes a vow: "We two are going to share the bed while we live and the same grave when we die."[60] To assure this union, Ruilang castrates himself and assumes the role of a wife. But others, jealous of the relationship, accuse Jifang of castrating a minor. When Ruilang reveals the truth and is arrested for self-mutilation (an "unfilial" act), Jifang takes his punishment. Dying of the beating, he commends his son to the sixteen-year-old: if the boy succeeds in his examinations, Jifang will feel at peace in the other world. Ruilang then dresses as a woman, assumes a feminine persona, and acts the role of the boy's mother. Like the mother of the philosopher Mencius, "she" moves three times—in this case to protect the handsome youth from distracting male love affairs. In the end, the boy does well in his examinations and wins a distinguished position.

Despite his initial expressions of disapproval, Li Yu teases his readers by Confucianizing the "southern mode," at once confirming and mocking accepted ideals. Just as the Greeks assimilated male homosexuality to the values of a warrior society, Li Yu assimilates the affair to a culture in which filial piety and scholarly achievement are prime virtues. Domesticity replaces the military setting, devotion is tested not on the battlefield but in the household. Li Yu remarks that his tale of Jifang and Ruilang exemplifies the virtues traditionally admired in husbands and wives. "My purpose in telling it," he remarks pertly, "is to make you open your sleepy eyes."[61] Yet he reiterates his initial objection to male love as "an unnatural development by certain ancients who traveled a deviant path." The "southern mode" would be fine if all lovers were as admirable as Ruilang and Jifang, but too often they "waste their essence and ruin their conduct to no purpose whatsoever."[62] Li Yu leaves unresolved the contradiction between the tenor of his romantic tale and his moralizing. Perhaps he feared the new Manchu censors and sought to deflect criticism with a conservative conclusion.

Another collection, *The Twelve Towers (Shier lou),* includes a much grimmer tale. In "The House of Collected Refinements," a handsome young man works in the shop of two connoisseurs who share his favors and to whom he is devoted. There, Quan attracts the attention of a ruthless official who, however, fails to seduce him. But the youth is lured to the home of a wealthy eunuch, who drugs him, has him castrated, and eventually delivers him to the official, whom he is now forced to serve. Eventually Quan exposes his new master's corrupt ways to the emperor and has the satisfaction of seeing him beheaded. Thereafter, he claims his skull and uses it as a urinal.[63] The story reflects abuses of the late Ming period: when men of rank were arrested, their sons were often enslaved and sexually abused by powerful courtiers.

Far more sympathetic in tone is Li Yu's play *Pitying the Perfumed Companion (Lian xiangban),* the most famous treatment of lesbian love in Chinese literature. Li was not only a story-teller; he was also a playwright who wrote dramas for his own troupe of young female singers and actresses. In this drama, supposedly based on an episode in his household, a young wife, Mme Fan, who is seventeen, meets a girl two years younger in a Buddhist convent. They fall desperately in love and take oaths of devotion before the Buddha in the presence of their approving servants. The girl laments that they must be separated and wishes they could be reincarnated as man and wife. In a charming scene they playfully try on a man's robes to see who might better fit the part. Then Mme Fan hits upon a more practical solution: she asks her husband to take the younger woman into the household as a concubine. He agrees, and the play ends happily.[64] Apparently this drama became a standard reference for lesbian devotion, for the artist Shen Fu (1763–c. 1812) makes reference to it in his *Six Chapters from a Floating Life,* a minor classic of Chinese autobiography. In this candid memoir Shen Fu tells how his sensitive and intelligent wife Yun fell in love with a beautiful and charming girl he had met at the house of a courtesan. When Yun proposes that he take her as a concubine, he asks, "Is my charming wife going to imitate the *Pitying the Perfumed Companion?*" "Yes, I am," she replies. But unfortunately Shen Fu is too poor to buy the girl, and she is sold to a wealthier suitor. Yun, we are told, remained devoted to her husband but died of grief.[65]

Li Yu, as we have seen, half accepts and half mocks the "southern mode." He writes (presumably) as an outsider. But was there a literature written by and for devotees of the cut sleeve, that is, by and for a specifically homosexual readership? Giovanni Vitiello has identified three collections of short stories from the late Ming period (c. 1628–1644) which appear to fall into this category. Two—*Forgotten Stories of Longyang (Lonyang yishi)* and *Fragrant Stuff from the Court of Spring (Yichun xiangchi)* exist only in single copies in Japanese libraries. Of the third collection, *Hairpins under His Cap (Bian er chai),* only two copies survive. No doubt this rarity is due to Qing censorship, which tried to suppress erotic fiction of every sort after 1714. One critic denounced all three collections as likely to corrupt readers even if the authors meant them as moral tales.[66]

Such an aim might perhaps be ascribed to an anonymous author of *The Forgotten Stories of Longyang,* twenty stories depicting the world of boy prostitutes, where men obsessed with boyish beauty pursue narcissistic youngsters interested only in money. Here the tone is often ironic or satirical.[67] But the four novellas that make up *Hairpins under His Cap* strike a radically different note. These are moral fables based on a boldly unconventional erotic psychology. In each story, passive partners suffer physical and psychological discomfort. In the end, however, their experiences are presented as exemplary and ennobling. The protagonists of the four tales endure progressively greater degradations, only to rise above them.

In the first story, the "Chronicle of Faithful Love" *(qingzhen)* a boy is seduced by a Hanlin academician he has grown fond of but feels violated and ashamed at having played a woman's part. The older man reassures him: "If we go by the logic of Reason then what we have done today is wrong; but if we use the logic of Love *(qing),* then we are right. For a man may become a woman and a woman may become a man."[68] The boy learns to accept and enjoy the physical side of passivity. Later, when his friend falls into disgrace, he leaves his family and position to follow him into exile. His love has enabled him to add the feminine virtue of *zhen* (fidelity) to the male virtues of the successful scholar-official.

In the final story, the "Chronicle of Marvelous Love" *(qingqi),* a brilliant youth sells himself to a brothel owner for money to save his family from disgrace. After suffering a brutal rape, he is ransomed by a chivalrous married man, who introduces him into his household disguised as a female concubine. When his benefactor is unjustly imprisoned with his family, the boy, disguised as a woman, smuggles his young son out of prison and, posing as a nun, raises him until he achieves distinction in his examinations. For this he is revered in his nunnery as a kind of female saint. Eventually he learns his true identity. As an immortal, he had been born as a woman but had rejected that life as too full of hardships. Reincarnated as a boy, he had been a beautiful transvestite prostitute, a devoted wife and mother, and finally a nun—the whole range of female experience he had tried to avoid. In the end he ascends to heaven with his pupil. Once more we have a Tiresias figure who incorporates virtues proper to both sexes.[69] The author of these remarkable fables remains unknown. He was also responsible for the four novellas published under the title *Fragrant Stuff from the Court of Spring.* These range from a story of redemptive love to a tale of boy-vampires who suffer grim retribution for their heartless exploitation of others.[70]

The acclaimed masterpiece of classical Chinese fiction is *The Dream of the Red Chamber (Honglou meng)* by Cao Xueqin (1715–1763), scion of a wealthy Qing family that fell into poverty. Known also in English as *The Story of a Stone,* its scores of minutely depicted characters provide an unparalleled panorama of the lives of masters, mistresses, and servants in an aristocratic household of the Manchu era. Cao Xueqin introduces homosexual episodes only incidentally, but his treatment is revealing. The pampered young hero Baoyu is surrounded by pretty young women—relatives and maids—with whom he flirts and intrigues. He also has a brief affair with a young actor: for this he is severely punished by his father, but this is because the boy is the favorite of a man of rank who can make trouble for the family. Baoyu's uncouth cousin, who pursues a handsome young man who has acted a girl's part in a play, is beaten up, not for his sexual interest in another male but for his aggressive boorishness.

On one occasion Baoyu comes across a young actress in the family's female troupe who has been caught burning "spirit money" to the dead in the garden. Baoyu befriends the girl and learns her story. She had played the "principal boy" in the company and was mourning the girl who played opposite her. "They became so accustomed to acting the part of lovers on the stage," a servant tells Baoyu, "that gradually it came to seem real to them and Nénuphar began carrying on as if they were really lovers." When her partner died, she had become distracted and cannot even now speak of her. Baoyu,

38. A Buddhist monk received in a wealthy man's house while his young companion is seduced by the owner. Silk painting from a private album, nineteenth century.

we are told, found a "strain in [his] own nature that responded to [this story] with a powerful mixture of emotions: pleasure, sorrow, and an unbounded admiration for the little actress."[71] The synopsis at the head of the chapter takes note of this response: "The cock-bird who mourns his mate is found to be a hen and a true heart is able to sympathize with a strange kind of love." Cao's sensitivity toward love between women stands in a striking contrast to such eighteenth-century European novelists as Diderot and Fielding.

• The Qing Dynasty •

The Dream of the Red Chamber shows us China in the most flourishing days of the Qing or Manchu dynasty. After the Ming regime disintegrated through maladministration, rugged warriors from the north captured Peking in 1644. This defeat by a foreign force prompted a reaction in morals. "Many Chinese conservatives blamed the loss of China to the alien Manchus on the hedonistic tendencies fostered by the Wang Yangming school of Neo-Confucianism. They therefore assigned to themselves the responsibility of re-

39. A male couple with two dogs. Silk painting from a private album, nineteenth century.

storing to China the more puritanical values of orthodox Confucianism, believing that such an effort could redeem China from its troubles."[72] The Manchu conquerors, well versed in Chinese culture, approved this program as a means of restoring order and sought to foster morality by legislation aimed at discouraging fornication and offenses with males *(jijian).*

The second Qing emperor, Kangxi, was a distinguished patron of Chinese scholarship, literature, and art and a formidable and effective ruler. He was also hostile to pederasty and boasted in an autobiographical sketch that he was not waited on by "pretty boys."[73] Kangxi was especially concerned about the purchase of girls and boys for sexual purposes: poor Chinese families often sold youngsters to acting companies or into concubinage or prostitution.[74] In 1679 extensive legislation was drawn up to check these abuses and confirmed in the Qing code of 1740.[75] It decreed the death penalty for the abduction and rape of males and for all relations with boys under twelve. It also penalized consensual relations: "Those who commit buggery *[jijian]* with consenting males shall be punished with the *li* [sub-statute] on military men and civilians who commit fornication, namely by 100 strokes of the heavy bamboo and wearing the cangue for one month."[76] (The cangue was a flat wooden board placed around the neck of an offender.) Since laws against fornication in China go back at least to the Tang code, this new law merely placed homosexual acts on the same legal footing as consenting heterosexual behavior. M. J. Meijer has noted that mixed couples were punished only if caught *in flagrante delicto,* and he conjectures that, by analogy, the same provision held for same-sex offences. There is no rhetorical denunciation of homosexuality as especially reprehensible or "unnatural"; it is simply treated on a par with sex between men and women.

To observers from England, such a mild law seemed startling. In 1898 a British commentator remarked: "It doubtless appears strange that abominable offences should, on the whole, be treated with but ordinary severity: but such offences are regarded as, in fact, less hurtful to the community than ordinary immorality."[77] How often these laws were enforced is unclear. Meijer found sodomitical rapes listed in the extensive published records of convictions but not consensual acts between adults. Vivien Ng has discovered one such conviction in the Qing period, but the case was a highly unusual one.[78]

As the eighteenth century progressed, however, Qing puritanism weakened and traditional Chinese patterns reasserted themselves. Indeed, Kangxi found his own son and heir sexually involved with palace officers, whom he ordered executed.[79] At least four of the eight Manchu rulers who succeeded him had homosexual affairs imputed to them. Kangxi's grandson, the emperor Qianlong (r. 1736–1796), rivaled his contemporaries Frederick the Great and Catherine the Great as an "enlightened despot" but outdid them as a parent by fathering twenty-seven children. But at sixty-five he fell in love with a handsome young courtier named Heshen, to whom he delegated much authority. (One tradition has it that Heshen reminded the emperor of one of his father's concubines whom he had loved in vain twenty years earlier.)[80] Unfortunately, Heshen, though affable and clever, was greedy and corrupt, and the country suffered severely while he enriched himself.

The seventh Qing emperor, Xianfeng, reigned in the troubled period from 1851 to 1861 when famines, the Taiping Rebellion, and European troops ravaged China. He had an affair with a leading *tan* actor of his day, Zhu Lianfeng, who committed suicide after a jealous friend made trouble.[81] Xianfeng's successor, Tongzhi, son of the notorious dowager empress, died in his teens. Though happily married, he is reputed to have had a brief romance with a young student.[82] The last emperor, Pu Yi, occupied the throne as a child from 1909 to 1912, became the Japanese puppet emperor in Manchuria in 1935, and ended his days as a "rehabilitated" citizen of the People's Republic working in the gardens of his former palace. He too has been described by his biographer as a devotee of the love of the "shared peach" and the "sheared sleeve."[83]

40. Man with a boy lowering a shade. Silk painting from a private album, nineteenth century.

Throughout the nineteenth-century foreign observers multiplied as European gunboats forced China to open her ports. Their reports on the country revealed the prejudices of their Western homelands. These post-Enlightenment responses, however, were more diverse than the Jesuits' in the seventeenth century. Since English homophobia was then reaching its zenith, we are not surprised to find John Barrow, secretary to the famous but ill-fated Macartney embassy of 1793, expressing himself in this vein in his *Travels in China* a decade later: "In China [the seclusion of women has the] effect of promoting that sort of connexion which, being one of the greatest violations of the laws of nature, ought to be considered among the first of moral crimes—a connexion that sinks the man many degrees below the brute. The commission of this detestable and unnatural act is attended with so little sense of shame, or feelings of delicacy, that many of the first officers of state seemed to make no hesitation in publicly avowing it."[84]

Napoleonic France, on the other hand, had ended executions and abolished criminal penalties for homosexual acts. The informed and dispassionate commentary of Jean-Jacques Matignon, a physician who served the French embassy in Peking in the 1880s, reflects this more enlightened Gallic view:

> Pederasty in China, as it was in Rome, is purely physical and not idealized, but purified by aesthetic sentiment, the love of beautiful forms . . . In China it is almost always a relation with a hireling, a servant or a professional who practices anal coitus for money . . . However, there is good reason to suppose that certain Chinese of intellectual refinement seek in pederasty the satisfaction of both the senses and the spirit . . . The Chinese often has a poetic soul: he loves poetry, music, the elegant phrases of the philosophers, things which one can not find among the fair sex in the Flowery Kingdom. So, if his means permit, he frequents the world of high masculine gallantry where he is sure to find young homosexuals *[pédérés]* . . . with literary knowledge. Public opinion is entirely indifferent to this kind of diversion and morality is not concerned about it: since it pleases the dominant partner and the passive one consents all is well. Chinese law does not like to involve itself with intimate affairs. Pederasty is even considered a matter of good form, an expensive taste and therefore an elegant pleasure.[85]

The only concern Matignon reported hearing in China was that these acts were "bad for the eyes."

• The Peking Stage •

In earlier times, literate Chinese would most often have associated homosexuality with rulers and their favorites, as in the anecdotes from the Warring States and Han dynasty. By the end of the eighteenth century there was another kind of archetypal couple: eminent scholar-officials and popular actors. The golden age of the country's most celebrated theater company, the Peking Opera, extended from the middle of the eighteenth to the middle of the nineteenth century. The major stars of this brilliant world were the men who played women's roles, the so-called *tan* actors. Of all the lovers in this new tradition, the most famous were the scholar Bi Yuan and the actor Li Guiguan.

Bi Yuan (1730–1797) was a scholar, a teacher, a government administrator, and a mentor to younger scholars and poets whom he sponsored, encouraged, and collaborated with. Bi Yuan served first at the Hanlin Academy, the imperial university, then as governor of Shanxi and Henan provinces, winning praise for his work in famine relief and flood control and his success in transporting troops and supplies during several rebellions. But in China, which honored the triumphs of scholarship as highly as victories in the field, his chief renown rested on his historical research on the Song and Yuan dy-

41. Chinese opera performers. German, book illustration, nineteenth century.

nasties and on ancient epigraphy.[86] A sketch of the life of Bi Yuan by Fang Ghao-ying, from which these facts have been gleaned, notes his hospitality to young scholars and hints obliquely at his sexual interests but is silent on his best-known relationship, that with Li Guiguan, who was so closely associated with him that when Bi Yuan made his brilliant success as an examinee they were feted by his friends as a couple.[87] Li, though an actor, was also engaged in scholarly pursuits: together they seem to have realized the ideal described by Matignon.[88]

By far the most successful *tan* actor of the period was Wei Changsheng, who was born about 1744 in Sichuan, dominated the Peking stage in the 1780s, and by his immense popularity made that city the unquestioned theatrical capital of China. Beloved for his magnanimous and sympathetic personality, he became a friend of the emperor's prime minister and favorite Heshen and, as one contemporary put it, "enjoyed from Heshen the favor of the cut sleeve."[89] Yet, popular as actors might be, their official status remained depressingly low, and their relations with officials were sometimes frowned on by the authorities. When a censor met Wei en route to the house of Heshen, he ordered him beaten "like a criminal."[90] As with most *tan* actors, Wei felt duty-bound to fulfill his filial obligations by marrying and rearing a family.

Wei's disciple Chen Yinguan succeeded his master as the foremost interpreter of female roles in his own day. His most celebrated amorous affair was with the scholar Li Caiyuan. Reversing the usual pattern, the youthful Chen paid Li's debts and made it possible for him to take his examinations.[91] The tradition of celebrated *tan* actors continued throughout the next century, when Zhou Xiaofeng and Chen Changchun dominated the stage in the 1820s and 30s and vied for the affections of the scholar Zhu Deshan. Indeed, the relation of Zhu and Zhou Xiaofeng, who won out in the contest, was likened to that of Bi Yuan and Li Guiguan.[92] Even in the turbulent twentieth century *tan* actors continued to enchant the Chinese public. One such performer, the brilliant Mei Lan-fang (1894–1961), toured Europe and the United States in 1930 to great critical acclaim, garnering university doctorates.[93]

The romantic associations of scholars and actors achieved their literary apotheosis in a substantial novel, as yet untranslated, which may be the most ambitious Chinese fiction on the theme. This is the *Pinhua baojian* of Chen Sen, a title which has been translated as *Precious Mirror for Gazing at Flowers* or, more prosaically, as *A Mirror of Theatrical Life* (1849). The novelist and literary historian Lu Xun, who lectured on the *Mirror* at Peking University in the 1920s, compared it, in his *History of Chinese Fiction,* to traditional tales of courtesan life, with their mixture of naturalism and pathos, a literary heritage that can be traced back to the Tang dynasty. Lu notes that at one time scholars had celebrated the passing of their civil service examinations by festivities graced by elegant demi-mondaines. But after 1426, when a reforming emperor forbade such frolics, scholars came to associate with handsome young actors who sang, danced, and were to some degree literate. Chen's novel describes their affairs, juxtaposing explicit sexual details with romance, realism with idealism. Lu was struck by the variety of its characters: "The author apparently believed that some actors were respectable, some disreputable, just as their patrons might be cultured or vulgar."[94] Defenses of male love are rare in Chinese literature, perhaps because it was so common. In Chen's novel, however, Tian Chun-hang delivers an apology in a style Walter Pater or Oscar Wilde might have appreciated:

> Elegant flowers, beautiful women, a shining moon, rare books, grand paintings—these beautiful things are liked by everyone. However, these beautiful things are not all combined. Favorites are like elegant flowers and not grass or trees; they are like beautiful women who do not need make-up; they are like a shining moon or a tender cloud, yet can be touched and played with; they are like rare books and grand paintings, and yet they can talk and converse; they are beautiful and playful yet they are also full of change and surprise . . . I do not comprehend why it is accepted for a man to love a woman, but it is not acceptable for a man to love a man . . . Passion is passion whether for a man or a woman.[95]

The novel tells the story of the love of the actor Du Qinyan for his patron, Mei Ziyu. Mei, who is married, falls ill; Du worries that Mei's wife will prevent him from seeing him. But when he arrives at his lover's home, she is friendly and sends him to Mei's room. Mei, on his deathbed in a semi-delirium, recalls the first days of their love. (The bemused Westerner may note that three years later, in 1852, Parisians were hastening to the theater to weep over Dumas's Lady of the Camelias.) The novel ends—literally—in a blaze of sentiment. The scholars and actors gather in the Nine Fragrances Garden and exchange complimentary poems. The thespians, who have given up the stage, burn their women's clothes and ornaments. The ashes soar to the sky: "Higher and higher they whirled, giving off a heady, intoxicating scent until they became mere dots of gold and vanished."[96]

While sodomites were being anathematized and persecuted in Europe as provokers of divine wrath, China looked upon the phenomenon of same-sex attraction calmly, as an inescapable fact of human existence. China, indeed, provides us with the longest documented period of tolerance in human history—two thousand years extending from 500 BCE to the fall of the Ming dynasty in 1644. And, though homosexuality was officially frowned on by the earlier Manchus, this disapproval seems to have been largely a formal gesture. In Chinese history and literature, until the end of the Imperial age and the triumph of Marxism, men who loved men were depicted as good or bad, sympathetic or self-seeking, honest or dishonest, talented or undistinguished, but not set apart as a race to be humiliated, denounced, or extirpated.

Under Communist rule, however, there has been a radical change. Chinese Communist officials, when queried by foreign visitors, until recently simply denied that homosexuality existed in China, the theory being that under a socialist economy social ills such as prostitution and homosexuality would vanish. As a result, a rich historical tradition has been lost. Though no explicit law forbids homosexuality, men have, in recent decades, been routinely imprisoned under vague charges of "revolting behavior" or "hooliganism."[97]

CHAPTER NINE

ITALY IN THE RENAISSANCE

1321–1609

A New Ethos and an Old

To most people the Renaissance signifies a dramatic rebirth of classical culture, first in Italy and later in the rest of Europe, and a weakening of religious influence on morals, philosophy, and art. One might expect this secularization and the new awareness of the role homosexuality had played in ancient Greece to bring about a new tolerance. To a limited degree this occurred. Scholars translated Plato, Xenophon, Lucian, and Plutarch, and the nature of "Greek love" became more fully understood among an intellectual elite. Artists, too, especially in Italy, were newly inspired by Greek homoerotic myths. Through their paintings, sculpture, poetry, and drama a surprising number of the creative geniuses of the Renaissance responded to these influences, inviting speculation about their own erotic interests. One painter, Sodoma, even wore his preference as a badge.

But this was only half the picture. The Renaissance did not see a lessening of punitiveness; rather, the age fostered new efforts at suppression unprecedented in their scope and virulence. This was true even in those Italian cities where the Renaissance was born. Indeed, it was especially true of them. Moreover, the Renaissance, preeminently a Latin phenomenon, was soon overtaken by the Reformation that convulsed northern Europe. In the end, more men and women fell victim to homophobia in the three centuries from 1400 to 1700 than in the Middle Ages, as Protestants and Catholics competed in enforcing harsh laws. In Spain, a vigorous branch of the Inquisition, organized by Ferdinand and Isabella, actively sought out sodomites, who were burned alongside religious heretics. The result was a paradox. The new intellectual and aesthetic freedom was accompanied by a wave of persecution that harassed and killed far more men and women than any previous age. This newly organized repression, which later spread to Spain and France, first took form in Italy.

• Repression in the Italian City States •

We have seen how the enthusiasm attending the inauguration of the Papal Inquisition in 1233 led to the founding, in cities such as Perugia and Bologna, of religious confraternities that took as their mission the tracking down of sodomites. Michael Goodich has suggested that these organizations, inspired by the new orders of preaching friars, were closely allied with the Guelph, or papal, party in Italy. In cities torn by fierce internal strife, the Guelphs were a middle-class mercantile faction bent on overthrowing aristocratic dominance. Its broad-based campaign for moral reform included "the active pursuit and persecution of heretics in accordance with papal instructions, legislation against usury and conspicuous consumption, and the realization of Christian morality in secular law through statutes against gambling, drinking, prostitution, abortion and sodomy."[1] The movement triumphed in a number of Italian cities in the 1230s; in some, friars took over the civil government, as Savonarola was to do two centuries later in Florence, and the way was clear for the reformers to achieve their aims.

New secular laws invoked the authority of scripture, the church fathers, canon law, and papal edicts. The first municipality known to have adopted the death penalty for sodomy was Bologna in 1259.[2] Bologna was of course a papal fief. Rome itself followed in 1363. So did Cremona (1387), Lodi (1390), and Milan (1476) in Lombardy; Padua (1329) and Bassano (1392) in the province of Venetia; Carpi (1351) and Parma (1494) in Reggio Emilia; and Genoa (1556) in Liguria.[3] Most of these laws prescribed burning for a first offense. A few cities had lesser penalties such as castration or fines. This was notably the case in Tuscany, a region of Italy that seems distinctive in its sodomy legislation. Fines were levied for first offenses in Pisa in 1286 and in Lucca in 1308. Florentine law condemned sodomites to castration in 1325 and later, as we shall see, experimented with many different scales of fines. Siena combined a monetary penalty with torture. A law of 1336 exacted a fine of 300 lire; but if this was not paid within a month, the convict was to be suspended by his "virile members" in the Campo del Mercato "and there remain hanging for an entire day."[4] The city of Treviso, near Venice, also included a peculiarly macabre provision, directed at women as well as men, in its statutes of 1574:

> If any person, leaving the natural use, has sexual relations with another, that is, man with a man, if they be fourteen years old or more, or a woman with a woman if they are twelve or more, by committing the vice of sodomy . . . the detected person, if a male, must be stripped of all his clothes and fastened to a stake in the Street of the Locusts with a nail or rivet driven through his male member, and shall remain there all day and

> all night under a reliable guard, and the following day be burned outside the city.[5]

Women were to be exposed to the same fate, barring the riveting. How often these horrendous laws were enforced in Italy's smaller cities we do not know. Our present knowledge of most jurisdictions remains sketchy, dependent on the chance survival of records and the vagaries of selective research.

• Death in Venice, 1342–1590 •

The exceptions are Venice and Florence. Here, the records are voluminous, and recent scholarship has thrown much light on these cities' attempts to extirpate sodomy. We now know that Florence (the smaller of the two) launched many more prosecutions, but punishment in Venice was far more savage. In each case the most intensive campaigns against sodomy came in the fifteenth and early sixteenth centuries. This is, of course, exactly the moment when the Renaissance produced its most brilliant achievements, as in Venice where the Bellinis, Carpaccio, Giorgione, and Titian flourished and adorned the city with their sumptuous masterpieces. In the fourteenth century the prosecution of sodomites in Venice had fallen under the jurisdiction of the so-called Signori di Notte (Lords of the Night), whose duty it was to deal with nocturnal disturbances and minor crimes of violence. The records of the Signori are fragmentary, but they provide some revealing details. The first known execution for sodomy in Venice took place in 1342, and at least thirteen cases were tried in the next sixty years.[6] Most convicted men suffered the standard fate—they were burned alive. Later this punishment was mitigated. Perhaps Venice's rulers found the screams of the dying unnerving: the place of execution was uncomfortably close to the city's chief administrative offices. At any rate, from 1446 onward the rite was changed, and victims were decapitated before their bodies were consigned to the fire.[7]

Suspects were tortured severely to obtain confessions. A man who withstood prolonged agonies without incriminating himself had some chance of escaping with his life; the man who sought to end his torment by confessing was almost certain to be burned. Some cases stand out in vivid detail. Rolandino Ronchaia was a strikingly effeminate man who made his living as a prostitute, concealing his true sex from his many clients. In 1354 he was convicted by the Signori and ordered to be burned alive between the Columns of Justice on the Piazzetta.[8] This "Little Square" is the open space before the Doge's Palace that connects Saint Mark's Square with the Grand Canal, the civic and ceremonial heart of Venice in the Middle Ages and the Renaissance, today a focus for casual tourism. The medieval Columns of Justice, dramatically visible from the lagoon, stand where they stood six hundred years ago, one surmounted by the winged lion of Saint Mark, the other by Saint Theodore and his crocodile. In all likelihood more homosexuals died on this spot than anywhere else in Europe before Hitler.

Trial records tend, inevitably, to dehumanize the accused, since the legal question was simply what organ entered which orifice. But a prosecution of 1357 allows us to see something of a human relationship behind the documents. A boatman, Nicoleto Marmagna, and his employee, Giovanni Braganza, had begun a love affair in Nicoleto's boat three or four years earlier. Nicoleto then took Giovanni into his family, marrying him to one of his nieces, while continuing the liaison. Under questioning, he tried to protect his lover by maintaining that Giovanni had only acquiesced under threats. But Giovanni admitted his willing participation, and both men were burned alive.[9]

In the fifteenth century Venice reached the height of her wealth and power, with a domain that included northeastern Italy, the Dalmatian coast, parts of Greece, and eventually Crete and Cyprus. In this heyday, Venice was widely admired not only for her external splendor but for the efficiency and stability of her government, which had a reputation for the strict and impartial enforcement of its laws. Most crimes were tried by lesser judicial bodies like the Signori di Notte. There was, however, an all-powerful Council of Ten primarily responsible for the safety of the state. Its preoccupation had originally been with two offenses: treason (a crime against the political integrity of the city) and counterfeiting (a crime against its financial integrity). Later, the council also took over from the Signori di Notte responsibility for punishing a third crime: sodomy. It may seem curious that sodomy should have been a concern of so august a body. This innovation is intelligible only when we grasp one cogent fact: because of religious fears, sodomy was also perceived as a substantial threat to national survival.

One reason for this new development was a sensational case that shook the state in 1407, implicating thirty-three Venetian citizens, no fewer than fifteen of them nobles, and for this reason regarded as too delicate for the Signori to handle. One nobleman, Claro Contarini, belonged to a famous family that had built the Ca' d'Oro on the Grand Canal and had supplied more members to the Council of Ten than any other. Contarini claimed he held minor clerical orders, a status that would have removed him to the jurisdiction of the more lenient ecclesiastical courts. Eventually it was proved that his claim rested on perjured testimony, and Claro was sentenced to be burned alive the next day "in the manner and form as were the other sodomites."[10]

The netting of so large a number of men, the frequent arrest of sizable groups throughout the rest of the century, and frequent references to their favorite meeting places suggests that a significant homosexual subculture existed in Venice.[11] But the most important consequence of the scandal of 1407 was to convince the Council of Ten that the Signori di Notte were not punishing sodomy with sufficient vigor. Complaining that they were not torturing men severely enough to obtain confessions, the council itself took over the prosecutions in 1418, in order to eradicate this vice "so that not only would no one presume to its practice but no one would even dare to mention it."[12] Prosecutions now increased: more than four hundred men were tried for relations with other males in the fifteenth century, and thirty-four for sodomy with women.[13]

What led to this ferocity? Venetian justice, if impartial, was often severe: poisoners and counterfeiters were also burned. But the enforcement of laws against sexual crimes presents an anomaly. If Venice had a reputation for law and order, it was also famous for the sexual opportunities it offered visitors: its courtesans were internationally renowned. The city licensed this activity, and the church accepted it. Augustine had argued that prostitution was a necessary evil that the state should tolerate to protect wives and virgins, and Aquinas had endorsed this view in his *Summa.*[14] Nor did Venetian law punish most other sexual activity harshly. Even when the victim was a female child, rape was typically punished with a few months in prison or at most one or two years.[15]

But homosexuality aroused a different concern. Repeatedly the Council of Ten affirmed that sodomites put the city in jeopardy, since God "destroyed and ruined by his judgment cities and peoples in which [these men] lived."[16] The council feared especially for the Venetian fleet, expressing surprise that, because of the extreme frequency of this sin, "divine justice has not sunk them."[17] In 1458, in a statement that confused biblical chronology, the council declared that God "brought down his wrath upon the cities of Sodom and Gomorrah and soon thereafter flooded and destroyed the whole world for such horrible sins."[18] The Venetians feared that their city would be submerged by the Adriatic, out of whose shallows it had arisen. Guido Ruggiero has concluded that a paranoia similar to "the witch scares that were to sweep Europe shortly afterward appears to have gripped Venetian authorities in the mid fifteenth century."[19]

But if Venice feared a wrathful and vindictive deity, why was this fear paramount at the moment of her greatest material, military, and artistic success? Should not these triumphs have assuaged the city's phobias? Instead, the opposite occurred. Once religious fear had taken over, civic success seemed irrelevant—indeed, the risk may have seemed greater because the society had so much to lose. We may speak of an "imperial anxiety." Any empirical test, such as a suspension of executions to see if they were really necessary, would have seemed too much of a gamble. In Venice the routine of slaughter became a kind of disaster insurance for the hard-headed businessmen and bankers who ruled the city.

Who were the men who suffered? Looking at the death sentences,

Ruggiero has concluded that "those executed represented a good cross-section of Venetian society."[20] Of all occupations, barbers led the list, apparently because the apothecary shops run by barber-surgeons were meeting places for a subculture. Besides the nobles and barbers, Patricia Labalme has also found "tailors, jewelers, fishermen, hatters, glass-makers, sellers of fruits and vegetables and wine, spice sellers, printers, censors, painters, cloth merchants, stone-cutters, a bombardier, a dancing master, a notary, and a government herald" in the records of the accused.[21] In 1406 a sizable reward of 2000 lire ($20,000?) was offered for any denunciation that led to a conviction. In 1455 two nobles were elected in each *contrada* (relatively small municipal areas) to monitor wine shops where "companions of inappropriate ages" were found together.[22] In 1444 schools of music and singing and gymnastics came under suspicion, and later schools of fencing and the abacus. The law ordered captains of the Council of Ten to "comb the city day and night with their associates and secret spies . . . searching for sodomites, for boys who were *patientes,* for companions of unequal age, surveying all shops, schools, porticos, taverns, brothels, and the homes of pastry chefs and prostitutes."[23]

The reference to "boys who were *patientes*" marks a changing attitude toward the culpability of youth in the fifteenth century. Earlier, boys and men who played a passive role had often gone unpunished. But in 1424 the council began to perceive young boys as willing accomplices, for money or affection, and ruled that boys between the ages of ten and fourteen should, if convicted, receive at least three months in jail and twelve to twenty lashes.[24] Children, like adults, were tortured. One youth of sixteen had his genitals severely mutilated and his arm so mangled that it needed to be amputated.[25] A later law of 1500 ordained that passive and active partners should suffer equally.

The Venetian authorities repeatedly discovered members of the clergy in the sodomite subculture but were vexed that they lay outside their jurisdiction. Men in holy orders could not be punished (apart from sentences of exile) except by church authorities, who ordinarily declined to degrade clerics—a measure that would have brought them within the reach of Venice's severe secular penalties. One senses that ecclesiastical bodies were uncooperative despite indignant protests from the council because public pilloryings or executions would have reflected on the morals of the church, which preferred to confine men to monasteries on bread and water. Nevertheless, we do hear of priests who suffered the death penalty. In their case this meant suspension in a wooden cage from the campanile in Saint Mark's Square, where they were left to die of starvation or exposure.[26]

The persecutions of the fifteenth century continued into the sixteenth, but with the new century penalties became less lethal. Exile and relegation to the galleys tended to replace burning—Venice needed sailors for her fleet. A more mundane rhetoric now warned that sodomy was a threat to population.[27] Nevertheless, horrendous punishments still occurred. In 1552 a man was dragged from the church of Santa Croce to the Rialto bridge, the scene of his crime, at a horse's tail. There, his hands were cut off. Then he was dragged to the Columns of Justice to be beheaded and burned.[28] Another burning took place in 1590.[29] Nevertheless, the anxiety that had grown with success seems to have declined as the fortunes of the city waned.

• Florence: The Price of Love, 1325–1542 •

Renaissance Florence provides a unique chapter in the history of homosexuality. Where the trajectory of fear and repression in Venice is clear and simple, the story in fourteenth- and fifteenth-century Florence is torturously complex. There, for a century or more, laws on sodomy were changed, on the average, more than once a decade and contain such elaborately gradated punishments that they resemble a kind of commercial tariff. These reflect an intrinsic polarity in Florentine culture, as clerical vehemence and a tacit tolerance struggled to reach compromises. The situation produced its own paradoxes. The resultant legislation reduced penalties far below Venetian lethality. But a vigorous attempt to control, rather than obliterate, sodomitical behavior led to a huge number of accusations and trials, all pointing to an extraordinarily high level of homosexual activity—a record excelling, in all likelihood, that of any other pre-modern European city.

The facts are remarkable and, at first glance, difficult to credit. But in the light of the extensive researches into civic documents by Michael Rocke, they appear incontestable. Rocke has documented over 2,500 convictions for sodomy in Florence for the period 1432 to 1502, the time when Florence's anti-sodomy campaign, like Venice's, was in full tide.[30] But this is only part of the story. Civic registers that survive for seventeen of the twenty-four years between 1478 and 1502 record 4,062 accusations, that is, about 160 a year.[31] Since only about twenty percent of those accused in these seventeen years were convicted, we may assume that about 12,500 men and boys probably came to the attention of the Officers of the Night (Ufficiali di Notte), as the city's sodomy police were called during these fateful seven decades. This is astonishing when we realize that Renaissance Florence after the Black Death was a comparatively small city.

Some resistance to morality may have been fostered by this plague, which struck Florence in 1348 and killed about 80,000 of its 120,000 citizens.[32] In its wake the young people in Boccaccio's *Decameron* (1348–1353) conclude that if life is short they should enjoy themselves all the more conscientiously. Not only do these tales excoriate the clergy as sexual hypocrites whose sermonizing is insincere, but many affirm the right of married women to sexual gratification if their husbands fail them, look sympathetically on premarital sex, and even make light of the sins of nuns.

Boccaccio's subversive ethic, however, stops short of condoning homosexuality, which is rarely mentioned in the *Decameron.* The opening tale is about a clever scoundrel who hoodwinks his confessor and is said to be "more fond of men" than "any base fellow."[33] Through a misunderstanding he comes to be revered, postmortem, as a saint. In the second tale the papal court at Rome is accused of enjoying sodomitic lust "without the least bit of remorse or shame."[34] Only in one story—the fifth on the tenth day—is homosexuality central. Pietro Vinciolo is a sodomite who neglects his wife's needs. When he finds her with a lover, she complains loudly of his inadequacy. They reach an accommodation, however, so that the next morning when the young man returns to the city square "he found himself not quite sure about which one he had been with more that night, the husband or the wife."[35] Though Boccaccio's portrait of Pietro is not sympathetic, he treats the scandalous *ménage à trois* with more amusement than indignation.

As in Venice, statutes against homosexuality in Florence were justified rhetorically on religious grounds. Sodomy, city authorities declared, was a most wicked crime that would bring God's wrath upon the city (1365); it would cause a terrifying judgment (1418); it was an "abomination, an offense against God, mortifying to the soul and harmful to the republic because of the evils it attracts" (1458). But if the religious impulse was strong, something in the local culture kept it from running to excess. The history of legislation shows a curious swing of the pendulum, and half a dozen antisodomite initiatives came to nothing. In 1325, four years after Dante's death, we find a series of elaborate laws which aimed at social control. These prescribed castration for native offenders, reserving burning for foreigners and vagabonds. Pimps, complicit fathers, and any man found alone in a garden with a boy in suspicious circumstances might be fined five hundred lire.[36] (This was a very substantial sum; one hundred lire was about the annual wage of a skilled workman.)[37]

In 1365 the pendulum swung back toward greater severity. A new law, warning of divine wrath, reinstituted burning as a punishment for a first offense. Boys under eighteen were exempted from the death penalty and might escape punishment entirely if they voluntarily denounced their lovers. But not all adolescents were treated leniently. In the same year the law was passed, a fifteen-year-old named Giovanni di Giovanni, accused of relations with "many men," was paraded through the city on an ass, publicly castrated, and then branded with a red-hot iron "in that part of his body where he permitted himself to be known in sodomitical practice."[38] Over fifty cases were prosecuted between 1348 and 1432, the majority involving violence or the abuse of children. But once again, there were exceptions. Two patricians, Salvestro di Niccolò Alamanni, thirty-six, and Jacopo di Amerigo da Verrazzano, seventeen, were convicted in 1404. They had conducted a love affair for two years, apparently with the connivance of their friends and relatives. This is one of the few cases in which court records document a strong emotional bond: Salvestro is quoted as saying his love for Jacopo meant more to him than his wife. The older man was given a huge fine, and both were exiled. Eventually the fine was drastically reduced and Jacopo's sentence remitted.[39] Undoubtedly, this leniency was due to family influence.

In 1403 conservative forces proposed setting up a special magistracy "to extirpate" the vice of sodomy, similar to the magistracy Venice was to establish fifteen years later.[40] This initiative was, however, neatly circumvented by a counter-proposal. The Signory did indeed set up a new department—the Officers of Decency. But the charge of this oddly named body was not to seek out sodomites but to open brothels for business and to recruit women to work in them. Apparently this was perceived as an alternative way of diminishing same-sex activity. In neighboring Lucca the sodomy police were also specially authorized to promote female prostitution.[41]

Twelve years later, in 1415, the faction favoring leniency won an important concession—a new law explicitly forbade the death penalty for a first offense. Instead, convicted men were assessed the huge fine of one thousand lire but could not be killed, mutilated, or exiled. Had the commune been shocked by executions it regarded as unwarranted? Even more curious, a provision forbade the removal of convicted sodomites from political office.[42] These two issues—whether sodomites should be put to death when there were no aggravating circumstances, or be deprived of the right to hold civic office—were to remain bones of contention in the next century.

Clerical opinion, however, was unanimous. In Dante's day the Dominican preacher Giordano da Pisa had sermonized (1305): "Oh how many sodomites there are among the citizens! Nearly all are dedicated to the vice, or at least the majority. Florence has become another Sodom."[43] The most impassioned attacks, however, came not from a native but from a citizen of neighboring Siena. Bernardino da Siena (1380–1444) won fame as a charismatic preacher who campaigned throughout Italy for new morals legislation. Pius II hailed him as a new Saint Paul. Bernardino inveighed against a variety of sins—blasphemy, the charging of interest, gambling, and the wearing of fine clothes—and called for harsh new laws. But he is perhaps most remarkable for the attention he paid to the sin of sodomy.

In some northern nations (such as England) preachers were solemnly warned against making even a single reference to this sin in the pulpit. Indeed, very few sermons are known to us, and Bernardino's record is unique: three sermons on the subject in Florence in 1424, another in 1425, and two in Siena in 1425 and 1427. Eager scribes took down these *prediche volgari*—preachings in the vernacular. Though a stern critic, Bernardino was also a close and candid observer; his diatribes provide insights into the role of homosexuality in Florentine life richer in detail than any other surviving literary sources. Bernardino justified this minute attention to his theme on the grounds of Tuscany's notorious reputation throughout Europe.[44] His extravagant-sounding claim is borne out by German usage. Throughout the Renaissance, Germans routinely called sodomites *Florenzer,* and even coined a verb, *florenzen,* "to florence."[45]

Bernardino's sermons are most revealing on Florentine parental attitudes. Mothers, he charged, sought to make boys as pretty as girls by dressing them in seductive finery, such as short doublets and "stockings with a tiny patch in front and another in back so that they show a lot of flesh for the sodomites."[46] As a result, Bernardino claimed, boys in alluring costumes presented a constant temptation in Tuscan streets; surely we can trust a saint's judgment here. Fathers, equally complacent, were happy to entertain their sons' lovers in their homes and took pride in their attentions.[47] In return, the lovers showered gifts of clothes and money upon the boys and might favor the family's civic ambitions. The boys, in turn, boasted their conquests and exploited older males who were "always irritated and upset, [they're] so afraid [they] will fall out of the good graces of the wicked *fanciullo.*" Handsome boys became idols for adoration: a man of this sort "servilely obeys the *fanciullo,* and does everything he can at his asking."[48]

Bernardino regards sodomites as a unique species, sees them as an identifiable faction within the body politic, and is less concerned with calling them to repentance than with extirpating them as a class. For him, the Tuscan sodomite has a distinct psychological profile. Typically he scorns women and does not marry. Women, in turn, hate sodomites—the enmity is mutual.[49] Far from seeing marriage as a cure, Bernardino warns women against marrying sodomites in the hopes of changing their behavior, since they are rarely cured and will only neglect their wives. Any unmarried man older than thirty-three is likely to be a confirmed sodomite and should be routinely excluded from public office.[50]

Bernardino decried Florentine lenience and demanded sterner measures. In Verona, he told his hearers, a man was quartered and his limbs hung from the city gates. In Genoa, men were regularly burned. He advised the Sienese to do the same "even if they had to burn every male in the city."[51] To edify his congregation, Bernardino described the burning of a sodomite in Venice. "I saw a man tied to a column on high; and a barrel of pitch and brushwood and fire, and a wretch who made it all burn, and I saw many people standing round about to watch."[52] Bernardino compared the spectators to the "blessed spirits of paradise [who] blissfully glory in witnessing the justice of God" punishing sinners in hell. So religious faith in this age anesthetized any sensitivity to human suffering.

In 1424 San Bernardino delivered three Lenten sermons on sodomy in

42. San Bernardino of Siena. Piero della Francesca, oil and tempera, c. 1455.

Florence.[53] It was in the course of these vivid preachments that he invited the worshipers in Santa Croce to express their disgust by spitting on the church floor. Still, the city took no immediate action. It was not until eight years later that the city changed its procedures. Like Venice, Florence took the fateful step, in 1432, of inaugurating its own special magistracy, the Officers of the Night, devoted specifically to the prosecution of male homosexuality.[54]

The rhetoric of the 1432 laws was less marked by hysterical fear than earlier statutes, however. The municipal authorities, Rocke suggests, seem at this point to have realized that sodomy could not be eradicated and that public opinion on the whole did not regard it as a major offense. On sentencing a man in 1436 the Ufficiali made a candid admission: "[The Officers of the Night] are watching with unceasing diligence so that the horrible crime of sodomy might be rooted out of the city and its territory, and they devote themselves to almost nothing else. Yet after all their labors, words, threats, and punishments against many persons, they believe it is nearly impossible for any good to come about, so corrupt and stained is the city."[55] The best that could be hoped for, they concluded, was that some men might be to some degree restrained.

So sodomy became a form of undesirable behavior—like drinking, gambling, or prostitution—to be regulated and taxed rather than eradicated. Under the draconian schedule of fines previously in force, it had been difficult to get convictions. Accordingly, the new law reduced the fine for a first offense to 10 florins, one-fifth what it had been.[56] This was still a very substantial fine: a skilled artisan in Florence in 1430 earned about 60 florins a year, wages having risen appreciably after the Black Death.[57] Florentine officials also experimented with another device. Boxes called *tamburi* (literally, drums) were set up for accusations before a number of churches.[58] To prevent revenge, the accusers' names were not to be revealed, but they could collect a percentage of any fine. The result exceeded expectations. So many accusations flooded in that the authorities suspected a sodomite plot to undermine the new system.[59] Inevitably false accusations were made out of malice, and the officers simply ignored many of the complaints. Still, the statistics are impressive. During the seventeen years for which these incriminating slips of paper survive, they average over 240 a year.

Unlike Venice, with its remarkably stable political system, Renaissance Florence was turbulent with class conflict. After a proletarian revolt had been put down in 1382, Florence was ruled by a Signory of eight wealthy businessmen, presided over by a Standard Bearer of Justice *(gonfaloniere di giustizia)* and assisted by various popular councils. In 1433, a year after the new Officers of the Night had been installed, Cosimo de' Medici was exiled as too favorable to the popular faction. But the next year he returned in triumph, and the golden age of Medicean Florence began. During the ascendancy of Cosimo (1434–1464), his son Piero (1464–1469), and his grandson Lorenzo (1469–1492), Florence grew wealthy and flourished, reaching its pinnacle of intellectual and artistic achievement.

During this Medicean regency the penalties for sodomy fluctuated with bewildering frequency. There were so many convictions under the 1432 law that the fine of 100 florins was judged insufficient, and in 1440 the tariff was increased.[60] But this proved counter-productive. The magistrates complained that the poor men who made up the bulk of those sentenced could not pay, and so they ceased assessing fines.[61] Income from fines dwindled to nothing, and the Convertite nuns (retired prostitutes who were supported by these moneys) were in danger of starvation.[62] One wonders if the hungry sisters, who had once been expected to seduce sodomites by their charms, were tempted to pray for more convictions. In 1459, as a result of this impasse, the fine for a first offense was drastically lowered by 90 percent, to 10 florins.[63] Convictions soared once more; in 1472 they amounted to 161, or one almost every other day.[64]

The increase in convictions in Florence seems to have had an effect in that skeptical city quite opposite to the similar rise in Venice. Instead of seeing homosexuality as a threat to the very existence of the state, the Florentines, now at the height of their prosperity and artistic eminence, looked on it for a time as a mere peccadillo. For the decade ending in 1492—the last years of Lorenzo de' Medici's rule—male love went all but unpunished.[65]

Who were the men involved? Dante identified the sodomites in his "Inferno" as famous writers and political and military leaders. Satirists like

Agnolo Firenzuolo wrote that figs (vaginas) belonged to the commons, but apples and peaches (buttocks) "to the great masters."[66] Later, Aristo was to complain that humanists were especially prone to "the most infamous of vices."[67] But the surviving records tell quite a different story. By far the greater number of convicted men, in fact, were poor and uneducated members of the working class. A law of 1459 declared that "nearly all those who are denounced or accused [to the Officers of the Night] of practicing such vices are very poor men, who cannot be punished in fines since they have no money."[68] Indeed, the six most common occupations of the 2,600 men whose occupations can be determined among those implicated from 1478 to 1502 were shoemakers (241), weavers (134), clothes dealers (125), butchers (97), barbers (95), and clergy (94).[69] The clergy presented special difficulties, since they could be punished only by the church, which was often unwilling to act. In 1470 the Officers of the Night issued a sharp rebuke to the archbishop of Florence: "Most reverend and just father . . . our magistracy is entrusted with . . . obviating as much as is possible, the horrible vice of sodomy. Wishing to fulfil part of our duty, we have arrested several young boys who have been sodomized not only by laymen but also by numerous priests. This was made known to the representative of your most reverend lord[ship], yet nothing has been done about it. For this reason we are most scandalized."[70] Contrary to the popular belief that pedagogues seduced their pupils, only twenty-one teachers appeared on the list.[71] Again, homosexuality has often been thought of as peculiarly associated with the arts; but only twenty-four painters' names appear, though goldsmiths, who also ranked as artists in Florence, provided forty more.[72] All in all, Rocke has identified men belonging to 350 occupations, a spectrum of pursuits stretching across the whole male working population.[73]

This is not to say that men of the higher orders were not denounced, arrested, and tried. Indeed, it was an embarrassment that, in 1432, the first man convicted under the new sodomy magistracy was Doffo di Nepo Spini, a recent Standard Bearer of Justice, the highest executive officer in the state.[74] Rocke's meticulous research has led him to estimate that members of more than half of the noble families of Florence appear in the lists of accused; these include some Medici.[75] Nevertheless, the documents confound a common theory that pederasty, historically, has been most common among cultured elites. History, which so often leaves the lives of the poor unrecorded, has, by opening bedroom doors in Florence, revealed that the working class was not mimicking upper-class decadence. Rather, where male homosexuality was concerned, it provided a majority of the participants. Perhaps we should reconsider Kenneth Dover's theory that working-class Athenians would have lacked the leisure to court boys. In Florence intimacies of the workplace, the tavern, and the street corner seem to have provided ample opportunity.

Was there a homosexual subculture in this paradise of art and commerce?

Rocke rejects the term as anachronistic. We have seen, however, that San Bernardino looked on sodomites as a race apart. And though most of the accused were men in their twenties and thirties who later married, Rocke was able to distinguish a relatively small number who seemed to fit this definition, a group who never married and were repeatedly convicted throughout their lives.[76] But this group was imbedded in a larger male culture that casually indulged in homosexual relations without a modern homosexual "identity" and came together at popular meeting places such as the Street of the Furriers, the Old Market, and favorite taverns.[77]

The tolerance of Lorenzo de' Medici's last years came to an end with his death. Once again the pendulum swung, this time as a result of a new and momentous religious campaign. In apocalyptic sermons that attracted huge crowds and spread panic through the city, Girolamo Savonarola, a Dominican friar from Ferrara, announced that the reign of Antichrist had begun and that the Second Coming would soon take place. Denouncing the new art of the Renaissance as shameless paganism, he predicted that Lorenzo and Innocent VIII would both die in 1492 and Charles VIII of France would invade Italy. His credibility was much enhanced when these prophecies proved true.

Savonarola's mission had a political as well as a religious side. Three themes dominated his preaching: opposition to the Medici as tyrants, reform of the Papacy, and the suppression of sodomy, if necessary by burning. Lorenzo's son, Piero de' Medici, had proved an inept ruler whose popularity was weakened when he made concessions to Charles. Finally, in November 1494, Piero fled, and a new republican government was installed under the control of Savonarola, who demanded from the pulpit that sodomites "be stoned or burned."[78] Though the new enactments did not go as far as the friar wished, they were markedly more severe than the Medicean legislation. Fines were abolished; first offenders were required to stand in the pillory and lose civic privileges; a second offense was to be punished by branding; a third by burning alive.[79] But, once again, Florentine public opinion exercised a restraining influence: denunciations dropped off dramatically. Citizens simply did not believe their sodomite neighbors should be treated so harshly. Realizing this, Savonarola conceded, "If you don't want to kill them, at least drive them out of your territory."[80] In June 1495 fines were once more introduced, and accusations again multiplied. Savonarola was unappeased, however, and continued to urge burning: "Make a pretty fire," he recommended in a sermon on the Psalms, "or two or three, there in the square, of these sodomites." "Don't punish with money or secretly, but make a fire that can be smelled in all of Italy."[81] Some months later a more drastic law gave the magistrates the power to prescribe death for the first conviction.

From the start, Savonarola had met with strong opposition, which, even under the new republic, often outran his popular support. But he was undaunted and called into question not just the probity of the Medici and local

43. Girolamo Savonarola. Fra Bartolomeo, oil, c. 1492.

clergy but the papacy itself. The new pope, Alexander VI, was alarmed when Savonarola allied Florence with France and invited Charles VIII to depose him. Savonarola was first forbidden to preach and then, when he ignored the decree, excommunicated. Throughout the turbulent days of the republic, Savonarola's fortunes varied with the election of state officials whose short terms insured frequent changes in policy. Amid this turmoil, sodomy prosecutions provided a barometer of Savonarola's popularity. In the two years from November 1495 to November 1497 some 731 men were accused, far above the average for the last half century.[82] Then in the last months of 1497 popular sentiment turned against the friar. A group of young men of mainly patrician background formed the Compagnacci to oppose Savonarola. Several of its leaders had faced sodomy accusations, and Rocke conjectures that the new laws had antagonized them.[83] This youth brigade succeeded in getting the age for admission to the Great Council lowered from twenty-nine to twenty-four and fomented a tumult at the prior's Ascension Day sermon on May 4. It was widely reported that a city official had remarked as the prior's power waned, "Thank God, now we can sodomize!"[84]

After Savonarola's excommunication on May 13, 1497, accusations of sodomy fell off; from November to May 1498 there was only one. When a Franciscan preacher challenged Savonarola to a trial by fire in the city center and he declined, his following began to dissipate. Shortly afterward he was arrested and tried for heresy and schism. On May 23, 1498, he was hanged and burned in the Piazza della Signoria. Jacopo Nardi tells us that a man from the crowd seized the torch from the startled executioner and lit the pyre, shouting that "the one who wanted to burn him was himself being put to the flames."[85] Sodomy was, it fact, the only crime Savonarola had especially wanted to burn men for. Giovanni Cambi, a contemporary chronicler, thought three things had brought about the prior's downfall: his attack on the papacy, his attack on the Medici, and his saying that "sodomites should be burned."[86]

In 1502, with the republic restored, the city abolished the Officers of the Night; the special magistracy had become an embarrassment by advertising the prevalence of sodomy in Florence.[87] Yet in the first half of the sixteenth century sodomy remained an important item on the Florentine legislative agenda. In 1512 some young noblemen seized the government palace and overthrew the republican regime, demanding among other things that the sentences of all men exiled or deprived of office for sodomy be revoked. When their candidate, Lorenzo's son Giuliano de' Medici, assumed power, he immediately granted these reprieves.[88] But when the Medici were overthrown again in 1527, the restored republican government marked the change by introducing new laws that blamed sodomites for provoking divine wrath and by instituting severer penalties.[89]

Florentine politics, ever unstable, brought back the Medici again in 1530.

44. The burning of Savonarola in front of the Palazzo Vecchio, Florence, May 23, 1498. Italian school, oil.

This time, however, the restoration was permanent: Cosimo I was created duke of Florence in 1537, and his descendants ruled the duchy for the next two centuries. Where earlier Medici had been, by and large, liberal in outlook, the duke was authoritarian and superstitious. When a lightning bolt damaged the cathedral dome, he took alarm. As the contemporary observer Bernardo Segni noted: "Duke Cosimo, extremely frightened, put himself in God's hands and supported by the clergy, created two very severe laws, one against blasphemy and the other against sodomy, imposing very harsh penalties on delinquents, even death."[90] At first, Segni tells us, the law was applied "with no little rigor." But Segni goes on to say that "within a short time [the laws] lost all their authority, not because of the duke's negligence but because of the negligence of the other magistrates and ministers of justice."[91] The new law of 1542 did not, however, fall totally into disuse: it was under this statute that Benvenuto Cellini was arrested in 1557.

• Donatello, Botticelli, Leonardo •

The criminal archives of the Italian Renaissance inevitably remain the preserve of the specialist. By contrast, the art of the *Rinascimento* is a heritage claimed by the entire civilized world. Museums display its triumphs with pride, and weighty tomes spread its images across our coffee tables. To experience the homoerotic side of this art, we do not need to study Italian or ferret out documents; we have only to turn the pages of these extravagant volumes. Few artifacts of the past reveal a homoerotic element at once so subtly pervasive and so accessible. Renaissance sculpture and painting enthusiastically revive pagan images, and Ganymede and Hyacinth reappear with Venus and Apollo. Even religious art takes on ambiguous overtones. Angels become teasingly androgynous, Saint Sebastians are beautiful naked youths, and even the austere John the Baptist is disconcertingly feminized by Leonardo and turned into a knowing street-boy by Caravaggio.

One of the most striking of these transformations is the bronze *David* of Donatello, now housed in the Bargello in Florence. Donato di Niccolò di Betto Bardi (c. 1386–1466) dominated quattrocento sculpture by virtue of his genius, the prodigality of his inventions, and his long life. He has been called a "pre-incarnation" of Michelangelo, who was born two years before he died and admired Donatello as his greatest predecessor. Giorgio Vasari, in his *Lives of the Painters, Sculptors, and Archetects* (1550), acclaimed him as an artist whose works approached the masterpieces "of the ancient Greeks and Romans more than any other."[92] Despite his fame and longevity, however, we know little of Donatello's private life, most of which was spent in Florence. Vasari spoke warmly of his goodness and generosity but deleted this encomium from his revised edition of 1568.[93] Donatello did not marry, choosing instead to live with other artists and his many young workshop assistants. In 1957 the art historian Horst Janson drew attention to three journal entries of uncertain authorship written a decade or so after Donatello's death which suggest that his emotional life was centered on these young men. "Donatello," we are told, "took particular delight in having beautiful apprentices. Once someone brought him a boy that had been praised as particularly beautiful. But when the same person showed Donatello the boy's brother and claimed that he was even prettier, the artist replied, 'the less long will he stay with me!'"[94] We learn also that Donatello guarded his finds with some jealousy: he "used to tint *[tingeva]* his assistants, so that others would not take a fancy to them."[95] These relations were sometimes tempestuous, though one drama ended in an anticlimax:

> Once [Donatello] had quarreled with a young disciple of his, who thereupon had run off to Ferrara. So Donatello went to Cosimo [de' Medici] and asked for a letter to the Count of Ferrara, insisting that he was going to

> pursue the boy, come what may, and kill him. Cosimo, familiar with Donatello's nature, gave him the letter but he also let the Count know, by a different route, what kind of man Donatello was. The Count then gave Donatello the permission to kill the boy wherever he might find him, but when the artist met his disciple face to face, the latter started to laugh and Donatello, instantly mollified, also laughed as he ran towards him.[96]

Cosimo must have understood that Donatello's amorous volatility would stop short of violence.

The Bargello *David* is today Donatello's most famous creation. Kenneth Clark has called it a "work of almost incredible originality."[97] A landmark in Renaissance art in several respects, it has been identified as the first free-standing nude in a thousand years. For the first time since antiquity we are asked to admire the beauty of a naked image. It inaugurates a major genre of Renaissance art, and inaugurates it in a homoerotic mode. This in itself is significant, given the anti-sodomy campaign that raged in contemporary Florence. Moreover, it does this by seizing upon a religious image and totally transforming it.

Traditionally, David had been represented as a bearded prophet-king with a harp or psaltery. But the bronze *David* is totally different. Its provocative nudity is emphasized, not diminished, by the floppy shepherd-boy's hat and military boots the boy wears. This is not Michelangelo's tense athlete, frowning as he concentrates on his task. This is an apprentice-model presenting himself shamelessly to our gaze as a seductive Ganymede. For Vasari the figure is "so natural in its lifelike pose *[vivacità]* and its rendering of the soft texture of the flesh *[morbidezza]* that it seems incredible to artists that it was not formed from the mold of an actual body."[98]

We do not know when the statue was cast. Most often it is placed in the 1430s, following Bernardino's sermons and after the inauguration of the Officers of the Night (1432). Surely it would have drawn some knowing smiles. Complacent Florentine youths had by then achieved international notoriety for, as the forthright saint had put it, "showing a lot of flesh for the sodomites." The statue's elegance, as Bonnie Bennett and David Wilkins have noted, "invites both the lingering gaze and a desire to touch."[99] One curious feature is the severed head of Goliath on which David stands, with its huge helmet crowned by a wing that "curves up to caress the inside of his thigh" almost to the buttocks. An allegorical scene on the helmet shows three winged boys pulling a chariot and two others doing homage to a man seated in it.[100] This has been called a "Triumph of Love" and associated with the symbolic chariot in the *Phaedrus.*

But the heavy vehicle depicted on the helmet does not speed airily along, and the putti bowing before the lumpish middle-aged figure seem mockingly ironic. Is Donatello inviting us to read David's triumph over the older man whose head he stands on as the triumph of an ephebe over a doting suitor, one of the men who, Bernardino complained, made fools of themselves over young Florentines? In Italian, as in English, a man can *perdere la testa* (lose his head). This "victorious" David looks forward not to Michelangelo's heroic *David* but to that sculptor's *Victory,* which also shows a handsome youth subduing an older man who has been identified with Michelangelo himself. Janson was right to call this David a "beau garçon sans merci."[101] The homosexual implications of the *David* seem clear, though at least one critic of note, John Pope-Hennessey, has demurred.[102]

No accusation against Donatello has been found in the Florentine archives, which during his lifetime are very incomplete. But if Donatello escaped notice, Botticelli was less fortunate. A terse summary of what was no doubt a more detailed charge appears in the records for November 16, 1502. It reads simply, "Sandro di Botticello si tiene un garzone": "Botticelli keeps a boy," a wording which suggests an ongoing relation.[103] The painter was then fifty-eight. Lacking particulars, art historians have been uncertain what to make of this notice. Jacques Mesnil, who discovered it in 1938, dismissed it as "a customary slander by which the partisans and adversaries of Savonarola abused each other."[104] Botticelli, despite the pagan exuberance of his *Primavera* and *The Birth of Venus,* had, later in life, become a ardent disciple of the friar, and Mesnil chose to regard the accusation as a malicious act by some opponent of the friar.

45. David. Donatello, bronze, 1440.

Botticelli, like Donatello, Leonardo, and Michelangelo, was unwed and expressed a strong aversion to the idea of marriage, a prospect he claimed gave him nightmares.[105] His workshop with its many apprentices had the reputation of a hangout for idlers. In 1473 one of these, a twenty-eight-year-old painter named Betto Pialla, was convicted of sodomy.[106] Mesnil, though he discounted the formal charge against Botticelli, nevertheless thought "woman was not the only object of his love."[107] He was led to this speculation by Botticelli's paintings: "The androgynous type of the angels of Botticelli, the grace of his figures of young boys, the profound beauty of certain of his figures of young men show him particularly sensible to the charm of adolescents."[108] Instances abound; one might cite the ambiguous angels who attend the Virgin in the *Madonna of the Magnificat,* the voluptuous naked war god sleeping by his clothed paramour in *Mars and Venus,* the artist's *St. Sebastian,* and the noble youth who looks upward in the left corner of the *Primavera.* Once again, as in ancient Athens, we may wonder whether Botticelli is expressing an aesthetic enthusiasm of his time and place or his private erotic sensibility. Opinion remains divided: André Chastel has called Mesnil's dismissal of the charge too glib, but Ronald Lightbrown in a recent study has agreed with Mesnil, ascribing the anonymous accusation to the "bitter party divisions of Florence."[109]

Leonardo was Botticelli's junior by eight years and an admirer of his art. Perhaps they met in the workshop of Verrocchio, where the tradition of handsome boy angels seems first to have blossomed.[110] It was while he was living with Verrocchio that Leonardo was accused of sodomy. On April 8, 1476, exactly a week before his twenty-fourth birthday, an anonymous denunciation appeared in the *tamburo* before the Palazzo Vecchio. It read:

> I notify you, Signori Officiali, concerning a true thing, namely that Jacopo Saltarelli . . . [who] dresses in black and is about seventeen years old . . . has been a party to many wretched affairs and consents to please those persons who exact certain evil pleasures from him. And in this way he has . . . served several dozen people about whom I know a good deal, and here will name a few: Bartholomeo di Pasquino, goldsmith, who lives in Vacchereccia. Leonardo di Ser Piero da Vinci, who lives with Andrea de Verrocchio. Baccino, a tailor, who lives by Or San Michele . . . Leonardo Tornabuoni, called *il teri;* dresses in black. These committed sodomy with said Jacopo, and this I testify before you.[111]

Jacopo's name was not unknown to the Ufficiali; another man had been convicted of sodomy with him in January of the same year.[112] The outcome of this new accusation, however, was conditional; Leonardo and the others were absolved provided that they "not be named again" *(ut ne tamburentur).* Nevertheless, the accuser repeated his accusation on June 7, this time in learned Latin. Paradoxically, the second verdict was identical with the first. Leonardo, a sensitive man, can only have been embarrassed and humiliated by his arrest, though his chagrin must have been lessened by the knowledge that scores of others had endured similar trials. Indeed, convictions in Florence had reached a record high (161) just four years earlier in 1472.[113]

We know, of course, far more about the life of Leonardo than we do about Donatello or Botticelli. The Saltarelli case first came to light in 1896. A dec-

46. Angels. Botticelli, detail from "Madonna of the Magnificat," tempera and oil, 1483.

ade later Sigmund Freud, alerted by this revelation, published his famous essay. Though Freud's elegant effort was more than a little bizarre in its theorizing, it made Leonardo's sexual nature a discussible subject and led to much debate. Associating homosexuality with femininity, critics now noted Leonardo's humane gentleness, his subtle psychological portraits of women, and his love for handsome and luxurious clothes.[114] But the man who painted the Mona Lisa also drew an extraordinarily violent cartoon for the *Battle of Anghiari,* and the designer of ducal interiors was also a skilled horseman whose strength amazed people. And though the fine arts have often been regarded as the special preserve of homosexuals, Leonardo was a pioneering anatomist and inventor who was employed by such ruthless Renaissance chieftains as Lodovico Sforza, Cesare Borgia, and Louis XII in a role many would regard as hypermasculine—that of military engineer.

More pertinent are Leonardo's intimate personal relations. Five years after his arrest he left to serve Lodovico for the next eighteen years in Milan. There, he painted the *Last Supper* and, in 1490 at the age of thirty-eight, took into his household a ten-year-old named Gian Giacomo Caprotti, whom he nicknamed Salai. Giorgio Vasari, in his life of the artist, calls him "a graceful and beautiful youth with fine curly hair, in which Leonardo greatly delighted."[115] The relation was to last out Leonardo's lifetime. Such devotion was more that an little unusual, given the boy's behavior. A year after his arrival, Leonardo wrote a lengthy account of his misdemeanors, calling him "ladro, bugiardo, ostinato, ghiotto"—thief, liar, obstinate, glutton.[116] Leonardo noted Salai's thefts of money or valuables on five separate occasions and the exorbitant cost of his year's wardrobe, which included twenty-four pairs of shoes. Obviously Salai had charm and beauty enough to make Leonardo overlook his "deviltries" and was as much a companion as a servant. At any rate, Leonardo's notebooks are full of sketches of curly-headed adolescents whom specialists believe to be the fetching youth.[117] Leonardo rented part of a vineyard in Milan to Salai's father, dowered his sister, and left him a share of his estate. He was at Leonardo's side for twenty-six years, almost to the very end, when he returned from France to Milan to care for some property the artist had given him.[118]

We do not know how Leonardo's immediate contemporaries regarded this affair. A curious document came to light in the British Museum a few decades ago, however. The author, the art theorist Gian Paolo Lomazzo (1536–1584), wrote several famous treatises, one of which had been translated into English and was familiar to Shakespeare. Lomazzo could not have known Leonardo, but he knew his younger disciples and may have had firsthand information. In this newly discovered dialogue Lomazzo unequivocally identifies Leonardo as homosexual. "Phidias" asks Leonardo if he has played with Salai "the game in the behind that the Florentines love so much":

> *Leonardo:* And how many times! Have in mind that he was a most beautiful young man, especially at about fifteen.
>
> *Phidias:* Are you not ashamed to say this?
>
> *Leonardo:* Why ashamed? There is no matter of more praise than this among persons of merit *[virtuosi]*. And that this is the truth I shall prove to you with very good reasons.

Leonardo even strikes a note of homosexual chauvinism: "Besides this, all Tuscany has set store by this embellishment, and especially the savants of

47. Saint John the Baptist. Leonardo, oil, c. 1515.

Florence, my homeland, whence, by such practices and fleeing the volubility of women, there have issued forth so many rare spirits in the arts."[119]

Salai was not Leonardo's only long-term companion. In 1508, now fifty-six, the master returned to Milan at the height of his fame as a painter and engineer. Visiting the villa of a nobleman in a nearby town, he met a son of the family whose age has been variously estimated from fifteen to eighteen and in effect adopted him.[120] Vasari, who interviewed Francesco Melzi in his old age, tells us he had been "a lovely child" when he met the artist, "who was very fond of him."[121] Intelligent, refined, courteous, and a competent painter, Melzi cared for the older man during his final illness at the court of Francis II and was his principal heir. His inheritance included Leonardo's numerous manuscript notebooks, which he preserved and edited. In a letter to Leonardo's brothers he described the older man's feelings for him as a "deeply felt and most ardent love" *(sviscerato et ardentissimo amore).*[122]

• Michelangelo: Love, Art, and Guilt •

Like other artists caught up in Savonarola's religious hysteria, Botticelli destroyed a number of his paintings. The last decade of the fifteenth century was a moment of high tension in Florence, when opposing currents mingled and clashed. One current was the humanism fostered and endowed by Lorenzo de' Medici, which centered on the Platonic Academy presided over by the Greek scholar Marsilio Ficino. The Academy made a special cult of the *Symposium,* and on November 7, the supposed date of Plato's birth and death, its members met to read the dialogue, which Ficino had translated. Ficino had also composed a lengthy *Commentary* (1469) that praised love between males: "The man enjoys the physical beauty of the youth with his eyes; the youth enjoys the man's beauty with his mind. The youth, who is beautiful in body only, by this practice becomes beautiful in soul; the man who is beautiful also in soul only, feasts his eyes upon bodily beauty."[123] But Ficino, who made it his life's task to reconcile Platonism with Christianity, rejected physical expression as a "wicked crime." "Love and the desire for physical union," he wrote, are "not identical impulses, but . . . opposite ones."[124] In this Platonic mode, Ficino loved Giovanni Cavalcanti, a younger member of the Academy, and wrote him rapturous love letters, published in Latin as the *Epistulae* in 1492. In this atmosphere, where male beauty was worshiped as a divine gift reflecting the supernal beauty of God, the teenage Michelangelo caught fire. But in 1491, a year before Lorenzo's death, Savonarola had begun his campaign against pagan art, nudity, and morals and inveighed furiously against Florence's sodomites. This was the second influence that shaped the genius of the adolescent Michelangelo, then an impressionable sixteen-year-old.

Michelangelo's temperament was tuned to respond strongly to each of these competing impulses. At fifteen, he had been discovered by the percipient Lorenzo, taken into his household, treated almost like a son at his table, and introduced to the circle of Ficino, Poliziano, and Pico della Mirandola. Here he was immersed in the art and mythology of Greek antiquity and exposed to Ficino's idealizing erotic theories. The aesthetic and amorous side of Michelangelo's nature came together in his enthusiasm for the beauty of young athletes; with his companions he made a bible of the *Symposium.* But he was also a devout Catholic with a wholly conventional sense of sin who responded to Savonarola's fiery sermons. Sixty years later he was to tell his biographer that the friar's voice still rang in his ears.

How was this conflict to be resolved? Michelangelo thought he had found the solution in Plato. Here was a philosopher who not only condoned the love of men but in the *Phaedrus* made it a transcendent value, while demanding a celibacy consistent with Christian teaching. Did Michelangelo succeed in realizing this ideal in his personal life? We shall explore this question later. It was, however, as a Platonic lover of men that Michelangelo presented himself to the public in sixteenth-century Italy.

In 1553 when Michelangelo was nearly eighty, his young disciple Ascanio Condivi published a *Life,* composed in a collaboration so close that it may almost be called an autobiography. In it Michelangelo touched on the attraction young men had for him in an apology carefully framed in religious terms:

> He has likewise read the Holy Scriptures with great application and study, both the Old Testament and the New, as well as the writings of those who have studied them, such as Savonarola, for whom he has always had great affection and whose voice still lives in his memory. He has also loved the beauty of the human body as one who knows it extremely well, and loved it in such a way as to inspire certain carnal men, who are incapable of understanding the love of beauty except as something lascivious and indecent, to think and speak ill of him. It is as though Alcibiades, a very beautiful young man, had not been most chastely loved by Socrates, of whom he was wont to say that, when he lay down with him, he arose from his side as from the side of his father. As for me, I have often heard Michelangelo discourse on the subject of love and have later heard from those who were present that what he said about love was no different than what we read in the writings of Plato.[125]

With these words the Dominican friar and the Greek philosopher are made to appear together as witnesses for the defense.

In Michelangelo's art the two impulses—Catholic orthodoxy and pagan enthusiasm for the male nude—sometimes alternate and sometimes combine. In Bologna, where he fled in 1494 when the Medici were overthrown by Savonarola, Michelangelo carved the likeness of a local saint, Proculus, whose furrowed brow is an image of adolescent anxiety, and on his return to Florence created his first masterpiece and most voluptuous male nude, the drunken *Bacchus,* whose dangling grapes are nibbled by a mischievous boy-satyr. In the two works that follow, the *Pietà* and the *David,* Christian and pagan aesthetic ideals coalesce. Both pay their respects to Faith and Eros. The superbly refined Christ that Mary holds in her arms has been shown by

48. Bacchus. Michelangelo, marble, 1497.

art historians to derive from images of the dead Adonis cradled by Venus, while the *David* that became Florence's civic emblem is no Jewish prophet but a Greek athlete in the full splendor of his physical prowess.

Sometimes the conflicting elements coexist in odd juxtaposition, as in the Doni tondo, where the Holy Family and a bug-eyed young Saint John are backed by a classical frieze of nude youths who might be lounging in a Greek palaestra. Their puzzling presence has inspired a dozen contradictory interpretations. One meticulous scholar has identified them as homosexuals awaiting purification through baptism.[126] This seems too explicit; the scene seems rather a generalized homage to the world of Plato, replacing the conventional shepherds or Magi we expect to find in such a painting. So, too, the ambitious tomb planned for Julius II was to have a stern Moses flanked with writhing, sensuous "Captives," strange companions for a lawgiver supposed to have condemned nakedness and male love equally. Sometimes these juxtapositions provoked scandalized protests, as with the giant *Ignudi* who punctuate the scenes of the Creation on the Sistine ceiling and the naked figures of the *Last Judgment,* whose sensual appeal almost led two Counter Reformation popes—Paul IV (1555–1559) and Gregory XIII (1572–1585)—to obliterate the painting.[127]

The images of Michelangelo's painting and sculpture are suggestive, but what of his life? Unlike most Renaissance artists, Michelangelo left an extensive literary record which throws much light on his erotic interests. Over 480 autograph letters survive, along with 800 addressed to him. In addition we have the manuscripts of over 300 poems. From this sizable body of material we are able to reconstruct in some detail his emotional attachments to other males.

Of these the most widely publicized in his lifetime was his love for Tommaso de' Cavalieri. Michelangelo met the young Roman noble in 1532 when he was fifty-seven and Tommaso twenty-three, and he was soon penning letters that reveal an infatuation. On January 1, 1533, Michelangelo wrote offering Tommaso some very fine drawings; the tone of the original draft of this letter is extravagant in the extreme. Michelangelo calls Tommaso "matchless and unequaled," the "light of our century, paragon of the world," and vows to devote to him "the present and the time to come that remains to me."[128] Another letter, dated July 28, speaks of the "boundless love" he bears Tommaso; he could as soon forget his name "as forget the food on which I live—nay, I could sooner forget the food on which I live, which unhappily nourishes only the body, than your name, which nourishes body and soul, filling both with such delight that I am insensible to sorrow or fear of death."[129]

Michelangelo also wrote several dozen love poems to Cavalieri, many of them sonnets. Praising Tommaso's "beautiful face" and "lovely arms" (86), he longs for physical intimacy, desiring to hold "my so much desired, my so

49. Ignudo. Michelangelo, fresco, Sistine Chapel, c. 1510.

sweet lord, / In my unworthy ready arms for ever" (70).[130] He wishes he were a silkworm so his dead remains might clothe and clasp his "beautiful breast with pleasure" (92). Borrowing from the *Phaedrus,* he represents his love as giving him wings on which to ascend to heaven (59, 87). But he goes beyond Plato in justifying his love on theological grounds: Cavalieri's beauty draws him to God who, "in His grace, shows himself nowhere more / To me than through some veil, mortal and lovely, / Which I can only love for being His mirror" (104). Here, Michelangelo is closer to the Sufist mysticism of medieval Persian homoerotic love poetry than to Shakespeare or ancient Greek literature.

Plato's conceit of love lending wings appears also in the drawings Michelangelo sent Cavalieri. Celebrated among Italian connoisseurs and copied many times, they have marked erotic associations. In the *Rape of Ganymede* an eagle carries off a full-bodied youngster to heaven. The Ganymede drawing is Michelangelo's only artwork on a classical homosexual theme. Renaissance interpretations of Jupiter's abduction of the boy were often blatantly sexual, but they could also be Neoplatonic, or even, through allegory, Christian. (Michelangelo's friend Sebastiano del Piombo jokingly suggested he might add a halo and pass off the design as Saint John the Evangelist in some church cupola.)[131] But a modern scholar has noted the peculiarly suggestive union of the bird and boy: "He confers on the eagle an anthropomorphic expression of passion: the bird seizes avidly in his talons the delicate body of the youth, and the bird's neck is stretched around his torso . . . The boy submits passively to the abduction and seems to be plunged in a dream of delights. From a distance the pair seem to form a single winged being—expressive of that mystic union of which Michelangelo speaks in some of his poems: 'One soul in two bodies became eternal, both rising to heaven with the same wings.'"[132] A bolder interpreter thinks the boy and bird are *in coitu.*[133]

In his love poems, Michelangelo takes an almost masochistic delight in being subject to Cavalieri, on whose name he puns (96):

> If capture and defeat must be my joy,
> It is no wonder that alone and naked,
> I remain prisoner of a knight-at-arms
> *(resto prigion d'un cavalier armato).*

It has been observed that Michelangelo's *Victory* depicts a young man vanquishing an older one whose face resembles the sculptor's. Though most commentators have regarded Michelangelo's relations with Cavalieri as Platonic, there is important evidence to the contrary. Frederick Hartt has noted that on August 2, 1533, Cavalieri wrote to Michelangelo, "I flee from evil deeds *(male pratiche),* and wish to flee them, for I cannot make love *(pratica)* with anyone but you."[134] One could hardly imagine a more direct avowal.

Like some other defenders of male love in Greece and Japan, Michelan-

50. The rape of Ganymede. Michelangelo, black chalk, c. 1533.

gelo downgrades the love of women, which he rejects as purely carnal: "This love for what I speak of reaches higher; / Woman's too much unlike; no heart by rights / Ought to grow hot for her, if wise and male; / One draws to Heaven, and to earth the other" (258). Though Cavalieri married four years after they met, he and Michelangelo remained friends to the end. Tommaso was present at Michelangelo's deathbed and afterward supervised the completion of his architectural projects in Rome.

Michelangelo was quite aware how his poems and art might be read by skeptical contemporaries. "The evil, foolish, and invidious mob," he feared, "May point and charge to others its own taste" (81). His prediction proved true. Pietro Aretino, Italy's most formidable satirist, angry that Michelangelo had not sent him drawings he thought worthy of his eminence, sent the artist an insolent warning. It would be better to send the drawings, he warned, "if only to silence evil tongues that maintain that only a Gherardo or Tommaso know how to command your courtesy."[135] He then added a direct gibe: "Even if you are divine you don't disdain male consorts."[136]

Two years later Benedetto Varchi lectured in Florence on Michelangelo's love poems and in 1550 published the lectures. Michelangelo was pleased and wrote to express his thanks. Varchi had described Cavalieri as a young nobleman of "incomparable beauty" and "such graceful manners, so excellent an endowment and so charming a demeanor that he deserved, and still deserves, the more to be loved the better he is known."[137] But if Michelangelo assumed that Varchi's respectful treatment of the poems would allay suspicion, he was more than a little naive. Giovanni Dall'Orto has shown how suspect the idea of Platonic love between men had become in Italy by this time. By the midpoint of the sixteenth century, Italian literary critics were quite inclined to regard Platonic love as simply a camouflage for homosexuality and "Socratic love" as an ironic euphemism.

Varchi's own career reveals how Platonic sentiments were being discounted. Varchi himself poured forth a deluge of sonnets to young boys while insisting on the chaste nature of his ardor. But Dall'Orto informs us that he "had a notorious series of homosexual liaisons . . . with well-known boys to whom he taught linguistics and a brand of popular neo-Aristotelian philosophy." In 1526 Varchi was attracted to Giuliano Gondi, who died soon after from wounds incurred in a street fight, and Gondi was succeeded by Lorenzo Lenzi and Giulio della Stufa.[138] Giulio was embarrassed by the poems he received and in 1553 warned Varchi that his protestations of chastity were mocked by other poets. One of them, Francesco Grazzini, had written in this ribald vein:

> O father Varchi, new Socrates . . .
> To you should come scores and scores
> Of pupils from all the world . . .
> Alcibiades and Phaedrus were perfect
> pupils, as Athens saw and knew,
> since they were handsome and young . . .
> His arms open and his trousers down: this is how
> your Bembo is waiting for you in the Elysian fields.[139]

Despite such scandals, Varchi was named consul to the Accademia Fiorentina and was accorded the honor of delivering the eulogy at Michelangelo's funeral in 1564. But the praise bestowed on him by a contemporary in

1583 was qualified by a reservation: "He was known, loved, and honored by all the main men of letters who lived then in Italy. But since he was always inclined to boy-love, and as he called them, *Platonic* [loves], often disguising the names of those he loved [in his poems], he greatly lessened the reputation that would have been rightfully appropriate."[140] All this suggests that Michelangelo and Condivi had been ill-advised to invoke Socrates and Alcibiades in the defense of Michelangelo's sexual purity in the 1553 *Life.* Such an appeal was, by that date, more likely to arouse than to allay suspicions.

Michelangelo's poems did not appear in print until 1623, when they were edited by his great-nephew. Their implications worried Michelangelo the Younger, who deliberately (like the first editor of Shakespeare's sonnets a few earlier later) changed the genders in some to the feminine and revised "resto prigion d'un cavalier armato," with its implied reference to a specific male, to read "I remain a prisoner of a heart armed with virtue."[141] In addition, the great-nephew added a candid manuscript note. Varchi, he complained, "did wrong in printing it according to the text. Remember well that this sonnet, as well as the preceding number and some others, are concerned, as is manifest, with a masculine love of the Platonic species." No accurate text of Michelangelo's poems appeared until 1863.

Vasari, in his *Lives,* was tactful in presenting Michelangelo's relation with Tommaso, whom he called a "Roman noble . . . for whom [Michelangelo] made stupendous designs in black and red chalk including a Rape of Ganymede, [and] the Vulture [sic] eating the heart of Tityus . . . Michelangelo drew a life-size portrait of M. Tommaso, his first and last, for he abhorred drawing anything from life unless it was of the utmost beauty."[142] Vasari mentions another recipient of important drawings by Michelangelo, a Gherardo Perini, who is apparently the Gherardo mentioned by Aretino in his insinuating letter. Little is known about Perini, though some mildly affectionate letters from Michelangelo to him dated 1522 have survived.

Michelangelo wrote several poems bewailing the sinfulness of his love affairs, which he feared would put his salvation at risk (20):

> Ah, Love how rapidly you do appear,
> Armed and powerful, reckless and audacious,
> And out of me you thrust
> The thought of death, even when it is timely . . .
> Cruel revenge accompanies great sin . . .
> How would you have me placed,
> So that my last day, [which should be good,]
> Should be the one of shame and of disaster?

Clearly, these fears reflect Michelangelo's awareness of his homosexual desires, which he would have seen as threatening the damnation he pictured so powerfully in the *Last Judgment.*

Michelangelo's Sistine frescoes are often regarded as the summit of Christian art. There is some irony here when we consider how this papal chapel, built in 1473, resonates with homoerotic associations. Indeed, two of the popes most closely associated with it were the target of gossip. Contemporary accounts call its creator, Sixtus IV, the lover of his handsome nephew Pietro Riario, whom he made a cardinal at the age of twenty-five and upon whom he lavished unheard of wealth, so that his extravagance was compared to a Roman emperor's. Sixtus is repeatedly called a "sodomite" in the diaries of Stefano Infessura, a charge usually discounted by modern historians since Infessura was "an ardent republican and the pope's political enemy."[143] But a century ago John Addington Symonds pointed out that the accusation appears also in the dispatches of the Venetian ambassador and is confirmed by the usually reliable diaries of Johann Burchard, the papal master of ceremonies.[144]

Nor was Sixtus the only suspect member of his family. Similar allegations were made about his nephew Julius II, the "warrior pope" who bullied Michelangelo into painting the Sistine ceiling. In 1511 Julius was condemned by the Council of Pisa as "this sodomite, covered with shameful ulcers."[145] The council had been convened by Louis XII, however, who was at war with Julius and wished to depose him, and so has no canonical standing. The charges were apparently inspired by Julius' fondness for Federigo Gonzaga, Francesco Alidosi, and other young men.[146] The diarist Girolamo Priuli also reported that Julius disported with Ganymedes "without shame" at Ostia and Città Castellana.[147] History has still to assess these rumors.

• Sodoma and Cellini •

The self-torturing Michelangelo presented himself to the world as a lover of male beauty who was platonically chaste. Giovanni Antonio Bazzi (1477–1549), more daring and more candid, startled his contemporaries by adopting—and has come down to posterity bearing—a provocative sobriquet, Il Sodoma, "the sodomite." Born at Vercelli near Milan, Bazzi may have studied under Leonardo during his stay in that city—a Leonardesque quality in his faces suggests this possibility. By 1500 he had settled in Siena and was soon the city's leading artist and a popular, if eccentric, local character. Exactly when he first adopted his opprobrious nickname is uncertain. But in 1513 he signed in this style, beside a marquis and a cardinal, when he entered a horse in the local *palio.*

Though the Renaissance has enjoyed a reputation (hardly deserved) for tolerance, Bazzi was unique in publicly acknowledging his sexual orientation; no other European of comparable note would do so again until André Gide. How did his contemporaries react? The record is decidedly checkered. Vasari, admitting that Bazzi was popular among the common people of

Siena, is sternly censorious: "His manner of life was licentious and dishonorable, and as he always had boys and beardless youths about him of whom he was inordinately fond, this earned him the name of Sodoma; but instead of feeling shame he gloried in it, writing stanzas and verses on it and singing them to the accompaniment of the lute."[148]

Vasari's notice appeared in 1568 shortly after the Council of Trent had finished its long labors, but even in the more liberal earlier part of the century public acceptance was uncertain. In Siena, Sodoma may have avoided harassment, but in Florence when another horse won a race in 1515 there was an ugly incident. Vasari gives this account: "The boys who used to call out the name of the victor after the trumpet had sounded asked him what they should cry, and when he replied 'Sodoma, Sodoma,' they repeated the name. But when some reverend men heard their shouts they began to say, 'What ribaldry is this? Why is such a name shouted in our city?' So before long poor Sodoma, his horse, and a baboon he had with him were stoned by the boys and the mob."[149]

The baboon may surprise the reader, but fondness for animals was another eccentricity for which Sodoma was notorious: "He loved to fill his house with all manners of curious animals, badgers, squirrels, apes, catamounts [mountain lions], dwarf asses, Barbary racehorses, Elba ponies, jackdaws, bantams, turtle-doves, and similar creatures . . . The animals were so tame that they were always about him, with their strange gambols, so that his house resembled a Noah's ark."[150]

Sodoma's contemporaries were not the only admirers embarrassed by his name. In 1908 a scholar, who published what is still the fullest scholarly biography in English, noted that many paintings and drawings "unquestionably his have been attributed to others, seemingly to save their reputations."[151] But even Vasari had to admit that Sodoma was highly regarded, despite the notorious unevenness of his work. Though he excoriated him for his "beastly" habits, extravagant dress, and lack of studiousness, he praised his poignant *Christ at the Pillar,* his swooning Saint Catherine of Siena, and his *Deposition from the Cross,* with its fainting Virgin and elegant legionnaires. Of Sodoma's *Saint Sebastian,* a male nude in a religious guise, John Addington Symonds wrote that it combined "the beauty of a Greek Hylas with the Christian sentiment of martyrdom."[152]

Called to the Vatican to join a galaxy that included Leonardo, Michelangelo, Raphael, Perugino, and Signorelli, Bazzi so pleased Leo X that the pope made him a Cavalier of Christ; henceforth the proud artist signed himself "Antonio Sodoma, Knight of Siena." He still had to face insults. When a Spanish soldier stationed in Siena in the army of the emperor treated him with contempt, Sodoma, who did not know his name, drew his face for identification. The Spanish governor had the man punished and, we are told, became Sodoma's friend and protector.[153]

51. Saint Sebastian. Sodoma, oil, c. 1525.

The persistent theme of Vasari's life is that Sodoma might have been a great painter had it not been for his buffoonery, laziness, and "bestial" pursuits. But his madness endeared him to some of his friends. Aretino, dropping his ironic style, wrote a warmly affectionate letter after they had been separated for thirty years.[154] Raphael admired him and defied the terrible Pope Julius II by declining to paint over his designs in the Vatican. It seems a paradox that in this cohort of bachelor artists, Sodoma should have been the only one to marry. The marriage seems not to have been very comfortable, but Vasari's assertion that Sodoma's wife left him because of his "bestialities" seems to be wrong. A tax report shows them sharing a house in 1541 when Sodoma was sixty-four. Nor is Vasari's contention that Sodoma died poverty-stricken because of his extravagances borne out by the records, which imply that he was reasonably well off. No doubt Vasari found that these stories fitted the moralizing vein of his narrative.[155]

Sodoma, despite his notoriety, kept clear of the law. Benvenuto Cellini (1500–1571) was not so fortunate. Born in Florence, he left his native city in 1519 to seek his fortune as a goldsmith in Rome and then with Francis I at Fontainebleau. His hasty departures from various locales had various causes—quarrels over pay, imagined slights, political changes, and, often enough, fights stemming from his stormy temperament. In 1545 he resettled in Florence to work for Duke Cosimo I, who welcomed the tempestuous artist. Cellini's stay was marked by no fewer than eleven trials for violent behavior.

Cellini was an ardent womanizer, and the famous autobiography, most of which he wrote in 1557–1559 while under house arrest, recounts his many affairs with models and courtesans. He was also susceptible to the charms of adolescent youths, who aroused depths of tenderness that are hardly to be found in his often brutal relations with women. Early in his autobiography he tells of his feelings for a fourteen-year-old Roman boy named Paulino:

> Paulino was the best-mannered, the most honest, and the most beautiful boy I ever saw in my whole life. His modest ways and actions, together with his superlative beauty and his devotion to myself, bred in me as great an affection for him as any man's breast can hold. This passionate love led me oftentimes to delight this lad with music; for I observed that his marvelous features, which by complexion wore a tone of modest melancholy, brightened up when I took my cornet, and broke into a smile so lovely and so sweet, that I do not marvel at the silly stories which the Greeks have written about the deities of heaven. Indeed, if my boy had lived in those times, he would probably have turned their heads still more.[156]

The "silly stories" of course included Ovid's tales of Ganymede and Hyacinth, which Cellini was to illustrate through his art.

This passion for boys was by no means always platonic. In January 1523,

52. Ganymede. Cellini, marble, 1525.

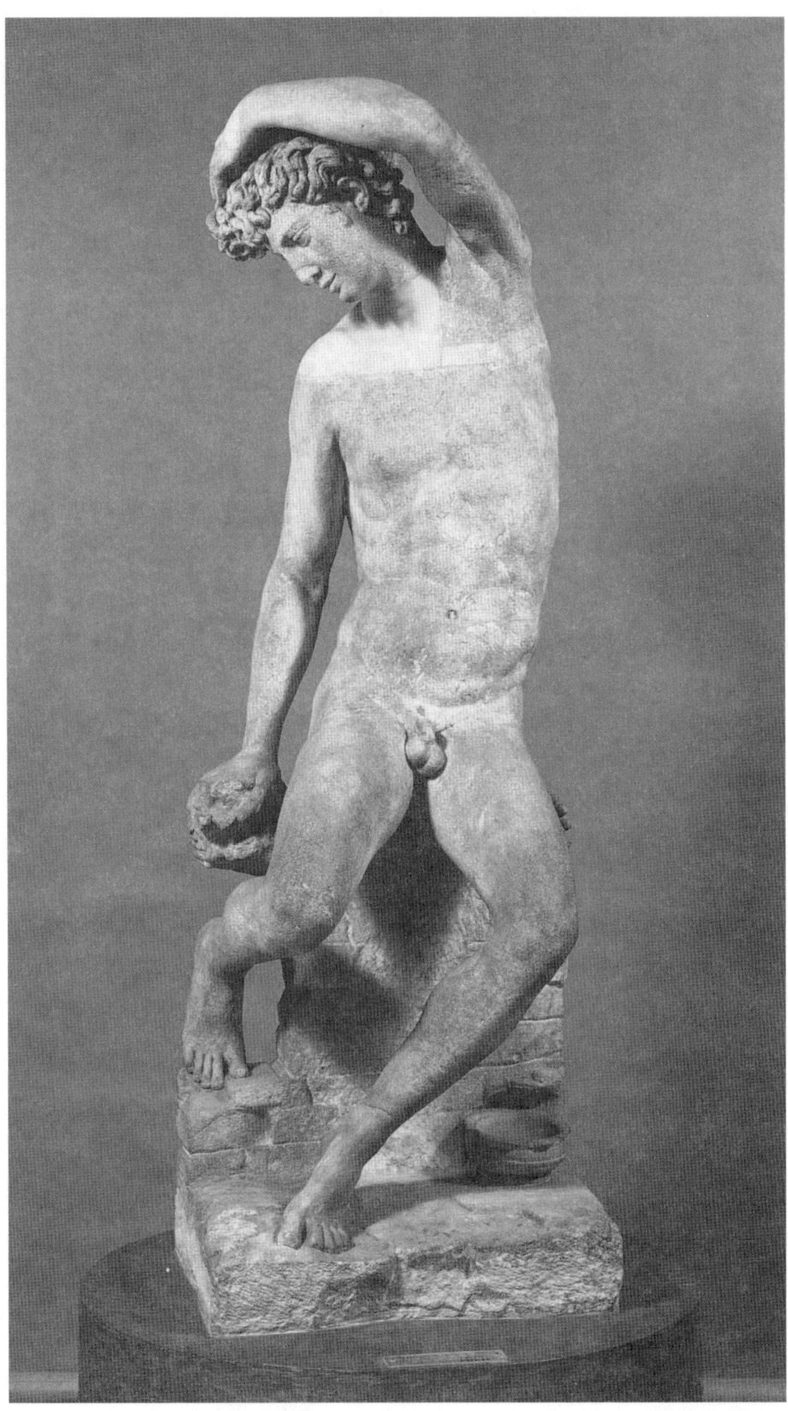

53. Narcissus. Cellini, marble, c. 1550.

during a brief return to Florence, Cellini and another man were convicted of sodomy with a boy named Domenico di Ser Giuliano da Ripa—presumably, from his name, a scion of the middle classes.[157] The trial took place during the first Medicean restoration of 1512–1527, which had, under pressure from its youthful supporters, reintroduced the pre-Savonarolan system of modest fines.[158] Cellini's penalty was twelve measures of flour, a relatively trivial sanction.

When Cellini returned once more to Florence in 1545 to work for the duke, he took the daring step of supplementing his work in gold by casting bronze statutes and carving marble. His first ambitious project was the bronze *Perseus,* a work which still holds a commanding place in the Loggia of the Lancers overlooking Florence's central square. While Cellini was at work on the *Perseus,* the duke showed him a fragment of an antique statue sent him as a gift: "When I had opened the box," Cellini tells us, "I cried to the Duke: 'My lord, this is a statue in Greek marble [it was in fact a torso], and it is a marvel of beauty. I must say that I have never seen a boy's figure so excellently wrought and in so fine a style among all the antiques I have inspected. If you Excellency permits, I should like to restore it—head and arms and feet. I will add an eagle, in order that we may christen the lad Ganymede.'"[159]

Cellini's rhapsodizing was followed by a tense moment when his *bête noire,* the sculptor Bandinelli, appeared on the scene and sneered at the fragment. Cosimo's entourage mischievously encouraged the rivals to spar, and Cellini, seizing the occasion with gusto, delivered a scathing dissertation on the faults of Bandinelli's *Hercules and Cacus.* The infuriated sculptor replied, "Oh sta cheto, sodomitaccio!" ("Oh shut up, you big sodomite!"). A public insult of this sort would ordinarily have moved Cellini to revenge, but violence in the duke's presence would have cost him dearly. Instead, he defused the situation with disingenuous banter: "You madman! You exceed the bounds of decency. Yet would to God that I understood so noble an art as you allude to; they say that Jove used it with Ganymede in paradise, and here upon this earth it is practiced by some of the greatest emperors and kings. I, however, am but a poor, humble creature, who neither have the power nor the intelligence to perplex my wits with anything so admirable."[160] The tension burst as the court exploded into wild laughter.

Cellini's restored *Ganymede,* which now stands in Florence's Museo Nazionale del Bargello, has none of the Platonic symbolism of Michelangelo's drawing. Here a mischievous pretty boy holds a goldfinch to tease the attendant eagle while he ruffles a neck feather with a finger of his other hand. Also inspired by homoerotic motifs are two other works which Cellini undertook not on commission but to please himself. The first was an *Apollo and Hyacinth,* in which the god, about to launch his discus, places one hand protectively on the head of the boy who crouches behind him. The other shows an elegantly posed *Narcissus,* arm flung over his head, gazing entranced at the face in the pool at his feet. Taken together, these three works make up a unique contribution to homoerotic Renaissance sculpture.

Like Donatello, Cellini often had young assistants working for him in his studio, and in his autobiography he often remarks on their beauty. Besides Paulino there was Ascanio, whom he calls "one of the handsomest boys in Rome." Cellini also speaks admiringly of Diego, a Spanish boy who lived next door, who had a "head and face far more beautiful than those of the antique Antinous."[161] On one occasion Cellini dressed Diego as a girl and took him to a party where other artists were parading their mistresses. Diego, whom Cellini called an "honest, virtuous, and studious lad," was the hit of the evening and the discovery of his sex provoked much amusement. But his employment of another boy, Cencio—"of extreme personal beauty"—caused a crisis.[162] Cencio's mother, a prostitute named Gambetta, egged on by Cosimo's jealous majordomo, tried to extract money by accusing Cellini of improper relations. In his autobiography Cellini claims that he confronted Cencio directly with the question: "You know, Cencio, whether I have sinned with you!" to which the weeping boy answered "No!"[163] Nevertheless Cellini, fearing prosecution, thought it wise to leave Florence for Venice, even though it meant suspending work on the *Perseus.*

Passionate, generous, tender, and dangerous when he felt himself injured, Cellini was not a man to restrain his sexual impulses. Like Michelangelo, he professed admiration for the sermons of Savonarola, but he did not agonize over his salvation. God, he felt, was on his side, despite a few homicides. Imprisoned in an unhealthy dungeon in Rome, Cellini claimed to have been comforted by divine visions which inspired his final masterpiece, the life-size marble *Crucifixion* now in the Escorial.

But if Cellini felt assured of God's favor, he had still to fear the civil authorities. The lenience of the early sixteenth century had given way to greater severity in Florence. When the second republic fell in 1530, the second Medici restoration did not manifest the liberalism of the first, and Duke Cosimo enacted harsh new laws on sodomy and blasphemy.[164] Cellini fell afoul of these shortly after his release from prison. The artist had taken a boy named Fernando into his service in 1551, left him a legacy in his will, and then, after a quarrel, revoked it in June of 1556. John Pope-Hennessy thinks this imbroglio may have inspired the subsequent prosecution of Cellini. For on February 27, 1557, it was charged that "for about five years he had held as his apprentice a youth, Fernando di Giovanni da Montepulciano, with whom he had carnal intercourse very many times and committed the crime of sodomy, sleeping in the same bed with him as if he were a wife."[165]

Forewarned, Cellini fled Florence but was recognized and captured before he could escape Tuscan territory. Confessing to "having sodomized the said Fernando," he was sentenced to four years in prison and the loss of his civil rights.[166] He spent another few weeks in the Stinche and was then released under house arrest on an appeal to the duke by the bishop of Pavia. It was to this enforced detention that we owe the incomparable autobiography. In July he began to dictate the manuscript to a fourteen-year-old amanuensis, and two years later he sent a draft to Benedetto Varchi. In 1563, two years after his release, he secretly married his maid and in his sixties produced four children to add to his illegitimate brood. Restored to civic honors, he bore with Varchi the prime responsibility for the arrangements for Michelangelo's funeral in 1564. He himself died seven years later, aged seventy-one.

• Rome and Caravaggio •

The Council of Trent, which was to define the Counter Reformation, met first in 1545 during the pontificate of Paul III. But Paul, for whom Michelangelo labored and Cellini designed coins and plate, was essentially a Renaissance pope. So was his successor, the pleasure-loving Julius III (1550–1555), whose homosexual affairs would be rehearsed with relish by Protestant polemicists for more than a century. But Paul IV (1555–1559) was a different sort. Sternly ascetic, he revived the Papal Inquisition to deal with Protestant heretics. Paul IV saw heresy everywhere, and according to the Catholic historian Ludwig Pastor, "An actual reign of terror began, which filled all Rome with fear."[167] Moreover, the jurisdiction of the Inquisition was now extended to cover such sexual offences as sodomy, bigamy, and rape.[168] How homosexuals fared in this atmosphere of fanaticism, which also marked the pontificate of Pius V (1566–1572)—who had himself served as inquisitor general before his election—scholarship has yet to tell us; there is no work on Rome and the papacy to match the researches of Rocke, Ruggiero, and Labalme on law enforcement in Florence and Venice.

Pius's successor, Gregory XIII, is chiefly known to history as the reformer of the calendar. But during his tenure an extraordinary episode took place of which we have a terse account in the dispatches of the Venetian ambassador Antonio Tiepolo in 1578: "Eleven Portuguese and Spaniards have been captured. They had assembled in a church near Saint John Lateran where they had performed some ceremonies of a horrible wickedness which sullied the sacred name of matrimony, marrying each other and being joined together as husband and wife. Twenty-seven or more, it is said, were discovered altogether on other occasions, but at this time they were not able to capture more than this eleven, who were given to the fire as they deserved."[169]

What makes this report truly remarkable is the claim that the victims had been married not in a secret ceremony but publicly in a Roman church. Did some priest actually perform a nuptial rite? Tiepolo seems to imply this. Given the unwavering hostility of church authorities to sodomy as the vilest of sins and the harsh temper of the times, this seems astonishing. John Boswell, in an intriguing book-length study, has investigated liturgies for what he calls, with some ambiguity, "same-sex unions." But these ceremonies, intended to establish bonds of "spiritual brotherhood" between male friends, are Greek and Slavonic rites deriving from Balkan churches of the tenth to thirteenth centuries and were hardly meant to condone sexual relations.

There is no reason, however, to doubt the ambassador's story. Montaigne, visiting Rome three years later, heard of the event as a recent sensation. His *Travel Journal* of 1580–81 confirms that the ceremonies were conducted in full seriousness and were an attempt, however foolhardy, to give dignity to relationships the men took seriously. Montaigne writes:

> On my return from Saint Peter's I met a man who informed me humorously of two things: that the Portuguese made their obeisance [to the Pope] in Passion week [that is, they suffered in making it]; and then, that on this same day the station was at San Giovanni Porta Latina, in which church a few years before certain Portuguese had entered into a strange brotherhood. They married one another, male to male, at Mass, with the same ceremonies with which we perform our marriage services, the same marriage gospel service, and then went to bed and lived together. The Roman wits *[esprits]* said that because in the other conjunction, of male with female, this circumstance alone makes it legitimate, it had seemed to these sharp folk that this other action would become equally legitimate if they authorized it with ceremonies and mysteries of the Church. Eight or nine Portuguese of this fine sect were burned.[170]

(The first edition of 1774 prints *esperis,* which editors have emended to *esprits* or *experts.* Boswell adopts the latter reading, but the first seems more in keeping with the tone of the passage, which puts forth the rationale as a joke.)

It is tantalizing not to know more about these men, but we can draw at least a few conclusions from these brief reports. First, expatriate Portuguese and Spaniards in Rome made up a social group sufficiently organized to form a small congregation in a Roman church. There, several—it is not clear exactly how many—were married by the rites usually reserved for legal matrimony. But what this "belle secte," as Montaigne calls them, looked upon as sanctification of their relationships as committed couples Church authorities saw as a blasphemous profanation of sacred rites. We can have no doubt that the burnings proceeded with full ecclesiastical approval. Presumably, they would have taken place in the ironically named Campo di Fiori (Field of Flowers). This was the traditional site of such executions in Rome, where a statue now stands to the philosopher Giordano Bruno, burned there in 1600.

Gregory's successor, Sixtus V (1585–1590), who had been a zealous officer of the Inquisition in Venice, put down a crime wave with such ferocity as to shock the Romans. A grim joke found "more severed heads . . . nailed to the

Sant'Angelo bridge than there were melons in the market stalls."[171] His severity also reached to consensual sex acts: he terrified the city by threatening death to Rome's adulterers. In June 1586 he burned not only a priest but also the boy who had sinned with him. Pastor tells us this pair were burned even though "both had voluntarily admitted their fault."[172]

Yet Rome, as the seventeenth century dawned, was not a narrowly puritanical city. Annibale Carracci, for instance, decorated the ceiling of the Farnese Palace with scenes from Ovid depicting every kind of amorous adventure, including the rape of a handsome Ganymede and the love of Apollo for Hyacinth.[173] Another prince of the church not averse to art with erotic—and especially homoerotic—overtones was Cardinal Francesco Maria del Monte, who became the first patron of Caravaggio. The greatest Italian painter of the new century, Michelangelo di Merisi da Caravaggio became known by the name of the town near Milan where he was born. At age nineteen he migrated to Rome, where he lived in the household of the cardinal, about whom one biographer wrote, "He loved the company of youths . . . [and at first] he gave no cause for censure, wisely keeping everything private. After Urban VIII's election [in 1623] . . . he dedicated himself openly to his tendencies."[174] Repeatedly in difficulties because of ruffianism, Caravaggio—a swaggering swordsman with the temperament of a mafioso—fled Rome for Malta in 1606 after killing a man in a brawl over a tennis game. There his skill as a painter earned him election to the Knights of Malta; nevertheless he was eventually jailed for an assault on a nobleman, after which he escaped to Sicily, where he painted some of his most powerful religious masterpieces.

We do not have the kind of legal and literary evidence for Caravaggio that we have for Leonardo, Michelangelo, and Cellini. We know only that in a trial for libel in 1603 a witness accused him of sharing a *bardassa* named Giovani Battista with his longtime friend Onorio Longhi. Caravaggio denied knowing the boy, however.[175] Yet modern art historians find a marked homoerotic element in his early paintings, fostered, it has been suggested, by the ambience of Del Monte's circle. These portraits depict "fleshly, full-lipped, languorous boys" who seem to solicit the onlooker with their offers of fruit, wine, flowers—and themselves.[176] Caravaggio's androgynous *Boy with a Basket of Fruit* begins the series. In the *Boy Bitten by a Lizard,* a girlish-looking youth recoils with effeminate alarm. One painting for Del Monte, the *The Musicians,* shows "pampered mignons" undressed or with clothes slipping from their shoulders, while the gender of the central figure in the *Luteplayer* has been debated since the artist's own day.

Most startling of all are his *Saint John,* which depicts a grinning street-boy in an exhibitionistic pose, embracing not the "Lamb of God" but a sexually mature ram, and *Amor vincit omnia,* in which a smirking urchin exposes himself shamelessly to our gaze. As Howard Hibbert has remarked, comparing Caravaggio's *Amor* with his namesake's *Ganymede,* "Michelangelo subli-

54. Bacchus. Caravaggio, oil, c. 1593.

mated the erotic story into a divine, quasi-Platonic metaphor of the aspiration of the soul to God. Caravaggio turned a pagan, heterosexual symbol that had become a cliché into a boy of the streets and an object of pederastic interest."[177]

According to an eighteenth-century manuscript, Caravaggio's interest in boys upset a teacher in Messina, whose pupils he followed on holidays "to observe the positions of these playful boys and to form his inventions."[178]

When the man complained, Caravaggio wounded him and had to flee once more, first to Naples, then to Port' Ercole on the coast of Tuscany, where he was imprisoned by mistake. Released, he wandered on the shore under the July sun, contracted a fever, and died in 1610 at the age of thirty-nine. His arresting art, ranging from portraits of youths like the ambiguous Uffizi *Bacchus* to coarse peasant figures in powerfully realized religious scenes, dramatically lit, and often startling in their realism, would influence a generation and win renewed appreciation from twentieth-century critics.

CHAPTER TEN

SPAIN AND THE INQUISITION

1497–1700

• The Spanish Inquisition •

In Tuscany, a modest degree of liberalism mitigated deadly laws and limited suffering. In Spain, no such restraint checked ecclesiastical fury or civic punitiveness. This was the nation of Christian Europe where hatred for homosexuals ran deepest and persecution was most intense. Political absolutism, historical racial conflicts, and popular superstition all conspired to fuel the fires of prejudice. In Castilian Madrid and Andalusian Seville, action by the secular authorities was merciless and swift. And in half the new state—in the provinces of Aragon, Valencia, and Catalonia—homosexual conduct was in the course of the century brought under the jurisdiction of Renaissance Europe's most formidable instrument of oppression, the Spanish Inquisition. Spain's Siglo de Oro, its splendid Golden Century, the zenith of its culture, wealth, and influence, was for homosexuals a Siglo de Terror.

In the final years of the fifteenth century, the unification of Spain under Ferdinand of Aragon and Isabella of Castile immensely increased royal power and limited feudalism. Unfortunately, the new royal authority was not exercised in the interests of toleration. So, in 1492, as Spain "liberated" the last Moorish kingdom and Columbus laid the foundation for the overseas empire, Jews who would not accept conversion were exiled. Though the power of the feudal nobles waned, medieval fear and superstition were not diminished. Instead, they grew stronger, as Ferdinand and Isabella created a new and distinctively Spanish Inquisition. A rage for conformity swept the country, fed by fears about the loyalty of the newly converted Jews and the remaining Moors and, as a new century dawned, by the rise of Protestantism in northern Europe. In this cauldron of religious and racial anxieties, Spain came to suffer what Ortega y Gasset has called "the great phobias of the collective imagination."[1] Outsiders of whatever kind fell under suspicion, and foreigners were especially suspect—Germans, French, and English of "Lutheranism," Italians and Muslims of *sodomia.*

55. Isabella of Castile and Ferdinand of Aragon. Juan de Flandes and Dutch School, oil, c. 1500.

The *Siete Partidas* (c. 1265) made natural disasters a sign of God's displeasure with sodomites, who now became scapegoats in times of distress. When a plague broke out in Barcelona in 1476, the local government burned five such men; others were to die there in 1493 and 1501.[2] The grotesquely cruel laws of Alfonso X had prescribed castration and suspension. We have an eyewitness description of their application by a German visitor in 1495. In the small southern port of Almería, recently freed from the Moors, Hieronymus Münzer saw six naked corpses "hanging upside down with their genitals about their necks." He was told they were Italians. But the penalty was not reserved for foreigners; later Münzer saw two Castilians suffer the same torment in Madrid.[3]

Burning may have been a less excruciating death. Ferdinand and Isabella were orthodox enough to favor it. At Medina del Campo in 1497 the Reyes Católicos issued a edict exacting this penalty. Its verbose rhetoric summed up the prejudices and fears of a thousand years:

> Since among the other sins and crimes which especially offend God Our Lord and bring infamy to the earth the crime committed against the natu-

ral order is especially notable, the laws must arm themselves with punishment against this abominable crime *[pecado nefando]* which it is not decent even to name, a destroyer of the natural order, punished by divine justice. Through it nobility perishes, courage is lost, and faith weakened. It is abhorrent to the worship of God Who in His indignation sends pestilence and other earthly torments. It gives birth to much opprobrium, insults the people and the land which tolerate it [Italy?], and merits the greatest punishment which can be inflicted for any deed . . . Because the penalties hitherto established are not sufficient to castigate and extirpate totally . . . such an abominable crime . . . we order and command that any person of whatever rank, condition, pre-eminence, or dignity who commits the abominable crime against nature, being convicted by that means which according to the law is sufficient to prove the crime of heresy or lese majesty ["injury to the state," that is, treason] shall be burned in flames of fire.[4]

A further clause allowed men to be burned even for attempts that fell short of consummation.[5] A provision that could be counted on to whet the appetite of Spanish kings for convictions made convicted men's goods forfeit to the royal treasury.[6]

Whereas popular feeling moderated punishments in Italy, mobs in Spain looked on sodomites with the same fierce detestation they felt for heretics, Jews, and Moriscos. This animosity was reflected in the rich vocabulary of colloquial abuse. Men suspected of homosexual inclinations were labeled *sodomitas* or *bujarrones* (from the Italian *buggiaron*). Especially degrading were the terms for men perceived as playing a feminine role—*bardaje* (from the Italian *bardassa*), *marica* ("little Mary"), and *puto* ("male whore"), the ultimate degrading insult. This last epithet was hurled derisively at an effigy of Isabella's brother, Henry IV of Castile, at the climax of a public ceremony of dethronement in Ávila on June 4, 1464.[7]

This hate also sparked one of the most famous episodes of Spanish social history, the revolt of the *Germanía* (Brotherhood) in 1519. In the city of Valencia an insurrection against the new young ruler, Charles I, took a revolutionary turn when the working classes, exasperated by low wages and laws banning unions, took up arms. On June 14 a Franciscan friar named Luis Castelloli preached an inflammatory sermon ascribing an outbreak of plague to God's wrath against sodomy. An excited mob hunted down four suspects, who were duly burned by the authorities on July 29. A fifth man held minor religious orders and was tried by an ecclesiastical court; when it prescribed a lesser penalty, the mob seized him, strangled him, and burned his body.[8] Fearing punishment, the leaders organized the *Germanía* to defend themselves, beginning a revolt it took Charles two years to subdue.

Harsh as the secular laws were, worse was to follow. The right of the Inquisition to burn sodomites rested on papal claims that were affirmed in an influential manual of procedure, the *Directorium inquisitorum* of Nicolas Eymeric. Eymeric, who had been inquisitor-general in Catalonia, wrote his manual at the papal court in Avignon in 1376. Reprinted many times, it remained a standard guide for procedure throughout the sixteenth and seventeenth centuries and made sweeping claims for papal authority. The pope might, Eymeric held, judge all Christian rulers and subjects in the light of biblical and canon law through the instrument of the Inquisition. Jews, Muslims, and other infidels did not generally come under its jurisdiction in matters of faith—an immunity they lost only upon conversion. But in certain questions of morals, he argued, all infidels, like all Christians, were subject to the judgment of the church, since Christ had delegated his divine power to judge all men to Peter and his successors, the Roman pontiffs: "It follows necessarily from these reasons that, by law if not in fact, the power of the pope extends over all men. By virtue of this power I do not see why the pope should refrain from punishing any heathen who violates natural law, since the latter does not know any other. The proof? God punished the Sodomites who sinned against natural law (Gen. 19). Now, the judgments of God are our examples! Consequently, why should the pope not proceed, if he has the means, as God proceeds!"[9] This breathtaking assertion claimed papal power of life and death over all sodomites, not only in Christian Europe but in lands of other faiths as yet unknown beyond the seas.

Eymeric justified ecclesiastical sanctions by appealing to the Sodom legend. But the pope's authority rested on his claim to be the vicar of Christ. Could not Jesus himself be represented as a homophobe despite his silence on the subject? An anonymous functionary of the tribunal at Valencia achieved this transformation in 1494 when he compiled a *Diccionario de los inquisidores* which drew on an obscure medieval legend that all homosexuals had died at the moment of Christ's birth. "The day of the birth of Our Lord Jesus Christ was prefigured according to Saint Augustine and Saint Jerome by the fire of Sodom, since all the sodomites in the world were annihilated on that night. The same Saint Jerome comments on Isaiah (VIII–X): 'The light was so potent that it destroyed all those who had engaged in that vice. It was the work of Christ. It carried out the extirpation of this filth from the face of the earth.'"[10] There is a mystery here. Modern research has found no source for the legend in the works of Jerome or Augustine, despite the specificity of the references, and has failed to trace it back beyond the early thirteenth century.[11] But this fantastic and ugly fable, which turned the prince of peace and good will into a mass murderer, gained a powerful hold on the Iberian imagination. It was repeated in a theological treatise by a Cuban archbishop as late as 1860.[12]

Nevertheless, the papacy did not always see fit to exercise its theoretical right to try sodomites through its inquisitors. It was an authority delegated to them on some occasions and withheld on others. Ferdinand and Isabella had in 1478 obtained papal sanction to set up a Spanish Inquisition whose primary aim was to enforce religious conformity among the Jews in Spain who had accepted Christianity. As a result of this campaign, thousands of Conversos, whose baptism had been coerced by force or fear, were burned on charges of having continued to secretly observe Jewish practices. Then, in January 1505, Ferdinand also issued a decree granting his new Castilian Inquisition authority to try sodomites.[13] A year later there was a spate of arrests in Seville; many men fled, but eventually twelve were convicted and burned by sentence of the local tribunal.[14] In 1509, however, the Supreme Council of the Inquisition in Madrid—commonly known as the Suprema—ruled that the organization should not be diverted from its primary task of hunting down heretics and Judaizers. Thereafter, the Inquisition in Castile left the prosecution of sodomites to the secular courts, whose own fervent piety and prejudice could be counted on to mete out a comparable severity.

In Aragon, by a "fateful accident," things took a different turn. William Monter, in his *Frontiers of Heresy*, has told the story in rich detail. What made the Spanish Inquisition unique was Ferdinand's determination to use it as an instrument of state power and national unity. Since the Inquisition had its headquarters in the Castilian city of Madrid, it was resisted by the provinces that made up the Crown of Aragon because they feared it would infringe on their local laws and liberties. (The Crown of Aragon consisted of the ancient kingdom of Aragon, Catalonia, the kingdom of Valencia on the east coat of Spain, the islands of Majorca, Sardinia, and Sicily, and the much-contested kingdom of Naples.) The Valencian and Aragonese opposition to Ferdinand had came from nobles who wished to protect their Converso and Moorish subjects. This struggle eventually involved the Aragonese Inquisition in sodomy prosecutions.

In Aragon the Inquisition had been opposed by a prominent Converso, Don Sancho de la Caballería. A grandson of a converted Jew, Don Sancho was nevertheless indubitably orthodox. Unable to bring a charge of heresy against him, the Saragossa tribunal accused him of sodomy and sought permission from Pope Clement VII to try him on the charge.[15] In 1524 the compliant pope issued a "hunting license" allowing three particular tribunals—those of Aragon, Valencia, and Catalonia—to try sodomites. Clement gave color to this new policy by associating the offense with the Moors: "We have learned, not without distress to our soul, that in the Kingdoms of Aragon and Valencia and in the Principality of Catalonia—as the world continually goes to the worse, alas—among some children of the infidels [Moors] the horrendous and detestable crime of sodomy has begun to spread and that if these debased kinds of men are not isolated they can drag down the faithful into this corruption."[16] Accordingly, Clement allowed the Inquisition in these three states—whose tribunals met in Saragossa, Barcelona, and the city of Valencia—to try sodomites.

This edict specified, however, that such trials must be conducted not by inquisitorial procedures but by the procedures laid down by local laws. Consequently, the accused was allowed to confront witnesses against him and was not to be tortured. Such was the power of the Inquisition, however, that the tribunals ignored this last provision and regularly tortured men to extract confessions. When finally, in 1593, a lawyer had the temerity to complain that such torture was illegal, the Suprema in Madrid replied that custom had long sanctioned its use.[17]

Don Sancho, whose arrest had inspired this extension of inquisitorial power, sought help from the archbishop of Saragossa, who intervened in his sentencing. The Inquisition, however, complained to the pope that his punishment was too lenient. Their victim, still in prison in 1531, cheated death by dying, but others accused of homosexuality were less fortunate. In 1541 a rural priest named Salvador Vidal was "relaxed" to the secular arm, "relaxation" being an ecclesiastical euphemism for handing a convicted man over for execution. (The church was not supposed to be responsible for the taking of life, but this was a hollow hypocrisy since it was well understood how the civic authorities would act.) In 1546 a layman was burned for sodomy at an *auto da fe* ("act of faith"). Others were publicly exhibited at *autos* after their convictions, then given long sentences as galley slaves. In 1558 the Saragossa tribunal burned four more sodomites at an *auto*—a lawyer, two priests, and a French shepherd boy.[18] As the successive campaigns against Judaizers, relapsed Moorish converts, and Protestant heretics achieved their ends by extirpating these dissenters, trials for sodomy—now interpreted as also including bestiality—formed a large part of the work of the three tribunals, which, in the last decades of the sixteenth century and the beginning of the seventeenth, were among the most active in Spain.

In 1571 the Suprema warned the Saragossa tribunal that "in sodomy trials the prisoners should not be promised mercy." The tribunal took the hint, and arrests accelerated. The next year twelve men were burned together at an *auto,* three for homosexuality and nine for bestiality. (To conform with Old Testament law, the "guilty" animals were executed along with the men.) On this occasion the Holy Office found it hard to provide enough wood for the simultaneous fires.[19] In the 1570s Saragossa tried over 100 men for sodomy and executed 36, mainly for bestiality. In the period from 1570 to 1630, when the Inquisition was most active in such matters, executions for sodomy (in both senses) in the Crown of Aragon outnumbered those for heresy. All told, about 400 men were tried and 70 executed for homosexuality in Aragon, Valencia, and Catalonia in this period.[20] If we count also the pre-1570 deaths in Saragossa and the dozen men burned in Seville in 1506, the Spanish Inquisition was responsible, during the period when it acted in such cases, for putting to death about a hundred men for sexual relations with other males.[21]

When we consider that the secular courts in such Castilian cities as Seville and Madrid each executed about an equal number, also under laws that were directly inspired by religion, it would appear that, after 1550, the number of men executed for homosexuality in Spain exceeded the number burned for Protestant heresies (about 200) in the sixteenth and seventeenth centuries.[22] Since those who endured other harsh punishments for homosexuality at the hands of the Inquisition outnumbered by four or five times those sentenced to death, the church must bear the guilt for having inflicted an enormous amount of unwarranted and atrociously cruel suffering. This was arguably the worst moment in the history of a mighty institution, which at its best was capable of producing great men, great art, and notable works of charity.

Though secular justice was also severe in the period, what distinguished the Inquisition was its calculated use of terror. *Autos* were entertainments for huge masses of people, and, like our contemporary sporting matches, embellished with gripping theatrical effects. "Crowds of familiars [lay officers] gathered from all over the district, dressed in the uniform of the Holy Office. Solemn processions with gigantic crosses and green candles advertised the main event. Specially dressed prisoners, sometimes with their crimes identified by placards around their necks [those condemned for sodomy bore the label *sodomita*], prostrated themselves before the Inquisitors in order to receive absolution . . . The general public *auto* seen here in full baroque flower was a truly remarkable event."[23]

But the professed aim of the inquisitors was less to punish the guilty individual than to strike fear in the multitude. Eymeric's manual, reissued in Rome in 1578 with the approval of Gregory XIII and a definitive commentary by Francisco Peña, a leading Spanish scholar of canon law, made this a first principle. "We must remember," Peña wrote, "that the chief purpose of the trial and death sentence is not to save the soul of the accused but to promote the public good and to terrorize the people *[ut alli terreantur]*."[24] Records for the first fifty years of the Inquisition, when there were a great many killings, are incomplete. But studies for the years from 1540 to 1700 provide a preliminary total of 44,000 trials.[25] The pervasiveness of the Inquisition in Spanish society was remarkable. The tribunal at Valencia alone had 1,638 "familiars," that is, associated laymen who served as spies and as police with the authority to arrest men and women.[26] They were usually common citizens—farmers and workmen who kept close watch on their neighbors' speech and actions even in the smaller villages. Under these circumstances, men who were attracted to other men, or women who loved women, lived in constant danger of denunciation.

As the case of Don Sancho had initiated prosecutions for sodomy in Aragon in 1524, so the trial of another nobleman inaugurated arrests in the kingdom of Valencia.[27] Once again the issue was raised as to whether the inquisitorial tribunal in Valencia had the right to try sodomites. The matter was settled by appealing to Clement VII's bull of 1524. Once the barrier was breached, cases multiplied. Two executions took place in Valencia in 1573; the men were Trinitarian monks.[28] (We may recall that Pius V's bull of 1568 made this possible.) During the next fifteen years about two dozen more men were executed for sodomy; about half the cases involved homosexuality. Then there was a lull in prosecutions: in the next three decades only four men died in Valencia.

Executions in Valencia resumed and reached their peak in the 1620s, culminating in mass executions in 1625. Though sixteen trials for sodomy had been held in 1622 and 1623, no one had been burned. Piqued by this apparent lenience, the Suprema in Madrid complained that the tribunal in Valencia was not applying torture with enough vigor. "Armed with such instructions, the Valencia Inquisition proceeded to torture its sodomy suspects more energetically over the next few years."[29] In 1625 six men identified a teenage prostitute who had slept with them. Under questioning, the youth, whose name was Nicolas Gonzales, implicated over sixty men and boys. Though under the age of majority at the time of his involvement, Gonzales was sentenced to death, and eleven other men were sent to the stake with him at a spectacular *auto de fe* in Valencia in November 1625. "The audience was treated to the unprecedented spectacle of a dozen men dressed in purple shirts, wearing the usual white miters on their heads, but with reddish collars and signs labeled with the single word *sodomita.* An eyewitness reported that it took 128 quintals of wood to burn them and seven hours to finish the job, 'something never seen or heard of in Valencia.'"[30] Seven of the men were slaves. As one of these, a forty-year-old Turk, complained, "You people have freedom and even bosses who will look out for you and get you off, but with us slaves it is just capture and burn straight away."[31]

The prosecutions for sodomy under the Aragonese inquisition reached their peak during the years 1570 to 1630. By Mary Perry's estimation "nearly 1,000 trials were held in these years [for homosexuality and bestiality] and more than 150 men died. In fact, in these jurisdictions during this period, as many men were executed on sodomy charges as on heresy charges."[32] In the extended period 1540 to 1700, Perry estimates there were 1,600 cases.[33] Now, however, in the wake of the Valencian holocaust, the Suprema's enthusiasm for burning sodomites began to wane, and it now forbade the exhibition of sodomites at public *autos.* In 1626 two men were quietly executed inside the Inquisition's palace "without making a noise." An execution in Valencia—of a Morisco slave for raping a Christian boy—took place two years later.[34] Henry Charles Lea records a burning at an *auto* in Barcelona in 1647.[35] But this by no means ended trials for sodomy. Lesser but severe sentences, including imprisonment, hundreds of lashes, long terms in the galleys, and fines and banishment, continued to be meted out. Lea counted exactly one hundred cases of sodomy before inquisitorial tribunals during the final period of their existence from 1780 to 1820.[36]

What of women who made love to other women in Hapsburg Spain? The Inquisition, like the civil authorities, seems rarely to have been concerned with cases of lesbianism. In 1560, however, several women in a town in Aragon were accused of engaging in such practices. The Suprema ruled, however, that the tribunal should not prosecute behavior unless an artificial phallus was used.[37] In this they were undoubtedly influenced by the opinions of secular jurists. The *Partidas* of Alfonso X had prescribed the death penalty only for men. But the standard gloss on the *Partidas,* published by Gregorio López in 1555, argued at length that the law applied to women by invoking the 1497 law of Ferdinand and Isabella which, as López argued, referred to "any person of whatever condition who has unnatural intercourse."[38] Antonio Gómez, the leading commentator on criminal law in Renaissance Spain, who was much cited by other European authorities of the day, held that if a woman had relations with another woman by means of any material instrument, both must be burned; otherwise, a lighter penalty was permissible.[39]

In the 1620s two women were sentenced to die in Castile by the secular courts; on appeal, the sentence was changed to 400 lashes and perpetual banishment. They were subsequently pardoned in 1625, on what grounds is not clear. Three decades later the Inquisition convicted a widow and a laundress who had been spied upon by neighbors in Saragossa. We do not know their fate.[40]

Among Spanish rulers, Philip II was especially determined to extend the Inquisition's power over sodomites. In the last years of his reign he asked Pope Clement VIII to grant jurisdiction over sodomites to the Spanish Inquisition in Sicily.[41] The conflict that consequently took place on that island between Spanish intolerance and Italian unwillingness to accept the church's teachings on sex is fascinating to observe. Spain of course controlled secular as well as inquisitorial justice in Palermo. (Sodomy, as we have seen, had been traditionally defined as *mixti fori*—a crime that could be punished by either the state or church.) Philip apparently thought the royal court in Palermo too lenient, for in 1569 he ordered the death penalty to be rigidly enforced, "without exceptions."[42] Still not satisfied, he arranged a concordat with the pope in 1597 transferring the offense to the Inquisition. Philip died the next year, however, and the Spanish viceroy, prompted by influential Sicilian nobles, persuaded the pope to revoke the edict.

The disparate views of Italians and Spaniards on homosexuality are dramatized in Sicilian heresy trials. Traditionally, fornication as such did not fall within the scope of the Inquisition. If someone expressed the belief that fornication was not a sin, however, this constituted a "heretical proposition" that might occasion a trial. When the Council of Trent inaugurated a new era of sexual puritanism, the Inquisition in Spain launched a campaign against such moral dissent, and many skeptics were disciplined. In Sicily, however, skepticism about the sinfulness of heterosexual relations was so common that the Inquisition hardly concerned itself with such cases. In this Italian milieu it was necessary, as William Monter has pointed out, to affirm that *sodomy* was not a sin in order to attract the attention of the Holy Office.

Prosecutions in Sicily reveal that a surprising number of Italians could be found who had made public declarations to this effect, even in the face of inquisitorial threats. Most often men defended anal relations with women as a legitimate means of birth control. In 1644, even after a long campaign against this particular heresy, a priest was condemned to five years in the galleys for publicly defending the view that "fornication was not sinful, or even sodomy."[43] The records of the Inquisition in Palermo indicate that some Italians enjoyed scandalizing conservative Spaniards: a serving man from north Italy appeared before the Inquisition after he voiced the opinion that homosexuality could not be sinful "because nature permitted it." One case throws an oblique light on the Roman marriages of 1578 by revealing a secret sympathy among some Italian clergy: a Franciscan friar had argued that homosexual love could be "holy and just." He was punished with a public whipping and a year's imprisonment.

Though the Sicilian Inquisition was denied permission to hear sodomy cases generally, it was allowed to discipline the men who made up its own large secular corps—the familiars. Indeed, it tried 173 accusations against such men in the period 1595–1635. "The defendants included a baron and a count, who were each fined and given long prison terms in Sicilian castles."[44] In the meantime, the royal court in Palermo implemented Philip's antihomosexual campaign through executions. A religious confraternity—the Bianchi (or "white" monks), officially the Order of the Most Holy Crucifix—ministered to condemned men. From their registry of the damned it has been estimated that about one hundred men were *impiccati e bruciati*, "hanged and burned," in Palermo between 1567 and 1640 for the "abominable sin."[45]

• Subcultures in Valencia and Seville •

If, to the above tally, we add arrests in such Spanish cities as Seville and Madrid (which we shall examine shortly), we may reasonably assume that trials specifically for homosexuality in mainland Spain in the sixteenth and seventeenth centuries numbered between one and two thousand. On the basis of this legal evidence, can we descry a homosexual subculture in Spain of the Siglo de Oro? Obviously, the difficulties in answering this question are formidable. In the midst of such persecutions, in which lives were quite literally at stake, one would expect homosexual coteries to be fear-obsessed and furtive to an extreme degree. Not until the twentieth century would homosexuals in Europe dare to form communities and openly document their own history. Given the high level of popular suspicion and organized surveillance, it would have been dangerous in Spain to keep a candid diary, to write intimate letters, or circulate poems like the sonnets of Michelangelo or Shakespeare. In contrast to persecuted religious sects, no family traditions would have handed down memories of these chilling times. The history of the crime "not to be named" was doomed to be inscribed almost entirely in the records of relentlessly hostile courts.

The records of the Inquisition, however, are extremely detailed and, from about 1550 on, have been meticulously preserved. One series of trials, those for sodomy in Valencia, has been scrutinized by the Spanish scholar Rafael Carrasco, who has tried to make out what they can tell us about the victims' daily lives. Clearly, such documents are of limited value: the questions posed by the inquisitors were routinely adapted to eliciting information about specific sexual acts. If the testimony seems focused at crotch level, this is because that was the focus of the clerics who conducted the interrogations. The accused were not asked how they saw or judged themselves or about ties of affection or loyalty, nor would they have been advised to volunteer such information. Under the circumstances, any attempt to describe what they saw as meaningful in their attachments would have smacked of heresy.

Carrasco has identified 259 trials for homosexuality in the records of the Valencian Inquisition from 1566 to 1775.[46] As we might expect, the men named constitute a full spectrum of the city's society. In contrast to Italian records in Florence and Venice, the most numerous occupational group (totaling forty-one) was made up of clergy—priests, seminarians, and (disproportionately) monks, who numbered twenty-nine. There were five noblemen and seven professionals (notaries, lawyers, or doctors), twenty servants, and an equal number of slaves. Seventy-nine men were artisans or unskilled workers. Another thirty-eight formed a floating population of soldiers, sailors, and vagrants in this swarming port city.[47] As we might anticipate, among foreigners, Italians provided by far the greatest number of victims (twenty-nine).[48]

These men, Carrasco tells us, can be divided, though not very precisely, into two groups: those whose relations with men were casual and opportunistic and those who manifested discernible or avowed inclinations for male partners, that is, men whom we might today designate as homosexuals. "It is clear that not all these secret seducers were frustrated heterosexuals or occasional lovers of whatever kind of satisfaction. Many confessed their erotic preferences without ambiguity."[49] Popular rage was strongest against the *maricas*—men who manifested feminine characteristics and were despised for their passive roles: "Between masculine men who sought their pleasure in whatever body, and those furtive men who hunted for the friendship of other

56. Auto da fe at Valladolid, May 1559. Contemporary Dutch print.

men the society established an important qualitative difference. The theological and legal point of view privileged the formal definition of the act of sodomy and condemned the first group without remission; popular sensibility on the contrary found in the second group much more motivation for hatred."[50]

Spain in the Renaissance was above all a society that looked at the world theologically; a scientific approach to human behavior was a much rarer thing. When seventeenth-century Spaniards did have occasion to write about homosexuality from a scientific point of view, however, they did what other medical men, materialist philosophers, or pseudo-scientists (such as astrologers) from the Greeks down to modern times have commonly done: they spoke of "inclinations," they diagnosed homosexuality as a peculiar psychological disposition, and they speculated about its causes. We may consider, for instance, the physiological speculations of Juan Huarte de San Juan. Huarte was a Basque physician who in 1575 published a work that became a minor classic of Spanish and Renaissance literature, reaching seventy editions before 1700 and influencing such thinkers as Montaigne, Bacon, Descartes, and Rousseau. Its title, *Examen de ingenios para las ciencias,* may be approximately rendered *A Study of Intellectual Aptitude for Learning.* Its fame was such that Shakespeare might have read an English translation published in 1594; Lessing produced a German version in 1752.

Huarte, very much the medical materialist, "explained" homosexual attraction in this fashion:

> In fact it happens thus: many times nature has made a female and it has been one or two months in the belly of the mother when the genital members, on some occasion, are unexpectedly subjected to much heat, and turn inside out and it becomes [in appearance] a man child. And afterwards we can clearly know to whom this transformation happens in the belly of the mother through certain movements which remain and are not decent in the male sex, but are womanish and effeminate *[mariosos]* and by a voice soft and musical; and such men are inclined to behave like women and fall ordinarily into the *pecado nefando.*[51]

Huarte then presents a parallel theory to explain the origin of lesbianism: cold can cause the genitals of a male fetus to turn inward, creating a child that is then taken for female while remaining psychologically male, that is, she behaves like a man and desires other women. In both cases we have not only a particular kind of behavior but the idea that this behavior follows from a certain sexual orientation. Sometimes the inquisitorial records reveal this kind of psychological self-definition on the part of the men questioned.

What kind of relations do the interrogations reveal? Some accusations were based on personal or political enmity, jealousy, or spite. But often men were apprehended for sexual encounters in public parks or gardens, inns or taverns, or monastery cells. These pairings were usually casual, but sometimes the men belonged to small groups whose members recognized each other by their gestures, mannerisms, speech, clothes, or hair styles. Carrasco concludes:

> The fact that sodomy was a practice open to masculine men who had nothing in common with *maricas* does not mean, of course, that it was not the amorous practice of those whom we would have to call homosexuals and not sodomites . . . There was in fact in [early] modern Valencia a complete crypto-society organized in a homosexual style . . . In the trials we see . . . small groups of men [whose] speech and manner of revealing themselves or signifying their femininity, and whose code for making approaches, reveal the existence of a true homosexual *ghetto.*[52]

From time to time wealthy and powerful men coerced their servants or underlings into granting favors or made advancement conditional upon them. Some clerical schoolmasters seduced boys in their charge. Affairs between strangers are often recorded. On one occasion two men who had been lifelong friends died together. Miguel Salvador de Morales and Baptista Tafolla had slept in the same room as children. When Tafolla returned from traveling in Italy, he sought out his old friend, who had become a Trinitarian monk. They were apprehended making love in Morales's cell and were burned in Valencia on June 25, 1574.[53] Other deaths were the result of what can only be called mad infatuations. José Estravagante, thirty-one, and Bartolomeo Teixidor, twenty, had been condemned to the galleys, the latter for sodomy, the former for another crime. There they conducted a brief passionate affair. Denounced to the Inquisition by their companions, they were resentenced and burned together in 1607.[54]

One group that faced harsh treatment at the hands of the Inquisition was Valencia's teenagers. Many of the pairings among males were of the man-boy pattern familiar in classical times and in Renaissance Italy. Moral attitudes toward the junior partners in such affairs have varied markedly from society to society. In ancient Crete some disgrace attended the boy who failed to form such an alliance. In fifteenth-century Venice, the authorities had at first punished only the active adult but later scourged and jailed consenting boys over ten. In our own society, the younger partner is routinely perceived as a victim and "survivor," even though some boys in fact may have welcomed such relations or sought them out. In Spain, generally speaking, few participants in homosexual acts were regarded as innocent, whatever their ages. William Monter has established that "nearly half of all sodomy defendants tried by the Inquisition were under the legal age of majority."[55] The extreme penalty of death was, however, in theory reserved for males who had reached a legally prescribed age. In Saragossa this was seventeen. But seven adolescents were burned for sodomy (of either kind) in the kingdom of Aragon in 1587 and two more seventeen-year-olds the next year.[56] "In 1584, a teenage Morisco, who had just been punished for heresy at a public *auto* in Aragon was caught making love in the Inquisition's jail immediately afterwards; he went to the galleys while his slave partner was executed."[57]

Some jurists held that the only way to stop pederasty was to burn young boys. Diego de Simancas, a counselor for the Suprema in Madrid in the late 1500s, took this view: "They told me in Rome that is was impossible in Italy to prevent or punish the abominable sin. I replied that it did not seem so to me, but that it would stop if they ordered and effected that any guilty boy should be burned for it unless he reported [the act] within a day after he had been violated. And from then on boys would know and acquire that fear which now in their thoughtlessness they hardly feel."[58]

In Valencia the legal age of majority was theoretically twenty-five, but this was often ignored.[59] In 1588 two twenty-year-old Moriscos, Gaspar Arrimen and Pedro Alache, were burned.[60] But even when minors escaped death, they often got very severe sentences. In 1625 a fifteen-year-old lacemaker was sentenced to 200 lashes and four years in the galleys and forced to watch his lover's execution.[61] When, two years later, a young itinerant French boy, Joan Beltrán, aged sixteen, was condemned in Valencia to six years in the galleys, the Suprema raised this already severe punishment to ten years, a sentence only the hardiest were likely to survive.[62] Given this record, we can understand the hysteria of a teenaged Neapolitan soldier who tried to escape from a city jail in Valencia in 1640 when some other Italians accused him of being a male prostitute. He was terrified "because he had seen a man burned at Madrid as a sodomite."[63]

The Inquisition did not burn men for the *pecado nefando* in Madrid or Seville, but secular justice was active in these cities. Seville, in particular, despite its many religious houses and ostentatious piety, was a lawless metropolis of 150,000, thronged by adventurers embarking for the new colonies or returning from them. Violence was common, prisons crowded, and executions so frequent that some priests found a lifelong vocation in attending the condemned. One of these, Pedro de León, served in the Royal Prison at Seville for thirty-eight years, from 1578 to 1616. To his *Compendio* (1619) we owe some unique insights into the life of that city's *sodomitas,* both as individuals and a clandestine community.

It has been estimated that the number of men burned for the *pecado nefando* in Seville during this period "easily amounted to a hundred."[64] Padre León had intimate conversations with fifty-four of these men during his chaplaincy and wrote up their stories in an "Appendix of the Convicted," where they make up about a sixth of his cases. A few minor sources also exist which fill in the short periods when Don Pedro was away from Seville—an anonymous manuscript entitled "Efemérides" ("Daily Reports") and a book on notable events in contemporary Seville by Francisco Ariño.

Unlike the purely judicial records of the Inquisition, Padre León's conversations with his *pecadores* reveal something of the social ambience in which they moved. Though his spiritual duty was to prepare them for dying as repentant Christians, he sometimes acted as an intercessor and protector. A notable instance occurred when a scandal broke out in 1585 involving a group Don Pedro called a *cuadrilla* or "little squad." One member was an effeminate transvestite named Francisco Galindo who denounced "many young men of good birth *[caballeritos]* in Seville and elsewhere, and also some religious." Ultimately eight men were burned. Many more might have been but for the intervention of Don León, who arranged for the implicated clerics to be turned over to their ecclesiastical superiors rather than suffer secular justice and then persuaded Galindo to rescind his accusations against some others, "saving many from the fire," among them several of "the most noble of Seville."

From the "Efemérides" we learn that other groups were not so fortunate. In 1588 and again in 1600 a sizable number of men—fifteen in each year—

were consigned to the flames, a pattern which would seem to indicate that homosexual subcultures in Renaissance cities continued to exist even under the most threatening and dangerous conditions.[65] León wrote that "this stain often falls on persons of high importance," including well-regarded clergy.[66] He had heard, outside confession, "many things about secular ecclesiastics and some regular clergy of decent families, and they themselves most honored and learned and even famous preachers, who provided unusually fine clothes for some youths with beautiful features, and entertained them like kings with picnics and dinners in their cells."[67]

But in contrast to the practice of the Inquisition in Aragon, few clergy were punished by the secular powers in Seville. One exception was Pascual Jaime, chaplain to the duke of Alcalá. Jaime had made himself conspicuous in the city by his elegant dress. Under torture he admitted that he had been engaged in homosexual behavior since the age of eight—he was then fifty-six. He "had such a passion and an inclination to associate with such youths that when he met with any of good appearance, even if they were ragged he took them home, cleaned them up, and dressed them handsomely at his own expense."[68] Since Padre Jaime was a well-known dignitary, his trial caused a great stir in Seville. He was formally degraded on a platform set up at the gate of the archbishop's palace, "relaxed" to the secular arm, and burned a few days later with a young partner who "cried like a boy."[69]

Torture was widely used in Seville, but especially in cases of *pecado nefando.* We are told that the authorities "placed no limits on the means; in this way they used the rack, the lash, fire, etc. In some cases this was a veritable martyrdom because they applied padlocked irons to the flesh which even led to the amputation of a hand . . . From this it happened that the pain of torture was greater than that of the fire, and many completely innocent men, overcome by the terror they experienced, confessed to whatever they were accused of."[70]

León, who had occasion to talk privately with the convicted men, came to the conclusion that some were innocent. He was especially distressed by the case of two peasant muleteers who had come to the city. One, suffering from diarrhea, took a novel medicine which caused pain in his *partes secretes* so that when his friend examined him at their inn, he cried out, "Be gentle; God, how it hurts." A chambermaid, seeing the man with his legs up, reported him to a magistrate; both men were burned on a charge of *pecado nefando,* despite the efforts of León and other Jesuits to intercede on their behalf.[71]

León also reported the unhappy case of Juan Duarte, Manuel López, Juan Pérez Mansilla, and Antón Morales, all of whom, he was convinced, were falsely accused in 1610. Tortured and forced to confess to a crime they had not committed, "they were immediately sentenced, and without any delay it was determined that the four should die in the fire. All along the route from

57. Inquisitorial torture. Eighteenth-century prints.

the prison to the place of execution, they made reiterated protestations of their innocence, but nothing and no one could prevent the carrying out of the sentence."[72]

Though the secular powers did not stage formal shows as impressive as the *autos* of the Inquisition, the march through the streets of Seville to the place of burning was an impressive rite. Mockery intensified the cruelty in the case of a Negro named Mayuca, who was outfitted with a fancy wig and elaborate fake lace and marched to the flames with two pretty boys who were painted and curled. If we can credit León, the sermons at the *quemadero* (burning place) sometimes attracted thousands of people. The Jesuit was especially proud of the effect of his preaching at Mayuca's burning. Despite his occasional attempts to mitigate harsh and precipitous justice, León was convinced that burning was necessary. He told men who were about to die that "without being turned to dust and ashes by the fire they would never amend, except through a miracle of God."[73]

In 1561 Philip II moved Spain's capital to Madrid. Though literary evidence of the treatment of sodomites in the city exists, it has not yet been collected and analyzed. Rafael Carrasco, however, has been able to make a "minimum estimate" of 100 to 150 deaths in Madrid during sixty-five years.[74] In December 1622, five young men were burned for the *pecado nefando.* Some details are poignant: according to a terse news item for March 1626, a young page accused of relations with Don Diego Gaytan de Vargas, a member of the Cortes family from Salamanca, denied the accusation in a loud voice in the streets "when they took him to burn." The anonymous reporter adds, "There was much pity throughout the capital."[75] Perhaps the painful impression produced by this episode helped influence the Suprema in Madrid to cease burning sodomites in *autos* a few years later.

• The Inquisition in Portugal •

Not all parts of the Iberian peninsula were as harshly savage toward men who consorted with men. After centuries of independence, Portugal came under Spanish control in 1580 and remained so until it revolted in 1640. The existence of a native Portuguese Inquisition during this period assured a pattern of oppression similar to that of Spain, but the toll of deaths was proportionately less. This fact, and the existence of a highly visible homosexual subculture in Lisbon, suggests that native folkways in Portugal were less fiercely hostile to male love than in Renaissance Spain. To some degree Lisbon appears to have paralleled contemporary Florence.

On paper, Portugal's laws were as draconian as Spain's. The *Afonsine Ordinances,* published in 1446 in the reign of Afonso V, prescribed burning for sodomy, "of all sins the most vile, unclean and foul," on account of which

58. Auto da fe in the Plaza Mayor, Madrid, June 30, 1680. Francisco Rizi, oil, c. 1680.

"God set the Flood upon the earth." The *Manuelinas* of Manuel I (1521) added confiscation of goods and infamy for the convict's descendants. Philip II, as active in his role as king of Portugal as he had been in Spain and Italy, commissioned a new set of laws, which were not, however, published until 1606, seven years after his death. These *Filipinas* remained in force until European revolutions ushered in a new order in the nineteenth century. Chapter 13 provided that "Any person, of whatever rank, who in any way commits the sin of sodomy, shall be burned and made dust by the fire so that his body and burial never have memory, and all his goods shall be confiscated by the Crown of our Kingdom, even if he have descendants, in which case his children and grandchildren shall be unworthy and infamous as the children of those who commit lèse majesté."[76]

Unlike the earlier ordinances, women were no longer excluded from the law, for, as the statute put it, "some commit the sin against nature with others and in the same manner as men." For mutual masturbation men might be sent to the galleys. Whoever knew and did not identify a sodomite would lose all his belongings and suffer perpetual exile. On the other hand, anyone who denounced a sodomite had the right, if the crime were proved, to receive half of the criminal's belongings; if he owned nothing, the Crown

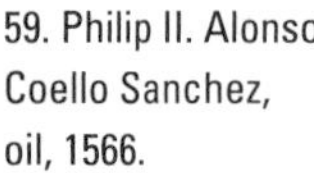

59. Philip II. Alonso Coello Sanchez, oil, 1566.

would reward the accuser with 100 cruzados. Curiously, no records of trials under these secular laws remain; perhaps, it has been suggested, they were destroyed, as in France and Scotland.

Of the consequences of religious bigotry, however, we have ample documentation. The Portuguese Inquisition had been established in 1536 by John III, a "fanatic of narrow mind and limited intelligence" who sought to imitate the Spanish institution in persecuting Jewish converts, who suffered henceforth in large numbers.[77] John also wished to use his new inquisitors to try sodomites, who in Portugal were known as *somítigos* or *fanchonos.* In 1547 sixteen men, servants from the royal palace and noble households, were exiled by the Inquisition.[78] John's brother Henry, a cardinal of the church who was also inquisitor-general and held this post even after he became king, obtained formal authority to act against homosexuals from Pius IV in 1562 and a dozen years later had the permission reconfirmed by Gregory XIII.[79] Yet despite this enthusiasm for punitive measures, arrests of sodomites in the sixteenth century led to only three burnings. The first took place in 1569; the victim was a mulatto cleric named Don Gaspar Lopes, who was also accused of Judaizing.[80]

This relative leniency does not seem to have been the result of any lack of candidates for punishment. As in Spain, the Portuguese Inquisition issued so-called edicts of faith which were read in churches and ordered the faithful to denounce any heretics or sodomites known to them among their neighbors and acquaintances. A period of grace followed during which people could earn lesser sentences if they confessed voluntarily. These appeals yielded ample fruit. The Brazilian anthropologist Luiz Mott has found 4,419 denunciations in a *Repertórios do Nefando* in the archives of the Torre do Tombo in Lisbon for the period from 1578 to 1794: in this enumeration Lisbon rivaled Florence.[81] The records of 479 inquisitorial trials provide a meticulous, richly detailed account of homosexual life in the Portuguese capital.

The picture reveals a large, visible, and at times exuberant subculture not subject to the popular animus found in Spanish cities. Many men—a surprising number of them clerics—were well known to their fellow citizens. Some were openly effeminate in voice and manner, wore women's ornaments, and used women's nicknames (Marica, Paula, and so on) in their private circles. One "falsetto singer of great beauty" worked as the servant of two inquisitors.[82] The cosmopolitan, multiracial nature of Lisbon fostered sexual diversity: "The contact of the Portuguese with innumerable people from Africa, Asia, and America, where homosexuality and transvestism were sometimes socially acceptable and even honored behavior, and the presence in the kingdom of large numbers of slaves and foreigners, made Lisbon in the XVI and XVII centuries not only a great Babel, but one of the principal Sodoms of Europe. Among the gays arrested by the Holy Office . . . 15% were blacks, Moors, Indians, Amerindians and mulattos."[83] A slave from Dahomey wore a woman's dress and competed with prostitutes in Lisbon's rowdy dockside district. In Portuguese Brazil a Negro who refused to dress as a man was in fact following the tradition of the *jimbandaa,* an order of transvestite sorcerers from Angola and the Congo.[84]

Certain houses in Lisbon were well known as meeting places and openly accommodated lovers seeking privacy. Even sacred precincts were put to use: from the archives of the Holy Office we learn that in the Patriarchal Cathedral *fanchonos* coupled "in the sacristy, inside the confessionals, behind the altars, in the bell tower, inside the cupboards for the ornaments, in the cloisters, in the cemetery, in the choir behind the organ, and inside the pulpits"—especially when two cathedral priests, one a canon and the other a curator, were members of the community.[85] Some priests were panderers and made their homes veritable brothels. One, the sixty-six-year-old Father Santos de Almeida, a royal chaplain, was accused of presiding over a "conventicle of *fanchonos.*"[86] Another leader of homosexual social life was Father Gregório Martins Ferreira, dean of Oporto Cathedral, who praised sodomy and sang songs satirizing his fellows to the accompaniment of the guitar.[87] Lisbon even acquired an openly gay institution, a group of dancers called the Dança dos Fanchonos, founded by a thirty-year-old mulatto named Antonio Rodrigues.[88] These men spoke of themselves as a "jurisdiction"—a confraternity of men with a distinct lifestyle and a strong sense of group identity.

Such flamboyant individuals have been likened to butterflies fluttering over the flames of a bonfire. Some were, quite literally, burned. Two of the dancers died agonizing deaths at the stake in 1621—in Portugal men were not strangled first but were burned alive. Father Santos perished similarly twenty-four years later.[89] All in all, some thirty men were burned by the Portuguese Inquisition for sodomy, most of them during the first half of the seventeenth century when the country was under Spanish rule.[90] The victims included four nobles, seven priests, seven teachers, several students and musicians, four slaves, three servants, three artisans, and a beggar. Five were mulatto, two black, and one a Turkish Muslim.[91] No lesbians were executed, though a number were arrested in Brazil.[92] After 1647 the inquisitors ruled that lesbian acts fell outside their jurisdiction. The last known execution of a *fanchono* by the Inquisition took place in 1671—the victim was a priest. (The last heretic was burned in Lisbon ninety years later.) In the eighteenth century, prosecutions fell off dramatically; there were only twenty-three trials, compared with 278 in the preceding hundred years.[93]

Besides burnings, Lisbon's sodomite subculture faced the constant threat of other cruel punishments. One hundred and sixty-five men were sent to the galleys, sometimes for ten years, in many cases for life.[94] There, discipline was harsh, food was vile and scanty, and mortality high, if not from hardships then from shipwreck or battle. Some men were captured by Moorish pirates, and it was not unheard of for a young galley slave to end up in the harem of a lordly *xerife* in Morocco or Algiers; some may have welcomed the promotion. Public whippings, regarded as a special indignity to be visited only upon the lower orders of society, were common, though less savage than in Spain. Many sentences were read publicly at *autos de fe* and routinely condemned a man's family to infamy for two or three generations. Exile to Portuguese colonies such as Angola or Brazil was common.

Torture, applied in about a sixth of the cases, was so severe as often to exceed the prescribed penalties for the acts the man was accused of. One standard form—water torture, by which water was poured into a suspect's mouth until he was near drowning—was occasionally used in sodomy cases. The commonest technique was the pulley "which involved the tying of the unfortunate's wrists behind his back with leather straps. He would be slowly lifted to the ceiling of the torture chamber by a pulley and then dropped, his fall ending just before he hit the ground, a procedure that would painfully dislocate most of his joints."[95] The rack, which involved the gradual tightening of straps around the arms and legs, was used on those judged too weak to survive the pulley—the old and infirm, women, and (usually) children.

A surgeon appointed by the Holy Office was always in attendance: the "humane" priests wished to avoid the shedding of blood or breaking of limbs. These ordeals were recorded in great detail—the fact that the scribes were paid by the page encouraged minuteness. Screams, pleas, and prayers were set down verbatim. Of the youngest of the sixty-nine sodomites whose sufferings are described—a ten-year-old named Brás Nunes—we read: "Restrained with straps and ropes, constantly calling upon the Holy Virgin Mother for compassion, he was tied and placed on the slab and raised up to the pulley at which point he was dropped."[96] Luiz d'Avelar, a servant in a noble household, was found to have a hernia and spared the pulley on this account.

> Placed upon the rack, he was stripped of his clothing and secured by double straps across his elbows, wrists and ankles. Since the criminal claimed to have nothing to confess the Inquisitor ordered the torturers to perform their duties and soon the straps across the criminal's left elbow, wrist, and ankle were tightened by one turn. The same procedure was performed on the right side, and the criminal would scream and call for Jesus to redeem him, for the Virgin of the Rosary to redeem him, and in this manner he was subjected to the ingenious treatment.[97]

One aged priest in his agony called upon his fellow priests "who were ordained as I was ordained" to have mercy upon him. Gradually, during the eighteenth century, these cruelties fell into disrepute. The Portuguese Inquisition effectively ceased to be active by 1794, though the institution was not formally abolished until 1821.

60. Inquisitorial scene. Domenico Beccafumi, drawing, early sixteenth century.

• Spain in the New World •

By the end of the sixteenth century Spain ruled a huge empire extending over five continents, a development that made Spanish policies on homosexuality of worldwide significance. Nowhere were they of more consequence than in Spanish possessions in the New World—in Mexico, the Caribbean, and Central and South America. Indeed, the sodomitical proclivities of American natives exercised a peculiar fascination over the Hispanic mind. In Spain and Rome a passionate debate took place concerning the legal, moral, and religious justifications for the Spanish conquest of the two new continents. Charges of cannibalism and human sacrifice were made against the native cultures, but sodomy was an offense which, if not quite so horrifying to European sensibilities, received even more attention as a sign of Indian depravity. The Spaniards—who knew only a world in which homosexuality was excoriated, feared, and all but hidden from public view—now encountered cultures where it was not only tolerated but openly avowed and, in certain areas of Central and South America, institutionalized.

In 1519 Hernán Cortés, newly embarked on his subjugation of Mexico, informed Charles V that "we have learnt and been informed for sure that they [the natives of Veracruz] are all sodomites and use that abominable sin."[98] This letter, printed in 1522, received wide circulation. Bernal Díaz del Castillo, who accompanied Cortés, recorded in his *True History of the Conquest of New Spain* (c. 1568) that Cortés and a friar who traveled with him repeatedly lectured the Indians on the wickedness of this sin and even went so far as to deplore its prevalence during an imperial audience with Montezuma in Mexico City. Díaz described "boys dressed in women's dresses who were earning their living in that perverted occupation" and Indian priests, the sons of chiefs, who kept no wives "but had the perverse occupation of sodomites."[99] Díaz appears to be speaking not of the Aztecs but of the Mayans and tribes on the south coast of the Gulf of Mexico, the first aborigines Cortés's party encountered. The reference to a homosexual priesthood is of special interest, since Díaz does not identify the men as transvestite shamans. Rather, they seem to have belonged to a tradition in which women were taboo for priests but same-sex liaisons were tacitly permitted, as in Buddhist Japan.

The Spaniards were also shocked to observe homosexual behavior elsewhere in the New World. Fernandez de Oviedo's *Natural History of the Indies,* the first official account of native customs, appeared in 1526 and was widely influential in forming Spanish opinion. Oviedo described a form of homosexuality among Carib tribes on the north coast of South America that seemed especially shocking:

> Very common among the Indians in many parts is the nefarious sin against nature; even in public the Indians who are headmen . . . have youths with whom they use this accursed sin, and those consenting youths as soon as they fall into this guilt wear *naguas* [skirts] like women . . . and they wear strings of beads and bracelets and the other things used by women as adornment; and they do not exercise in the use of weapons, nor do anything proper to men, but they occupy themselves in the usual chores of the house such as to sweep and wash and other things customary for women.[100]

The Spaniards had, in fact, encountered a cultural tradition unknown to Europe but common to many Indian tribes in North and South America: publicly recognized gender-role reversal. The Spanish called these men *bardajes,* passive sodomites. Later, French explorers in North America called them *bardaches,* a word which in a slightly variant form *(berdaches)* has entered the vocabulary of modern anthropology.[101]

Oviedo's generally negative picture of native life was seized upon to justify Spanish rule and the expropriation of Indian wealth and land. In 1547 a Spanish intellectual named Juan Ginés de Sepúlveda used Oviedo's damning information in his *Treatise on the Rightful Causes of the War against the In-*

dians, where one speaker gives a concise rationale for the conquest of the New World:

> [These are] the reasons upon which you . . . found the justice of the war waged by the Spaniards on the barbarians: the first is their being barbarous, uncivilized and unhuman men by nature serfs [this argument is taken from Aristotle's defense of slavery in his *Politics*]; the second . . . to banish nefarious intercourse [sodomy] and the amazing crime of devouring human flesh, crimes which offend nature; . . . the third to free from serious offences very many innocent mortals whom the barbarians immolated every year; the fourth to propagate the Christian religion wherever the occasion presents.[102]

Such arguments had wide influence among those who undertook to defend the conquest. A report by Bishop Tomás Ortiz to the Council of the Indies in 1525, emphasizing the sodomitic proclivities of the Caribs, had persuaded Charles V to rule that these Indians should be slaves on the grounds that they were irrational creatures and hence subhuman.[103]

But the position that Indians were not human beings inevitably appalled many clergy who had lived among them: had they been baptizing animals without souls? Theologians were prepared to join battle on this ground. In 1537 Paul III issued two papal bulls declaring that the Indians were indeed rational beings, and in that same year the eminent Spanish theologian Francisco de Vitoria addressed Spanish claims in lectures at the University of Salamanca. (Vitoria, who lived a century before Hugo Grotius, has been called the true founder of international law.) He argued that "the Emperor [Charles V] is not the ruler of the whole world," hence Indians should not be deprived of their land and possessions. Vitoria directly attacked the idea that sodomitical behavior justified conquest: "Christian princes cannot wage war on the infidels on account of sins against nature . . . that is to say, because of the sin of sodomy rather than on account of the sin of fornication."[104] Vitoria gave point to his contention by drawing an acerbic analogy with contemporary European politics: "On the same ground it should follow that the king of the French could make war on the Italians because they commit sins against nature."

Despite Vitoria, the charge of sodomy remained a popular argument for Spanish hegemony. In his famous defense of the Indians presented to Charles V in 1542, Bartolomé de Las Casas was at pains to refute it. It was an accusation "the Apostle of the Indians" vehemently denied: "They [the Spaniards] have defamed them a thousand times and accused them of being infected with sodomy; but this charge is a great falsehood and wickedness."[105] If some writers exaggerated by making sodomy a practice universally approved in the Americas, Las Casas erred on the other side. The truth, as so often, was mixed: some native cultures did condone homosexuality, others did not. Even after his categorical denial, Las Casas himself was forced to admit that homosexuality was institutionalized in Mayan society.

Indeed, he later gives an interesting account of the Mayan myth of the origin of same-sex love, which, like the Greeks, the Mayans ascribed to their gods, whom Las Casas demonizes:

> It was always held among them [the Maya of Vera Paz in Guatemala] as a great and nefarious sin until a demon [a god] appeared under the disguise of an Indian named Cu, and in another language Chin, and in others Cavil and Maran, who induced them to commit it, as he himself executed it with another demon; from there it happened that some of them did not consider it sinful . . . Due to this fact some parents provided their youngsters with a boy to use for a woman, and if someone else got at him he was ordered to pay for him in the same way as they did in respect of women when someone raped his neighbor's wife.[106]

Since chroniclers who were pro-Indian minimized the extent of homosexuality in America while their opponents often maximized it, it is difficult to arrive at a clear picture of Indian cultures. Though the Mayans and Caribs—the first peoples the Spanish encountered—were tolerant and even in some cases approving of same-sex relations, the two most powerful American peoples, the Aztecs and the Incas, seem to have been hostile, and the overall picture is distinctly checkered.

The Franciscan friar Bernardino de Sahagún arrived in Mexico shortly after the conquest and spent the remainder of his long life "writing an exhaustive anthropological study of the Aztecs."[107] Echoing the style of their Nahuatl language, he reported (c. 1565) that among the Aztecs, "The sodomite is an effeminate, a defilement, a corruption, filth; a taster of filth, revolting, perverse, full of affliction. He deserves laughter, ridicule, mockery . . . Womanish, playing the part of a woman, he merits being committed to flames."[108] Sahagún does not, however, give a specific Aztec law. Neither does Las Casas. However, Jerónimo de Mendieta, another Franciscan who studied Nahuatl and in 1596 made an extensive list of Aztec laws, stated that "those who committed the nefarious sin, agent and patient, died for it."[109]

In addition, we have a very explicit description of the punishments exacted by the Chichimecs, the people who occupied the Valley of Mexico before the Aztecs, by a native writer, Fernando de Alva Ixtlilxochitl (1606). Its details are precise enough and sufficiently remote from European traditions to carry conviction: "The nefarious sin was punished in two ways: the one acting as a female had his entrails removed from the bottom, was tied down to a log and the boys from the town covered him with ash, until he was buried; and then they put a lot of wood [on top] and burnt him. The one acting as a male was covered with ash, [and] tied down to a log until he died."[110] Yet, having surveyed the multiplicity of conflicting reports that had reached him, the Spanish historian Antonio de Herrera, writing in 1601, registered some doubts: "Though some people say in Mexico that those who committed the nefarious sin were put to death, others say they did not pay attention to it for punishment" but merely held such men in contempt.[111]

The ferocity of Inca repression in Peru, however, is well documented. Here, half a century before Pizarro's triumph, two cultures with antithetical attitudes collided. The Mochicas who flourished in Ecuador from 400 to 1000 and the Chimú who succeeded them are both famous for their sophisticated pottery, much of it startlingly erotic. Oral and anal intercourse, mainly heterosexual but occasionally homosexual, are freely represented on hundreds of pieces, while vaginal relations are the exception.[112] By contrast, the Incas of Peru, who conquered the Chimú in 1466, punished homosexual relations harshly.

Cieza de León, in his richly detailed *Chronicle of Peru* (1553), recounts a common legend: according to the Chimú, sodomy had been introduced into the land by certain giants who had landed on the coast near Puerto Viejo. Lacking women, they consorted with each other and were destroyed by a fearful "fire from heaven." This last touch suggests a conflation of a native myth with the Sodom story, the kind of mixing of traditions that often casts doubt on Hispanic accounts of native beliefs. Cieza de León emphatically denies that the Incas were sodomites, however. The pre-Columbian Inca rulers, he reports, so abominated sodomy that on this account they launched a campaign of extermination among the Chimú. In the end there was only one man left alive for every fifteen women.[113] But despite his impassioned rhetoric, Léon makes one revealing admission. The Inca rulers seemed to have sanctioned sodomy in a special religious context:

> As for those who served as priests in the temples, with whom it is known that on feast days the headman had carnal knowledge, they did not think that they were doing wrong or committing a sin, but did this as a sacrifice prompted by the devil [a native god]. It might even be that the Incas were unaware that such a thing was done in the temples; and if they overlooked certain things, it was so that they would not be disliked, and they may have felt that it was enough for them to order that the sun and other gods were worshiped everywhere, without taking measures to forbid ancient religions and customs the loss of which is like death itself to those born in them.[114]

Here is a unique effort to see things from a native point of view.

But if the native rulers of Peru were willing on occasion to look the other way, this would have been unthinkable for their Spanish conquerors, who from the start treated native sodomites with extreme brutality. An early episode, first recounted in the writings of Pietro Martire d'Anghiera, an Italian serving in Spain as councillor of the Indies, is the most notorious. In the 1516 edition of his *Decades* he tells the story of Vasco Nuñez de Balboa, who in 1513 had arrived at the court of a native king in Panama. When Balboa found the king's brother surrounded by men "smooth and effeminately decked" who engaged in sodomy, he had forty of them "given for a prey to his dogs."[115] The scene was memorialized in a famous engraving published in Frankfurt in 1590 as an illustration in Théodore de Bry's monumental collection of accounts of the New World entitled *Historia Americae.* The plate shows elegantly clad Spanish soldiers posing superciliously while their hunting dogs sink their fangs into the limbs and throats of the naked Indians who writhe in agony before them. These fierce mastiffs haunted the European imagination as striking images of Spanish barbarism in the Americas and found a place in twentieth-century Mexican murals protesting the cruelties of the conquest.

Balboa's savagery did not shock other Spaniards, however. Antonio de la Calancha, rector of an Augustinian college in Lima in 1622, praised Balboa, calling his giving the Panamanians to be savaged by his dogs a "fine action of an honorable and Catholic Spaniard."[116] In sixteenth-century Peru, Spanish magistrates energetically persecuted sodomite natives. Cieza de León recounts that Juan de Olmos, the chief justice at Puerto Viejo, had "burnt great numbers of these perverse and devilish Indians."[117] In 1580 the inquisitorial tribunal in Lima sought authority to try sodomy cases, but this was denied them by the Suprema in Madrid; consequently punishment was meted out by the secular rulers.[118]

In Mexico, a similar pattern was established. Official inquisitorial tribunals in Lima and Mexico City had been created in 1569 by Philip II. In earlier days inquisitorial powers in Mexico were exercised by the local bishops, such as Archbishop Juan Zumárraga (1536–1543), who interpreted them as covering a wide range of sexual offenses. An examination of the trials conducted by Zumárraga has revealed that "homosexuality was a prime concern of the [episcopal] inquisition," which inflicted "stiff fines, spiritual penances, public humiliation, and floggings" for sexual sins.[119]

A century later, in 1662, the Mexican Inquisition complained that homosexuality was common, especially among the clergy, and asked for jurisdiction on the grounds that the secular courts were not sufficiently vigilant. The request was denied.[120] In fact, the civil authorities, under the duke of Albuquerque, had recently been extremely active, indicting a hundred men for sodomy and executing a substantial number:

> On Tuesday, November 6, 1658, at eleven in the morning, fifteen men were taken from the royal jail of this court, fourteen to be put to death by burning, and the remaining one, because he was a boy, was given two hundred lashes and sold to a brick layer for six years, all of them for having committed the sin of sodomy with one another over many years.[121]

In Mexico City heretics were burned in the Alameda, now a popular park near the city center, sodomites at another *quemadero* in the subdivision of San Lázaro. We are told that the strangling of the fourteen men proceeded at

61. "Balboa throws the Indians who have committed the abominable crime of sodomy to be torn to bits by his dogs." Théodore de Bry, engraving for *America,* 1590.

a leisurely pace throughout the day, finishing at eight in the evening when the attendant crowd was entertained by seeing the bodies set afire.

Spanish authority in the New World suppressed human sacrifices to native deities but instituted its own blood sacrifices to religious and sexual orthodoxy. Observing these holocausts, Protestant Europe looked with horror on the "Black Legend" of Spanish cruelty in the Americas but accepted as a matter of course the burning of sodomites sanctioned by its own biblical traditions. Indeed, in the following centuries Protestant states were to prove the more lethal staging ground for executions as the number of burnings began to diminish in the Catholic south.

CHAPTER ELEVEN

FRANCE FROM CALVIN TO LOUIS XIV

1517–1715

• Outings, Protestant and Catholic •

Christian scruples made Renaissance Europe a far more homophobic society than, for instance, contemporary China and Japan. Yet despite the uniformly condemnatory rhetoric, legal oppression varied greatly from country to country. Fiercest in Spain, it was severe in France and Italy, rare in England, and seems to have been almost totally lacking in such northern states as Russia, Denmark, and Sweden. Denmark had no sodomy law till 1683 or known prosecutions before 1744. In Sweden there were none before 1600 and very few after.[1] Russia, where male relations seem to have been surprisingly open in the 1600s and 1700s, did not have a sodomy statute until 1832.[2] Even in those Latin countries where regular enforcement of the laws advertised the prevalence of male pairings, differences were noted. Thus the French scholar Joseph Scaliger (1540–1609), reputedly the most erudite man in Europe, quoted, in Italian, a common proverb: "In Spagna gli preti, in Francia i Grandi, in Italia tutti quanti" ("In Spain the priests, in France the nobles, in Italy everyone").[3]

Modern research lends Scaliger's quip some credence. Priests who would have been quietly relegated to monasteries in France or Italy were far more likely to be publicly burned in homophobic Spain, and records show that homosexual conduct was widely spread through all classes in Italian cities. Moreover, the privileged status of the French aristocracy did assure their immunity. In France the full force of the law fell on members of the middle and lower classes, whose more modest status made them flammable.

Though the French invasion of Italy in 1494–1516 devastated the peninsula, it spread an appreciation of Italian art through Francis I's patronage of Leonardo and Cellini. But the homoerotic side of the Italian Renaissance had little influence on French culture. The vogue of Ficino's male-oriented Platonism did not cross the Alps. When the cult of Platonic love did reach France and England, it was through such works as Baldassare Castiglione's

The Courtier (1528), where Pietro Bembo's celebrated discourse on love restricted it to love between men and women. In this version it became a convention guiding the amours of literate lords and ladies, void of its original homoerotic overtones.[4]

Indeed, French judgments of Italy, like Rome's of ancient Greece, were sharply ambivalent. The aristocracy might collect Italian art and imitate Italian architecture, but to the conservative bourgeoisie Italy was the suspect home of luxury and sexual license. Homosexuality, in particular, came to be called *le vice italien,* or alternatively *le vice ultramontain* ("across the Alps"). Henri Estienne, member of a Protestant family long famous as printers and humanists, lamented in 1566, "Is it not a great pity that some who before setting foot in Italy abhorred even the mention [of sodomy], after having lived there, enjoy not only the words but even put them into practice, and avow this among themselves as if this was something they learned at a good school?"[5]

The spread of Protestantism in France caused a series of civil wars that erupted intermittently for over a generation and reached a murderous climax in the Saint Bartholomew's Day Massacre of 1572. This deadly rivalry exacerbated homophobia, since each side used accusations of sexual vice to denigrate the other. The ritual of reciprocal "outings" pitted English, German, and French Protestants against Italian, German, and French Catholics and made itself most sharply felt in attacks on the person of a French king with an ambiguous lifestyle who had the ill-fortune to antagonize both sides.

It is not surprising that Protestants fired the first shots, directing them at the papacy. The popes, after all, were members of a sodomitical nation. The denunciation of the warrior pope Julius II as a "sodomite covered with shameful ulcers" by the abortive Council of Pisa (1511), though motivated by that pope's French and imperial enemies, gave ammunition to Protestant reformers a decade later.[6] But the scandal that Calvinists and Lutherans fixed on with the greatest relish was the elevation of Julius's protégé Julius III to the papacy in 1551. Julius III had presided over the opening session of the Council of Trent six years earlier while still a cardinal. But he, as pope, was more interested in his private pleasures than in church reform. That he made his fifteen-year-old favorite, Innocenzo, a cardinal despite his obscure birth and disreputable manners caused widespread scandal even in Catholic Rome. There, satirists hailed the youth, who was by no means attractive in appearance, as "the new Ganymede." A popular Protestant commonplace book, Thomas Beard's *Theatre of God's Judgment* (1597), took note of the relation, with typical exaggeration, denouncing Julius as a lustful satyr whose "custome was to promote none to Ecclesiasticall livings, save only his buggerers: amongst whom this holy father (contrary to the Suffrages of the whole colledge) would needs make Cardinall."[7] This was only one of a flood of Protestant attacks spanning more than a century.

As late as 1696 the French encyclopedist Pierre Bayle devoted a substantial entry on Julius in his *Dictionnaire historique et critique,* quoting from ecclesiastical historians, Catholic and Protestant, who had chronicled Julius's "unbridled passion."[8] (Bayle, whose own upbringing had been Protestant, was a pioneer in calling for toleration for Catholics, Protestants, and freethinkers alike.) He quotes the moderate Catholic historian Jacques-Auguste de Thou to the effect that Julius, on his election, devoted himself to "voluptuous pleasures" with his "Monkey" (Innocenzo), whom he had raised to high office.[9] Bayle also repeats the words of the Swiss Protestant Thomas Erastus, whose bias had no doubt sharpened his pen:

> This boy had remained in Bologna [where Julius had been legate], so that Julius, who did not want to bring him to Rome before he had raised him to the cardinalate and needed a little time to obtain agreement to this promotion, suffered all the rigors of his absence, and sought the best remedies he could find. He was only happy when he heard news of his Innocenzo, and he demanded them from all who could give them. He had him come near to Rome so he could conveniently go to see him; and having him brought once secretly to the city, he waited at the windows with all the impatience of a man whose mistress had promised him a night. He was heard to say that the principal reason he rejoiced in being pope was that it gave him the opportunity to benefit Innocenzo; and that he was less obliged to the cardinals for making him pope than for agreeing to the promotion of Innocenzo to a cardinal's hat. He made him his principal minister and the intercessor for all those who sought his favors.[10]

Even the *Oxford Dictionary of Popes* (1986) candidly admits that Julius "created scandal by his infatuation with a fifteen-year-old youth, Innocenzo, picked up in the streets of Parma, whom he made his brother adopt and named cardinal."[11]

Faced with this onslaught, Catholics sought to even the balance by "outing" Calvin's chief aide, Théodore de Bèze, who had succeeded him in Geneva in 1564 and was commonly called the "Protestant Pope." In his youth Bèze had published Latin verse that might have issued from the pen of a Tibullus or a Marbod of Rennes. One elegy showed the poet torn between his love for a young man and a young woman: "I embrace now him and now her."[12] In the event, he chooses Audebert; if Candida complains, he will stop her mouth with a *basiolo imo*—a deep kiss. Jérome Bolsec, in his hostile *Life of Bèze* (1584), denounced these lines as "lascivious, absolutely shameless, and detestable."[13] A dozen other partisans took up the point with glee. One, Claude de Sainctes, wrote, "Instead of your Audebert, you now have embraced Calvin, and so have substituted a spiritual male-whore for a carnal one, thus being still what you were—a sodomist."[14]

Protestant controversialists found a riposte in the poetry of Giovanni

Della Casa, archbishop of Benevento, much hated as the censor of heretical books and watchdog of orthodoxy. They were happy to discover among his literary works a poem they cited as "De laude Sodomiae" ("In Praise of Sodomy"). In fact, as William Schleiner has shown, there was no such poem.[15] What Della Casa did write, and had published in 1538, many years before he became an archbishop, was a long risqué burlesque entitled "Capitolo del Forno" ("Verses on the Oven") in which he called intercourse a "divine trade" *(mestier divino)* and spoke enthusiastically of women's "two ovens." In his own defense Della Casa was reduced to pointing out, rather lamely, that he had celebrated heterosexual, not homosexual, sodomy.

• Calvinism and Repression •

Ultimately the rise of Protestantism led to greater religious and moral freedom in Europe, but its immediate effect was to sharpen sexual repression, especially in Calvinist countries. Fornication and adultery were vehemently condemned and conformity enforced by public rituals of humiliation and occasional executions. Though sodomy was routinely denounced, the enforcement of sodomy statutes in Calvinist states appears to have been erratic (as in sixteenth- and seventeenth-century Scotland and Holland) or entirely lacking (as in Cromwell's England). One Protestant jurisdiction, however, does stand out as notably severe in its punishments, namely, Calvin's Geneva.

Nowhere did the Reformation triumph so definitively as in French-speaking Geneva. Under Calvin's leadership, the Genevans established a theocracy that subjected every aspect of life to a stern code inspired by the Old Testament. During the proceeding century, we know of six sodomy trials in the city. In the 125 years following Calvin's triumph there were sixty—thirty ending in burnings, beheadings, drownings, and hangings.[16] If we consider the small size of the city—Geneva had only about 12,000 inhabitants when Calvin took office—the actual rate of executions far surpassed that of the Inquisition in contemporary Spain.

A trial in 1555 reveals the thinking of Calvinist judges. A young French printer had attacked his roommate, who aroused the house by crying out. Three jurists—all religious refugees from France—were consulted. The first declared that "this sin ranks among the most execrable, prohibited by both divine and human laws, such that the Lord showed the rigor of his judgment . . . by burning five cities for it."[17] He argued that the man deserved to die but that, since the attempt did not succeed, he might be given a lesser penalty. The second, quoting Genesis and Saint Paul, recommended burning. The third agreed, since under Roman law an attempt was equivalent to the act itself. The man was hanged.

The most intense punitive activity in Geneva came in the 1560s when authority passed into the hands of Bèze, in the 1590s, and in 1610. After 1560

62. Richard Puller von Hohenberg and his servant, Anton Mätzler, burned at Zurich, September 24, 1482. Dietrich Schilling, manuscript illustration, *Die Grosse Burgunder-Chronik,* c. 1483.

the population doubled as Protestants fled a France torn by religious strife. In this period six Frenchmen and an Italian were banished for homosexual acts and another four Frenchmen were drowned, including a twenty-year-old student. There were also three executions for bestiality and one for lesbianism, an offense that was rarely prosecuted. When in 1568 a woman confessed to an affair, the Consistory sought learned advice as to how the crime should be dealt with. Germain Colladon, the city's most distinguished legal authority, justified the death penalty on the basis of the *Constitutio criminalis Carolina,* the imperial code that had been formally adopted in 1532 at the

Diet of Regensburg.[18] This code, popularly known as the *Carolina* after the reigning emperor, Charles V, had ordained the death penalty by burning for "anyone committing impurity with a beast, or a man with a man, or a woman with a woman."[19] The *Carolina* was to have a major influence in Germany and elsewhere until the French Revolution. On its authority, the woman in question was put to death by drowning.

An accident of battle led to five burnings in 1560: at war with the duke of Savoy, the Genevans had captured a fort with Turkish galley-slaves. "Of the thirty-odd Turks who fell into Genevan hands, three confessed that they habitually engaged in homosexuality and were promptly burned for it, along with two French Catholics whom they implicated."[20] Before 1600 nearly all the men put to death for sodomy had been foreigners—French, Italians, or Germans, many of them religious refugees. In 1610, however, a leading local official confessed, under torture, to homosexual acts with more than twenty men "ranging from magistrates to gamekeepers." Eleven were tried; four were burned and the rest banished. Executions continued until 1662; then prosecutions decreased dramatically as religious fervor ebbed.

In Flanders, also, the fires of religious hatred flamed and consumed sodomites. During the fourteenth and fifteenth centuries there had been at least twenty-eight executions in Antwerp, Brussels, Ypres, Mechelen, and Louvain. In the wake of the Reformation, violent warfare in the Low Countries set native Protestants against Catholics supported by Spanish power. Protestants, predictably, sought to discredit their foes by portraying monasteries as hotbeds of sodomy. In 1578 several Franciscans were burned in Bruges; in Ghent, where the authority of the Catholic bishop had been replaced by a Protestant Committee of Eighteen, an unusually large number of executions took place: eight more Franciscans and six Augustinians were burned at the stake.[21] A contemporary engraving by Nikolas Hogenberg, captioned "Execution for Sodomitical Godlessness in the city of Bruges," shows two monks bound to posts on a platform in the city square in a kind of alcove made of combustible twigs. Another monk mounts the steps to take his place beside them. Two others are being lashed on a stage in the foreground as a crowd looks on.[22]

What part religious animosity played in prosecutions in France is less clear. France provides a unique source, however—a statistical record of trials compiled by the parlement of Paris, which served as an appeals court for most of the northern two-thirds of the country. During the period 1565–1640, the parlement reviewed 176 sodomy sentences, 121 of them capital. In the end there were 77 executions.[23] Probably about a dozen of these were for bestiality, then severely punished in France.[24] Since the era of most intense prosecutions began about 1530 and ended about 1680, we may therefore hazard a rough guess that about 150 men and women were executed for sodomy in France in the sixteenth and seventeenth centuries. Since the country

63. "Execution for sodomitical godlessness in the city of Bruges." Nicolas Hogenberg (1500–1539), engraving.

had about fifteen million inhabitants, this rate would be considerably lower than Spain's, perhaps only one-third or one-fourth as great.

Details about sixteenth-century trials are usually sketchy. We do, however, have some information about lesbian prosecutions. Of Françoise de L'Étage and Catherine de la Manière we know only that they were tried and acquitted at Bordeaux in 1533.[25] Henri Estienne mentions a woman from Fontaines who disguised herself as a men, married another woman, and was burned alive *(toute vive)* about 1535 for the "wickedness which she used to counterfeit the office of a husband."[26] Montaigne, who was fascinated by sexological details, recorded another case of cross-dressing a few days after he set out on his trip to Italy in September 1580. At Vitry-le-François, a small town on the Marne, he recorded a tragic story which hints at the existence of a small rural lesbian community.

> A few days before [we arrived] there had been a hanging at a place called Montier-en-Der, near here, upon this occasion: Seven or eight girls around Chaumont-en-Bassigni plotted together a few years ago to dress up as

> males and thus continue their life in the world. One of them came to this place . . . earning her living as a weaver, a well-disposed young man who made friends with everybody . . . Later he went to the said Monter-en-Der, still earning his living at the said trade, and fell in love with a woman whom he married and with whom he lived four or five months, to her satisfaction, so they say. But she was recognized by someone from the said Chaumont, the matter was brought before justice, and she was condemned to be hanged, which she said she would rather undergo then return to a girl's status; and she was hanged for using illicit devices to supply the deficit in sex.[27]

In the next century most of the trials we know of were instigated by parents who complained that their children had been abused.[28] But not all parental complaints were well-advised. At Tours in 1666 a silk merchant charged that a co-worker had "furtively carried off" his twenty-one-year-old son. The accused man, Antoine Mazouër, who was forty, claimed the father had beaten his son excessively, that he had sought refuge with him, that he was caring for him as a father, and that nothing sexual had taken place. The son's testimony is missing from the published records, but apparently he confessed that the relation was sexual and voluntary, since the older man was burned alive and the younger one strangled.[29]

• Henry III and the Mignons •

Montaigne, in his *Essays,* discusses Greek homosexuality but pointedly avoids the subject in contemporary France: as the supporter of a monarch perceived as conspicuously bisexual, he may have felt it discreet to be silent.[30] Of all French kings, Henry III is perhaps the most puzzling personality. Hailed as a hero at eighteen after victories over the Huguenots at Jarnac and Moncontour, he was elected king of Poland in 1573, only to return to France a few months later to succeed his brother Charles IX. Now the young warrior's style changed dramatically. Preferring the society of poets and men of letters, he eschewed the martial exercises regarded as essential for a French king and appeared at court dressed "like a woman," with abundant cosmetics and strings of pearls.[31] Henry alternated between bouts of hard work and fits of indolence so prolonged he seemed to have retired from public life. Loving fine clothes and extravagant display, and frequently indulging in wild debauches, he did penances so extreme that he was accused of living *en capucin*—like a monk or hermit.[32]

Henry also surrounded himself with handsome, athletic, swashbuckling young men from the minor nobility who imitated his style of dress, makeup, and adornment. Pierre L'Estoile, whose journals give us our most intimate view of the age, described them as wearing "velvet bonnets like the

64. Henry III of France. Jean Decourt, oil, c. 1580.

whores in the brothels."[33] These transvestite musketeers were the notorious *mignons* on whom Henry lavished enormous treasure. Despite the novelty of his wardrobe, Henry was highly intelligent, charming people with his affable and courteous manners and, in an age of fanaticism, remaining moderate and conciliatory, a trait that drew Montaigne and L'Estoile to his side: indeed, L'Estoile thought that in better times Henry might have made a good king. But in fact his reign was one of the most disastrous in French history. His most authoritative modern biographer has likened him to a doomed Shakespearean prince, who combined Hamlet's brilliance with the weakness of a Henry VI.

The religious civil wars that wracked France made Henry's position all but impossible and ensured that his sexual behavior would surface as a political issue. In 1572, at twenty-one, he had supported the Catholic side in the Saint Bartholomew's Day Massacre. This and his victories over them earned him the hatred of the Huguenots. It was a Huguenot poet-historian, Agrippa d'Aubigné, who did most to create the image of Henry as a latter-day Nero or Sardanapalus, of doubtful gender and sodomitical proclivities, "a King-Woman, or better, a Man-Queen."[34] In his *Universal History* d'Aubigné wrote, "You would hear it said aloud that from the time that this prince had prostituted himself to unnatural love, and had even turned his pleasures to passive rather than active, one noted the loss of that courage which had been seen before the birth of these enormities."[35]

But fate decreed that Henry would suffer even more at the hands of pious Catholics. Extremists objected to the peace he made with the defeated Huguenots in 1576 and formed a Holy League under the leadership of the duc de Guise. Henry, however, outmaneuvered the duke by putting himself at the head of the league and disbanding it. Personal attacks by Catholic writers intensified greatly in 1584 when Henry's younger brother died and the childless king, the last of the Valois line, recognized his distant cousin, the Protestant Henry of Navarre, as his heir. A modern researcher has estimated that in the next five years, before his assassination, some 900 pamphlets vilified Henry, a record even for that age of vitriol.[36] Of all the charges—tyranny, heresy, sorcery, and sodomy—the last seemed the least refutable, since appearances so obviously supported it.

The attacks were first directed against the so-called *mignons*, who were characterized either as *mignons d'état* (youths who supported Henry politically) or *mignons de couchette* ("bedroom favorites"). Outraged by the wealth bestowed on them, critics poured forth scurrilous verses. One sonnet denounced them as "shameless Ganymedes."[37] Another praised one mignon (Saint-Luc) for his bravery in war but charged another (Quélus) with winning advancement only through *son cul* (his ass).[38] When the mignons, barefoot and clad in sacks with holes for their heads and feet, marched with Henry in a penitential procession, lashing their backs, one wit opined that they should have aimed their blows lower.[39]

A dozen or more men were designated *mignons* during the king's reign. The first made up a quartet of favorites in 1573—Quélus (or Caylus), François d'O, Saint-Luc, and Saint-Sulpice.[40] A quarrel arose with another brawling young nobleman named Bussy d'Amboise, a favorite of Henry's brother, who was attacked and killed for mocking these "mignons de couchette."[41] A few months later a greater carnage took place when Quélus, with two friends, Maugiron and Livarot, fought a supporter of the duc de Guise and his seconds. Two men were killed on the field; another died the next day. One of the dead was Maugiron, who may have been Quélus's lover. The wounded Quélus lingered for a month, tenderly nursed by the king.[42] The grief-stricken Henry raised a monument with marble statues of the couple in the church of Saint Paul in Paris.[43]

The attacks on the mignons inevitably touched the king as the flood of cartoons, engravings, satirical poetry, and pamphlets, grew. One scurrilous pamphlet, *Les propos lamentables de Henri de Valois (The Deplorable Behavior of Henry of Valois)* had Henry confess that he was an adulterer, a rake, incestuous, and a sodomite.[44] A contemporary French account of Edward II's love for Piers Gaveston (*Histoire tragique et mémorable de Gaverston* [sic], 1588) drew ominous parallels with the fate of that ill-starred monarch.[45] A satirical engraving of a "hermaphrodite" mocked the ambiguous fashions of Henry's court with verses declaring, "I am not a male or a female . . . Which of the two shall I chose? . . . It is better to be both—one gets from that a double pleasure."[46]

But did Henry in fact have sexual relations with his mignons? Pierre Chevallier, whose biography is the most detailed modern study, has argued that there is no proof that would stand up in a court of law. But surely this is an unreasonable standard for historical biography. Henry's stereotypical lifestyle, his fondness for group orgies with the mignons, his masochistic guilt, and the intensity of his emotional involvements with his handsome young followers, some of whom he addressed by feminine nicknames, all suggest some sexual involvement. The Savoyard diplomat de Lucinge reported that Henry had been initiated into homosexuality by René de Villequier, a member of his suite in Poland: "He has been imbued by him with the vice which nature detests which he could not unlearn . . . I will say only that his cabinet has been a real harem of all lubricity and lewdness, a school of sodomy, where filthy revels have occurred which all the world has known about."[47] Chevallier discounts this evidence, but it seriously undermines his thesis that Henry's homosexuality remained latent. Lucinge's claim that it was Villequier who first led the king to experiment with homosexuality is borne out by the testimony of Henry's devoted supporter Jacques-Auguste de Thou in his *History of His Own Times,* published in Latin between 1604 and 1608.[48]

In 1588 Henry's fortunes took a turn for the worse. By now allied with Henry of Navarre against Henry of Guise in the War of the Three Henrys, he was driven from Paris by a mob that expressed its hate for the mignons by smashing the statues of Quélus and Maugiron. In December Henry ordered the assassination of Guise and his brother, the Cardinal of Lorraine. For this, Sixtus V excommunicated him. Shortly thereafter he was stabbed to death by a fanatical monk ardently committed to the Holy League, and the throne of France passed to the unequivocally heterosexual Henry IV. Épernon and another mignon, Bellegarde, were present at Henry's deathbed; twenty-one years later they took the lead in interring his body in a royal tomb in the church of Saint Denis, a service his heir had neglected to perform.

• The Poets' Revolt •

Henry IV is said to have brought France's religious wars to an end in 1592 with a *bon mot,* "Paris is well worth a mass." But this was an act of political expediency and hardly a triumph for Catholic piety. Not until 1615 were the canons of the Council of Trent accepted in France. Some commented drily

65. Young noblemen carousing. Jean de Saint-Igny, pen drawing, early seventeenth century.

that this was now appropriate, since *le vice ultramontain* had already crossed the Alps. Henry himself was no model of chastity; his court swarmed with mistresses and royal bastards. Protestant dissent, along with the disillusionment bred of three decades of religious wars and the new materialist philosophies spawned in Italian universities, all contributed to produce an era of anarchic skepticism. In short, the mood of literary Paris from 1600 to 1620 prefigured Restoration England after the fall of the Puritans. In this heady atmosphere of revolt, some poets took the daring step of openly avowing their sexuality in mocking rhymes.

Théophile de Viau was born in 1590 to a Protestant family that belonged to the *petite noblesse* of Gascony. Handsome, irreverent, and charming, he was the best and most popular French poet of his time. Ninety-three editions of his poems appeared before the end of the century, five times the number of his closest rival, Malherbe. Théophile, as he was usually called, wrote rhapsodically of nature and of erotic adventures, sometimes romantic, sometimes scabrous. His associates were dubbed *libertins*—the epithet implied first of all theological heterodoxy and only secondly sexual license. They looked "not to God and the Church, but to Nature—a Nature governed ultimately by an unalterable Destiny, and seen as a liberating force, far superior to the dogmas of revealed religion."[49] To achieve happiness, they proposed that men and women should follow their instincts. Théophile endorsed this philosophy in his *First Satire:* "J'approuve qu'un chacun suive en tout la nature."[50] For Théophile, the "natural" included both heterosexual and homosexual desire.

Théophile's verse included philosophical and mythological poems, pastorals, epigrams, and light-hearted tavern verse declaimed to intimates in Paris's smoke-filled cabarets. Some of these rhymes mocked religious beliefs, more sang of forbidden love. In 1619 the "prince of libertines" was exiled from Paris for "verses unworthy of a Christian." At the same time, he met and fell in love with a beautiful and talented nineteen-year-old aristocrat, Jacques Vallée des Barreaux, with whom he exchanged amorous letters in Latin. The name carried a warning—Des Barreaux's great-uncle, Geoffroy Vallée, had been burned for atheism. The young poet likewise scorned religion and was recklessly defiant of conventional opinion. Their ill-fated and sometimes tormented alliance has been likened to that of Oscar Wilde and Lord Alfred Douglas in late Victorian England.[51]

Théophile's tavern poems reflect the spirit of Villon and Rabelais, treat sex and its attendant disabilities with a cynical wit, and are liberally sprinkled with the obscenities common to their milieu. His homosexual poems owe something to Martial and Petronius but are touched by an affability hardly to be found in these predecessors. They are not pederastic but reflect a kind of humorous male camaraderie. One poem breaks with convention by adding contemporaries to the standard classical references. It is a plea to an aristocratic lover slow to redeem a promise:

> Appolon avec ses chansons
> Desbaucha le jeune Hyacinthe,
> Si Corridon fout Aminte
> César n'aymoit que des garçons.
>
> On a foutu Monsieur le Grand,
> L'on fout le Comte de Tonnerre.
> Et ce savant roy d'Angleterre
> Foutoit-il pas le Boukinquan?

Je n'ay ni qualité ni rang
Qui me donne un marquis pour garse.
Et tu sais pourtant bien que j'arse
Aussi fort qu'un Prince du sang.[52]

("Apollo with his songs seduced young Hyacinth; if Corydon fucked Amyntas, Caesar loved only boys. Monsieur le Grand [Bellegarde] was fucked, so was the Comte de Tonnerre, and this learned King of England [James I]—didn't he fuck Buckingham? I have neither birth nor rank to merit a marquis for a whore; you know well, however, that I get as stiff as any royal prince.")

Such poems might circulate in private or be recited to groups of intimates; publishing them was far more risky. Jesuit reformers, determined to stamp out religious deviance and moral dissent, attacked Théophile as an atheist—someone who took an Epicurean and materialist view of the universe. In 1619 the Italian philosopher-priest Lucilio Vanini had had his tongue torn out and been burned alive in Toulouse on such a charge. Public avowals of homosexuality could expose one to similar danger. When Père Garasse, a crusading Jesuit, attacked him in a book denouncing libertine writers and a warrant was issued for his arrest, Théophile fled, hoping to escape to the Netherlands.

Tried *in absentia* in Paris, he was condemned to be burned alive for "impieties, blasphemies, and abominations."[53] Lacking the poet, the authorities put a wicker effigy in the flames. Captured, Théophile would have suffered in the flesh if influential friends had not intervened to bring about a new trial. A young man named Louis Sageot, a dependent of Père Voisin, another Jesuit who assisted Garasse in the prosecution, declared in court that Théophile had written a poem complaining that he always caught infections when he avoided the "carnal company" of boys.[54] Things looked bad for Théophile, who had been so demoralized by his harsh prison conditions that he had tried to starve himself to death. But when he confronted his accuser, revealing how he had discovered him in an act of sodomy, Sageot broke down and admitted he had perjured himself at the behest of Voisin. Des Barreaux then testified that Voisin had solicited him when he was a pupil at a Jesuit college. The case collapsed, the former verdict was rescinded, and Voisin was exiled in disgrace. Théophile was sentenced to banishment, but the decree was not enforced. He died a year after his ordeal in 1626, his health undermined by his two years' incarceration. Des Barreaux, with whom he had been reunited, was at his side.

Though the prosecution had failed, it effectively ended the age of open libertinism. The combination of theological and sexual heterodoxy proved too explosive in the face of a Catholic reaction that was daily gathering force in France. Théophile escaped incineration only by converting to Catholicism, practicing its rites assiduously, and denying at his trial authorship of his erotic poems and any heretical interpretations of his other writings. Théophile was not without courage—he refused to implicate friends who had written some of the poems ascribed to him at his trial. We may forgive him for declining martyrdom.

Des Barreaux survived his lover for forty-seven years, dying in 1673. Insouciant about his duties in the Paris parlement, he bore two titles: Théophile's widow and *l'Illustre débauché.* A ribald popular song of the day claimed he knew "all the new pleasures" of sodomy.[55] Another member of Théophile's circle succeeded the poet as Des Barreaux's boon companion. This was Denis Sanguin de Saint-Pavin, who had unimpeachable aristocratic credentials. Dubbed the king of Sodom, he bore the title nonchalantly, protected by his rank and social position as Sodoma had been by his talent in Italy a century earlier. As a "commendatory" abbé, he had no particular religious duties, led the life of a gentlemanly dilettante, and was cordially received in the salons of Madame Sévigné and the Marquise de Rambouillet for his affable wit.

Saint-Pavin wisely forbore to publish his poems, though he recited them to intimate circles; most remained in manuscript until the twentieth century. In one rhyme he congratulated Des Barreaux on his retirement to a monastery with novices: "Qu'il est heureux dans ses caprices! / Il peut trouver en mesme lieu / Et son salut et ses délices!" ("How lucky he is in his whims! / He can find in the same place / Both his salvation and his pleasures!").[56] In poem after poem he proclaimed the legitimacy of sexual pleasure. At seventy-three he wrote to the exiled marquis de Jarzé: "Where you dwell, free from the smarting cares which torment courtiers, go court the shepherdess, or even, if you will, the shepherd; . . . and give yourself wholly to the pleasures which accord with your desires. Do not listen to Morality. Nature, more liberal, more often grants us a hundred things which are forbidden. She alone, in her great book, teaches us how to live."[57] It was a paradox typical of an age in which aristocratic status meant everything that the homophobic Louis XIV made Saint-Pavin his honorary chaplain in 1668.[58]

• Louis XIII, the Just •

Saint-Pavin's office, accorded him in the year before he died, was an honorary one that conferred no power. Libertine poets like Théophile were often protected by powerful nobles, but their role in society was marginal. And, like other members of the middle and lower classes, they risked punishment. One of them, Claude Le Petit, wrote a half-admiring, half-mocking sonnet on the burning of a sodomite friend in 1661; a year later he was himself burned alive for publishing obscene verses. "He died," wrote an unsympathetic spectator, "with the same so-called fortitude as that other wretch whose inclinations he shared."[59]

Yet ironies abounded. In modern democracies homosexuals have rarely governed. But in monarchies where power was hereditary, there was always the possibility that a ruler would turn out to be homosexual or bisexual. A man or woman whose behavior the church and state damned might hold supreme authority. Sodomites were expected to remain invisible, but Renaissance kings and queens lived the most public of lives. Such an anomaly was bound to create paradoxes. At no time do these appear more vividly than at the beginning of the seventeenth century. In 1610 the nine-year-old Louis XIII succeeded his father Henry IV, who, like Henry III before him, had been assassinated by a fanatical Catholic. At that moment in European history, one "sodomite," James I, ruled England, Scotland, and Ireland; another, Rudolph II, presided over the Holy Roman Empire; and France had its second homosexual king within a generation.[60]

Louis XIII's relations with his father had been close and affectionate, only occasionally interrupted by princely tantrums. His feelings toward his mother were distinctly cooler. Marie de' Medici ruled as regent for several years; but when Louis was fifteen her unpopular advisor, Concini, was assassinated, his wife burned for sorcery, and the queen herself forced into exile. Almost as important in Louis' upbringing was his personal physician, Jean Héroard. He had been present at Louis' birth and was at his side for more than twenty years, during which time he kept an almost hourly account of Louis's medical treatment and personal behavior. As a result, we know more about the childhood and adolescence of Louis XIII than of any other historical figure.

Louis was made aware of his sexuality almost as soon as he could talk. In the free-spoken, ribald court of Henry IV he learned that the first duty of a dauphin was to make another dauphin. He was taught to call his penis the *mignon d'Infante*—the infanta's delight, since a Spanish princess was his preordained bride. But even in infancy it soon became clear that Louis was much more drawn to men than to girls. The gossipy Tallemant des Réaux wrote that "the King gave his first sign of affection for anybody in the person of his coachman, Saint-Amour. After that he showed kindly feeling for Haran, the keeper of his dogs."[61] At ten the boy's strong emotional need to attach himself to an older man showed in the passion he developed for his falconer, Charles d'Albert de Luynes, who was thirty-three. Louis moved Luynes into an apartment directly over his in the Louvre, visited him at all hours of the day and night, and saw far more of him than of Anne of Austria, whom he married at fourteen. Luynes, an ambitious member of the lesser nobility without any exceptional talents, was gentle and paternal in his relations with the young king, who, distrustful of his own judgment, in effect let him rule the realm.

If Louis shared Henry III's interest in men and the same devout religiosity, he was in most ways his opposite. Caring nothing for clothes or art or literature, he was devoted to hunting and warfare and led his armies in the field.

66. Louis XIII as a youth. Frans Pourbus the younger, c. 1616.

Though he insisted on royal protocol, Louis was hardly regal in his tastes—he was skilled at many handicrafts, grew peas for the market, and learned to lard veal, all to the scorn of his courtiers. Henry had been suavely articulate; Louis stammered, spoke little, and was often morose and sulky. His chastisement of any who violated royal authority won him the title Louis the Just, but his justice was sometimes edged with cruelty. Nevertheless, since he lacked the stigma of femininity and was unquestionably devoted to the Catholic cause, he did not suffer the abuse Henry III had borne.[62]

Héroard's journal routinely recorded Louis's boyhood orgasms; we learn that the royal marriage was not consummated on the wedding night. Three years later Luynes carried the weeping king to Anne's bedchamber and all but threw him into bed.[63] When Luynes died of fever in 1621, the grieving Louis (then twenty) became melancholic and depressed. By now convinced of the wisdom of keeping his emotional life separate from politics, he resolved that no new favorite would play a role in his administration, a rule he kept rigorously. Then, in 1624 Louis made the crucial decision of his reign when he installed Cardinal Richelieu as his chief advisor. Richelieu, well aware of the king's predilections, seems to have been concerned only that his attachments be to men who were politically innocuous.

Richelieu made France the most powerful nation in Europe, supplanting Spain. The state within a state the Huguenots had set up at La Rochelle was dismantled after a devastating military campaign, the nobility were ruthlessly brought into subjection to the throne, and Hapsburg power, which threatened France on both its eastern and southern frontiers, was checkmated. Louis' personal life was less successful. Lacking mistresses, he was called Louis the Chaste. But such a title, in religiously heterosexual France, was inevitably tinged with irony. It was almost twenty years before renewed relations with Anne led to the birth of a son, who was to become Louis XIV. In the meantime, Louis's emotions were fixed on a series of young men. The first was an athletically handsome equerry, François de Baradas. This liaison moved a grandson of Henry III's favorite Saint-Luc to pen an irreverent rhyme: "Become a bugger, Baradas, / if you are not already one, / like Maugiron, my grandfather, / and La Valette."[64] Tallemant des Réaux. whose sketch of Louis in his *Historiettes* is maliciously mordant, wrote that the king "loved Baradas violently; he was accused of committing a hundred filthy acts with him."[65] Baradas was not very intelligent, however, and lost favor by fighting a duel after dueling had been forbidden by royal decree.[66]

Louis's last favorite was the handsomest, the most glamorous, and the most tragic. Richelieu made the mistake of introducing his protégé Henri Coiffier de Ruzé, marquis of Cinq Mars, to the king when Louis was thirty-eight, Cinq Mars nineteen. The spoiled young aristocrat was beautiful and splendidly dressed, a form of ostentation that embarrassed the modest Louis. But the gloomy king was captivated and rejuvenated by the dashing youth, and the court was amazed to see him dancing and carousing. This union of opposites did not proceed smoothly, however. Louis's letters to Richelieu are filled with anguished complaints about the distress their lovers' quarrels caused him. Louis protested after a typical contretemps: "I haven't slept a wink all night and am really upset."[67] The court could not help but take notice. "The king loved M. le Grand ardently," one courtier wrote.[68] Tallemant's account of the affair is more explicit. He describes how another courtier (whom he names) surprised Cinq Mars as he was anointing himself from head to foot with jasmine oil. "A moment after came a knock. It was the King. It would appear . . . he was anointing himself for a contest." Again, on a royal journey, the king "sent M. le Grand to undress, who returned adorned like a bride. 'To bed, to bed,' he said to him impatiently . . . and the mignon was not in before the king was already kissing his hands."[69] Cinq Mars, who was himself an ardent womanizer, merely tolerated these passionate attentions.

Louis warned the young man that if he ever had to choose between them, he would support Richelieu. Cinq Mars was unwise enough not to believe him. He plotted with the king's brother, Gaston, to stage a *coup d'état* with the aid of Spanish troops and assassinate the cardinal. Richelieu discovered the plot and tricked the conspirators into confessions. Wearied with his favorite's vagaries, Louis, true to his word, put considerations of state before tender feelings. On August 12, 1642, the intrepid Cinq Mars was beheaded for treason at Lyon. Shortly before the event, Louis is said to have remarked: "M. le Grand will soon be passing his time very badly."[70] Some members of the court thought him inhumanly cold. A royal historiographer, predictably, praised the king for subordinating personal considerations to the good of the realm. Louis the Just outlived his lover by only nine months.

• Monsieur and Madame •

French tradition—priding itself on its achievements in literature, art, and architecture and on its triumphs on the battlefield—calls the age of Louis XIV *le Grand Siècle,* the Great Century. For the historian of morals and of homosexuality, it is an age of great ironies, embracing at the same time pious conformity and extreme freedom. It is also an age with unparalleled sources of information about the private lives of men and women, for the French aristocracy developed a new passion—the writing of personal memoirs. (Such revelations, however, were not meant for immediate scrutiny; most did not see the light until the nineteenth century.) The *historiettes* of Tallement des Réaux; the *romans* of Bussy-Rabutin; the memoirs of Saint-Simon, of the marquis de Sourches, and of Giovanni Battista Primi Visconti; and the letters of the duchesse d'Orléans take us freely into the bedrooms of the *grand monde.* The kind of intimate details the Inquisition recorded in Spain were preserved in France by lordly candor. The subject of male love, taboo in middle-class company, was freely canvassed in more sophisticated circles.

Louis XIV, the Sun King, who came to the throne at the age of five in 1643 and ruled till 1715, typifies the age's contradictions. Contemporaries testify unanimously to the strength of his homophobia.[71] Yet Louis had a homosexual father (Louis XIII), a homosexual uncle (César de Vendôme, whose Hôtel de Vendôme in Paris was popularly known as the Hôtel de Sodome), a flamboyantly homosexual brother (Philippe d'Orléans), and a son (the comte de Vermandois) whom he punished for his affairs with other youths. French society reflected these contrasts. The open libertinism of Théophile's circle had vanished. Outward conformity and shows of piety became the norm, especially after 1680 when Louis XIV gave up his mistresses and fell under the influence of Madame de Maintenon. Publicly, the morals campaign waged by the Jesuits and the Company of the Holy Sacrament appeared to have triumphed, but it was often the triumph of Tartuffe.

In 1682 a court scandal erupted which suggested that sodomy deserved its name as *le beau vice,* that is, the vice of the fashionable world. A few years earlier a number of young rakes at the summit of French society had inaugurated a club described in an essay provocatively titled "La France devenue italienne." This intriguing sketch, whose details appear to mix fact with fancy, was most widely disseminated as an appendix to Bussy-Rabutin's *Histoire amoureuse des Gaules,* a *roman à clef* about erotic intrigues at Versailles. It opened with a cool declaration: "The facility of all the women had made their charms so scorned by young men that they were hardly held in regard any more at court; debauchery reigned there more than in any place in the world, and though the King had professed many times an inconceivable horror for these sorts of pleasures, it was only in this that he could not be obeyed."[72]

The youths, it was claimed, formed a secret brotherhood *(confrérie)* led by the duc de Gramont, the marquis de Manicamp, the chevalier de Tilladet, and the marquis de Biran, all of whom contended for leadership. In semblance, it was modeled on the Order of Saint Lazare and took as its emblem a young man trampling a woman underfoot in the style of Saint Michael trampling the devil. A set of ordinances were drawn up which purportedly required the initiation of novices at the hands of "grand priors" and the total avoidance of women.[73] These tongue-in-cheek rules exhibit a certain dry irony—they could be read as the regulations of an ascetic brotherhood. According to the account, the group met with unexpected success: "After they had accomplished these holy mysteries, each returned to Paris, and someone not having kept the secret, it soon became common talk what had happened at the country house [where they had met to avoid Louis's surveillance] so that some inflamed by their inclinations and others by the novelty of the affair hastened to join the order."[74]

Among them was the fifteen-year-old comte de Vermandois, Louis's son by Louise de la Vallière. A strikingly beautiful boy, the prince had been legitimatized and destined for high office, but when another young, handsome, and popular prince of the blood, the prince of Conti, joined, Louis became aware of the group and moved angrily to punish its members. Vermandois was whipped in the royal presence and exiled. Conti permanently lost favor. The king's wrath descended also on the prince de Turenne, the marquis de Créqui, the chevalier de Sainte-Maure, the chevalier de Mailly, the comte de Roucy, the vidame de Laon, and the comte de Marsan, all of whom were sent into exile.[75]

But these trials were as nothing compared with what Louis had to bear at the bejewelled hands of Philippe d'Orléans (1640–1701), who, as was customary with the brother next in line to the king, was known simply as "Monsieur." As a child his delicate beauty had led his mother, Anne of Austria, to call him "my little girl," and he was encouraged to wear women's clothes.[76] But Philippe's femininity, marked from birth, seems to have been an essential part of his nature. He was fascinated with women's dresses and adornments, loved jewels, perfumes, huge wigs, colorful ribbons, high heels, and malicious gossip. In his teens he attended a ball with a female cousin, both dressed as shepherdesses.[77] Throughout his life he lived surrounded, on the one hand, by virile young men and, on the other, by effeminates who shared his tastes. One contemporary called him "the silliest woman who ever lived."[78]

The first love of his life was the comte de Guiche; they met clandestinely at the house of the mother of Philippe's transvestite friend, the abbé de Choisy.[79] When Philippe was married off to Charles I's daughter, Henrietta, Guiche seduced the susceptible duchess, and husband and wife found themselves vying for the attentions of the same man. (In this age, bisexuals of Guiche's sort were said to be *au poil et à la plume*—"after fur and feathers," like versatile huntsmen.) But the great love of Monsieur's life was another Philippe, the chevalier de Lorraine, an angelically handsome but penurious nobleman of princely rank. In 1668 Lorraine moved into the most luxurious apartment in the Palais Royal, Philippe's Paris residence. There he exploited his position during thirty tempestuous years, exacting huge sums from Philippe for himself and for his own lovers and mistresses. From then on Lorraine was recognized as a kind of *maîtresse en titre* ("official mistress"). Saint-Simon, in his famous memoirs, called him "always the publicly recognized master of Monsieur's household."[80]

Surprisingly, the man who seemed more concerned with beauty patches than feats of arms proved an effective warrior. The abbé de Choisy wrote of Monsieur that "I have seen him during campaigns for an entire fifteen hours on horseback," risking not only his life but his complexion to sun and gunsmoke.[81] On April 11, 1677, during the war with Holland, Philippe was given credit for defeating the forces of William III at the battle of Cassel. Even Saint-Simon, whose sketch of Monsieur is acidly critical, admitted that he showed "much valor."[82]

Though Madame de La Fayette wrote that "the miracle of inflaming the heart of this prince was not reserved for any woman," Philippe was required to produce Bourbon heirs.[83] When Henrietta died, he was married to Elizabeth-Charlotte, daughter of the Elector Palatine, henceforth known as "Madame." The second duchess's fifty years of correspondence describing the amours of her husband and dozens of other men in France and throughout Europe has been aptly called "an encyclopedia of homosexuality." Perceptive and humorous, peppery and humane, and candid to an incredible degree, the letters of "Liselotte" to friends and relatives in Germany, France, England, and Spain are a major source for our knowledge of private life at the court of Louis XIV. Her temperament complemented her husband's: while he advised the ladies of the court on their coiffeurs and diamonds, she went riding and hunting with the king. Monsieur freely discussed his love

67. Philippe, duke of Orléans, "Monsieur." Antoine Mathieu the elder, oil, c. 1665.

entanglements with his wife, who, despite her pious German Lutheran background, was determined to handle the matter diplomatically.

The duchess hated Lorraine, who she felt tried to turn her husband against her, and feared that the immense sums Monsieur spent on his lovers would impoverish her and their children. Because of this anxiety, relations with Philippe were often edgy: "It is in vain that I do my best to persuade him that I don't want to trouble him in his divertissements and his love for

68. Elisabeth Charlotte, duchess of Orléans, "Madame." Hyacinthe Rigaud, oil, 1713.

men, he believes always that I want to prevent his giving all his goods to his gallants." Nevertheless, she took pains to keep on speaking terms with his lovers: "I don't wish any harm to the mignons," she wrote to her aunt Sophia, the electress of Hanover, "and I chat amicably and politely with them."[84] At other times she felt that piety and sodomy had coarsened court life—the new moral code made it difficult for young men and women to converse freely, and male attachments diverted men from women.[85] When, after the birth of three children, Philippe suggested separate bedrooms, Madame was relieved at not having to face pregnancy again. Liselotte was, in fact largely indifferent to sex and broke the rules by taking no lovers.

Madame shared these details with her correspondents, most of whom she felt were naively ignorant of male love. "On this matter," she informed her half-sister Amelise in the Palatinate, "I have become so knowledgeable in France that I could write books on it."[86] In 1705 she essayed a typology: "Where have you been hiding, you and Louise, that you know so little of the world? . . . Anyone who would detest all who loved boys could not be friends with . . . six persons here. There are all kinds of them. There are some of them who hate women like death and can only love men. Others love men and women; my Lord Raby [an English visitor] is of this number. Others love only children of ten or eleven years, other youths from seventeen to twenty-five years and these are the most numerous."[87] She tried to explain how devout Christians squared their behavior with their faith:

> Those who have that taste and who believe in Holy Scripture suppose that it was only a sin as long as there were few men in the world and what they practised could hurt the human race . . . But now that the world is completely populated they consider it a simple divertissement. They hide it as much as they can in order not to scandalize the common people, but they speak openly of it among people of quality. They consider it a delicate refinement *[gentillesse]* and do not fail to say that since Sodom and Gomorrah God our Lord has no longer punished anyone for this reason. You will find me very well-informed on this matter; I have heard it talked about often since I have been in France.[88]

When Amelise assumed that Catholics, who did not read their Bibles, necessarily fell short of Protestant standards of morality, Madame replied tartly:

> If you do not wish to be shocked by people, dear Amelise, surround yourself with few of them. Reading the Bible will not do anything. Ruvigny, who was one of the elders of the church of Charenton, is one of the worst of the clique. He and his brother La Caillement are Protestants and always read the Bible but do worse than any of those who are here, and understand very well the jokes when one pokes fun at them. La Caillemont said "I have to love men, since I am too ugly to be loved by women." There are also many in Germany who practice this debauchery. Count von Zinzendorff, who was the Emperor's envoy here, changed color whenever he saw a well-made page and was so excited that it was a shame to see . . . Believe me one finds such sodomites *[solche Benjametter]* in all countries.[89]

Philippe died suddenly in 1701, but in the twenty-one years that remained to her Madame often returned in her letters to the subject of her marriage. She wrote to her aunt in Hanover, soon to be named heiress to the

English throne: "Monsieur often plagued and worried me, but only out of weakness and too great a devotion to those who assisted his pleasures."[90] Eventually, however, there had been a reconciliation. Philippe had wearied of the chevalier de Lorraine, realizing at last that his attachment was entirely self-interested. To Princess Caroline of Wales (later queen as the wife of George II) Madame wrote in 1716, "I won Monsieur over during the last three years of his life. We even used to laugh together about his weaknesses . . . He [now] had confidence in me and always took my side, but before that I used to suffer dreadfully. I was just beginning to be happy when the Almighty took poor Monsieur from me."[91]

There is much besides Madame's revelations to suggest that Scaliger's remark about nobles in France was more than speculation. The historian Primi Visconti (1648–1713) reported that the marquis de la Vallière had tried to seduce him by reciting the *mot* in French: "Monsieur, en Espagne les moines, en France les grands, et en Italie tout le monde." But when he told his friend the abbé del Carretto of this incident, the abbé replied that "it is necessary to have compassion because men with such an inclination are born with it as poets are born with rhyme."[92] Here is an epochal change.

Madame's age is the first since classical times in which we can document a sophisticated tolerance among knowledgeable men and women in Western Europe. When someone asked Mademoiselle de Gournay (Montaigne's literary executrix) if sodomy was a crime, she replied, "God forbid that I condemn what Socrates practiced."[93] Bussy-Rabutin roused the ire of Louis XIV by chronicling the amours of the court too explicitly in his *Histoire amoureuse.* But his *roman à clef* contains a revealing anecdote. When Bussy (who appears as a character in his own novel) encounters the comte de Guiche and the comte de Manicamp in bed, he remarks philosophically: "As for me, I do not condemn your manners; everyone must manage in his own way *[chacun se sauve à sa guise]*; but I do not reach beatitude by the road you take."[94]

• Six Generals •

Under the *ancien régime* the clergy, like the aristocracy, were usually free from criminal sanctions, since the police routinely referred errant priests to their ecclesiastical superiors, who took care to minimize publicity. There were many scandals involving clergy of all ranks, from abbés to cardinals.[95] No group, however, aroused as much suspicion as the Jesuits. As a foreign order closely allied with the Italian papacy and as Europe's most celebrated schoolteachers, they were routinely accused of pederasty in jokes, ribald songs, and innuendoes. Voltaire played this game with relish in his campaign against ecclesiastical tyranny. Though there were indeed many scandals, the order's egregious reputation was undoubtedly inflated by anti-clerical prejudice.

Surprisingly, another institution surpassed the church in notoriety in the reign of the Sun King—namely, the army. In its entry under *Vice ultramontain,* the compendious *Dictionnaire du Grand Siècle* (1990) lists four leading French generals and two of their most renowned antagonists. These were, respectively, the prince de Condé, the maréchal de Luxembourg, the duc de Vendôme, and the marquis de Villars, and their opponents, William III and Prince Eugene of Savoy.

Louis de Bourbon, prince de Condé, known to history as the Grand Condé, was hailed as the French Alexander. Descended from an uncle of Henry IV, he was the second prince of the blood and might have inherited the throne if Louis XIII had not belatedly fathered two sons. Condé won his epithet when, at twenty-one, he overwhelmed the Spanish army—the most formidable in Europe—at the battle of Rocroi on May 19, 1643, and five days after the accession of the five-year-old Louis XIV established France as the most powerful state on the continent. Condé maintained his reputation throughout a lifetime of military successes in France and Germany. When he died forty-four years later, Louis XIV (whom Condé betrayed before his death) lamented that he had lost "the greatest man in my kingdom."

Much better educated than most aristocrats, Condé was skilled in mathematics, law, and history. When he retired in 1675 to his estate at Chantilly, where Théophile had found sanctuary fifty years before, he became an arbiter of literary taste and held court splendidly for such friends as Racine, Boileau, and La Bruyère. Totally disdainful of convention, he had in his younger days been the patron of the surviving circle of libertine poets at the Pomme de Pin. The abbé Saint-Pavin, the acknowledged king of this Sodom, welcomed him to the group with some ironic flattery. Condé had been repeatedly compared to Julius Caesar as a soldier and statesman. Saint-Pavin drew another comparison between them: "For your honor I am jealous: / this parallel gives me pain, / Caesar, just between us, / was also a bugger like you, / but never so great a captain."[96]

Long after Condé's death Madame explained his preferences: "In the army he was used to young cavaliers; when he returned he could not tolerate women."[97] Nevertheless, one famous beauty tried to seduce him. When they parted, Ninon de Lenclos is supposed to have remarked that the duke must be strong, a sly reference to the Latin proverb *Pilosus aut fortis aut libidinus* ("A hairy man is either strong or lustful").[98] A fellow general, the comte de Coligny-Saligny, the devoted friend in his youth, praised Condé's wit and his courage but swore "on the Holy Gospels that I hold in my hand" that he was a sodomite.[99] A doggerel Latin rhyme represented Condé and companion facing a flood on the Rhone. When Condé feared they might drown, his friend reassured him: "Our lives are safe, for we are sodomites—we can perish only by fire."

But in 1681 Louis's conversion to piety and monogamy signaled a triumph at court for the Jesuits and ecclesiastical orthodoxy. Courtiers must have wondered whether this turn of affairs would threaten Louis's nonconformist generals. Others, especially the Jansenists and Huguenots, soon felt the growing bigotry—most Protestant churches were closed, and Louis publicly bound himself to extirpate heresy. The brutal *dragonnades* billeted soldiers in Huguenot households, where every kind of torture and outrage was encouraged. When the Edict of Nantes, by which Louis's grandfather Henry IV had sought to protect the rights of Protestants, was formally revoked in 1685, the resulting persecution was, in the eyes of one famous French historian, "worse than the Revolutionary Terror of 1793."[100] Huguenots, forced to receive the Eucharist, protested what they considered an act of idolatry by spitting out the wafers and were burned alive for sacrilege.

Doctrinal and moral intolerance went hand in hand. On Christmas day, 1684, the Jesuit father Pierre Bourdaloue, Louis's favorite preacher, in a sermon before the king suggested that Louis, having extirpated heresy and sacrilege, might extend his power to the bedrooms of Versailles and other "monstrous things": "Scripture forbids me to name them, but it is sufficient that Your Majesty knows and detests them . . . They will not withstand your disfavor nor the weight of your indignation, and when you will it these vices, shameful to the name of Christianity, will cease to outrage God and to scandalize men. It is for that, Sire, that heaven has placed you on the throne."[101]

Louis sought to act. He warned his brother to discipline his servants, but it was reported that when he approached his war minister, the formidable Louvois undertook to persuade the king that sodomite generals "were worth more to His Majesty than if they loved women," since these could take their lovers on campaigns, while the others "could not be detached from their mistresses" in Paris.[102]

If Louis prided himself on his defense of the faith, he was even prouder of France's new military glory: for him, victorious generals trumped crusading preachers. He soon had need of them to support his growing aggression in the Rhineland. In 1685 the death of Madame's brother, the Elector Palatine, led Louis to make claims based on his sister-in-law's rights of inheritance. His subsequent devastation of the Palatinate horrified Europe and led the angry Madame to confront Louvois for atrocities committed in her name. In the same year William III of the Netherlands was able to persuade the Catholic emperor and the Catholic elector of Bavaria to join Protestant Germans and Swedes in the League of Augsburg to oppose Louis. Louis's leading general in the ensuing war was the duc de Luxembourg (1628–1695).

Luxembourg, a younger cousin of Condé, had been raised with him and shared his libertine tastes. He aided him in the whirlwind conquest of the Franche-Comté in 1668 and seven years later was named a marshal of France, despite his deformed back. In the War of the League of Augsburg he defeated William at Leuze (1691), Steenkirk (1692), and Neerwinden (1693). He collected so many enemy banners for display in Paris that he was known as the "tapissier of Notre Dame." When William complained, "I can never beat that cursed humpback," Luxembourg replied, "How does he know I have a hump? He has never seen my back."[103] Primi Visconti noted in his *Mémoires sur la cour de Louis XIV:* "The marquis de Montrevel had introduced me to Luxembourg and apprized me how the young and handsome Tallart, the son of madame de La Baume, was in the campaign more to serve the general than the king. Luxembourg, Créquy, La Vallière and Seignelay formed a society in which the first two were actors, the other two submissives *[courtisans]*."[104] The duc de Tallart later became a field marshal.

In her correspondence the duchess of Orléans speaks of Luxembourg's rival, William III of Orange, as a typical lover of men.[105] She had known him as a child in The Hague, where they turned somersaults on the palace's Turkish carpets; she was seven, William nine, and a marriage between them was regarded as a possibility. Madame always retained a lively regard for William, whose "grandeur of soul" she admired, despite the fact that he was the recognized leader of Protestant Europe against her brother-in-law.[106] The perception she and others shared of William's homosexuality was based largely on his attachment to a Dutch nobleman, William Bentinck, who had become his page at fifteen and a life-long valued friend and adviser. Apparently Bentinck (whom William had made earl of Portland after he assumed the English throne) felt less constrained in Paris than in Holland and Britain, for when he was sent to France as ambassador in 1697, Madame remarked, no doubt with some exaggeration, that "all those who came with my lord Portland" were openly involved in same-sex relations.[107]

William's second love was another young Dutchman, Arnold Joost Keppel, who consoled him in his final years. When Madame heard that Keppel had almost "died of grief" at the king's death in 1702, she remarked sadly, reflecting on the self-seeking greed of Monsieur's lovers, "We have hardly seen any similar friendship here in my husband's circle."[108] We will see, in our next chapter, how his English subjects regarded William III's male involvements.

Homosexual generals were to play a leading part in the next great war to engulf Europe, the War of the Spanish Succession, which broke out in 1702. Chief among these were the duc de Vendôme (1654–1712) and his cousin, Prince Eugene of Savoy (1663–1736), who fought against the French. Vendôme was the grandson of a bastard son of Henry IV, César de Vendôme, who himself had a reputation for sodomy. He won early fame fighting in Holland and Alsace and shared in Luxembourg's defeat of William III at Steenkirk. A ribald rhyme inspired by his success in Spain in 1697 noted his sexual preference: "He took the pox and Barcelona / And each from the wrong side."[109] Despite his known predilection for passive sodomy, he was highly popular with his troops, the French court, and the common people of Paris. He was also popular with the peasants on his estate at Anet, whom he rewarded for their sexual services with gold coins; with these they paid their rent.[110]

The duc de Saint-Simon, who was jealous of Vendôme—he was incensed that someone from an illegitimate line should enjoy such favor at court—expressed his amazement at Louis's partiality: "What is marvelous to one who knew a king . . . full of a just and indeed singular horror of the inhabitants of Sodom and even for the least suspicion of that vice, [is that] M. de Vendôme was more filthily immersed in it all his life than anyone, and so publicly that he made no more of it than of the most trifling and most ordinary gallantry, without the king, who had always known this, ever finding it offensive nor being any the less well disposed to him."[111] Yet adoring crowds swept the duke along with enthusiastic acclamations in the street, besieged his carriage, and applauded him at every turn. When he arrived at a performance of Lully's *Roland* given to honor him, "everyone fell to clapping their hands and crying: *Vive Vendôme!* until the opera began; after the end of which the same *vive Vendôme!* recommenced."[112] Saint-Simon complained that Vendôme was treated by everyone like a demigod; he decried this "universal madness" and lamented that Louis "seemed to remain king only to exalt him the more."[113]

When Europe's refusal to accept Louis XIV's grandson Philip as heir to the Spanish throne led to the War of the Spanish Succession, Vendôme was sent to oppose Prince Eugene in Italy. He fought him to a draw at Luzzara in 1702 and beat him again at Cassano three years later. In the Low Countries he was himself decisively defeated by Marlborough and Eugene at Oudenarde in 1706, but he recouped his reputation in Spain. Summoned there by Philip in 1710 when his situation seemed desperate, he was, in Voltaire's phrase, "worth an army."[114] When Vendôme died two years after, the grateful Philip, who realized he owed his crown to him, had him buried with high honors in the Escorial. So the sodomite-hero lay next to Don Juan of Austria, the victor of Lepanto, in a monastery-palace in the land of the Inquisition.

Charles Louis Hector de Villars (1653–1734) sprang from the minor nobility of Lyon and won his dukedom on the battlefield. He has been called "the last of the great generals of Louis XIV."[115] Fiery, spirited, and daring to a degree that often tried the nerves of the admiring king, Villars was dismissed by Saint-Simon as a conceited, swashbuckling romancer. But Saint-Simon was a sedentary civilian. At the outbreak of the War of the Spanish Succession, Villars won a great victory at Friedlingen in Alsace in 1702 and was hailed as the savior of his country. But when France, bled white and impoverished by the interminable wars spawned by Louis XIV's expansionist policy, sued for peace in 1708, the Allies' terms were so harsh that Louis made a pathetic appeal to the nation to fight on. France rallied to him; and Villars, after the indecisive bloodbath at Malplaquet, beat Eugene at Denain in 1712. Villars was fêted as the hero of the Peace of Utrecht (1713), which ended the war and recognized Philip as king of Spain. During his long life—he fought his last campaign at the age of eighty—the marshal was adored by his soldiers. Occasionally, despite his reputation as a womanizer, he returned the compliment. Madame reported that his true passion was for young men and that "the pretty prince d'Eisenbach" had threatened the national idol with his baton on receiving an unwelcome "declaration of love."[116]

The most famous antagonist of these generals, whom Napoleon ranked as one of the greatest military geniuses of all time, was Prince Eugene of Savoy. His statue stands in the Heldenplatz in Vienna as one of Austria's national heroes. Though he divides this honor with the Archduke Karl (who fought Napoleon), he was not a Hapsburg. Eugene, the scion of a junior branch of the dukes of Savoy, was born and educated in France. Puny, frail, and sickly, he was snubbed by everyone, including the king. The unfeeling Madame called him "nothing but a dirty, very debauched boy who gave no promise of being any good. He had a small, snub nose; [though] his eyes were not bad and showed intelligence."[117] Destined for the church, he wore a black clerical outfit from the age of five and a tonsure; Louis called him "le petit abbé." But Eugene rebelled, sought a military command, and when it was denied by the contemptuous king, sought service under the emperor in Vienna. Louis was to regret his refusal.

Eugene fought in the relief of Vienna and regained Belgrade from the Turks in 1688. In 1697 he liberated Hungary. Made supreme commander at thirty, he led the Austrian forces in the War of the Spanish Succession, defeating the French in Italy. In 1704 Eugene and the duke of Marlborough won a great victory on the northern front at Blenheim. His later successes in Italy ensured that Austria would control the northern half of the country till Garibaldi's day. The prince was the nemesis of the French king, whom he hated. His victory at Oudenarde, coming after the enormous loss of men at Malplaquet, forced Louis to sue for peace; Eugene dictated the terms. When the Spanish empire was partitioned after the Peace of Utrecht, he became governor of what had been the Spanish Netherlands (now Belgium), then imperial viceroy in Italy.

The austere severity of his character later in life and his avoidance of women—he never married—gave him a reputation as an ascetic. Madame, however, painted a lurid picture of his youth in France: uncharitably, she called him a "little slut" and wrote that "he often played the woman with young people" to earn desperately needed money.[118] A scholar and a connoisseur, Prince Eugene filled his magnificent palace in Vienna, the Belvedere, with sculpture and paintings, and his books formed the nucleus of the Austrian national library.

• Les Lesbiennes •

But what of women who loved women in this world of kings, libertine poets, aristocratic license, and unceasing warfare? The literate medieval world knew of such women principally through Ovid and Martial or from learned treatises on theology or the law. The Renaissance added to this meager knowledge a rediscovered Sappho and Lucian's vignettes in his *Dialogues of the Courtesans.* Then, in the age of Shakespeare, an enterprising Frenchman who had led an active life at court, fought in many bloody campaigns, and traveled widely wrote a unique commentary on women who were attracted to women—the first since antiquity. The writer was the abbé Brantôme (1540?–1614), whose racy pages, for all the limitations of their male viewpoint, constitute a pioneering document in the history of sexology. They are novel in another respect. Hitherto, scholars had referred to lesbians routinely by the Greek-derived term *tribade.* Brantôme was the first writer to use the modern word *lesbienne* as a synonym, though the term did not gain wide acceptance until the nineteenth century.[119]

French Renaissance scholarship had brought Sappho's Greek texts into European notice once more by publishing editions with translations. Hitherto Sappho had been known chiefly through Ovid's *Heroides,* in which the lovelorn poet, scorned by the youthful ferryman Phaon, leaps from the Leucadian cliff. Then, in 1546, Robert Estienne printed Sappho's famous "Ode" ("He is more than a hero") in his edition of the Greek rhetorician Dionysius of Halicarnassus, who had quoted it; and a decade later his son, Henri Estienne, published a full edition of Sappho with Latin translations. Inevitably these new publications challenged scholars to interpret Sappho's erotic psychology. The attendant moralizing provides a unique view of attitudes toward lesbian love in France. Henri Estienne, for example, assumed that Sappho had led a respectable life until her husband's death and then began her "shameless promiscuity" with the (perhaps legendary) Phaon and a long list of "beloved girls."[120]

French translations in the years immediately following introduced Sappho to a wider public. In 1555 the poet Louise Labé hailed her as a precursor but discreetly ignored her "sapphism." So did Madeleine de Scudéry in her immensely popular pseudo-historical novel *Le Grand Cyrus* (1649–1653). Scudéry presents Sappho as passionately devoted to her circle of female friends, but her only lover is Phaon.[121] The Hellenist Tanneguy La Fèvre was more candid in his *Brief Lives of the Greek Poets* (1664). Le Fèvre informs us that Sappho "was of a very amorous disposition, and that, not being satisfied with that which other women find in the company of men . . . she wanted to have mistresses."[122] This willingness to admit Sappho's love for women without moral censure is all but unique, however. The most influential treatment of Sappho's love life was published in 1681 by Le Fèvre's daughter, Anne Le Fèvre Dacier, a renowned and erudite classical scholar in her own right. But Madame Dacier blanks out all hints of lesbianism, dismissing, without saying what they were, the "calumnies" with which envious rivals "attempted to blacken her."[123]

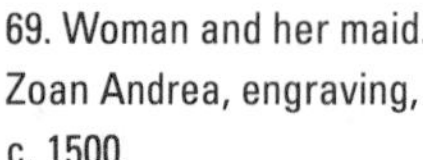

69. Woman and her maid. Zoan Andrea, engraving, c. 1500.

Pierre Bayle remarked in his *Dictionnaire* that Dacier had "tried to render the fact uncertain," but he has no doubt that Sappho's poems to women imply "concupiscent love."[124] But despite this demurrer, it was Dacier's image of Sappho—Sappho the lover of Phaon—that was to dominate, until the nineteenth century, the immense fictional and dramatic literature she inspired in France. In the Enlightenment Sappho is not the singer of the love of women but—with Racine's Phèdre, whose most famous speech echoes Sappho's "Ode"—the archetype of the woman despairingly in love with an indifferent male.

Given this censure and evasion, it is a surprise to come upon the detailed and nonjudgmental treatment of lesbianism in Brantôme's *The Lives of Gallant Ladies.* Despite his nominal ecclesiastical status, Pierre de Bourdeille, abbé and seigneur de Brantôme, was a soldier-courtier, very much a man of the world, and in his *Lives* an indefatigable recorder of feminine amours. A friend of Marguerite of Navarre, he had accompanied Mary Queen of Scots on her return to Scotland and visited England, Italy, Spain, Portugal, and Morocco. After suffering a riding accident in 1583, he devoted his retirement to writing his candid and scandalous comments on French manners and morals. His most ambitious book, which he entitled simply *Dames,* did not appear until 1666, half a century after his death.

The book's opening chapter sets the tone: "On Ladies Who Make Love and Their Cuckold Husbands." We would hardly expect male homosexuality to figure here, but Brantôme is as meticulously exhaustive as any academic sexologist. Some men in Italy, he claimed, deliberately make themselves cuckolds in order to seduce their wives' lovers—a depravity he deplores. In fact he treats all male amours with scorn: "There never was either a b—— *[bougre]* or a sodomist *[bardache],*" he tells us, "who was upstanding, valiant and great-hearted except the great Julius Caesar so that by the great dispensation of the Almighty such loathsome persons *[abominables]* are all marked and most disapproved of." If such men flourish, he warns ominously, "God awaits them and in the end we shall see them get their due."[125]

There is a striking discrepancy between Brantôme's attitudes toward male homosexuality and lesbianism. Though his approach is casually informal, his sources are comprehensive and include Sappho, Martial, Juvenal, and Lucian, the reports of contemporaries in France and abroad, and his own personal observations. He starts with the Greeks:

> It is said that Sappho of Lesbos was a very fine mistress of this trade, indeed, what is more, that she invented it, and since her the ladies of Lesbos have imitated her in it and continued in it to this day . . . And women of the sort who like this practice will not let other men touch them, but yield themselves to other women, just as if they were men, and these are called *tribades,* a word derived, so I have been told by Greeks, from *tribo, tribein,* which means to rub or fret or mutually fret and those who play at this game of *donna con donna,* as seen today, are called in French *fricatrices.*[126]

Sometimes, he thinks, lesbianism is the result of sexual deprivation, as in Turkey and Greece, where women are kept in seclusion. But women in Italy and Spain had told him of courtesans who have love affairs with other women. He admits too that "in our own France such women are quite common," though he thinks such practices have only recently been introduced from Italy.[127] Some of these women, he tells us, have quickly abandoned lesbianism when they found male lovers. Others, who have denied serious lesbian interests, he believes to be in fact secretly bisexual.

70. Women bathing. Jean Mignon (after Luca Penna), engraving, c. 1540.

In his French text Brantôme calls these women *ces lesbiennes,* inaugurating a new usage.[128] But his personal judgment is lenient, even admiring. "Unmarried girls and widows," he thinks, who do not wish to risk pregnancy or abortion, "may be excused for liking such frivolous, vain pleasures, and preferring to give themselves to each other and so get rid of their heat." In so doing they offend God less and are "not such whores that way as if with men, just as there is a great difference between actually pouring water into a pot and merely moistening it round and about."[129] This insouciant stance would hardly have recommended itself to contemporary theologians or jurists, who routinely favored burning.

In Brantôme's view, husbands whose wives have affairs with other women do not share the disgrace of cuckolds, and he claims to know men who are relieved that their wives have chosen female rather than male lovers.[130] Brantôme even affects to admire lesbians above other women. Women who favor women, he contends are "more courageous and plucky than [others], as indeed I have known some to be both in body and spirit."[131]

• Queen Christina •

Brantôme boasted that some of the unnamed women who appeared in his anecdotes were of princely rank. But since women were less likely to occupy thrones in early modern Europe than men, there were few whose sexuality came under the kind of scrutiny visited on Henry III and Louis XIII. One seventeeth-century queen did, however, become the object of international comment—namely, Queen Christina in Sweden.

Her father, Gustavus Adolphus, had been Protestant Europe's leading general in the Thirty Years' War and her mother a conventional German princess. But from an early age Christina shone as a cosmopolitan whose affinities were with classical antiquity and the *Grand Siècle,* not with the Bible and Swedish Lutheranism. French was the language she preferred to speak and in which she wrote her letters, essays, and memoirs. Her admiring father, anticipating he would have no son, gave her the education of a prince. She was trained, like a boy, to ride and hunt and shoot. "In this," Christina wrote in her autobiography, "my inclinations were wonderfully in agreement with his intentions. I had an aversion and an invincible antipathy to all that women are and say."[132] This female male chauvinist became an expert horseman, swordsman, and hunter. In 1632, when Gustavus Adolphus died fighting in the battle of Lützen, Christina inherited the throne at the age of six. At eighteen she was proclaimed "king" and began to wear various items of male attire—boots, hats, and doublets: here was a Henry III in reverse. Ten years later she had left Sweden to live the rest of her life in France and Italy.

Few rulers have been better trained or embraced their studies with such enthusiasm. In her youth she read and worked twelve hours a day and claimed to have made do with three or four hours' sleep. Besides French and Swedish, she spoke German, Italian, Flemish, Spanish, and Latin, the language of diplomacy. She took up Greek with avidity and learned some Hebrew and Arabic. It was said she had a better understanding of Plato and Tacitus than many specialists. She was also an ardent patron of science, philosophy, art, music, and the theater. Seeking mentors of her own intellectual rank, she induced several of Europe's leading savants to suffer Stockholm's dark and icy winters, including Grotius, Salmasius, Comenius, and Descartes, who did not survive a bout of pneumonia. Among her other correspondents were Bayle, Gassendi, the Great Condé, and Anne Le Fèvre Dacier. She knew too much to rule Sweden.

Nevertheless, Sweden's greatest statesman, Count Axel Oxenstierna, tutored her for many years on the labyrinthine politics of a Europe bitterly divided by dynastic ambitions and religious hatreds. She listened with admiration to his wisdom, absorbed his lessons, and set out to oppose his war policy when she came of age. In 1647, appalled at the bickering that was delaying

71. Queen Christina. Sébastien Bourdon, oil, c. 1653.

peace after three years of stalled negotiations with Spain and the emperor at Osnabrück, the twenty-one-year-old queen sent a royal command to the Swedish delegates that effectively ended the Thirty Years' War, perhaps the bloodiest and most destructive struggle Europe had ever seen. For this she "earned the gratitude of the voiceless suffering millions in Europe and in her own country."[133]

Was Christina beautiful? She did not resemble Greta Garbo, who played her in a famous film. Her mother, she wrote, "could not bear me, because I was a daughter and ugly."[134] She had fine large eyes, un-Swedishly black, a hawklike nose, and a large mouth, and she was usually untidy and disheveled, pointedly neglecting her clothes. She disliked mirrors, since "they had nothing agreeable to show her."[135] Diplomats diplomatically skirted the question of her appearance; you forgot it, they agreed, when you heard her rich voice and became aware of the scope of her knowledge and her commanding intelligence. One discriminating Frenchwoman thought that, with her slight build, she looked "like a pretty boy."[136] Her wit could be deadly. Told that

Charles I had lost his head, she wondered whether it would be missed, since he had used it so rarely. She was not a conventional monarch. But Milton praised her, and Andrew Marvell thought her fit to rule a universe.

Foreign chancelleries buzzed with speculations about the queen's ambiguous style. Montecuccoli, the sophisticated imperial ambassador, thought her entirely unlike a woman, and a priest at the Spanish embassy agreed: "There is nothing feminine about her except her sex; her voice, her manner of speaking, her walk, her style, her ways are all quite masculine . . . Though she rides on a side-saddle she holds herself so well and is so light in her movements that unless one were quite close to her, one would take her for a man."[137] John Thurloe, Cromwell's secretary of state, reported: "We hear stories of the Queen of Sweden and her Amazonian behavior, it being believed that nature was mistaken in her, and that she was intended for a man, for in her discourse, they say she talks loud and sweareth notably."[138]

She was quite as heterodox in religion. From childhood she had, she confessed, "a deadly hatred for the long and frequent sermons of the Lutherans" and suspected that hell-fire was an invention to deceive and control people.[139] Her reading of the classics and contemporary scientific philosophy had confirmed her native skepticism. In 1652 she wrote to the Landgrave Frederick of Hesse, "I shall not go into the disputes now raging between the Lutheran and the Catholic ministers of the gospel. I myself believe in a third religion, which having found the truth has cast aside the beliefs of these established churches," that is, she was a free-thinker.[140]

Christina was carried a step further by her association with her French physician Pierre Bourdelot, who shocked the Swedes by his avowed disbelief. Bourdelot had been a member of the prince de Condé's libertine circle at Chantilly. But when Condé himself finally met the ex-queen in Antwerp in 1655, he was alarmed by what he regarded as her dangerous candor. He described her as one who "recognized neither God nor religion, who had only libertine discourses in her mouth, and who moreover even justified the vices of all the nations and sexes [presumably pederasty and lesbianism] . . . The bad reputation which she gained (although as you know I am not scrupulous) grieved me because I had her interests very much at heart and I liked her personally."[141]

Was Christina a lesbian? The record is complex, but the consensus of modern biographers favors that view. In 1651, when she was not quite twenty-five, she startled Europe by announcing that she planned to abdicate. She had earlier, in preparation for this, persuaded the Swedish Riksdag to recognize her cousin, Charles Gustavus, as heir to the throne. Three years later in a moving ceremony which made hardened statesmen and sturdy peasants weep, she gave up the throne. A few months after her uncrowning—she had lifted the crown from her own head when no one present was willing to perform the act—the former queen, now safely out of

Sweden, caused a second sensation: the daughter of the man who had been Protestantism's foremost champion converted to Catholicism and went to live in Rome.

Why did she take these two steps, which puzzled everyone? Despite opposition from a fractious nobility, she was a superbly trained, conscientious, remarkably hard-working, and relatively successful ruler. Certainly it would have been impossible to convert to Catholicism and still rule Sweden—Catholicism was forbidden by law. Later, Christina promoted the idea that she had given up her throne for her new faith. But the fact is that she first contemplated abdicating very early—in 1646, just before she turned twenty.[142] Indeed, she seems not to have become seriously interested in Catholicism until six years later, when she opened secret communications with the Jesuits. Her decision to abdicate seems to be more closely connected with another development that was noticed in 1646—her pronounced aversion to the idea of marriage.[143]

At sixteen she was in love, or thought herself in love, with her cousin Charles Adolphus and considered marrying him.[144] She was also attracted to various handsome, dashing young courtiers, and there were rumors of affairs, even with the Spanish ambassador. She bestowed such large estates and fortunes on her favorites that it caused much criticism. But it is unlikely these were passionate involvements. Christina protested that "she felt such a repulsion toward the marital state that she would rather choose death than a man" and was apparently repelled by the idea of intercourse. She told the French ambassador that "she would never submit to be treated the way a peasant treats his field when planting seeds."[145] Eventually she had a painful interview with her cousin in which she told him she no longer felt bound by her youthful declarations.

It would appear that a crisis had occurred shortly before the queen's twentieth birthday. The most likely explanation lies in the attachment she formed with a young woman named Ebba Sparre early in 1645. Later in life Christina wrote over a thousand maxims that were not published until after her death. Pierre Bayle thought them "as fine as La Rochefoucauld's."[146] Among them we find: "Love is the essentially Protean element of Nature, an element which conceals itself behind many guises."[147] Ebba, a lady-in-waiting and the daughter of one of Christina's councilors, was strikingly beautiful, of a gentle, affectionate disposition, with considerable intelligence and charm. With her Christina laid aside the scorn she ordinarily displayed for her own sex. She called her "la belle Comtesse," or simply Belle, and introduced her to the English ambassador (a representative of the Puritan Commonwealth) as her "bedfellow" whose mind was "as beautiful as her outside."[148]

The Englishman was not shocked—royalty in this age often had same-sex bedmates. Gustavus Adolphus had them, and so later did Peter the Great. But Peder Juel, the sober Danish envoy to the Swedish court, wrote home that she had "hidden the beautiful Ebba Sparre in her bed and associated with her in a special way."[149] A German observer writing about the queen's sexual inclinations in 1685 thought "the Swedes were far too primitive and stupid to understand her."[150] However, at least one Swedish nobleman did leave on record his concern. In 1653 Ebba was married to Jacob De la Gardie, though she continued to associate as closely with the queen as before. Jacob's brother Magnus, who earlier had been himself highly favored by Christina, wrote that he was surprised his brother allowed this, considering the "gossip to which it gives rise among so many people."[151]

When Christina left Sweden after her abdication in 1654, she cut her hair short and donned men's clothes as soon as she crossed into Denmark, freely expressing her joy in her new liberty. Her keenest regret at leaving the country seems to have been parting from the woman she had shared her life with for so many years. From Brussels, she wrote: "My happiness would be second to none if I was allowed to share it with you and if you could witness it. I swear to you that I would merit the envy of the gods if I could enjoy the pleasure of seeing you . . . I will carry with me even after death the noble passion and tenderness that I have always shown to you."[152] After her splendidly triumphant reception in Rome as Catholicism's most distinguished convert, she still felt a gnawing loneliness. A letter written in 1656, addressed "à la Belle," reads: "How happy I would be if it was permitted for me to see you, Belle, but I am condemned to the fate of loving you always, esteeming you always, but seeing you never."[153] A year later she wrote from Italy:

> Now that, in the most civilized part of the world I have seen the most beautiful and the most charming members of our sex, I can claim with even greater assurance that I have seen no woman who can compete with you, for you are charming above them all . . . But even if I must face the fact that I may never see you again, I am equally sure that I will always love you, and you are cruel if you doubt this fact. You should not doubt a friendship which has persisted through an absence of three years; and if you remember the power you have over me, you will also remember that I have been in the possession of your love for twelve years; I belong to you so utterly, that it will never be possible for you to lose me: and only when I die, shall I cease loving you.[154]

Christina hoped to see Ebba again when she visited Hamburg in 1661; the reunion did not come about, and Ebba died the next year.

Christina's life was not a tragedy like Henry III's. After her abdication it could only be a long anticlimax. But she enjoyed her role at the center of the cultural life of Rome, where she founded and presided over learned academies, produced operas and plays, and expanded her distinguished art collection of masterpieces by Rubens, Titian, Veronese, Correggio, and Tintoretto. At the same time she startled the Romans by removing the fig leaves from the statues in the Farnese Palace and giving free rein to her Rabelaisian wit. Anxious popes wondered what the Queen of Sweden might do or say next to startle the pious. Many, aware of her irreverent skepticism, regarded her conversion as insincere; the debate continues to this day. Perhaps she thought it a small price to pay for admission into this sophisticated cultivated society, so rich in music and beauty, where appearances were everything and a philosophical libertinism could comfortably exist with an outward conformity.

Eventually she found her way into the letters of Madame, who recorded that she "was given to all kinds of debauchery, even with women. If she had not been so intelligent no one would have put up with her." Madame rashly concluded that "she owed her vices to the French, and above all to old Bourdelot, who had been Condé's physician."[155] After Christina's death in 1687 Madame's son, the regent, bought her art collection. Its fine female nudes, some of which had been looted by Gustavus Adolphus' troops from the imperial galleries in Prague when the Swedes captured that city in the Thirty Years' War, came at last to decorate the walls of the Louvre. Christina herself was rewarded with a tomb in Saint Peter's.

CHAPTER TWELVE

ENGLAND FROM THE REFORMATION TO WILLIAM III

1533–1702

• Silence and Denial •

To leave Latin Europe and cross the channel to England at the start of the Reformation is to enter a different world. Whatever their private behavior, men and women in Tudor and early Stuart Britain were not inclined to any revealing discussion of homosexuality. Not for them the too-knowledgeable sermons of a Bernardino or the candor of a Montaigne, a Brantôme, or a Duchesse d'Orléans. If Europeans quipped about sodomy in Italy, Spain, and France, Englishmen were sure their land was free from such pestilence. As good Protestants, they might have excepted, on reflection, some "papistical monks" who had vanished with the dissolution of the monasteries.

Whether "unnatural" sin should be publicly noticed had long troubled writers on morality. Some French Protestants thought the Catholic confessional with its probing questions about sex too likely to suggest enticing novelties to the ignorant, and they even expressed doubts, on the same grounds, about public executions for sodomy.[1] In England the tradition strongly favored silence. A Shropshire cleric named John Mirk, writing his *Instructions for Parish Priests* in doggerel verse in 1400, forbade any mention of this sin from the pulpit: "Thow schalt thy paresch no thynge teche: / Ny of that synnë no thynge preche."[2] Chaucer, in *The Canterbury Tales,* makes his parson call sodomy an "abhominable synne, of which that no man unnethe [scarcely] oghte speke ne write."[3]

Like other nations, the English maintained that homosexuality was a foreign importation. A parliament in Chaucer's day (1376) blamed Lombard merchants for having "lately introduced into the land a very horrible vice which is not to be named," implying that it would otherwise have been unknown.[4] Sir Edward Coke repeated this theory in all seriousness in his *Institutes* of 1628. This need to expatriate the origins of homosexuality led Jeremy

Bentham, a century and a half later, to remark dryly that "reasoners like Dr. Coke would fetch over instruction in this mystery upon rafts from Florida or Mexico if they did not hear by good luck of its being practiced a little nearer."[5] In our own times, visitors to Communist Russia and Communist China were routinely told that homosexuality existed only in decadent capitalist states. What Marxist orthodoxy supposedly ensured in socialist societies, Britain's superior Protestant morality was held to guarantee in Elizabethan and Jacobean England.

When John Harris preached on "The Destruction of Sodom" in 1628 before the House of Commons, he deplored British sinfulness generally but made only the briefest mention of sodomy—"a sin none but a devil, come out of Hell in the likeness of a man, dares to commit." Harris solemnly assured his hearers that the "*Peccatum nefandum,* that sin not fit to be named, the high hand of God hath kept out of our country."[6] Members familiar with the court of James I (just three years dead) must have struggled to suppress a smile at this naiveté. But however naive Harris's remark was, we must recognize a genuine national myth, one which would for two more centuries perceive homosexuality as ineffably alien, bizarre, diabolical, and, above all, un-British.

• Monasteries and the Law •

This willed blindness, however unrealistic, had one fortunate result. England was spared the burnings and hangings then common in Italy, Spain, Portugal, and France. No records of sodomy trials have been found in the fourteenth or fifteenth centuries. Indeed, England had no formal legislation until 1533. In that year the parliament of Henry VIII made "buggery" a felony punishable by hanging "without benefit of clergy." This last clause meant that a man in holy orders—or anyone who could translate a few verses from the Latin psalter—might escape execution for murder but not for sodomy.

It has usually been assumed that sodomy, like incest and adultery, had been left to the ecclesiastical courts, which, as guardians of sexual morality, could have claimed jurisdiction. But an assiduous researcher has found only one sodomy case among 21,000 trials in the London church records from 1470 to 1516, on which occasion the accused was simply excommunicated when he failed to appear.[7] Apparently neither secular nor religious courts had acted, for parliament took note of a gap in the law in the preamble to its new statute. "There is not yet," it noted, "sufficient and condign punishment appointed and limited by the due course of the laws of this Realm, for the detestable and abominable Vice of Buggery committed with mankind or beast."[8] The law was subsequently interpreted as criminalizing anal intercourse with men or women but not acts between women. In this last respect it differed significantly from continental codes.

But why did parliament act in 1533? One impetus was Henry VIII's struggle with the papacy. Frustrated by the pope's refusal to grant him a divorce from Queen Katherine, Henry sought to exploit the anti-clerical spirit of the time, which had been fanned by Luther and the newly emerging Protestant sects. Parliament began, in 1532, to limit the jurisdiction of ecclesiastical courts. The new law making buggery a statutory offense would seem to fit into this campaign. In 1533 Henry married Anne Boleyn, and the next year parliament passed the Act of Supremacy which made the king the new head of the English church. When some priests refused to accept the new order, Henry had them hanged and disemboweled as a warning.

Henry was now all-powerful in church affairs. But he was also bankrupt, and the great wealth of the monasteries proved a temptation. Since the monastic orders still had considerable popular support, Thomas Cromwell, Henry's agent in these efforts, sought a way to discredit them. If charges of sexual immorality—and especially of sodomy—could be brought, their wealth could be pillaged more easily. In 1543 Henry revealed his thoughts on this matter in a letter to the earl of Arran, then regent in Scotland, whom he advised to send a commissioner to the Scottish abbeys with secret orders to "examine all the religious of their conversation and behavior in their livings, whereby if it be well handled, he shall get knowledge of all their abominations," after which he and his nobles might safely seize their lands "to their great profit and honor."[9] (In this age "conversation" meant not speech but acts, especially sexual intimacies.)

Henry's advice was based upon what had happened in England. In 1535 Cromwell sent agents to make formal "visitations" of England's monasteries to determine their assets, uncover superstitions, and report on sexual misconduct. The monks were subjected to much rough bullying by the rapacious visitors in order to elicit confessions. As a result, the documents they produced, called the *Comperta* (or "Disclosures"), caused a sensation. The Protestant bishop Hugh Latimer tells us that "when their enormities were first read in the Parliament House, they were so great and abominable that there was nothing but: "*Down with them!*"[10] We may guess what provoked the uproar when we read a typical entry in the *Compendium Compertorum:* "*Rufford.*—6 sod[omites]. Incontinence, Thos. Doncaster, abbot, with 2 married women, and 4 others; 6 seek release [from vows]. Superstition: Virgin's milk . . . Rents 100£; debt, 20£."[11] In 175 entries we find over 180 monks designated as "sodomites." Given the English horror of sodomy, this would have seemed a truly damning record.

Nevertheless, the designations are ambiguous. "Sodomy" in the Renaissance most often meant homosexuality, but it could also refer to heterosexual anal intercourse, to bestiality, and, more rarely, to masturbation, the three other sins Aquinas had designated as "sins against nature." But it is likely masturbation was the sin most often confessed. The second entry in the

Comperta, for the monastery of Repton, has this note: "Thomas Rede, subprior, and three others, named as sodomites *per voluntarias pollutiones,"* indicating that voluntary pollution, or masturbation, was at issue. Another entry reads "Sod., 4 *per voluntariam pollucionem* and 4 with boys."[12] This suggests that the unqualified notation, "sod."—the form that occurs most often—might mean either masturbation or same-sex relations.

In only a dozen cases is the reference to homosexuality unequivocal. But a hasty or a tendentious reading of the *Comperta* might easily leave the impression that a very large number of monks had confessed to same-sex relations. We may wonder whether the confusion was accidental or calculated. In either case, the report dealt religious houses in England a deadly blow. Within a few years the monasteries were dissolved and their wealth transferred to Henry and those nobles and lawyers who had supported his policies.

We have no record of the act of 1533 being used against individual monks, though its existence must have strengthened the king's hand. Nevertheless, the plundering of these ancient institutions was often unpopular, since they had traditionally provided charity, education, and hospitality. In northern England a violent rebellion challenged Henry's action. It was in connection with this revolt that we find what seems to be the only formal charge of sodomy on record in Henry's reign. Lord Hungerford, who had been a close companion of Henry in his youth and an associate of Cromwell's, was convicted of treason and of sodomy with his male servants. In addition, he was accused of employing a priest who had criticized the "plucking down of abbeys."[13] This was the crux of the matter; the sodomy charge appears to have been brought to bolster a case that was primarily political. Hungerford was beheaded on Tower Hill on July 28, 1534, the same day as his former patron, Thomas Cromwell, who had also lost the favor of the brutal and tyrannical king.

Before his fall, Thomas Cromwell had sponsored a learned and energetic reformer who wrote anti-Catholic plays. John Bale (1495–1563) had been a Carmelite friar for twenty-four years before he converted to Protestantism, married, and devoted the rest of his life to attacking the Catholic Church. In an age notable for theological rancor, his "coarse and bitter" attacks were unequaled in their acerbity.[14] Bale's Protestant morality plays were outspoken vehicles for his campaign against the papacy. His "comedy," *The Three Laws of Nature, Moses, and Christ, Corrupted by the Sodomites, the Pharisees, and Papists* (c. 1536), was a shot fired in this war. Among its characters was "Sodomismus," who appeared on stage robed "like a monk of all sects." Sodomismus is not, however, a theatrical representation of a Tudor homosexual but a figure out of medieval allegory, representing sexual "sins against nature" in the broader sense, an eternal figure like the Wandering Jew, associated with the Flood (which he caused), with Onan (who signified masturbation), with the citizens of "Sodom and Gomor," with famous Greeks and

Romans, and finally, in the contemporary world, with monks and Catholic prelates, including "Pope July"—"which sought to have, in his fury, / Two lads, and to use them beastly, / From the cardinal of Nantes."[15] Here, Pope July is not Julius III, whose partiality for boys made him a target for Protestant invective later in the century, but his more famous patron Julius II, who had died in 1513.

The issue of clerical celibacy had created much theological rancor. Since monks like Luther broke their vows by marrying, Protestant ardor could be discounted as carnal lust. Married reformers like Bale counter-attacked aggressively, painting the Roman clergy as men who forewent "honest marriage" for sodomitical pleasures. In 1546 Bale published *The Actes of the Englysh Votaryes* (monks) in which he attacked the entire priesthood as "none other than sodomites and whoremongers all the pack."[16] One understands, on reading these intemperate pages, how the bishop came by his nickname "bilious Bale." Bale probably did more than any other English writer to link homosexuality with Catholicism.

The effects of Bale's labors can be seen in Robert Burton, a reclusive Oxford clergyman-scholar whose *Anatomy of Melancholy* (1621) describes and analyzes what we now call mental depression. But Burton digresses upon a thousand topics, and his chapter on "love melancholy" yields a catalog of sexual deviations, including (in Latin) the fullest discussion of homosexuality published by an English writer prior to the nineteenth century, though this amounts to a mere page and a half. After identifying Greek and Roman rulers and writers and modern Turks and Italians as especially given to the vice, he turns to England: "And terrible to say, in our own country, within memory, how much that detestable sin hath raged. For, indeed, in the year 1538 [sic], the most prudent King Henry the Eighth . . . inspected the cloisters of . . . priests and votaries, and found among them so great a number of wenchers, gelded youths, debauchees, catamites, boy-things, pederasts, sodomites (as it saith in Bale), Ganymedes, &c., that in everyone of them you may be certain of a new Gomorrah."[17]

When Henry VIII's daughter Mary succeeded to the throne in 1553, Catholicism was restored and parliament repealed Henry's sodomy law along with most of the legislation passed by Protestant parliaments. This change was cited to suggest that Catholic policy was tolerant of sodomites, an absurd accusation if we compare law enforcement in England with contemporary Catholic states.[18] It is ironic that the law annulled by Mary's parliament was revived under Elizabeth because of charges against a clergyman who was, in fact, a Spanish Protestant. In 1563 Casiodoro del Reina, a distinguished scholar who served a refugee church in London, was accused of sodomy with Jean de Bayonne, a seventeen-year-old in his congregation. Assuming that sodomy was a capital crime in England as in France and Spain, Reina and the boy fled to the continent.[19] The scandal seems to have reminded the authorities of the deficiency in English law, for on January 12 of the next year they reinstated the statue of Henry VIII, alleging that its repeal had emboldened "divers evil disposed persons . . . to commit the said most horrible and detestable Vice of Buggery," though Reina's guilt was by no means clear.[20]

The Elizabethan statute had a long life. Its language remained unchanged until life imprisonment was substituted for the death penalty in 1861. In that form it survived until 1967, when homosexuality was decriminalized on the recommendation of the Wolfenden Committee. In Elizabeth's reign, however, the statute seems scarcely to have been enforced at all, if we may trust the fragmentary legal evidence. Men could be tried for sodomy at county assizes or, after 1563, by justices of the peace at Quarter Sessions, but the only county with complete records—Essex—had no cases at the Quarter Sessions in the period from 1556 to 1680, and just one at the Assizes, in 1669.[21] Though convictions appear sporadically in several counties after 1600, only one has been so far been traced in the age of Elizabeth.[22]

Nevertheless, scores of men would be hanged under this law, chiefly in the eighteenth and nineteenth centuries, and many hundreds more imprisoned. Moreover, its worldwide influence would be enormous, for it set the pattern for England's vast empire, including Canada, Australia, New Zealand, and the American colonies. These have now abandoned such statutes, but discriminatory laws deriving from the English buggery statute still survive in India, Malaysia, Nigeria, Kenya, Tanzania, and Uganda, and in dozens of island dependencies from Papua New Guinea to the Caribbean. They have darkened the lives of millions.

✦ Elizabethan Literature ✦

After Henry VIII's semi-Reformation, the Protestant interlude of Edward VI, and the Catholic reaction of "Bloody" Mary, the English Renaissance came to fruition in the first great flowering of English literature under Elizabeth. Like its counterpart in Italy, the "new learning" drew its inspiration from the rediscovery of Greece, whose myths and literature provided new perspectives on human behavior. Among the discoveries was the fact of Greek homosexuality, now known at first-hand rather than through the filters of Ovid and Virgil. In Elizabethan London, as in fifteenth-century Florence, a new enthusiasm for Greek art promoted a distinctive cult of beauty that did not exclude the beauty of young males, while the knowledge of classical ideals of male love derived from Plato and Plutarch created new tensions and ambiguities.

Secondary education in Tudor England, for the privileged minority who had access to it, meant primarily the study of Latin. In 1531 Sir Thomas Elyot's influential *Book Named the Governor* (that is, the Tutor) warmly recommended the study of such poets as Ovid, Catullus, and Martial despite their "lascivious" nature.[23] Elizabethan schoolboys from seven to seventeen were set to read and imitate these authors as daily chores. Shakespeare's "small Latine" would not have been small by modern standards and would have encompassed erotic verse by poets like Horace and Virgil, who wooed both genders. To have mastered classical Latin was to have received a reasonably candid sexual education from poets who were unabashedly libertine and bisexual. It is a fact that an English schoolboy in Shakespeare's day would have learned far more about homosexuality from his classroom reading than a student in the age of Kinsey.

Literary critics and moralists felt obliged to protest. Sir Philip Sidney in his famous *Defense of Poetry* deplored the "abominable filthiness" he found "authorized" in the *Phaedrus* and *Symposium,* where, he complained, Plato "feigns many honest burgesses of Athens to speak of such matters that, if they had been set on the rack, they would never have confessed them"—presumably he meant in contemporary England.[24] Frances Meres, whose *Palladis Tamia (Treasury of Wisdom)* was the first English book to list Shakespeare's plays, moralized in medieval fashion by comparing homosexuality with interest on money: "As pederasty is unlawful because it is against kind; so usury and increase by gold and silver is unlawful, because against nature; nature hath made them [both] sterile and barren."[25] In his *Anatomy* Burton regretted that Plato had "delighted in Agathon, Xenophon in Clinias, Virgil in Alexis, Anacreon in Bathyllus."[26]

Elizabethan poets, beauty-drunk, were wont to toy with what Gregory Bredbeck has called a decorative or "ornamental homoeroticism."[27] Even the most admired poem of the age, Edmund Spenser's *Faerie Queene,* is full of details whose ambiguous erotic implications have puzzled readers. In his "masque of Cupid" Spenser compares an allegorical figure to two famous *eromenoi:*

> The first was Fancy, like a lovely boy,
> Of rare aspect, and beauty without peer,
> Matchable either to that imp [child] of Troy,
> Whom Jove did love and choose his cup to bear,
> Or that same dainty lad which was so dear
> To great Alcides [Hercules], that when as he died,
> He wailèd womanlike with many a tear.[28]

Sylvanus' Cyparissus (1.6.17) and Apollo's Hyacinth (3.11.37) make their appearance, and Cupid sports "wantonly" with Adonis in the latter's mystical garden (3.6.49). But Spenser's devotion to chastity is quite as strong as his passion for beauty, and we are apparently not to read these passages as condoning Greek love.

Nevertheless, the 1590s seem to have inaugurated a unique brief flowering of genuinely homoerotic English poetry. To this decade belong Marlowe's *Hero and Leander* and *Edward II* and Shakespeare's sonnets. It also saw the publication of the pastorals and sonnets of Richard Barnfield, in which the shepherd Daphnis pours out his feelings of love for a beautiful boy with an impassioned directness that has tempted readers to identify the poet with the lovelorn swain.

Richard Barnfield was born in Staffordshire in 1574 and attained a modest reputation on the basis of two slim volumes containing his "Ganymede" poems. At the age of twenty he published *The Affectionate Shepherd, Containing the Complaint of Daphnis for the Love of Ganymede,* which opened with these startling lines:

> Scarce had the morning star hid from the light
> Heaven's crimson canopy with stars bespangled,
> But I began to rue th' unhappy sight
> Of that fair boy that had my heart intangled;
> Cursing the time, the place, the sense, the sin;
> I came, I saw, I viewed, I slippèd in . . .
> If it be sin to love a lovely lad,
> Oh then sin I, for whom my soul is sad.[29]

When the poem was attacked for depicting this courtship, Barnfield replied that he aimed at "nothing else but an imitation of Virgil in the second Eglogue of Alexis," a defense that surely begged the question.[30] Thomas Warton, in the eighteenth century, thought that "a writer of the present age who was to print love-verses in this style would be severely reproached and universally proscribed," and in 1816 another British littérateur lamented that their "sexual perversion" matched Shakespeare's sonnets.[31] Barnfield, for his part, retired from London to his native county, married, and produced no more poetry to delight—or trouble—critics.

• Christopher Marlowe •

Christopher Marlowe, England's first great poet-dramatist, was also a controversial figure. Like Sodoma in Italy, Marlowe was unique in the England Renaissance in tacitly avowing his interest in his own sex. The parallel with Théophile de Viau in France a generation later is even more telling: both were double heretics—in sex and religion. Though he entered Cambridge in 1580 with a scholarship for students contemplating holy orders, Marlowe won notoriety as a militant atheist. For this, his one-time friend and fellow-dramatist Thomas Kyd denounced him to Elizabeth's Privy Council. Marlowe, Kyd wrote, had been used "to jest at the divine scriptures, gibe at prayers, and strive in argument to frustrate and confute what hath been spoke or writ by prophets and by such holy men."[32] Another informer, Richard Baines, sent the council a fuller account of Marlowe's heresies. He had called Moses a "juggler" (deceiver) and claimed that "the first beginning of Religion was only to keep men in awe." Baines also reported on Marlowe's sexual heterodoxies: the poet had avowed that "all they that love not tobacco and boys were fools" and that "St. John the Evangelist was bedfellow to Christ and leaned always in his bosom [and] that he used him as the sinners of Sodoma."[33] With "trembling," Thomas Kyd verified this last point: "He would report St. John to be our saviour Christ's Alexis . . . that is, that Christ did love him with an extraordinary love."[34] Perhaps Marlowe's radical repudiation of Christianity owed something to his homosexuality. How could he compound with a religion which so thoroughly condemned and scorned men of his sort?

Marlowe's career as a poet and playwright was precocious, brilliant, and tragically brief. The premier of his spectacularly successful *Tamberlaine* may have taken place while he was still in Cambridge. Soon he was hailed as the "Muses' darling" and praised for his "mighty line." A rival rhymester, Michael Drayton, found in his imaginative verse "those brave translunary things, / That the first poets had." But though Marlowe set a new standard for dramatic poetry and pointed the way for Shakespeare (who was his exact contemporary), his protagonists were, from a contemporary English point of view, disturbingly alien: a barbaric Scythian conqueror *(Tamberlaine),* a proto-Shylock *(The Jew of Malta),* an effeminate French king (Henry III in *The Massacre at Paris*), a magician allied with a devil *(Doctor Faustus),* and a homosexual English monarch *(Edward II).*

Marlowe's life, like his dramas, was turbulent and violent and skirted an Elizabethan underworld of government spies and confidence men. In 1589, two years out of Cambridge, he was attacked in the streets by a man whom a friend killed on the spot. Thomas Kyd described him as "intemperate and of a cruel heart," but Marlowe had friends who disagreed. The satirist John Marston suspended his usually jaundiced view of mankind to call him "kind Kit Marlowe," and the publisher Edward Blount spoke of him as one "who has been dear to us" and noted the affection his patron, Thomas Walsingham, had borne for him. But some Cambridge students, writing about 1600, expressed the consensus, which combined admiration for Marlowe's genius with horror at his life and opinions: "Pity it is that wit so ill should dwell, / Wit lent from heaven, but vices sent from hell."[35]

When some atheist writings were found among Thomas Kyd's papers, Kyd claimed, after torture, that they were in fact Marlowe's. As a result, a warrant was issued for the poet's appearance before the Privy Council. This was no light matter. Another Cambridge graduate, Frances Kett, had been burned in 1589 for denying the divinity of Christ. Marlowe's own death, however, intervened before he could be questioned. On May 30, 1593, having spent the day drinking with three men in a tavern at Deptford near London, Marlowe, then twenty-nine years of age, had become embroiled in an argument over the reckoning. Seizing one man's dagger, he found it turned against him so that it pierced his skull. The man was Ingram Frizer, a part-time spy and petty swindler. Frances Meres, describing the episode five years later, thought there was a sexual side to the imbroglio: Marlowe, he wrote, "was stabbed to death by a bawdy serving man, a rival of his in his lewd love."[36] There is no hint of this in the detailed coroner's record, however; the quarrel appears to have involved only unpoetical shillings and pence.

Marlowe's poetry and plays reveal his fascination with male love. His early drama *Dido, Queen of Carthage* tells the familiar story from the *Aeneid* but opens with a very un-Virgilian scene in which Jupiter is discovered "dandling Ganymede upon his knee." When the boy complains of Juno's jealousy and begs for a present, the amorous god replies: "What is't, sweet wag, I should deny thy youth? / Whose face reflects such pleasure to mine eyes."[37] The interlude ends when Venus complains that Jupiter is neglecting her favorite, Aeneas, to play "with that female wanton boy."

Marlowe's most famous poem also reveals a homoerotic sensibility. *Hero and Leander* is an exuberant work whose élan and sly wit make it the most readable of Elizabethan poetic narratives. The tale describes the love of Hero, ambiguously described as "Venus' nun," and the young Leander, who swims the Hellespont to visit her. Its debt to Ovid is clear, but it also owes something to those late Greek prose romances that were eagerly read in translation by the Elizabethan public. The poem opens with an elaborate description of Hero's ornamented gown; the description of Leander, by contrast, ignores the vesture for the youth:

> His dangling tresses that were never shorn,
> Had they been cut, and unto Colchos borne,
> Would have allured the vent'rous youth of Greece,
> To hazard more than for the Golden Fleece . . .
> His body was as straight as Circe's wand;
> Jove might have sipp'd out nectar from his hand.
> Even as delicious meat is to the taste,
> So was his neck in touching, and surpass'd
> The white of Pelops' shoulder. I could tell ye
> How smooth his breast was, and how white his belly,
> And whose immortal fingers did imprint
> That heavenly path with many a curious dint
> That runs along his back . . .

If the Elizabethan cult of male beauty sanctioned this catalogue of Leander's physical charms, the Greek setting allowed Marlowe to emphasize the appeal they might have had for other males:

Had wild Hippolytus Leander seen,
Enamour'd of his beauty had he been;
His presence made the rudest peasant melt,
That in the vast uplandish country dwelt . . .
For in his looks were all that men desire.[38]

And, as the Greek novels had, on occasion, allowed for a same-sex subplot, so Marlowe incorporates a homoerotic episode in his poem. When Leander swims to visit Hero at Sestos, the sea god Neptune is entranced:

With that he stripp'd him to his ivory skin,
And crying, "Love, I come," leapt lively in.
Whereat the sapphire-visag'd god grew proud [sexually
excited]
And made his capering Triton sound aloud,
Imagining that Ganymede, displeas'd,
Had left the heavens . . .
The lusty god embrac'd him, call'd him love,
And swore he never should return to Jove.

Marlowe cleverly equates the swirling waves with the playful advances of the god:

He watch'd his arms, and as they open'd wide
At every stroke, betwixt them would he slide
And steal a kiss, and then run out and dance,
And as he swam cast many a lustful glance,
And threw him gaudy toys to please his eye,
And dive into the water, and there pry
Upon his breast, his thighs, and every limb,
And up again, and close beside him swim,
And talk of love. Leander made reply,
"You are deceiv'd, I am no woman, I."
Thereat smil'd Neptune.[39]

An English youth might have responded in this naive fashion—but a Greek? Leander escapes Neptune, and the adolescent lovers consummate their romance. Here Marlowe's contribution to the poem breaks off, death having intervened. George Chapman finished the tale to the final tragedy of Leander's drowning, but, not surprisingly, we find no more submarine erotics.

• The Tragedy of Edward II •

In 1592 or shortly after, Marlowe wrote his most poignant tragedy, *Edward II,* and another poet, Michael Drayton, made Edward's lover, Piers

Gaveston, his subject in a narrative poem. What provoked this interest in an unlucky fourteenth-century king whose doomed love was a story well dimmed by time? We may find a hint in the book that was Marlowe's and Drayton's chief source: Holinshed's *History of England, Scotland and Ireland.* As early as 1583, Elizabeth's agent Sir Francis Walsingham had warned the seventeen-year-old king of Scotland, James VI, about unscrupulous favorites, citing Edward II's ill fate.[40] Four years later the execution of his mother, Mary Queen of Scots, made James heir to the English throne. A revised edition of Holinshed (1587) lamented that James was swayed by favorites of "base lineage" who "keep his majesty thrall to . . . their abominable and execrable" deeds.[41] Marlowe, who was knowledgeable about foreign affairs, would have been keenly aware of James's reputed inclinations. In his report on the poet's heterodoxies, Thomas Kyd made the claim that Marlowe had planned to serve "the k[ing] of Scots."[42]

So James was likened by some prescient contemporaries to his Plantagenet ancestor, whose disastrous reign ended bloodily for him and his friends. In medieval chronicles Edward II appears as an inept ruler led astray by favorites unwisely endowed with wealth and power. The first was Piers Gaveston, son of a Gascon knight, whom Edward met in 1298 when he was fourteen and Piers a year or so older. Ironically, the prince's father, the redoubtable warrior-king Edward I, had chosen Piers as a model companion. It was a fateful moment: "Upon looking on him," wrote an early chronicler, "the son of the king immediately felt such love for him that he entered into a covenant of constancy, and bound himself with him before all other mortals with a bond of indissoluble love, firmly drawn up and fastened with a knot."[43] The intensity of this all-consuming passion alarmed observers. Fourteenth-century chroniclers are rarely given to psychological analysis. But the author of the Malmesbury *Life of Edward II* (c. 1326?) felt a need to explain the king's infatuation: "Indeed I do not remember to have heard that one man so loved another. Jonathan cherished David, Achilles loved Patroclus. But we do not read that they were immoderate. Our king, however, was incapable of moderate favor, and on account of Piers was said to forget himself, and so Piers was accounted a sorcerer."[44]

What kind of man was this monarch who affronted everyone by making a friend of modest rank a "second king"? Marlowe's *Edward II* paints him as an aesthete who relished elegant, erotically ambiguous courtly masques. "Music and poetry," we are told, are "his delight." But contemporary accounts describe him as "tall, muscular and good-looking" and only moderately intelligent.[45] The Malmesbury *Life* calls him "robustus" (literally, like an oak). Another contemporary, the Lanercost chronicler, complained "that [Edward] had devoted himself privately from his youth to the arts of rowing and driving chariots, digging pits and roofing houses; also that he wrought as a craftsman with his boon companions by night, and at other mechanical arts . . .

wherein it [did] not become a king's son to busy himself."[46] When Pope John XXII wrote to rebuke Edward, it was not for sexual sins but for such plebeian pursuits. In retrospect Edward appears more like a Wyoming rancher than an Oscar Wilde, more a Louis XIII than a Henry III. Gaveston, his lover, is portrayed in the chronicle of Geoffrey le Baker as "graceful and agile in body, sharp witted, refined in manners [and] sufficiently well versed in military matters."[47]

Eventually, Edward I had some second thoughts about the fascinating Gascon. When the prince gave Gaveston a title traditionally resolved for royalty, the angry king exploded, tore out his son's hair, and exiled the favorite. When the patriarch died a few months later, Edward's first act was to recall Gaveston and heap honors upon him. He shocked the English barons by making him Lord Chamberlain and earl of Cornwall and giving him his niece in marriage. The man they looked on as an alien upstart worsened matters by behaving with calculated arrogance, and as a crowning insult, he defeated them in tournaments.

When the king went to France to marry Philip the Fair's daughter Isabel, Gaveston was named regent, another indication that Edward thought him a "second self." Returning with his bride, Edward greeted Piers at Dover with "kisses and repeated embraces" and "a singular familiarity."[48] At the coronation a few weeks later Gaveston offended the nobles by his presumptuous attire—royal purple rather than their more modest cloth-of-gold. Edward was so much more attentive to him than to the queen—a mere child of twelve—that her royal uncles left the feast in protest.

For the next four years Gaveston's status caused unceasing quarrels between the king and the barons. Twice more exiled at the barons' insistence despite strong protests from Edward, Gaveston was formally indicted for misadvising his royal master and denounced as "an open enemy of the King and his people."[49] No hint was placed on record that the king and Piers were lovers, despite their open infatuation. Finally, when he returned from his second exile in 1312, Gaveston's enemies captured and beheaded him at Warwick Castle. Edward, we are told, mourned for his friend as David had mourned for Jonathan.[50]

History was not on Edward's side. His defeat by the Scots at Bannockburn in 1314 dealt a deadly blow to his prestige. When Edward chose new advisors, he showed himself once more unwise; the Hugh Despensers, father and son, belonged to a noble English family but proved so avaricious and tyrannical that they provoked another civil war. Edward's alienated wife, who had begun an affair with Roger Mortimer, now took the field against him in a campaign that would earn her the epithet "she-wolf of France."[51] When her forces landed in England, barons and people, smarting under the Despensers' misrule, rallied to her side.

Edward was captured, imprisoned in Kenilworth Castle, and forced to re-

72. David and Jonathan, David and Saul (bottom); allegorical figures of "Friendship" and "Hate" (top). Manuscript illustration, *La Somme le roy,* c. 1300.

sign the crown to his fifteen-year-old son. The Despensers were seized and brutally dispatched. Though there is far less evidence for an emotional involvement with the younger Hugh than with Piers, a grisly detail in Jean Froissart's famous *Chronicles* (c. 1380?) is explicit. Froissart tells us that Hugh's penis and testicles were severed and burned before his face "because he was and had been a heretic and a sodomite, so that public rumor of it had run through all England, and even about the king."[52]

Edward's own sufferings are vividly described by Thomas de la Moore, a minor official who was a witness to his abdication at Kenilworth and whose account of the king's last days strongly influenced Elizabethan chroniclers. Edward's captors, fearing he would be rescued by his friends, dragged him from castle to castle by night, bare-headed and in tatters, treating him with deliberate brutality. Finally, according to accounts de la Moore claimed to have heard from Edward's tormentors, he was moved to Berkeley Castle, fed bad food, kept awake at night by drums, and put in a room over rotting carrion.

When the king survived these tortures, he was subjected to a particularly horrible death: "On the night of October 11 [1327] while lying in on a bed [the king] was suddenly seized and, while a great mattress . . . weighed him down and suffocated him, a plumber's iron, heated intensely hot, was introduced through a tube into his secret parts so that it burned the inner portions beyond the intestines."[53] This method, de La Moore tells us, was devised so the body would not reveal an outward wound. But it is hard not to see some measure of erotic symbolism in this sadism.

As Edward's agony advances, de la Moore's account takes on a distinctly religious overtone, modulating finally into full-blown hagiography: "In this way the very vigorous warrior was overpowered and a loud cry was heard within and outside the castle . . . as of someone suffering a violent death. This cry of the dying man moved many in Berkeley and certain men in the castle, as they themselves have declared, to compassion and prayers for the departing sanctified soul." There follows an astonishing apotheosis: "Thus he held the world in contempt as his master, namely Christ, once held the world in contempt. The highest heaven received into the kingdom of the angels first the forerunner, who was rejected by the nation of the Jews, and now his follower, who was abused by the nation of the English."[54] The hypocritical queen gave her dead husband an ostentatious funeral in Gloucester Cathedral, where his recumbent image remains as one of the masterpieces of English Gothic art. Three years later the young Edward III seized power, executed Mortimer, and immured his mother in a Norfolk castle.

The dead king's tomb became a saint's shrine favored, monkish chroniclers complained, by wives who liked to gad about on pilgrimages. Queen Philippa and the royal family themselves fostered the cult of the murdered monarch. Edward's great-grandson, Richard II, even launched a serious campaign to have him canonized; in 1395 he sent Boniface IX a book of Edward's "miracles."[55] Not surprisingly, some clergy objected. In the same year, Thomas de Burton, abbot of Meaux in Yorkshire, deprecated the growing cult and gave a specific reason for denying the dead king a halo. "King Edward himself delighted excessively in the vice of sodomy," Burton wrote, "and all his reign was devoid of good fortune and blessings."[56] Finally, the word had been set down unequivocally by an English scribe. It had taken the prospect of a sodomite saint to provoke this candor.

Marlowe's drama, written shortly before his own death in 1593, is the most famous work inspired by Edward's tragedy. Inevitably, it has commanded attention as the only Elizabethan drama with a homosexual protagonist and, indeed, the only English play to touch on the theme of same-sex attraction in anything more than a peripheral way before the twentieth century. That said, a question arises: would Elizabethan audiences have recognized it as such, given English reticence and the remoteness of their perceptions from our own?

So oblique are the hints in Holinshed and Stow that only a sophisticated few in the first audiences for Marlowe's tragedy would have anticipated a play about a sodomite monarch. Marlowe's own treatment of the subject did not connect up with the Elizabethan perception of sodomy as something "filthy," "diabolical," "Romish," and "unnatural," though the jealous queen's comparison of herself to Juno upset by Jove's preference for Ganymede (1.4.178–180) might have aroused suspicions. To the modern reader, the elder Mortimer's catalog of male couples (1.4.390–400), recited to persuade his nephew to tolerate Edward's infatuation with Gaveston, may look like a piece of pro-gay rhetoric:

> The mightiest kings have had their minions:
> Great Alexander loved Hephestion;
> The conquering Hercules for Hylas wept;
> And for Patroclus stern Achilles drooped . . .
> Then let his grace, whose youth is flexible
> And promiseth as much as we can wish,
> Freely enjoy that vain light-headed earl,
> For riper years will wean him from such toys.

But we must bear in mind that English tradition often desexualized classical myths or historical relationships.

Is Marlowe's portrait of the king a negative or positive one? Edward is infatuated with Gaveston, frivolous and irresponsible, inexpert at politics, and cruel to a wife who dotes on him and is jealous of her male rival. But he gains our sympathy when he falls from power and the queen plots his death. Gaveston is ambitious, self-seeking, and willful but devoted to the man whose love eventually costs him his life. Edward, asked why he loves Piers, replies simply, "Because he loves me more than all the world" (1.4.77). By the end of the play the queen and Mortimer look diabolical, and Edward, whose torture and murder closely follow Thomas de la Moore's account as retold by Holinshed, looks more and more pitiful. Charles Lamb thought that Edward's death in Marlowe's play aroused "pity and terror beyond any scene ancient or modern."[57]

Charles Forker has called *Edward II* "unique in English Renaissance drama for its non-satiric and humane portrayal of explicit homosexual emotion."[58] But how "explicit" the play was remains a question. Its message was muted, unavoidably, given the prejudices of the times. Had Marlowe made it clearer that Edward's love for Gaveston was "sodomitical," he could hardly have avoided some stereotyped moral condemnation. This he was unwilling to provide.

Michael Drayton took a different approach in his narrative poem, *Peirs Gaveston* (sic). Drayton was a gentlemanly poet of unimpeachable respectability and orthodoxy who lived a totally undramatic life: in short, Marlowe's opposite. But, encouraged by the success of Marlowe's play, he had his own poem ready for the press a few months after the dramatist's demise. In three hundred dulcet stanzas, the ghost of Gaveston appears from purgatory to tell his story and bewail his fate.[59] Drayton departs from Marlowe and his historical sources, however, by making Gaveston strikingly beautiful (lines 115–118) and rhapsodizes on the power of male beauty to inspire male love in lines reminiscent of Plato (169–214):

> O heavenly concord, music of the mind,
> Touching the heart-strings with such harmony,
> The ground of nature, and the law of kind,
> Which in conjunction do so well agree,
> Whose revolution by effect doth prove,
> That mortal men are made divine by love.

His poetic narrative allowed Drayton more freedom in describing the physical details of the love affair than would have been acceptable on the stage. Hence the erotic temperature is several degrees warmer than in Marlowe, as in this declaration by Gaveston (227–228, 233–234):

> My breast his pillow, where he laid his head,
> Mine eyes his book, my bosom was his bed . . .
> His love-sick lips at every kissing qualm
> Clung to my lips to cure their grief with balm.

Drayton then likens the youths' love-making to Venus "sporting" with Adonis—ardors which lead to a sinful consummation (295–298):

Our innocence, our child-bred purity
Is now defiled and as our dreams forgot,
Drawn in the coach of our security [false self-assurance]
What act so vile that we attempted not?

Marlowe seems to have relied entirely on Elizabethan accounts of Edward's life. Drayton, however, tells us that he carefully culled John Stow's collection of rare fourteenth-century manuscripts for historical details.[60] There he may have encountered the *Chronicle of the Abbey of Meaux,* with its reference to Edward's sodomy. At any rate, Drayton finally brings himself to use the word (1267–1270):

Some slanderous tongues in spiteful manner said
That here I lived in filthy sodomy,
And that I was King Edward's Ganymede,
And to this sin he was enticed by me.

This points directly to Edward's sexual relations with Gaveston. But Drayton could only do this because he was willing, as Marlowe was not, to make the expected negative judgment.

• Shakespeare's Sonnets •

Shakespeare learned much about versification from Marlowe, whose "mighty line" was the rage when Shakespeare began his own play writing. In dramaturgy, too, the debt of *Richard II* to *Edward II* is obvious. And in *As You Like It* he saluted Marlowe by quoting the most famous line from *Hero and Leander:* "Dead shepherd, now I find thy saw of might, / 'Who ever lov'd that lov'd not at first sight?'" (5.3.81–82). But does England's, and the world's, most famous writer belong to the roster—by no means small, if we include Greece, Rome, medieval Islam, China, and Japan—of literary men who have fallen in love with both sexes?

The point has been argued among Shakespeare scholars for the last two centuries. By 1944 the editor of the Variorum edition of the Sonnets could summarize, in an appendix, the conflicting views of nearly forty commentators. The controversy began in 1780 when George Steevens expressed his distaste for sonnet 20, in which Shakespeare notoriously describes his young friend as his "master-mistress." "It is impossible," Steevens vituperated, "to read this fulsome panegyrick, addressed to a male object, without an equal mixture of disgust and indignation."[61] To this, Edmund Malone, the leading Shakespeare scholar of the day, replied: "Some part of this indignation might perhaps have been abated, if it had been considered that such addresses to men, however indelicate, were customary in our author's time, and neither imported criminality nor were esteemed indecorous."[62]

But the genie would not go back into the bottle; the battle was joined and has raged hotly ever since. Early in the nineteenth century Samuel Taylor Coleridge protested that Shakespeare's love was "pure" and there was in his writings "not even an allusion to that very worst of all possible vices."[63] Continental critics were not so sure. A French reviewer of the sonnets wrote in 1834: "*He* instead of *she?* . . . Can I be mistaken? Can these sonnets be addressed to a man? Shakespeare! Great Shakespeare? Did you feel yourself authorized by Virgil's example?" A generation later, Austria's leading dramatist, Franz Grillparzer, also had doubts about Malone's thesis: "To vindicate Shakespeare, since a great part of his sonnets are addressed to a *male* person, the interpreters adduce from his dramas many passages in which the word 'lover' is used by man to man for 'friend,' 'favorite,' 'devotee.' But in all these instances, *beauty* is never the cause of the affection."[64] And so it has gone.

We may wonder, in retrospect, why the controversy did not surface until 164 years after Shakespeare's death. This delay was caused by the peculiar publication history of the sonnets. They first appeared in 1609 in an unauthorized edition by the bookseller Thomas Thorpe, dedicated to a mysterious "Mr. W. H." Anyone reading Thorpe must have seen that the collection consisted of 126 love poems to a young man followed by 26 sonnets to a married woman (the so-called "dark lady") which tell the story of a passionate love affair consummated and regretted. But Thorpe's edition seems to have been little known and may even have been quietly suppressed. In 1640 it was succeeded by another by John Benson which effectively supplanted it.

But Benson scrambled the order of the sonnets, gave them fanciful titles, and changed some pronouns from masculine to feminine so it would be possible for a reader to assume that nearly all the poems were inspired by the "dark lady." It was not until 1780, when Malone's reprint of the original 1609 edition revealed the true state of affairs, that Steevens raised the alarm. Let us look at sonnet 20, which ignited the debate:

A woman's face, with nature's own hand painted,
Hast thou, the master-mistress of my passion—
A woman's gentle heart, but not acquainted
With shifting change, as is false women's fashion;
An eye more bright than theirs, less false in rolling,
Gilding the object whereupon it gazeth;
A man in hue all hues in his controlling,
Which steals men's eyes and women's souls amazeth.
And for a woman wert thou first created,
Till nature as she wrought thee fell a-doting,

And by addition me of thee defeated,
By adding one thing to my purpose nothing.
But since she pricked thee out for women's pleasure,
Mine be thy love, and thy love's use their treasure.

This sonnet follows sonnet 17 in which Shakespeare urges the young man to marry so he may perpetuate his beauty by begetting beautiful children. The first sonnets are avuncular in tone, but by sonnet 13 Shakespeare has begun to call the young man "dear my love," and in 15 he declares that he himself is at "war with Time for love of you," that is, he wishes to make him immortal through his poetry. In sonnet 18 he drops the theme of procreation and writes an unabashed love poem, one of the many that have led critics to hail the sonnets as the "greatest love-poetry in the world":[65]

Shall I compare thee to a summer's day?
Thou art more lovely and more temperate.

Then, two sonnets later, Shakespeare calls the young man his "master-mistress."

Commentators have repeatedly tried to relate Shakespeare's love for the young man to the cult of Renaissance friendship. Thus Douglas Bush in his preface to the 1961 Pelican edition of the sonnets: "Since modern readers are unused to such ardor in masculine friendship and are likely to leap at the notion of homosexuality . . . we may remember that such an ideal—often exalted above the love of women—could exist in real life, from Montaigne to Sir Thomas Browne, and was conspicuous in Renaissance literature." Bush cites *Euphues,* Sidney's *Arcadia,* the fourth book of *The Faerie Queene,* and some of Shakespeare's plays.[66] But we have only to look at Montaigne to see the difference. The Frenchman is at pains to distinguish his ideal of friendship from "that other, licentious Greek love," on the grounds that Greek love was love not for an equal but for someone younger, and inspired specifically by male beauty.[67]

Shakespeare, for his part, complains that his love gives him sleepless nights, causes sharp anguish and fearful jealousy, and torments him as friendship hardly could (27, 28). He speaks to the young man as a courtly lover to his mistress, calling him the "lord of my life" to whom he is bound in "vassalage" as a slave (26, 57, 58). C. S. Lewis, who did not argue for a homosexual interpretation of the sonnets, nevertheless found their language "too loverlike for ordinary male friendship" and was finally forced to admit that "I have found no real parallel to such language between friends in sixteenth-century literature."[68] (Lewis overlooked Michelangelo, who died in 1564, the year of Shakespeare's birth.)

But could such a love for a beautiful youth exist without a sexual basis? In sonnet 20 Shakespeare faces this issue, aware that the young man must, after all the copious praise, be uneasy about its root, and attacks the question by introducing a conceit. He imagines that Nature had originally intended to make a woman and had then found herself in love with her creation. To resolve this (lesbian) dilemma, she adds a penis—which Shakespeare declares to be "to my purpose nothing." But though he rules out sexual relations with the refurbished youth, he makes a startling suggestion. The young man should have sexual relations with women but love only him: "Mine be thy love and thy love's use their treasure." Love only me, but sleep with women: this is a radical proposal from which modern readers are likely to recoil with confusion.

Did some current such as had inspired Ficino's theory of Platonic love in Renaissance Florence a century earlier touch Shakespeare? It is worth noting that Edmund Spenser's editor, the mysterious "E. K.," defending Spenser from the charge of pederasty in *The Shepheardes Calender* (1579), held that the kind of male love described in Plato, Xenophon, and Maximus of Tyre was "much to be allowed and liked of" and not to be confused with the "execrable and horrible" sin of sodomy.[69] Here was at least one English theorist who was willing to admit the acceptability of an ideal Platonic love between males.

It is natural that critics rejecting a homosexual reading of the sonnets should seize on sonnet 20 as settling the issue. But does it? We may recall that Socrates in the *Phaedrus* presents his ideal lovers as achingly desirous of each other but determined to frustrate this sexual impulse. And Xenophon, in his own *Symposium,* presents a whole group of men all ardently "in love" with other men but committed to limiting their sexual experience to women. In sonnet 20 Shakespeare rules out physical relations, but he does not deny that he feels desire. Indeed, Shakespeare describes the feelings aroused by the young man's beauty as exactly the kind of "passion" a beautiful woman might inspire, and then writes repeatedly in this vein throughout the rest of the sonnets. In the light of these expressions, the only candid approach is to call the poems homoerotic in this Platonic—or more specifically, Xenophontic—sense. As such, they remain undoubtedly the most distinguished love poetry written by one man to another.

• James VI and I •

Christopher Marlowe never went to Edinburgh to serve King James—his violent death intervened. James, at the age of thirty-six, succeeded Elizabeth on the English throne in 1603. He had been James VI of Scotland since infancy, following the deposing of his mother, Mary Queen of Scots. John Knox had preached at his coronation to a court and populace that was Puritanical and lawless, impoverished and brutal. Of the six rulers of Scotland who preceded James, all but one had died violent deaths. His own father,

Henry Darnley, was murdered a few months after his birth and his mother forced to flee when she married the earl of Bothwell, the suspected murderer. Two men who were regents during James's childhood were assassinated; one was his grandfather.

The childhood of the precocious boy-king, who had a passion for books, was lonely and loveless. His tutor, George Buchanan, was one of Europe's most distinguished humanists, but his treatment of James was crudely harsh. When Lady Mar, James's foster mother, objected to his beating the "Lord's anointed," Buchanan replied, "I have beat his arse; you may kiss it if you like." At an unusually young age James ended the regency and left the bleak austerity of Stirling Castle to make a formal entry into Edinburgh. There, he was welcomed and feted unwontedly, and there he met for the first time his father's cousin, Esmé Stuart, seigneur d'Aubigny, his nearest male relative.

Esmé (or Aimé) Stuart was a French lord familiar with the elegant court of Henry III, a world as different from Calvinist Scotland as could be imagined. Sir James Melville, a Scots noble who had served Mary, called him "of nature upright, just, and gentle."[70] But it was assumed he had been sent by the Guises to aid the Scottish Catholics and give support to Mary, then a prisoner in England. His respectful manners, handsome looks, fine clothes, and personal charm dazzled the young king; this was a ray of Gallic sunshine in Scotland's gloom. In an unexpected turn of events, the thirteen-year-old boy fell passionately in love with the smiling Frenchman, who was thirty-seven, married, and the father of five children.

Amorous involvements with handsome male favorites were a recurrent pattern in James's life. A seventeenth-century commentator wrote of the king: "From the time he was fourteen [sic] years old and no more, that is, when the Lord Aubigny came into Scotland . . . even then he began . . . to clasp some one *Gratioso* in the embraces of his great love, above all others."[71] Lacking parents or siblings or a sympathetic older friend and starved for affection, James was publicly demonstrative in a way that startled onlookers. An English observer described him as "in such love with him [Aubigny] as in the open sight of the people oftentimes he will clasp him about the neck with his arms and kiss him."[72]

James showered favor on his kinsman, making him a gentleman of the bedchamber, privy councilor, earl, and finally (1580) duke of Lennox—Scotland's only duke. In his new role, Lennox was faced with a dilemma; he had come as a Catholic agent highly suspect in Presbyterian Scotland; now he was chief advisor to a boy who was emotionally and politically dependent upon him. Which loyalty would be paramount? Though motives are often hard to ascertain in Renaissance political life, where dissimulation was taken for granted, the evidence suggests he chose loyalty to James. The teenage king instructed Lennox in the doctrines of Calvinism, and the duke made a public profession of the new faith. But the Scottish Kirk remained distrustful

73. James I as a youth. Oil, artist unknown.

of the suave foreigner, and when Lennox had the earl of Morton, a former regent, tried and beheaded on a charge of treason, the Scottish nobles took alarm and conspired to oust him.

In the Raid of Ruthven, James was lured to Ruthven Castle as a guest but then kept prisoner for ten months by the so-called Lords Enterprisers, who forced him, much against his will, to banish Lennox.[73] The duke made a melancholy journey back to France but kept up a secret correspondence with the king. Lennox told him, truly enough, that he had given up wife, children, and country "to dedicate myself entirely to you"; he prayed to die for James to prove "the faithfulness which is engraved within my heart, which will last forever."[74] "Whatever might happen to me," he wrote, "I shall always be your very faithful servant . . . [you are] he alone in this world whom my heart is resolved to serve. And would to God that my breast might be split open so that it might be seen what is engraven therein."[75]

James was devastated by the loss of the man who had been his family, friend, lover, and mentor, whom he would never see again. Lennox died in France after several months' illness, having received a cool reception as an apostate Catholic. He might have saved face by claiming that his conversion had been a political ruse; instead, he refused the sacraments and died in the reformed faith. This spared James much embarrassment, for he had repeatedly vouched for the sincerity of his lover's conversion. Just sixteen when this first and most poignant of his love affairs came to an unhappy end, James memorialized it in an allegorical poem called "Ane Tragedie of the Phoenix" (1583), which likened Lennox to an exotic foreign bird of unique beauty killed by envy. Lennox left him, as a final gift, his embalmed heart.

Was the affair consummated? Recent biographers have thought it was.[76] The Scottish ministry was warned that the duke sought to "draw the King to carnal lust."[77] Lennox, a sophisticated member of the French aristocracy under Henry III, would have understood the boy's emotional and physical needs. Scottish opinion, on the other hand, saw homosexual relations simply as the work of the devil. Two executions had taken place in 1570, when James was four. Scotland had no sodomy statute, but in a Calvinist nation such a law was not deemed necessary; the indictment, we are told by a nineteenth-century jurist, was simply "founded on the divine law where it is declared in Leviticus xx."[78] On September 1, two men, John Swan and John Litster, described as "smiths and servants to Robert Hannay," were burned in Edinburgh on Castle Hill.[79] An anonymous *Historie and Life of King James the Sext* describes their exposure to public scorn: "First, they were detained in prison for the space of eight days upon bread and water; then they were placed at the market place with the inscription of their fault written on their forehead; after that they were placed in the kirk to repent before the people three several Sundays; fourthly, they were ducked in a deep loch over the head three several times; and last of all bound to a stake and fire kindled about them where their bodies were burned to ashes to the death."[80] In 1630 another man, Michael Erskine, accused "of divers points of witchcraft and filthy sodomy," was condemned "to be worried [strangled] at ane staik while [till] he be dead, and thereafter his body to be burnt to ashes."[81]

As king, James was of course expected to produce heirs to continue the dynasty. In 1589 he married Anne of Denmark. Anne was pretty but had no intellectual interests, preferring music, dancing, and court masques. The marriage produced seven children, the last born in 1607. But James had by then lost interest in his wife, and the couple drifted apart. Anne lived a rather sad, reclusive life, appearing at court functions only occasionally.

Apart from his loves, what kind of man was this first king of "Great Britain"? He was remarkably learned in Greek, Latin, Hebrew, history, and theology and not a little vain about his erudition, which won him the title "the wisest fool in Christendom." He thought scholarship his true vocation and would have liked to have been a university savant. A man of peace whose policies left Scotland more secure and prosperous than it had been for several centuries, he quickly ended England's longstanding war with Spain. Anthony Weldon, whose essay on James's idiosyncrasies is more than a little malicious, called him a "peaceable and merciful Prince"—"such a King I wish this Kingdom have never any worse."[82] In appearance he looked somewhat portly, since he wore a doublet padded against stilettos. (During his reign two French kings were stabbed to death by Catholic fanatics and William of Orange shot.) He had a "pawky" sense of humor, and courtiers were troubled to think twice about his deadpan jokes. James published books on kingship, demonology, and religion and an attack on tobacco. In Scotland he promoted trials for witchcraft, but later, in England, he came to the conclusion that much evidence against witches was fraudulent, and he pardoned most of the women and men who had been convicted. His greatest literary achievement was vicarious: the commissioning of the translation that became known as the King James Bible.

James was well aware, as he put it, that "a king is as one set upon a stage whose smallest actions and gestures all the people gazingly do behold."[83] But this only underlines the irony that a king who claimed to rule by divine right as God's viceroy repeatedly showed, in full view of his subjects, inclinations toward what they regarded as the most diabolical of vices. Though the topic was banned from public discourse, Englishmen had now to face the reality that their new monarch was suspect. Francis Osborne noted in a memoir not published until Cromwell's day:

> The love the King showed [men] was as amorously conveyed as if he had mistaken their sex and thought them ladies, which I have seen Somerset and Buckingham labour to resemble in the effeminateness of their dressings; though in w[horish?] looks and wanton gestures they exceeded any part of womankind my conversation did ever cope withal. Nor was his love, or whatever else posterity will please to call it . . . carried on with a discretion sufficient to cover a less scandalous behaviour; for the king's kissing them after so lascivious a mode in public, and upon the theater, as it were, of the world, prompted many to imagine some things done in the tiring house that exceed my expressions no less than they do my experience, and therefore left them upon the waves of conjecture, which hath in my hearing tossed them from one side to another.[84]

A coded diary entry by Sir Simonds D'Ewes, written in 1622 when the antiquarian was a law student in London, is colored by D'Ewes's Puritan leanings. This conversation with a friend reveals how strong a hold the fear of divine retribution still had on the popular imagination: "I discoursed with him [of things] that were secret, as of the sin of sodomy, how frequent [!] it was in this wicked city, and if God did not provide some wonderful blessing against it, we could not but expect some horrible punishment for it; especially it being, as we had probable cause to fear, a sin in the prince as well as the people, which God is for the most part chastiser of himself, because no man else indeed dare reprove or tell them of their faults."[85]

James sought to deflect criticism by adopting a severe stance vis à vis the law. His book on kingship, *Basilikon Doron,* lists sodomy among those "horrible crimes which ye are bound in conscience never to forgive," along with witchcraft, willful murder, incest, poisoning, and counterfeiting.[86] For this he earned the scorn of Jeremy Bentham, who in an unpublished manuscript denounced James as a hypocrite.[87] Here, however, the king may be simply following Scottish tradition. But James also singled out the crime in a letter to his chancellor Lord Burleigh in 1610. It was customary to issue a general pardon at the conclusion of a session of parliament. James, nevertheless, directed Burleigh to make an exception in cases of sodomy so "no more colour may be left to the judges to work upon their wits in that point."[88] Apparently English judges had been interpreting the Elizabethan law in a way that made it difficult to convict. It is hard to forgive the king this harshness toward a crime with which he was so closely associated.

James's principal favorite during his first years in London was Robert Carr, son of a Scots laird whom he made a gentlemen of the bedchamber. His good looks caused much comment, but his intelligence was limited; he could be affable but also petulant and insolent. Carr's downfall came through a woman he fell in love with, the young, beautiful, and unscrupulous Frances Howard. Unfortunately, she was already married. After a scandalous divorce, which James facilitated by packing a court of bishops, the two were wed in a lavish ceremony over which the king presided. At that time (1613) he also made Carr earl of Somerset. Carr's best friend, Sir Thomas Overbury, who hated Frances and had vehemently opposed the marriage, had died in the Tower a few weeks earlier, but little notice had been taken of the event.

During the next two years, however, the king's relations with Carr became increasingly troubled. James describes the difficulties in a letter that runs to five printed pages and must be the most detailed analysis of a male love affair gone bad the century provides. James acknowledges the benefits he felt he had derived from their intimacy: "For I am far from thinking of any possibility of any man ever to come within many degrees of your trust with me, as I must ingenuously confess ye have deserved more trust and confidence of me than ever man did: in secrecy above all flesh, in feeling and unpartial respect, as well to my honour in every degree as to my profit. And all this without respect either to kin or ally or your nearest and dearest friend whatsoever . . . And in these points I confess I never saw any come towards your merit."[89]

But now "strange streams of unquietness, passion, fury, and insolent pride" have threatened their love. Carr has rebuked the king "more sharply and bitterly than ever my master [Buchanan] durst do." Loud words have passed between them which others have heard. In the past James had "dissembled [his] grief thereat only in hope that time and experience would reclaim and abate that heat which I thought to wear you out of by a long-suffering patience and many gentle admonitions." James's wounded spirit shows itself in his complaint that Carr had for a long time been "creeping back and withdrawing yourself from lying in my chamber, notwithstanding my many hundred times earnest soliciting you to the contrary."[90] At this critical point, the Overbury scandal burst upon the world when an underkeeper of the Tower revealed that Carr's new wife had plotted to poison the prisoner. James insisted that Carr face a trial, and when his wife confessed her guilt, both were sentenced to death. James commuted the sentences, but the pair remained in the Tower for seven years.

The great love of James's last dozen years was more fortunate. George Villiers was the impecunious son of a Leicestershire baronet. James met him in 1614 when Villiers was twenty-two, just as his feelings for Carr were turning sour. Even the puritanical D'Ewes was entranced by Villiers' beauty, reporting that: "I most earnestly viewed him for about half an hour's space at the least . . . I saw everything in him full of delicacy and handsome features."[91] Francis Bacon commended him to the king as of "a safe nature, a capable mind, an honest will, generous and noble affections, and a courage well lodged."[92] His sweetness of manner and devotion charmed James, and his rise was swift. In 1615 James knighted him; eight years later he was the first commoner in a century to be made a duke. Ultimately, he was the most powerful of James's favorites and the man whose affectionate devotion brought him the most satisfaction. But the enormous wealth James lavished upon Buckingham and his greedy relatives undermined the favorite's—and the king's—popularity.

Buckingham adroitly won over Anne, who addressed affectionate letters to him expressing the hope that he would continue "always true" to her husband. If James's letters to Robert Carr are unique records of pain and anxiety, the letters to and from Buckingham are more remarkable still for the candor with which they reveal their intimacy. Buckingham's biographer, Roger Lockyer, thinks the affair became sexual in August 1615 at Farnham Castle, on the basis of a letter from the duke referring to the event: "Sir, all the way hither I entertained myself, your unworthy servant, with this dispute, whether you loved me now . . . better than at the time which I shall never forget at Farnham, where the bed's head could not be found between the master and his dog."[93] James, in turn, addressed Buckingham by many epithets—child, friend, sweetheart, wife, ransacking the vocabulary of familial intimacy to describe his feelings for him and declaring that "I desire only to live in this world for your sake, and . . . I had rather live banished in any part of the earth with you than live a sorrowful widow's life without you."[94]

During the first years of his ascendancy Buckingham had no direct influence on politics, but in 1619 he played a prominent role in the negotiations for the marriage of Prince Charles to the Spanish infanta. As the two young men were about to depart on an unprecedented visit to Madrid, James suffered much distress. "I am now so miserable a coward," James wrote to Buckingham, "as I do nothing but weep and mourn; for I protest to God I rode this afternoon a great way in the park [with] . . . the tears trickling down my cheeks, as now they do that I can scarcely see to write. But alas, what shall I do at our parting?"[95] Returning, Buckingham wrote that he would make speedy haste "to lay myself at your feet, for never none longed more to be in the arms of his mistress . . . My heart and very soul dances for joy, for the change will be no less than to leap from trouble to ease, from sadness to mirth, nay from hell to heaven. I can not now think of giving thanks for wife or child, my thoughts are only bent on having my dear dad and master's legs soon in my arms."[96]

When they were reunited in England, "the Prince and the Duke being on their knees, the king fell on their necks and they all wept."[97] The Spanish marriage, which had been unpopular, fell through amid much rejoicing in England, but the journey cemented a strong friendship between Charles and Buckingham. Two years later James died, with Buckingham at his side. During the troubled opening years of his reign, Charles kept Buckingham on as his chief advisor. Their policies proved controversial, and in 1628 the duke was assassinated by a disgruntled veteran, who later apologized for an act he had come to regret as misguided.

• Francis Bacon •

When James I revisited Scotland in 1617, Francis Bacon ruled England in his absence as lord keeper. This marked the pinnacle of a career that was shortly to take a dramatic downward turn. Bacon had been born in 1561; Shakespeare and Marlowe in 1564; James in 1566: was there some conjunction of the stars? In his teens he spent three years in the suite of the English ambassador at the court of Henry III and the flamboyant mignons. At twenty he began a career in parliament, where he served for four decades. Advancement was slow under Elizabeth; but under James I Bacon rose rapidly, becoming solicitor general in 1606, attorney general in 1613, and chancellor in 1618. In 1621 he was made viscount St. Albans. In his writings on religion and government Bacon usually advocated liberal policies. Nevertheless, in his official capacities he routinely supported James against parliament, defended the unpopular monopolies the king granted his favorites, and, like many, perhaps most, judges of his time, accepted money from litigants whose cases he was trying. Hence, when parliament rebelled against James in 1621, it charged his lord chancellor with taking bribes. Bacon signed a confession admitting to the offenses, claiming only that he had not let the gifts influence him. Fined a huge sum, he spent four days in the Tower. James remitted the fine, and the chastened ex-chancellor retired to his luxurious country estate to devote the rest of his life to his first love, philosophy.

Bacon's philosophical program was as idealistic as his political career had been compromised. Having taken, as he put it, "all knowledge for my province," he aimed to promote the welfare of mankind by encouraging scientific discovery and experiment. He had set forth this mission in the *Advancement of Learning* (1603–1605), mapping out research projects that would improve human health and welfare. Though cautiously respectful of religion, he argued that science should seek purely secular explanations for natural phenomena, free from prejudice and superstition. Bacon looked to physics and mathematics as the exemplary sciences, but he also recommended the study of human behavior, that is, of sociology and psychology. His success was unexampled. Of all the Englishmen of his age, he made the greatest impression on European thought, and eventually on the world. He has been called the single most influential writer of the second millennium, as Saint Paul was of the first. The Royal Society was founded in London in 1660 to carry out his program, which heralded the Enlightenment and the Age of Reason. He stands at the head of the English philosophical tradition, which was later to encompass Hobbes, Locke, Berkeley, Hume, and Mill.

With a life so embroiled in politics and rich in ideas, Bacon's biographers have found little space to devote to the private man. But what we do know is revealing. His favored servants lived in affluence, keeping coaches and racehorses, and it was thought he found his lovers among them. Little information survives about his attachments, however; we cannot trace the trajectory of his affections as we can with the extraverted James. In this matter, Bacon cultivated secrecy and discretion and, in his writings, struck a pose of moral conservatism. In *The New Atlantis,* his prescient vision of humanity's technological future, Bacon exalts the traditional family and assures his readers that this utopia "has no touch" of "masculine love."[98] But the historian Arthur Wilson noted in 1653 that Bacon's generosity to his "young, prodigal, and expensive" servants "opened a gap to infamous reports."[99] More pointedly, John Aubrey wrote, in the manuscript of his *Brief Lives* (not, however, published until the nineteenth century), "He was a *paiderastes,*" adding that "his Ganymedes and favorites took bribes; but his Lordship always gave judgment *secundum aequum et bonum* [according as was just and good]."[100]

No illuminating details have been found in Bacon's own correspondence. But a letter from his mother to his brother Anthony is suggestive. "I pity your brother," she wrote in 1593, when Bacon had not yet achieved fame, "yet he pitieth not himself but keepeth that bloody Percy . . . as a coach companion and bed companion—a proud profane costly fellow, whose being about him I verily fear the Lord God doth mislike and doth the less bless your brother in credit and otherwise in his health."[101] At that time not all bed companions were assumed to be lovers, but we may note that Lady Bacon feared divine disfavor, as Simonds D'Ewes feared it later for King James. Despite her disapproval, Henry Percy remained with Bacon until the end of his life, a trusted servant and friend, to whom he bequeathed a hundred pounds in his will.

In some autobiographical notes the hostile Simonds D'Ewes made a revealing comment on Bacon's style of life after his fall:

> For whereas presently upon his censure at this time his ambition was moderated, his pride humbled, and the means of his former injustice and corruption removed, yet would he not relinquish the practice of his most horrible and secret sin of sodomy, keeping still one Godrick, a very effeminate faced youth, to be his catamite and bedfellow, although he had discharged the most of his other household servants: which was the more to be admired [wondered at] because men after his fall began to discourse of that his unnatural crime which he had practiced many years . . . And it was thought by some that he should have been tried at the bar of justice for it, and having satisfied the law most severe against that horrible villainy with the price of his blood; which caused some bold and forward man to write these verses in a whole sheet of paper, and to cast it down in some part of York House in the Strand, where Viscount St. Alban yet lay—"Within this sty a hog doth lie / That must be hanged for sodomy."[102]

Though D'Ewes's animus against Bacon had its roots in political and religious hatred, his report has a specificity which suggests that it is substantially accurate.

Did the ex-chancellor really stand in danger of hanging? Probably not, though an English peer and an Irish bishop would be executed for sodomy within the next two decades. That his brother Anthony narrowly escaped this fate, however, we know from records in France. Anthony never married and was always on close terms with his brother. Living in France as an intelligence agent for Sir Francis Walsingham, he had visited Montaigne and made a friend of Henry of Navarre (later Henry IV). But in 1586 he was convicted of sodomy in Montauban, a Huguenot town in southern France. His alleged partner had been a page named Isaac Burgades, who, it was charged at the trial, had declared that "there was nothing wrong in the practice of sodomy" and that "Théodore Bèze of Geneva approved of it."[103] Anthony was found guilty; we do not know the sentence. Presumably it was burning: a priest named Benoist Grealou had been burned alive for the same offense at nearby Cahors in 1563. Fortunately, Henry intervened on the grounds that the Englishman's punishment might strain relations with Elizabeth and that a foreigner should not be subject to all the "harshness of French justice."[104] Anthony returned to England, joined his brother in the Essex circle, and died of illness in 1601 two months after the earl's execution for treason.

• Puritanism and the Restoration •

The great drama of seventeenth-century England was the rise of Puritanism, its triumph in 1649 after a civil war and the execution of the king, and its collapse a decade later with the restoration of Charles II. The Puritans, when they came to power, made the enforcement of sexual morality a priority, punishing fornication and treating adultery as a capital offense. In this they followed their co-religionists in New England. There, Puritan legislators had attempted to enforce Old Testament codes through their own laws. One preamble declared that "Jehovah the Great Law-giver . . . hath been pleased to set down a Divine Platform, not only of the Moral, but also of Judicial laws suitable for the people of Israel."[105] Accordingly, when the colony of Massachusetts Bay enacted its first "Body of Laws and Liberties" in 1641, it incorporated not the Elizabethan sodomy statute but the 2000-year-old language of Leviticus verbatim: "If any man lieth with mankind as he lieth with a woman, both of them have committed abomination, they both shall surely be put to death."[106] Other colonies copied the Bay Colony code, and this Hebraic formula remained on the books in Connecticut until 1822.

Rhode Island's law cited Saint Paul's animadversion on "vile affections" from Romans 1:26; New Haven went further in 1655 by using the same passage to justify the death penalty for lesbianism, a unique development in the English-speaking world.[107] In Pennsylvania, William Penn's "Great Law" of 1682 reflected Quaker humanitarianism, which opposed capital punishment. It reduced the penalty for sodomy to six months' imprisonment—an unheard of leniency, which, however, the English government nullified some years later. Hangings in the colonial period were infrequent; nevertheless, in 1776 at the time of the American Revolution all thirteen colonies had capital laws. In a new nation which affirmed a right to "life, liberty, and the pursuit of happiness," black slaves were denied liberty, and sodomites—in theory at least—lost the right to life. (In Virginia Thomas Jefferson sought, unsuccessfully, to mitigate this harshness by substituting castration for hanging.)[108] In Puritan England it was not necessary to introduce a new law, since the biblical penalty was already available. Yet there was no persecution of sodomites such as took place in Calvin's Geneva, and no executions are recorded under Cromwell.

Though prosecutions for sodomy were rare in seventeenth-century England (unlike Latin Europe), two sensational trials attracted attention. The first was especially bizarre. In 1631 the earl of Castlehaven was accused of allowing two servants with whom he was sexually involved to rape his wife.

The attorney general remarked that sodomy was so rare "that we scarce hear of it"; he called it a "pestiferous and pestilential" offense that, unpunished, would "draw from heaven heavy judgments upon this kingdom." He reported King Charles's desire that "his throne and people" might be cleansed from "the guilt of such abominable impieties" and voiced collective fears by quoting Leviticus: "By these abominations the land is defiled; and therefore the Lord does visit this land for the iniquity thereof."[109] Castlehaven was convicted and beheaded, and the two servants who had given evidence against him were hanged despite a promise of immunity. The scabrous elements of the Castlehaven trial made it attractive as judicial pornography; several manuscripts of the testimony survive and two pamphlets made the details public in 1699 and 1710.

Such records are not available for the trial of John Atherton, bishop of Waterford and Lismore in Ireland, who was convicted of sodomy and hanged on the Gallows Green in Dublin in 1640. In this case, crucial facts still remain a mystery. The execution of a bishop for sodomy was a truly sensational event, unimaginable under ordinary circumstances. But these were not ordinary times. Atherton owed his appointment as bishop to the earl of Strafford, whom Charles I had named as his lord lieutenant in Ireland and who acted vigorously and effectively as the king's agent. Six months after Atherton's death, the Puritan parliament in London, over the passionate objections of Charles, sent the unpopular earl to his death on the scaffold. Five years later, Strafford's friend Archbishop Laud met the same fate, and in 1649, at the end of a bitter civil war, Charles himself. Atherton had the ill luck to be caught early in a vortex of this maelstrom.

Atherton was a skilled ecclesiastical lawyer who had aroused the enmity of the powerful earl of Cork by the campaign he waged to recover church lands the earl had appropriated in Ireland. On appointing Atherton, Strafford had boasted that Cork would think "the devil is let loose upon him."[110] But Atherton's suits threatened a multitude of landowners, Protestant and Catholic alike, and his overreaching greed made him heartily disliked. When the Irish parliament rebelled against Strafford's policies on June 16, 1640, one piece of business it took up was a petition from Atherton's tithe collector, John Child, who accused the bishop of "fornication and adultery, and claimed to have committed sodomy with him."[111]

Atherton's conviction three weeks later led to a shameful scene in Dublin on December 5, when the bishop dangled from the end of rope for nearly an hour as friends held down his hands to shorten his agony. For the Puritans, the death of a bishop under such degrading circumstances was a matter for satisfaction, and the Anglican episcopacy was abolished in 1643. The first account of Atherton's case, a brief anonymous piece of doggerel entitled *The Life and Death of John Atherton, Lord Bishop of Waterford and Lismore* (1641), featured a woodcut of the prelate with a noose about his neck. Reflecting the

74. "The life and death of John Atherton." Anonymous pamphlet, 1641.

anti-episcopal bias of the times, it adjured bishops to shun avarice, extortion, lust, buggery, incest, rape, and adultery and painted Atherton's story in lurid colors, accusing him of seducing some sixty-four women and, like "a devil from th'infernal Pit," "taking a male fiend / To sodomize with him."[112] The "fiend" was John Child who was himself hanged at Bandonbridge near Cork in March 1641.

But was Atherton guilty of sodomy? Child, on the scaffold, affirmed that he had given false testimony against him. Thomas Carte in his *Life of the Duke of Ormonde* (1737) claimed that Atherton's suits against the earl of Cork had led to his death, averring that he "fell a sacrifice to that litigation rather than to justice, when he suffered upon the testimony of a single witness that deserved no credit."[113] Other eighteenth-century commentators disagreed.[114] But the author of the 1882 article on Atherton in the *Dictionary of National Biography*—still the only generally accessible account of his life—

thought Atherton's repeated declarations that "he deserved death," along with his statement that he "applauded God's justice" in his sentencing, were "incompatible with the idea that Atherton was the innocent victim of a vile conspiracy."[115]

The author of this essay drew his conclusions from a substantial pamphlet that appeared a few weeks after the bishop's hanging. The use of Atherton's hanging to defame the hierarchy had prompted Archbishop Ussher, head of the Church of England in Ireland, to ask his chaplain Nicholas Barnard to reply. Barnard's daunting task was to turn the scandal into an occasion for edification. We may admire the skill he brings to a seemingly impossible task. His effort, published as *The Penitent Death of a Woeful Sinner,* is a powerful narrative that takes us through the last week of the condemned man almost hour by hour. As a historical document, however, it leaves much to be desired, since it almost completely obfuscates the details of Atherton's trial and conviction.

Barnard portrays Atherton as a man wracked by remorse springing from his fear of damnation. Though the bishop had defended himself aggressively at his trial, now, we are told, he "made a sorrowful, large confession of his vileness."[116] Atherton's self-abnegation, as Barnard presents it, is extreme. But though Barnard dramatizes the bishop's guilt for his unscrupulous litigation and his neglect of his clerical duties, he avoids any reference to his sexual sins, except for the "reading of naughty books" and "viewing of immodest pictures."[117] His account of the bishop's lengthy speech at the gallows shows a thoroughly penitent man, dignified and eloquent, asking forgiveness of others and welcoming his ignoble death as the just reward for his sins. In the end, we are told, many in the crowd who had come to gloat and jeer wept aloud.

Reading this, we naturally assume that the bishop feels guilt for the (here) unspecified crime for which he was sentenced. Thus it comes as a shock when Barnard records this declaration: "He said it was *digitus dei* [the finger of God], the justice of which he fully and solemnly acknowledged . . . at that instant he heard the Jury had returned him guilty, though he denied then (as he did now) the main thing in the Inditement [sodomy] which the law laid hold of, and which has been since confirmed by the confession of his chief accuser at his execution also."[118] Atherton is concerned not with human justice in the law courts but with what he calls "God's justice." He declares that he was not guilty of the sodomy charge but that his conviction is providential on account of his *other* sins.

The intensity of the bishop's self-loathing seems remarkable if he did not see himself as guilty of some such heinous sin as sodomy, though an extensive career of adultery, fornication, and incest might account for it. The Irish historian Aidan Clarke, the only scholar to have thoroughly examined the bishop's case in recent times, thinks Atherton was not guilty of the charge

75. John Wilmot, Earl of Rochester, with a monkey. Artist unknown, oil, c. 1675.

against him. The strongest arguments for this view are the declarations Atherton and Child reportedly made at the point of death. In the minds of seventeenth-century Christians, perjury at such a moment would have assured damnation. If we weigh all the details of a very imperfect record, it is difficult not to conclude that the bishop's hanging was a flagrant abuse of the sodomy law for political purposes.

With the death of Cromwell, the tide turned against Puritanism, and Restoration England celebrated its overthrow by revolting against sexual repression. Charles II set the pace with his troop of mistresses; it was said that courtiers were politically suspect if they failed to follow his example. This was a rare moment when political conservatism marched with libertinism. Nor was all the sinning heterosexual. Samuel Pepys tells us that his friends assured him "that buggery is now [1663] almost grown as common among our gallants as in Italy, and the very pages of the town begin to complain of their masters for it."[119]

The most notorious of all the Restoration rakes was, of course, the earl of Rochester. Witty and dissipated, and a favorite at Charles II's court, Rochester was much involved with women—with a wife in the country and a string of mistresses in London. But his correspondence and poems make it clear that he was openly bisexual. A letter to his close friend Henry Savile praised "the pretty fool, the bearer," who was, in fact, Rochester's French valet, Jean Baptiste de Belle-Fasse, of whom he wrote: "The greatest and gravest of this Court of both sexes have tasted his beauties, and I'll assure you Rome gains upon us here in this point mainly, and there is no part of the Plot carried with so much secrecy and vigour as this. Proselytes of consequence are daily made."[120] The reference is to the so-called Popish Plot of 1678 which allegedly aimed to assassinate Charles II and place his Catholic brother James on the throne: Rochester facetiously claims that the Jesuits aspired to subvert England sexually as well as politically.

Rochester's verses, which circulated widely in manuscript but were not published until his death in 1680, treat sex with brutal candor. Coition with women is his main theme, but a number of poems reveal his versatility, as in "The Disabled Debauchee," where a superannuated rake recalls an escapade with his mistress:

> Nor shall our love-fits, Cloris, be forgot,
> When each the well-look'd link-boy strove t'enjoy,
> And the best kiss was the deciding lot,
> Whether the boy fucked you, or I the boy.[121]

(A link boy was a boy hired to carry a torch through London's dark streets.) In another lyric Rochester assumes the character of a woman-despising pederast:

> Love a woman! you're an ass.
> 'Tis a most insipid passion . . .
>
> Then give me health, wealth, mirth, and wine,
> And if busy love intrenches [encroaches],
> There's a sweet soft page of mine,
> Does the trick worth forty wenches.[122]

Rochester is also often assumed to be the author of a bawdy extravaganza entitled *Sodom, or The Quintessence of Debauchery,* though the authorship is much disputed. The tone of this priapic farce may be gathered from its cast: Bolloxinian is king of Sodom, the queen is Cuntigratia. The lusty king, who "eats to swive, and swives to eat again," is bored with his marital duties and issues a proclamation in favor of buggery. The desperate women order dildoes and embark on a campaign to bed the men who scorn them. Bolloxinian is delighted with a gift of forty striplings from the king of Gomorrah, but sexual disease lays the men low, and Flux, the royal physician, delivers the wholly conventional moral:

> To Love and Nature all their rights restore—
> Fuck women and let buggery be no more,
> It doth the procreative end destroy,
> Which Nature gave with pleasure to enjoy.[123]

But the defiant king, as reckless as Don Juan, declares: "I scorn the gift [of a wife], I'll reign and bugger still." Demons shriek, and fire and brimstone rain down as the curtain falls. In an epilogue, the women of the court declare themselves better partners since they are sexually insatiable. These characters are not people but vocal private parts. With *Sodom* a writer tried to exorcise one of the most potent myths of Puritanism by turning it into ribald fantasy.

• Between Women •

If the English were reticent about male homosexuality in the reigns of Elizabeth and James, the silence about women who were attracted to other women was even more complete. Lesbianism was not a matter for the law, and Britain had no Queen Christina. Indeed, one French visitor, the count de Gramont, remarked that the English were "yet so uncivilized as never to have heard of that refinement of love of ancient Greece."[124] Knowledge of lesbianism was confined primarily to the relatively few readers able to decipher the erotic works of Sappho, Lucian, Ovid, and Martial.

Yet early in the seventeenth century, in a verse letter to John Donne, his friend Thomas Woodward, by a fantastic conceit, chose to call their mutual inspiration "a chaste and mystic tribadry," that is, a lesbian affair, in which his Muse "rubb'd and tickled" Donne's to "spend some of her pith."[125] In the 1590s when these lines were written, Donne was a member of the Inns of Court in London where university graduates studying law prided themselves on their literary sophistication. It was presumably in this intellectually adventurous milieu that Donne wrote "Sappho to Philaenis," a remarkable poem celebrating lesbian love. (Here Donne follows Martial in using "Philaenis" as a generic term for a lesbian.)[126] In "Sappho to Phaon," Ovid had shown Sappho in love with a handsome young ferryman for whom she has abandoned her female lovers. Donne inverts Ovid. In his monologue, Sappho dismisses her feeling for Phaon and justifies her all-absorbing love for another woman.

One wonders how Donne came to write such revolutionary lines, totally at odds with the moral and religious beliefs of his age. "Sappho to Philaenis" flies directly in the face of orthodoxy by treating admiringly a kind of love routinely denounced as unnatural. Why, Donne's Sappho asks, should she "admit the tillage of some harsh rough man" when a woman's love leaves no damning evidence, only "sweetness."

> And between us all sweetness may be had,
> All, all that Nature yields, or Art can add.
> My two lips, eyes, thighs, differ from thy two,
> But so as mine from one another do,
> And, oh, no more; the likeness being such,
> Why should they not alike in all parts touch?
> Hand to strange hand, lip to lip none denies;
> Why should they breast to breast, or thigh to thighs?[127]

"Sappho to Philaenis" extols lesbian love because it rests not on difference but on "likeness."

Donne's attitude toward male homosexuality seems to have been conventionally negative.[128] Janel Meuller has suggested that Donne framed his ideal of erotic equality in female terms because lesbianism, rarely spoken of, was less criticized than male love in his day.[129] But in fact "tribadism" met with strong disapproval. In his book on famous women, Donne's contemporary Thomas Heywood spoke of the "preposterous and forbidden luxuries [lusts]" imputed to Sappho.[130] Most likely Donne, who was strongly attracted to women, simply found it easy to sympathize with their feeling for each other. He would not be the only heterosexual male who has found lesbianism imaginatively exciting. Later in his career when Donne took holy orders and became an Anglican dean, he would have had no choice but to endorse Paul's strictures. But as a young poet free of such constraints he achieved an act of imaginative sympathy that set aside centuries of prejudice.

In late seventeenth-century England, three women poets—Katherine Philips, the duchess of Newcastle, and Aphra Behn—have a place in the literary history of lesbianism. Of these, Katherine Philips is the most ambiguous. Hailed as the "English Sappho," Philips addressed poems to women that suggest attachments passionate enough to qualify as love affairs. In 1648 Katherine, who was sixteen, had married James Philips, who was fifty-four, but her personal life was largely focused on a "Society of Friends," mainly female. On these she lavished her affections, calling herself "Orinda" and addressing them by pastoral epithets in the *précieuse* style made popular in England by Charles I's French queen, Henrietta Maria. Her first passion was for Mary Aubrey ("Rosania") of whom she wrote: "She hath a face so eminently bright / Would make a lover of an anchorite . . . / For every glance commits a massacre" (34).[131] When Rosania married, Katherine denounced her as a "lovely apostate" (38). Katherine then transferred her affections to Anne Owen, whom she called "Lucasia." In "To My Excellent Lucasia, On Our Friendship" (36), Philips borrows the style of John Donne's love poems to express her new ardor:

> I did not live until this time
> Crown'd my felicity,
> When I could say without a crime,
> I am not thine but thee.
> This carcass breath'd and walk'd and slept,
> So that the world believ'd
> There was a soul the motions kept,
> But they were all deceiv'd.
> For as a watch by art is wound
> To motion, such was mine.
> But never had Orinda found
> A soul till she found thine.

The intensity of Katherine's feeling for her own sex in this fine poem would suggest a parallel with Shakespeare's sonnets. But unlike Shakespeare, Philips distinguishes between friendship and love—friendship is "love refin'd and purg'd of all its dross," stronger than passion but "not so gross" (64). Philips died of smallpox in London during the Great Plague of 1664; she was thirty-one. John Dryden and Jeremy Taylor admired her poems, and Abraham Cowley, praising her, took care to say she lacked Sappho's "ill manners." To her contemporaries she was not only "The Matchless" but also "The Chaste" Orinda. Whether her poems belong to the new tradition of romantic friendship between women or whether they reveal a lesbian element in her psyche remains an open question.

A verse play by the duchess of Newcastle raises the issue of lesbianism more pointedly. Margaret Lucas, lady-in-waiting to Henrietta Maria, had married William Cavendish, marquis (later duke) of Newcastle, in 1645; she was twenty-two, her husband fifty-one. Unlike Katherine Philips, who in everything conformed punctiliously to the decorum of her age, the duchess was a notable eccentric. She wore a mixture of men's and women's clothes that set off her fine figure and featured a startling décolletage. Instead of curtsying, she made masculine bows. Queen Christina, who met the duchess in Antwerp the year after she left Sweden, would have recognized a kindred spirit. Her appearance in print was a further provocation, since for a woman avowedly to seek fame as an author was seen as another kind of "immodesty." In 1668 the duchess published a collection of "dialogues upon several subjects" in the form of fanciful plays. One philosophical romance, *The Convent of Pleasure,* has the distinction of being the first work by an Englishwoman to touch on the issue of love between women in a direct way.

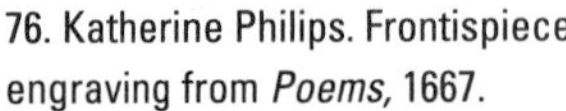
76. Katherine Philips. Frontispiece engraving from *Poems,* 1667.

In this utopian fantasy, Lady Happy shuns the male sex and retires to a convent which is not ascetic but sumptuously luxurious. Immured and manless, the ladies watch grim tableaux on the sufferings of women who marry. When a visiting princess of truly "masculine presence" joins the company and asks leave to dress as a man in a play, Lady Happy is willing to oblige. Alarmed when she finds herself falling in love with "her," she has a consoling—and revolutionary—thought: "Why may not I love a woman with the same affection I could a man?"[132] This is far from Iphis's lament.

The two women soon move beyond platonism. A stage direction tells us that they "embrace and kiss and hold each other in their arms" (4.1). Soon they are observed kissing "with more alacrity than women use, [with] a kind of titillation" (5.1). In Restoration comedy, male same-sex episodes are treated as ridiculous or indecent. In the *Convent of Pleasure* the woman-with-woman encounter is presented in a romantic light. For this reason the play

77. Aphra Behn. James Fittler (after Thomas Uwins), engraving, published 1822.

has been hailed as "an extraordinarily subversive lesbian romance" by Emma Donoghue, even though, to accord with convention, the duchess has the princess turn out to be a prince.[133]

Aphra Behn was an even more unconventional figure. Reared in Dutch Surinam and married briefly to a Dutch merchant, Behn served as an English spy in Antwerp, wrote a novel *(Oroonoco)* with a black slave as hero, and by dint of a dozen or so successful comedies became the first Englishwoman to live by her pen. Contemporaries praised her as an androgyne of "a female sweetness and a manly grace" whose poetry joined "the beauties of both sexes."[134] Most of her erotic verse is directed to men, but some shows a fascination with women which suggests she was bisexual. "To the Fair Clarinda, who made love to me, imagin'd more than Woman" abounds with ambivalences. The "Incomparable Aphra" could play with gender ambiguities as freely as Shakespeare had in his "master-mistress" sonnet.

Fair, lovely maid, or, if that title be
Too weak, too feminine for nobler thee,
Permit a name that more approaches truth,
And let me call thee lovely charming youth.
This last will justify my soft complaint,
While that may serve to lessen my constraint;
And without blushes I the youth pursue—
When so much beauteous woman is in view.[135]

Behn is cleverly making use of conventions in order to undermine them. To call Clarinda a "fair maid" fails to do her justice, since she also has the noble attributes of a young man. But if she is really a young man, then Aphra can with propriety address a love poem to her. On the other hand, Clarinda's female status obviates any moral censure, since the love of women for women is conventionally seen as sexless. Behn delights in having it both ways:

Against thy charms we struggle but in vain:
With thy deluding form thou giv'st us pain,
While the bright nymph betrays us to the swain.
In pity to our sex sure thou wert sent,
That we might love, and yet be innocent.
For sure no crime with thee we could commit;
Or if we should—thy form excuses it.

But Behn could also be more direct in voicing her feelings for another woman. A poem published in 1692, three years after her death, bears a title that is itself a confession: "Verses designed by Mrs. A. Behn to be sent to a fair Lady that desired she would absent herself to cure her love." It begins:

In vain to woods and deserts I retire,
To shun the lovely charmer I admire . .
In vain in grottos dark unseen I lie,
Love pierces where the sun could never spy . . .
The more I struggl'd, to my grief I found
Myself in Cupid's chains more surely bound.[136]

This poem, which uses Ovidian verse to rewrite Ovid in the spirit of Sappho, may be the first in English in which one woman unambiguously declares her infatuation with another. As such it trod a dangerous line. Yet, despite her Bohemian life and well-publicized amours, Behn was buried in Westminster Abbey when she died in 1689.

• William III in England •

We have already observed William of Orange as a general on the European stage. But what did the English make of him when he became their king in

1689? This was a title to which he had two claims. His wife Mary II was James II's eldest daughter, but his mother was another Mary Stuart, daughter of Charles I. Moreover, since his mother was also the daughter of Henrietta Maria, sister to Louis XIII, she was a first cousin to Monsieur. Thus, William was related to homosexual royalty on both the Stuart and Bourbon sides of his mother's family. Two other leading generals of the day, the Great Condé and the duc de Vendôme, belonged to cadet branches of the Bourbon dynasty. That these men who favored their own sex were accepted leaders in seventeenth-century Europe must have given William reassurance. There was, however, an important difference: the prince and the duke were free-thinkers in Catholic France; William was a devout Protestant called to rule a country that defined same-sex love as a Latin and popish vice.

His father, William II of Orange, had died of smallpox in 1650 a week before his son was born. The princes of Orange had by tradition been "stadtholders"—national magistrates who led the Dutch army in times of war. But the nation's burgess leaders, desiring to limit aristocratic influence in the republic, denied the young man the post. Not until France invaded the Netherlands in 1672 and panic ensued was he given command. The young general rebuilt the disorganized Dutch forces, drove back the French, and won the title "Redeemer of the Fatherland." Henceforth, William's chief aim was to counter the aggressions of Louis XIV. His ability to do this was appreciably strengthened in 1688 when leading English dissidents invited him to overthrow his uncle and father-in-law, James II, whose pro-Catholic policies had caused general alarm. So the Dutch Calvinist leader of Protestant Europe now became, for his English supporters, the acclaimed "savior" of Anglican England, and for their opponents, James's partisans, a foreign usurper whose sexuality was suspect. A Jacobite satirist affected surprise at this paradox:

> For the case, Sir, is such,
> The people think much,
> That your love is Italian, your government Dutch.
> Ah! who would have thought that a Low-Country stallion
> And a Protestant Prince should prove an Italian?[137]

William III was sober, serious, and as taciturn as his famous ancestor William the Silent. He was not, however, a puritan or bigot. Trained for war and statesmanship, he had little time for literature but a passion for art and architecture. Intelligent, judicious, and self-controlled, his manners were not ingratiating, and his reserve alienated the English political class, who never developed the warm regard for William they felt for his wife, Mary. In the field, despite much energetic valor, he was defeated at Steenkirk in 1692 and Landen in 1693 before he triumphed at Namur in 1695. Nevertheless, he successfully contained Louis by keeping together a difficult coalition of Protestant and Catholic states during several long campaigns. Bishop

78. William III. Sir Godfrey Kneller, oil, late seventeenth century.

Gilbert Burnet, who had known William for sixteen years and understood his sexual nature, wrote in his *History of His Own Times:* "I considered him as a person raised up by God to resist the power of France, and the progress of tyranny and persecution. The series of the five princes of Orange, that was now ended in him, was the noblest succession of heroes that we find in any history . . . After all the abatements that may be allowed for his errors and faults, he ought still to be reckoned among the greatest princes that our history, or indeed that any other, can afford."[138] French captains at Versailles, who had often fought him, admired him as "the finest prince in the world."[139]

William had married his cousin in 1677 in order to ally England with the Netherlands in the struggle against the French. But he soon developed a strong affection for Mary, who fell deeply in love with him. This did not, however, keep him from a ten-years' attachment to Elizabeth Villiers, one of her ladies in waiting, who was witty and intelligent and commonly perceived as his mistress. But William's strongest and most enduring bonds throughout his lifetime were with men. Of these, the most important was William Bentinck, a Dutch aristocrat a year older than William who had entered his household as a page at the age of sixteen. Like William, he was serious, capable, and conscientious; he soon became his closest friend, advisor, and trusted political intimate, a role he was to play for three decades. When at age twenty-five the prince's life was threatened by smallpox, his doctors, following a custom of the day, decreed that a young man of his own age should share his bed "to draw off the fever."[140] Bentinck, who had faithfully attended William in the sickroom, volunteered. The prince recovered; Bentinck himself contracted the disease but survived.

Their intimacy continued after William assumed the throne in England, where his enormous grants of land and mansions to his Dutch favorite aroused strong criticism in parliament. Then in 1692 a young Dutchman named Arnold Joost van Keppel attracted William's attention. Keppel was twenty-three, handsome, and in every way Bentinck's opposite, being lively and amusing and a keen womanizer. Soon Keppel had more access to the king than the older man, and Bentinck's apartments in Kensington Palace with their private door into William's were reassigned to Keppel. When Mary died from smallpox in 1694, the king, who had slept in his wife's room on a pallet for many days during the illness, was genuinely sick from grief. In this crisis he came to depend still more on the younger man.

The situation was not helped when the two favorites, who jarred on each other, quarreled in public. Bentinck, now earl of Portland, was reputedly the richest subject in Europe. Gifts were now also showered upon Keppel, who was granted a peerage as earl of Albemarle. Angry and jealous, the normally phlegmatic older man asked the king to relieve him of his court appointments so he might retire to private life. When William pressed him for an explanation, Bentinck's reply was a bombshell:

> Sire: it is your honour that I have at heart, and the kindnesses which Your Majesty shows to a young man and the manner in which you appear to authorize his liberties and impertinences make the world say things which I

> am ashamed to hear, and from which I believe you to be as far removed as any man in the world. I thought it was only the ill-intentioned in England who invented these outrageous things, but I was thunderstruck to find that The Hague and the army furnished the same sort of discourse and tarnished a reputation that has never before been subject to such attacks.[141]

Clearly, rumors of a love affair between the king and Keppel were circulating not only among William's enemies in England but also in his native Netherlands and in an army passionately devoted to the house of Orange. William, who still valued Bentinck highly, was greatly upset at the idea of parting from his friend of thirty years. He assured him that "I love you as tenderly as I have done all my life, though you will not believe it," and fashioned this reply:

> You tell me that you believe I am as far removed as any man in the world from the foul suspicions people are spreading about me, and you conclude that until you see the end of what is destroying me, you will show me by your withdrawal the sorrow you feel, and that it depends on my wisdom and prudence to protect my reputation. Assuredly this has always been very dear to me, but it seems a most extraordinary thing that one may not feel regard and affection for a young man without its being criminal. Whatever I can reasonably do to avoid such horrible calumnies I will do; but I confess I cannot understand your wanting to withdraw for such a reason. If it becomes known, as it will, it can only do me great harm, and as for you, everyone will blame your conduct extremely.[142]

We may note that Bentinck, in this exchange, affects not to believe the rumors, and the king, while deploring them, stops short of a clear denial. However, Bentinck's statement that the king had "never before been subject to such attacks" was inaccurate. Such attacks had in fact existed in abundance and had involved Bentinck himself.

The homosexuality of William's great-grandfather James I had never become a public issue in England, comment being confined to secret diaries and memoirs published after James's death. But by William's time the situation had changed. Free-spoken Restoration poets and dramatists had weakened the silence taboo and made the pretense that homosexuality was unknown in England difficult to maintain. More significant in the king's case was the virulent political atmosphere: the new parties (Whigs and Tories) were bitterly divided as to whether the Catholic James should be excluded from the throne. As in France under Henry III, a deadly national quarrel with its roots in religion led satirists to publicize a monarch's sexual preferences, a subject usually regarded as too delicate to broach.

Modern biographers of William III have avoided quoting these satires. Their wit is often feeble and their verse execrable, and the king's admirers, respecting him as a soldier, statesman, and Christian, have routinely dismissed them as politically motivated. Granted that the poems are indeed "singularly coarse" and vitriolically partisan, nevertheless the fact that they are monotonously reiterative on this theme should give us pause. We cannot simply assume on a priori grounds, as their editor does, that they are "probably groundless."[143]

Such attacks began to appear shortly after William's coronation in 1689 and named Bentinck as his lover. "The Coronation Ballad" is a parody of Bishop Burnet's coronation sermon by a Jacobite sympathizer who accuses the king of "buggering" Bentinck.[144] In these poems Bentinck is sometimes a "catamite," more often a "bardash," the English variant of the French *bardache*—a passive homosexual. "The Reflection," a poem attacking parliament for dethroning James II, proclaimed that "William van Nassau with Benting Bardasha/ Are at the old game of Gomorrha."[145] Another Jacobite satire called Bentinck the "catamite who rules alone the state"; several reiterated an ancient old association by accusing William of "playing the Italian" with his friend.[146] "Jenny Cromwell's Complaint against Sodomy" pretended to express the outrage of London prostitutes, alarmed that William had introduced a competitive vice. It began with a parody of Dryden's "Absalom and Achitophel":

> In pious times, ere bug-ry did begin,
> When women only ruled at in and in,
> [Then] Britons did encounter face to face,
> And thought a back stroke treacherous and base.[147]

The great preponderance of allegations of homosexuality focused on Bentinck. After 1692, however, as Keppel became influential, some pointed to him. One satire represented him and two other young courtiers as competing for favors from William:

> In love to his minions he partial and rash is,
> Makes statesmen of blockheads, and Earls of bardashes,
> His bed-chamber service he fills with young fellows,
> As Essex and Windsor, which makes Capell [sic] jealous.[148]

Clearly these lampoons, all of which try to ridicule, threaten, or degrade William by appeals to homophobic sentiment, come from sources inimical to the king for political reasons. But there is also evidence that originates with William's admirers.

We have already heard the testimony of the duchess of Orléans. As a granddaughter of James I's daughter Elizabeth, the unlucky queen of Bohemia, Madame took a keen interest in English affairs. She had romped with William as a child in The Hague and looked on bemusedly as her female relatives tried to arrange a marriage. Once settled in Paris with Monsieur, she followed William's career with curiosity, comparing him favorably with the hapless James II, now an exile at Versailles. Heedless of Catholic prejudice, she even defended him against a hostile abbé. "I would find the prince of Orange as wicked as you do," she told him, "if he had not been called and put on the throne by a people of his religion who believed themselves to have suffered enough oppression."[149]

"Liselotte" identified William as a homosexual repeatedly in her correspondence. In 1689 she wrote to her beloved Aunt Sophia in Hanover a bit superciliously, "We are told that the women of a small county in Ireland have revolted against King James and taken up arms for the Prince of Orange. It must be for the honour and glory alone, for no one can say that he has any kindness for their sex—he is believed to have very different inclinations."[150] When William turned out to be an affectionate husband, she wrote again in 1695: "It is true that people here think of King William as belonging to that brotherhood, but they say he is less taken up with it now."[151] But in 1701, a year before his death, she made him an archetype by speaking of men "who share the inclinations of king William."[152] This was not simply gossip picked up in Monsieur's circle; she claimed to have discussed homosexuality in England with English visitors.[153] Despite Madame's knowledge of the king's tastes, she expressed regret that she had not married him. In 1697 she wrote of the widower: "I have a true esteem for King William and if it is true that he wants my daughter, I should like it with all my heart."[154] However, she thought it unlikely he would marry again.

In the modern Netherlands homosexuality is no longer a damning stigma, and Henri and Barbara Van der Zee have been willing, in their dual biography of William and Mary, to accept the evidence for William's nonconformist orientation.[155] But for his principal English and American biographers the notion of a homosexual hero has seemed an intolerable contradiction. Stephen Baxter expresses admiration for William's political and military career but dismisses the charge of homosexuality as a "foul rumour" invented by William's French enemies.[156] According to Baxter, the calumny only gained currency in England after the king's apartments were connected by a private door to Keppel's, an arrangement Baxter explains by assuming the king needed his aide's assistance when he worked late at night.[157] Nesca Robb's authoritative biography at least attempts to review some of the evidence. But she is equally dismissive of the theory that William was a "pervert."[158] Her article on William III in the 1995 edition of the *Encyclopedia Britannica* sums up this Anglo-American consensus by declaring categorically in its concluding sentence, "A legend of William's homosexuality does not stand up to examination."[159]

It is William's friend and defender Bishop Burnet who has given Anglophone biographers most pause. In his laudatory *History* Burnet makes this cryptic remark: "He had no vice, but of one sort, in which he was very cautious and secret."[160] The standard response of those determined to avoid the slur of homosexuality has been to link these words to William's reputed affair with Elizabeth Villiers. To support this view, Robb cites an early sketch of the king's character written by Burnet in 1686–87 when he was an exile in Holland and later published as a *Supplement* to the *History.* There Burnet is a bit more forthcoming: "If he [the king] has been guilty of any of the disorders that are too common to princes, yet he has not practised them as some to whom he is nearly related have done, but has endeavoured to cover them; though let princes be as secret as they will in such matters they are always known."[161] H. C. Foxcroft had admitted in the 1902 edition of the supplement that these lines had "been open to the most sinister misconstructions" and invoked the Villiers affair to explain them.[162] Robb, taking the same tack, adds: "Neither the Nassaus nor the Stuarts were notoriously homosexual, and the reference is obviously to the Villiers scandal."[163] But this is to overlook not only James I but, more pertinently, William's homosexual Bourbon relatives, especially the notorious Monsieur.

How did the king's contemporaries respond to Burnet's "no vice, but of one sort"? In the case of Jonathan Swift we know the answer. Swift wrote many barbed comments in the margins of Burnet's *History* when it was published in 1723. Opposite "No vice, but of one sort" he observed indignantly, "It was of two sorts—*male* and *female*—in the *former* he was neither cautious nor secret." When Burnet calls the earl of Albemarle "King William's constant companion in all his diversions and pleasures," Swift responds, "very infamous pleasures."[164] Biographers favorable to the king have simply dismissed Swift's notes as Tory prejudice.

There is, however, an important passage in the *Supplement* that Baxter, Robb, and others have ignored. Speculating (before 1688) as to what might keep William from succeeding to the English throne, Bishop Burnet saw three difficulties. First, Dutch republicans would not want their stadtholder to assume royal rank. Second, the English would be leery of a foreign prince with a standing army of 30,000 at his command. Then he adds, "This and another particular, that is too tender to be put in writing, are the only things that can hinder him from being the greatest king that has been for many ages."[165] The editor of the *Supplement,* taking alarm at this admission, suggests that Burnet may once more be referring to Elizabeth Villiers. But this is to overlook the manners of the age. Augustus II of Saxony was elected king of Poland despite his reputation as the father of more than 300 illegitimate offspring. Louis XIV in France and Philip IV in Spain also fathered numerous bastards. If the English, who had tolerated the many mistresses of Charles II and James II, had been willing to consider only monogamous candidates for the throne, their choice at the end of the seventeenth century would have been difficult indeed. Even a bishop could hardly have believed they would so limit themselves. In 1714 George I of Hanover succeeded

Queen Anne despite the very visible German mistresses he brought to England. Bisexuality, however, was a more serious matter. As one epigrammatist hostile to William put it: "If a wily Dutch boor for the rape on a girl / Was hanged by the law's approbation, / Then what does he merit that buggers an Earl?"[166] The knowledge that the candidate he enthusiastically supported as king belonged to a class of men who were liable to an ignominious death at the hands of the public executioner might well have given Burnet pause.

William III's real achievements as a monarch have made it hard for admiring historians to acknowledge his sexual nature. Though the aristocratic class that controlled the English parliament disliked him as a foreigner who favored Dutch aides and was engrossed in international affairs, he was popular with the common people. He not only rebuilt the Dutch army so that it was capable of fending off Louis XIV, he also created a powerful English force to head a European coalition that opposed the growing power of France. In Ireland, on the other hand, "King Billy" left a mixed legacy. By defeating James II at the Battle of the Boyne he became the idolized hero of the Ulster Protestants and a symbol of tyranny to Irish Catholics. Yet William himself had favored a peace of reconciliation that Irish Protestant intransigence prevented.

Where other Stuart kings, like Charles I and James II, had moved England toward the absolutism of France, Spain, and Austria, William III accepted legal limits to royal power and in doing so established a liberal political system "that was to be the wonder of eighteenth-century Europe."[167] The Declaration of Rights to which he assented as a condition of assuming the throne created a precedent for the Bill of Rights in the American Constitution. To nineteenth-century liberal historians like Macaulay he was England's greatest king, whose Dutch heritage showed at its best in his treatment of religion: William favored religious rights for Protestant dissenters and for Catholics. The Toleration Act of 1689 provided the first legal guarantee of religious freedom in England, and press censorship was allowed to lapse in 1695, fifty years after Milton published his *Areopagitica.* At the end of the seventeenth century William III stood preeminent among the statesmen of Europe.

Arnold van Keppel, despite his debonair manners, proved an efficient, loyal, and devoted aide. His grief when the king died moved Madame to comment that none of her husband's lovers had been of this caliber. William Bentinck, despite his jealousy, remained in William's service, serving brilliantly in Paris in 1697 as the ambassador who negotiated the Peace of Ryswick. He met Madame, who noted the number of homosexual English aristocrats in his entourage.[168] The king died five years later, holding his hand. May we not acknowledge William III's achievements—and the fact that he was a committed Christian whom Bishop Burnet could praise as a man "raised up by God"—and at the same time recognize him as one of the greatest men in British history who have loved other men?

CHAPTER THIRTEEN

PRE-MEIJI JAPAN

800–1868

• Europe Discovers Japan •

After observing Renaissance Spain, France, and Italy with their virulent prejudice and grim executions, we must remind ourselves how differently nations outside the Christian West might view same-sex relations. Among them, China, as we have seen, provided a relatively tolerant milieu for male love affairs during this same era, informally institutionalizing such attachments and producing subtle and sympathetic works of fiction which explored their psychological complexities in ways that removed them from the realm of the demonic. Yet there was another culture even more striking in the contrast it presented to early modern Europe: this was Japan before the Meiji restoration of 1868.

For centuries Japan had existed on the periphery of Europe's consciousness only as Marco Polo's fabled but unvisited islands of Cipango. Then in the early 1540s some shipwrecked Portuguese sailors stumbled, in an almost literal sense, upon the country. At the end of the decade, Saint Francis Xavier, who had been serving as a Jesuit missionary at Goa in India, set sail for the new-found land, inspired by the glowing accounts he had heard of its inhabitants. Ten weeks in Satsuma on the western coast of the island of Kyushu convinced him they had not been overpraised. The people, he reported enthusiastically, "are the best who have as yet been discovered, and it seems to me that we shall never find among heathens another race to equal the Japanese."[1] Their sociability and good manners charmed him, their military ethic and sense of honor appealed to him as a Spanish aristocrat, and their eagerness to learn about Christianity flattered him. Other Jesuits wrote enraptured reports on the beauty of Japanese temples and gardens.

One custom, however, marred the picture. When Xavier visited the monks of the Zen monastery at Hakata, he found—to his horror—that "the abominable vice against nature is so popular that they practice it without any feeling of shame."[2] The monks had welcomed the missionaries in friendly fashion, thinking at first they might be some unknown sect of Indian Buddhists, but Xavier was too shocked for civility. He "loudly condemned the superior and the other monks for committing, shamelessly, such an odious and abominable crime."[3] He was shocked again to find that male love was also common among the samurai warriors who ruled the district. At Yamaguchi the local lord or daimyo, Ouchi Yoshitaka, received him warmly, keen to hear the doctrines of the *kirishitan.* A translator read a Japanese version of the Ten Commandments and appended a fiery denunciation of the sin of Sodom, which he called "more unclean than the pig and lower than the dog and other animals without reason."[4] Ouchi was understandably angry at this crude outburst, and the Jesuits, whom he peremptorily dismissed, feared they might be killed.

Further acquaintance convinced other Jesuits that male love was not merely a local but a national tradition—one the Japanese thought natural and meritorious. This astounded the followers of Loyola, who (forgetting the Greeks) had theorized that reason alone without revelation would convince men of the nefariousness of such conduct. Alessandro Valignano, a Jesuit administrator who visited Japan several times between 1579 and 1603, summed up the missionaries' views in a report to his superiors:

> Even worse [than adultery] is their great dissipation in the sin that will not bear mentioning. This is regarded so lightly that both the boys and the men who consort with them brag and talk about it openly without trying to cover the matter up. This is because the bonzes [priests] teach that not only is it not a sin but that it is even something quite natural and virtuous and as such the bonzes to a certain extent reserve this practice for themselves. They are forbidden under grave penalties by ancient laws and customs to have the use of women and so they find a remedy for their disorderly appetites by preaching this pernicious doctrine to the blind pagans . . . Their great influence over the people, coupled with the customs handed down by their forefathers, completely blinds the Japanese, who consequently do not realize how abominable and wicked is this sin, as reason itself plainly shows.[5]

At first Catholic missions met with some success. They endured for nearly a century before Christianity was extirpated with horrible cruelties by the Japanese, who feared its converts might, as in the Philippines, provide a base for European conquest. During this time the Jesuits repeatedly blamed the Japanese for three special sins: idolatry (that is, Buddhism), abortion, and sodomy. How, we may ask, did this last "sin," which the Japanese called *nanshoku,* or the "love of males," become an honored way of life among the country's religious and military leaders so that its acceptance paralleled, and in some respects even surpassed, ancient Athens?

• The Buddhist Priesthood •

Verifiable, as opposed to legendary, Japanese history hardly exists before 552, when Buddhism was first introduced from China. Being a less developed culture with no written language, the Japanese took far more from the Chinese than the Romans did, for instance, from the Greeks. With Buddhism came a flood of other influences: calligraphy, art, and literature, the idea of a centralized imperial state, and, later, Confucian philosophy and Taoist beliefs about sex. For several hundred years, educated Japanese males so favored the Chinese language for their serious literary efforts and imitated Chinese literary models so slavishly that it was left to women, like the Lady Murasaki and Sei Shōnagon, to create the first masterpieces of Japanese vernacular literature.

As a result of these influences, Chinese traditions of the love of the cut sleeve and the shared peach helped establish the legitimacy of male love in Japan. Of this favorable culture the West has remained largely ignorant, for only recently have Japanese and American scholars brought to light this fascinating forgotten world. "The Japanese *nanshoku* tradition," Gary Leupp tells us, in his wide-ranging historical survey, "drew heavily upon that of the Chinese. Tokugawa works [1603–1868] on the topic repeatedly allude to famous homosexual relationships in the Chinese past, to continental homoerotic literature, and to Taoist and *yin-yang* theories of sexuality."[6] Seventeenth-century Japanese sources cite the chivalry of the emperor Ai, the love of the duke of Wei for Mizi Xia, and of the Han emperors for such favorites as Jiri and the musician Li Yannian.[7]

Moreover, unlike Republican Rome, Japan does not seem to have had any countervailing negative native traditions to overcome. Homosexuality was not, as in Rome, associated with slavery. Japanese Shintoism was principally concerned with propitiatory rites and ceremonies; its mythology fostered nationalism through the cult of divine emperors, but it had no special code of morals and seems to have regarded sex as a natural phenomenon to be enjoyed with few inhibitions. Phallic shrines dotted the countryside. Premarital virginity was not rigidly insisted upon, and freeborn boys did not lose status if they had adult lovers. Early law codes penalized incest and bestiality but not homosexual relations. The gods of the Shinto pantheon were themselves highly sexual. In later times, some came to be seen as "guardian deities" of male love. These myths were not normative, however, like the stories of Ganymede and Hyacinth in ancient Greece and seem not to have arisen until the Tokugawa period.[8]

Some Japanese accounts placed the beginnings of *nanshoku* in the eighth and ninth centuries, but these reputed instances seem problematic and uncertain.[9] One early tradition of consequence, however, held that homosexuality had been "invented" by the bodhisattva Monju or Monjushiri. Bodhisattvas were Buddhist saints who had achieved enlightenment on earth but who, out of compassion, delayed their assent to Nirvana in order to help others achieve this goal. Monju was specifically the bodhisattva of wisdom. Here is a parallel with China's Yellow Emperor.

By far the most important tradition, however, ascribed the introduction of male love to the Buddhist sage Kūkai, who, after his death, came to be known as Kōbō Daishi ("The Great Teacher"). Kūkai, perhaps Japan's most revered religious figure, was an ascetic monk who in 806 returned from two years of study in Tang China to found Shingon ("True Way") Buddhism in Japan. In time he became a semi-legendary figure, a cultural hero who combined the renown of a Saint Patrick and a Leonardo. Kūkai wrote many influential religious texts, won fame as an artist and calligrapher, oversaw major engineering works, created (it was said) the syllabary that was used to adapt Chinese ideographs to the Japanese language, and founded a monastery on Mount Kōya which remains to this day one of Japan's chief religious centers.

That the Japanese in the course of time associated male love with Kōbō Daishi indicates the prestige of the "Way of Youth," as it came to be called. There is an exuberant reference to this tradition—the earliest known—in a Chinese poem by the famed Zen monk Ikkyū, who lived from 1394 to 1481:

> Monju, the holy one, first opened this path;
> Kōbō of Kongō [Kōbō Daishi] then revived it.
> Without male and female,
> its pleasures are like an endless circle;
> men shout with pleasure when they attain entrance.[10]

Then in 1676 a literary scholar named Kitamura Kigin put together an anthology of poems and stories celebrating male love, which he entitled *Wild Azaleas.* His title came from a wistful poem ascribed to Shinga Sōzu, one of Kūkai's ten chief disciples, which Kigin took as an emblematic expression of male love:

> Memories of love revive
> like wild azaleas bursting into bloom
> on mountains of evergreen;
> my stony silence only shows
> how much I love you.[11]

Kigin's preface to his anthology, justifying *nanshoku* in a Buddhist context, confirms the details of Valignano's negative report a century earlier but strikes a decidedly different note:

> It has been in the nature of men's hearts to take pleasure in a beautiful woman since the age of male and female gods, but to become intoxicated by the blossom of a handsome youth . . . would seem to be both wrong and

> unusual. Nevertheless, the Buddha preached that Mt. Imose [associated with heterosexual love] was a place to be avoided and the priests of the law entered this Way [*wakashudō,* "the Way of Youth"] as an outlet for their feelings, since their hearts were, after all, made of neither stone nor wood. Like water that plunges from the peak of Tsukubane to form the deep pools of the Minano River, this love has surpassed in depth the love between women and men in these latter days. It plagues the heart not only of courtier and aristocrat (this goes without saying) but also of brave warriors. Even the mountain dwellers who cut brush for fuel have learned to take pleasure in the shade of young saplings.[12]

This preface overleaps a millennium and a continent to reveal an ethos we have not encountered since the dialogues of Plato and Plutarch.

Despite the crucial role of Buddhism in determining Japanese attitudes toward male love, the earliest affairs we can document involve not monks but aristocrats of the classical Heian period, which stretched from 794 to 1185. Courtiers who attended the emperor at his court at Heian-an (modern Kyoto) were not samurai warriors (who did not appear in Japan until later) but sensitive aesthetes for whom good taste in poetry, calligraphy, dress, and perfumery was paramount. Nowhere is this world reflected more brilliantly than in "The Tale of Genji" by Lady Murasaki. Despite its hyper-refined personae, this enormously complex novel is a psychological masterpiece that traces the course of many love affairs in its thousand pages. Only once, however, does Murasaki touch on same-sex attraction. In chapter two the irresistibly handsome and cultivated Prince Genji pursues a young married woman, using her brother as a go-between. The boy—"a particularly attractive lad of perhaps twelve or thirteen"—is "of a quiet, pleasant disposition" with "some aptitude for the classics."[13] Much taken with Genji's good looks, the boy is eager to carry his letters. When his sister rejects the prince, Genji's disappointment, we are told, "had the boy on the point of tears." Finally the frustrated amorist turns to the brother: "'Well, you at least must not abandon me.' Genji pulled the boy down beside him. The boy was delighted, such were Genji's youthful charms. Genji, for his part, or so one is informed, found the boy more attractive than his chilly sister."[14] Murasaki presents her hero's bisexuality perfectly casually, but this is an unique episode in the book's fifty-six chapters.

Lady Murasaki is thought to have written "The Tale of Genji" about 1020 or 1030. Records of love affairs between men begin to appear in courtiers' diaries shortly after. Gary Leupp identifies them in the diaries of Ōe Tadafusa (1040–1111), Fujiwara Yoringa (1120–1156), and Fujiwara Kanezane (1147–1207). In Heian times, the Fujiwara family was the most prominent in Japan, maintaining its power by marrying its daughters to successive emperors. Some entries are remarkably candid, as Leupp tells us: "Yoringa, for example, mentions sexual encounters with several partners, ranging from menservants to aristocrats. The first of these occurs in 1142, when the young Yoringa summons a dancer to his home at midnight. Twice in 1147 he mentions going to bed with such entertainers, and on the fifth day of the first month of 1148 he writes, 'Tonight I took Yoshimasa to bed and really went wild: it was especially satisfying. He had been ill for awhile and resting, so tonight was the first night [since his recovery].'"[15] Yoringa's diaries also identify two Heian emperors, contemporaries of England's Norman kings, who slept with boys—Shirakawa (r. 1073–1087), a strong-willed ruler who dominated Japan for forty-three years after his retirement, and his grandson Toba (r. 1107–1123), a devout Buddhist.

During Japan's middle ages, however, it was love affairs between Buddhist monks and monastic acolytes, known as *chigo,* that are most prominent. Specific terms, which Leupp has traced to the early 1100s, distinguished the lovers: the older monk was known as a *nenja,* the teenage boy as a *nyake.* Later, other expressions arose: "By the seventeenth century the senior partner was called the 'older brother' *[anibun]* and the junior, the 'younger brother' *[otōtobun];* the relation itself was called a 'brotherhood bond' *[kyōdai musubi].* The pair ritually swore loyalty to one another, and, at least in later periods, documented their relationship with a written oath."[16] We may note the parallels with ancient Greece and imperial China.

The vast collection of tales from India, China, and Japan compiled about 1100 and known as the *Konjaku,* whose stories (in twenty-eight volumes) exceed the thousand and one tales of the *Arabian Nights,* also records male loves. So do the *Tales from Uji,* dated a century later. One of these recounts, with some psychological acumen, the story of Fujiwara no Zōyo, high priest of a temple near Kyoto, who died in 1116. Enamored of a novice who is a popular dancer and acrobat, Zōyo persuades him to become a priest so that he may always be near him. The boy, out of affection for the older man but against his own inclination, agrees and puts on priestly dress. The affair wanes, however, until one day the high priest asks the boy to put on the clothes he wore when they first met and to dance for him. When he does, their love revives, and the priest regrets having induced the boy to leave his secular calling.[17]

The same period also produced some of the greatest masterpieces of Japanese erotic art. These *shunga* scrolls appeared in large numbers and freely depict every kind of sexual activity, combining explicitness with a high degree of artistry. "To the traditional Japanese," a modern encyclopedia tells us, "sex was neither a romantic ideal of love nor a phallic rite of the gods; it represented simply the joyful union of the sexes and a natural function. *Shunga* were thus considered a normal subject of the Japanese artist, no more improper or degrading than the painting of a nude or a classical love scene seemed to a Western contemporary."[18] Many scrolls portray homosexual behavior, nearly always in the form of anal intercourse. The most notable of these, historically and artistically, is the so-called *Acolyte's Scroll (Chigo no sōshi),* now housed in the Daigoji Treasure House at the Sambōin Temple south of Kyoto. Art historians have suggested that, barring its subject, the *Acolyte's Scroll* might well have been ranked as a National Treasure.[19]

Closely identified with *nanshoku* was Zen Buddhism, introduced in 1236 from China, where it had already been cultivated for many centuries. Its austere discipline appealed to the new samurai warrior class, and Zen consequently attained a special political significance. In addition, Zen had an immense effect on Japanese secular culture, influencing poetry, painting, calligraphy, landscape gardening, and the ritual of the tea ceremony. Zen monks who composed poetry usually wrote in Chinese and, unlike their Chinese counterparts, made male love an important theme in their work. Katō Shūichi, in his history of early Japanese literature, notes: "The development of this kind of homosexual poetry and prose was one of the great contributions made by the Zen Sect to the culture of Japan in the Muromachi period." Katō quotes a poem from the *Ryūsuishū* (1462) of Tōshō Shūgen, whose imagery transports us to Ming China:

> We passed the night in the same bed,
> And now looking at the pale moon at dawn through the window
> Our two shadows fall on the curtain,
> A pair of mandarin ducks.
> I would celebrate the night's joy of love forever.
> Our temple is like Kimshan Temple on the Yang-Tse.[20]

The most notable medieval Japanese literary works treating of male love, however, are the so-called *chigo monogatari,* or acolyte tales, which portray the loves of Buddhist priests or monks for boys in monasteries. Margaret Childs has put us in her debt by translating two of the most poignant stories—the "Tale of Genmu" and *Aki no Yo no Nagamonogatari (A Long Tale for an Autumn Night).* The "Tale of Genmu" (which has a postscript dated 1486 but is likely older) is a story of a love affair imbued with Buddhist religious feeling.[21] The monk Genmu sees a youth at a vow-taking ceremony whose beauty overwhelms him: "The luster of his disheveled hair brought to mind cherry blossoms drooping under a spring rain on a quiet evening, or the limp branches of a willow at dawn. No word or picture could have conveyed his loveliness. He was a truly elegant sight."[22]

The departure of the boy, Hanamatsu, from the shrine is delayed by a snowfall, and he and Genmu spend an evening composing linked poems. Returning to his hut "with love-stricken heart," Genmu finds that "the image of the boy with whom he had fallen in love displaced all his pious thoughts."[23] But when, at the youth's invitation, he returns at night to Hanamatsu's monastery, he can find no shelter except a deserted hall, where he hears the eerie sound of a flute, "delightful and frightening." The player is Hanamatsu, and once more they spend the long night composing poems. Then the boy gives him the flute and disappears.

In the morning Gemnu learns that Hanamatsu had died seventeen days earlier avenging his slain father: he, Gemnu, had passed the night with a ghost. Genmu is overcome with grief and guilt and feels some religious compunctions: "In anguish and sorrow he reflected: 'I stupidly let myself become entangled in an attachment, in a romantic passion, and so have encountered a spirit . . . If we would just stop long enough to think about it, the fact that we must all grow old and die is only too obvious . . . I was deluded! How ashamed I am! The *Lotus Sutra* repudiates love for novices and youths as something to be avoided. Genshin, in the *Teachings Essential for Rebirth* . . . asserts that such love is punished in the third hell. Could it lead to anything but continued rebirth in this world?'"[24] The Lotus Sutra, an early Indian work, deprecated the love of youths; Genshin was a Japanese priest whose *Teachings* (984) were widely known in later centuries, though his negative judgment on *nanshoku* was all but ignored.[25]

Worshiping at Kōbō Daishi's shrine on Mount Kōya, Gemnu meets a young monk of twenty who turns out to be Hanamatsu's slayer. The youth and beauty of his victim have already aroused the young man's remorse and led him to take up a religious life. He and Genmu grieve and practice religious austerities until they die, some forty years later. They achieve Buddhahood in the Western Paradise, sharing the same lotus seat throughout eternity. It is then revealed that Hanamatsu was in fact a manifestation of the bodhisattva Monju, who had chosen this means to bring both men to enlightenment. The story rests on a paradox inconceivable in medieval Christianity—the forbidden love affair had led to salvation.

It has been suggested that the tale of Genmu was influenced by *A Long Tale for an Autumn Night,* which appears in a manuscript written some time before 1377.[26] Master Keikai is a high-ranking priest and teacher who has gained literary fame and military honor for the "fierce courage [of] his conquering sword."[27] But he is ashamed of neglecting his religious duties for these worldly pursuits and goes to pray for salvation to the bodhisattva Kannon at Ishiyama. (Kannon was the bodhisattva of "infinite compassion," whom Japanese Christians identified with the Virgin.) At the shrine he falls in love with a beautiful aristocratic youth of sixteen. Despite the boy's own deeply pious nature, he returns Keikai's affection and visits his room at night:

> They wept as they opened their hearts to each other. Sincere were the vows they expressed as they lay together. Nor were their sweet words of love exhausted when in the cold room, their dreams were suddenly shattered. Short of time, their tears impossible to quench, they listened resentfully to the chirruping of a bird perched on a bamboo branch that announced the

> break of day . . . The light of the dawn moon broke into the room from the west window. In the youth's eyes, framed by his sleep-tousled hair, was a slightly bewildered look. At this sight and the thought of how he would miss the youth, the Master felt that he could not survive a separation.[28]

Despite Buddhism's formal proscription of *nanshoku,* there is no reference to any moral conflict in this particular tale.

But when the boy leaves his monastery to return the priest's visit, he is waylaid by goblins who keep him prisoner for months in a gloomy cave. His fellow monks blame the monks of Keikai's monastery for his disappearance, and a bloody feud breaks out in which thousands die. On escaping, the boy finds his monastery reduced to ashes. He drowns himself, and Keikai finds his discarded clothes on the bank of the stream. Mourning his dead lover, he becomes a solitary hermit "wakened from the dreams of the floating world." The patron spirit of his monastery then reveals the divine plan: "Keikai's enlightenment was accomplished by the Ishiyama Kannon's manifesting herself as a youth."[29] These events, and Keikai's exemplary life, lead to the salvation of many others. Once again, a romantic love affair has worked a religious miracle.

• Samurai and Shoguns •

In the next stage of Japanese history the love of youths was to take on political and military significance as a crucial element in a feudal warrior society. Feudalism attained dominance in Japan in the twelfth century for the same reason it arose in Europe—because of the breakdown of an effective central authority. The Heian emperors in Kyoto lost control of the country, their administrations ceased to function, and local lords took command. Violent disturbances marked the reign of the emperor Go-Shirakawa (r. 1156–1158), who like many of his predecessors ruled most potently after his official retirement—in this case for an additional thirty-four years. A devout Buddhist and a fine musician, Go-Shirakawa fell in love with the youthful Fujiwara Nobuyori, whom he raised to a position of power. The affair ended tragically, however: the young man was executed in 1159 when he betrayed the emperor during the Heiji rebellion.[30]

The Heiji rebellion proved to be a definitive event in Japanese history. It ended with the triumph of the warlord Minamoto Yoritomo, whose power Go-Shirakawa recognized in 1192 by naming him shogun, or military commander. For over 600 years men holding this title acted in the name of emperors who became ceremonial puppets. To escape the influence of the court aristocracy, Yoritomo set up his headquarters at Kamakura, a town 150 miles to the east, on a bay near modern Tokyo, inaugurating the so-called Kamakura age of Minamoto shoguns, which lasted until 1333.

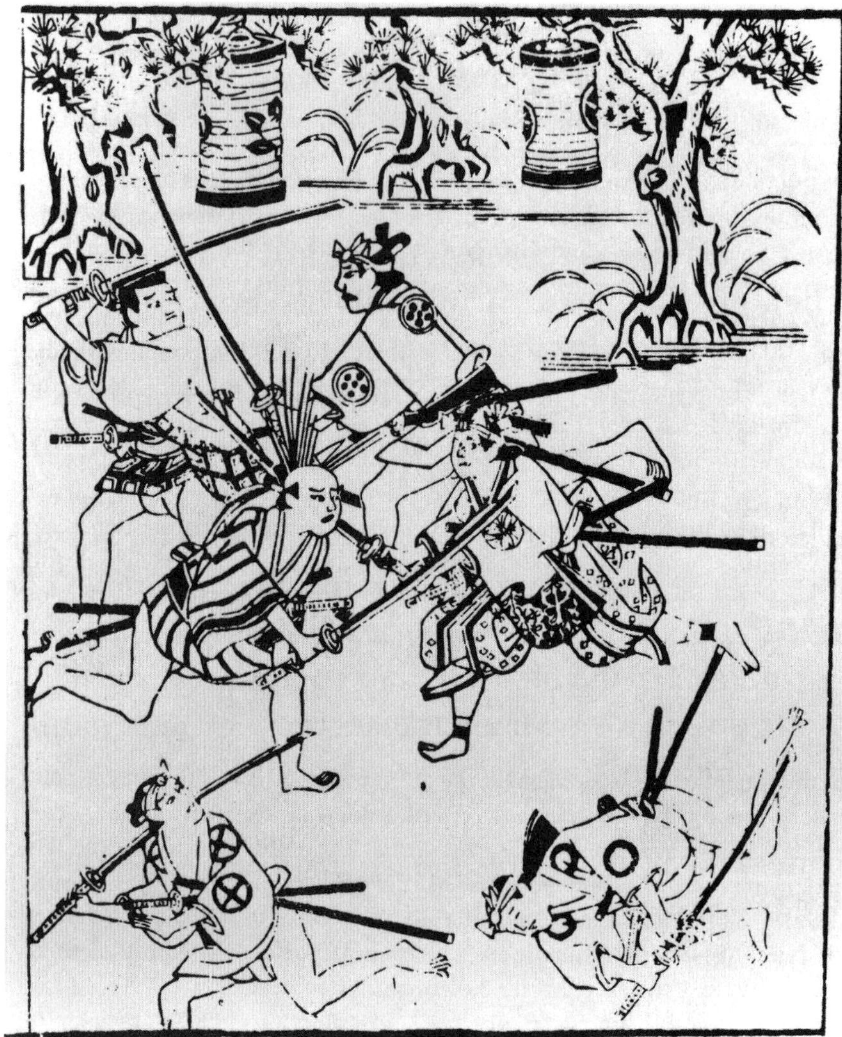

79. A Samurai and his lover fight off their enemies. Illustration, Saikaku, *Great Mirror of Male Love (Nanshoku ōkagami)*, 1687.

This redoubtable founder of Japan's first military government has been described as an "unloved figure" in Japanese history. One of the few humanizing touches in the story of his triumph was his relation with his lover Yoshinao, a young officer in the Imperial Guard.[31] In this as in so much else, Yoritomo set a significant precedent. In the following war-torn centuries handsome young men played an important part in many shoguns' lives. Such youths were not frail and delicate flowers like the temple acolytes but were, more often, apprentice warriors. They were called *wakashu,* and love for them was known as *wakashudō* or simply *shudō.* As in Greece, the lover was supposed to prove himself by a willingness to die for the beloved. A seventeenth-century defender of male love claimed (erroneously) that the lover for whom the Chinese emperor Ai had cut his brocaded sleeve had sacrificed himself for the emperor and had thus inspired the tradition of "a retainer's committing suicide to follow his lord to the grave in both China and Japan." In fact, as we have seen, the young man was killed by hostile members of the court after Ai's death. Nevertheless, the spokesman for *nanshoku* declares that "most of those who storm the battlefield, warding off the enemy and accompanying their lords to the end, are the lords' male sex-partners *[gomotsu]*."[32]

But in real life feudal obligations and the demands of idealized love might well conflict. A samurai might fall in love with a page who was his overlord's bedmate. Or his duty to his lord might require him to kill his lover or someone close to him. An exemplary tale of this sort is Ihara Saikaku's "Tragic Love of Two Enemies," from his *Tales of the Samurai Spirit* (1688). After Senpatji is ordered by his feudal lord to kill his best friend, the friend's widow retires to a remote province where she bears a son named Shynosuke. Years later Senpatji, unaware of their identity, comes upon the woman and the boy living in poverty; struck by their personal refinement, he rescues them and falls in love with the son. When the mother realizes who Senpatji is, she orders the boy to kill him. Shynosuke protests that he cannot kill their benefactor, but Senpatji protests, "I am happy to die at your hands. Come, kill me, and avenge your father." The mother overhears and tells them, "I admire you both. Each is a man of honor. Love each other again for this one night. I wish to grant you such an interval." The grim tale ends when the mother enters the room in the morning and sees that "Shynosuke had pierced Senpatji's heart with his sword which passed through his own breast and out at his back."[33]

As in ancient Greece, Japanese culture idealized *shudō* as a source of morality and military courage. In 1482, at the moment when Ficino was expounding Platonic love in Florence, a Japanese essayist named Ijiri Chusuke wrote:

> In our empire of Japan, this way flourished from the time of the great Master Kōbō particularly. And in the abbeys of Kyoto and Kamakura . . . and in the world of the nobles and warriors, lovers would swear perfect and eternal love, relying on no more than their mutual goodwill. Whether their partners were noble or common, rich or poor, was absolutely of no importance. Consequently, some abandoned their property or lost rank as a result of their passion, while others gained a fine position or acquired a name thanks to their love . . . This way must be truly respected and it must never be allowed to disappear.[34]

The anonymous treatise *Shin'yu-ki* (*Records of Soulmates,* 1643) appealed to the Buddhist concepts of compassion *(jihī)* and sympathetic love *(nasake).*

It made sensitivity to a lover a religious duty which some may have found difficult to abide by: "There are few beautiful young men who have soul. This confirms the proverb that beauty is in general soulless. He who is born infirm may perhaps have been beautiful in his previous life and yet did not respond to his admirer. Such physical deformity is the result of a lack of soul in a previous life . . . Even if you are unable to take him who loves you into your heart, you should try and make *giri* [obligation] your rule of conduct."[35] Other moralists thought *shudō* was necessary to promote "gentleness of speech" and the "refinement of polite behavior," even arguing that "if you learn the teachings of the Buddha and expect to achieve Awakening, you will surely practice *shudō*. For this way is really like that of the true Awakening in that we may give ourselves wholly to it."[36]

But what of the older partner? If the boy was to cultivate *nasake* and *giri* (love and duty), what qualities should mark the ideal *nenja?* Tsuneo Watanabe has summarized the ideals set forth in a book called *Nanshoku jussum no kagami* (*A Ten-Inch Mirror for Male Love,* 1687):

> So, in order to reward the *wakashu* for his *giri,* the *nenja* is duty-bound to see to his education. "It is a grave fault not to teach a *wakashu* to distinguish between the true and the false. This must never be forgotten." "If a *wakashu* is unreasonable, we can imagine the soul of his lover." He who cannot educate his beloved is not fit to practise *shudō.* We may conclude then, setting aside for a moment the question of its practical realization, that after a long period of development, the Japanese tradition of homosexuality finally reached the level of the erotic pedagogy of Ancient Greece.[37]

When we try to trace Japanese male love in the shogunate, we find much drama but hardly this high idealism. The rule of the Minamoto shoguns came to an end when the emperor Go-Daigo restored imperial power in 1333. But Go-Daigo was betrayed by his chief supporter, Ashikaga Takauji, who set up a rival emperor five years later and became the new shogun. Takauji now moved his military headquarters from Kamakura to the Muromachi district of Tokyo, which gave its name to a new period of Japanese culture (1338–1573). Muromachi Japan produced fifteen Ashikaga shoguns, six of whom, including Takauji, are known to have had *wakashu* lovers.[38] If we include also the Tokugawa shoguns who succeeded them in the seventeenth and eighteenth centuries, we may conjecture that at least half of the twenty-six shoguns who ruled Japan from 1338 to 1837 had male love affairs.[39]

Constantly bedeviled by bloody struggles for power, the Ashikaga shogunate eventually lost control of a country which sank into anarchic civil war. Nevertheless, Muromachi Japan shone with cultural achievements which set the norms for Japanese art and literature. The age reached its first zenith under Takauji's grandson Yoshimitsu, who reigned from 1367 to 1394 and then from retirement to 1408. Though Yoshimitsu was an able leader who consolidated Ashikaga power, he won his greatest fame by his patronage of art and scholarship in a court which in some respects paralleled the court Cosimo de'Medici would preside over in Florence a generation later. This golden age produced the brilliant Kitayama era, named after the district in Kyoto where Yoshimitsu built himself a splendid palace in which to enjoy his very active retirement. Here, the culture of Buddhist monks, of the ancient Heian aristocracy, and of the new military leaders coalesced and flourished. This Japanese renaissance was notable for the "Five Mountain" poetry of Zen Buddhism, for its ink painting, its architecture (most notably the Golden Pavilion that Yoshimitsu built on his Kitayama estate), and above all for the development of Nō drama into a sophisticated literary form.

Yoshimitsu's son Yoshimochi, the fourth Ashikaga shogun (r. 1395–1428), loved a young samurai named Akamatsu Mochisada, a prince of the powerful Akamatsu family. A fifteenth-century history tells the tale: "A very beautiful young man [Mochisada] was granted three provinces simply through the homosexual favors of the lord [Yoshimochi]. Proud of this favor, he conducted himself in such an arbitrary manner that he committed injustices that caused everyone to frown; but no one dared accuse this favorite lover. However, Akamatsu Mitsusuke, head of the clan of the Akamatsu, considering this [misconduct] a dishonor to the clan, brought many great lords to his side and issued an accusation against Mochisada, who was unable to deny his guilt."[40] This forced the hand of Yoshimochi, who ordered his lover to commit *seppuku.* The shogun never forgave Mitsusuke and until his death bore a bitter hatred.

Yoshimochi's younger brother, Yoshinori (r. 1429–1441), had been a Buddhist monk since the age of ten. When, at thirty-five, he unexpectedly became shogun, he laicized himself and proved to be a surprisingly strong ruler. Yoshinori enjoyed the performances of young entertainers at the temples and brought them into his palace retinue, where they had no choice but to share his bed. But a passionate affair with a young man was to cost Yoshinori his life. Once again, Akamatsu Mitsusuke played a fateful role. When Yoshinori made plans to bestow three provinces belonging to Mitsusuke on his young lover, Mitsusuke, in revenge, invited Yoshinori to a banquet in Kyoto and killed him.[41]

More disasters followed under Yoshinori's successor as the fortunes of the Ashikaga family took an ominous turn and incessant feuds erupted finally into a fierce rebellion, the Ōnin War of 1467–1477, at the end of which Kyoto lay in ruins. Not until a century later was unity restored following the campaigns of the "three heroes of unification," the great warlords Oda Nobunaga, Toyotomo Hideyoshi, and Tokugawa Ieyasu. Finally, in 1603, the Tokugawa dynasty of shoguns came to power, and a desolated country entered upon an unprecedented two and a half centuries of peace.

⋅ Nō Drama and Kabuki ⋅

The world's oldest extant professional theater is the Nō theater of Japan. Nō developed out of a crude mixture of popular folk dances, religious dances, and acrobatics that bore the undignified name of *sarugaku*—literally, "monkey music." Its transformation into a highly stylized aristocratic art of ceremonious refinement took place in the fourteenth century and owed much to a shogun's love for a boy actor.

In 1374 the twelve-year-old Zeami performed before Ashikaga Yoshimitsu. This was a defining moment in the history of Japanese drama, for Yoshimitsu—himself only seventeen—was highly appreciative of the beauty and talent of the young boy. From this attachment sprang 500 years of shogunal patronage of what had been hitherto an undistinguished entertainment. With Yoshimitsu's encouragement, Zeami raised the literary level of Nō and wrote a score of its major classics. Nevertheless, Yoshimitsu's close ties with the actor-playwright did not go uncriticized. When, four years after their first meeting, the young shogun witnessed a traditional festival in the company of his handsome favorite, a nobleman named Go-oshikō Kintada disapproved: "The child from the Yamato *sarugaku* troupe . . . was called to join him, and he followed the proceedings from the shogun's box. The shogun has shown an extraordinary fondness for him ever since. He sat with the boy and shared drinks with him. *Sarugaku* like this is the occupation of beggars, and such favor for a *sarugaku* player indicates disorder in the nation."[42] A sexual relationship would not have disturbed Kintada, but Yoshimitsu's treating a boy who ranked as an outcast as a social equal was galling to his aristocratic pride.

Nijō Yoshimoto, the court's senior statesman and himself a respected poet, was more sympathetic and seems indeed to have been as overwhelmed by the young actor-dramatist's charms as the shogun, as a surviving letter suggests:

> Should [Zeami] have time, please bring him over with you once again. The entire day was wonderful and I quite lost my heart. A boy like this is rare—why, look at his *renga* [linked verse] and court kickball, not to mention his own particular art! Such a charming manner and such poise! I don't know where such a marvelous boy can have come from . . . I should compare him to a profusion of cherry or pear blossoms in the haze of a spring dawn . . . It's no surprise that the shogun is so taken with this boy . . . In spite of myself, I feel as if the flower of the heart still remains somewhere in this fossilized old body of mine.[43]

Yoshimoto is reputed to have formed Zeami's subtle and allusive poetic style by educating him in the Japanese classics. His plays remain the seminal works of Nō drama, an austere art which, with its esoteric poetry, highly stylized gestures, and glacial pace, still commands a devoted audience in Japan.

Though a Japanese bibliography lists seventeen Nō plays which treat the theme of male love, the subject has been little explored.

The origins of kabuki were, if anything, even less respectable than Nō. In 1603, in a dry riverbed in Kyoto, a temple attendant named Okuni performed dances whose appeal was more sexual than religious. An immediate sensation, she organized a troupe of women whose performances advertised their availability as after-hours prostitutes. Quarrels broke out over the women, and in 1629 the government banned the so-called women's kabuki, a term that signified "eccentric" or "off-beat" and carried a hint of titillating improprieties. It was replaced by the boy's kabuki, in which boys in their early teens played the roles of both sexes and were, like their predecessors, on call for private intimacies. A seventeenth-century account noted that "they have produced a theater called *wakashu* kabuki in which the dancers are young men. Many men were so enchanted by their charms that they ended up swearing their eternal love and becoming ill by seriously wounding their arms," as a proof of their devotion.[44] Since the samurai fought just as tempestuously over the boys as they had over the women, in 1652 the *wakashu* kabuki was also banned.

The government now insisted that kabuki roles should be played by "adult" men, that is, males over fifteen who had shaved the forelocks that were traditionally worn by Japanese youths. They also required that kabuki plays should be more than erotic come-ons and should have regular plots. These changes and the fact that performing in kabuki might now be a lifelong profession helped turn it into a serious art with highly accomplished practitioners. Eros, however, was wilier than the authorities. The younger actors, wearing purple scarves to hide the embarrassment of their shaven pates, continued to allure patrons. The novelist Ihara Saikaku was amused at one unexpected result of the ban on forelocks. "Theater proprietors and the boys' managers alike," he wrote, "were upset at the effect it might have on business, but looking back on it now the law was probably the best thing that ever happened to them. It used to be that no matter how splendid the boy, it was impossible for him to keep his forelocks and take on patrons beyond the age of twenty. Now, since everyone wore the hairstyle of adult men, it was still possible at age 34 or 35 for youthful looking actors to get under a man's robe."[45]

Some kabuki players carried the gender ambiguities of the stage into real life. These were the men who played women's roles, the so-called *onnagata* or *oyama*. Writing on his art, one successful female impersonator held that "one cannot become an excellent *oyama* without living as a woman in ordinary life. In fact his masculinity betrays itself easily in him who makes an effort of will to become a woman on the stage."[46] These popular stars often dressed as women at home and on the street and attracted lovers of both sexes, like their counterparts in the Peking Opera. Eventually skilled male

80. Onnagata actor as a singing girl. Torii Kiyotune, silk painting, eighteenth century.

"actresses" of sixty came to play nubile girls of sixteen, to the critical acclaim of connoisseurs.

We are told that *shudō* pieces once performed on the kabuki stage "are now lost and have passed from the modern repertoire."[47] An eighteenth-century treatise, *The Actors' Analects,* assures us that they had once been popular and that the actors who played the boys' parts were even more in demand than the *onnagatta.* "In plays in former times the theme of male love very often occurred. Principal actors playing young men often received larger salaries [even] than those playing women. At that time homosexual love was the rage in all the quarters of the town."[48]

Within the theater and outside, prostitution thrived and even set standards of taste in high society. One moralist complained that daimyo and women of rank now copied the speech and manners of actor-prostitutes.[49] With the coming of peace, cities grew at a remarkable rate, as samurai were required to move from their rural estates into towns. In 1550 few cities in Japan had over 50,000 inhabitants. By 1700 Edo, with a million inhabitants, was perhaps the world's largest city, and with this urban growth a large and wealthy business class arose. In the Confucian social hierarchy such merchants, regarded as mere unproductive traders, ranked at the bottom of the social scale below the samurai, the food-growing peasants, and the artisans. Denied any political power, they had the wherewithal to enjoy themselves amply in the new civic pleasure quarters which the samurai were in theory forbidden to enter. In contrast with Europe, where the new middle class provided the backbone for puritanical religious movements, the Japanese middle class were unabashed hedonists, while many samurai, impoverished by peace and falling agricultural prices, lived in penury in the new money economy. It was the middle class which provided the chief patrons for kabuki theater, for shops selling art works, and for the brothels with their cultivated courtesans of both sexes.

In France and other European countries, male homosexuality was decried as an aristocratic vice. By contrast, in the new cities of Japan the new middle class was eager to embrace this samurai tradition. But these relationships fell short of the heroic warrior ideals of earlier ages; rather than "brotherhood bonds," they were frequently commercial transactions, sometimes glamorous, sometimes sordid. In Edo, fourteen wards featured *nanshoku* teahouses,

81. Monks entertained by visiting actor-prostitutes. Urushiya Ensai, *The Pickled Bud of Male Love (Nanshoku ki no me-zuke)*, 1703

with boys in residence or on call.[50] Most famous was the Yoshichō district, with over a hundred boy prostitutes. Some commanded high fees that might amount to half a year's salary for a samurai's servant. Many prostitutes were established or apprentice actors connected with the theaters, whose polished manners and fashionable, expensive wardrobes were much in demand. A guidebook published in 1768 listed a sampling of 232 boys in Edo, 85 in

82. The entertainment district in a Japanese city. Silk painting, artist unknown.

Kyoto, and 49 in Osaka.[51] Smaller cities and villages also provided solace, especially those near monasteries where pilgrims might stop. Besides priests and samurai, their patrons might include "peasants, packhorse drivers, river forders, woodcutters and fishermen."[52] In Edo, male prostitution seems to have reached its heyday in the mid 1780s; by 1830, after a series of reforms, it was estimated to have declined by 90 percent.[53]

• A Debate and an Anthology •

Tokugawa Japan produced a remarkable harvest of literature on male love, unsurpassed in any culture since ancient Greece. Moreover, since these writings took the form of prose fiction, they give us a uniquely intimate sense of the men's personal lives and social circumstances. In no other society of premodern times do we have so immediate an experience of the thoughts and feelings of men who loved other men. But this is not all the picture. There are also documents that, like the dialogues of ancient Greece, argue the moral, aesthetic, and social merits of male love. These discussions, which pit heterosexual and homosexual antagonists against each other, inevitably call to mind Plutarch and "Lucian," and one is often struck by the similarity of their arguments. At the same time, the context remains quintessentially Japanese, with its moonlight and cherry blossoms and appeals to Buddhist and Confucian ideals.

One anonymous example of this genre, which has been translated by Gary Leupp, bears the title *Denbu monogatari,* literally, *A Boor's Tale.* Thought to have been composed about 1640, it is in fact not a tale but a dramatized argument. Like Plutarch's dialogue on love, it features men in a social setting, in this case bathing in a river to escape the summer's heat. One laments the rage for the love of youths—a friend of his has become "crazy over young men," courting them and pining over impossible passions. Other men, he reports, are swearing vows of eternal love and mutilating their arms and thighs as pledges. They regret the night's short span, have "passionate hearts agitated like the deep Yoshino river," and are disconcertingly open about their affections—"walk[ing] around together, in the gaudiest costumes, holding hands, practically shouting, 'Look at us!'"[54]

When one man objects, "What useless passions such people have! How much better to enjoy the Way of Women, which has delighted people from antiquity!" four or five angry boy lovers challenge him to a sword fight. But as in Plutarch, violence gives way to debate. The narrator proposes the topic: "Is the Way of Women truly vulgar and the Way of Youths really more refined?" as the swordsmen had argued. This hardly sounds impartial, but determined to keep the peace, he admonishes the group: "Let's see whose logic is superior and be tolerant toward the weaker argument!"[55]

The boy lover's speech reveals an aestheticism peculiarly Japanese, and quite un-Hellenic. The "Way of Youth," he argues, is more refined because it is "usually preferred by high-ranking samurai and priests. Really, a youth's elegant form, when he's dressed in beautiful clothes, decked out in gold and silver and sporting the great and small swords, is like the willow-tree bending in the wind. You invite him to view cherry-blossoms, or the moon; or you take him along to an incense-guessing party."[56] To appear on a sight-seeing jaunt holding a courtesan's hand would, on the other hand, cause a public scandal and disgrace one's parents.

The woman lover (who throughout the debate is invidiously called "the boor") replies that affairs with boys may be appropriate for high-ranking samurai but not for the speaker, who is apparently a bourgeois townsman. Moreover, boy lovers, he claims, are often grimy, uncouth, warlike types. (Perhaps this is a reference to the many impoverished soldiers without a position in the new society.) Moreover, these boys suffer pain during intercourse. "When their parents inquire, 'Why do you walk as though you were being stuck with a bamboo cane?' they can't explain what's ailing them. They just blush with embarrassment."[57] In the past men have squandered their wealth on female prostitutes, but now they waste it on infatuations with actors in the new youths' kabuki. Priests may love boys, but this is only because they are forbidden women.

But what of the merits and demerits of women and family life? The men who founded Japan's Buddhist sects, the boy lover contends, despised women because they are more prone to evil than men; children, moreover, are an eternal encumbrance. The boor counters by appealing to Confucius, who stressed the need to continue the family line.[58] Boys cannot bear children, and parents are naturally upset if their sons shun marriage. Sons can ensure a family's salvation by becoming priests or avenge wrongs done their fathers. Women are not inelegant; some have been distinguished poets. The most famous lovers in Japanese literature, such as the "Shining Genji," have loved women. Were they boors?

In the end, as we might expect, neither side convinces the other, though the woman lover's arguments are set forth at greater length and conclude the debate. A Confucian upholder of the family would no doubt prefer them, as a Buddhist aesthete might incline the other way. The narrator, however, is under no illusion that "logic" will finally determine men's sexual choices; we recall his plea for tolerance. Night falls with no decision, and the men hurry back to their village to continue the argument another day.

Debates about *nanshoku* were popular and reveal the existence of men who identified themselves as definitely homosexual and were ready to defend their preference. But did they form a community with a special identity? The anthology compiled by the distinguished Tokugawa critic Kitamura Kigin (1625–1705), which we have already sampled, suggests they did. Hitherto, poetry and tales of male love had been intermixed in volumes containing poems and stories about women. But Kigin attempts to define a distinct historical literary tradition that homosexual men could regard as validating their lifestyle.

Kitamura Kigin was a scholar who had written a major study of the "Tale of Genji," biographies of exemplary women, and a study of women poets, and a teacher whose knowledge of classical Japanese literature brought him appointment as official tutor to the shogun's family. His anthology of homosexual themes, *Wild Azaleas* (*Iwatsutsuji,* 1676), derived its title, as we have seen, from a poem by a ninth-century religious teacher. "It was this poem," he wrote, "that first revealed, like plumes of pampas grass waving boldly in the wind, the existence of this way of love, and even serious people came to know and practice it."[59] In most of Kigin's thirty-four poems and sixteen tales, priests and monks express their tender feelings for temple acolytes in idealized relationships that are not explicitly sexual. For example, a tenth-century poem by Gon no Sōzu Yōen laments the failure of a boy named Tatsu to make a promised visit:

> If you had been the moon
> slowly crossing the great sky
> Over our lovers' rendezvous,
> I might have seen your reflection
> in my tear-soaked sleeves.[60]

Kigin's poems derive from the first eight official imperial anthologies, ranging in date from 905 to 1205, and from other early sources. The prose works include summaries of *A Tale for a Long Autumn Night,* the story of Zōyo from the *Tales from Uji,* and other tales of priests and *chigo,* none later than 1510. Kigin, who was determined to give an air of classical dignity to his work, declined to include more modern fiction as too well known and too sensational. He did not attempt to publish his manuscript; but when his book appeared in print in 1713, it enjoyed considerable popularity and was frequently reprinted, the last edition dating from 1849, almost on the eve of Commodore Perry's arrival in Tokyo Bay.

• Saikaku's *Great Mirror* •

Classical Japanese literature and art reached a new golden age in the so-called Genroku period, a term applied specifically to the years 1688–1704 or, more broadly, to the century from 1650 to 1750. It was a prosperous and "liberated" age of extravagance and self-indulgence, infatuated with the refined and ephemeral beauty of the "floating world." Its chief poet was Matsuo Bashō, its chief playwright Chikamatsu, its chief novelist Ihara Saikaku. The first two remained in favor in later times, but Saikaku, despite his contemporary popularity, had faded from view by the nineteenth century, and in the 1930s his erotic tales were censored by Japan's military ruling clique. Only since World War II has his full stature been appreciated. Among earlier Japanese novelists, he is now ranked next to Murasaki.

Saikaku was born in 1642 in Osaka, Japan's principal commercial center, and died in 1693. His background was middle class, and much of his fiction treats of the new mercantile world that developed spectacularly under Tokugawa rule. The son of a well-to-do merchant, he soon grew bored with trade and turned to poetry. Saikaku first won literary fame as a composer of linked *haikai,* and in one unbelievable but well-documented feat he composed an astounding 23,500 verses within twenty-four hours. He published no fiction until he was forty, when he had a huge popular success with his *Life of an Amorous Man,* whose hero begins his busy sex life at seven. At fifty-four he takes time to tally his conquests, which outdo Mozart's Don with a

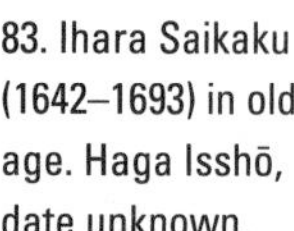
83. Ihara Saikaku (1642–1693) in old age. Haga Isshō, date unknown.

total of 3,742 women—and 725 boys. Other books followed in rapid succession, including *The Life of an Amorous Woman;* its heroine is a kind of Japanese Moll Flanders who begins as a fashionable courtesan and ends as a streetwalker. Then in 1687 Saikaku turned to a different theme with the publication of a collection of forty short tales entitled *The Great Mirror of Male Love (Nanshoku Ōkagami),* the most substantial literary work on male homosexuality to appear in any language before modern times.

The *Great Mirror* is divided into two parts: the first twenty tales center on the love of samurai for boys of their own class, the last twenty on kabuki actor-prostitutes. The samurai tales offer variations on the theme of heroic sacrifice but are often edged with a wry irony that humanizes the characters. A typical situation involves a beautiful boy beloved of a daimyo, who shares his lord's bed out of feudal duty but longs for a "real" lover of his own choosing. In "Within the Fence" (1:3) Tamanosuke tells the servant who accompanies him to the lord's court: "I suppose my mother asked you not to deliver love letters from my male admirers. It would be heartless of you not to convey them to me, regardless of the status of their senders. I was blessed to be born into this world of humanity with looks that men find agreeable. It would be terrible to earn the reputation of a 'heartless youth,' as the Chinese boy Yu Hsin was called."[61] Tamanosuke "yearned to be on a lover's secret rendezvous." He becomes his lord's favorite but soon finds a samurai with whom he forms a bond, even though both know this may spell their doom. Apprehended, they beg to be allowed to commit *seppuku* together; pardoned, they are forced to separate.

Korin, in another tale (2:2), is not so fortunate. He defiantly tells the daimyo who loves him: "Forcing me to yield to your authority is not true love. My heart remains my own, and if some day someone should tell me he truly loves me, I will give my life for him."[62] When he later refuses to reveal his lover's name, he is put to death, and the lover commits suicide at his tomb. But not all the boys resent their lord's attentions. Sometimes, the boy sincerely loves the daimyo and feels betrayed when his affections turn elsewhere (2:1).

These tales of heroic devotion fulfill Japanese stereotypes, but Saikaku is not a narrowly formulaic writer. Jinnosuke and Gonkurō in "Love Letter Sent in a Sea Bass" (1:4) are exemplary samurai heroes who face death together against overwhelming odds, but this does not prevent the jealous youth from writing a petulant letter to his lover with a long list of grievances. Nor are all the heroic lovers samurai. Seihachi, a hairdresser, gains fame when he rescues his lover (a samurai's son) from violent monks bent on raping him (3:1). In "Aloeswood Boy" (2:4) a shopkeeper's son falls in love with a merchant who has stopped briefly at the family's incense store. When the boy becomes ill with love-sickness, his despairing middle-class parents seek out the stranger. Even the convention that routinely paired a man in his twenties with a youth in his teens is not universally held. In "Two Old Cherry Trees Still in Bloom" (4:4), two men, now sixty-six and sixty-three, who had eloped together as teenage pages, live in obscure poverty. Still in love, one of them continues to play the role of "younger brother." Their extreme aversion to women is presented farcically: they sweep and purify their doorstep after women have set foot on it.

This misogynist theme pervades the *Great Mirror* in ways that have puzzled commentators. It seems hard to reconcile with Saikaku's own life and his other writings, which depict love between men and women without bias. Married to a young wife who died at twenty-five after bearing him several daughters, Saikaku mourned her loss poignantly in a series of poems before assuming a monk's robes for the remainder of his life. Yet the brief preface to the *Great Mirror* dismisses women as fit only "for the amusement of retired old men in lands lacking handsome youths." The first "story," entitled "Love: The Contest between Two Forces," is in fact an essay in which Saikaku assumes the persona of a fanatical champion of boy love who despises women. But the essayist's logic seems deliberately absurd. He interprets Japanese myths in a bizarre fashion, invents preposterous etymologies, ascribes love affairs to famous writers who had none, and makes men lovers who lived hundreds of years apart. This fierce misogynist even castigates a

84. A "woman-hater" chases away three women. Illustration, Saikaku, "Two Old Cherry Trees Still in Bloom," 1687.

character of Saikaku's own creation—Yonosuke, the "hero" of *The Life of an Amorous Man*—for favoring women. Yet misogyny appears in other contexts that are not clearly ironic.[63]

On the other hand, not all the stories show an anti-woman bias. In "Drowned by Love" (4:1) a man falls in love with an entrancing woman whom he marries; when she dies, he is grief-stricken and only then does he, like Orpheus in the Greek legend, turn to the love of boys. Saikaku is kaleidoscopic rather than consistent. He has no compunction about changing opinions from story to story; in one mood he reflects one point of view, in another another.

The tales of kabuki prostitutes lead us into a different world, one Saikaku knows intimately and is fascinated by. Though he complains of the rising cost of this "new craze"—spendthrift priests, he claims, have driven prices up—he is much taken by the boys' beauty and charm and by their skill in the theater and in bed. His portrait of this world mixes sentiment and realism. Hatsudayū (5:1) falls in love with a samurai who has saved him from a bullying boor; when the man disappears, the handsome dancer, a "thoughtful gentle-hearted youth," laments his loss and becomes a monk on Mount Kōya. It is, moreover, part of the boys' code not to reject anyone sincerely in love with them. When a seventy-year-old miser appears smitten, the generous Shizuma (5:2) offers himself to the man, only to discover he has sought him out on behalf of his lovesick daughter. Though "worried what others would say" about his deviation, he agrees to sleep with her. Sennojō, a popular *onnagata,* keeps a diary recounting how he turned "brawny samurai . . . into purring pussycats, breathed sophistication into earthy farmers, made Shinto priests cut their thick hair more stylishly, and put *hakama* [trousers] on Buddhist abbots."[64] But when one former lover becomes an impoverished flint-seller who sleeps under a bridge, Sennojō tries to rescue him and renew their relation, only to be rejected by the homeless derelict, who has lost all feeling for him.

Most of the boys in Saikaku's story bear the names of real actors on the Kyoto, Osaka, and Edo stages. An Edo guidebook of 1662 corroborates his description of the enthusiasm these actors aroused: "When these youths, their hair beautifully done up, with light make-up, and wearing splendid padded robes, moved slowly along the runway singing songs in delicate voices, the spectators in front bounced up and down on their buttocks . . . [and others] shouted: 'Look, look. Their figures are like emanations of the deities.'"[65] Nevertheless, the guidebook denounced the boys as scoundrels who fleeced and ruined their patrons, mere "prostitutes, having as their chief aim to seduce men and to take things," a view endorsed by other Tokugawa moralists, who tended to treat the boys as a pariah class.[66] But Saikaku eulogizes one boy actor, Heihachi, who excelled in warrior roles (6.5) and gave himself "for love not pay, to men who yearned for him."[67] When an infatuated farmer cut off his finger and threw it on the stage as proof of his love, "Heihachi handled the matter magnificently, increasing the good repute of boy love by his actions." His skill in the arts of both war and love made him, we are told, "a worthy model for all the boys of Japan."

Sometimes the patrons of the youthful actors express compunctions about their use of them as sexual objects. The narrator of one tale (8:3) confesses:

85. A man relaxes with a female prostitute and a handsome youth. Nishikawa Sukenobu, print, Kyōhō-era (1716–1735).

86. Brothel customer with a female prostitute watches a male youth writing. Okumura Masanobu, print, c. 1740.

87. An actor-prostitute charms a client with agreeable conversation. Print from Kitagawa Utamaro, *The Pillow Book (Uta Makura)*, 1788.

"In my 27 years as a devotee of male love I have loved all sorts of boys, and when I wrote down their names from memory the list came to 1,000. Of all these, it was with only a very few that I shared a sense of honor and masculine pride; the others were working boys who gave themselves to me against their will. When you consider their suffering in aggregate, it must have been considerable."[68] In atonement he donates one thousand papier-mâché figures of boys to a Buddhist temple, hoping these will one day be recognized as "holy work" sacred to "the Male Love Sect." Saikaku concedes that these boys might be teased and humiliated to amuse a patron or forced to entertain drunken customers or repulsive old men with unbrushed teeth and odoriferous leather stockings. One story is pointedly titled "Fireflies Also

Work Their Asses at Night" (7:1). Nevertheless, the protagonist of this tale forgets the agony of his trade "when he saw the love-lorn faces of men and women gazing after him on his way home and could hear their countless cries of admiration. It filled him with a sense of pleasure and pride in his own beauty, and this alone made him willing to bear his bone-grinding regimen."[69] Saikaku was never willing to limit himself to a simplistic view.

In this brilliant, refined, and tolerant milieu, we have, not surprisingly, evidence of a self-conscious subculture. Though the *Great Mirror* occasionally portrays bisexual behavior, it is noteworthy that Saikaku more often depicts devotees of male love as a class who think of themselves as exclusive in their preferences, stress this exclusiveness by calling themselves "women haters" *(onna-girai),* and form a unique community—a "male love sect." No other early society shows this phenomenon quite so clearly as seventeenth-century Japan, and no writer documents it so fully as Saikaku in the *Great Mirror.*

• Tokugawa Finale •

The shogun who ruled during the Genroku period (in its narrower sense) was Tokugawa Tsunayoshi, whose reign, extending from 1680 to 1709, made him a contemporary of Louis XIV and William III. Tsunayoshi was a paradoxical figure, at once humane and tyrannical, an ardent Confucian heedless of the Confucian principle of moderation. Like other shoguns of his line, he headed a regime that was a military police state. A disgruntled English merchant, writing in 1614, called Japan "the greatest and powerfullest tyranny that ever was heard of in the world."[70] But if political opposition was ruthlessly suppressed, the government allowed freedom elsewhere. Twenty-four pleasure districts with theaters, teahouses, and brothels were licensed in cities and towns as safety valves to defuse unrest. In 1616 the so-called Legacy of Ieyasu (named after the first Tokugawa shogun) had conceded that "courtesans, dancers, catamites, streetwalkers, and the like always come to the cities and prospering places of the country. Although the conduct of many is corrupted by them, if they are rigorously suppressed [more] serious crimes will occur daily."[71] Augustine and Aquinas would have agreed, barring the "catamites."

Though samurai were limited to Spartan lives under military discipline and forbidden to visit the pleasure quarters, idle warriors seeking amusement ignored the laws and wore wide sedge hats to hide their faces in the theaters. We have seen how their brawls caused the closing first of the women's and then of the boys' kabuki. In 1648 an unenforceable edict admonished men not to "make outrageous *shudō* propositions, or lose one's head over *wakashū.*"[72] Five years later the warning was repeated: "As in the past, to make or even to accept *nanshoku* propositions is strictly forbidden." But no persecution ensued to match the burnings and hangings in contemporary Europe. Given the popularity of male love at all levels of society, it is hard to believe this proscription was taken very seriously. Like the many sumptuary laws that forbade the wearing of fine clothes by the merchant class, they seem to have been ignored or interpreted leniently.[73]

Such moralizing edicts had little influence on high-ranking samurai and less on the shoguns themselves, whose lives fell almost uniformly into a bisexual pattern. Indeed, of the eleven Tokugawa rulers between 1603 and 1837, eight seem to have had male love affairs.[74] Of the remaining three, one died at seven and another was a life-long invalid. Tokugawa Ieyasu, the warrior who unified Japan and founded the dynasty, had seventeen children by his nineteen wives and concubines but was nevertheless criticized "for spending too much time disporting with boys."[75] One of his beloved pages was Ii Manchiyo, scion of a powerful clan who were among his chief supporters in his struggle for leadership.[76]

Ieyasu's son Hidetada, a contemporary of James I, also had several page-boy lovers. One relationship ended tragically when he ordered the youth to commit *seppuku* because of an affair with a daimyo.[77] Hidetada's son Iemitsu persecuted Christianity to the point of extinction in Japan and in 1639 inaugurated the Seclusion Policy which was to keep Japan isolated from the rest of the world for two centuries. As a boy, Iemitsu had loved an older manservant, Sakabe Gozaemon, whom he had known since childhood. "Imetsu, as the 'younger brother,'" we are told, "offered himself physically, giving pleasure to Gozaemon, the 'elder brother.'" But the affair soured, and the sixteen-year-old Iemitsu killed his twenty-one-year-old lover "for a real or imagined offense while the two . . . were relaxing in a bathtub."[78] His personal enthusiasm for the kabuki theater probably postponed the abolition of the boy's kabuki, which did not take place until 1652, the year after his death.

Of all the Tokugawa shoguns, it was the contradictory Tsunayoshi whose homosexual involvements were most numerous and remarkable. The most learned and scholarly of the shoguns, Tsunayoshi's impressive achievement was to convert Japan's samurai from volatile swordsmen into a well-educated civilian bureaucracy. Aspiring to be a sage-ruler who would wed Buddhist compassion with Confucian wisdom, Tsunayoshi began well, building temples and promoting scholarship and education in the Confucian classics. On succeeding to power in 1680, he improved the conditions of prisoners and arranged for help for abandoned children.[79] But he lacked restraint, and his very benevolence became oppressive. He issued many laws for the protection of animals, birds, and even fish and was especially concerned for the welfare of dogs, imprisoning thousands of men for mistreating them. Since the dog was Tsunayoshi's natal sign, wits came to wish he had been born in the year of the tiger or dragon, creatures less common in Japan.

Tsunayoshi's passion for boys was also extravagant, and he often chose his official aides from among his male pages. One page, Yanagisawa Yoshiyasu, the son of a poor samurai, eventually became his chief minister and lifelong companion. An eighteenth-century manuscript, published after the Meiji Restoration, stated: "The ruler liked sex with males. From among the sons of daimyo and *hatamoto* [the officer corps] down to soldiers and housemen, no matter how humble, if they were handsome, he appointed [his] attendants."[80] It listed nineteen such favorites; modern research has enlarged the total to 130. The most favored boys lived at Yoshiyasu's residence and made up a kind of harem, closely chaperoned and separated from their families. Their rewards, in the form of gifts, honors, and fiefdoms, could be large: many commoners became daimyo with much political power. Boys who declined to serve, however, were subject to exile. We may compare this situation with the European harems of Charles II, Augustus of Saxony, and Louis XV. The situation was different, however, in that royal mistresses did not themselves hold posts. Here was a unique experiment in "pedocracy." Critics disapproved not the homosexuality but the democratic mixing of young commoners and Nō actors with aristocratic scions.

Not all the love between men in the Genroku age was shadowed by the arbitrariness of shogunal power. Matsuo Bashō, its foremost poet, mourned in his *Saga Diary* (1691) a young disciple with whom he had shared intimacy:

> In dreams I cried out something about Tokoku, and I awoke in tears . . . For me to have dreamed about him must surely have been a case of what they call a "dream of longing." He was so devoted to me that he traveled all the way to my home town of Iga Ueno to be with me. At night we shared one bed, and we got up and lay down at the same time. He helped me, sharing the hardships of my journey, and for a hundred days accompanied me like my shadow. Sometimes he was playful, sometimes sad—his solicitude impressed itself deep in my heart. I must have had such a dream because I cannot forget him. When I awoke I once again wrung the tears from my sleeves.[81]

Bashō was a lover of quiet who sought seclusion, even from his many disciples. The Genroku theater, on the other hand, exploited current tragedies and scandals and sometimes dramatized the opposing pull of homosexual and heterosexual attachments. Chikamatsu's *Love Suicides in the Women's Temple* (1708) opens in a temple on Mount Kōya, a site traditionally associated with Kōbō Daishi and boy love, as the opening lines remind us:

> On Kōya the mountain
> Where women are hated
> Why does the maiden-pine grow?
> Yet even if the maiden-pines
> Were all rooted out,
> Would not the stars of love
> Still shoot through the night?

Then follows: "More fitting than pine, than plum or willow, is the minion cherry, the temple page, for his love is the way of Monju . . . spread by the Great Teacher [Kōbō Daishi], the love of fair youths respected even by the laity: this is the home of the secrets of pederasty."[82]

Despite these traditions, Kumenosuke, a nineteen-year-old page at the temple, has committed the unforgivable sin of falling in love with a woman. When his lover, a senior priest at the shrine, berates him, he meekly replies, "If I go to Oume and break with her will you be as kind and loving as you used to be?"[83] But Kumenosuke, who cannot bear to forsake Oume, is expelled from the mountain in disgrace, and the drama ends tragically when the pair commit suicide. Such "boy and girl" suicides were a popular theme in kabuki theater and in the puppet plays that competed with them in the early eighteenth century. It is worth noting, however, that the first double suicide to gain public attention was that of two young samurai lovers in 1640.[84] Eventually, finding that life was imitating art and too many couples were dying together, the government banned the subject in 1723.

The theme of male love survived in the kabuki theater as late as the nineteenth century. *The Scarlet Princess (Sakura Hime Azuma Bunshō),* a tragedy by Nambuko Tsuruya and others, first produced in 1817, opens with a dramatic prologue. The monk Seigen and the temple page Shiragiku stand on a cliff traditionally associated with lovers' suicides and agree to die together. The page throws himself into the sea, but at the last moment Seigen loses his nerve and fails to follow him. In the play, which takes place seventeen years later, the boy is reincarnated as the Princess Sakura. Seigen's anguished but unrequited love for the beautiful princess, which eventually causes his death, is a punishment for his cowardice, a working out of Buddhist karma.[85] Two other plays by Nambuko—*White Waves of the Flowers of Chigogafuchi* (1817) and *The Asakusa Miracle* (1829)—also feature male love affairs.[86]

Fiction on male love themes continued to flourish after the death of Saikaku. His follower Ejima Kiseki, who had himself exhausted his middle-class inheritance in the pleasure quarters of Kyoto, wrote his *Characters of Worldly Young Men* in 1715. One sketch involves the rakehell heir of a rich merchant, "who had never cared for women: all his life he remained unmarried, in the grip of intense passions for one handsome boy after another."[87] Hiraga Gennai (1726–1779) belonged to a higher social class. A *rōnin* or masterless samurai who became a scholar of Western learning, he conducted experiments with thermometers and electricity and published important works on botany and zoology. He won his greatest fame, however, as a writer of comic fantasies such as *Nenashigusa* (*Rootless Weeds,* 1763). No translation as yet exists, but Gary Leupp has provided a synopsis of this remarkable *jeu d'esprit:*

> It begins in hell, where a twenty-year-old novice monk has just arrived after wasting away for the love of the popular actor Segawa Kikunojō. His

> crimes include squandering his superior's fortune, selling the brocade curtains of his temple's altar, and pawning a precious statute of Amida Buddha—all to finance his trips to Sakai-chō to purchase Kikunojō's favors.
>
> The devils accompanying the hapless monk observe that he has sinned against his superior. They note, however, that nowadays the clergy patronize courtesans and ignore the monastic dietary rules, "so this monk's passion for actors seems a comparatively minor sin." They suggest a slight reduction in the youth's punishment. However, Enma, the king of hell, will not be persuaded to apply a more lenient treatment. "His sin," he declares, "may seem minor, but it is not." He lists the evil effects of homosexual passion, ranging from hemorrhoids to political rebellion, and orders that henceforth *nanshoku* is to be strictly forbidden.[88]

But when Enma examines a portrait of Kikunojō the monk has brought with him, he is so smitten by the actor's beauty that he falls off his throne in excitement. He decides to leave hell, find the young man, and "share his pillow." Dissuaded from so drastic a course, he finally arranges that the Dragon King will engineer Kikunojō's death by drowning. The rest of the rollicking tale describes farcical efforts to effect the drowning with the aid of erotically insidious water-sprites. The book was a great popular success.

Tsunayoshi's heir was his nephew Ienobu, the sixth Tokugawa shogun (r. 1709–1712), who won applause by revoking his predecessor's harsh laws on dog abuse and restoring Japan's finances, which Tsunayoshi had damaged by his debasement of the currency. Ienobu's closest personal tie was with his lover Manabe Akifusa, the son of a Nō actor. As the shogun's principal confidante, Akifusa attended him for thirty years, finally as grand chamberlain. A contemporary described Akifusa as "rather like a jewel, beautiful, gentle, and modest, and yet with a fine grasp of reality."[89] Ienobu's political mentor, Arai Hakuseki, a stern Confucian who regretted Akifusa's lack of learning, nevertheless praised him highly: "From his childhood Lord Akifusa had no free time, and thus was unable to engage in study, but there was something very fine about his character; there were ways in which he could stand unashamed before the gentlemen of old."[90]

The Japanese enthusiasm for the delights of the pleasure quarters suffered some restraint in the reign of the next adult shogun, Tokugawa Yoshimune, a distant relative who succeeded Ienobu's son, a boy who died at seven. Energetic and capable, he instituted drastic economic reforms and reduced expenditures, lived in Spartan frugality, and on occasion appeared in cotton clothes and straw sandals. This shogun frowned on men who wasted their wealth on courtesans or patronized elegant male actors. But when Yoshimune died in 1751, a reaction set in against this unwonted austerity, and Japan entered an era that has been compared to rococo France under Louis XV. Teahouses for prostitutes of both sorts once again proliferated, and writers like Hiraga Gennai were the rage. Like Tsunayoshi and Ienobu, the powerful eleventh shogun Tokugawa Ienari (r. 1786–1837) was an enthusiast for Nō drama. He ruled Japan for fifty years, sired fifty-five children by forty consorts, yet at the same time chose male lovers from among the Nō actors.[91]

On Ienari's death new economic and moral reforms sought once again to curb extravagance, and teahouses for pleasure were closed during the Tenpō era (1842–1843). But in the long run these efforts too were ineffective. It was not the actions of government authorities but exposure to Western mores that changed the attitudes of a thousand years in Japan. In 1859, six years after Commodore Perry arrived in Tokyo, Japanese ports were opened to trade, and Western influence became paramount. Fearful of suffering the humiliation China had experienced in the Opium Wars, the Japanese hastily began to modernize. Feudalism, traditionally hospitable to male love as a bond between warriors, ended with the Meiji Restoration of 1868 which abolished the shogunate and returned power to the emperor. Finding that foreigners were shocked by phallic shrines, explicitly erotic art, and such customs as public mixed-sex nude bathing, the Japanese became self-consciously embarrassed about many indigenous ways. Like the Jesuits of the Counter Reformation, Victorian visitors were especially horrified by Japan's acceptance of male love. This was now seen in racial terms as a typical "bad sterile aberration" of "non-European people."[92] Japan's cultural elite quickly accepted these European views and began to decry "evil customs" of the past, despite lingering allegiance to the ideals of *nanshoku* in the army and among university students.

Western laws on homosexuality were briefly adopted. Since the new German empire seemed to offer the most appropriate model for a state that sought to be modern, scientific, and militaristic, Japan in 1873 followed the Prussian code by making homosexual relations between men a crime.[93] However, the penalty was limited to ninety days' incarceration. (England's contemporary statute provided for life imprisonment.) Ten years later, on the advice of a French legal consultant, the law was repealed and never restored.[94]

Though homosexuality in twentieth-century Japan has not met with the extreme religious and moral condemnation common in the West, it has been tacitly ignored as something not to be publicly acknowledged or discussed. A famous modern novelist like Yukio Mishima felt constrained to make his "Confession" (as he called it) from behind a "Mask." Knowledge of the role of male love in the nation's historical and literary past has largely been lost. Japanese gays and lesbians are expected to marry and carry on homosexual affairs discreetly behind a façade of conformity. As elsewhere in those parts of the world open to new liberalizing influences in the post-Stonewall era, however, change is taking place. In 1994 Tokyo held its first gay pride parade, and popular attitudes are beginning to be more accepting as discussion becomes more open.[95] So does the East unlearn the lessons the West has taught.

CHAPTER FOURTEEN

PATTERNS OF PERSECUTION

1700–1730

• Policing Paris •

During the eighteenth century China and Japan showed little awareness of the continent that boasted it had attained the "Age of Reason." In sharp contrast, European intellectuals used their new knowledge of the high civilizations of the East to demonstrate what might be achieved in lands lacking Christian revelation. A new skepticism arose, fostered by Newtonian science and humanitarian disgust at the cruelty and fanaticism of the religious wars that had devastated Europe in the previous century. In France, a new breed of "philosophers" preached religious tolerance, condemned laws punishing heresy and witchcraft, and deplored cruel penalties for other crimes. How did homosexuals fare under this new dispensation?

Paradoxically, they did least well in the countries that, in 1700, had the most liberal political traditions, namely, England and the Netherlands. Indeed, Protestantism, the new faith that had promoted religious freedom in Europe, produced in this era a climate more fiercely condemnatory of "sodomites." It was absolutist France which, in the years before the Revolution, gradually abandoned lethal measures, substituting less drastic forms of social control. In eighteenth-century Paris energetic police surveillance largely replaced *les bûchers,* though occasional burnings still took place.

The English thought sodomy could tempt only "a devil out of hell." The French, by contrast, came to see "nonconformist" sex as an illicit pleasure to which the aristocracy had already succumbed. The masses, on the other hand, were regarded as comparatively untainted. Dire punishments for the nobles, it was argued, would not only undermine the social order by revealing the derelictions of the ruling class but would corrupt the young and ignorant in the lower ranks of society. Consequently, aristocratic sodomites were not publicly chastised but were, as before, exiled to their country estates and deprived of royal favor.

Louis XIV had died in 1715, to be succeeded by his five-year-old great-grandson. The ensuing regency under Madame's son Philippe d'Orléans was notorious for its sexual license. Once more, as in the old king's youth, homosexuality flourished in court circles. In 1726 a middle-class lawyer, Edmond-Jean-François Barber, noted in his journal: "For a long time the vice [of sodomy] has reigned in this land, and recently it has been more fashionable than ever. All the young seigneurs are ardently given over to it, to the great chagrin of the ladies of the Court."[1] One philosophical lady—the duchesse de la Ferté—noted the alternating tastes of French kings, remarking that "Henry II and Charles IX loved women, and Henry III mignons; Henry IV loved women, Louis XIII men, Louis XIV women." Now she wondered if "the turn of the mignons had come again."[2]

But by 1722 even the free-living Philippe felt compelled to act when a group of young nobles staged a party in the park at Versailles. According to the maréchal de Richelieu, it ended in "Greek orgies" under "the very windows" of the boy king.[3] At a council called to consider the affair, an exasperated regent declared, "We must send a rude summons to these seigneurs and tell them that they were not showing the best of taste." Informed that they had formed a "brotherhood" *(confrérie),* he ordered it dissolved and a number of youths exiled.[4] When the young Louis XV, asked why so many youths had disappeared from the court, he was told they had "pulled up fences in the gardens."[5] A cautious nobleman remarked that, "as this vice is unknown among the people," it was necessary to mete out a punishment "that afforded no scandal."[6]

In the 1660s the city of Paris had organized its first police force to control seditious meetings and disorderly mobs and to patrol the streets and markets of the capital. Under Marc-René d'Argenson, who served as its lieutenant-general from 1697 to 1718, it was expanded enormously to include both official spies and an army of volunteer informers who reported on the private lives of citizens. The surveillance of sodomites now became an accepted function of the police, which created patrols *(patrouilles de pédérastie)* much as Florence had done three hundred years before. But instead of boxes for anonymous accusations, the Paris police employed *agents provocateurs* (popularly known as *mouches*—"flies") who roamed the streets inviting solicitations by loitering in known cruising places and giving the impression they were seeking partners. Many were handsome young prostitutes whom the police dealt with leniently in return for cooperation in this kind of entrapment. The voluminous records of arrests and interrogations, preserved in the Bibliothèque de l'Arsenal and the Archives Nationales and extensively studied by Michel Rey, Maurice Lever, and Claude Courouve, provide a detailed picture of homosexual life in the streets and taverns of eighteenth-century Paris.

There was also a conceptual shift. At the beginning of the century the police had functioned as a kind of moral auxiliary to the church. Officers lectured sodomites, asked when they had last been to confession, and referred them to the appropriate clerical authorities. In turn, the abbé Théru, professor at the Collège Mazarin, spied for the police for several decades, denouncing many of his fellow clergy and demanding the harshest penalties, such as burning or deportation. "Good laymen such as you," he told the police when accusing a fellow abbé in 1725, "have to act as apostles and angels of God."[7] But by 1740 theological influence in French society had waned, and this religious approach began to seem outmoded. A significant change appears in the vocabulary of the police reports. "Sodomites" now become *pédérastes,* a secular term used not just for the lovers of boys but for homosexuals generally. They are also called *infâmes* (an expression derived from legal tradition) or, more poetically, *les gens de la Manchette,* literally, "people of the [lace?] cuff." The origin of this latter expression, found in satirical verse as early as 1726, is unknown.[8] Since the expressions *chevaliers de la Manchette* and *l'ordre de la Manchette* were also commonly used, Michel Rey has conjectured that it may have been coined in mocking imitation of some aristocratic order, such as England's Knights of the Garter.[9] In fact, some daring street-boys did dress in an aristocratic style that made them immediately suspect.

The thousands of police reports that survive for the period 1723 to 1749 reveal a substantial Parisian subculture.[10] Certain streets and parks were especially frequented—among them busy thoroughfares like the Pont Neuf and Saint Germain and avenues along the Seine. There was also much activity on the Champs Elysées, in the Tuileries gardens, the Luxembourg palace, and the Palais-Royal, milieus traditionally reserved for well-dressed members of the upper classes. In such places strollers made eye contact, asked for the time or tobacco, and at nightfall made suggestive gestures, sometimes exposing themselves in pissoirs and dark alleys.[11] Since 1706 "assemblies" of men had met in the taverns of the Saint Antoine district. By 1748, Rey reports, "one can count no fewer than eight taverns" where men gathered, ate, drank, danced, and found sexual partners.[12] Some groups adopted rituals that imitated courts, convents, or societies of freemasons. If some men dressed as women and used women's names and effeminate mannerisms, others felt uneasy in such a setting and objected to such affectations. In these societies middle-class businessmen and artisans predominated. Of 234 men arrested in 1749, 129 were craftsmen and merchants, 58 servants, and only 28 of the nobility or gentry; about one-third were married.[13] Some innkeepers allowed men to bring pick-ups to their taverns and rent private rooms: in the same year a dozen wine sellers were arrested for *pédérastie.*[14]

Such police records are, inevitably, dehumanizing in their narrow focus on illegal acts and rarely tell us about the emotional bonds these men formed: private feelings were not at issue. Popular scorn and a sense of shame made male love wholly clandestine. We no longer find coteries of avowed sodomites such as had formed around Théophile de Viau, the Great Condé, and

Saint-Pavin a century earlier, and there was little sense of solidarity. The police routinely led men to betray their friends and lovers by threats of dire punishment or promises of leniency, which might or might not be kept. Resistance was rare but not unheard of. One *mouche* reported to the police that a harness-maker's assistant named Veglay who often appeared in public places with a dozen or so other *infâmes* "had said that he had been summoned by the police and had appeared before a monsieur Chaban; that this gentleman had wanted to intimidate him by threatening him with prison in order to make him tell the names of those with whom he had infamous commerce, but that Veglay having responded defiantly, he had dismissed him, and that the best way to behave was never to disclose one's friends."[15]

In such humiliating grillings men were hardly likely to open their hearts. Yet some reports do reveal affectionate ties. One lackey told a priest "that he had always encountered much difficulty in finding a friend with a good disposition, with whom he could have established a pleasurable relationship which might last." Sometimes this desire for companionship strikes a poignant note: a police spy recounted how a man he met told him that "he wanted very much to get to know me, and that we would live together like two brothers, that he would pay for half of the room, that we would eat and drink together." Two servants who had slept together for two years "were unable to fall asleep without having mutually touched each other and without having performed infamous acts. It was almost always necessary for Duquesnel to have his arm extended along the headboard, under Dumaine's head. Without that Dumaine could not rest."[16]

In 1726 Barbier could still declare in his journal that most people did not even know what the crime of sodomy was.[17] But Théru, more knowledgeable in these matters and aware of how many Parisians were involved, worried that reputable citizens might come out of the closet if the police relaxed their control: "If one spares the corruptors too much . . . there will be great disorders . . . because all kinds of people will take off their masks, believing that everything is permitted for them, and they will organize leagues and societies, which will be disastrous, with respectable people in the lead. I have already heard of one, and when I am better informed about it, I will warn the magistracy."[18] The abbé's "league," if it really existed, remains unknown to history. Perhaps some men did indeed speculate privately about the possibility of organizing to oppose police oppression, but they did not act.

Nevertheless, the rising number of arrests made it difficult to maintain that the *le beau vice* was confined to the *beau monde.* Jean-Charles-Pierre Lenoir, lieutenant-general of police in 1775, reported that even half a century earlier the police estimated the number of sodomites in Paris at over 20,000.[19] And Mouffle d'Angerville, in his *Mémoires secrets* for October 1784, wrote that "the police commissioner Foucault, who died recently, had responsibility for this party and had shown his friends a great book in which were inscribed all the names of pederasts known to the police. He claimed that there were almost as many of them in Paris as prostitutes; that is to say, almost 40,000."[20] Since the population of Paris in the eighteenth century stood at about 600,000, this latter figure is likely an exaggeration: it would imply that about 20 percent of the adult men in the city were seeking male partners. Still, it was difficult to imagine any longer that homosexual inclinations were confined to the aristocratic few. Mouffle d'Angerville was forced to admit that "this vice, which used formerly to be called *le beau vice* because it affected only noblemen, intellectuals, or Adonises, has become so popular that today there is no rank of society, from dukes to footmen and the common people, that is not infected."[21]

Why, then, did Parisian sodomites not organize, as the abbé Théru had feared they might, to oppose police entrapment, blackmail, and harassment? Even if we take a more conservative estimate of their numbers, they would have made a formidable party with members at every level of society. It is difficult to speculate, but we may note that some crucial elements were lacking in the historical situation. The German homosexual rights movement of 1897 and the American "homophile" movement of 1950 were sparked by the statistical studies of Magnus Hirschfeld and Alfred Kinsey which suggested that homosexual behavior, far from being exotically rare, was much more common than generally imagined. But these findings were publicized by social scientists favorable to reform. In eighteenth-century France, only the police had the pertinent knowledge, and they were not about to use it to press for social change. The idea of human rights was still embryonic among French citizens: not until 1789 did the epochal Declaration of the Rights of Man appear. Even though reformers argued, in effect, that these rights encompassed a right to sexual privacy, few took seriously the idea that homosexuals were an oppressed minority.

In the meantime punishments were still formidable. Men were routinely entrapped and arrested, some simply for conversations "in suspect places at untimely hours."[22] Young first offenders were often scolded, made to sign a statement that they would not cruise the streets again, and released. Foreigners were deported and provincials sent back to their native regions "under the surveillance of bailiffs, provincial officials, or bishops." Those whom the police thought might seduce the young were relegated to the hospital-prison in Bicêtre, a place much feared because of its high mortality. Here they might linger for weeks or months or even decades if their families wanted them detained. Some were deported to the Indies. One eighteenth-century practice would startle the Pentagon: "in times of war" a convicted homosexual "could be released by enlisting in the army."[23]

Beyond these lesser punishments there stood always the risk of fire. Leviticus and the Code of Justinian continued to be cited in law books, which still called sexual relations between men or between women a violation of divine as well as human law. Though burnings for sodomy were rare in eighteenth-century France, the threat was kept alive by at least half a dozen well-publicized cases. In all but two of these, there was some aggravating circumstance, such as kidnapping or murder. In 1720 Philippe Basse and Bernard Mocmanesse went to the stake, but they were also convicted of blasphemy, itself a capital crime. Benjamin Deschauffours, who had kidnapped boys and sold them to aristocrats, had also been accused of killing one. Because of the large number of men involved (some 200) and their high rank (one was the bishop of Laon, another was a count and a *cordon bleu*—a Knight of the Order of the Holy Ghost) the government wished to hush up the affair.[24] But the chief of police insisted on making an example, and Deschauffours was burned in the Place de Grève in 1726. The burning had the desired effect, and for some time Parisian sodomites were especially fearful.

This brutal and sordid affair had an odd sequel: Deschauffours had an apotheosis as a martyr to a severe and archaic law. In 1733 a whimsical pamphlet entitled *Anecdotes pour servir a l'histoire secrète des Ebugors (bougres)* depicted him as the champion of an oppressed class: "Fourchuda [Deschauffours], celebrated inhabitant of Spira [Paris], who in his zeal in defending a large army of Ebugors, was taken prisoner in the struggle, was condemned and thrown into the fire by the order and judgment of the principal partisans of the Cytherans."[25] (The Greek island of Cythera was traditionally associated with heterosexual love, as in Watteau's painting.)

Among the manuscripts of the Bibliothèque Nationale there exists also an imaginary dialogue entitled *L'Ombre de Deschauffours* ("The Ghost of Deschauffours"), dated 1739, in which Deschauffours discourses in hell with a police officer, various nobles and churchmen, and a hustler of his acquaintance.[26] Most of the skit is given over to humorous persiflage: Deschauffours, for instance, feels he is in a strong position in hell since he has the support of the ample Jesuit contingent there. (On the night of his death a Jesuit college also burned down: wits had suggested that a spark from his pyre had ignited it as a judgment.)[27] But the satiric dialogue also attacks the police for corruptly enriching themselves through bribes and for "persecuting" men whose tastes do not correspond to theirs. Deschauffours is made to defend human diversity: "You are absurd to want to reform the tastes of human kind. I, who have never liked bitches or cunt, am I for that reason not to like *bardaches?* Each to his taste, one man drinks, the other eats. In nature each has his inclination." Another hell-dweller agrees: "Our friend is right. Why the devil should anyone want to dispute tastes and complexions. Inclination takes its direction at the moment of birth. How can you want to reform it when you have no power over it?"[28]

A less well publicized but more pitiful case was that of two workmen, Bruno Lenoir and Jean Diot, who were apprehended by the watch on the night of January 4, 1750, "committing crimes," as the magistrate put it, "which propriety does not permit us to explain in writing." One of the men was described as drunk—presumably Lenoir. The sentence, delivered on June 5, condemned them to be "burned alive, with their trial records, and their cinders then scattered on the winds, and their goods confiscated by the King."[29] Apart from this decree, few references to the men have come down to us. But the lawyer Barbier, who had thought the death penalty would not be carried out, has left an account in his journal:

> Today, Monday July the sixth, they burned publicly in the Place de Grève those two workers, namely, a joiner's assistant and a butcher, eighteen and twenty years old, whom the watch found one night openly committing the crime of s[odomy]. There was apparently a little wine at play to push the effrontery to this point . . . Since some time passed after the sentencing without an execution it was believed that the penalty had been commuted because of the indecency of these kinds of examples which indeed teach the young what they know nothing about . . . [But] since these two workmen had no connection with persons of distinction, either at Court or in the city, and since they have apparently not named anyone [of rank], this example was made with no further consequences.
>
> The fire was composed of seven wagons of brushwood, two hundred faggots and straw. They were attached to two stakes and strangled beforehand, and were immediately burned with shirts impregnated with sulphur. They did not publicly cry the sentence [as they had with Deschauffours] apparently in order to avoid mentioning the name and nature of the crime.[30]

Perhaps the executions were due to the peculiarly volatile situation in Paris in the summer of 1750. Barbier reported that the police had been earning bounties by kidnapping children who were sent to Louisiana as silk workers. Beginning with homeless urchins, they went on to seize boys and girls on errands or on their way to church, and serious riots broke out in protest.[31] The burning of the two sodomites may have been calculated to intimidate the populace and restore order.

This was to be the last execution in France for relations not involving violence. (The last man burned for sodomy, in 1784, was a Capuchin monk who had made a murderous attack on a young boy.) Though conservative jurists continued to justify the punishment in legal texts, French public opinion became more and more averse to burning. There was a growing awareness that homosexuality could not be eradicated and that savage punishments were archaic. The typical Frenchman looked on "pederasts" with a mixture of amusement, disgust, and disdain but opposed harsh penalties. As one humorist writing at the outbreak of the Revolution put it, "Brûler, c'est bien sérieux!" ("Burning, that's really serious!") "Who," he asked, "would denounce a man who you'd have to burn if he were convicted?"[32] Satirical pamphlets would spoof the idea of sodomites formally demanding their rights before the National Assembly, but their ribaldry was mixed with a certain indignation at past "martyrdoms."

• "Reforming" Britain •

In England the current of feeling ran strongly in the opposite direction. The rate of executions increased significantly, mounting until it reached its peak early in the nineteenth century. Unlike the French, the British did not regard more police surveillance as an adequate response to homosexuality: instead, it was seen as a menace to be extirpated by draconian measures. Jeremy Collier, an Anglican priest best known for a dyspeptic attack on the Restoration stage, struck the keynote in an essay published in 1698. Expressing satisfaction that sodomites faced hanging, he fulminated: "Such monsters ought to be the Detestation of Mankind, pursued by Justice and exterminated from the Earth."[33]

Indeed, this animus seems to have intensified as the century progressed. Where French thinkers thought the death penalty a barbarous anachronism, English journalists regretted that sodomy could not be more severely punished. In 1750 the political journal *Old England* addressed the subject. The paper's most famous contributor was Lord Chesterfield, a friend of Montesquieu and an admirer of Voltaire, but its stance on homosexuality was hardly cosmopolitan. The editor, who argued that sodomites deserved something worse than mere hanging, spoke with impassioned rhetoric that shows the height homophobic feeling could reach in Britain:

> The very Mention of this detestable Vice is shocking to human Nature, and shakes the Soul of even great Sinners . . . This shocking Vice was for some time charged as peculiar to Roman Catholic Countries, among Convents, Seminaries, and other Societies of Men, where no Women were admitted . . . But since the Reformation, all Protestant Countries, and more especially this Island, have been by common Consent acquitted of the Imputation of it . . . But the Abomination is [now] notorious: Our Courts of Justice have had it before them. We have seen the filthy Delinquents under Punishment for it. 'Tis therefore too big to be hid under a Bushel.
>
> Tho' Death is the penalty which our Laws inflict on this crime, yet a simple Deprivation of Life by the Hand of Justice is not adequate to the Heinousness of it. It deserves something more exemplary personal. 'Tis true our laws and our Nature abhor cruelty in Executions . . . and yet in Cases of High Treason the Criminal is to be dismembered alive and his Entrails cast into the Fire before his Eyes . . . and a woman who murders her husband is to be burnt alive. And what is the Abomination we are speaking about but High Treason? And that too in a higher degree still—Treason

> against the Majesty of Heaven, and Murder of the very Essence of Procreation!—this Subject swells under my Pen.[34]

This same editor (who wrote under the pseudonym Argus Centoculi) could argue for more humane prisons for other offenders. But having to admit that homosexuality existed in England seems to have roused a special rage. The loss of a cherished myth awakened a kind of ferocity. As in Spain under the Inquisition, intolerance became a badge of virtue and brutality a point of national pride.

What had occurred to change the traditional perception and keep the level of hatred so high? There were three things. First, London was now the largest city in Europe, and its sizable homosexual subculture could no longer be overlooked. Second, journalists publicized its existence in sensational accounts in the press.[35] And finally, the newly founded Society for the Reformation of Manners made the tracking down of sodomites a major aim, seeking convictions that would lead to their exposure in London's pillories or to hangings at Tyburn.

The recognition of a visible gay subculture in England was a novelty—and a shock. In the late seventeenth century club life in London had experienced remarkable growth. After the Restoration, hundreds of coffeehouses sprang up, attracting men who shared common interests. At first the patrons were businessmen, political cronies, or members of various professions. Later, clubs proliferated to accommodate men of every conceivable taste or interest, and at the beginning of the eighteenth century men who were attracted to other men began to gather in coffeehouses and taverns willing to serve them.

These rendezvous are first described in a book that is largely humorous—Ned Ward's *History of the London Clubs* (1709). The author, himself a gregarious tavern owner, includes such whimsicalities as the Lying Club, the No Nose Club, the Beggars' Club, the Surly Club, and the Farting Club. When, however, he comes to describe effeminate men in what he calls "the Mollies Club," Ward's tone changes from humorous to indignant:

> There are a particular Gang of Sodomitical Wretches in this Town, who call themselves Mollies, and are so degenerated from all masculine Deportment, or manly Exercises, that they rather fancy themselves Women, imitating all the little Vanities that custom has reconcil'd to the female Sex, affecting to speak, walk, talk, tattle, courtesy, cry, scold, and to mimick all manner of Effeminacy that has ever fallen within their several Observations, not omitting the Indecencies of lewd Women, that they may tempt one another, by such immodest Freedoms, to commit those odious Bestialities, that ought forever to be without a Name.[36]

Ward describes a mock lying-in and a mock-christening in a broadly satirical way that suggests a fair amount of literary invention. But the most interesting feature of the sketch is the interpretation Ward gives to these men's be-

88. Catherine Hayes, burned for the murder of her husband while two sodomites hang in the background, May 9, 1726. Engraving from *The Malefactor's Register.*

havior. Their femininity is interpreted as a conscious effort "to extinguish that natural Affection which is due to the fair Sex, and to turn their juvenile Desires towards preternatural [unnatural] Pollutions."[37] The mollies are perceived not as men whose personal tastes led to a feminine lifestyle but as malicious women haters. For more than a century the term "misogynist" was to serve British journalists as a synonym for homosexual, on the assumption that only men who despised women could love their own sex. Bisexuality was ignored, as was the fact that the vast majority of men who were tried for sodomy looked and behaved much like the average London tradesman or workman.

Ward's equation of homosexuality with misogyny was adumbrated by a broadside ballad of 1707 entitled "The Women-Hater's Lamentation," which cast women as victims of the sodomites' willful disdain. The verses describe "the fatal end of Mr. Grant, a Woollen-Draper, and two others that Cut their Throats or Hang'd themselves in the Counter [jail]; with the Discovery of near [a] Hundred more that are Accused for unnatural despising the Fair Sex, and Intriguing with one another."[38] As a rationale for hanging, this pseudo-feminist argument even made its way into eighteenth-century law books.[39] By adopting it, men of the world discovered a new justification for old prejudices and could pose as chivalrous defenders of women.

Before London journalists exposed the mollies' clubs, an educated Englishman would hardly have had a stereotype for a "sodomite." What common image would have fitted a rakehell bisexual like Rochester, the ultra-feminine Monsieur, and William III? Insofar as the man in the street thought of sodomites at all, he would have imagined them as dim, monkish figures haunting continental cloisters. Now, to his chagrin and horror, they were a local reality, mainly lower- or middle-class Londoners who were indubitably Protestant and incontestably English. In his meticulously documented study of this subculture Rictor Norton finds it was made up principally of servants, artisans, merchants, barbers, tavern keepers, porters, skilled workers (from silk weavers to blacksmiths), and "not a few foot soldiers, but relatively few schoolmasters and gentlemen of independent means."[40]

The convictions which first brought these sodomites into public notice in London were the work of the Society for the Reformation of Manners. In 1690, in the wake of the evangelical enthusiasm inspired by the Glorious Revolution, clergy and laity joined to agitate for the enforcement of laws on morality. Their particular concerns were such offenses as drunkenness, prostitution, blasphemy (swearing and cursing), and profanation of the Lord's Day (by selling goods on Sundays). The movement was a reaction to the Restoration just as the Restoration had been a reaction to Puritanism. But now loyal Anglicans worked with Puritan dissenters in voluntary associations throughout the country, recruiting informers and distributing blank warrants for arrests. As the movement grew, it succeeded in securing the conviction of a large number of men and women—the society's annually published blacklist (printed in Gothic "black letter") averaged about two thousand names and gave a new term to the language. By 1738 the society reported that it had prosecuted 101,683 persons in forty-four years, an impressive number by any standard.[41]

Behind this effort for moral improvement lay a paranoia based on superstition. A special Providence had saved England from the Armada and the Gunpowder Plot. But would it save her from the armies of the Louis XIV, who might restore James II or his son and initiate an anti-Protestant terror in the British Isles? An earthquake had recently devastated Jamaica, and tremors had been felt in London: could this be a sign of divine wrath? Unpunished vices, the society warned, could provoke God "to send down his Judgements on a sinful Nation."[42] John Disney's *Second Essay upon the Execution of the Laws against Immorality* (1710) argued that convictions for "the horrid Sin of Sodomy" were especially desirable "because this Sin draws down the Judgments of God upon the Nation where 'tis suffered in a very particular Manner."[43]

Most of the petty crimes the society focused on brought only small fines or short jail terms. But, uniquely, sodomy was a felony for which men could be hanged. In 1698 an agent of the society entrapped a naval commander named Captain Edward Rigby.[44] His conviction brought much publicity: Rigby was set in the pillory, heavily fined, and given a prison sentence which, however, he escaped by fleeing abroad. Encouraged by this success, the society now launched a campaign to apprehend others. A pamphlet entitled *The Sodomites' Shame and Doom* "by a Minister of the Church of England" warned that "Your Names and Places of Abode are known" and would "be visited by such as may bring your Crimes to just Punishment"—that is, "to the Gallows, which our Laws have justly appointed to your Sin."[45]

The campaign netted a good many victims in the next few years. Four sodomites were sentenced to hang at the Maidstone Assizes in Kent in 1702. A satire entitled "The He-Strumpets" (1707) mentions forty arrests and three suicides.[46] The "Women-Hater's Lamentation" had claimed that one hundred men had been entrapped by the society's agents, but this may be an exaggeration. By 1710 the society was able to boast that, through the activities of its informers, "our streets have been very much cleansed from the lewd night-walkers and most detestable sodomites."[47] Norton has suggested that the prosecutions had an unintended effect—actually stimulating the growth of London's subculture by advertising the existence of meeting places.

Despite the arrests, molly houses actually grew in number to more than a score. Twenty years later came the most notable raids: "On a Sunday night of February, 1725/26, a squadron of police constables converged upon the molly house kept by Mother Clap in Field Lane, Holborn . . . All the avenues of escape being blocked, by the early morning hours the rooms had been emptied of 40 homosexual men—'notorious Sodomites' in the language of the day—who were rounded up and hauled off to Newgate prison to await trial. By the end of the month several more molly houses had been similarly raided, and . . . three men were subsequently hanged at Tyburn."[48] The news of these trials prompted a storm of abuse in the popular press. One writer proposed that anyone convicted of sodomy should be castrated in open court and "the Hangman sear up his Scrotum with a hot Iron."[49]

The Society for the Reformation of Manners continued to congratulate itself on its success in hunting down men. In 1727, the bishop of Saint David's praised its "laudable Diligence" in bringing "those abominable wretches who are guilty of the Unnatural Vice . . . to condign Justice."[50] Nevertheless, the society's days were numbered as its unpopularity grew. Riots broke out when it tried to close brothels in poor districts. Its informers were accused of bribery and extortion; as a result, their paid testimony came to be distrusted. Daniel Defoe complained that "they were Zealous against the poor Drury Lane Ladies of Pleasure and the Smithfield Players and Poets were sensible of their Resentments . . . but Cheating, Bribery, and Oppression found no zealous Reformers."[51] In other words, the society penalized the poor while leaving rich and aristocratic sinners undisturbed. Despite decades of efforts to enforce the laws, vice seemed as prevalent as ever. By 1738 the society was formally dissolved. But the fierce prejudice aroused by the clergy and the press did not disappear with its demise. It remained in full force, and even intensified. Not until 1835, in a decade of far-reaching political and legal reforms, did executions come to an end.

• Souls in Exile •

Given this fervor for persecution, it is illuminating to reflect how far, at this moment, the East differed from the West. As concern about male effeminacy grew in England, ambiguously gendered performers reigned as popular favorites at the Peking Opera and in the kabuki theaters of Tokyo. And as the English middle class organized to hang sodomites, a passion for handsome youths became fashionable in the middle class of urban Japan. Cultural traditions and religious influences could hardly have diverged more dramatically.

We must wonder how England's rhetoric of abuse affected sensitive individuals in this age which was, in this matter at least, the reverse of "enlightened." Thomas Gray (1716–1771) lived as a scholarly recluse at Cambridge and won European acclaim, through one slim volume, as the most distinguished poet of his generation. A shy, affectionate man, his emotional life centered on intense male attachments. Gray's letters to Horace Walpole, whom he had met as a schoolboy at Eton College, have been called "love letters, full of expressions of endearment."[52] Writing to Walpole, then a fellow-student at Cambridge, Gray calls him half his soul, tells him "I am starving for you," and recounts how he haunted his dreams.[53] Though naturally witty and humorous, Gray suffered all his adult life from persistent depression. What he wrote of the rustic poet in his famous "Elegy" might have been said of himself: "Melancholy marked him for her own." Indeed, his letters to friends dwell persistently on his low spirits.

The scholarly Gray buried himself in dead languages to escape present pain, discovering that Anacreon and Virgil did not share English prejudices.

89. Thomas Gray. John Giles Eckhardt, oil, 1748.

In 1739 Walpole, who as the son of England's prime minister enjoyed a social position and wealth far beyond Gray's, invited him to join him on the Grand Tour, then a required part of the education of any upper-class youth. For young men who loved other men, such journeys had a special significance, for they revealed that continental societies did not everywhere seethe with indignation at sodomites. Finally the two friends came to rest in Florence, a city given over, as another traveler put it, to "love and antiquities."[54] Florence was indeed a favorite refuge for Englishmen who would have been scorned had their sexual preferences been exposed at home. The last Medici duke, Gian Gastone, had been popular among its tolerant citizens despite his open predilection for young boys. There also Sir Horace Mann, the English envoy who owed his appointment to Walpole, held open house at his villa for a congenial circle of bachelor visitors.[55]

Something—we do not know what—caused an estrangement between the two men, and Gray returned alone to England. His affections now turned to another Etonian friend, the twenty-four-year-old Richard West, to whom Gray also wrote letters with markedly amorous overtones.[56] But West, who was sickly and delicate, died suddenly. Gray mourned him in a Latin poem and an English sonnet, both published posthumously. He now resigned himself to a life of discontented gloom, brightened by occasional flashes of wit, as in his "Ode" on the death of Walpole's favorite cat. He can hardly have been cheered by reading contemporary satires. Here are the punishments a minor poet, Thomas Gilbert, proposed for sodomites in his "A View of the Town" (1735):

> Let Jesuits some subtler pains invent,
> For hanging is too mild a punishment;
> Let them lay groaning on the racking-wheel,
> Or feel the tortures of the burning steel,
> Whips, poisons, daggers, inquisitions, flames:
> This crime the most exalted vengeance claims.[57]

Gray's despairing view of life is revealed in his "Ode on a Distant Prospect of Eton College," with its bitter epitaph from Menander: "I am a man; that is sufficient reason for being miserable." This powerful poem, written when Gray was only twenty-six, depicts schoolboys naively happy in a juvenile paradise where "ignorance is bliss." But Gray contemplates the grim fate that may await them in later years: "These shall the fury Passions tear, / The vultures of the mind, / Disdainful Anger, pallid Fear, / And Shame that lurks behind," mixed, for good measure, with "bitter Scorn" and "grinning Infamy." Here is the pessimistic note of A. E. Housman (another closeted Cambridge don) sounded in the formal diction of the eighteenth century.

Gray's mood brightened for a while when, at fifty-three, he fell in love with Charles Victor de Bonstetten, a genial Swiss youth of "exceptional good looks and the most captivating personal charm."[58] Gray had invited Bonstetten to study with him in Cambridge, a place the bemused Swiss likened to a dreary monastery, with its celibate teachers and black-robed students. Gray was swept away by the young man's adulation of his poetry and learning and by his beauty, enthusiastic nature, and devotion to study: "I never saw such a boy," he told a friend, "our breed is not made on this model."[59] Bonstetten, in turn, wrote to his father "when Mr. Gray talked to me I felt palpitations, I was moved as if I had heard the voice of a god." It was a perfect *erastes-eromenos* match.

When Bonstetten was forced to return to France, the aging poet poured out his heart: "Remembrance is now the only satisfaction I have left. My life now is but a perpetual conversation with your shadow . . . I can not bear this place where I have spent tedious years within less than a month, since you left me."[60] They planned to meet again in Switzerland, but Gray, who was in poor health, died the next summer. Sixty years later, Bonstetten, in his *Souvenirs,* wrote of Gray as a man who had exiled himself from his own nature in "the arctic pole of Cambridge."[61]

Other vulnerable intellectuals also suffered secretly. Horace Walpole, as the son of England's most powerful politician, had an assured rank in society and amused scores of correspondents with his witty letters, which fill forty-eight volumes in the Yale edition. But his lifelong love for his cousin Henry Seymour Conway went unreciprocated—Conway thought "the avowing of a passion for a youth . . . notoriously impious and contrary to nature."[62] On his return from Italy, Walpole wrote to Mann that he "never was happy but at Florence" and "had a million times repented returning to England, where I never was happy, nor expect to be."[63] When Walpole publicly defended Conway, who had been dismissed from a public post, he was attacked as "a being whom, if naturalists were to decide on, they would most likely class him by himself; by nature maleish, by disposition female, so halting between the two that it would very much puzzle a common observer to assign him to his true sex."[64]

More daring, and more lucky, was Lord John Hervey. Though his personal enemies made much of his effeminacy—Lady Mary Wortley Montagu famously opined that the world consisted of three sexes, "men, women, and Herveys," and Alexander Pope, joining the gay-baiters, satirized him as "Sporus," Nero's catamite-wife, in his *Epistle to Dr. Arbuthnot*—Hervey braved opinion by openly sharing a "common home" with his lover, a member of parliament named Stephen Fox. But Hervey, a courtier close to George II and Queen Caroline, had an unassailable status.[65]

William Beckford was less lucky. Son of a lord mayor and heir to the greatest fortune in England, Beckford was a leader of London's gilded youth, a talented musician, and the author of a famous oriental romance, *Vathek,* written in French in 1782. But an intense, feverish affair with the young William Courtney (sixteen at the time) erupted in scandal. On November 27, 1784, the *Morning Herald* published these damning words: "The rumour concerning a Grammatical Mistake of Mr. B.—and the Hon. Mr. C—, in regard to the genders, we hope for the honour of Nature originates in Calumny! For however depraved the being must be, who can propagate such reports without foundation, we must wish such a being exists, in preference to characters who, regardless of Divine, Natural and Human Law, sink themselves below the lowest class of brutes in the most preposterous rites."[66] These few lines, at once supercilious and portentous, were enough to ensure that Beckford, then twenty-four, would suffer total ostracism in English society for the remaining sixty years of his life. A generation later, Byron, setting out on his travels, visited the mansion near Lisbon where the famous recluse had lived in exile. A great admirer of *Vathek* and himself bisexual, Byron saw in Beckford an alter ego whose fate he might share. In a draft of *Childe Harold* he took note of his disgrace, using the mandatory rhetoric of the day:

> Unhappy Vathek! In an evil hour
> Gainst Nature's voice seduced to deed accursed,
> Once Fortune's minion, now thou feelst her Power!
> Wrath's vials on thy lofty head have burst.
> In wit, in genius, as in wealth the first,
> How wondrous bright thy blooming morn arose!
> But thou wert smitten with unhallowed thirst
> Of nameless crime, and thy sad day must close
> To scorn and solitude unsought—the worst of woes.[67]

After years abroad, where the English still kept him quarantined, Beckford returned to England to build the monumental Fonthill Abbey. There he lived in splendor with a magnificent art collection, shunned and unvisited, as mysteriously isolated as Howard Hughes in our own day. In a letter to one of his daughters, Beckford revealed the depths of his bitterness: "I have been hunted down and persecuted these many years. I have been stung and lacerated and not allowed opportunities of changing the snarling barking style you complain of, had I ever so great an inclination. If I am shy or savage you must consider the baiting and worrying to which I allude—how I was treated in Portugal, in Spain, in France, in Switzerland, at home, abroad, in every region."[68] In 1816, in the decade when English homophobia may be said to have reached its zenith, Beckford wrote in his journal: "Tomorrow (according to the papers) they are going to hang a poor honest sodomite. I should like to know what kind of deity they fancy they are placating with these shocking human sacrifices."[69]

If the English fury against homosexuals had its roots in theology, anxieties about masculinity intensified it. Randolph Trumbach has traced changing perceptions of effeminacy in an instructive series of essays. Early in the eighteenth century "beaus" and "fops" were ridiculed for the time they spent making themselves elegantly presentable. But it was assumed that they did this to attract women—they were "ladies' men." After the sensational exposure of the mollies in the London press, however, over-refinement and feminine interests came to stigmatize men as sodomites.[70] Sensational pamphlets like *Hell upon Earth, or the Town in an Uproar* (1729) denounced mollies as "effeminate Villains" who should die "unpitied and unlamented."[71] Another, *Satan's Harvest Home* (1749), listed among "Reasons for the Growth of Sodomy," the "effeminate" custom of men kissing each other (a common English custom at the beginning of the century), Italian opera, and the sending of young boys to "Girls Schools," an emasculating experience the author feared would sap Britain's military might.[72] Sodomy was now a growing menace about which the English had become acutely self-conscious.

So, in Tobias Smollett's novel *Roderick Random* (1748), Captain Whiffle is presented as a perfumed dandy, careful of his complexion, who swoons at the fumes of a sailor's tobacco and maintains with the ship's surgeon "a correspondence not fit to be named."[73] The portrait is both hostile and funny. Later, the book's hero applies to Lord Strutwell, a potential patron with none of the popular stigmata. But Strutwell defends sodomy, citing Greek and Latin writers. In response, the horrified Roderick strikes up the national theme: "Eternal infamy his name confound / Who planted first this vice on British ground!"[74] The couplet was in fact Smollett's own, from his satire "Advice" (1746), but the conviction of the foreignness of homosexuality was as old as the Plantagenets.

Abuse of sodomites became a way for Englishmen to affirm their manhood and allay any suspicions about their own sexuality. Nowhere was this more vividly dramatized than at public pilloryings. Exposure could be a vindication or a doom. Daniel Defoe, pilloried for a satire on the church, was pelted with flowers.[75] But someone who was an object of popular hatred, as were sodomites, might be in danger of his life. If there was not sufficient evidence to convict for sodomy, men were often found guilty of the "attempt," a crime for which the standard punishment was the pillory, where, Jeremy Bentham reported, a man might "have a jaw broken or eye beat out"—or worse.[76] When in 1727 Charles Hitchen, a colleague of the notorious "thief-taker" Jonathan Wild, was condemned to the pillory for attempted sodomy, he wore armor to protect himself. But a howling mob tore off this protection and, "after half an hour, when it seemed that Hitchen might be dying, the Under-Sheriff was obliged to take him down."[77]

William Smith, condemned in 1780 to stand in the pillory in Southwark for the same offense, died on the spot, either from the violence of the enraged crowd or the tightness of the pillory around his neck. Edmund Burke was brave enough to protest in parliament on the grounds that the pillory was not supposed to be a death sentence. For his pains he was vilified in the press as a defender of sodomites. "Every man applauds the spirit of the spectators," the *Morning Post* assured its readers, "and every woman thinks their conduct right. It remained for the patriotic Mr. Burke to insinuate that the crime these men committed . . . deserved a milder chastisement than ignominious death."[78] Editors who had proposed making the penalty for sodomy something more horrific than hanging now clamored for the death penalty for the attempt.

Eventually English extremism caught the attention of Europe. Foreign visitors were especially shocked by the role women played in this violence. The popular dogma that sodomites were women-haters now bore lethal fruit.

Street women, chiefly prostitutes and fishwives, were encouraged to lead the attack by hurling stones, filth, and rotten vegetables; in their new role as agents of morality they returned upon the defenseless sodomites the scorn society commonly visited on them. Wilhelm von Archenholz, a Prussian visitor, informed his countrymen in 1787 that "since English women are so beautiful and the enjoyment of them is so general, the revulsion of these Islanders against paederasty passes all bounds." A sodomite's sentence to the pillory, he assured them, "is almost as good as death."[79] Even Casanova, in his memoirs, labeled the English "irrational" on this subject.[80] In France, a movement for law reform had gradually gained support in the course of the century. In 1785 the scientist-reformer Condorcet proposed decriminalizing sodomy and protested, in the name of humanity, England's use of the pillory: "The law of England, which exposes guilty men to the violence of the mob, and above all the women who torment them, is at the same time, cruel, indecent and ridiculous."[81] In 1810 a pillorying in central London of a group of homosexuals whose trial had received sensational publicity drew an unprecedented crowd estimated to number between thirty and fifty thousand.[82] Finally, six years later, parliament abolished the use of the pillory in such cases.

• A Witch Hunt in the Netherlands •

In the eighteenth century the Dutch Republic challenged England's proud boast that it was the freest country in Europe. During their eighty-years' struggle with Spain, the United Provinces were a haven for Spanish and Portuguese Jews, French Huguenots, English Puritans, and even Catholics. The Dutch East India Company had established trade links with half the world, so that all faiths rubbed shoulders in the markets of Amsterdam, where Mammon competed with Jehovah and Muslims could worship in the only mosque in Christendom. Despite clerical opposition, Spinoza published biblical studies challenging the very bases of Christianity, and many of the most radical authors of the Enlightenment found publishers in The Hague or Amsterdam. Superstition too seemed to have abated: the last burning for witchcraft had taken place in 1595; such trials did not end in England until 1712 and in France until 1718. Given this record of toleration, it is an irony of history that the most deadly persecution of homosexuals known to us before Hitler took place in the Netherlands in the eighteenth century.

It began in 1730 when two men were arrested for sodomy in the provincial capital of Utrecht. They implicated a twenty-two-year-old exsoldier and gentleman's servant named Zacharias Wilsma, who had been intimately associated with homosexual circles in several cities.[83] Wilsma, in turn, identified some 140 other men. As a result, investigations followed in Amsterdam, The Hague, Rotterdam, Haarlem, and Leiden. Soon, to an extent unprecedented in European history, the republic was engaged in a witch hunt for sodomites that engulfed the entire country. Eventually the search spread to many smaller towns, including Delft, Groningen, Heusden, Kampen, Leeuwarden, Middelburg, Naarden, Ryswyk, Schieland, Utrecht, Vianen, Voorburg, Woerden, Zutphen, and Zwolle.[84] In the end, about 250 trials took place.[85] More than a hundred men who had fled the country were condemned in absentia and permanently exiled. Of those who faced their judges, at least seventy-five were executed.[86]

Since the seven United Provinces were only loosely federated, there was no uniform criminal code. Each province had its own laws, and individual cities had their own jealously defended local statutes, though the "Carolina" (Charles V's imperial code of 1532, which made sodomy a burning matter) was recognized in some jurisdictions. In those with no explicit laws it was nevertheless assumed, on biblical grounds, that sodomy was a capital crime. When the States of Holland, the Netherlands' most populous province, issued a "Placard" on July 21, 1730, to be displayed in public places, the justification for the arrests was wholly religious:

> Be it known herewith to everyone that we have perceived, to our most heartfelt grief, that in addition to other transgressions of God's most sacred laws, whereby his just wrath towards our dear Fatherland has been inflamed time and again, some terrible atrocities have been committed for some time past in our dear states of Holland and West Friesland, offending Nature herself, and that many of our subjects have turned so far away from any fear of God as audaciously to commit crimes which should never be heard of, on account of which God Almighty had in earlier times overturned, destroyed, and laid waste Sodom and Gomorrah.[87]

In the hope that God would not "punish the iniquity of our land with his terrible judgments, and spew forth the land and its inhabitants [Lev. 18:28]," the decree ordered that convicted men should be publicly executed, but it left the means to individual judges.

Not surprisingly, since arrests and executions had already taken place, many men had already fled the country. Consequently, it was ordered that any who "without apparent good cause" had left their homes since May 1 should be exiled if they failed to explain their absence. Most wealthy or influential men who were implicated did escape abroad. But an alderman from Delft, a city father from Haarlem, and Frederick van Reede van Renswoude, an eminent diplomat and president of the Knightly Order of the States of Utrecht were charged.[88] The majority of those convicted, however, were of humbler rank: "couriers, apprentices, seamen, coachmen, house servants, house decorators, spice merchants, tanners, coopers, innkeepers, wine merchants, florists, [and] weavers."[89] What provoked such unprecedented severity on so broad a scale?

Today, in many Western nations, it is commonplace for homosexuals to form associations for recreational, political, or religious purposes or to provide social services. But in 1730 in the Netherlands, the discovery of social networks occurred through lurid revelations in an atmosphere of religious hysteria. In this light, these associations seemed a veritable Satanic fifth column threatening the very existence of the state. The "enormity" of the discovery created a mood of panic in the masses and the elite alike. Like the English, the Dutch saw sodomy as a peculiarly Catholic sin from which Protestants were exempt. Both peoples believed their holiness had vouchsafed them a special protection from Spanish power and French aggression. Might not such horrible sins cause God to abrogate the divine covenant that had protected them?

A fact of physical geography also obsessed the Dutch imagination. The threat of annihilation seemed especially plausible since so much of the Low Countries lay below the level of the North Sea. The ancient tradition that sodomy caused Noah's flood helped stoke the fears of 1730. Serious floods had plagued the country as recently as 1728. When a hitherto unknown species of woodworm caused large portions of the dykes to collapse in the winter of 1731, it looked as though the ominous warnings of the Placard had proved all too accurate. Clergymen hastily published sermons with such titles as *The Worm a Warning to the Feckless and Sinful Netherlands* and *The Finger of God: Holland and Zealand in Great Need from this Hitherto Unheard of Plague of Worms.*[90] Like fifteenth-century Venice, the Netherlands were a successful commercial empire that feared a sudden watery extinction.

Hitherto sodomy had been the "unmentionable crime," and trials and executions had often been secret. Now a flood of legal and religious treatises, pamphlets, broadsheets, and doggerel verse poured forth. Anti-Catholic writers reminded readers that Rome was the *catamitorum mater,* and there were the inevitable references to Julius III, to Archbishop della Casa, and to Sixtus IV, who, it was popularly claimed, had given his cardinals license to commit sodomy during hot weather. Protestants were supposed to do better. "The reformed Christians or Protestants," one clergyman wrote, "are proud not only because they received a greater revelation than others of the eternal light, but because they have improved the moral standard which was terribly decayed especially in the clergy."[91] Leonard Beels's *Sodom's Sin and Punishment* (1730) reveled in enumerating catastrophes ascribable to divine wrath—the spire of the cathedral in Utrecht had collapsed in 1674, an earthquake had been felt in 1692, the town of Stavoren had disappeared beneath the waves in 1657 in a flood, which, it was claimed, had drowned 100,000.[92]

In the seventeenth century the Dutch republic had enjoyed its Golden Age as a major European power preeminent in trade, finance, industry, and agricultural production. But after 1713, following the Peace of Utrecht, the

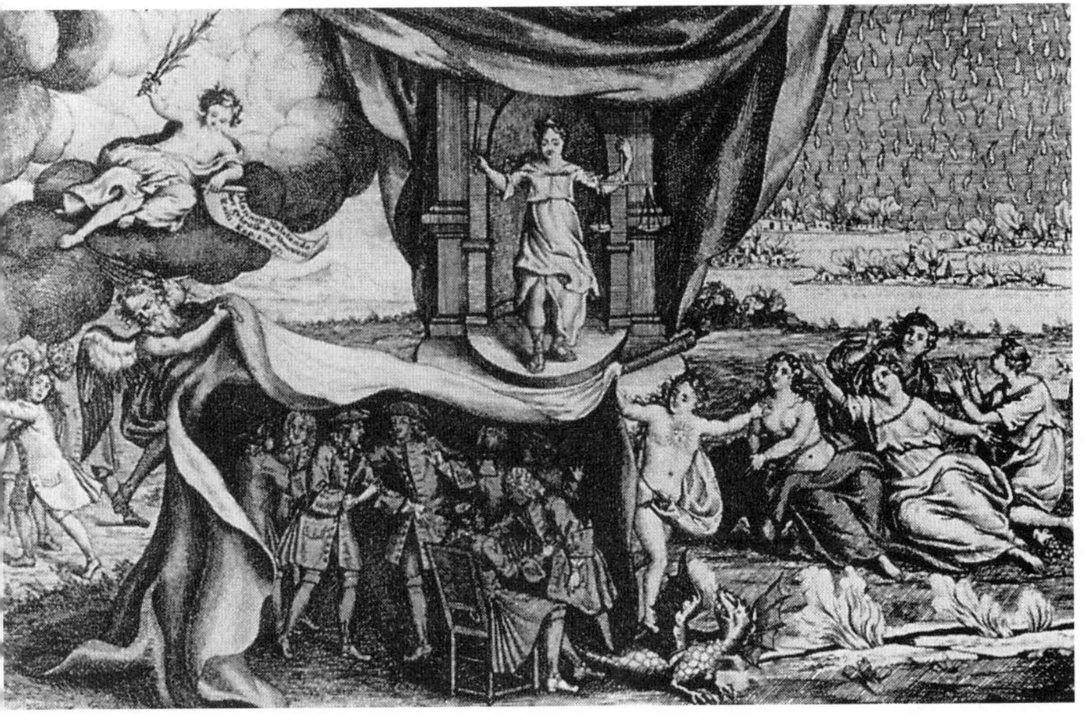

90. "Justice Triumphant." Engraving, Amsterdam, 1730.

Netherlands underwent a steep decline in military and political prestige. The Amsterdam Stock Exchange slumped as commercial rivals like England now surpassed the Dutch, and anxiety grew. In these circumstances sodomites were convenient scapegoats. In one poem of 1730 a ruined merchant and an unemployed tradesman complained: "You [sodomites] are the source of the decay."[93] Edward Coke, in the third part of his *Institutes* (1644), had proclaimed that "the sodomites came to this abomination by four means—by pride, excess of diet, idleness, and contempt of the poor."[94] This adroitly turned Ezekiel's four causes of Sodom's fall (16:49) into four causes of sodomy. So wealth, high living, and a failure to provide charity were perceived as promoting homosexual behavior. The remarkable prosperity that had itself been the sign of divine favor had, theologians argued, all too easily led to sodomy, which was in turn to blame for the country's economic decline.

Dutch artists also commented on the sensational revelations. One striking engraving—*Justice Triumphant*—combined Baroque allegory with contemporary scenes. Justice with her scales looks down from above as Divine Wrath trails a banner with words from Paul. Below, an old man and a naked woman (Time and Truth) pull aside a curtain to reveal a sodomite club where four well-dressed couples discuss the startling news. In the background fire rains down upon the cities of the plain as—a Dutch touch—the waters of the Dead Sea rise to inundate them.

Grimmer and more explicit in its realism is a series of scenes in an engraving entitled *Timely Punishment Decreed for the Abominations of the Most Godless and Damnable Sinners.* In the first scene two men quit an elegant salon, hand in hand; then they are shown fleeing their homes, leaving wives and children behind. Arrested in the street, they next appear in prison lamenting their fates. The last and most elaborate scene shows a huge crowd in the city square in Amsterdam, where five men dangle from a gallows, two are garroted on posts, and another pair drown in barrels. At the side, bodies of dead men burn on a grill, while in the foreground a skeleton holds a scroll showing ships taking corpses to be thrown into the sea.

These pictures are chillingly close to reality. As we have seen, methods of execution were varied. Here are the fates of five men who suffered in Amsterdam:

- Pieter Marteyn Janes Sohn and Johannes Keep, decorator, strangled and burned, June 24, 1730
- Maurits van Eeden, house servant, and Cornelius Boes, eighteen, Keep's servant, each immersed alive in a barrel of water and drowned, June 24, 1730
- Laurens Hospuijn, chief of detectives in the Navy, strangled and thrown into the water with a 100-pound weight, September 16, 1730[95]

Another thirteen perished in The Hague:

- Jan Backer, middleman for hiring of house servants, and Jan Schut, hanged and burned, June 12, 1730
- Frans Verheyden; Cornelis Wassermaar, milkman; Pieter Styn, embroider of coats; Dirk van Royen, and Herman Mouillont, servant, hanged and afterward thrown into the sea at Scheveningen with 50-pound weights, June 12, 1730
- Pieter van der Hal, grain carrier; Adriaen Kuyleman, glove launderer; David Munstlager, agent; and Willem la Feber, tavern keeper, hanged and thrown into the sea at Scheveningen with 100-pound weights, July 21, 1730
- Antonie Byweegen, fishmonger, hanged, then burned to ashes, July 21, 1730
- Jan van der Lelie, hanged and thrown into the sea, September 24, 1731

Inevitably, news of executions on this scale made an international sensation. French, English, Irish, German, and even colonial American newspapers were full of the scandal and reported the arrival of fleeing refugees. The English press, hardly favorable to sodomites, nevertheless accused Dutch tribunals of procedures that might jeopardize the innocent.[96] The States of Holland sent formal protests asking the English government to suppress the newspapers, but the charge that stung most sharply—that Dutch courts imitated the Inquisition in their use of torture—could hardly be denied, since this was routine in sodomy cases.

The persecution of 1730 provoked a reign of terror that lasted in the Netherlands for more than a year. The spectacle of men hanged, burned, and drowned in city after city spread fear far and wide. The anxiety of apprehension, the strain of standing trial, the agony of torture, the pangs of death on the scaffold or in the dungeons of prisons where men sentenced to the stake were first strangled, the indignity of seeing friends' bodies treated as refuse to be burned or thrown into the sea: all these were part of a repulsive national ordeal. Nowhere, however, were the horrors of the panic so potently realized as in the small village of Faan in the northeastern province of Groningen.

Like the Salem witch hunt of 1692, the persecution at Faan had a political side and was exacerbated by village feuds and rivalries. Its instigator was Rudolph de Mepsche, the local judge or *grietman.* De Mepsche, the lord of Oosterdeel-Langewoldt, a domain that included Faan and five other villages, had lost power a few years before to a rival provincial dignitary, Maurits Clant, lord of Hanckema.[97] Opinion in the district had been inflamed by one of de Mepsche's supporters, a local cleric named Henricus Carel van Buyler, who in 1731 published a book whose title, *Helsche boosheit van grouwelyke zonde van sodomie (The Hellish Wickedness of the Horrible Sin of Sodomy),* conveyed its fanatical spirit. Van Buyler perceived the sodomy trials as proof of a diabolical conspiracy by popes and Jesuits to exterminate the human race; he favored harsh public punishments, holding that boys as young as twelve might be put to death, and denounced any who challenged his views as "advocates for Satan's realm."[98]

But despite van Buyler's superheated imagination, Faan was in fact a small farming community with no known connections to a national sodomite network. The events in Faan began in April 1731 (after trials elsewhere had largely ceased) with the interrogation of a blind boy of thirteen who had accused another boy of the same age.[99] The pair named seventeen others, mainly youths between fifteen and twenty with whom they claimed to have engaged in sex play. By the end of May the net had spread wider: six middle-aged farmers were apprehended, four of them supporters of Maurits Clant. Eventually, thirty-six men were held, many of them brought to confess "by often unbearable torture."[100] On September 21 twenty-four men and boys were sentenced, all but two to death. How many were really guilty is uncertain. Desperate relatives and neighbors sought in vain to appeal the sentences. So apprehensive was de Mepsche of a public revolt that he stationed a regiment of soldiers in the village.[101] The body of one man who had died in prison before the verdicts could be announced was hung head-down from

91. "Timely punishment depicted as a warning to godless and damnable sinners." Engraved broadsheet, Amsterdam, 1730. (1) Two men leave a meeting-place on hearing of the persecution. The allegorical figure of a woman with a serpent's tale represents "abominable sin." (2) The two men flee their homes. The figure symbolizes despair. (3) The suspects are arrested in the street. The figure stands for terror. (4) The convicted men await execution in prison. The figure holds a grill on which their bodies will be burned. (5 and 6) The city square in Amsterdam where sodomites are being hanged, drowned in barrels, and garrotted and their bodies burned. The skeleton holds a scroll showing ships taking bodies to be thrown into the sea. The seated man holds the flaming sword of "Divine Justice."

the public gallows. Then on September 24 the remaining twenty-one were strangled and publicly burned. Of those executed, nine were in their teens; one boy was fifteen, another fourteen.[102]

As late as April 1732 twelve men were still in prison awaiting trial, and more arrests were threatened. Then, when another man died—clearly as a result of torture—the provincial government intervened and brought charges of malfeasance against de Mepsche. Public opinion now turned decisively against the magistrate, his aides, and van Buyler. The judge who had been a

figure of terror now became an object of scorn and hatred. "In the years to follow, de Mepsche became known in popular legend as a brute and a scourge and an executioner of innocent people."[103]

No such reaction occurred in other parts of the republic, however, where prosecutions, though dire, were less concentrated. Despite some concerns by the ruling oligarchy about adverse effects on trade, mass arrests were made intermittently later in the century—in Amsterdam in 1764, in several other cities in 1776, and in The Hague and Utrecht in 1797.[104] By now silence and secrecy had given way to anxious speculation about the significance of this persistent phenomenon. Inevitably, the discovery that so large a number of men were sexually involved with other men and the realization that sodomite networks, despite judicial terrorism, continued to exist as part of the human landscape led to changes in popular perceptions. Sodomy, once simply a nefarious sin into which Satan might trap any erring individual, now became the propensity of a recognizable species—"that damned seed," as one author put it, "about which one to his grief has heard so much in these sad days," a uniquely different sort of man, with his own stereotyped characteristics.[105] Thus a forensic specialist writing in 1768 advised his readers that sodomites could be identified by their effeminate posture, languishing glances, and affected speech.[106]

In time these men, too, came to see themselves differently and to feel that their condition was a natural phenomenon, not a sign of damnation. One clergyman on trial argued that his inclinations were "proper to his nature," since they were due to his mother's longing for her absent husband while she was pregnant. This theory did not recommend itself to the authorities, who rejected out of hand any argument that seemed to diminish the guilt of the individual.[107] But other men with strong religious convictions refused to consider their homosexuality at odds with their religious faith. Gerrit van Amerongen, a member of a homosexual circle in The Hague, defiantly maintained at his trial in 1776 that men like him were "born" with their dispositions and could be as loving in their relationships as any "man and wife." As time passed, such men were reassured by the knowledge of how many others shared their orientation. In 1797 one told a friend, "It is a weakness you and I share with thousands of others," and Jan van Zaanen, in 1826, wrote to his lover in Amsterdam, "It is a weakness that is innate and God has created no human being for his damnation."[108]

Despite the adverse climate of opinion, a movement for reform slowly gathered momentum. In 1777 Abraham Perrenot, a legal adviser to Stadtholder William V, published an anonymous treatise entitled *Nadere Bedenkingen over het straffen van zekere schandelijke misdaad (Further Thoughts about the Punishment of a Certain Shameful Crime)* in which, echoing the reforming ideas of the Enlightenment, he argued that homosexual relations which did not involve the seduction of the young should not be punished.[109] Judges became less willing to impose the death penalty, substituting instead long sentences of imprisonment—often thirty or fifty years. The last execution for sodomy in the Netherlands—perhaps the last to take place on the continent of Europe—occurred in 1803.

A new Dutch penal code of 1809 substituted lengthy prison terms for relations between consenting adults, retaining the death penalty for the seduction of minors. The disruptions of revolution and war, however, prevented its coming into effect; and when France annexed the country in 1810, the Napoleonic Code was introduced. Henceforth homosexual relations between consenting adults ceased to be a crime at all in the Netherlands.

Since World War II, Amsterdam, reflecting the liberal views of Dutch society generally, has distinguished itself as the European city most strongly supportive of the rights of its gay and lesbian citizens. Near the Anne Frank house a civic monument commemorates men and women who have suffered from homosexual oppression, memorializing, along with those who perished in Nazi concentration camps, the victims of the terror of 1730.

CHAPTER FIFTEEN

SAPPHIC LOVERS

1700–1793

• Law and Religion •

A new awareness of male homosexuality in England in the eighteenth century brought another startling realization: women too might be attracted to their own sex. We have noted the Gallic irony of the comte de Gramont, who thought the court of Charles II "so uncivilizd as never to have heard" of such romantic possibilities.[1] What had caused this blindness? Largely it sprang from differences in law and religion. Henry VIII's "buggery" statute penalized anal intercourse, whether same-sex or heterosexual, but took no account of encounters between women. As a result there were no trials to publicize them, as there were on the Continent. Moreover, Protestant clergy asked no intimate questions in the confessional and consequently lacked the knowledgeableness of Catholic priests.

Even Catholic priests, however, were often confused in the matter. In 1700 the distinguished Franciscan theologian Ludovico Maria Sinistrari set out to elucidate the problem in a monumental treatise on criminal and canon law *(De delictis et poenis).* Here, in eighty-two paragraphs of legal Latin, Sinistrari gave an account of procedure in male sodomy trials and, in addition, provided far more information about the theologico-legal aspects of lesbianism than any previous writer. Indeed, the erudite monk took professional pride in noting that even "very learned" confessors admitted to confusion about female sodomy.[2] Sinistrari's approach was at once conservative and novel. Professing the traditional view that lesbian acts merited burning, Sinistrari drew on new medical research, especially Gaspar Bartholin's study of female anatomy, to present a new view as to what constituted the offense. Jurists had maintained that, penetration being necessary to constitute the crime, women could be executed only if they used artificial instruments, as in the case of two Spanish nuns who had been burned (paragraph 11). Sinistrari ingeniously argued, however, that the crime could occur only if one woman possessed a clitoris long enough to penetrate another (14–22). He conjectures that female circumcision was practiced in Egypt and Ethiopia because of the prevalence of this anomaly, which he believes is rare in Europe (16). Hence, he advises (24):

> If women are accused of a crime of this kind, the Judge is bound to have the female body inspected by a jury of matrons. For if these find the [enlarged] clitoris, and it be proved the women lay together, and the matrons' corroborations side with the crime, there is a presumption that they made use of it for the heinous delinquency: just as it is legally presumed from a man's sleeping with a woman that they have fornicated. [Then] it is necessary to have recourse to torture, that the Judge may find out whether the unmentionable crime was committed. This case may readily fall out in Communities of women [nunneries], though it is a well known fact that it has taken place more than once even between lay and secular women.

Sinistrari, who had taught law at Padua and served in Rome as consultor to the Supreme Tribunal of the Holy Inquisition, was known in private life for his witty urbanity. About sodomy, however, he was not urbane. Sinistrari agreed with Saint Augustine that the severest penalties ought to be "irremissibly inflicted even though the majority of the population was guilty of this transgression" (50). Were not Sodom's citizens punished *in toto?*

Despite this severity, Sinistrari's views, if accepted, would have had the beneficent effect of making convictions for lesbianism rare or impossible. Unfortunately, in the case of Catharina Margaretha Linck, sentenced to death in Germany in 1721, they did not prevail. Linck's career is a remarkable tale, with enough adventures, mishaps, and scandals to supply a picaresque novel. (The trial records, taken from the Prussian Secret Archives, were first published in 1891 by F. C. Müller in a journal of forensic medicine.) The illegitimate daughter of a widow who placed her in an orphanage in the Saxon city of Halle, Catherine Margaret had, by the end of her teens, served (in male disguise) in the Hanoverian, Prussian, Hessian, and Polish armies. Deserting frequently, she had escaped execution only by revealing her sex. Her religious experiences were equally varied. Joining a Quaker-like sect called the Inspirants, she had ecstatic seizures, became a prophetess, and assured a rich merchant of Nuremberg he could walk on water. (His buoyancy proved inadequate.) Back in her native Saxony, she worked as a weaver for three or four years, dressing sometimes as a man, sometimes as a woman.

In 1717 at Halberstadt, a small town forty miles from Halle, Linck "married" another Catherine Margaret, surnamed Mühlhahn, who at eighteen was five years her junior. At this point she dressed and behaved to all appearances like a man and in the bedroom used a "leather instrument." The marriage was stormy, with quarrels that sometimes led to violence, but the couple stayed together for four years. Finally, her suspicious mother-in-law beat and stripped her to establish beyond a doubt that she was a woman. At her trial, Mühlhahn claimed to have been for a long time ignorant of her partner's real sex. Linck, however, maintained that both mother and daughter had known the truth before the marriage. Asked how she justified her misdeeds, she declared that Satan had possessed her when she married as a man and committed "abominable sodomy." For this, she lamented, "she deserved death tenfold." Her defense counsel, however, asked for a sentence of life imprisonment for Linck and requested that Mühlhahn be released, since she had already spent time in prison and had suffered "extreme depression caused by her wanting to come to the aid of the accused."[3]

The trial records of 1721 are remarkable not only for bringing to life the story of this tumultuous woman who seems to have stepped out of the pages of some rogue novel but also for revealing the workings of a legal system trying to decide how lesbian acts should be defined and punished. The trial court at Halberstadt recommended the death penalty. The Judicial Faculty at Duisburg agreed, recommending that Linck be hanged and her body burned and that her lover be tortured "to get at the truth in her case." But the jurists who prepared the final report to the king noted various other options, among them Article 116 of the code of Charles V which made burning alive the penalty and Saxon traditional law (as expounded by Benedict Carpzow in his standard treatise on the subject) which prescribed "the sword" for male or female sodomy.[4]

Punctiliously, the jurists also asked what, in fact, was female sodomy? Did Paul's mention in Romans 1:26 of women who left "the natural use" really refer to lesbianism or could he perhaps have had in mind bestiality, which the Old Testament clearly condemned? Or could he, they asked, using the new approach suggested by Sinistrari, have had in mind African women "with a so-called flaw of nature, a very large clitoris," who might have been capable of penetration? In the end, they rejected both lines of defense and concluded that "all interpreters" of Romans 1:26 had taken Paul's words to mean relations between women. As for artificial instruments, Paul could well have known them since Aristophanes mentions them (as *olisboi*) in his comedies. Indeed, women who use them, they declared, "behave much more unnaturally than the African women, who, after all, use members with which nature endowed them, merely in a wrong and improper way."

A merciful minority of the jurists thought the death penalty not applicable since "with these types of instruments actual fleshly union is not possible, much less can semen be released—both processes being required for the real offense . . . of sodomy." Since scripture nowhere explicitly requires the death penalty for female couples, they argued that the penalty might be reduced to flogging. But the majority, more traditionally minded, voted for death "by the sword"—the Saxon mode.[5]

The final judgment was left to the king. Unfortunately, the ruler of Prussia in 1721 happened to be Frederick William I, the notoriously irascible Soldier

King, father of Frederick the Great. Frederick William had earlier issued an edict "that all gypsies found within the boundaries of his kingdom were to be strangled, while sodomites would be burned alive."[6] Consequently, Catharina Margaretha Linck was beheaded and her lover sent to prison. This is the last known execution for lesbianism in Europe and a striking anomaly in an age which had—at least in the case of women—let such savage punishments fall into desuetude.

No comparable drama took place in England, though accounts of cross-dressing females occasionally appeared in the press. Most told of women seeking lost husbands or lovers or wishing to follow male occupations, such as soldiering or sailing. Sometimes, however, an erotic element entered the story when they married other women and cohabited with them. In 1746 no less an author than Henry Fielding paused in the writing of his masterpiece *Tom Jones* to produce a fictionalized account of such a case, though his anonymous catchpenny effort of twenty-three pages, entitled *The Female Husband, or the Surprising History of Mrs. Mary, alias Mr. George Hamilton,* was not definitely identified as his until the twentieth century.[7]

Fielding's story—one part fact to ten parts fiction—was inspired by a brief paragraph in a Bath newspaper which told how one Mary Hamilton "otherwise George, otherwise Charles Hamilton, was try'd for a very singular and notorious Offence." She had espoused "one Mary Price, who appeared in Court and deposed that she was married to the said Prisoner . . . and lived as such for about a Quarter of a Year, during which Time she, the said Price, thought the Prisoner a Man, owing to the Prisoner's using certain vile and deceitful Practices, not fit to be mentioned."[8]

Between 1740 and 1840 several famous French novelists treated lesbian themes, notably Diderot (in *La Religieuse*), Théophile Gautier (in *Mademoiselle de Maupin*), and Balzac (in *The Girl with the Golden Eyes*). Fielding's novelette—a kind of lesbian *Moll Flanders*—is a unique English example of the genre, differing from its Gallic counterparts both in its picaresque realism and its harsh moralizing. It opens with a paean to heterosexuality, qualified with British caution: "That propense inclination . . . implanted in the one sex for the other [is], when govern'd and directed by virtue and religion, productive not only of corporeal delight, but of the most rational felicity." Fielding, however, strikes an alarmist note: "But if once our carnal appetites are let loose, without these prudent and secure guides . . . there is nothing monstrous and unnatural which they are not capable of inventing, nothing so brutal and shocking which they have not actually committed."[9] Yet despite his drumfire of moral disapprobation, Fielding projects himself into the emotional life of his anti-heroine with remarkable immediacy. Here, for what may be the first time in modern European fiction, readers are invited to imagine how women might experience passionate love and devotion for other women and find this love rewarding.

Fielding introduces Mary Hamilton as a virtuous innocent with a warm affection for Anne Johnson, a woman aflame with "enthusiasm" for the new sect of Methodism. Anne soon converts her young friend both to Methodism and to the lesbian amours that she had "learnt and often practiced at Bristol with her methodistical sisters" (31). When Anne heartlessly deserts her for an eligible male, the grief-stricken Mary behaves as the "fondest husband" might on losing a "beloved wife." On a whim, she dresses as a man and sails for Dublin in the guise of a Methodist preacher. There, a wealthy widow, Mrs. Rushford, finds this "beautiful youth of eighteen" quite to her taste and, at sixty-seven, is embarrassingly eager for matrimony. Tempted by the fortune, George-Mary marries her, planning to satisfy her new wife "by means," Fielding remarks, "which decency forbids me even to mention" (37). The ruse succeeds, and the widow enthusiastically boasts of her new mate's prowess. But when she accidentally discovers her true sex, she flies into a comic rage, and the "female husband" hastily flees the scene.

Now fully embarked on her rogue's career, she passes herself off as a doctor, elopes with a young girl in Devonshire, is again unmasked, and has to escape once more. Finally, she meets Mary Price (or "Molly") of the newspaper account, a barely literate girl "about eighteen years of age and of extraordinary beauty." "With this girl," Fielding tells us, "hath this wicked woman since her confinement declared she was really [as] much in love as it was possible for a man ever to be with one of her own sex" (43). When the "doctor" proposes marriage, Molly's mother happily approves, while the bride was "so extremely enamoured, that I question whether she would have exchanged the Doctor for the greatest and richest match in the world" (46). Fielding assures his readers that "the newly married couple not only continued, but greatly increased the fondness which they had conceived for each other" (47). Molly, for her part, naively reports the sexual side of the marriage as more than satisfying. But this happy interlude ends when someone recognizes the pseudo-husband, and Molly's mother obtains a warrant for "his" arrest.

In real life the Hamilton case caused some confusion, since no English law covered lesbian relations. On November 3, 1746, the Bath newspaper Fielding used as his source reported: "There was a great Debate for some Time in Court about the Nature of her Crime, and what to call it, but at last it was agreed that [Mary Hamilton] was an uncommon notorious Cheat [a fraud], and as such was to be publickly whipp'd in the four following Towns, Taunton, Glastonbury, Wells and Shipton-Mallet, [and] to be imprisoned for six Months."[10]

Mary's punishment in *The Female Husband* is similar: she is to be whipped in "four market towns" in Somerset and to be imprisoned. Such whippings would have been inflicted at intervals of several weeks, presumably to allow time for partial healing. Fielding is more sensitive to the aesthetic injury than to the cruelty of this treatment, commenting only that "those persons who have more regard to beauty than to justice could not refrain from exerting some pity toward her, when they saw so lovely a skin scarified with rods in such a manner that her back was almost flayed" (50). In the end, Fielding degrades Mary by having her ask her jailer to procure a young girl to "satisfy her most monstrous and unnatural desires." Perhaps he felt he had gone too far in revealing how women might find fulfillment in such love affairs. As Emma Donoghue has pointed out in her study of eighteenth-century England, "A lesbian reader of *The Female Husband* would learn that she was not monstrous, only immoral, at times distinctly heroic—and most importantly, that there were 'others' out there whom nothing could deter."[11]

Despite Fielding's dire example, not all "female husbands" suffered the fate of Mary Hamilton. In 1760 the *London Chronicle* reported that Barbara Hill, whose true sex came to light when she tried to enlist as a soldier, had been married for five years to a woman "with whom she has lived very agreeably ever since" and that her partner had "come to town in great affliction, begging that they might not be parted."[12] The account makes no mention of any legal punishment and is sympathetic in tone. Two months later the paper reported that a certain Samuel Bundy had been exposed as a woman and jailed in Southwark "for defrauding a young woman of money and apparel by marrying her." The "wife" apparently repented bringing the charge, for the paper noted that "there seems a strong love, or friendship on [her] side, as she keeps the prisoner company in her confinement." When she failed to press charges, the judge took no action beyond burning the "husband's" male clothes. In 1764 the *Chronicle* reported the death of a woman who had posed as a male farmer throughout her life and had been "married" to another woman for twenty years. Such marriages, when no outrageous fraud was involved, seem more often to have been regarded as curiosities rather than as crimes.[13] English popular attitudes toward female couples in amicable relationships seem to have been, on the whole, less uniformly hostile than Fielding's tale might lead one to expect.

Though lesbianism was theoretically a capital crime in the Dutch republic, where Charles V's law of 1532 prevailed, we have no record of executions in that country. In 1606 Maeyken Joosten, who had been married for thirteen years and had four children, fell in love with a young girl, married her, and was convicted of having "had sexual contact with [her] in every manner as if she were a man." The prosecutor, warning that such deeds "brought down the anger of God upon cities and countries," recommended that she be "bound and put alive into a sack and choked in water." Nevertheless, her punishment was reduced to a whipping and exile.[14]

A more notorious case was that of Hendrickje Lamberts van der Schuyr, who had served in the Dutch army as a man and fought at the siege of Breda in 1637. Hendrickje owed her fame to Nicolaas Tulp, a distinguished Dutch physician immortalized in Rembrandt's *Anatomy Lesson,* who had given a first-hand description of her case in his *Observationum medicarum* (1641), where he diagnosed her as a hermaphrodite. The twenty-seven-year-old Hendrickje lived in Amsterdam and had an ongoing relationship with a forty-two-year-old widow. Tried for "having entered into a relationship . . . against all natural order," Hendrickje was whipped and exiled.[15]

In the eighteenth century, prosecutions for lesbianism all but ended. An exception occurred in the years 1795–1798 when some eight impoverished working-class women were tried and imprisoned in Amsterdam for terms of two to twelve years.[16] With the adoption of the Napoleonic Code in 1810, same-sex relations, whether female or male, ceased to be crimes in the Netherlands.

• Romance and Innuendo •

In England lesbian love affairs took on a paradoxical aspect. Women like Mary Hamilton might be severely punished, but at the same time a cult of romantic friendship between women flourished, and genteel ladies might still affect to disbelieve in the possibility of physical relations. Sometimes this disbelief might be simply a *faux naif* posture, cloaking a malicious intent to defame, as in Delariviere Manley's sensational novel, *The New Atalantis* (1709). In this roman à clef, Manley, a Tory propagandist, portrayed a "new Cabal" of women who were prominent Whigs. After revealing that the cabal has been suspected of "criminal" diversions, Manley affects to reject the calumny. Some critics, she declares, "pretend to find in these [women] the Vices of old Rome reviv'd, and quote you certain detestable Authors, who (to amuse Posterity) have introduc'd you lasting Monuments of Vice, which could only subsist in Imagination, and can in reality have no other Foundation than what are to be found in the Dreams of Poets."[17]

The disclaimer, however, is entirely disingenuous since Manley goes on to provide many details that suggest the women are lesbians. The cabal has a secret Bower of Bliss where men are excluded, allows marriage only as a necessary evil, examines novices to see if their "Genius" (inclinations) fit them to join the group, and reserves their most tender kisses and rapturous embraces for one another. One aristocratic couple wanders, disguised as men, through the "gallant quarter of the city" seeking adventures with "Creatures of Hire" who obliged their titled companions' "peculiar Taste" by "all the Liberties that belong to Women of their loose Character and Indigence."[18] Thus, while ostensibly deprecating popular suspicions, the author amply validates them.

Manley and her publisher suffered brief imprisonment for this veiled satire. But since she had taken the precaution of identifying her characters only by Italian and Spanish pseudonyms, she was soon released. A French translation added a convenient key—British libel law did not reach to Paris. Titillated scandal-lovers devoured half a dozen editions in English, French, and German.[19]

Manley's personae were limited to "Persons of Quality," that is, of rank. Two women of quality who do not appear in her "new Cabal" were Queen Anne (r. 1702–1714) and her elder sister Mary II, wife of William III. Both were the daughters of Anne Hyde, the duchess of York, in whose circle intense involvements between women seem to have flourished. One of her ladies, Anne Killigrew, wrote notable love poems to a woman we know only as Eudora and was compared to Sappho and Katherine Philips.[20] But it was the two young princesses, Mary and Anne, whose passionate attachments to other women are most fully documented, since royal correspondence has survived when other letters have vanished. In 1673, when she was eleven, Mary performed in a court masque on the legend of Calisto, a nymph who served Diana. In the traditional myth, an enamoured Jupiter woos Calisto in the shape of her mistress. Inevitably, the situation suggested a lesbian seduction. Mary, as Calisto, was required to call out: "She raves, I to the nymphs for aid must call, / Or she will do some horrid act I fear, / Help, help, my goddess is distracted here."[21]

Two years later, there was an ironic reversal. "In her stage role of Calisto," a recent biographer tells us, Mary "had blushed when wooed by one of her own sex; in real life she fell unashamedly in love with another girl, Frances Apsley, nine years her senior, the beautiful daughter of Sir Allen Apsley, keeper of the King's hawks."[22] Inspired by the French romances popular at the time, Mary wrote passionate letters to Frances, whom she addressed as her adored "husband." (For many years these letters were thought to be addressed to William III.) Isolated at Richmond Palace from the rakes of Charles II's court, Mary poured out her starved affections. "You shall hear from me every quarter of an hour if it were possible," she wrote Frances, "all the paper books in the world would not hold half the love I have for you, my dearest, dearest, dear Aurelia." In a ecstasy of self-abnegation, Mary called herself "your humble servant to kiss the ground where you go, to be your dog in a string, your fish in a net, your bird in a cage, your humble trout." "O have some pity on me," she begged, "and love me again or kill me quite with your unkindness for I cannot live with you in indifference."[23] Two years later, Mary married William, much against her will; soon, however, she came to love her serious-minded husband, and her feelings for Frances faded into a calm friendship.

Emotional attachments to women seem to have played a much more important part in the life of Mary's younger sister, Queen Anne. Anne also fell under the spell of Frances and, again borrowing the style of literary romance, wrote to her as "Ziphares," a man "who pined for a sight of his 'faire Semandra.'"[24] But Anne's strongest feelings were inspired by Sarah Churchill,

92. Queen Anne. Michael Dahl, oil, c. 1705.

Duchess of Marlborough, who as the queen's confidante for two decades was to play a major role in British politics. In their remarkable correspondence, Anne insisted they lay aside all distinctions of rank; so Sarah became "Mrs. Freeman" and Anne "Mrs. Morley." Repeatedly, Anne assured Sarah how "passionately I am yours."[25] Unlike her lively sister Mary, Anne was reserved and taciturn and was dominated by the handsome, intelligent, imperious Sa-

93. Sarah Churchill, Duchess of Marlborough. Bernard Lens the younger, miniature watercolor, 1720.

rah. In 1692 when Mary had insisted that Anne (then twenty-seven) dismiss Sarah from her suite for political reasons, since her husband, John Churchill, had fallen out of favor, Anne openly rebelled, defied her sister, and assured Sarah, "I am more yours than can be exprest and had rather live in a Cottage with you than reign Empresse of the world without you."[26] "Let them do what they please, nothing shall ever vex me, so I can have the satisfaction of seeing dear Mrs. Freeman; and I swear I would live on bread and water between four walls with her without repining."[27] Anne's loyalty to her friend caused a serious rift with Mary and William, whom she was to succeed on the throne.

Finally, in 1702 William died and Anne was free to elevate Sarah to a position of real political power as groom of the stole and keeper of the privy purse, in which posts Sarah kept Anne loyal to Lord Churchill, who—now raised to high eminence as the duke of Marlborough—replaced William as leader of the European Grand Alliance against Louis XIV in the bloody War of the Spanish Succession. But all did not go smoothly. A serpent appeared in Eden in the person of Abigail Masham, a poor relation of Sarah's who held the modest office of a royal bedchamber woman. Tiring at last of the domineering duchess, Anne turned to the more modest Abigail, who served surreptitiously as a backstairs liaison with Tory leaders bent on peace.

When Sarah realized the extent of Abigail's influence and her place in Anne's affections, her rage erupted in an angry letter that accused the queen of lesbian tendencies. "I remember you said . . . of all things in this world you valued most your reputation, which I confess surpris'd me very much that your Majesty should so soon mention that word after having discover'd [revealed] so great a passion for such a woman [Mrs. Masham], for sure there can be no great reputation in a thing so strange and unaccountable . . . nor can I think the having no inclination for any but one of one's own sex is enough to maintain such a character as I wish may still be yours."[28] We are reminded of Bentinck's jealous letter to William III. The duchess had already shown Anne a scurrilous ballad, probably written by Sarah's own secretary, Arthur Maynwaring:

> Whenas Queen Anne of great Renown
>   Great Britain's Scepter sway'd
> Besides the Church, she dearly lov'd
>   A Dirty Chamber-Maid . . .
> Her Secretary she was not,
>   Because she could not write;
> But had the Conduct and the Care
>   Of some dark Deeds at night.[29]

In 1710 Anne dismissed Sarah from her court and supported the Tories in negotiating an end to the war, despite repeated threats of blackmail from the duchess.[30] So the embittered relations of these three women affected the destiny of Europe. It seems highly unlikely, whatever Anne's "inclinations," that anything sexual took place; Anne was a model of devout piety, invalided by the time of her succession (at thirty-seven) after eighteen pregnancies. But it is remarkable that the duchess should have raised the charge of lesbianism at all in a land where the possibility of Sapphic love was barely acknowledged, and in light of Anne's earlier passionate attachment to herself.

Yet despite the rumors that circulated about royalty, female pairs might, if they maintained a façade of genteel respectability, be acclaimed, after the fashion of the day, as idealized "romantic friends." This was the case with Sarah Robinson Scott, who, having won modest fame as a writer of novels and histories, left her husband and went to live with her friend Barbara Montagu in a village near Bath, where they founded an institution for poor girls. A decade later Scott published a novel, *A Description of Millennium Hall,* based on their experiences, which became "the *vade mecum* of romantic friendship." In the novel, two women renounce matrimony and retire to the country to engage in "aesthetic pursuits and civilized enjoyment," much like the ladies in the duchess of Newcastle's utopian convent.[31]

Life having inspired art, this popular work of fiction now inspired numerous imitations in real life. As Lillian Faderman shows in her full and fascinating account of these romantic pairings, real and fictive, by far the best known "romantic friends" were the Ladies of Llangollen. Eleanor Butler and Sarah Ponsonby were aristocratic Irishwomen who, at age thirty-nine and twenty-three, disguised themselves as men and eloped not once but twice. Despairing of seeing them married, and convinced of the strength of their passion, their families finally provided them with small allowances and allowed them to settle in Wales.

Their unladylike bid for independence might have been expected to rouse social hostility, but the current stereotype of ideal female friendship made them icons rather than pariahs. "When I first heard of them I was disposed to be captivated by anything so romantic," wrote Lady Louisa Stuart in 1782, four years after their elopement.[32] Even Byron, when, as a college student he fell in love with a younger boy, cited "the Ladies" as an ideal same-sex couple in a letter to a sympathetic woman friend.[33] Eventually, they corresponded with Queen Charlotte, won a pension from George III, and became the rage not only in Britain but in Europe. Their modest cottage in a picturesque Welsh valley, where they charmed everyone and shared the same bed for fifty-three years, was visited by an impressive list of celebrities, among them the duke of Wellington, William Wilberforce, Sir Walter Scott, Robert Southey, Madame de Genlis, Prince Paul Esterhazy—even the young Charles Darwin. Poets were much given to eulogizing them. Anna Seward, whose own love for her friend Honora Sneyd inspired a series of sonnets modeled on Shakespeare's, devoted a whole volume of poems to their praise. In 1827 William Wordsworth addressed them as "Sisters in love, a love allowed to climb / Ev'n on this earth, above the reach of time."[34]

Their bucolic paradise was not without a thorn or two. Today they would be seen as a lesbian couple in the style of Gertrude Stein and Alice B. Toklas,

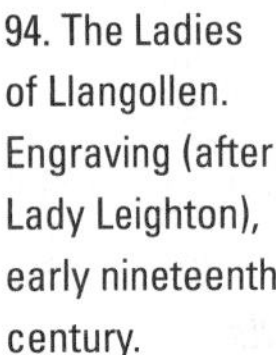

94. The Ladies of Llangollen. Engraving (after Lady Leighton), early nineteenth century.

but suspicions of this sort were far less common before the age of Freud, and their conventional conservatism in matters social and political insulated them from criticism. But in 1790 the *General Evening Post* maliciously described Eleanor Butler as a "tall and masculine" personage who "wears always a riding habit, hangs her hat with the air of a sportsman in the hall, and appears in all respect as a young man, if we except the petticoats which she still retains."[35] The outraged ladies wrote to their friend Edmund Burke about an action for libel. But Burke advised against this (he had himself sued the press for sexual innuendoes a decade before), assuring them that their reputation was such that no one would take notice of such calumnies. He was almost right.

Prominent among the Ladies' admirers was Hester Thrale (later Mrs. Piozzi), the friend and biographer of Dr. Johnson, who esteemed them as "the fair and noble recluses."[36] Given that redoubtable lady's repeated condemnations of male homosexuality, this enthusiasm may seem surprising. Indeed, Mrs. Thrale ranks with the duchess of Orléans a century earlier in the assiduity with which she set about unmasking contemporaries in her "Thraliana." But whereas the duchess, writing at the court of Louis XIV, looked on with bemused interest, Thrale's diaries reveal the prejudices of her nation sharpened by her own Protestant piety. She lamented the spread of "unnatural Vice among Men (now so modish)" and in April 1789, three months before the fall of the Bastille, commented: "Nature does get strangely out of Fashion sure enough: One hears of Things now, fit for the Pens of Petronius only, or Juvenal to record and satyrize: The Queen of France is at the head of Set of Monsters call'd by each other Sapphists, who boast her Example, and deserve to be thrown with the He Demons that haunt each other likewise, into Mount Vesuvius."[37]

Hester Thrale had earlier violated the ethos of her class by marrying an Italian musician named Gabriel Piozzi, causing many of her friends (including Dr. Johnson) to disown her. But a stay in Italy merely confirmed her moral insularity. "This Italy is indeed a Sink of Sin," she lamented in June 1786, "our Beckfords . . . run away at least from the original Theatre of their Crimes, & do not keep their Male Mistresses in Triumph like the Roman Priests and Princes."[38] She was especially astonished at the popularity of the elderly cardinal of York, "who kept a Catamite publicly at Rome while I was there, tho' a Man of the best Character possible for Piety & Charity, with which, as a Person said to me—that Vice has nothing to do. They consider'd it as mere Matter of Taste."[39] (The cardinal, Henry Stuart, was the younger brother of "Bonnie Prince Charlie" and the last Stuart claimant to the English throne.) England, she concluded patriotically at the end of her moralizing, "is the very best part of Europe to live in, for almost every Reason."[40]

In 1795 when Mrs. Thrale heard a clergyman preach an Advent sermon on how "Christianity had mended the World in general & how the Vices of the Ancients were unknown in Modern Times," she thought him absurdly naive.[41] ("Poor dear Man" was her comment.) Obsessed with the application of biblical prophecies to contemporary life, Mrs. Thrale fitted her view on homosexuality into her historical world picture. The growth of offenses "towards God & Reason, & Religion & Nature" which she perceived to be taking place confirmed her belief that the world would end in the year 2000, consumed by fires supernatural rather than volcanic.[42] Even warm personal friendship could not dull her gratification at punishments she felt were divinely ordained. When she heard a (false) report that her once dear friend George James had been guillotined in Brittany, she exclaimed in triumph, "See how Vengeance does pursue the Guilty!!!"[43] Reading Mrs. Thrale helps us understand how executions for sodomy in England could reach unprecedented numbers in the next forty years, even as they declined elsewhere.

Lesbianism especially fascinated her, and she took note of a new word for the enormity. This "horrible Vice," she writes, "has a Greek name now & is call'd Sapphism" and is growing in prevalence: "The Queen of France was all along accused, so was Raucoux [Raucourt] the famous Actress on the Paris Stage." Moreover, she admits its existence even in England: "'tis now grown common to suspect Impossibilities—(such I think 'em)—whenever two Ladies live too much together." Bath, she reports "is a Cage of these unclean Birds."[44] So was "that House of Miss Rathbone's" where several women "lived in sinful Celibàt" (that is, unmarried).[45] Mrs. Siddons, the famous tragedienne, had told Mrs. Thrale that "her Sister was in personal Danger once from a female Fiend of this Sort."[46] Growing ever more alarmed, she begins to suspect her most intimate acquaintances: "Why was Miss Weston so averse to any marriage I am wondering . . . and why did [she] make such an Ado about little Sally Siddons's Wit & Beauty & Stuff? The Girl is just like any other Girl—but Miss Weston did use to like every Girl so . . . Colonel Barry . . . had a good Escape of Miss Trefusis if all be true."[47] Finally, even the Ladies of Llangollen fell under suspicion. A recently published diary note by Mrs. Thrale condemns them as "damned Sapphists" and reveals that some ladies refused to spend the night at their famous cottage unless they were accompanied by gentlemen.[48]

Anne Seymour Damer (1749–1828) was an aristocrat, a scholar, and an amateur actress. Her lifelong passion, however, was sculpture, in her age regarded as an unwomanly pursuit involving hard and dusty work. Her cousin and mentor Horace Walpole, impressed by her intelligence and learning, introduced her to Sir Horace Mann as one who "writes Latin like Pliny and is learning Greek" and compared her modeling (hyperbolically) to Bernini's.[49] Granddaughter of one duke and sister-in-law to another, Anne married John Damer at eighteen and separated from him seven years later. She lived for another half century, winning modest fame for a bust of Nelson, two monumental masks that still adorn a Thames bridge at Henley, and a colossal statue of George III. Cosmopolitan in outlook, she traveled much in France and Italy, met Josephine, and sculpted a bust of Charles James Fox for Napoleon.

Anne Damer's social eminence—she knew Reynolds, Nelson, and Mrs. Siddons—together with her intense friendships with young actresses made her a focus for sexual gossip. The ever-vigilant Mrs. Thrale condemned her as "a lady much suspected of liking her own Sex in a criminal Way" and recorded a "droll but bitter Epigram" penned by Mrs. Siddons's husband:

> Her little Stock of private Fame
> Will fall a Wreck to public Clamour,
> If Farren leagues with one whose Name
> Comes near—Aye very near—to *Damn her.*[50]

Mrs. Thrale, as we have seen, regarded lesbians as "female Fiends." Joseph Farrington, diarist and fellow artist, harrumphed at Anne's "singularities."

95. Anne Damer and Mary Berry at Strawberry Hill. Richard Cosway, drawing, c. 1800.

"She wears a Man's Hat and Shoes," he complained, "and a Jacket also like a Man's—thus she walks about the fields with a Hooking-stick."[51] When Anne's special friend, Elizabeth Farren, the leading comic actress of the day, was pursued by the earl of Derby who wanted to marry her, the author of a satire entitled *The Whig Club* (1794) commented maliciously: "Tho' the vanity of the comedian must be interested in the event, her amorous passions are far from awakened by the idea . . . she is supposed to feel more exquisite delight from the touch of the cheek of Mrs. D——r than from the fancy of any *novelties* the wedding night can promise."[52]

Another pamphlet, running to twenty-three pages of satirical verse, must have made Damer uncomfortable, though its treatment of lesbianism was more jocular than hostile. The pseudonymous author of *A Sapphick Epistle from Jack Cavendish to the Honourable and Most Beautiful Mrs. D***** (c. 1777) informs us that "Miss Sappho was the first young classic maid that bestowed her affections on her own sex . . . She was the first Tommy the world has upon record; but to do her justice, though here hath been many Tommies since, yet we have never had but one Sappho."[53] (In eighteenth-century slang, "Tommy" was the female counterpart of "Molly.") The tone of the verse is rollickingly ribald, in marked contrast to Mrs. Thrale's religious rancor or Fielding's censoriousness:

When Sappho, the fair Lesbian belle,
    Had gain'd the knack to read and spell;
    She woo'd the Graces all;
No wench of Mytilene's Town,
Or black, or fair, or olive brown,
    Refus'd her amorous call.[54]

Anne Damer appears in the poem to warn women that male lovers mean pregnancy, childbirth, and a "thousand other woes"; her own country estate, on the other hand, is extolled as a "a mountain of delight . . . taste, elegance and Sapphick love."[55] The poet's posture is that of a lovesick admirer who is archly knowledgeable about Damer's European travels and her penchant for "the maids of warm Italia's Land."[56] In the 1780s William Beckford was to face ostracism and exile for his presumed sexual deviance, yet despite these satirical shafts and the hostility of Mrs. Thrale, Anne Damer's place in British society remained secure. Horace Walpole, who had written to Horace Mann that "I love her as my own child," made her his executrix and heir to his neo-Gothic country house at Strawberry Hill.[57]

• A Nun and an Actress •

Despite the occasional satire and the suspicious Mrs. Thrale, lesbianism in England remained largely out of the public eye. In France at the end of the century it was more open, especially among actresses who led public lives and belonged to an occupation not too far removed in respectable eyes from prostitution. It was even to play a part in scandalous revolutionary pamphlets that denounced the alleged erotic excesses of an unpopular queen.

In the early years of the eighteenth century Marc René D'Argenson, head of the Parisian police from 1697 to 1718, was much more concerned with controlling male homosexual behavior in the streets and taverns of Paris than with lesbianism, which he treated with discretion. "The notorious Mme. Murat was not formally charged, in spite of repeated warnings. The Lieutenant général, taking account of her birth and connections, judged that she and her kind were best dealt with by exile or confinement to any convent that would have her."[58] Whereas sodomites might still be burned at the stake, lesbians were dealt with like streetwalkers, debauched actresses, or unruly courtesans and charged with minor offenses. Women of the lower classes were briefly jailed. In aristocratic society, a *lettre de cachet* might be obtained by an irate father or husband to immure a woman who had affronted conventional morality. By this means, the marquise de Listenoy was briefly detained in 1730 at Vesoul, along with her lover Mme de Saint-Lambert and a little girl who "called one of them *papa* and the other *maman*."[59]

Romantic female friendship inspired as much enthusiasm in France as in England, and it is often a puzzle to say when it was colored by erotic feeling. Famous bluestockings like Mme de Staël (who was amicably separated from her husband) and Juliette Mme Récamier (whose marriage was a mere formality) addressed each other in rapturous terms despite their love affairs with Benjamin Constant and Chateaubriand. After their first meeting in 1798 Mme Récamier wrote "from then on I thought only of Mme de Staël," and Mme de Staël replied: "I love you with a love surpassing that of friendship . . . I go down on my knees to embrace you with all my heart." And later, "You are in the forefront of my life . . . It seemed to me when I saw you that to be loved by you would satisfy destiny."[60]

Male observers responded variously to such passions. In Rousseau's *La Nouvelle Héloïse,* the heroine, Julie, falls in love with her tutor, Saint Preux. But her confidant, Claire, hesitates to marry because her love for Julie so exceeds her love for her man. "The most important thing in my life," she tells her, "has been to love you. From the very beginning my heart has been absorbed in yours." Saint Preux feels some envy but sympathetically shares their feelings, which he finds erotically arousing: "Nothing, no, nothing on earth is capable of exciting such a voluptuous sensibility as your mutual caresses; and the spectacle of two lovers has not offered my eyes a more delicious sensation."[61] Rousseau's rapturous celebration of passionate emotion and romantic invocations of nature made the novel a literary sensation when it appeared in 1761.

By contrast, when Denis Diderot observed Sophie Volland's intimacies with her sister Mme le Gendre, he was tormented by jealousy.

> I am obsessed [he confessed to Sophie] and do not know what I'm writing . . . I see by the letter you've scribbled that Madame le Gendre is or will be with you incessantly. I have become so sensitive, so unjust, so jealous . . . I am ashamed of what is happening to me, but I don't know how to prevent it. Your mother maintains that your sister likes amiable women, and it is certain she likes you very much; and then that nun for whom she had such a penchant and then that voluptuous and tender manner with which she leans sometimes leans towards you. And then her fingers oddly squeezed between yours.[62]

Diderot's letter is of special interest since it was written in 1760 when he was at work on *The Nun,* a novel that offers a gripping (and complex) picture of lesbianism in a French convent. The book was inspired by a hoax. Hoping to lure a friend back to Paris, Diderot wrote him letters purportedly from a nun who sought assistance in having her vows revoked. The hoax was soon abandoned, but it inspired Diderot to compose a fictional memoir by the imaginary woman, whom he named Suzanne Simonin.

Diderot's *roman à thèse* was meant to question the wisdom of locking up young women like Suzanne in convents when they had no vocation and were unwilling prisoners. Though it makes a strong case against the unnaturalness and petty tyranny of convent life, *La Religieuse* is not, however, a facile exercise in anti-clericalism: Suzanne is a pious Catholic, and her religious enthusiasms are presented with surprising sensitivity. The book recounts her experiences under three mothers superior. The first, a kindly and devout woman, dies and is succeeded by a sadistic tyrant. Fortunately, a sympathetic lawyer has Suzanne transferred to another house where the new superior is frivolous and lacking in clerical dignity but good-natured and popular. She makes a pet of Suzanne, kisses and caresses her, praises her figure when she undresses her, and swoons ecstatically when she performs at the keyboard:

> Then I played some pieces of Couperin, Rameau, and Scarlatti, during which she lifted a corner of my collar and rested her hand on my bare shoulder, with the tips of her fingers touching my breast. She was sighing and seemed oppressed, breathing heavily. The hand on my shoulder pressed hard at first but then ceased pressing at all, as though all strength and life had gone out of her and her head fell on to mine. Truly that harebrained woman was incredibly sensitive and had the most exquisite taste for music, for I have never known anybody on whom it had such an extraordinary effect.[63]

Suzanne frankly enjoys the gifts and affection showered on her by this woman with "lovely cheeks, red lips, and a handsome head" and when she asks, "Sister Suzanne, do you love me?" she replies innocently, "How could I fail to love you? I would have to be the very soul of ingratitude" (137). When the superior experiences a second orgasm during their mutual caresses, the naive nun does not interpret the episode as erotic: she thinks the other woman has fainted from some strange malady. Moreover, the joy the superior has discovered in her love for Suzanne transforms life in the convent. "The community," she reports, "had never been happier than since I joined it" (147).

But when Suzanne tells her confessor of the older woman's endearments, he calls her "a libertine, a wicked nun, a pernicious woman, a corrupt soul" and forbids Suzanne to be alone with her again (162). Since he refuses to explain what the danger is, Suzanne rejects his advice as too severe. Nevertheless, she refuses to see the superior again in private. The latter protests, "I esteem and love [some] more than others. That is all my crime" (165–167). Deprived of Suzanne's company, she falls into a demented lovesickness, so that Suzanne hears her "heartrending wailing" in the corridors at night and is "filled with pity." The older woman becomes erratic and reclusive, turns severely pious, then frenzied, as her melancholy breeds an acute sense of guilt. In a paroxysm of remorse she scourges herself and begs the other nuns to "trample me underfoot" (172).

A new confessor, Dom Morel, admits to Suzanne his lack of any religious vocation. Like his predecessor, he warns her of the older woman but again refuses to explain—there is such a thing as "poisonous knowledge." Unsatisfied with these evasions, Suzanne asks pointedly, "How can the endearments and caresses of a woman be dangerous to another woman? . . . Where is the evil of loving each other, saying so and showing it? It is so delightful!" (176). But when she overhears the superior tell Morel, in portentous tones, "Father I am damned," she is terrified and feels a strong revulsion. The superior falls ill, becomes delirious, sees "angels descending in wrath" to drag her to hell, and dies murmuring "I am lost! . . . tell her I love her" (179–182). Suzanne escapes from the convent with Dom Morel, only to be assaulted by her rescuer. She dies in Paris, in wretched squalor, helpless and despairing.

Diderot's tale, whose psychological subtlety owes much to Samuel Richardson, whom Diderot admired greatly, is both compelling and unsettling. In contrast to Fielding's clear condemnations, his story is full of disorienting uncertainties that are never resolved. It was, moreover, not published until 1796, a decade after the author's death. The editor of Diderot's collected works proposed suppressing the "disgusting amours of the Superior," which, he thought, even dissolute men would find "chilling and meaningless" and honest women "revolting or unintelligible."[64] During the Bourbon Restoration the novel was twice banned. One eminent Victorian, Lord Morley, writing in 1878, commented on the lesbian theme: "It is appalling, it fills you with horror, it haunts you for days and nights, it leaves a kind of stain on the memory."[65]

Today, French and American critics have differed sharply about *La Religieuse.* Marie-Jo Bonnet, in a searching critique, calls the novel "the most beautiful portrait in male literature of one woman in love with another."[66] Lillian Faderman, in contrast, has labeled Diderot's depiction of lesbianism "vicious and pathological."[67] Inevitably, one must concede that Diderot's choice of a naive narrator who, even at the story's end, has not yet grasped what lesbianism is makes it difficult to determine his own point of view. Yet we may feel that each of these judgments is too extreme. The mother superior seems too troubled a personality for her love story to be called "beautiful." On the other hand, she is not a sinister villain who plots to ensnare her victim by trickery or threats. Frustrated in love and subject to theological terrors, she seems less a vicious woman than a weak and pitiable one caught in an emotional turmoil that destroys her. Obviously, Diderot's novel shows that he could all too easily imagine women falling in love with other women. Did he see such love as always doomed to defeat and tragedy? We do not know.

In the 1770s, a decade after Diderot wrote *The Nun,* lesbianism was to become a widely recognized phenomenon in Parisian life, as anonymous journalists exploited the theme. By this time numerous clandestine periodicals circulated in ways designed to baffle government control. The most influential of these, the *Mémoires secrets* of Bachaumont, Mouffle d'Angerville, and Pidsanat de Mairobert provided much uncensored political, literary, and theatrical gossip. In July 1774 it reported, "The vice of the tribades is becoming very fashionable among the ladies of the Opera: they make no mystery of it and treat this peccadillo with pretty condescension."[68] The *Mémoires* named Sophie Arnould, the leading singer of the day, who had triumphed in the premieres of Gluck's operas, and Françoise Raucourt of the Comédie-Française, "who is mad about her own sex and has renounced the marquis de Bièvre to give herself over to it more freely." A more reputable private news sheet, the *Correspondance littéraire,* edited by Grimm and Diderot, suggested that lesbian groups in Paris were well organized, though still clandestine: "There exists, it is said, a society known by the name of the Lodge of Lesbos, but their assemblies are more mysterious than those of the Free Masons have ever been. There one is initiated into all the secrets which Juvenal describes so frankly and naively in his 16th satire . . . It is said that our superb Galathée [Raucourt] is one of the chief priestesses of the Temple."[69]

Françoise Raucourt was the stage name of Françoise-Marie-Antoinette Saucerotte, who in 1762 at the age of sixteen had made her sensational debut as Dido in a performance that roused wild enthusiasm. Critics raved about her beauty, her voice, and the polished maturity of her acting. Melchior Grimm predicted she would be the *gloire immortel* of the French theater. A contemporary source reported: "Servants sent to secure places discharged their mission at the risk of their lives; several were carried away in an unconscious state, and one is said to have died."[70] Françoise's male lovers were succeeded by women on whom the teenage actress spent a fortune: the *Correspondance* quoted her as saying she now understood how women had ruined so many young men.[71] With two or three houses, a dozen horses, fifteen servants, and debts equal to one hundred times her annual salary, she was bankrupt at twenty and had to flee to Brussels. Rescued from her embarrassments by a "benevolent hand," she found herself boycotted by her colleagues at the *Comédie,* who refused to accept her back into the troupe "because the misconduct and libertinism of this actress were repugnant to the decency of the company."[72] But Marie Antoinette interceded and persuaded the king to order her reinstatement. When she appeared again as Dido, there were hisses; however (according to the *Mémoires*), her partisans "applauded her noisily and the demoiselle Arnould, with a number of other tribades, organized a cabal in the orchestra for their illustrious sister."[73]

In the 1780s a flood of subversive literature held authoritarian hierarchies and traditional morality up to ridicule. Libertine writers turned from philosophy to farce, from theory to epigrams, from discussions of virtue to defenses of what had been called vice. Imprisoned in 1777 by a *lettre de cachet,* the twenty-eight-year-old Mirabeau, who had already written several pornographic novels, occupied himself by composing an *Erotika Biblion* which arrived—via Plato—at some startling conclusions: "But there are women who love other women? Once more, nothing could be more natural: these are the halves of former females who were doubles. In the same way certain males who were the doubles of other males have retained an exclusive taste for their own sex. There is nothing strange about this . . . See how the extent of our knowledge effects the extent of our tolerance! I wish these ideas would inspire moral preachers."[74]

Mirabeau's libertine treatise appeared in 1783, by which time lesbians had no longer to fear the fire, the noose, or even the whip; the era of legal sanctions was past. A year later the *Mémoires* declared, "Tribadery has always been in vogue among women as homosexuality *[pédérastie]* among men; but one did not flaunt these vices with so much scandal and notoriety as today. As the former is not punished by the laws, it is less surprising. Consequently our prettiest women give themselves over to it, glory in it and make it a point of pride!"[75] Journalists now seemed readier to relish the scandal than to register indignation. A few continued to denounce lesbianism as the "most hideous" taste in the world and an infectious madness, but such language was beginning to sound archaic.[76]

Raucourt herself was saluted as "the most famous of our modern lesbians" by the *Correspondance littéraire.*[77] Belatedly learning tact and discretion, the grand tragedienne at last propitiated her colleagues and regained her popularity. The hostility she next faced was political rather than moral. Imprisoned as a royalist in 1793, she escaped the guillotine only because a sympathetic clerk destroyed her dossier, which had been marked with a red "G." Napoleon, a warm admirer, gave her a handsome pension and made her the head of a French troupe sent to dazzle Italy. Her later appearances in Paris met with great success.

During her days in prison, Raucourt had met a witty and attractive young woman named Marie-Henriette Simonot-Ponty, with whom she shared a lasting attachment and a home in the country. When they were separated, Raucourt wrote passionately to her lover, assuring her "you are so necessary to my existence that far from you I am nothing but a shadow"—"I will love you until my last day."[78] Ponty was, indeed, with her when she died in 1815. Like her life, Raucourt's death was also an occasion for scandal. When the curé of her parish refused to perform the burial service, a mob estimated at 15,000 threatened to break down the church door and hang him from a lamppost. To quell the riot, Louis XVIII was forced to send a priest from his household to officiate.

• The Ill-Fated Queen •

The fate of the another woman associated by the French public with lesbianism was much grimmer. In the mid and late eighteenth century, the French

96. Marie Antoinette, Queen of France. Elisabeth Vigée-LeBrun, oil, 1783.

monarchy came under attack in a flood of scurrilous pamphlets that sought to undermine its dignity and authority. These scabrous publications at first highlighted the promiscuity of Louis XV with his numerous mistresses and his notorious Deer Park. Then, when Marie Antoinette succeeded her grandfather-in-law in unpopularity, they focused on the sexual exploits of the young queen, whom copper engravings pictured in erotic postures with her alleged female favorites. Terry Castle has summarized these salacious attacks:

> In the years leading up to the Revolution, anti-royalist propagandists elaborated on the charge [of lesbianism] in a host of secretly published pornographic *libelles* [lampoons] designed to inflame public sentiment against her. In the anonymous *Portefeuille d'un talon rouge* (1779) and the *Essai historique sur la vie de Marie Antoinette* (1781), for example, the queen was accused of bringing the vice of "tribadism" with her from Austria into France and of having affairs with the Comtesse de Polignac and Mme Balbi. In the scurrilous *Amours de Charlot et de Toinette* (1779), she was depicted in "criminal" embraces with the Princesse de Lamballe. And in the grossly obscene *Le Godmiché royal* (1789) . . . she was shown deploying a dildo on her female lover "Hébée" (Polignac or Lamballe) after complaining about her husband's impotence—a motif revived in the equally scandalous *Fureurs utérines de Marie Antoinette, femme de Louis XVI* of 1791.[79]

The first three pamphlets antedate the Revolution by as much as a decade. In 1775 Marie Antoinette, then just twenty and queen for only one year, wrote to her mother, Empress Maria Theresa in Vienna: "They have been liberal enough to accuse me of having a taste for both women and lovers."[80] The queen, who disdained public opinion, showed little concern, but the empress was horrified at the allegations. A year later, the *Mémoires secrets* took note of the hostile campaign, deploring some "execrable couplets" that "criminally misrepresent the friendship of the queen for madame the Princesse de Lamballe."[81]

What led to this cascade of abuse? Its first source seems to have been disaffected courtiers who were jealous of the favors the queen had bestowed on two women friends. The Princesse de Lamballe had been one of the few Frenchwomen to show Marie Antoinette affection when she had arrived in France as the fourteen-year-old bride of the dauphin. Attractive, with luxuriant blond hair and blue eyes, the young princess, who had been widowed at eighteen on the death of her dissipated husband, became Marie Antoinette's life-long confidante and the superintendent of the royal household, a highly lucrative post. More dangerous was the raven-haired Comtesse de Polignac. Coming upon this angel-faced beauty in 1775, the susceptible young queen experienced what has been called a "superheated falling in love."[82] But the comtesse's vulturous relatives shut out the older nobility, who became hostile and spread malicious gossip. It is said that the comtesse cost the French state more than Mme de Pompadour, who had been mistress to Louis XV.[83]

Extra fuel was added to the fire when the queen became the patroness of Sophie Arnould at the Opéra and Françoise Raucourt at the Comédie Française. Soon speculation about Marie Antoinette's love affairs had become an international phenomenon. By the spring of 1789 her lesbian propensities were so taken for granted that Mrs. Thrale could, as we have seen, report that "the Queen of France is at the Head of a Set of Monsters call'd by each other Sapphists."[84] This, however, was a wild exaggeration; three or four

97. The Princess Lamballe (1749–1792). Antoine-François Callet, oil, date unknown.

women certainly attracted the queen, but there was no such open circle at court as there was in Parisian theatrical circles.

Was there any truth in these rumors? The queen's enemies at court and, later, among the revolutionists were convinced of her sexual iniquity. After the Bourbon Restoration in 1815, her royalist defenders, who regarded her as a saint and martyr, indignantly repudiated these "infamous accusations," and her modern biographers have likewise tended to see them as fabrications.[85] Stefan Zweig, writing in 1932, reminded his readers that Louis had for seven years tried but failed to consummate the royal marriage. The queen, he thought, "at this juncture involuntarily turned towards a woman friend."[86] But in the end Zweig was inclined to interpret her attachments as schoolgirl crushes. More recently Joan Haslip (1987) has agreed with Zweig.[87] Nevertheless, Marie Antoinette remained, among lesbians, a potent symbol of same-sex love. In 1825 the lesbian diarist Anne Lister visited the queen's cell in the Conciergerie with her lover, who had dropped the queen's name as a clue to her sexual interests when they first met.[88]

But whatever the ideology of her traducers, there is no doubt as to the queen's unpopularity. Pretty, frivolous, and wildly extravagant, with no political knowledge, sense, or wisdom, Marie Antoinette was perceived as a treacherous foreigner who favored the interest of her Austrian relatives and opposed any move toward economic or political reform. After 1789 the hatred became more violent, and the radical press painted her as a modern Messalina or Fredegund. The result was that her friends and associates became special objects of popular hatred during the Revolution.

This animus provoked a horrifying episode during the first hours of the September Massacres of 1792. The Princess de Lamballe had loyally returned to Paris to be near her royal mistress despite the queen's pleas that she seek safety. She was one of the first aristocrats to fall victim to the Terror. On September 3 a drunken mob burst into the courtyard of the Temple, where the deposed king and queen were imprisoned, dragging a naked, headless trunk by the legs, whose genitals, according to some accounts, were hideously mutilated. One man waved the severed head of Marie de Lamballe on the end of a pike. "Their wish was, they explained, to mount the stairs into the tower, taking their trophies with them, that they might compel the queen to kiss the lips of her intimate."[89] Fortunately, the commander of the guard was able to deflect the brutal crowd to the Palais Royal. When the queen learned what was happening, she fell into a deep faint, the only time, her daughter later claimed, that she had seen her mother lose her composure during any of her tribulations.

Jacques-René Hébert, the most virulent of the Jacobins, had denounced the princess, in his gutter news sheet *Père Duchesne,* as the queen's lesbian friend, "a coryphée of the orgies of the Trianon."[90] Jules Michelet, in his monumental *Histoire de la Révolution française* (1850), suggested that a morbid curiosity about these rumors "was perhaps the principal cause of her death" and that the killers had stripped her body "expecting to find on her some shameful mystery which would confirm" them.[91] Some of these details are now discounted as unhistorical embroiderings of a legend, but it is hard to imagine that the incensed mob's sadism did not have, as one motive, "the overthrowing of Lesbos."[92]

98. The head of Princess Lamballe paraded before the Temple where Marie Antoinette was held, September 2, 1792. Contemporary engraving.

99. The execution of Marie Antoinette, October 16, 1793. Charles Monnet, engraving.

A year later Marie Antoinette stood trial as an enemy of the Revolution. Though the verdict was a foregone conclusion—the second Reign of Terror was under way—an elaborate indictment was drawn up by the prosecutor, Fouquier-Tinville. Accused of conspiring with France's enemies to defeat the revolutionary armies, the queen also faced a sensational sexual accusation. At the trial Hébert produced a letter his captors had persuaded her eight-year-old son to sign accusing his mother of practicing indecencies with him. But this charge had the unexpected result of creating an reaction in the queen's favor when, appealing to the women in the court, she indignantly denied the allegation. She may then have expected that the court would raise the issue of lesbianism. But here the trial took a bizarre turn, for Fouquier-Tinville, instead of taking the accusatory pamphlets at face value, set forth the strange theory that the queen herself had "actually pushed perfidy and dissimulation so far as to print and distribute . . . works in which she herself was depicted in a most undesirable light . . . in order to lay a false scent and to persuade the foreign powers that she was being grossly maligned by the French."[93] Perhaps Fouquier-Tinville feared the wild extravagance of the material would undermine the government's case. The next day, on October 16, 1793, the executioners held up the queen's severed head before the crowds in the Place de la Révolution. Madame de Polignac, who had escaped the Terror, died in Vienna a year later.

CHAPTER SIXTEEN

THE ENLIGHTENMENT

1730–1810

• Montesquieu and Beccaria •

In the second third of the eighteenth century France experienced an intellectual upheaval that was to drastically alter the political, legal, and moral landscape. Montesquieu and Voltaire, returning from their visits to England, sang the praises of British political and religious freedom. Step by step age-old opinions were called into question by one writer after another, despite state censorship and the threat of the Bastille. A tyrannical church which had torn out the tongues of blasphemers, cast the corpses of actors and actresses into quicklime in unhallowed wastelands, broken Protestant "heretics" on the wheel, and burned speculative books on science and philosophy now came under fire from skeptics who published their works anonymously in liberal centers like Amsterdam or Geneva. They were called "philosophes," but they were not philosophers in the classical academic sense; rather, they were rationalists who dared to subject traditional religious, political, and moral issues to critical scrutiny, in the light of science, history, and reason.

Many were deists, or even, as the century progressed, atheists, who dared to challenge the basic theological and moral tenets of Christianity. One of the more militant of these was Jean-Baptiste de Boyer, marquis d'Argens, a retired military officer who became a minor luminary at the court of Frederick the Great. D'Argens earned an international reputation in 1736 with his *Lettres juives,* the pretended reports of two Jewish merchants to a rabbi in Cairo. The book was larded with a strong dose of anti-clericalism, but his broadside hit home. "A mistaken zeal for exterminating our nation, and certain Nazarenes who were considered heretics," writes one of the Jews, "first served as the pretext for establishing the Inquisition."

> But the imbecilic people did not see that this single matter would carry after it all the others. For, what deeds, good or bad, do not lead back to religion? Judaism, heresy, the observance of all the precepts of Nazarene law,

> oaths, crimes against divine worship, bigamy, sodomy, theft from churches, insults against priests and monks, sorcery, and finally many other things which are connected with Nazarene belief. The people, astonished, realized too late the exorbitant power they had given the monks. But they had neither the strength nor courage to rescind it.[1]

To many philosophes in the Age of Reason, the Bible as a code of morals seemed often barbaric, and the God of the Old Testament an archaic tribal deity, merciless toward enemies of the Jews and to the Jews themselves when they disobeyed his sometimes savage commands. Inevitably, the treatment of homosexuals—which d'Argens noted glancingly in his list of clerical tyrannies—also came into question. By the end of the century a momentous change took place: in 1791 French law, which for centuries had condemned sodomites to the stake, was reformed so that homosexual relations ceased to be a crime at all.

Nevertheless, progress toward legal reform was slow and halting, and even when relief from legal ferocity arrived, ancient prejudices remained. In the eighteenth century the status of the homosexual in French society was always a peripheral issue, never becoming the center of a public debate for the simple reason that, in an age of revolution, too many other matters preempted the attention of reformers, and in their scattered references the need for change was more often implied than openly advocated. This caution is exemplified in the most influential political essay the century produced, Montesquieu's *The Spirit of Laws* (1748). Montesquieu's magnum opus, on which he had labored for twenty years, undertook to examine the laws, customs, and political systems of Europe and Asia, both modern and ancient, on a comparative basis, evaluating each nation and culture disinterestedly. Though firmly opposed to bigotry and superstition, Montesquieu trod warily and was only moderately liberal in his conclusions.

In Book XII of *The Spirit of Laws,* after short chapters on heresy, sorcery, and treason, Montesquieu devoted a single page to "The Crime against Nature." Since Montesquieu knew he must take powerful negative emotions into account before he could break new ground, he disclaims any desire to diminish the "horror" that sodomy inspires. Yet he warns that this horror may be abused by tyrants who may seek convictions for secret crimes by dubious means. Then, by noting that witchcraft, heresy, and sodomy are the only three crimes still punished in France by fire, Montesquieu, by implication, places sodomy among what were now commonly perceived as archaic ecclesiastical offenses.

Finally, he looks for sociological causes for male homosexual behavior—causes that were mundane rather than demonic—and finds different influences in different states at different times: naked athletics in ancient Greece, the scarcity of women in polygamous Asiatic societies, and the sequestering

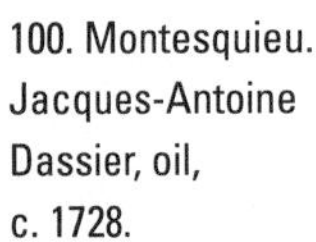

100. Montesquieu. Jacques-Antoine Dassier, oil, c. 1728.

of young males in single-sex schools in France. Taking the view that it is more important to change social conditions that might foster homosexuality than to punish it, Montesquieu ends by analogizing it to such commonplace "vices" as prostitution, which are controlled not by burning but by police surveillance. Despite his initial disclaimer that he is not trying to change public sentiment, he has in fact degraded sodomy from a horrific theological offense to a minor social problem.[2]

But what Montesquieu does not say is even more significant than what he does. His essay is most radical in what it omits. He does not mention Sodom or Leviticus, references that were still routine in French legal treatises. In this he went well beyond the famous *Encyclopedia.* This monumental work, in which the philosophes sought to codify the new dispensation of rational criticism, remained brutally orthodox in its entry on "Sodomy": "This crime took its name from the city of Sodom which perished by fire from heaven because of this abominable disorder which was common there. Divine justice has pronounced the penalty of death against those who soil themselves with this crime (Leviticus xx)."[3] Montesquieu, by contrast, mentions only one reason for discouraging male homosexuality, a wholly secular one: he worries that it may give "to one sex the weaknesses of the other," that is, passive homosexuality may feminize men. Montesquieu's critical skepticism did not extend to gender roles.

Did Montesquieu really regard male homosexuality with horror? Most likely his opening disclaimer was the strategic feint of a reformer trying to change his readers' minds about a long-standing taboo. But one crucial difficulty kept him and the philosophes from tackling the problem more aggressively—the lack of any clear conception of sexual orientation, a conception that has in our century proved critical in changing social attitudes. Montesquieu thought of sexual desires as fluid, and he rashly predicted that, with only a moderate amount of discouragement, same-sex love would vanish before the superior attractions of heterosexuality.

The influence of *The Spirit of Laws* in Europe and America was immense: its ideas proved basic even for the United States Constitution. Its primary focus, however, was on politics rather than criminal law. For law reform, the seminal book was that of an Italian disciple, Cesare Beccaria. *Of Crimes and Punishments,* published in 1761 when the young aristocrat was only twenty-three, took Europe by storm. Its great success lay in showing that the same critical method the philosophes had applied to science and religion might be systematically applied to criminal law. The opening sentence reveals Beccaria's radical spirit: "A few remnants of the laws of an ancient predatory people [the Romans], compiled by a monarch who lived twelve centuries ago in Constantinople, mixed subsequently with Lombardic tribal customs, and bound together in chaotic volumes of obscure and unauthorized interpreters—these form the tradition of opinions which in a large part of Europe is still accorded the name of law."[4] Here was a clarion call to reject "the dregs of utterly barbarous centuries."

Beccaria's novel ideas soon became the common coin of legal thought: the accused should be regarded as innocent until proven guilty, judges should not interpret laws arbitrarily, punishments should be proportional to crimes and no more severe than was necessary to achieve their purpose, which should be deterrence, not revenge. Beccaria argued against the death penalty and, in his most impassioned chapter, denounced judicial torture, still commonly in use on the Continent. It was largely due to his influence that by 1789 torture had disappeared as a routine practice in European courts.

On homosexuality Beccaria had little to say—a mere paragraph in a chapter on "crimes difficult to prove" which dealt primarily with adultery and infanticide—and what he does say closely echoes Montesquieu. He suggests that "Attic venery" *(l'attica venere)* springs not so much from "the satiety of pleasures" as from the confining of "ardent youth" to single-sex colleges and religious seminaries. The law should concentrate on prevention rather than punishment. He does make one further point, however: men accused of this crime in Italy are often subjected to "torments that triumph over innocence," that is, they confess to crimes they did not commit in order to escape pain they cannot bear.[5]

• Frederick the Great •

The influence of the philosophes was not confined to the middle and lower classes, who, indeed, were often devoutly hostile to their radicalism. It impinged also on the remarkable constellation of "enlightened despots" who, in the late eighteenth century, graced thrones in absolutist states. Not the least of these was Frederick II of Prussia. His father, the redoubtable Frederick William, was anything but enlightened. We may recall his edict of 1725 ordering that "all gypsies found within the borders of his kingdom were to be strangled, while sodomites would be burned alive."[6] In cases where leniency was recommended the Soldier King overruled the courts, as with Catherine Margaret Linck. Between 1700 and 1730 nine men were executed for bestiality, three for relations with other men.[7] Viewed in historical perspective, of course, the king's homophobia is not without its irony. Frederick William could not have foreseen that his "effeminate" heir, who was thirteen when he issued his harsh anti-sodomy command, would become the hero of an admiring nation and would win from the rest of Europe—where respect for his military genius and "enlightened" intelligence was mixed with shock at his lack of scruples—the epithet "the Great."

As with William III, Frederick's biographers have often shrunk from facing the facts of his sexual nature. Prussian patriots like Leopold von Ranke and Heinrich von Treitschke (who admired Frederick as a nation builder) simply avoided the subject. In England, the hostile Macaulay hinted at "vices from which History averts her eyes, and which even Satire blushes to name."[8] But a decade later Frederick's champion, Thomas Carlyle, in his monumental eight-volume biography (1852–1865), denounced such rumors as "thrice-abominable" falsehoods.[9] And Will Durant, whose excellent account of Frederick must be the most widely read in our (or any) age, delivered a Scotch verdict, perhaps intimidated by Carlyle's vehemence: "He was suspected of homosexuality, but of this we have only surmise."[10]

Yet the contemporary evidence is overwhelming, including an abundance of statements from friendly sources. For example, the Prince de Ligne, who fought Frederick in battle but delighted in his company, reported a conversation about handsome young men: "I spoke as a connoisseur [that is, from a aesthetic point of view]; he as an amateur."[11] And Voltaire, who, at the beginning of their friendship lost no occasion to flatter Frederick, sent the king a clever poem comparing him to Julius Caesar:

> J'aime César, ce bel esprit,
> César dont la main fortunée,
> À tous les lauriers destinée,
> Agrandit Rome, et le prescrit
> Un autre ciel, une autre année.
> J'aime César entre les bras
> De la maitresse qui lui cède;
> Je ris et ne me fâche pas
> De le voir, jeune et plein d'appas,
> Dessus et dessous Nicomède.[12]

("I love Caesar, that brilliant man—Caesar, whose fortunate hand, destined to win all the laurels, makes Rome great and ordains for it another sky and another year. I love Caesar in the arms of the mistress who yields to him. I laugh and am not perturbed to see him, young and attractive, above and under Nicomedes.") Voltaire meant that he preferred the Caesar who reformed the calendar—and Caesar the bisexual lover—to the military adventurer. Translated, this meant that he applauded Frederick's sponsorship of the Berlin Academy of Science and took a tolerant view of his sexuality, while decrying the rape of Silesia.

Frederick's case is unique for his age in one regard: his sexual orientation was explicitly canvassed by a biographer immediately after his death. In 1788 Dr. Johann Georg Zimmermann, who had attended the king during his last illness, published his *Conversations,* in which he set about to scotch the rumors of Frederick's "Grecian taste in love." Zimmermann admitted that "Voltaire, la Beaumelle, the Duke de Choiseul, innumerable Frenchmen and Germans, almost all the friends and enemies of Frederick, almost all the princes and great men of Europe, even his servants—even the confidants and friends of his later years, were of opinion that he had loved, as it is pretended, Socrates loved Alcibiades."[13] (Laurent La Beaumelle was a minor poet who had added some incriminating lines to *La Pucelle,* Voltaire's ribald mock-epic about Joan of Arc; the witty duc de Choiseul, French minister for foreign affairs, had bombarded Frederick with epigrams as well as canon.) Zimmermann's strange conjecture was that Frederick merely pretended to "this vicious failing" in order to contradict another rumor: that he had been emasculated. A reputation as an active sodomite was, he assumes, less damning in the king's eyes. Hence, Zimmerman argues,

> we find that he encouraged the spreading of [this suspicion] wide abroad, with all the powers of royalty, not only by honoring with particular favors young men who, by their beauty and daily intercourse with the king, raised

> such a suspicion, but chiefly and above all by granting leave to the bookseller Bordeaux, at Berlin, almost under the windows of his palace, to print the *Pucelle d'Orléans,* adulterated by La Beaumelle. In this publication, printed in Berlin, with the king's approbation, we find the most impudent and satiric passage, which with the highest cynic perspicuity and clearness charges the king with the Grecian taste in love.[14]

According to Zimmermann's convoluted theory, Frederick believed he had been medically castrated as a result of a botched cure for gonorrhea. But Zimmermann thought that the aggressive virility of "the greatest and most intrepid hero of his age" made it impossible that this had happened. The operation, he thinks, had not left him emasculated, though Frederick himself(!) did not realize this. Apart from the prima facie unlikelihood of this idea, it is on record that court physicians examined Frederick's corpse and took special note of his genital integrity.[15]

But what in fact do we know about Frederick's relations with young men? And how did these affairs affect his life and reputation? The record is one of intrigue, ardent friendships, casual affairs (if we are to believe Voltaire), and tragedy. The details are well documented by eighteenth-century writers, some hostile but not all. Occasionally we have evidence from Frederick's own hand. From the start, the story is bound up with the young prince's relationship with his violent father.

It is no exaggeration to speak of Frederick's childhood and youth as hellish. His father, Frederick William I, was eccentric to the verge of dementia. His principal passion in life was his regiment of "giants," tall soldiers whom he collected from all over Europe, sometimes having them kidnapped. Irritated by any trifle, he struck men across the face with his cane and kicked women in the street when he lost his temper, which was often. Determined to restore the treasury depleted by his own spendthrift father, he distinguished himself by his miserliness, and his children were often starved or fed spoiled food. Macaulay wrote that "Oliver Twist in the parish workhouse" was a petted child "compared with this wretched heir apparent of a crown."[16]

Frederick William was particularly incensed by his son's disdain for things military. (Young Frederick had called his uniform a "shroud.") The king despised learning and especially hated French culture. But Frederick played the flute, loved French literature, wrote French poetry, wore his hair exasperatingly long in the French style, and favored elegant French clothes. The angry king denounced his son's "lascivious and womanly activities," calling him "an effeminate boy, without a single manly inclination, who cannot ride nor shoot."[17] On occasion, servants had to brave his wrath to save Frederick from his father's fists or sword; once he attempted to strangle him.[18] Inveterately sanctimonious, Frederick William justified his wrath by appeals to religion, a habit that must have strengthened the boy's agnosticism.

The first friendship to arouse suspicions was with his father's page, Peter

Christoph Keith. The prince was sixteen, Keith a year older. Frederick's sister Wilhelmine, his devoted companion and closest ally, wrote that the two "soon became inseparable. Keith was intelligent, but without education. He served my brother from feelings of real devotion, and kept him informed of all the king's actions." Then she added, mysteriously, "Though I had noticed that he was on more familiar terms with this page than was proper in his position, I did not know how intimate the friendship was."[19] The king, alarmed, sent Keith into exile. But Frederick William was no luckier with a young officer he appointed as a companion responsible for his son's morals. Frederick was soon sending Lieutenant Borcke fervent love letters. "Nobody loves and esteems you as I do," he wrote. "Give me in return half the friendship I bear you." "My wearisome affection breaks from me and discloses to you the feelings of a heart filled with you, and which cannot be satisfied save in knowing that you are fully convinced of the tender friendship with which it adores you."[20]

More significant, and finally more tragic, was another attachment Frederick formed this same year (1728). Hans Hermann von Katte, six years his senior and the son of a Prussian general, loved music and French literature and was as derisively skeptical as the prince. Katte served as the teenager's confidant and protector, standing guard during his flute lessons, and their friendship seems to have blossomed into a love affair. But Frederick's relations with his father had by now become intolerable. "We have accursed scenes here every day," he complained to Borcke. "I am so tired of them that I had rather beg my bread than live any longer on this footing." Frederick William, for his part, had taken to taunting and humiliating his son in public. "Had I been treated so by my father," the king declared, "I would have blown my brains out, but this fellow has no honor, he takes all that comes."[21]

It is not surprising that the desperate Frederick laid plans to escape from Prussia. But the plot misfired. Frederick was caught as he was about to cross the border, and Katte was arrested as his accomplice. The king had both court-martialed for desertion. Katte was sentenced to life imprisonment, but the court refused to judge the prince. The king, outraged at this leniency, ordered Katte executed and the prince imprisoned. Katte's sentence aroused widespread protests even in autocratic Prussia, but the king was adamant. A startled Frederick was roused at five on a November morning and ordered to look out the window of his cell. When his friend appeared in the courtyard, the prince called out, "My dear Katte, a thousand pardons." Katte called back, "My prince, there is nothing to apologize for." Then he knelt and was beheaded; before the sword fell, Frederick fainted.[22]

The shattered prince, bereft of freedom and self-respect, had no choice but abject surrender to the will of the king. Nevertheless, imprisonment was easier to bear than life with his father. His jailors were tolerant and sympathetic, and at Cüstrin Frederick found two life-long friends. Dietrich Lieutenant Count von Keyserling was a civilized young man who shared Frederick's enthusiasms. Frederick gave him the romantic nickname of Césarion, and he became a fixture in his life. It was Keyserling who was later sent to woo Voltaire to Potsdam. At least some observers suspected Frederick and Keyserling were lovers. The marquis de Valory, French ambassador at Frederick's court, reported that the two spent hours together and that Frederick forbade his friend to go near the window "as he did not wish him to be seen and talked about."[23] When he moved into his new palace at Sans Souci, Frederick celebrated the occasion in French verse, at once pedestrian and ardent: "In this new palace of noble architecture / the two of us will enjoy complete liberty / in the intoxication of friendship! / Personal ambition and enmity / will be accounted the only sins against nature."[24]

In 1731, shortly before his release from prison, Frederick made another friend who was also to serve him for many years. This was Michael Gabriel Fredersdorf, a private in the Prussian army and an accomplished flautist, who became Frederick's valet and factotum, responsible for the royal theater and opera. He was four years older than the prince, clever, well-mannered, and strikingly good-looking. Voltaire, who later observed the relationship at first hand, wrote slyly in his *Mémoires:* "This soldier, young, handsome, well made, and who played the flute, served to entertain the prisoner in more than one fashion."[25] This was to prove the longest attachment of Frederick's life. Eventually Frederick made him chancellor and shocked Prussia's class-conscious aristocracy by giving the peasant's son an estate. Later, when Fredersdorf proposed to marry, the king wrote with cynical candor: "Have your marriage ceremony today rather than tomorrow if that will contribute to your care and comfort; and if you want to keep a little page and a little scout with you as well, do so."[26]

As heir to the Prussian throne, Frederick had no choice but to marry when his father commanded. Unfortunately, Elizabeth Christine of Brunswick-Bevern, the ordained bride, was totally lacking in wit and intellect. Frederick spoke of suicide and wrote to Wilhelmine, "There can be neither love nor friendship between us." He told another acquaintance that the marriage would be "Good morning, Madame, and *bon voyage*."[27] After he became king, he gave his wife a separate palace in Berlin and contrived to see as little of her as possible. The queen of Prussia never saw the inside of the splendid rococo palace Frederick built at Potsdam, where he lived with his male friends in a court devoid of women. But the neglected queen always remained pathetically loyal to the man she called "the dear Prince whom I love and adore."[28]

But what of Frederick's soubriquet? Was he truly "great"? He was unique as the only modern (that is, post-classical) homosexual to win that epithet. But as such he embodies fascinating contradictions. As a youth he fitted a certain stereotype—the long-haired aesthete-dandy, wittily skeptical, devoted to literature and music. Traditionally, this stereotype has been set

101. Execution of Hans Hermann von Katte, November 16, 1730; Katte, shortly before his death (inset). Engraving, nineteenth century; engraving (after George Lisiewsky), 1730.

against another—the aggressively masculine male who is a successful military leader or tough-minded man of affairs. But Frederick embodied both antitheses, and to a remarkable degree. On becoming king, the pacifist who had written the *Anti-Machiavel* developed into Europe's most formidable warrior and a statesman often accused of Machiavellian diplomacy. But devoted as he was to war and realpolitik, Frederick continued to pour out poetry in French (some six volumes in his collected works) and regularly gave concerts as a flautist that were applauded by some of the age's most discriminating music critics.[29] Between battles, he composed over a hundred flute concertos, sonatas, and symphonies (some of them still performed), and gave Bach the daunting theme for his *Musical Offering*.

As for his claim to "greatness," most modern biographers, lacking Carlyle's enthusiasm for Frederick's Prussia, have rendered a mixed judgment. Throughout his life he remained a humanitarian who favored freedom and tolerance. Before his accession in 1740 reformers like Voltaire regarded him as Europe's best hope. "The philosophers and the men of letters," D'Alembert told him, "in every land have long looked upon you, Sire, as their leader and model."[30] In some respects he fulfilled these expectations. As king he introduced religious toleration, acted to make the press freer, ended judicial torture, mitigated harsh penal laws, and freely granted asylum to refugees with whom he disagreed—for instance, Rousseau and the Jesuits. Yet when he felt the safety of the state was at issue he was merciless, and the man who had abolished torture impassively witnessed brutal punishments for breaches of military discipline.

Frederick sought to lure distinguished scientists, philosophers, and literary men to Potsdam, and he assembled there a brilliant entourage, with such savants as Maupertius, d'Argens, Algarotti, and La Mettrie. Finally he attracted Europe's most famous citizen, Voltaire. Under Frederick's patronage the sciences flourished in Prussia, and its educational system became the best in Europe. Nowhere else in Germany could Immanuel Kant have published his critiques of religion without fear of censorship. Frederick's poetry is negligible, but his histories, seven volumes in elegant and incisive French prose, have commanded respect, especially his *Histoire de mon temps.* Showing scant respect for his fellow princes, whom he characterized as mainly "illustrious imbeciles," he favored "philosophical" history in the style of Voltaire: "To follow the discovery of new truths, to grasp the causes of change in morals and manners, to study the process by which the darkness of barbarism has been lifted from the minds of men—these surely," he wrote, "are subjects worthy to occupy all thinking men."[31]

In law reform he was open to the influences of such enlightened thinkers as Montesquieu and Beccaria. "Princes," he wrote, "are born to be judges of the people"; "everything that makes them great has its origin in the administration of justice."[32] He insisted that he himself was not above the law and

102. Frederick the Great and Voltaire at Sans Souci. P. C. Baquoy, engraving (after N. A. Monsiau), date unknown.

often took the side of his poorer subjects against his judges. In 1730, a decade before his accession, a Prussian named Andreas Lepsch had been burned at the stake for sodomy. As a king advocating law reform, Frederick opposed such horrors, repeating (somewhat disingenuously) an argument that was a commonplace of his age: "It is undeniable that through frightful public capital punishments [for sodomy] many young and innocent spirits, who naturally want to know the reason for such a terrible execution, . . . will be scandalized rather than improved, and it is even possible evil tendencies may be awakened in them, tendencies of which they had previously no inkling."[33] At the beginning of his reign and again at the end, Frederick appointed committees of leading jurists to reform the laws. The second committee did not complete its work till 1794, eight years after his death. Its new code reduced the punishment for sodomy from burning to imprisonment for a year or more, whipping, and banishment.[34]

In politics Frederick's influence was retrograde. Though he admired the English constitution, he strengthened Prussia's rigid caste system which denied power to the middle classes. By making the Junker military aristocracy paramount, he prevented any movement toward democracy, a stultification that was to have disastrous effects for Germany and Europe. But Frederick's record in war, if morally dubious, was personally heroic: he risked his life in battle repeatedly and had half a dozen horses shot from under him. In the Seven Years' War (1756–1763) Prussia faced an unprecedented coalition that included France, Austria, Russia, Sweden, and Saxony. The spectacle of Frederick's taking on these armies one by one and surviving victorious after many vicissitudes is one of the epics of military history. His victories over the French and Russians in 1757 established his reputation as the greatest general of his time. In the end, he transformed a despised minor state into a great power, doubling its population and tripling its armed forces.

But there are many "buts." The seizure of Silesia was an unscrupulous stroke that ultimately drenched Europe in blood. And the mighty army Frederick created was to become, in later centuries, the potent instrument of Bismarck and Hitler. One may wonder whether his military victories and will to power were spurred by his sense of the anomalous role of the homosexual in eighteenth-century Europe and by his father's contempt for the sensitive boy he despised as an effeminate weakling. Perhaps Frederick's greatest achievement was that, while achieving "greatness" according to the military-monarchal standards of his society, he nevertheless retained to the end, in a climate that was so scornfully hostile, an exceptional degree of urbane humanity.

• The Vagaries of Voltaire •

Voltaire's quasi-love affair with the "non-conformist" Frederick was one of the most fascinating episodes in a long and dramatic life. His views on same-sex love, however, were neither simple nor consistent. It was a theme Voltaire touched on often in a literary career extending over six decades, first in a discursive poem, then in two important "philosophical" essays, and repeatedly in his correspondence, polemics, and moralizing tales. He had several homosexual friends of note and some enemies whose tastes he pointedly dwelt on. Yet few authors can have revealed so many contradictions. His first sustained, and least prejudiced, comment appeared in verses dated 1714, when Voltaire was twenty. The *Anti-Giton* derives its title from the boy in Petronius's *Satyricon* whose name in early eighteenth-century France had become a synonym for a handsome young homosexual.[35] Its target was a fashionable young marquis who headed a coterie in the French theater.

The treatment of "l'amour anti-physique" (anti-natural love) in the poem is playfully satirical: the lines are addressed to a favorite actress whose theater, dedicated to the god of love, has been invaded by a "culte hérétique." Voltaire plays with the legend of Sodom but will not countenance the idea of a supernatural disaster. More wit than moralist, Voltaire in the *Anti-Giton* depicts male love in a way that is not wholly unappealing. Indeed, he associates it with heroism and high culture, as in these lines:

Ainsi que Loth chassé de son asile,
Ce pauvre dieu courut de ville en ville:
Il vint en Grèce, il y donna leçon
Plus d'un fois à Socrate, à Platon;
Chez les héros il fit sa résidence
Tantôt à Rome, et tantôt à Florence;
Cherchant toujours, si bien vous l'observez,
Peuples polis et par art cultivés.

("Chased like Lot from his asylum, / the poor god [of anti-natural love] fled from city to city. / He came to Greece, and there gave lessons / more than once to Socrates and Plato. / He made his home with heroes / sometimes at Rome, and then at Florence, / seeking always, you may well note, / peoples who were civilized and cultivated in the arts.")[36] Thus, it is not surprising, Voltaire concludes, that this love now flourishes in Paris, the modern rival of Greece and Italy.

In the published version of the poem Voltaire does not name the man he is attacking, but a manuscript identifies him as Philippe Égon, marquis de Courcillon (1687–1719). Voltaire finds him a quite attractive young man: "He [anti-natural love] takes the form of a handsome marquis / with a agreeable bearing, a refined air, and clever speech. / Thirty mignons follow him laughing; / Phyllis ogles him and sighs as she retreats."[37] Other versions of the poem sang the marquis's praises more fully. He is "broad-chested, well-made and handsome," "desire and mischief shine in his eyes," "he is blithe and talks engagingly."[38] In fact, Voltaire, whose satire was often malicious, seems much taken with his victim and even adds a sympathetic touch—

Courcillon had lost a leg in battle. What then, is his error? Voltaire's standard is purely literary. "L'amour anti-physique" is condemned solely for failing to conform to the canons of gallantry set by Racine: "This false Love struts at all hours / in the theater dedicated to the muses, / where, led in triumph by Racine, / gallant Love chose his abode." There is no vitriol here; Voltaire's satire is far gentler than Juvenal's or Alain de Lille's. He ends with his own gallant gesture, imploring a famous actress, Adrienne Lecouvreur, to use her charms to lead theater-goers back to orthodoxy. Voltaire's views would not always be so urbane.

Among Voltaire's most notable homosexual friends were Count Francesco Algarotti, the marquis de Villette, and Frederick the Great; among the enemies he accused of the vice were the detested Abbé Desfontaines and the critic Élie Fréron, upon whom Voltaire bestowed such epithets as "viper," "thief," "toad," "drunkard," "ugly Giton," and "vermisseau né du c[ul] de Desfontaines" ("worm born in the ass of Desfontaines").[39] In 1735 Algarotti was a guest of Voltaire and his mistress, Mme du Châtelet, for six weeks at the latter's chateau. The cosmopolitan count was a handsome twenty-three-year-old Venetian who charmed both his hosts and shared their wide-ranging enthusiasms for science and literature. Voltaire described him as a "young man who knows the language and customs of every country, who makes verses like Ariosto, and who knows his Locke and Newton."[40] In England Algarotti entranced both Lady Mary Wortley Montagu and Lord Hervey. Later, he was recruited for Frederick's free-thinking circle of scholars in Berlin where, as Voltaire put it, there were "neither women, nor priests."[41]

In the summer following Algarotti's visit, Voltaire himself was flattered to receive his first letter from Frederick, then crown prince of Prussia, who saluted his writings as "treasures of the mind" and begged for his unpublished manuscripts.[42] Voltaire, no mean flatterer himself, replied, calling Frederick a "philosopher prince, who will make men happy."[43] Both agreed in deploring superstition and persecution. Soon Frederick was begging Voltaire to "leave your ungrateful country and come to a land where you will be adored."[44] Voltaire, in return, assured the prince, "You think like Trajan, you write like Pliny, you speak French like our best writers . . . Under your auspices Berlin will be the Athens of Germany, and, it may be, of Europe."[45] Inspired by Voltaire, Frederick wrote his *Anti-Machiavel,* deploring kings who placed "the fatal glory of conquerors [above] that won by kindness, justice, and clemency."[46] (Given Frederick's later career, there was some irony here.) Voltaire contributed a preface to the pamphlet and had it published anonymously in The Hague. When Frederick became king of Prussia in 1740, he eagerly arranged a meeting with Voltaire at Cleves, where each managed to fascinate the other. After a second meeting, Voltaire assured the new monarch in mocking verse that his equation of Berlin with Athens had proved apt: he had seen Algarotti at Frederick's court embracing a young Frenchman—"le beau Lujac, son jeune ami"—as he imagined Socrates might have made love to Alcibiades.[47]

Voltaire's friendship with the king was an intense and enduring passion, though often clouded with storms. A curiously amorous note pervaded the relationship from its earliest phases. "For four years you have been my mistress," Voltaire wrote the king in 1740. But for the moment, he explained, he must return to Mme du Châtelet: "Yes, I go to the knees of an adored object, / But I leave behind what I love."[48] He addresses Frederick as "grand roi, charmante coquette" ("great king, charming tease") and declared that he would like to spend the rest of his life at his feet.[49] The ardor is passionate enough, but it does not seem to have been erotic. Though he frankly and explicitly acknowledged the homosexual ambience of Frederick's court, Voltaire takes care to distance himself from it: "As for me, quite uninterested / in these affairs of Greece, / conscripted only by Frederick himself, / I left my studies and my mistress."[50]

Voltaire spent another six weeks in the company of the Prussian king in 1743. The fascination persisted: Frederick continued to press Voltaire to remain with him permanently, assuring him when Voltaire complained of an obnoxious French bishop, "The bishops here are all good fellows—some make love before and some behind but none would persecute anyone."[51] The attractions of Berlin were obvious: freedom to publish, intimate association with a congenial and all-powerful monarch who was witty and affectionate, music and theater, and lively free-spoken intellectual give-and-take at royal suppers. This feast looked like Versailles without its ecclesiastical censors. Seven years later, facing more hostility from the French authorities and sensing that his affair with Mme du Châtelet had come to an end, Voltaire made a momentous decision. He announced he would devote the rest of his life to Frederick in Berlin. In a letter to his niece he called this step a "marriage after the flirtations of so many years" and described himself approaching the altar with a palpitating heart.[52]

The lifetime lasted three years and was a protracted tragicomedy. Voltaire caused an embarrassing scandal by illegally purchasing foreign bonds, and he publicly declared war on another imported intellectual, Maupertuis, the proud head of Frederick's new Berlin Academy. When Voltaire finally left Berlin, Frederick's agents in Frankfurt treated him roughly until they retrieved some compromising poems Frederick had loaned him. Nevertheless, the two resumed their fervent correspondence. It continued until Voltaire's death twenty-five years later. At the end of his life Voltaire summed it all up. "It was," he wrote in a generous mood, "a lovers' quarrel: the harassments of courts pass away, but the nature of a beautiful ruling passion is long-lasting."[53]

The rapprochement, however, did not keep Voltaire from writing frankly, with feline wit, about Frederick's homosexuality in his *Mémoires* (1759). The king, he recorded, slept in Spartan style on a simple army cot, but "when His Majesty was dressed and booted, the Stoic gave some moments to the sect of Epicurus; he had two or three favorites come, either lieutenants of his regiment, or pages, or haidouks [Hungarian infantrymen], or young cadets. They took coffee. He to whom the handkerchief was thrown stayed another quarter of an hour in privacy."[54] (In Turkish harems, the woman chosen to sleep with a sultan was presented with a handkerchief.)

Before Voltaire left Potsdam, Frederick encouraged him to set forth his views on religion, morals, and society in a *Philosophical Dictionary,* which, however, he did not publish until 1764. It contained an entry on "Amour" (devoted not to gallantry but to animal behavior!) and another on "Amour nommé socratique" ("So-called Socratic love"). The *Dictionary* was one of Voltaire's most successful polemical fireworks, emended, extended, and reprinted often during his lifetime and later. Its essay on homosexuality was probably the eighteenth century's most widely read pronouncement on the subject. The modern reader, however, may find its emphasis puzzling and its tone disconcertingly homophobic.

To comprehend Voltaire we must understand several controversies, personal and philosophical, that the poet was engaged in. The earliest version of the essay began by asking, "How did it come about that a vice which would destroy mankind if it were general, that a sordid outrage against nature, is still so natural? It seems the highest degree of deliberate corruption, and yet it is the ordinary lot of those who have not yet had the time to be corrupted."[55] That is to say, why is it that young schoolboys often find each other desirable? Voltaire, we must recall, was a deist; morality, he thought, derived not from divine revelation but from universal laws implanted in the hearts of all by a benevolent Creator. All civilizations, Voltaire argued, have recognized property rights and solemn oaths and condemned injurious lies, slander, murder, or poison.[56] Voltaire came to see certain sexual acts as also violating "natural law"—including some kinds of incest and homosexuality. Since schoolboy amours seemed to contradict this theory of an innate repugnance, Voltaire felt compelled to explain them on a "natural" basis. His answer: "Often, for two or three years, a young man resembles a beautiful girl, with the freshness of his complexion, the brilliance of his coloring, and the sweetness of his eyes; if he is loved it is because nature makes a mistake; homage is paid the fair sex by attachment to one who owns its beauties, and when the years have made this resemblance disappear, the mistake ends."[57]

Voltaire was unhappy with the idea that his heroes the Greeks could have approved of sexual affairs between men. "I cannot bear," he wrote, "to hear anyone say that the Greeks authorized this license." But Voltaire's theory of history and morals was highly dogmatic. In his *Philosophie de l'histoire* he had argued that Herodotus's account of religious prostitution among the Babylonians could not be credited because such an institution would have violated natural law; he cannot believe "that there has ever been a civilized nation which made laws against morals."[58] As Voltaire's contemporary Melchior Grimm complained, "Voltaire thinks one can doubt the authenticity of reported facts which are not in conformity with right reason."[59] Solon, Voltaire declared, could not have favored same-sex relations in his maturity despite his youthful homoerotic verse. But assuming that Solon, like Théodore de Bèze, to whom he compares him, would have repudiated his early homoerotic poetry hardly takes into account the differences between Solon's Greece and Calvin's Geneva. Finally, however, Voltaire's commitment to law reform briefly overcomes his prejudices. In a footnote he condemned burning as too severe a penalty: "That is too much . . . we should proportion punishments to crime; what would have Caesar, Alcibiades, Nicomedes, king of Bithynia, Henri III, king of France, and so many other kings have said?"[60]

This note also takes aim at an old enemy, the Abbé Desfontaines, who, he tells us, "was at the point of being roasted on the Place de Grève." Voltaire had been a friend of Guyot Desfontaines, whom he had rescued from imprisonment on charges of sodomy by interceding with the Paris police. But when Desfontaines later criticized a tragedy by Voltaire, the poet was enraged at his ingratitude. A lengthy war began in which the two exchanged scurrilous insults. (Voltaire even added lines to the *Anti-Giton* vilifying this "filthy pedant.") It was a contest hardly creditable to either man and deplored by their friends. Yet poisonous scandal-mongering was common to both clerics and anti-clericals in this age. In a letter to the police the Abbé Théru, whom we have met earlier as an assiduous informer, incriminated Voltaire:

> It is said that S[ieu]r Arouet de Voltaire is disposed to solicit the liberty of his dear and intimate friend the abbé Guyot Desfontaines, and that if he does not dare do this openly he will use the credit of several persons of consideration and authority; but if one informs himself about the life this poet has led since he left the College of the Jesuits and if you examine the people he has associated with, you will have no regard for his pleas nor for those of his friends, and you will regard him and his friends as very much suspect.[61]

Théru suggests that Voltaire is a sodomite because he had close social relations with a group he had spied on. It is hard to know what to make of this accusation. Some biographers think Voltaire may have been involved in same-sex relations as a young man.[62]

Later, Voltaire read Beccaria's book and took up the cause of law reform in earnest, writing a preface to a French translation and a commentary. In 1777, when the Société Économique of Berne offered a prize for a model criminal code, Voltaire contributed money for the project and wrote an essay of his own entitled *Prix de la justice et de l'humanité.* There Voltaire traced the history of sodomy legislation, deploring the fact that the *Établissements* of Saint

Louis were used "to burn alive a few unfortunates convicted of this filth" and arguing that such deeds might more fittingly "be shrouded in the shadows of oblivion than be illuminated by flaming faggots before the eyes of the multitude."[63]

This final essay reveals once more Voltaire's ambivalence, laced as it is with anti-homosexual rhetoric. Voltaire calls sexual relations between men "a turpitude which dishonors human nature" and declares that "this vice unworthy of mankind is unknown [!] in our harsh climate."[64] Nevertheless, by this time Voltaire was once again on warm terms with Frederick, and one of his most intimate new friends was a young aristocrat whose homosexuality he was well aware of. Voltaire flattered the marquis de Villette as a poet, calling him "the French Tibullus," thanked him for coming to "cheer him up" in his retreat at Ferney in 1765, and recruited him as a philosophe.[65] Yet the numerous scurrilous attacks launched against the marquis had made him arguably France's most visible homosexual, and Voltaire joked freely about Villette's preferences in the letters he wrote him.[66] He sought, somewhat optimistically, to redirect his interests by marrying him to an attractive young protégée also resident at Ferney. The pair nursed Voltaire lovingly in his old age, and he died, in 1778, at their home in Paris. Villette kept his heart in an urn inscribed "Son esprit est partout et son coeur est ici" ("His spirit is everywhere; his heart is here"). We shall find Villette playing an active role in the oncoming Revolution.

What then are we to make of Voltaire's inconsistencies? He seems to have been attracted to and enjoyed the company of handsome, clever, young homosexuals, relying on them for help and support. Modern slang unkindly calls women who enjoy the company of gay men "fag hags"; we may perhaps think of Voltaire as a kind of male counterpart. The *Anti-Giton* is only superficially disapproving, and his letters to Frederick and Algarotti assume a casual, jocular complicity. Yet his two published essays, despite their argument for law reform, are unequivocally condemnatory, denouncing homosexuality as a "disgusting abomination" that threatens the existence of the race. Is this simply the common hypocrisy which assumes a libertine flippancy about sex in private (male) circles and a canting solemnity on public occasions? Or is something more at work?

Part of the answer may lie in the additions Voltaire made when he revised his essay on Socratic love. He strengthened the censorious tone, so at odds with the man-of-the-world insouciance of his letters, by adding a prefatory comment: "If the love called Socratic and Platonic was only a decent sentiment, one must applaud; if it was a debauched love one must blush for Greece."[67] More significantly, he strongly amplified the essay's anti-clericalism, adding (in 1771) a pointed reference to a Carmelite priest in his own neighborhood who had been accused of seducing his pupils. From this incident he generalizes: "These amusements have been common enough between teachers and schoolboys. The monks responsible for educating the young have always been somewhat addicted to pederasty. This is the necessary consequence of the celibacy to which these poor men are condemned . . . a strange choice for a teacher, to be chaste or a sodomite."[68]

Voltaire's philosophical tales, highly popular in his own day, harp persistently on the same theme. In the most famous of these, *Candide,* he repeatedly associates the Catholic clergy with sodomy, tracing Pangloss's syphilis back to a page "who had received it from a Jesuit" and making Cunegonde's haughty brother owe his clerical office to an older Jesuit who had found him "very pretty."[69] The adolescent hero of the *Voyages de Scarmentado* meets a teacher in Rome who is anxious to put him "in the category of his mignons," and when the handsome hero of *La Princesse de Babylone* visits that city, men in red and purple "throw soft glances at him" and murmur praises of his beauty.[70]

Like the sixteenth-century Protestant fanatic John Bale, Voltaire found it expedient to use the charge of sodomy against the Catholic clergy. That his campaign fed vicious prejudice that made life difficult for many who did not have the secure positions of Frederick, Algarotti, or Villette seems not to have occurred to him. Indeed, Voltaire seems hardly to have thought of homosexuals as a category at all and drastically underestimated their numbers in Paris and France generally. But just as he shamelessly used popular anti-Semitism to undermine the Old Testament (and the Christian faith that drew on it), so Voltaire had no scruples about using popular homophobia in his war against "l'infâme."

• Diderot and Sade •

Voltaire wrote as a moralist and law reformer. Denis Diderot, the prime mover behind the *Encyclopedia* and the philosophe who stood next to Voltaire in contemporary reputation, approached sex primarily as a psychologist. An atheist and materialist who sought to "explain" homosexuality as a human phenomenon, Diderot felt challenged by the newly published accounts of North America by French explorers. Sixteenth-century observations of Indian life had prompted theological debates about the legitimacy of Spain's New World conquests. Diderot, instead, chose to speculate on the "causes" of what he called "le goût antiphysique des Américains" ("the unnatural taste of Americans") in an exhaustive catalogue:

> I believe that it is necessary to look for the cause in the heat of the climate, in the scorn for the weaker sex, in the insipidity of pleasure in the arms of a woman exhausted by fatigue, in the inconstancy of tastes, in the bizarre whims which impel men generally to the less common sexual enjoyments, in the search for sexual pleasure easier to imagine than it is de-

> cent to explain, perhaps in a conformation of organs which establish better proportions between American men than between an American man and an American woman—a disproportion which would cause both the disgust of Americans for their women and desire of American women for Europeans. Moreover, would not the hunts which sometimes separate men and women for entire months, lead men to approach men?[71]

Before we smile at this desperate roster of "causes," we should pause to recall the multitudinous theories spawned, in the wake of Freud, by twentieth-century psychiatry.

Most often Diderot perceives sex as an anarchic force seeking pleasure as its end and only incidentally fostering procreation. His most searching critique of sexuality is to be found in a dialogue he wrote in 1769 and appended to *D'Alembert's Dream* as the "Sequel to the Conversation." In this after-dinner chat D'Alembert's mistress, Julie d'Espinasse, and Dr. Bordeu (in real life Diderot's personal physician) discuss sex taboos, self-consciously aware of their intellectual daring. The doctor, who considers above all the health and happiness of the individual, objects when Mlle de L'Espinasse uses the expression "contrary to nature." Such language, he thinks, is illegitimate, and he takes a stand opposing Voltaire's theory of a universal natural law governing sexual relations: "Nothing that exists can be either against nature or outside of nature, and I don't even make an exception of chastity or voluntary continence, which would be the most heinous of crimes against nature if it were possible to sin against nature or commit crimes against it."[72] Masturbation, for instance, routinely decried as "unnatural" by moralists, is pleasurable, relieves a "plethoric condition," and avoids the dangers of adultery or infection.[73]

But what of non-procreative acts involving two persons instead of a single individual? "I ask you therefore, what will be the verdict of common sense as between two acts, both equally limited to the satisfaction of lust, both capable only of giving a wholly non-utilitarian pleasure, but of which one gives only pleasure to the one who does it and the other gives pleasure both to him and to a being of *the same* or of the opposite sex?"[74] Diderot's doctor conceives same-sex relations not as love but as makeshift expedients or mere lust inspired by youthful male beauty. At the end of the conversation, when Mlle L'Espinasse asks, "What's at the bottom of these sexual perversions?" Bordeu abruptly downgrades homosexual acts to a medical problem: "Invariably [!] they are traceable to a weakness in the nervous organization of young persons or the rotting of the brain in old people. In Athens they were brought about by the seductive power of beauty, in [papal] Rome by the scarcity of women, and in Paris they are caused by fear of the pox. Good-by, good-by."[75] Diderot was well aware that his sexual radicalism might provoke

103. Denis Diderot. Louis Michel van Loo, oil, 1767.

attacks: his manuscript was not published until 1830, forty-six years after his death.

Like Voltaire, Diderot was not above charging men he pilloried in satires with homosexuality, as in his verses on Frederick the Great.[76] Diderot himself, however, seems to have been susceptible to what Bordeu had called the "seductive power" of handsome youths, as passages in his art criticism suggest. Though Diderot thought Christian art offered more opportunity for tragic themes, he argued that classical art produced greater pleasure: "There is no comparison between our saints, our apostles, and our sadly ecstatic virgins, and those banquets of Olympus where muscular Hercules, leaning on his club amorously regards delicate Hebe . . . where the Master of the gods, intoxicating himself with the nectar poured to the brim by the hand of a young boy with ivory shoulders and alabaster thighs, makes the heart of his jealous wife swell with chagrin."[77] But Diderot goes further. In his *Essai sur peinture (Essay on Painting)* he imagines a hypothetical biblical scene—the wedding at Cana—in this classical bisexual mode: "Christ, half tipsy, somewhat nonconformist, would have glanced at the bosom of one of the bridesmaids and at Saint John's buttocks, uncertain if he would remain faithful to the apostle with the chin shaded by light down."[78] In England, a "nonconformist" meant a non-Anglican, usually a member of a puritanical sect. In eighteenth-century France, by an ironic contrast, *nonconformiste* came to mean a sodomite and was so defined in editions of the Jesuits' *Dictionnaire universel.*[79] We may note that Diderot here uses it to describe a psychological disposition.

In a letter to his mistress, Sophie Volland, Diderot expatiated on the way candid autobiographies might illuminate human nature. But who, he asks, would have the courage to keep "an exact register of all the thoughts of his mind, of all the movements of his heart, of all his pains, of all his pleasures?" It would be easier, he thinks, to record great crimes than sentiments that are "obscure, vile and low," to avow murderous thoughts than to confess that "one day when I was in a bath among a large number of young men, I noticed one of surprising beauty, and I could not keep myself from approaching him."[80] This sounds like a veiled confession, muted by shame and fear. Was Diderot, one wonders, himself "somewhat nonconformist," a closet bisexual?

Like their antagonists the Jesuits, the philosophes were themselves often charged with sexual nonconformity. Another euphemism for homosexuality in eighteenth-century France was "the philosophical sin." Originally, this term referred to Greek philosophers such as Socrates, but it also came to suggest a link between free thought and homosexuality in the lives of the philosophes. Today one hardly associates pornography with cerebration, but in eighteenth-century France radical thinkers wrote pornography not just to titillate but as an intellectual challenge to conventional morality. D'Argens, Diderot, and Mirabeau all wrote erotic fiction, sometimes with lesbian or male homosexual characters who defended their tastes. The clerical narrator in the anonymous *L'Histoire de Dom Bougre* (1741) asks the reader to look upon antiphysical pleasures without "prejudice": "Go to the schools of the most famous sages of Greece, go to those of the most upstanding people of our time, you will learn how to live."[81] Typically, this tale may be read either way—as a defense of homosexuality or an exposé of priestly corruption.

But the most notable wedding of lurid pornography with extravagant intellection must be the marquis de Sade's *Philosophy in the Bedroom,* a novel in which an orgy is interrupted for the delivery of a revolutionary manifesto—"Yet Another Effort, Frenchmen, If You Would Become Republicans." It includes a bold program of law reform:

> But sodomy, that alleged crime which will draw the fire of heaven upon cities addicted to it, is sodomy not a monstrous deviation whose punishment could not be severe enough? Ah, sorrowful it is to have to reproach our ancestors for the judiciary murders in which, upon this head, they dared indulge themselves. We wonder that savagery could ever reach the point where you condemn to death an unhappy person all of whose crime amounts to not sharing your tastes. One shudders to think that scarce forty years ago the legislators' absurd thinking had not evolved beyond this point. Console yourselves, citizens; such absurdities are to cease: the intelligence of your lawmakers will answer for it.[82]

The four pages Sade devotes to the subject are lucid and passionate, the polemic of a man who, here at least, sounds rational and informed. They recapitulate traditional "philosophical" arguments forcefully, revealing Sade's fierce individualism and his courageous willingness to speak out whatever the personal cost. The "pamphlet" reflects the revolutionary boldness of the times—Sade appears to have written it early in 1793, shortly after the execution of Louis XVI.

Sade cites the customs of ancient Crete, Greece, Rome, Gaul, and Persia and adds, from modern anthropology, reports about the Indians of Louisiana and Illinois, the blacks of Angola, and Algerian Muslims. This is commonplace enough. What is novel is the force of the rejection of the idea that sodomy is contrary to nature. Like Diderot, Sade argues that "no inclinations or tastes can exist in us save the ones we have from Nature."[83] These desires are "le résultat de l'organisation"—the result of our constitution—"to which we contribute nothing and which we cannot alter. At the most tender age, some children reveal that penchant and it is never corrected in them."[84] Here, for the first time in a published plea for law reform, the idea of what we would today call sexual orientation emerges clearly. "We must demand enough wisdom and enough prudence of our legislators," Sade concludes, "to be entirely sure that no law will emanate from them that would repress these trifling acts which being determined by constitution . . . cannot render the person in whom they are present any more guilty than the person whom Nature has created deformed."[85]

Yet despite Sade's eloquence and erudition, his arguments would have carried little weight. First, his reforming "pamphlet" was inserted in a pornographic tale. Second, it is marred by the marquis's typical extravagance. Since republican civic virtue "demands new laws," Sade opposes penalizing theft (which redistributes income), rape (which Nature has sanctioned by creating men stronger than women), or even murder (which is natural in the animal world and approved in some societies). He argues for enforced prostitution of women "of all ages" on the grounds that state brothels will keep men engrossed in sensual pleasure and prevent them from revolting against a republican government. Indeed, most of "Another Effort" runs counter both to common sense and humanity. In such a context, few readers would have noticed that the pages on sodomy are, in fact, telling and reasonable.

Nor would Sade's personal history have recommended him as an advocate. He had been twice imprisoned for whipping unwilling prostitutes, and in Marseilles in 1772 he had been condemned to be burned at the stake for sodomy with a manservant. Lacking the culprit, the court burned an effigy. His "sadistic" novels—*Justine, Juliette,* and *The 120 Days of Sodom*—were notorious. Though the pampered aristocrat became an ardent reformer and actually held public office during the Revolution, he spent the last thirteen years of his life locked away in asylums as an alternative to imprisonment for writing *Justine. Philosophy in the Bedroom* first appeared in print in 1795 as a "posthumous" work "by the author of *Justine.*" In fact, Sade did not die till 1814.

• Toward Reform •

There was some irony here. Sade seems to have been unaware that the law against sodomy had been repealed two years before he wrote his impassioned appeal. The change was made without public debate and went unheralded in the press. As late as 1807, police who apprehended men for homosexual acts were ignorant that the law no longer provided a basis for any charges.[86] The new Code Pénal de la Révolution, promulgated in 1791, had in fact abolished the offense. How had this epochal development come about?

In the 1780s criminal law reform triumphed in many European countries, first of all in states ruled by enlightened despots like Frederick the Great in Prussia, Leopold II in Austria, and Catherine the Great in Russia, and aroused much debate in England and France. By the end of the decade the momentum for reform in France had become irresistible. From their scattered provinces members of the three estates forwarded *cahiers* (notebooks) to the National Assembly with proposals for new laws. Though the abolition of the sodomy statute received little public attention, it seemed a logical step. First, burning at the stake was now regarded as barbaric and archaic. (The last burning for sodomy had taken place in 1783, as we have seen, but the case involved a murderous stabbing of a teenager by a former Capuchin monk.[87]) Second, there was a strong consensus for abolishing "religious" offenses such as heresy, sorcery, blasphemy, and sodomy. Finally, there was a predisposition in favor of personal freedom and against punishing "victimless" crimes. This principle was set forth most notably in the fourth clause of the Declaration of the Rights of Man passed by the National Assembly on August 26, 1789, which defined liberty as the right "to do anything that does not injure others."[88]

One preeminent revolutionary leader summed up the national consensus in his *Plan de législation criminale* (1790). This was Jean-Paul Marat, the leader of the radical Jacobins, whose inflammatory speeches provoked the September massacres of 1792 and who was himself assassinated by Charlotte Corday a year later. In a note on sodomy and bestiality, Marat echoed Montesquieu and Voltaire. Though male love is "an indecent love which nature rejects" and "a revolting crime which must inspire only horror," it should be "left in the shadows" for fear of enlightening the innocent. Marat did make one novel suggestion, however: "If it is nevertheless necessary to punish these crimes when they are known," their perpetrators "should be regarded as insane, and only merit in this regard to be condemned to asylums *(petites maisons)*."[89] (Here was a hint psychiatry would take up a century later.)

When freedom of the press was achieved in France in 1789, an unprecedented flood of pamphlets followed. Some treated male relations with jocular irony. Of these *jeux d'esprit,* the most elaborate appeared in 1790 and was entitled *Les Enfants de Sodome à l'Assemblée Nationale, ou Députation de l'Ordre de la Manchette aux représentants de tous les ordres.* (It was mischievously identified as originating "chez le marquis de Villette, Grand-Commandeur de l'Ordre"—that is, from the residence of Voltaire's friend.) The anonymous author proposed that, at this moment of revolutionary fervor, members of the order should organize and demand their rights. But the humorist had his tongue in his cheek. "Thanks to the lights of philosophy," a spokesman for the Order declares, "the times are much changed; we will no longer suffer the shame of seeing Italy march gloriously alone towards the perfection of this science."[90] The Order must oppose prejudice and barbaric laws and reveal that "great men have been for the most part Unnaturalists *[Anti-physiciens]* and that this famous and illustrious Order can equal in numbers and quality those of Malta and of the Holy Spirit." There follows a mock bill of rights to be presented to the National Assembly by a delegation headed by Villette ("a bugger if there ever was one") and supported by leading churchmen, aristocrats, actors, physicians, lawyers, merchants, a locksmith, and a seller of lemonade, all identified by name. The author has a detailed knowledge of homosexual milieus in Paris and, indeed, raises important questions of justice. But the pervasive mockery, mixed with bawdy wit, reveals a Gallic unwillingness to take the matter quite seriously.

The man most often attacked for his sexual preferences in the war of pamphlets was Villette. The marquis was a leading member of the Club of 1789, a journalist who wrote for the *Chronique de Paris,* and a deputy to the National Convention in 1792, where he served on the foreign affairs committee. In June 1790 he had gained public attention by suggesting that Louis XVI be reduced to a mere figurehead without power. In the ensuing debate he was denounced as a man "unnatural" in all things—"tastes, inclinations and actions."[91] In partisan eyes, left and right, he became a new Henry III. The *Children of Sodom* identified the former marquis as a disciple of Voltaire, claiming that the philosopher himself had played "such games" in his youth and established a "new Gomorrah at Ferney."[92] A year later a scurrilous pamphlet entitled *Vie privée et publique de ci-derrière marquis de Villette* reviewed the homosexual side of Villette's life in scabrous detail.

The conservatives' use of such charges to discredit the Revolution prompted a friend of Villette's to reply. This defense, unique in its detailed discussion of the role male love might play in society, was the work of Anacharsis Cloots, one of the most colorful figures to occupy the public stage during the French Revolution. A nobleman of Dutch descent but a fervent Jacobin, the baron was a citizen of the small principality of Cleves, at this time part of Prussia. On June 19, 1790, Cloots's cosmopolitanism led him to make a memorable theatrical gesture: he led a delegation of men from thirty-six nations to the bar of the National Assembly to proclaim the world's allegiance to the Declaration of the Rights of Man. Thereafter he was known as "l'Orateur du genre humain"—"the Spokesman for the Human Race"—and in March 1791 he answered a Prussian critic in an essay to which he gave the same title.

This wide-ranging manifesto, which appeared four months before the new penal code, mixed conventional liberal doctrines with a uniquely candid view of same-sex love. Cloots was defiantly utilitarian: "Consult reason in dictating your code and you will efface a number of mortal and venial sins from your barbaric catechism . . . What is virtue? What is vice? . . . Everything useful to society is virtue, everything harmful is vice."[93] These principles, Cloots admits, will lead to a conclusion some will think shocking—there should be no sexual offenses "apart from rape, abduction, seduction or adultery." He even dares to invoke the amorous attachments his readers may have had to other youths: "It is good to soften the severities of legislators by reminding them that friendship, at a young age, has its kisses, its tears, its effusions similar to love."[94]

Cloots then adds a long footnote to vindicate Villette and to tally the social benefits of same-sex attachments:

> If Achilles loved Patroclus, if Orestes loved Pylades, if Aristogiton loved Harmodius, if Socrates loved Alcibiades, etc. were they for this less useful to their native lands? The charms of Briseis would have cost the taking of Troy without the charms of Patroclus. And the Athenians would have languished longer under the tyranny of the Pisistratids without the intimate

> union of two virtuous lovers who were declared to be the liberators of their native land. People speak often about nature without knowing her, they fix her limits arbitrarily; they do not know or pretend not to know that it is impossible to act contrary to it.[95]

Cloots adds an interesting observation: no secondary school, he tells us, is exempt from homosexual behavior since "nature is universal." "I was brought up by priests in Brussels, by Jesuits in Mons, by ecclesiastics in Paris, by the military in Berlin and I found Lesbos everywhere." Nevertheless, Cloots declares, to lay suspicion to rest, "The revolution absorbs all my leisure, and we have need for all our vital spirits for so beautiful a cause." Alas, two years later the "beautiful cause" claimed his life at the height of the Terror. Cloots was executed on Robespierre's orders with other dissenting Jacobins on March 24, 1794.

Cloots's essay is notable for its imaginative sympathy and for avoiding the abusive vocabulary that Montesquieu, Voltaire, Marat, and even Diderot had employed. More characteristic of the age is the note to Voltaire's *Prix de la justice et de l'humanité* that Condorcet added in the monumental Kehl edition of Voltaire's works (1784–1789). There he took the crucial step of calling for total decriminalization of sodomy but balanced his legal liberalism with conventional expressions of distaste: "Sodomy, when there is no violence, cannot fall within the scope of the criminal law. It does not violate the rights of any other man. It has only an indirect influence on the good order of society, like drunkenness, or the love of gambling. It is a low, disgusting vice whose proper punishment is scorn. The penalty of fire is atrocious . . . For the rest, we must not forget to remark that it is to superstition that we owe the barbarous use of this punishment."[96] Condorcet had been cofounder of the *Chronique de Paris* with Villette and one of the brightest stars of the Enlightenment—as a mathematician, social theorist, and architect of France's new secular educational system. He too fell victim to the Terror. Villette, more fortunate, escaped the guillotine by dying a natural death in July 1793.

But before the dance of death began, progress had taken place. The Constituent Assembly passed its radical criminal law reform measures in two stages. On May 23, 1791, Le Pelletier de Saint-Fargeau reported on the preparation of the drafts, which, he assured his hearers, punished only true crimes and not those artificial offenses "created by superstition, feudalism, the tax system, and despotism."[97] He did not name these pseudo-crimes, but they would certainly have included heresy, blasphemy, and sodomy. The new municipal police code (July 19–22) covered misdemeanors, the new penal code (September 25–October 6) felonies. As for sex crimes, the penal code listed only rape, and the police code only public indecency, the selling of obscene prints, and the debauching of minors (child prostitution). Neither code mentioned sodomy—formerly a capital offense, now, by implication, no crime at all.

The decriminalization of sodomy in 1791 had far-reaching consequences, since the Napoleonic Code of 1810 retained the innovation. The influence of the latter proved crucial throughout Europe, providing a model for states that sought to move beyond feudalism. Not only was it promulgated in countries occupied by Napoleon (such as the Netherlands), but it became the model for Catholic states that revised their criminal codes later in the nineteenth century, among them Bavaria, Spain, Portugal, and the new kingdom of Italy. Beyond Europe, its example led to the deletion of sodomy statutes from the penal codes of the newly emerging republics of Central and South America and the colonies that made up France's extensive empire in Africa, Asia, and the Pacific. For homosexuals in France and a host of other nations, the threat of execution or lengthy imprisonment was now obsolete.

We should not overestimate the change. Public opinion in France still reflected the moral disapprobation of the philosophes, and sodomites were still the object of scorn and derision. Napoleon, whose decisions in such matters were final, allowed the decriminalization of 1791 to stand in his new code but echoed the national ambivalence. Though sodomy was no longer a crime, sodomites remained subject to police surveillance that was arbitrary and oppressive and might involve blackmail. Napoleon himself approved such an approach when he reviewed a case in 1805. "We are not," he told his minister of justice, "in a country where the law should concern itself with these offenses. Nature has seen to it that they are not frequent. The scandal of legal proceedings would only tend to multiply them. It would be better to give the proceedings another direction."[98] Thus the emperor endorsed the replacement of a harsh penal code with administrative measures by which the police, acting independently of the courts, detained men briefly in prison or prescribed internal exile. Indeed, this remained the routine in France for almost two centuries. The special department set up by the police in Paris to control homosexuals was not abolished until 1981.[99]

• Bentham vs. Blackstone •

As the threat of death was lifted in France, it grew greater in England. To the English, French revolutionary reforms often looked less like the triumph of reason than the folly of a nation that had escaped Catholic superstition only to embrace godless immorality. In Britain, Enlightenment thinkers remained silent on sodomy law reform: none dared openly speculate on sexual morality in the style of Cloots or Diderot. The silence taboo held firm, national sentiment was hostile to change, and religious convictions still colored legal thought. Though eighteenth-century Europe hailed Edinburgh as the Athens of the North, the article on sodomy in the third edition of the *Encyclopedia Britannica,* published there in 1797, was more redolent of John Knox than Montesquieu. As to punishment, it declared succinctly: "There is no statute in Scotland against Sodomy; the libel [legal indictment] of the crime is therefore founded on the divine law, and practice makes its punishment to be burnt alive."[100]

Edward Gibbon, though a religious skeptic, left no doubt as to his stand in his *Decline and Fall of the Roman Empire* (1776–1788). In chapter 44 of his monumental work, Gibbon introduced his discussion of Justinian's harsh laws with an emphatic expression of distaste: "I touch with reluctance, and dispatch with impatience, a more odious vice [than adultery] of which modesty rejects the name and nature abominates the idea. The primitive Romans were infected by the example of the Etruscans and Greeks."[101] Though he deplored the dubious accusations brought by Justinian and Theodora, Gibbon refused to accept Montesquieu's views on law reform: "A French philosopher has dared to remark that whatever is secret must be doubtful, and that our natural horror of vice may be abused as an engine of tyranny. But the favorable persuasion of the same writer that a legislator may confide in the taste and reason of mankind is impeached by the unwelcome discovery of the antiquity and extent of the disease."[102] Gibbon's knowledge of the widespread acceptance of same-sex relations in ancient Greece and Rome, in China, and in the Americas did not lessen his belief in criminal sanctions. In private life, he was quite as adamant. When William Beckford sought asylum in Switzerland, the historian, then domiciled at Lausanne, insisted that the British rule of ostracism be maintained on foreign soil and publicly scolded a young Englishman who had the temerity to visit the distinguished millionaire.[103]

William Blackstone's magisterial *Commentaries on the Laws of England* (1765–1769) is a work whose influence on English and American law can hardly be overestimated. Blackstone's condemnation was as merciless as Gibbon's, just as remote from continental thinking, and a powerful force for conservatism throughout the Anglo-Saxon world. Portentously, Blackstone called sodomy a crime "of so dark a nature that the accusation if false deserves a punishment inferior only to the crime itself." Then he added: "I will not act so disagreeable a part, to my readers as well as myself, as to dwell any longer on a subject, the very mention of which is a disgrace to human nature. It will be more eligible to imitate in this respect the delicacy of our English law, which treats it, in its very indictments, as a crime not fit to be named: '*peccatum illud horribile, inter christianos non nominandum.*'"[104] As to punishment, Blackstone was resolutely theological: "This [offense] the voice of nature and of reason and the express law of God, determine to be capital. Of which we have a signal instance, long before the Jewish dispensation [that is, Leviticus] by the destruction of two cities by fire from heaven, so that this is an universal, not merely a provincial, precept."

Blackstone's great antagonist was the utilitarian philosopher Jeremy Bentham, who did not share his uncritical admiration for British law as largely beyond improvement. Indeed, reform of Britain's lethal and archaic penal code was a prime concern throughout Bentham's long life (1748–1832). In his early twenties he had already begun to draft a new criminal code, but the hostile reaction to the French Revolution in the 1790s paralyzed all reform in Britain. Consequently, Bentham's eminence as a thinker was first recognized in Latin countries like France and Spain. Napoleon hailed his *Introduction to the Principles of Morals and Legislation,* first published in French in 1789, as "a work of genius" and drew on it in preparing his own code.[105] When liberalism took hold in Spain in 1812, the Cortes asked for Bentham's aid in revising the nation's penal laws; so did several of the new republics of Central and South America where Bentham was acclaimed as "el legislador del mundo" ("the lawgiver of the world"). Finally, with the fading of anti-French feeling and the passage of the Reform Bill in 1832, the influence of Bentham's ideas was also enormous in Britain and America; he was by far the most important reformer England ever produced.

Unfortunately, Bentham's views on sodomy law reform lay hidden in unpublished writings which amply testify to the strength of British homophobia. In these voluminous notes, Bentham lamented the impossibility of any rational discussion in England and blamed especially the press: "In all other parts of the field of morality—public and established religion out of the question—the press has for this century or more been practically free. But, in effect, upon this it neither is nor ever has been practically free. A battery of grapeshot composed of all the expressions of abhorrence that language has given birth to is by each newspaper and every other periodical kept continually playing upon this ground." Indeed, Bentham felt that anyone challenging received opinion could expect to be personally attacked: "No wonder that down to this instant [1816] no man with the torch of reason in his hand should have found nerve to set foot on it. 'Miscreant! You are one of them then.' Such are the thanks which any man [would receive] who should attempt to carry upon this part of the field of morality those lights to which all other parts are open."[106]

As early as 1774, Bentham had sketched out some notes on homosexual law reform, citing classical antiquity and Enlightenment principles. A decade later he wrote an essay on "Paederasty" which argued powerfully for a change in legal and social attitudes. Same-sex relations, Bentham maintained, give pleasure to those who engage in them and cause no harm to others. To counter Montesquieu's argument that they impart to men the "weakness" of women, he cited famous Greek and Roman generals. To Voltaire's contention that homosexuality threatened the very existence of the human race, he replied that ancient Greece, despite the popularity of male love, suffered from over- rather than under-population.[107] Nor would Bentham tolerate the

104. Jeremy Bentham. Henry William Pickersgill, oil, c. 1829.

epithet "unnatural." Those who use it mean only that a sexual act is non-procreative. But if we call all pleasurable activities that are not physiologically necessary unnatural, we would have, for instance, to apply the term to a taste for music.[108]

Bentham was prepared to do battle on a remarkable number of fronts, and even to take the offensive. Though he lacks the word, Bentham has a clear conception of what we now call homophobia. For Bentham it was not homosexuality that needed explaining but this irrational "antipathy," akin to the unreasoning aversion that leads some people to kill harmless animals like toads and spiders.[109] Moral philosophers who denounce pleasure—including sexual pleasure—do so from a foolish pride which seeks admiration for the exercise of asceticism. A God who wanted us to eschew pleasure would be a malevolent being, since Bentham thinks pleasure good and suffering evil.[110] The Sodom story, so often invoked to justify the death penalty, makes reference, Bentham pointed out, not to consensual relations but to the threat of rape.[111] Playing on British distaste for Catholic persecution, Bentham compared England's blind hatred for pederasts to the hatred that led the Inquisition to burn Moors and Jews.[112]

Even in France or Italy, Bentham's passionate defense would have been exceptional. In Georgian England the public airing of such views was unthinkable. In a page of minute jottings he agonized over the risks: "To other subjects it is expected that you sit down cool, but on this subject if you let it be seen that you have not sat down in a rage you have given judgment against yourself at once." "When a man attempts to search this subject it is with a halter around his neck. On this subject a man may indulge his spleen without control. Cruelty and intolerance, the most odious and most mischievous passions in human nature, screen themselves behind a mask of virtue."[113] On one occasion Bentham encountered prejudice face-to-face in a British judge who had just sentenced two men to hang for "an offense of the sort in question." Bentham was deeply shocked by his demeanor. "Delight and exultation," he tells us, "glistened in his countenance; his looks called for applause and congratulations at the hands of the surrounding audience."[114]

When peace with France followed the battle of Leipzig in 1814, Bentham once more took up the topic. His project this time was nothing less than a book-length critique of biblical teachings. Under the title *Not Paul but Jesus,* it was to contrast a humane Jesus who rejected asceticism and was silent on the subject of homosexuality with a Paul whose denunciation was "vehement."[115] By 1818 Bentham had written five hundred folio pages that went far beyond decriminalization. Here, male love with its "bonds of attachment" becomes an unequivocal good in its own right.[116] In the decade that, to judge from the increased rate of executions and the tone of the national press, was the most hostile in British history, Bentham leapt ahead a century and a half to the Gay Liberation ethos of 1969.

Bentham especially protested the use of traditional pejorative language. Such terms as "abomination" and "perversion," he complains, hopelessly prejudice debate. "It is by the power of names, of signs originally arbitrary and insignificant," he notes, "that the course of imagination has in great measure been guided."[117] To avoid such pitfalls Bentham did what German sexologists did at the end of the nineteenth century when they first attempted to write about homosexuality from a scientific point of view. He tried to create a neutral vocabulary, coining such expressions as "the improlific appetite" and (echoing Beccaria) "the Attic mode."[118]

Bentham wrote assiduously but with deepening despair. "Never did work appear," he declared, "from which at the hand of public opinion a man found so much to fear, so little to hope."[119] Indeed, English popular feeling against sodomites had grown ever stronger during the period when Bentham wrote on the subject. It attained a kind of hysteria during the Regency (1810–1820), when brutal pilloryings in the heart of London drew enormous crowds seething with hostility and all but shut down city business. Between 1806 and 1835 over sixty men were hanged in England and another twenty in the navy, a much greater number than in any earlier century.[120] Indeed, this punitiveness reached its peak at a time when executions had ceased elsewhere in Europe. (The last known execution on the Continent occurred in the small town of Schiedam, near Rotterdam, in 1803.)[121] Given these conditions, it is not surprising that none of Bentham's writings on the subject saw print until well into the twentieth century.

The Enlightenment and the cataclysm it provoked had varying effects in Europe. In revolutionary France, anti-clerical feeling was strong enough to sweep away sodomy laws, and those Catholic lands on the Continent that came under the anti-feudal and anti-ecclesiastical influence of the Napoleonic Code shared in this liberalization. Police surveillance continued, however, with little to check arbitrary enforcement, since few men dared complain of entrapment, bribery, or police brutality. In Protestant countries, where the tyranny of the church had been less severe, there was no general reaction against statutes that were religious in origin. After Frederick the Great's death, laws against consensual relations continued to be enforced in Prussia. With German unification, they were extended in 1871 to jurisdictions such as Catholic Bavaria, where they had been dropped under the influence of Napoleonic law. As a result, Germany, Britain, and the United States retained their statues on sodomy until late in the twentieth century, a pattern that had a curious consequence in Nazi Germany. In a treatise designed to provide a rationale for more severe laws, the jurist Rudolf Kläre gave a racial interpretation to European traditions. Kläre argued that Teutonic jurisdictions (such as Germany, England, and the forty-eight American states that followed English law) were morally superior to decadent Latin countries (such as France, Spain, Italy, and Poland) which no longer punished homosexual acts.[122] With some revisions that widened its scope, the historical Article 175 of the German Imperial Code became a potent instrument of Nazi policy. It is estimated that over 50,000 homosexuals were convicted during Hitler's regime and that as many as 15,000 may have died in death camps.[123] The law was not abolished until 1969. In England, the death penalty survived until 1861, when it was changed to life imprisonment. Thus amended, the statute of Elizabeth remained in force for another century until 1967, when parliament abolished it after a decade of debate spurred by the Wolfenden Report.

In the United States matters took a different turn. The American Revolu-

105. Charing Cross pillory. August Charles Pugin and Thomas Rowlandson, illustration for R. Ackermann, *Microcosm of London,* 1808.

tion fostered no campaign to get rid of church-inspired laws similar to that waged by the philosophes. Nevertheless, in the nineteenth century the death penalty for sodomy was abandoned state by state, although South Carolina kept it on the books until after the Civil War.[124] Not until the publication of the Kinsey Report in 1948 and the subsequent recommendation of the American Bar Association (1961) that laws on private consenting sexual relations between adults be dropped did the decriminalization of homosexuality move ahead. A wave of law reform in the 1960s and 1970s wiped sodomy laws from the books of most northern, western, and midwestern states. In half a dozen other states, supreme courts declared sodomy laws unconstitutional. Unfortunately, the United States Supreme Court, alarmed at the controversy over its decisions on school prayer and abortion, failed to follow suit. In *Bowers v. Hardwick* (1986) it upheld the constitutionality of sodomy statutes by a vote of five to four, though Justice Lewis Powell, who cast the deciding vote, later admitted that he had "made a mistake."[125] As a result, sixteen American states entered the third millennium with laws that a moderate reformer like Montesquieu thought archaic a generation before the French Revolution. Then, on June 26, 2003, the United States Supreme Court, ruling on a Texas law, overturned *Bowers.* America now joins Europe, where the forty-five countries that make up the Council of Europe, from Lutheran Iceland to Muslim Azerbaijan, have abolished this ancient stigma.

CONCLUSION

Our story concludes here, at the moment when executions finally cease in Europe. Looking back over twenty-four centuries, what pattern can we see in the dozen societies we have examined? Most striking, certainly, is the divide between those that called themselves Christian and those that flourished before or independently of Christianity. In the first we find laws and preaching which promoted hatred, contempt, and death; in the second, varying attitudes, all of them (barring Islam, which, like Christianity, inherited the lethal tradition of the Hebrew scriptures) to a radical degree more tolerant.

In sharp contrast stands ancient Greece, in this matter at an unimaginable distance from the three great Abrahamic religions. Institutionalized in Sparta, extolled in Athens on account of its tyrannicide-heroes, and exploited in Thebes as the basis for that city's redoubtable Sacred Band, love between males was honored as a guarantee of military efficiency and civic freedom. It became a source of inspiration in poetry and art, was applauded in theaters and assemblies, and was enthusiastically commended by philosophers who thought it advantageous for young males to have lover-mentors. Indeed, the Platonic school, whose rejection of physical relations was hardly shared by Greek society as a whole, figuratively exalted the male Eros to the skies.

In Rome no comparable idealization held sway. Male homosexuality was not in itself a cause for condemnation, since relations with slaves were legally and socially acceptable. But the association of homosexuality with slavery made the passive role, according to the rules of Roman sexual politics, unacceptable to a freeborn Roman, since it compromised his status as a dominant male. Accusations of passivity might lead to a loss of civic rights *(infamia)* and were common coin in Roman politics, leaving few leaders in the late republic and the early empire untarred. Nevertheless, nearly every Roman poet of note wrote love poems to boys, and Virgil in the *Aeneid* attempted to naturalize "Greek love" in the story of Nisus and Euryalus. He did not succeed, though the Greek ideal gained some favor in second-century Rome. Yet the *cinaedus* ("faggot") remained an object of popular contempt, and this special form of homophobia—which condemned one partner but not the other—helped pave the way for the death penalty at the beginning of the Christian era.

It is when we turn from the classical world to societies influenced by biblical law that we find a great divide. The roots of Levitical ferocity toward male lovers remain obscure, though their likeliest origin appears to have been rivalries with Near Eastern cults that honored transvestite shamans. Whatever its source, the virulence of the Mosaic dispensation is all but unique among ancient religions. Under its influence, Philo of Alexandria—the only ancient Jewish writer whose surviving works treat the subject in detail—could invite mob violence by urging that suspect effeminate men should not be allowed "to live for a day or even an hour." Unfortunately, with the ascendancy of Christianity, this deadly tradition which held that all male homosexuals should be ruthlessly exterminated became dogma in European states for some fourteen centuries.

Philo's wish seems to have been realized under Constantine, Rome's first Christian emperor, who, we are told, exercised his authority by exterminating the effeminate priests Philo had inveighed against in Egypt. Such a campaign accorded with the endorsement of the Levitical death penalty by such early Christian writers as Tertullian, Eusebius, and the authors of the Apostolic Constitutions. It was also furthered by the fateful transformation of the Sodom story in religious teaching from a tale of selfish greed and mistreatment of aliens to an indictment of all consensual homosexual acts. By 390 the fanatical emperor Theodosius felt it incumbent to rid Rome "of the poison of shameful effeminacy" by consigning passive men to "avenging flames in sight of the people." At that same moment Saint John Chrysostom, preaching in Christian Antioch, called for all homosexuals to "be driven out and stoned," an inflammatory cry of hate that bore terrible fruit in the Eastern Empire when Justinian launched his bloody campaign against bishops, rich laymen, and political enemies a century later, causing the death of many.

Justinian's laws, which cloaked avaricious cruelty in the language of pastoral solicitude, generalized the Sodom legend by blaming homosexuals for "earthquakes, famine, and pestilence." Such fears were to proliferate in Western Europe in the Carolingian age. So the Council of Paris (829), terrified of marauding Vikings and Saracens, predicted defeat by the infidel if sodomitical sins were not punished and called for the death penalty, quoting Saint Paul's dictum in Romans that such deeds were "worthy of death." By a further turn of the screw, the Middle Ages linked homosexuality with doctrinal heterodoxy, speaking of "heresy of the spirit" and "heresy of the flesh." As a result, thirteenth-century religious confraternities in Italian cities were enjoined to deliver both kinds of sinners to the newly inaugurated Papal Inquisition. This linkage also gave color to Philip IV's persecution of the Templars, in which the double accusation of sodomy and heresy was used to destroy the order and deliver their wealth into his hands. In Spain, Ferdinand and Isabella burned sodomites and confiscated their estates; in Protestant England, Henry VIII's agents used the charge of sodomy to justify his pillaging of the monasteries. Two centuries later Montesquieu had ample cause to deplore the abuse of sodomy laws by tyrants.

During the Middle Ages and Renaissance, harsh legal sanctions against homosexuality routinely found their justification in Christian teaching. Angry sermons spewed hate, predicted catastrophes, blamed sodomites when these occurred, incited mobs, called for stonings or burnings, and expressed gratification when these took place. How did a church which taught mercy and compassion justify such extreme measures? The adoption of the death penalty by the priestly authors of Leviticus may have been no more than contingent; nothing in the theology of ancient Judaism made this inevitable. No reason is given for such severity other than calling lying with a man an "abomination," a term used so generally of anything disapproved that we can only speculate as to the roots of the prejudice.

Medieval Christianity, by contrast, prided itself on reconciling faith and reason. Hence Thomas Aquinas felt the need to present a rationale for making homosexuality a horrendously serious sin. He did this by appealing to the Greco-Roman notion of natural law and calling all non-procreative sex acts treasonous rebellion against God. As church and state, recovering from the chaos of the Dark Ages, became more efficiently organized in the thirteenth century, men could be more systematically hunted down by inquisitors or civic officers. So a contemporary English legal treatise decreed, in one sweeping ordinance, that "the inquirers of Holy Church" should seek out apostates, heretics, and sodomites to put them to death. This was also an age of codifications, when sodomy laws were first systematically incorporated into collections of statutes in England, France, Spain, and Italy. These laws routinely invoked Leviticus, quoted Paul, and played on superstitious fears. Some were ingenious in their cruelty, as in the case of the *Fuero Real* of Alfonso X of Castile (1255), which ordered that convicted men should be castrated and then, three days later, hung by their legs until they died.

Nor were these idle threats. Though records are often scant and research has just begun, we know of executions in medieval Switzerland, in Spain, in the Low Countries, in France, and in Italian cities, most notably Venice. In the name of Christianity San Bernardino promoted executions in fifteenth-century Siena, and Savonarola in Florence. Nowhere, however, was the church's involvement in the persecution of homosexuals more direct than in Spain during the most active years of the Spanish Inquisition. In Aragon, Catalonia, and Valencia more than a thousand men were tried by the Inquisition for sodomy, and in certain decades more were executed for sexual than for doctrinal heresy. The secular authorities were also active in France and elsewhere in Spain, convinced that the burning of sodomites had the full backing and approval of the ecclesiastical authorities.

Not only Latin Christendom witnessed these persecutions, which must have made life a fearful trial for many: the Bible-centered faith of Protestants committed them to a similar routine of terror. Executions became commonplace under Calvin and his successors in Geneva, and in the Netherlands a nationwide pogrom was launched so that, as the authorities put it, "God might not punish the iniquity of the land with his terrible judgments." Nor is there any doubt that executions in England, which reached their peak in the early nineteenth century, were the result of a century of campaigning by clergy who called upon the nation to "exterminate the monster."

It can hardly be argued that these horrors were a necessary stage in the development of civilized societies. In China and Japan the philosophical wisdom of Confucianism and the religious teaching of Buddhism did not foster them. Indeed, China was more tolerant than ancient Rome, lacking that empire's deep-seated fear of male effeminacy; and Japan, in its Samurai code, produced an ethos remarkably akin to that of classical Greece. In contrast, to look back on the history of homosexuality in the West is to view a kaleidoscope of horrors: Justinian's castrated bishops; the dangling corpses of Almería; the burning of the "married" couples in Renaissance Rome; the priests starved to death in cages in Venice's Saint Mark's Square; women burned, hanged, or beheaded on the charge of lesbianism; men tortured and burned by the Spanish Inquisition; Indians savaged by Balboa's mastiffs or burned in Peru; the deaths at the *quemadero* in Mexico City; the men and boys of Faan; and the scores of men and adolescents hanged in Georgian England. All these atrocities were committed with the certainty that they were the will of God, necessary to stave off the kind of disaster that had overwhelmed the Cities of the Plain.

Homosexuals, of course, have not been the only victims of faith-inspired intolerance. Historically, crusades against heretics, Muslims, Jews, and witches—all justified on biblical grounds—led to far more deaths than laws against homosexuality. Cruel and unjust institutions such as slavery were, in the not-too-distant past, defended by theologians, including Protestant clergy in the United States. But religious leaders also deplored such crimes and today decry them. It is to the credit of Christianity that it has been able to abandon convictions strongly held for centuries, admitting past errors and seeking reconciliation. So the Vatican has expressed regret for anti-Semitism and the persecution of religious dissent, and America's Southern Baptists for their endorsement of slavery in the nineteenth century and racial segregation in the twentieth.

The debt owed by civilization to Christianity is enormous. How can we not be grateful for its works of compassion, its service to education, and its contribution to the world's treasury of great art, architecture, and music? We must recognize those church leaders who throughout the ages have worked for peace and the alleviation of human oppression, and give thanks for the countless priests, nuns, and Protestant clergy who have labored selflessly—sometimes at the cost of their lives—in the service of humanity. A religion that preached both love and hate has left most of the hate behind. Christianity has proved itself a creed with a conscience, not lacking in men and women of good will. Even in the case of homosexuality there have been Christian Christians, though they are still a prophetic minority disconcerting to church officialdom.

About the future one may be modestly hopeful, though the controversy will doubtless be long and impassioned. But scholarship has now brought to light the long sad record of oppression and abuse, and men and women who call themselves Christian can no longer plead ignorance or avoid the burden of a deplorable, long-obscured past.

NOTES

Preface

1. Statement of the International Theological Commission, "Memory and Reconciliation: The Church and the Faults of the Past," December 1999, pp. 2, 16.

1. Early Greece: 776–480 BCE

1. Forster, p. 51.
2. Percy (citing H. Michell), p. 75.
3. Sergent, pp. 262–265.
4. 178–179; *Dialogues,* p. 510.
5. Snell, p. 15.
6. Aeschines, p. 115.
7. Sargent, p. 207.
8. *Iliad* 16:97–100.
9. Clarke, p. 384.
10. Percy, pp. 29–35.
11. *Politics* 1272a 12, p. 67.
12. Strabo 10.4.21; 5:155–159.
13. Percy, pp. 73–74.
14. "Lycurgus" 18.4; *Lives* 1:265.
15. *Lacedaemonians* 2.14; *Scripta Minora,* p. 149.
16. Dover, p. 187.
17. Ibid., pp. 185–190.
18. Percy, p. 59.
19. Pauly 16:1889–1890.
20. *Moralia* 760EF; 9:375–377.
21. Athenaeus 601F; 6:243.
22. Dover, p. 187.
23. Percy, p. 114.
24. Buffière, p. 90.
25. Theocritus, p. 48.
26. Robinson and Fluck, p. 1; Percy, pp. 118–120.
27. Robinson and Fluck, pp. 132–136.
28. Ibid., frontispiece.
29. Dover R934.
30. Ibid. B65, R651.
31. Ibid. R547.
32. Ibid. R598.
33. Notopoulos, p. 408.
34. Bowra, p. 178.
35. *Greek Lyric* 1:79–81.
36. Ibid. 1:93–95, 147.
37. Sappho, pp. 23–24.
38. *Greek Lyric* 1:21.
39. "Lycurgus" 18.4; *Lives* 1:265.
40. Brooten, "Paul's Views," pp. 65–70.
41. *Lucian* 7:379–385; "Affairs" 28; 8:195.
42. *Greek Lyric* 1:3.
43. Ibid. 1:7.
44. Ibid. 1:203.
45. Gubar *passim.*
46. Cather 1:147.
47. *Tusculan Disputations* 4.33; p. 411.
48. Horace Odes 1.32; *Greek Lyric* 1:231–233.
49. *Lyra Graeca* 2:83.
50. Ibid. 2:89.
51. Buffière, p. 252.
52. Eglinton, p. 250.
53. *Hesiod/Theognis,* p. 100–101.
54. Ibid., p. 105.
55. Ibid., p. 145.
56. Ibid., p. 146.

57. *Greek Lyric Poetry*, p. 100.
58. *Hesiod/Theognis*, p. 142.
59. "Solon" 1.2–4; *Lives* 1:405–407.
60. *Athenian Constitution* 17.2; p. 53.
61. Buffière, p. 245.
62. "Aristides" 2.3; *Lives* 2:217.
63. Pausanias 1.30.1; 1:165.
64. Thucydides 6.54–59; 3:277–285.
65. Athenaeus 695B; 7:225.
66. Herodotus 6.123; 3:277.
67. Thucydides 1.20; 1:35–37.
68. Herodotus 6.109; 3:265.
69. Arrian, *Anabasis* 4.10.3; 1:371.
70. Demosthenes 280; p. 431.
71. Brunnsåker, p. 43.
72. Stewart, p. 72.
73. 182; *Dialogues*, pp. 513–514.
74. *Moralia* 760C; 9:373.
75. Athenaeus 602C; 6:247.
76. Buffière, p. 114.
77. Xenophon, *Anabasis* 7.4.7; 3:309–311.
78. Athenaeus 226C; 3:197.

2. *Judea: 900* BCE*–600* CE

1. Boswell, p. 100.
2. *Doe v. Commonwealth*, p. 1201.
3. *Bowers v. Hardwick*, p. 196.
4. Blackstone 4:216.
5. Plant, pp. 89, 99.
6. Orbach, p. 377.
7. Loader, pp. 31–34.
8. Bailey, pp. 2–4.
9. Orbach, p. 353.
10. *Babylonian Talmud: Sanhedrin* 109a; 14:749.
11. *Midrash Rabbah: Leviticus* 4.1; 4:48–49.
12. *Babylonian Talmud: Sanhedrin* 109b; 14:751–752.
13. Ibid. 109b; 14:752.
14. Ibid.
15. *Babylonian Talmud: Baba Bathra* 12b; 13:62; *Kethuboth* 103a; 9:654.
16. *Midrash Rabbah: Genesis* 50.7; 4:438.
17. Matthew 10:15; Mark 6:11; Luke 10:12.
18. Thomas, p. 425.
19. Yamauchi, *passim.*
20. Herodotus 1.199; 1:251–253.
21. Strabo 8.6.20, 4:191; 6.2.6, 3:83; 11.14.16, 5:341; Barton 6:674–675.
22. Pope, p. 415.
23. Fry, *passim.*
24. Williams, *passim.*
25. Graillot, *passim.*
26. Lucretius, *De Rerum Natura* 2.598–643; pp. 143–145; Ovid, *Fasti* 4.237–373; pp. 205–215; Lucian, *Syrian Goddess* 15; pp. 55–56.
27. Augustine, *City of God* 7:26; 2:469.
28. Apuleius, *Golden Ass* 8.26–29; pp. 389–395.
29. Bailey, p. 52.
30. Orbach, p. 356.
31. Boswell, p. 99.
32. Bailey, pp. 50–51; Dion, pp. 44–45.
33. *Babylonian Talmud: Sanhedrin* 54b; 14:367–368.
34. Nachmanides 5:288.
35. Philo 3.37–38; 7:499.
36. Licht, pp. 124, 128.
37. Goodenough, pp. 33–34.
38. Philo 3.40–42; 7:501.
39. Ibid. 3.39; 7:499.
40. *Babylonian Talmud: Yebamoth* 76a; 8:512–513.
41. Crompton, "Myth," *passim.*
42. *Midrash Rabbah: Leviticus* 23.9; 4:299.
43. *Babylonian Talmud: Sukkah* 29a; 6:130.
44. Ibid. *Kiddushim* 82a; 11:422.
45. Ibid. *Horayoth* 13a; 15:97.
46. *Midrash Rabbah: Lamentations* 1.16.45; 7:124–125.
47. Goldin, p. 25.
48. *Babylonian Talmud: Sanhedrin* 45a; 14:295.
49. Steakley, *Homosexual Emancipation*, p. 88.
50. *Third Pink Book*, p. 294.

3. *Classical Greece: 480–323* BCE

1. Athenaeus 601E; 6:243.
2. Africa, p. 405.
3. Pindar 10.105; p. 119.
4. Athenaeus 601D-E; 6: 241–243 (rev.).
5. Bowra, pp. 275, 413.
6. Athenaeus 601A; 6:239.
7. Symonds, "A Problem," pp. 197–198.

8. Ibid., p. 198 (rev.); Athenaeus 602E; 6:249.
9. Ibid. 602E; 6:249.
10. Symonds, "A Problem," p. 199.
11. Athenaeus 603E; 6:253.
12. "Pericles" 8.5; *Lives* 3:25.
13. Athenaeus 604D; 6:257.
14. Ibid. 604E; 6:259.
15. "Protagoras" 315d; *Dialogues* 1:140.
16. *Moralia* 770C; 9:435.
17. Dio Chrysostom 12.51–52; Richter, p. 220.
18. Pliny 34.19.54; 9:167.
19. *Institutio Oratoria* 12.10.9; Richter, p. 220.
20. Pausanias, "Boeotia" 9.34.1; 4:323.
21. Ibid., "Elis 2" 6.10.6, 15.2; 3:61–63, 91.
22. Ibid., "Elis 1" 5.11.3; 2:439.
23. *Exhortation* 4; p. 121.
24. Sergent, p. 181.
25. Dover, p. 136.
26. Ibid., p. 137.
27. Ibid.
28. Ibid., p. 146.
29. Diogenes Laertius 3.29; 1:303.
30. Greek Anthology 7.99; Africa, p. 409.
31. "Symposium" 181b–d; *Dialogues,* 1:512–513.
32. Ibid.
33. Ibid. 191e–192a; 1:523.
34. Ibid. 191c; 1:522.
35. Ibid. 192a; 1:523.
36. Dover, p. 142, n. 10.
37. "Symposium" 192a–e; 1:523–524.
38. Diogenes Laertius 4.21; 1:399.
39. "Phaedrus" 247d; *Dialogues,* 3:154.
40. Ibid. 254e; 3:161.
41. Ibid. 255b; 3:162.
42. Ibid. 255e; 3:163.
43. Ibid. 256c; 3:163.
44. Durant 2:523.
45. "Laws" 8.836c; *Dialogues,* 4:403.
46. Ibid. 1.636d; 4:202.
47. Ibid. 8.836b–c; 4:403.
48. Ibid. 8.836c; 4:403.
49. Ibid. 8.836d; 4:403.
50. Ibid. 8.840a; 4:407.
51. Ibid. 8.838c; 4:405.
52. Ibid. 8.838c; 4:405.
53. "Symposium" 1.8–10; pp. 384–385.
54. *Anabasis* 7.4; 3:311.
55. "Economist" 12.14; *Works* 3 (1): 255–256.
56. Diogenes Laertius 5.22, 24; 1:465, 469.
57. *Politics* 1272a25; p. 67.
58. Ibid. 1311a31; p. 233.
59. *Nicomachean Ethics* 7.5.3–5; p. 403.
60. *Problems* 4.26; 1:127–129.
61. *Politics* 1269b23; p. 60.
62. Plutarch, *Moralia* 1044B; 13(2):501.
63. Sextus Empiricus 3.246; 1:491.
64. Ibid. 3.245; 1:489.
65. Diogenes Laertius 7.17; 2:129.
66. Athenaeus 563E; 6:45.
67. Sextus Empiricus 3.200; 1:461.
68. Diogenes Laertius 7.129; 2:235.
69. *Tusculan Disputations* 4.34.72; p. 411.
70. Buffière, p. 477, n. 36.
71. Durant 2:652.
72. Aeschines 29; p. 29.
73. Ibid. 132; p. 107.
74. Ibid. 137; p. 111.
75. Ibid. 141–152; pp. 113–123.
76. Ibid. 136; p. 111.
77. "Constitution" 2.12; *Scripta minora,* p. 147.
78. "Pelopidas" 18.4; *Lives* 5:385.
79. Ibid. 19.1; 5:387.
80. Ibid. 17.6; 5:383.
81. "Comparison of Pelopidas and Marcellus" 1.1; *Lives* 5:523.
82. "Boeotia" 9.13.11; 4:231.
83. Athenaeus 605A; 6:261.
84. Diodorus 15.39.2; 7:57.
85. Ibid. 15.88.2; 7:199.
86. Nepos 15.3.102; p. 169.
87. *De Oratore* 3.34.139; 2:111.
88. "Pelopidas" 33.1–4; 5:425–429.
89. Ibid. 28.5, 35.3–7; 5:411, 431.
90. Diodorus 15.87.6; 7:197.
91. *Moralia* 761d; 9:381.
92. "Boeotia" 9.15.6; 4:239.
93. "Arcadia" 8.11.9; 3:403.
94. Dio Chrysostom 49.5; 4:299.
95. "Pelopidas" 26.5; 5:407.
96. Ibid. 18.2; 5:385, also *Moralia* 761b–c; 9:379.
97. Ibid. 18.5; 5:385–387.
98. "Boeotia" 9.40.10; 4:361.

99. Weeks, p. 122.
100. Green, p. 164, pl. 208.
101. *Politics* 1311a31; p. 233.
102. Diodorus 16.93.5–6; 8:97.
103. *Politics* 1311b6; p. 234.
104. "Alexander" 22.4; *Lives* 7:285.
105. Athenaeus 603b: 6:251.
106. Herodotus 1.135; 1:177.
107. Curtius 6.5.23; 2:47.
108. "Alexander" 67.4; 7:413.
109. Athenaeus 603b: 6:251.
110. Diodorus 17.37.6; 8:223–225.

4. Rome and Greece: 323 BCE–138 CE

1. *Braggart Soldier* 1111–1114; p. 95.
2. Lilja, p. 31; Cody *passim.*
3. Polybius 31.25.6; 6:213.
4. Suetonius 1.49.4; 1:69.
5. Valerius Maximus 6.1.5; 2.5.
6. Ibid. 6.1.9; 2.11; Livy 8.28.1–8; 4:109.
7. Gray-Fow, *passim;* Lilja, pp. 112–121.
8. Valerius Maximus 6.1.7; 2:7.
9. *Letters to his Friends* 8.12.3, 8.14.4; 2:163, 171.
10. Suetonius "Domitian" 8.3; 2:355.
11. Juvenal 2.44, p. 21; Richlin, "Not before . . ." 3:569–571.
12. *Institutio Oratoria* 4.2.69; 2:87.
13. Seneca the Elder, *Controversiae* 4, Preface 10; 1:431 (rev.).
14. Plutarch, *Lives* "Sulla" 2.4, 36.1; 4:329, 439; "Pompey" 48.7; 5:243.
15. *Cicero* "Verrine Orations" 2.1.24.62, 2.2.78.192; 2:187, 499.
16. Ibid. "In Catalinam" 2.5.8, 2.23–24; 10:57, 71.
17. Ibid. "Pro Sestio" 17.39; 12:85.
18. Josephus 15.29–30; 6:273.
19. *Cicero* "Philippics" 2.18.45; 15:109.
20. Ibid. 2.34.86; 15:149.
21. Ibid. 13.8.17; 15:563.
22. Lucretius, *On the Nature of the Universe* 4.1053; p. 163.
23. Ibid. 4.1065–1076; p. 163.
24. *Tusculan Disputations* 4.32.68–69; pp. 407–409.
25. Ibid. 4.33.70; p. 409.
26. Virgil 5.293–295; p. 135.
27. Ibid. 9.175–184; p. 265–266.
28. Ibid. 9.430–437; p. 275.
29. Suetonius "Vergil" 9; 2:467.
30. Ibid.
31. Virgil 9.450–455; p. 276.
32. *Greek Anthology* 12:157; 4:363.
33. Ibid. 12:86; 4:323.
34. Aulus Gellius 19.9.12; 3:385.
35. Ibid.19.9.14; 3:385.
36. *Callimachus* 30; p. 157.
37. Ibid. 43; pp. 165–167.
38. *Catullus* 5; p. 7.
39. *Poetry* 48, p. 69.
40. Tibullus 1.1.75–77; p. 35.
41. Ibid. 1.4.9–14; p. 43.
42. Ibid. 1.4.39–48; p. 44.
43. *Callimachus* 53; p. 175.
44. Theocritus 7.56, 7.99; pp. 30–31.
45. Ibid. 5.116–117; p. 24.
46. Ibid. 13.8–9; p. 49.
47. Ibid. 12.1–16; p. 47.
48. Suetonius "Vergil" 9; 2:467.
49. Satire 1. 2.114–119; *Works,* p. 21.
50. Ibid. 2.3.325; p. 72.
51. *Odes* 4.1; pp. 265–267.
52. Arnold, p. 349.
53. *Letters* 7.4.6; cited by G. Williams, p. 215.
54. *Loves* 1.1.19–20; p. 15.
55. *Metamorphoses* 10.190–195, p. 240.
56. Ibid. 9.718–722; p. 231.
57. Brooten, *Love Between Women,* p. 46.
58. *Controversiae* 1.2.23; 1:87.
59. Howell, pp. 297–299.
60. *Lucian* "Dialogue of the Courtesans" 5; 7:381.
61. Ibid. "Affairs of the Heart" 28; 8:195.
62. Petronius 75; p. 76.
63. Seneca, *Epistulae* 95.24; 3:73.
64. Petronius 81; p. 83.
65. Ibid. 114; p. 128.
66. Gibbon, ch. 3; 1:92n.
67. Suetonius 1.49; 1:65–69.
68. Ibid. 2.68, 71; 1:229, 233.
69. Ibid. 3.43–44; 1:353–355.
70. Ibid. 4.36; 1:461.
71. Ibid. 6.28–29; 2:131–133.
72. Ibid. 7[1].22; 2:225. 7[2].2; 2:229. 7[3].3,12; 2:255, 265–267.
73. Ibid. 8[2].1,7; 2:321, 329.

74. Ibid. 8[3].1; 2:341.
75. *Juvenal* 2.13; p. 19.
76. Ibid. 6.34–35; p. 87.
77. Martial 12.18; 3:105.
78. Gibbon, ch. 3; 1:95.
79. Dio 68.7.3; 8:371.
80. Ibid. 68.7.4; 8:373.
81. *Scriptores* 4.5, 14.9–10; 1:13, 47.
82. Lambert, p. 119.
83. *Scriptores* 14.6; 1:45.
84. Dio 69.11.2–4; 8:445–447.
85. Symonds, *Sketches* 3:193.
86. Lambert, p. 201–203.
87. Ibid., p. 207.
88. Ibid., p. 193.
89. Ibid., p. 7.
90. Ibid., pp. 181–182.
91. Ibid., p. 189.
92. Ibid., p. 187.
93. Ibid., pp. 184–185.
94. Ibid., p. 7.
95. Ibid., p. 216.

5. Christians and Pagans: 1–565 CE

1. John 8:3–11.
2. *EH* 2:1093.
3. Mark 5:1.
4. Matthew 4:25.
5. John 13:23; 20:2; 21:7; 21:20.
6. Crompton, *Byron,* p. 281.
7. Matthew 10:15; Mark 6:11; Luke 10:12.
8. Greenberg, p. 199.
9. Aristaeus 152; *Old Testament Pseudepigrapha* 2:23.
10. Pseudo-Phocylides 191; ibid. 2:581.
11. "Sybilline Oracles" 3:596–599; ibid. 1:375.
12. *Wisdom of Solomon* 14.23–27; pp. 269–270.
13. Bailey, p. 175.
14. Knox, p. 355.
15. *Christ the Educator* 2.10.92; p. 170.
16. Ibid. 2.10.95; p. 173.
17. Ibid. 2.10.86; pp. 166–167.
18. Ibid. 3.3.22; p. 217.
19. Ibid. 3.3.20; p. 216.
20. Ibid. 3.3.23–24; p. 219.
21. Tertullian 1.29.4; 1:83.
22. Eusebius, *Préparation* 13.20.7; p. 455.
23. *Oxford Dictionary of the Christian Church,* p. 76.
24. "Apostolical Constitutions" 6.28; 17:173.
25. Bullough, ch. 7.
26. Greek Anthology 5.19, 1.139; 5.232, 1:245.
27. Aelian, p. 8.
28. Athenaeaus 601E–F; 6:243.
29. Ibid. 602D; 6:247–249.
30. Ibid. 602E, 603E-604F; 6:249, 253–261.
31. *EH* 1:87–88.
32. Aelian 12.1; pp. 355–357.
33. Ibid. 2.21; p. 93.
34. Apuleius 12; pp. 35–36.
35. *Moralia* 750B; 9:315.
36. Ibid. 750C; 9:315. 751A; 9:319.
37. Ibid. 751B; 9:319.
38. Ibid. 751C; 9:321.
39. Ibid. 751E; 9:323.
40. Ibid. 751E-752A; 9:323–325.
41. Ibid. 755F; 9:345.
42. Ibid. 757F; 9:357.
43. Ibid. 760B–C; 9:373.
44. Ibid. 761B; 9:379.
45. Ibid. 761C; 9:379–381.
46. Ibid. 761D; 9:381.
47. Ibid. 761D; 9:383.
48. Ibid. 765B; 9:403.
49. Ibid. 766E; 9:413.
50. Ibid. 766E–F; 9:413–415.
51. Ibid. 769B–D; 9:429.
52. Ibid. 770C; 9:435.
53. Flacelière, p. 24.
54. Jones, p. 180; Lucian 8:147.
55. Jones, pp. 177–179.
56. Lucian, "Affairs" 13; 8:171.
57. Ibid. 19; 8:181.
58. Ibid. 24; 8:187.
59. Ibid. 28; 8:195.
60. Ibid. 27; 8:193.
61. Ibid. 33; 8:201
62. Ibid. 36; 8:207.
63. Ibid. 38; 8:211.
64. Ibid. 45; 8:219.
65. Ibid. 48; 8:225.
66. Ibid. 47; 8:227.

67. Ibid. 51; 8:229.
68. Ibid. 53; 8:231.
69. Ibid. 52; 8:231.
70. *Moralia* 712C; 9:83.
71. Xenophon of Ephesus, p. 181.
72. Ibid., pp. 169–170.
73. Achilles Tatius 1.7–8, 12–14; pp. 23–25, 37–47.
74. Ibid. 2.35.1; p. 121.
75. Nonnus 10.196–198; p. 343.
76. Ibid., 10.264–271; p. 347.
77. Boswell, pp. 33–34.
78. Sentences 5.4.14 = Digest 47.11.2; *Civil Law* 10:327.
79. Dalla, p. 127; Cantarella, p. 224.
80. Bailey, p. 68 n. 4; see Institutes 4.18.2; *Civil Law* 2:175.
81. Digest 3.1.6; *Civil Law* 3(2):4.
82. Richlin, "Not Before," p. 556.
83. Sentences 2.26.13; Dalla, p. 109.
84. Eusebius 3.55; *Select Library* [2nd ser.] 1:534–535.
85. Ibid. 4.25; 1:546.
86. Firmicus Maternus 16.4, 29.1–3; pp. 78, 114–116.
87. Ibid., p. 14.
88. Ibid. 6.6; pp. 56–57.
89. Ibid. 4.2; pp. 50–51.
90. Minucius Felix 28.10; p. 105.
91. Firmicus Maternus, p. 9; 12.2; p. 67.
92. Bailey, p. 70, as revised by Boswell, p. 123, n. 9
93. Ibid., p. 123 n. 9.
94. J. H. Smith, pp. 145–146.
95. Hyamson, p. 83.
96. Cf. Hyamson, pp. 82–83; Greenberg, p. 230.
97. Gibbon, ch. 27; 2:56.
98. Theodoret 5.17; p. 219; Theophanes 62B; 1:113; Zonaras 13.18.11–12; 3:86.
99. *Theodosian Code* 9.7.6; p. 232.
100. Bailey, pp. 9–28.
101. Philo 26.133–136; 6:69–71.
102. Clement, *Christ the Educator* 3.8.44; p. 235.
103. *City of God* 16.30; p. 743.
104. *Confessions* 3.1(1); p. 35.
105. Ibid.
106. Ibid. 4.4(7); pp. 56–57.
107. Ibid. 4.4(9); p. 57.
108. Ibid. 3.8(15); p. 46
109. Harkins, p. xxxviii.
110. Flannery, p. 50.
111. Ibid., p. 52.
112. Harkins, p. x.
113. Homily 5 on Titus; *Select Library* [1st ser.] 13:538.
114. "Discourse . . . against the Greeks" 49; *Saint John Chrysostom Apologist,* p. 103.
115. *Against the Opponents* 3.8; p. 140.
116. Homily 8 on Thessalonians; *Select Library* [1st ser.] 13:358.
117. Ibid.
118. Homily 4 on Romans; ibid. 11:356.
119. Ibid. 11:357.
120. Ibid. 11:358.
121. Institutes 4.18.4; *Civil Law* 2:175
122. Malalas 18.168; p. 436; *PG* 97:644.
123. Boswell, p. 172.
124. Gibbon, ch. 44; 2:838–839.
125. Theophanes 151D; 1:271; *PG* 108:408.
126. Cedrenus 1.368C; 1:645–646.
127. *Procopius* 11.34–36; 6:141.
128. Novella 142; *Civil Law* 17[7]:161.
129. Novella 77; *Civil Law* 16[7]:288.
130. Ibid.
131. Dalla, pp. 203–204.
132. Ibid.
133. Novella 141; *Civil Law* 17[7]:160.
134. Ibid. 17[7]:161.
135. *Procopius* 19.11; 6:231.
136. Ibid. 20.9–10; 6:237.
137. Ibid. 20.11–12; 6:237–239.
138. Flannery, p. 138.
139. Durant 4:114.

6. Darkness Descends: 476–1049

1. Salvian, pp. 212–214.
2. Gibbon, ch. 16–18.
3. Tacitus, "Germania" 12; p. 281.
4. Ammianus Marcellinus 31.9.5; 3:445.
5. Bleibtreu-Ehrenberg, p. 36.
6. Gade, p. 132.
7. Greenberg, p. 245.
8. Goodich, pp. 72–73; Boswell, p. 177, n. 27.
9. Thompson, p. 191.
10. *Lex Visigothicorum* 3.5.4; Bailey, p. 92.
11. Thompson, p. 243.
12. Ibid., p. 247.
13. Bailey, p. 93.

14. Canon 3; Bailey, p. 93.
15. *Lex Visigothicorum* 3.5.7; Bailey, pp. 93–94.
16. Laeuchli, p. 86, n. 65.
17. Ibid., p. 134.
18. Clement, *Christ the Educator* 3.4 (29); p. 223.
19. Percival, p. 70.
20. Bailey, p. 88.
21. Ibid., pp. 86–89.
22. Payer, p. 170, n. 117.
23. 5; Bieler, p. 71.
24. 2, 3; ibid., p. 75.
25. 3; ibid., p. 97.
26. 8–9; ibid, p. 115.
27. 10.2, 6–9; ibid., pp. 127–129.
28. 1.12; McNeill and Gamer, p. 185.
29. Boswell, p. 182.
30. Payer, p. 135.
31. Bailey, pp. 94–95.
32. "Karoli Magni Capitularia" 49; p. 57.
33. Boswell, p. 182; Payer, p. 58.
34. "Concilium Parisiense," p. 634.
35. Amann, p. 215.
36. Twomey, p. 207; Ginzberg 5:178, n. 26.
37. *PL* 97:109–110.
38. Ibid. 97:866.
39. Ibid. 97:842–843.
40. R. I. Moore, p. 92.
41. Bleibtreu-Ehrenberg, p. 220.
42. *PL* 97:909.
43. Ibid. 97:910.
44. Bleibtreu-Ehrenberg, p. 227.
45. Koran 7.80–81, 11.78–83, 15.51–74, etc.
46. Ibid. 4.16; Schild, p. 181.
47. *Encyclopaedia of Islam* 5:777b.
48. Ibid. 5:777a.
49. Greenberg, pp. 178–181; Crompton, *Byron,* pp. 111–118.
50. Giffen, p. 99.
51. Ibid., p. 86.
52. Ibid., pp. 10–11.
53. Ibn Hazm, tr. Arberry, pp. 21–22.
54. Ibid., p. 76.
55. Ibid., p. 23.
56. Ibid., p. 35.
57. Ibid., p. 31.
58. Ibid., p. 90.
59. Capellanus, p. 35.
60. Ibn Hazm, tr. Arberry, p. 222.
61. Ibid., p. 225.
62. Monroe, p. 172.
63. Ibn Hazm, tr. Nykl, p. 181.
64. Ibn Hazm, tr. Arberry, p. 267.
65. Ibid., p. 243.
66. Ibid. p. 249.
67. *Encyclopaedia of Islam,* 5:777b.
68. Ibn Hazm, tr. Arberry, p. 259.
69. Ibid., tr. Nykl, p. 200.
70. Ibid., tr. Arberry, p. 258.
71. Hrosvitha, pp. 129–153.
72. Lévi-Provençal 2:173, n. 4.
73. Nykl, p. 143.
74. Ibid., p. 156.
75. Ibid., p. 157.
76. Daniel, "Arab Civilization," p. 10.
77. Nykl, p. 156.
78. Daniel, p. 10.
79. Nykl, p. 22.
80. Ibid., p. 39.
81. Ibid., p. 59.
82. Ibid., p. 268.
83. Ibid., p. 283 and 280–298 *passim.*
84. Ibid, p. 252.
85. Roth, "Deal Gently," p. 28, nn. 34–35.
86. Ibn Sa'id, pp. 4, 5, 89, 69.
87. Lane, p. 13.
88. Ibid., p. 7.
89. Roth, "Deal Gently," p. 20.
90. Ibid., pp. 42–48.
91. Ibid., p. 31.
92. Maimonides, *Guide* 3.49; 3:262–263.
93. Maimonides, *Code* 1.1.14; p. 13.
94. Monroe, pp. 372–374.
95. Greenberg, pp. 186–187.
96. Ibid., p. 177.
97. *PL* 132:331–334; Goodich, pp. 25–28.
98. *PL* 140:923–933; Goodich, p. 28.
99. *PL* 161:682–688; Goodich, pp. 31–32.
100. Bullough, p. 382.
101. *PL* 187:1498; Goodich, pp. 32–33.
102. Lea, *Inquisition of Spain* 4:362.
103. Thielicke, p. 276.
104. Cf. Agnos.
105. Peter Damian, pp. 27, 29, 32–33.
106. Ibid. 1; p. 29.
107. Ibid. 15; p. 61.
108. Ibid. 16; p. 63.
109. Ibid. 16; p. 65.
110. Ibid. 2; p. 31.

111. Ibid. 21; pp. 76–77.
112. Ibid. 23; p. 83.
113. Ibid., pp. 95–96.

7. *The Medieval World: 1050–1321*

1. Stehling, *Poems,* p. 31.
2. Ibid., p. 33.
3. Ibid., p. 35.
4. Ibid., pp. 37–39.
5. Boswell, pp. 221–226.
6. W. Daniel, p. 40.
7. Stehling, "To Love a Boy," p. 152.
8. Baudri, p. 112.
9. Ibid., p. 183.
10. Stehling, *Poems,* pp. 59–61.
11. Ibid., p. 57.
12. Ibid., pp. 69–73.
13. Ibid., pp. 131–135.
14. Ibid., p. 113.
15. Ibid., p. 121.
16. Boswell, p. 265.
17. Stehling, *Poems,* p. 93.
18. Boswell, p. 215.
19. Eadmer, *Life,* p. 64.
20. William of Malmesbury, p. 337.
21. Ordericus 4:189.
22. Barlow, p. 109.
23. Eadmer, *History,* p. 50.
24. Bailey, p. 124.
25. Boswell, pp. 218–219; McGuire, *passim.*
26. Southern, pp. 150, 152; Boswell, p. 218.
27. Bailey, p. 125.
28. Barlow, p. 106.
29. Bailey, pp. 125–126.
30. Richard 1:17.
31. Canons 8–11; Bailey, p. 96.
32. 37; Goodich, p. 42.
33. *Dictionary of the Middle Ages* 3:638.
34. Goodich, p. 43.
35. *Dictionary of the Middle Ages* 4:538.
36. Aquinas 2a2ae. Qu. 154, art. 12, reply 4; vol. 43:249.
37. Boswell, p. 313.
38. Aquinas 1a2ae. Qu. 94, art. 3, reply 2; 28:85.
39. Curran, p. 130.
40. Bagemihl, p. 12.
41. Ibid., pp. 20, 488.
42. Aquinas, 2a2ae. Qu. 153, art. 2, reply; 43:193.
43. Ibid., 2a2ae Qu. 154, art. 12; 43:247.
44. Ibid.
45. Noonan, p. 242.
46. Curran, p. 127.
47. Canto 11, 1.50.
48. *Politics* 1.10, 1258b34; p. 270.
49. Panormitanus, cited by Boswell, p. 331.
50. Nelson, p. 100.
51. Goodich, p. 82.
52. O'Brien, p. 77.
53. Ibid., pp. 86–87.
54. Barber, *Trial,* p. 249.
55. Ibid., p. 61.
56. Cf. Legman.
57. B. Hamilton, p. 83.
58. Barber, *Trial,* p. 56.
59. Ibid., p. 57.
60. Ibid., p. 116.
61. Ibid., p. 106.
62. Ibid., p. 157.
63. Ibid., pp. 229–230.
64. Barber, "Molay," p. 123.
65. Ibid., p. 121.
66. Gade, p. 129.
67. Ibid., p. 124.
68. Ibid. p. 131.
69. Ibid., p. 126.
70. Muyart, pp. 509–510.
71. Viollet 2:147–148.
72. Laurière, cited by Viollet 4:36–37.
73. *Philosophical Dictionary,* p. 79.
74. Viollet 1:161.
75. Rapetti, p. 279.
76. Beaumanoir, p. 304.
77. Bouteiller, p. 870.
78. Brillon 6:216.
79. Ibid. 1:42.
80. *Fleta,* p. 90.
81. *Mirror,* p. 53.
82. *El Fuero Real* 4.9; *Los Códigos* 1:412.
83. *Partidas* 7.21; *Los Códigos* 4:424.
84. Van Kleffens, pp. 255–282.
85. Ibid.
86. Bailey, p. 154.
87. "Annales Basileenses," p. 201; cited by Boswell, p. 293, n. 73.
88. Warnkönig 3(2):76.

89. Videgáin Agós, p. 116.
90. Ibid., pp. 53, 116, 254.
91. Ibid., p. 116.
92. Courouve, "Sodomy Trials," p. 21.
93. Goris, p. 203.
94. Osenbrüggen, p. 290.
95. Ruggiero, *Boundaries,* pp. 115–116.
96. Ibid., p. 127.
97. Bailey, p. 161.
98. See Chapter 1.
99. Rapetti, p. 280.
100. Berners, pp. 725–727.
101. 115. Aquinas, 2a2ae, Qu. 154, art 11, reply; 43:245.
102. *Codex* 9.9.20; *Corpus iuris* 2:375.
103. Cino da Pistoia 2:546.
104. Bartholomaeus 4: no pagination.
105. Herman, p. 86.
106. Cormier, pp. 218–219.
107. Ibid., p. 220.
108. Marie de France, p. 112.
109. Alain de Lille, pp. 3–4.
110. Guillaume de Loris, p. 1.
111. Ibid., pp. 323–324.
112. Wilkinson, pp. 184–185.
113. *Ovide moralisé* 10.2519–2534; 4:71.
114. Cf. Kay, Pézard.
115. Canto 11, 1.48; p. 105.
116. Canto 6, 11.79–80; p. 68.
117. Canto 15, 11.81–84; p. 138.
118. Canto 15, 11.106–107; p. 139.
119. Coulton 4:699.
120. Canto 15, 1.114, p. 139; Boccaccio, *Esposizioni,* p. 681.
121. Canto 16, 11.59–60, p. 144.
122. Rocke, "Sodomites," p. 7.
123. *EH* 1:295.
124. *Commento* 1:375.
125. Avalle, p. 81.
126. Coulton 4:700.
127. Boswell, p. 375, n. 50.
128. Villani 8.92; pp. 377–381.
129. Canto 20, 11.91–93; p. 178.

8. *Imperial China: 500 BCE–1849*

1. Bullough, p. 247.
2. Ruan and Tsai, pp. 21–22.
3. Han Fei Zi, p. 78.
4. *Zhanguo ce,* p. 449.
5. Hinsch, p. 53.
6. See Wuxia Ameng.
7. Ibid., p. 22.
8. Han Fei Zi, p. 78.
9. *Zhanguo ce,* p. 449.
10. Hinsch, pp. 24–25.
11. *Zhanguo ce,* p. 62.
12. Han Fei Zi, p. 46.
13. Ibid., p. 43.
14. *Zhanguo ce,* pp. 227–229.
15. Hinsch, pp. 35–36.
16. Sima Qian 2:419.
17. Ibid.
18. Ibid.
19. Hinsch, pp. 47–48.
20. Xiaomingxiong, pp. 48–50.
21. Hinsch, pp. 41–42.
22. Ban Gu 3:38–39.
23. Hinsch, pp. 44–46.
24. Van Gulik, p. 48.
25. Ibid., p. 250.
26. Eberhard, pp. 63–64.
27. Xiaomingxiong, pp. 63–65.
28. Bullough, p. 362; Senelick, p. 60.
29. Hinsch, pp. 346–347.
30. Holzman, pp. 123–124.
31. *New Songs,* p. 231.
32. Ibid., pp. 200–201.
33. Van Gulik, p. 122.
34. Ibid., p. 207.
35. Hinsch, p. 87.
36. Ibid., p. 92.
37. Ibid., p. 93–94.
38. Spence, *Memory Palace,* p. 226.
39. Xiaomingzong, pp. 127–133.
40. Goodrich 1:314.
41. Xiaomingxiong, pp. 129–133.
42. Hummel 1:190.
43. Xiaomingxiong, pp. 135–137.
44. Vitiello, "The Dragon's Whim" 78:363.
45. McMahon, p. 77.
46. Vitiello, "The Dragon's Whim" 78:363.
47. Boxer, p. 223.
48. Spence, *Memory Palace,* p. 221.
49. Ibid., p. 228.
50. Ibid., p. 203.
51. Ibid., p. 220.
52. Chan, p. 70.
53. Spence, *Memory Palace,* p. 227.
54. Lowry, pp. 12–13.
55. Ibid., p. 143.
56. Wuxia Ameng, pp. 104–105.

57. Lowry, p. 143.
58. Hinsch, pp. 134–136.
59. Li Yu, *Silent Operas,* p. 101.
60. Ibid., p. 118.
61. Ibid., p. 103.
62. Ibid., p. 134.
63. Li Yu, *A Tower,* pp. 83–115.
64. Hanan, *Li Yu,* pp. 159–161.
65. Shen Fu, pp. 53–57.
66. Vitiello, "Exemplary Sodomites," p. 40.
67. Ibid., ch. 2.
68. McMahon, p. 74.
69. Ibid., pp. 75–78; Vitiello, "Exemplary Sodomites," ch. 3.
70. Ibid., ch. 4.
71. Cao Xueqin, ch. 58; 3:132–133.
72. Ng, "Late Imperial China," p. 501, n. 25.
73. Spence, *Emperor of China,* p. 129.
74. Ibid., p. 127
75. Meijer, p. 109.
76. Ibid., p. 112.
77. Alabaster, p. 369.
78. Ng, "Rape Laws," p. 69.
79. Hummel 2:924.
80. Xiaomingxiong, p. 164.
81. Chou, p. 91.
82. Ibid.
83. Brackman, p. 121.
84. Barrow, pp. 149–150.
85. Matignon, pp. 264–265, 267.
86. Hummel 2:622–625.
87. Mackerras, p. 93.
88. Xiaomingxiong, p. 20.
89. Mackerras, p. 93.
90. Hinsch, p. 155.
91. Ibid, p. 100.
92. Mackerras, p. 141.
93. Scott, pp. 107–113.
94. Lu Xun, p. 320.
95. Hinsch, p. 159.
96. Lu Xun, p. 322.
97. Hinsch, p. 163.

9. Italy in the Renaissance: 1321–1609

1. Goodich, p. 79.
2. Rocke, "Male Homosexuality," p. 5.
3. Dahm, pp. 439–443; Kläre, p. 64.
4. Bowsky, p. 5.
5. *Statuta . . . Tarvisii,* pp. 187v–188.
6. Labalme, p. 241, n. 108.
7. Ibid., p. 242.
8. Ruggiero, p. 136.
9. Ibid., pp. 115–116.
10. Ibid., pp. 129–131.
11. Ibid., pp. 135–145.
12. Ibid., p. 133; quotation from Labalme, p. 224.
13. Ruggiero, table 6, pp. 128, 119.
14. Bullough, *Women and Prostitution,* p. 76.
15. Ruggiero, p. 93.
16. Ibid., p. 189, n. 9.
17. Ibid., p. 189, n. 10.
18. Ibid., p. 109.
19. Ibid., p. 140.
20. Ibid., p. 124.
21. Labalme, p. 231.
22. Ibid., p. 226.
23. Labalme, pp. 226–227.
24. Ibid., p. 236.
25. Ruggiero, p. 125.
26. Labalme, p. 239.
27. Pavan, p. 275.
28. Labalme, p. 242.
29. Ibid., p. 243.
30. Rocke, "Male Homosexuality," p. 13.
31. Rocke, *Friendships,* p. 10
32. Ibid., p. 28.
33. Boccaccio, *Decameron,* p. 23.
34. Ibid., pp. 34–35.
35. Ibid., p. 376.
36. Rocke, *Friendships,* pp. 21–22.
37. Goldthwaite, p. 437.
38. Rocke, *Friendships,* pp. 22, 24.
39. Ibid., pp. 24–25.
40. Ibid., p. 30–31.
41. Ibid., p. 46.
42. Ibid., p. 32.
43. Rocke, "Male Homosexuality," pp. 6–7.
44. Rocke, *Friendships,* p. 37.
45. Grimm 3:1817.
46. Rocke, *Friendships,* p. 38.
47. Ibid., p. 39.
48. Rocke, "Sodomites," p. 15.
49. Rocke, *Friendships,* p. 40.
50. Ibid., p. 41.

51. Ibid., p. 43.
52. Bernardino 2:66.
53. Rocke, *Friendships,* p. 36.
54. Ibid., p. 45.
55. Ibid., p. 59.
56. Ibid., p. 51.
57. Goldthwaite, pp. 430, 438.
58. Rocke, *Friendships,* p. 49.
59. Ibid., p. 55.
60. Ibid., p. 58.
61. Ibid., pp. 62–63.
62. Ibid., p. 62.
63. Ibid., p. 63.
64. Ibid., p. 159.
65. Ibid., p. 200.
66. Ibid., p. 136.
67. Durant 5:576.
68. Rocke, *Friendships,* p. 63.
69. Ibid., table B.13, p. 250.
70. Ibid., p. 139.
71. Rocke, "Male Homosexuality," table 15, p. 322.
72. Ibid., p. 327.
73. Ibid., p. 321.
74. Rocke, *Friendships,* p. 56.
75. Ibid., p. 141.
76. Rocke, "Male Homosexuality," p. 412.
77. Rocke, *Friendships,* pp. 154, 160.
78. Ibid., p. 205.
79. Ibid., p. 206.
80. Ibid., p. 207.
81. Rocke, "Male Homosexuality," p. 484, n. 54.
82. Rocke, *Friendships,* p. 212.
83. Ibid., p. 222.
84. Ibid., p. 221.
85. Ibid., p. 223.
86. Ibid., p. 221.
87. Ibid., pp. 224–225.
88. Ibid., p. 229.
89. Ibid., p. 231.
90. Ibid., p. 233.
91. Ibid., pp. 234–235.
92. Vasari 1:301.
93. Bennett and Wilkins, p. 7.
94. Janson, p. 85.
95. Ibid.
96. Ibid.
97. Clark, p. 54.
98. Janson, p. 78.
99. Bennett and Wilkins, p. 219.
100. Janson, pl. 34b.
101. Ibid., p. 85.
102. Rocke, *Friendships,* p. 289, n. 119.
103. Ibid., p. 298, n. 121.
104. Mesnil, p. 154.
105. Lightbrown, p. 44.
106. Mesnil, p. 204, n. 83.
107. Ibid., p. 128.
108. Ibid., p. 207, n. 126.
109. Chastel, p. 290, n. 4; Lightbrown, p. 302.
110. Chastel, p. 294.
111. Payne, p. 28.
112. Rocke, *Friendships,* p. 298, n. 120.
113. Ibid., p. 64.
114. Durant 5:215–216.
115. Vasari 2:163.
116. Payne, p. 100.
117. Pedretti, p. 154.
118. Payne, p. 101.
119. Eissler, pp. 150–151, n. 2.
120. Payne, p. 242; Pedretti, p. 142.
121. Vasari 2:163.
122. Payne, p. 292.
123. Ficino, p. 147.
124. Ibid., pp. 130, 208.
125. Condivi, p. 105.
126. D'Ancona, p. 47.
127. Brandes, pp. 163–164.
128. *Letters* 1:193.
129. Ibid. 1:184.
130. The numbering of the poems is keyed to Creighton Gilbert's translation.
131. Panovsky, p. 213.
132. De Tolnay, p. 112.
133. Liebert, p. 278.
134. Hartt, "Review," p. 250.
135. Brandes, p. 349.
136. *Poetry* (tr. Clements), p. 144.
137. Condivi, p. 144n.
138. Pope-Hennessey, p. 254.
139. D'all Orto, "Socratic Love," p. 57.
140. Ibid., p. 59.
141. Symonds, *Michelangelo,* pp. 127–128.
142. Vasari 4:172.
143. Durant 5:396; Kelly, p. 250.
144. Symonds, *Renaissance* 1:388n.
145. Garde, p. 251.
146. Creighton 4:130, n. 3; Shaw, p. 187.

147. Sternweiler, p. 144.
148. Vasari 3:285.
149. Ibid. 3:289.
150. Ibid. 3:285–286.
151. Cust, p. 23.
152. Ibid., p. 174.
153. Ibid., pp. 198–199.
154. Ibid., pp. 235–236.
155. Ibid., pp. 237–238.
156. Cellini, pp. 34–35.
157. Pope-Hennessy, p. 28.
158. Rocke, *Friendships,* pp. 229–230.
159. Cellini, p. 353.
160. Ibid., p. 357.
161. Ibid., pp. 177, 51.
162. Ibid., p. 155.
163. Ibid., p. 342.
164. Rocke, *Friendships,* pp. 232–233.
165. Pope-Hennessy, p. 253.
166. Ibid., p. 254.
167. Pastor 14:287.
168. Durant 6:925.
169. Boswell, *Same-Sex Unions,* p. 265, n. 14.
170. Montaigne, pp. 954–955.
171. Durant 7:241.
172. Pastor 21:92.
173. Martin, p. 83.
174. Hibbard, p. 30, n. 14.
175. Ibid., p. 306.
176. Posner, p. 302.
177. Hibbard, p. 157.
178. Ibid., p. 386.

10. Spain and the Inquisition: 1497–1700

1. Carrasco, p. 42.
2. Monter, *Frontiers,* p. 280.
3. Ibid.
4. Carrasco, pp. 40–41.
5. Tomás y Valente, p. 227.
6. Carrasco, p. 41.
7. T. Miller, p. 173.
8. Lea 4:362–363.
9. Eymeric, p. 76.
10. Carrasco, p. 39.
11. *EH* 2:869.
12. Fraxi, 2:69.
13. Carrasco, p. 11.
14. Lea 4:362.
15. Monter, *Frontiers,* pp. 276–278.
16. Carrasco, p. 58.
17. Monter, *Frontiers,* p. 76.
18. Ibid., pp. 280–281.
19. Ibid., pp. 282–283.
20. Ibid., p. 288.
21. Ibid., pp. 280–281.
22. Durant 6:641.
23. Monter, *Frontiers,* p. 57.
24. Eymeric, p. 130.
25. Monter, *Frontiers,* p. 29.
26. Carrasco, p. 14.
27. Monter, *Frontiers,* p. 283.
28. Ibid., p. 137.
29. Ibid., p. 140.
30. Ibid., p. 303.
31. Ibid., p. 141.
32. Ibid., p. 288.
33. Perry, p. 71.
34. Monter, *Frontiers,* p. 142.
35. Lea 4:367.
36. Ibid. 4:371.
37. Monter, *Frontiers,* p. 282.
38. Crompton, "Myth," p. 18.
39. Tomás y Valente, p. 228.
40. Monter, *Frontiers,* pp. 316–317 and n. 35.
41. Lea 4:365.
42. Ibid. 4:364.
43. Monter, *Frontiers,* p. 175.
44. Ibid., p. 287.
45. Ibid., p. 289; Cutrera, pp. 128–203.
46. Carrasco, p. 38.
47. Ibid., p. 167.
48. Ibid., p. 172.
49. Ibid., p. 135.
50. Ibid., p. 48.
51. Ibid., p. 46, n. 65.
52. Ibid., pp. 134–135.
53. Ibid., p. 117.
54. Ibid., p. 119.
55. Monter, *Frontiers,* p. 290.
56. Ibid., p. 296.
57. Ibid., p. 293.
58. Carrasco, p. 19.
59. Ibid., p. 59.
60. Ibid.
61. Ibid., p. 80.
62. Ibid., p. 64.

63. Monter, p. 298.
64. Herrera Puga, p. 305.
65. Ibid., pp. 293, 296.
66. Ibid. p. 314.
67. Ibid., p. 316.
68. Ibid., p. 312.
69. Perry, p. 81.
70. Herrera Puga, p. 325.
71. Ibid., pp. 329–330.
72. Ibid., pp. 328–329.
73. Ibid., p. 324.
74. Gonzales Palencia, p. 289.
75. Ibid., p. 133.
76. Trevisan, pp. 66–67.
77. Lea 3:238.
78. Mott, "Justitia," p. 706.
79. Lea 4:365.
80. Mott, "Justitia," p. 710.
81. Ibid., p. 709.
82. Mott, "Pleasures," p. 87.
83. Ibid., p. 86.
84. Ibid., p. 87; Trevisan, p. 55.
85. Mott, "Pleasures," p. 89.
86. Ibid., pp. 91–92.
87. Ibid., pp. 93–94.
88. Ibid., p. 90.
89. Ibid., pp. 90–92.
90. Mott, "Justicia," Quadro IV, p. 737.
91. Ibid., pp. 728–729.
92. Ibid., p. 707; Trevisan, p. 54.
93. Ibid., Quadro I, p. 736.
94. Ibid., Quadro IV, p. 737.
95. Ibid., p. 712.
96. Ibid., p. 713.
97. Ibid., p. 714.
98. Guerra, p. 52.
99. Ibid., pp. 123–124.
100. Ibid., p. 55.
101. Dynes, *Homolexis,* pp. 19–20.
102. Guerra, pp. 80–81.
103. Ibid., p. 52.
104. Ibid., pp. 61–62.
105. Ibid., p. 69.
106. Ibid., p. 70.
107. Ibid., p. 112.
108. Ibid., p. 26.
109. Ibid., p. 24.
110. Ibid., p. 160.
111. Ibid., p. 154.
112. Ibid., p. 257.
113. Ibid., pp. 92–93, 271.
114. Ibid., p. 93.
115. Ibid., p. 48.
116. Ibid., p. 190.
117. Ibid., pp. 90, 141.
118. Lea 4:364.
119. Greenleaf, pp. 108, 132.
120. Taylor, "Homosexuality," p. 17.
121. Taylor, "El Ambiente," p. 18.

11. France from Calvin to Louis XIV: 1517–1715

1. *EH* 1:311, 2:1268.
2. *EH* 2:1135; Karlinsky, p. 349.
3. Schleiner, p. 48.
4. Meylan, *passim.*
5. Estienne 1:175.
6. Garde, p. 251.
7. Schleiner, p. 54.
8. Bayle 8:455.
9. Ibid.
10. Ibid.
11. Kelly, p. 263.
12. Schleiner, p. 44.
13. Ibid., p. 47.
14. Garde, p. 289.
15. Schleiner, p. 52.
16. Monter, "Switzerland," p. 43.
17. Ibid., p. 46.
18. Ibid.
19. Crompton, "Myth," p. 18; *EH* 2:1199.
20. Monter, "Switzerland," p. 44.
21. *EH* 1:123–24.
22. Beurdeley, p. 120.
23. Soman, p. 36, n. 7.
24. Lever, p. 95.
25. Ibid., p. 88.
26. Estienne 1:178.
27. Montaigne, pp. 869–870.
28. Lever, pp. 91–94.
29. Hernandez, pp. 30–35.
30. Montaigne, pp. 138, 642, 680.
31. L'Estoile, p. 142.
32. Ibid., p. 446.
33. Ibid., p. 122.
34. Teasley, p. 21.
35. Von Römer, "Heinrich der Dritte," p. 615.
36. Teasley, p. 17.

37. L'Estoile, p. 232.
38. Ibid., p. 154.
39. L'Estoile, p. 328.
40. Chevallier, *Henri III,* p. 418.
41. L'Estoile, p. 181.
42. Cady, "Henri III," p. 131.
43. Von Römer, "Heinrich der Dritte," pp. 643–646.
44. Cameron, p. 17.
45. Teasley, p. 23.
46. Cameron, p. 83.
47. Chevallier, *Henri III,* p. 433.
48. Von Römer, "Heinrich der Dritte," p. 608.
49. Maber, p. xxii.
50. Ibid., p. 37.
51. Daniel, *Hommes,* pp. 12–13; Beurdeley, pp. 113–115.
52. Viau, pp. 103–104.
53. Lachèvre 1:142.
54. Ibid. 1:256.
55. Tallemant (ed. Adam) 2:933, n. 7.
56. Collins, p. 177.
57. Ibid., p. 174.
58. *Gay and Lesbian Literary Heritage,* p. 629.
59. Beurdeley, p. 120.
60. Garde, p. 313.
61. Tallemant, *Portraits,* p. 16.
62. But see Daniel, *Hommes,* p. 21, n. 30.
63. Moote, p. 144.
64. Daniel, *Hommes,* p. 22.
65. Tallement (ed. Adam) 1:339.
66. Moote, pp. 165–166.
67. Ibid., p. 286.
68. Ibid., p. 285.
69. Tallement, *Portraits,* pp. 25–26.
70. Moote, p. 289.
71. Van der Cruysse, p. 160.
72. Bussy-Rabutin (ed. Livet) 3:345.
73. Lever, pp. 158–160.
74. Bussy-Rabutin (ed. Livet) 3:356–357.
75. Lever, pp. 160–162.
76. Van der Cruysse, p. 157.
77. Ibid., p. 159.
78. Daniel, *Hommes,* p. 34.
79. Ibid., pp. 163–164.
80. Ibid., p. 165.
81. Van de Cruysse, p. 160.
82. Ibid.
83. Ibid., p. 164.
84. Ibid., p. 179.
85. Orléans, *A Woman's Life,* p. 87.
86. Van der Cruysse, p. 178.
87. Ibid., p. 181.
88. Ibid., p. 180.
89. Ibid., p. 181.
90. Orléans, *Letters,* p. 99.
91. Ibid., pp. 181–182.
92. Primi Visconti, *Mémoires,* p. 136.
93. Dewald, p. 117.
94. Bussy-Rabutin (ed. Adam), pp. 143–144.
95. Daniel, *Hommes,* pp. 46–47, 51–52; Lever, pp. 234–237.
96. Collins, p. 178.
97. Van der Chruysse, p. 173.
98. Lever, p. 154.
99. Ibid.
100. Durant 8:71–72.
101. Bourdaloue 10:42–43.
102. Van der Cruysse, p. 286; quotation in Lever, pp. 166–167.
103. Garde, pp. 384–385.
104. Primi Visconti, p. 144.
105. Van der Cruysse, p. 178; Orléans, *Letters,* p. 52.
106. Van der Cruysse, p. 326.
107. Ibid., p. 181.
108. Ibid., p. 426.
109. Lever, p. 174.
110. Daniel, *Hommes,* p. 40.
111. Saint-Simon 2:693–694.
112. Ibid. 2:1510.
113. Ibid. 2:698.
114. *Dictionnaire du Grand Siècle,* p. 1575.
115. Garde, p. 412.
116. Lever, p. 175.
117. Frischauer, p. 34.
118. McKay, p. 10.
119. Bonnet, p. 35.
120. DeJean, pp. 30, 37.
121. Ibid., pp. 103–110.
122. Ibid., p. 55.
123. Ibid., p. 57.
124. Bayle 13:94.
125. Brantôme, p. 118.
126. Ibid., p. 129.
127. Ibid., p. 130.
128. Ibid., pp. 130–131.

129. Ibid., p. 135.
130. Ibid.
131. Ibid., p. 129.
132. M. L. Clarke, p. 228.
133. Masson, p. 72.
134. Goldsmith, *Christina,* p. 10.
135. Masson, p. 82.
136. Goldsmith, *Christina,* p. 207.
137. Ibid., p. 74–75.
138. Masson, p. 220.
139. M. L. Clarke, pp. 233–234.
140. Goldsmith, *Christina,* p. 177.
141. Åkerman, pp. 3–4.
142. Masson, p. 99.
143. Ibid., p. 87.
144. Ibid., pp. 63–64.
145. Goldsmith, *Christina,* pp. 72–73.
146. Åkerman, p. 308.
147. Goldsmith, *Christina,* p. 66.
148. Masson, p. 201.
149. Ibid., p. 186.
150. Goldsmith, *Christina,* p. 72.
151. Masson, p. 187.
152. Ibid., p. 230.
153. Ibid., pp. 263–264.
154. Goldsmith, *Christina,* pp. 69–70.
155. Orléans, *Correspondance* 1:279.

12. England from the Reformation to William III: 1533–1702

1. Estienne 1:140.
2. Mirk, p. 80.
3. Chaucer, p. 258.
4. *Rotuli* 2:332.
5. Crompton, *Byron,* p. 53.
6. Harris, pp. 9, 34.
7. Wunderli, pp. 83–84.
8. Bailey, p. 147.
9. Knowles, p. 204.
10. Coulton, 4:68.
11. *Letters and Papers,* 10:138.
12. Ibid. 10:137, 138.
13. Ibid. 15:215–216, 458.
14. *DNB* 1:962.
15. Bale, *Dramatic Writings,* p. 23.
16. Bale, *Actes,* no pagination.
17. Burton 3.3.1.2, p. 652.
18. Wyatt, p. 156.
19. Kinder, pp. 28–31, 119–120.
20. Bailey, pp. 149–150.
21. Bray, *Homosexuality,* p. 39.
22. Ibid., pp. 71, 128n.44.
23. Elyot 1.13, pp. 47–48.
24. Sidney, pp. 40, 6.
25. Bredbeck, p. 5.
26. Burton 3.2.1.2; p. 652.
27. Bredbeck, p. 92.
28. Spenser, *Faerie Queene* 3.12.7, p. 169.
29. Barnfield, pp. 79–80.
30. Ibid., p. 116.
31. Ibid., p. 23.
32. Brooke, p. 107.
33. Ibid., pp. 98–99.
34. Ibid., p. 107.
35. Marlowe, *Poems,* pp. xxii–xxiii.
36. Brooke, p. 114.
37. Ibid., pp. 130–132.
38. Marlowe, *Poems,* pp. 8–10.
39. Ibid., pp. 33–35.
40. Read 2:218.
41. Marlowe, *Edward the Second,* p. xx.
42. Boas, p. 243.
43. J. S. Hamilton, p. 13.
44. Monk of Malmesbury, p. 15.
45. Prestwick, p. 79.
46. "Lanercost Chronicle," p. 270.
47. J. S. Hamilton, p. 13.
48. Ibid., p. 47.
49. Bingham, *Edward II,* p. 66.
50. Monk of Malmesbury, p. 30.
51. Thomas Gray, "The Bard" (1757).
52. Froissart, p. 92.
53. De la Moore, p. 318.
54. Ibid., p. 319.
55. Steel, p. 122.
56. Thomas de Burton, p. 355.
57. Marlowe, *Edward the Second,* p. 83.
58. Ibid., p. 85.
59. Drayton 1:162.
60. Ibid. 1:208.
61. Rollins 1:55.
62. Ibid.
63. Rollins 2:232–233.
64. Ibid.
65. J. D. Wilson, p. xvii.
66. Pequigney, p. 64.
67. Montaigne, p. 138.
68. Lewis, p. 503.
69. Spenser, *Minor Poems,* p. 18.

70. Melville, p. 236.
71. Bergeron, *Royal Family,* p. 29.
72. Bingham, *James VI and I,* p. 162.
73. Ibid. p. 168.
74. Ibid., p. 152.
75. Bergeron, p. 32.
76. Willson, p. 36; Bingham, p. 132.
77. *Calendar of the State Papers* 6:149.
78. Erskine 1:1203.
79. Pitcairn 2(1):491, n. 1.
80. *Historie,* p. 64.
81. Hume 1:469.
82. Weldon, pp. 9, 58.
83. Kernan, p. 19.
84. Osborne 1:274–275.
85. D'Ewes, *Diary,* pp. 92–93.
86. James I, p. 20.
87. Crompton, *Byron,* p. 42.
88. Akrigg, p. 315.
89. Ibid., p. 336.
90. Ibid., pp. 336–337.
91. Bergeron, p. 162.
92. Ibid., p. 163.
93. Lockyer, p. 22; Ross Williamson, p. 235.
94. Akrigg, p. 431.
95. Ibid., p. 386.
96. Ibid., pp. 177–178.
97. Ibid., p. 174.
98. Cady, "Renaissance Writing," p. 18.
99. A. Wilson, p. 159.
100. Aubrey, p. 11.
101. Bacon 8:244.
102. Bray, "Friendship," p. 14.
103. Du Maurier, p. 66.
104. Ibid., p. 67.
105. Crompton, "Colonial America," p. 278.
106. Ibid., p. 279.
107. Ibid., p. 281.
108. Ibid., pp. 282–283, 293.
109. Bingham, "Deviant Sex," pp. 455, 459–460.
110. A. Clarke, p. 50.
111. Ibid., p. 45.
112. *Life and Death,* p. [6].
113. *DNB* 1:688–689.
114. *Biographia Britannica* 1:246–254.
115. *DNB* 1:689.
116. Barnard, p. 6.
117. Ibid., p. 14.
118. Ibid., pp. 25–26.
119. Pepys 4:209–210.
120. Rochester, *Letters,* p. 230.
121. Rochester, *Poems,* p. 99.
122. Ibid., p. 25.
123. Rochester, *Sodom,* pp. 57, 113–114.
124. A. Hamilton, p. 243.
125. Donne, *Satires,* p. 212.
126. Allen, p. 190; Vessey, pp. 79–91.
127. Donne, *Complete Poems,* p. 76.
128. Donne, *Sermons* 5:259.
129. Mueller, p. 194.
130. Heywood, p. 394.
131. Philips 1:118–119.
132. Newcastle, p. 32.
133. Donoghue, p. 227.
134. Stiebel, p. 232.
135. Behn, *Poems,* p. 74.
136. Ibid., p. 75.
137. *Poems on Affairs of State* 5:38.
138. Burnet, *History,* p. 703.
139. *Calendar of the Manuscripts* 3:278.
140. J. Miller, p. 55.
141. Robb 2:398.
142. Ibid. 2:399.
143. *Poems on Affairs of State* 5:57.
144. Ibid. 5:42.
145. Ibid. 5:60.
146. Ibid. 5:122, 221.
147. Rubini, p. 381.
148. *Poems on Affairs of State* 5:38.
149. Orléans, *Lettres françaises,* p. 146.
150. Orléans, *Letters,* p. 52.
151. Ibid., p. 70.
152. Van der Cruysse, p. 178.
153. Ibid., p. 181.
154. Ibid., p. 383.
155. Van der Zee, passim.
156. Baxter, pp. 462, 111.
157. Ibid., p. 350.
158. Robb 2:450, 448.
159. *New Encyclopedia Britannica* 12:669.
160. Burnet, *History,* p. 439.
161. Burnet, *Supplement,* pp. 191–192.
162. Ibid., pp. 191–192n.
163. Robb 2:402.
164. Swift 5:285, 259.
165. Burnet, *Supplement,* p. 193.

166. *Poems on Affairs of State* 5:153–154, n. 23.
167. J. Miller, p. 203.
168. Van der Cruysse, pp. 181, 426.

13. Pre-Meiji Japan: 800–1868

1. Boxer, p. 37.
2. Watanabe, p. 20.
3. Ibid., p. 21.
4. Ibid.
5. Cooper, p. 46.
6. Leupp, p. 13.
7. Ibid., p. 214; Ihara, *Great Mirror,* pp. 51–52.
8. Leupp, p. 33.
9. Watanabe, p. 32; Leupp, p. 23.
10. Schalow, "Kūkai," p. 216.
11. Schalow, "Invention," p. 13.
12. Ibid., p. 10.
13. Murasaki, p. 41.
14. Ibid., p. 48.
15. Leupp, pp. 25–26.
16. Ibid., pp. 43–44.
17. *Collection,* p. 250.
18. *Kodansha Encyclopedia* 7:187.
19. Leupp, pp. 40, 45–46.
20. Katō, p. 283.
21. Childs, *Rethinking Sorrow,* p. 26.
22. Childs, "Genmu," p. 40.
23. Ibid., p. 42.
24. Ibid., p. 50.
25. Genshin, p. 33.
26. Childs, *"Chigo Monogatari,"* p. 129.
27. Ibid., p. 133.
28. Ibid., p. 139.
29. Ibid., p. 150.
30. Leupp, p. 26.
31. Ibid., p. 54.
32. Ibid., p. 214.
33. Ihara, *Comrade Loves,* pp. 45–47.
34. Watanabe, p. 109.
35. Ibid., pp. 110–111.
36. Ibid., p. 113.
37. Ibid.
38. Leupp, pp. 52–53.
39. Ibid., pp. 53–55.
40. Watanabe, p. 49.
41. Ibid. pp. 49–50.
42. Hare, p. 16.
43. Ibid., pp. 17–18.
44. Ibid., p. 82.
45. Ihara, *Great Mirror,* pp. 214–215.
46. Watanabe, p. 86.
47. Ihara, *Great Mirror,* p. 42.
48. *Actors' Analects,* pp. 41–42.
49. Ogyū, p. 55.
50. Leupp, p. 66.
51. Ibid., p. 71.
52. Ibid., p. 77.
53. Ibid., pp. 74, 77.
54. Ibid., pp. 205–206.
55. Ibid., p. 207.
56. Ibid., p. 208.
57. Ibid., p. 209.
58. Ibid., p. 212.
59. Schalow, "Invention," p. 10.
60. Ibid., p. 15.
61. Ihara, *Great Mirror,* p. 64.
62. Ibid., p. 98.
63. Ibid., pp. 237, 273, et passim.
64. Ibid., p. 205.
65. Shively, *"Bakufu,"* p. 240.
66. Ibid., p. 241, n. 32.
67. Ihara, *Great Mirror,* p. 245.
68. Ibid., p. 293.
69. Ibid., pp. 251–252.
70. Leupp, p. 156.
71. Shively, "*Bakufu,*" p. 242.
72. Leupp, p. 161.
73. Ibid., pp. 161–163.
74. Ibid., pp. 53–55.
75. Leupp, p. 54; Shively, "Tsunayoshi," p. 97.
76. Leupp, p. 136.
77. Ibid., p. 54.
78. Ibid., p. 144.
79. Shively, "Chikamatsu," p. 161.
80. Shively, "Tsunayoshi," p. 98.
81. Keene, *Travelers,* p. 303.
82. Chikamatsu, p. 132.
83. Ibid., p. 140.
84. Leupp, pp. 196–197.
85. Brandon, p. 254f.
86. Leupp, p. 92.
87. Hibbett, p. 88.
88. Leupp, p. 87.
89. Nakai, p. 54.
90. Ibid.
91. Leupp, p. 158.

92. Bleys, p. 187.
93. Watanabe, p. 121.
94. Hawkins, p. 37.
95. S. D. Miller, p. 7.

14. Patterns of Persecution: 1700–1730

1. Barbier (Feb. 1726), p. 16.
2. Marais (Aug. 1722) 2:322.
3. Courouve, *Vocabulaire,* p. 121.
4. Ibid., p. 83; Rey, "Sodomites," p. 23.
5. Marais 2:321.
6. Rey, "Police," p. 134.
7. Ibid., p. 133.
8. Courouve, *Vocabulaire,* pp. 118, 156.
9. Rey, "Lifestyle," p. 188.
10. Rey, "Police," pp. 130–131.
11. Rey, "Lifestyle," pp. 180–181.
12. Ibid., p. 186.
13. Ibid., p. 187.
14. Ibid., p. 180.
15. Courouve, *Vocabulaire,* p. 141.
16. Rey, "Lifestyle," pp. 185–186.
17. Barbier (Feb. 1726), p. 17.
18. Rey, "Police," p. 134.
19. Ibid., p. 137.
20. *Mémoires secrets* 23:204.
21. Ibid.
22. Rey, "Police," p. 143.
23. Ibid.
24. Barbier (Feb. 1726), pp. 16–18.
25. Rey, "Police," p. 136.
26. Courouve, "Les Gens de la Manchette," appendix.
27. Barbier (Feb. 1726), pp. 17–18.
28. Courouve, *Les Gens* (Scene 5), p. [27].
29. Courouve, *L'Affaire Lenoir-Diot,* pp. [3–4].
30. Barbier (July 1750), pp. 252–253.
31. Ibid. (May 1750), pp. 242–251.
32. Coward, p. 240.
33. Collier, p. 154.
34. Argus Centoculi, pp. 1–2.
35. Patterson, pp. 257–259.
36. *Columbia Anthology,* p. 209.
37. Ibid., p. 211.
38. Norton, p. 52.
39. Crompton, *Byron,* pp. 50–51.
40. Norton, p. 12.
41. Burtt, p. 43, n. 10.
42. Ibid., p. 49.
43. Disney, pp. 206–207.
44. Norton, pp. 44–48.
45. *Sodomites' Shame,* p. 2.
46. Norton, pp. 50–51.
47. Ibid., pp. 51–52.
48. Ibid., p. 54.
49. Ibid., p. 67.
50. Ibid., p. 68–69.
51. Burtt, p. 59.
52. Bentman, p. 204.
53. Gray, *Correspondence* 1:21, 15.
54. Rousseau, p. 174.
55. Ibid., pp. 181–185.
56. Bentman, pp. 206–208.
57. Gilbert, p. 283.
58. Ketton-Cremer, p. 246.
59. Ibid., p. 250.
60. Gray, *Correspondence* 3:1127.
61. Ketton-Cremer, p. 253.
62. Walpole 37:8.
63. Ibid. 19:448, 486.
64. Rousseau, p. 173.
65. Halsband, pp. vii, 176, 88–89, 101.
66. Fothergill, p. 172.
67. Byron 2:18.
68. Beckford, p. 13.
69. Alexander, p. 194.
70. Trumbach, p. 134.
71. *Hell upon Earth,* p. 42–43.
72. *Satan's Harvest Home,* pp. 47, 51–55.
73. Smollett, ch. 35, p. 199.
74. Ibid., ch. 51, p. 310.
75. McLynn, p. 282.
76. Crompton, *Byron,* p. 22.
77. Howson, p. 288.
78. Crompton, *Byron,* p. 33.
79. Ibid., p. 22.
80. Casanova 1:261.
81. Voltaire, *Oeuvres complètes* (ed. Beaumarchais) 29:323, n. 17.
82. Crompton, *Byron,* p. 164.
83. Van der Meer, "Sodomy," p. 159.
84. Von Römer, "Der Uranismus," pp. 393–417.
85. Schama, p. 602.
86. Van der Meer, "Sodomy," p. 141.
87. Crompton, "Genocide," p. 86.
88. Van der Meer, "Persecutions," pp. 278–279.
89. Schama, p. 603.

90. Ibid., p. 607.
91. Lombardi, p. 75.
92. Ibid., pp. 72–73.
93. Ibid., p. 52.
94. Coke, p. 59.
95. Crompton, "Genocide," p. 88.
96. Ibid., p. 76.
97. Noordam, "Rural Areas," p. 98.
98. Lombardi, p. 87.
99. Boon, p. 243.
100. Noordam, "Rural Areas," p. 99; Boon, p. 243.
101. Van der Meer, "Sodomy," p. 190.
102. Crompton, "Genocide," pp. 89–90.
103. Boon, p. 245.
104. Van der Meer, "Sodomy," p. 141.
105. Ibid., p. 210.
106. Ibid., p. 192.
107. Ibid., pp. 200–201.
108. Ibid.
109. Hekma, pp. 443–444.

15. Sapphic Lovers: 1700–1793

1. Ballaster, p. 14.
2. Sinistrari, par. 7.
3. Eriksson, pp. 34, 37.
4. *Practicae novae imperialis Saxonicae rerum criminalium* (1652), *Pars* II, *Qu.* 76
5. Eriksson, pp. 38–40.
6. Evans, p. 118.
7. Baker, p. 214.
8. Castle, "Matters not Fit," p. 605.
9. Fielding, p. 29.
10. Baker, p. 222.
11. Donoghue, p. 80.
12. Ibid., p. 67.
13. Ibid.
14. Dekker and van de Pol, pp. 59, 79–80.
15. Ibid., pp. 52, 79.
16. Van der Meer, "Tribades," pp. 444–445.
17. Manley 1:574–575.
18. Ibid. 1:576–581.
19. See also Ballaster, pp. 13, 32–33; Donoghue, pp. 232–241.
20. Donoghue, pp. 113–114.
21. E. Hamilton, p. 27.
22. Ibid., p. 31.
23. Ibid., pp. 31–33.
24. Gregg, p. 21.
25. Brown, p. 97.
26. Gregg, p. 88.
27. Brown, p. 56.
28. Gregg, pp. 275–276.
29. *Poems on Affairs of State* 7:309.
30. Gregg, pp. 328–329.
31. Faderman, pp. 103–106.
32. Mavor, p. 62.
33. Crompton, *Byron,* p. 102.
34. Faderman, p. 121.
35. Ibid., p. 124.
36. Ibid., p. 125.
37. Thrale 1:517, 2:740.
38. Ibid. 2:640.
39. Ibid. 2:874–875.
40. Ibid. 2:640.
41. Ibid. 2:949.
42. Ibid.
43. Ibid. 2:868.
44. Ibid. 2:949 and n. 3.
45. Ibid. 2:868.
46. Ibid. 2:949.
47. Ibid. 2:868 and n. 3.
48. Donoghue, p. 150.
49. *DNB* 5:450.
50. Thrale 2:770.
51. Benforado, p. 52.
52. Ibid., p. 23.
53. Donoghue, pp. 262–263.
54. *Sapphick Epistle,* p. [6].
55. Ibid., p. 15.
56. Ibid., p. 20.
57. Benforado, p. 19.
58. Coward, p. 245.
59. Ibid., p. 246.
60. Faderman, pp. 79–80.
61. Ibid.
62. Diderot, *Correspondance* 3:74.
63. Diderot, *The Nun,* pp. 134–135.
64. Bonnet, pp. 96–97.
65. A. M. Wilson, pp. 387–388.
66. Bonnet, p. 107.
67. Faderman, p. 43.
68. Bonnet, p. 113.
69. Ibid., p. 108.
70. H. N. Williams, pp. 149, 151.
71. Bonnet, p. 139.
72. Ibid., pp. 140–141.
73. Ibid., p. 141.
74. Ibid., p. 111.

75. Ibid., p. 114.
76. Merrick, p. 41.
77. Ibid., p. 43.
78. Ibid., p. 45.
79. Castle, *Apparitional Lesbian,* pp. 128–130.
80. Haslip, p. 84.
81. *Mémoires secrets* 9:48.
82. Zweig, p. 121.
83. Ibid., p. 122.
84. Thrale 2:740.
85. Castle, p. 131.
86. Zweig, p. 120.
87. Haslip, pp. 84, 137.
88. Castle, p. 261, n. 56.
89. Zweig, p. 375.
90. Haslip, p. 270.
91. Michelet 1:1082, 1499 n. 1.
92. Bonnet, p. 165.
93. Zwieg, p. 431.

16. The Enlightenment: 1730–1810

1. D'Argens, p. 272.
2. Montesquieu 12.6, 1:207–208.
3. *Encyclopédie* 16:266.
4. Beccaria, p. 3.
5. Ibid., p. 85.
6. Evans, p. 118.
7. Steakley, "Prussia," p. 164.
8. Macaulay 1:496.
9. Carlyle 5:343.
10. Durant 10:496.
11. Henderson, p. 47.
12. Voltaire, c. June 15, 1743; *Works* 92:374.
13. Zimmermann, p. 132.
14. Ibid., p. 136.
15. Henderson, p. 46.
16. Macaulay 1:495.
17. Asprey, p. 48.
18. Ibid., p. 47.
19. Ibid., pp. 42–43.
20. Ibid., p. 45.
21. Ibid., p. 60.
22. Ibid., p. 70.
23. Ibid., p. 83.
24. Steakley, "Prussia," p. 168.
25. Voltaire, *Mémoires,* pp. 25–26.
26. Goldsmith, p. 79.
27. Ibid.
28. Durant 10:495.
29. Ibid. 10:496.
30. Ibid., 10:497.
31. Ibid., 10:528.
32. Evans, p. 121.
33. Ibid., p. 122.
34. Steakley, "Prussia," p. 171.
35. Courouve, *Vocabulaire,* pp. 118–120.
36. Voltaire, *Oeuvres* (ed. Moland) 9:562–563.
37. Ibid. 9:563.
38. Ibid. 9:565.
39. *Dictionnaire des lettres françaises,* p. 507.
40. Nov. 3, 1735; *Works* 87:241.
41. Voltaire, *Mémoires,* p. 45.
42. Aug. 8, 1736; Voltaire, *Works* 88:28.
43. c. Sept. 1, 1736; ibid. 88:44.
44. Apr. 7, 1737; ibid. 88:283.
45. c. Jan. 1, 1737; ibid. 88:179–180.
46. Durant 9:446.
47. Voltaire, *Works* 91:376.
48. c. Dec. 1, 1740; ibid. 91:371.
49. Dec. 31, 1740; ibid. 91:391.
50. Dec. 15, 1740; ibid. 91:377.
51. Mitford, pp. 127–128.
52. Oct. 13, 1750; ibid. 95:368.
53. Mason, p. 69.
54. Voltaire, *Mémoires,* p. 43.
55. Voltaire, *Philosophical Dictionary,* p. 76.
56. Voltaire, *Oeuvres* (ed. Moland) 19:605.
57. Voltaire, *Philosophical Dictionary,* pp. 76–77.
58. Ibid., p. 79.
59. Voltaire, *Works* 59:65.
60. Voltaire, *Philosophical Dictionary,* p. 79n.
61. c. May 25, 1725; ibid. 85:248.
62. Mason, pp. 51–54.
63. Voltaire, *Oeuvres* (ed. Moland) 30:570.
64. Ibid. 30:569–70.
65. *Dictionnaire des lettres françaises,* p. 1333.
66. Merrick, p. 32.
67. Voltaire, *Oeuvres* (ed. Moland) 17:179.
68. Ibid. 17:182.
69. Voltaire, *Romans et contes,* ch. 4, p. 153; ch. 15, p. 179.
70. Ibid., p. 135; ch. 9, p. 396.

71. Diderot, *Oeuvres* 10:86.
72. Diderot, *Rameau's Nephew,* p. 179.
73. Ibid., pp. 176–177.
74. Ibid., p. 179. Italics added.
75. Ibid., p. 182.
76. Diderot, *Oeuvres* 10:863–869.
77. Ibid. 10:185.
78. Ibid. 6:287.
79. Courouve, *Vocabulaire,* p. 164.
80. July 14, 1762; Diderot, *Oeuvres* 5:666.
81. Ragan, p. 19.
82. Sade, *Complete Justine,* p. 325.
83. Ibid., p. 326.
84. Ibid.; Sade, *Oeuvres* 3:552.
85. Sade, *Complete Justine,* p. 329.
86. Courouve, "Law Reform," p. 10.
87. Lever, pp. 384–387.
88. *Constitutions,* p. 59.
89. Marat, pp. 103–104.
90. Lever, p. 389.
91. Courouve, "Law Reform," p. 9.
92. Merrick, p. 39.
93. Cloots, p. 123.
94. Ibid., p. 124.
95. Ibid., pp. 124–125, n. 1.
96. Voltaire, *Oeuvres* (ed. Moland) 30:570, n. 4.
97. Sibalis, p. 82.
98. Ibid., p. 92.
99. Fillieule and Duyvendak, p. 183.
100. Crompton, *Byron,* p. 14, n. 5.
101. Gibbon 2:837.
102. Ibid. 2:838.
103. Crompton, *Byron,* pp. 233–234.
104. Blackstone 4:125–126.
105. Radzinowicz, p. 359, n. 5.
106. Crompton, *Byron,* pp. 44–45.
107. Bentham, pp. 396–398.
108. Ibid., p. 402.
109. Ibid., pp. 94, 106.
110. Ibid., pp. 95–96.
111. Ibid., p. 106.
112. Ibid., p. 98.
113. Ibid., pp. 384–385.
114. Crompton, *Byron,* p. 21.
115. Ibid., p. 40.
116. Ibid., ch. 7.
117. Ibid., p. 262.
118. Ibid., p. 271.
119. Ibid., p. 255.
120. Ibid., pp. 16–18, 163–168.
121. *EH* 2:887.
122. Kläre, ch. 6, 7.
123. Steakley, *Emancipation,* p. 111; Lautmann, p. 146.
124. Crompton, "Colonial America," p. 288.
125. Jeffries, p. 350.

BIBLIOGRAPHY

Abbreviations

DNB	Dictionary of National Biography
EH	Encyclopedia of Homosexuality
JH	Journal of Homosexuality
PG	Patrologiae Graecae
PL	Patrologiae Latinae

Sources and Suggested Reading

Achilles Tatius. Tr. S. Gaselee London: W. Heinemann, 1917.

The Actors' Analects. Tr. C. J. Dunn and B. Torigoe. New York: Cambridge University Press, 1969.

"Admonitio generalis." In *Monumenta Germaniae historica. Legum sectio II: Capitularia regum Francorum.* Ed. A. Boretius. Vol. 1: Part 1. Hanover: Hahn, 1881. P. 57.

Aelian. *Historical Miscellany.* Tr. N. G. Wilson. Cambridge: Harvard University Press, 1997.

Aeschines. *The Speeches of Aeschines.* Tr. C. D. Adams. Cambridge: Harvard University Press, 1968.

Africa, Thomas. "Homosexuality in Greek History." *Journal of Psychohistory* 9 (1982): 401–420.

Agnos, Peter, ed. *The Queer Dutchman Castaway on Ascension.* New York: Green Eagle Press, 1978.

Åkerman, Susanna. *Queen Christina of Sweden and Her Circle: The Transformation of a Seventeenth-Century Philosophical Libertine.* New York: E. J. Brill, 1991.

Akrigg, G. P. V., ed. *Letters of James VI & I.* Berkeley: University of California Press, 1984.

Alabaster, Ernest. *Notes and Commentaries on Chinese Criminal Law.* London: Luzac, 1899.

Alain de Lille. *The Complaint of Nature.* Tr. D. M. Moffat. New York: Henry Holt, 1908.

Alexander, Boyd. *Life at Fonthill 1807–1822.* London: Hart-Davis, 1957.
Allen, D. C. "Donne's 'Sapho to Philaenis.'" *English Language Notes* 1 (1964): 188–191.
Amann, Émile. *L'Époque carolingienne.* Paris: Bloud et Gay, 1947. (*Histoire de l'Église,* vol. 6.)
Ammianus Marcellinus. Tr. J. C. Rolfe. 3 vols. Cambridge: Harvard University Press, 1935–1939.
"Annales Basileenses." In *Monumenta Germaniae historica. Scriptores.* Ed. G. H. Pertz. Vol. 17. Hanover: Hahn, 1861.
Apollodorus. *The Library.* Tr. Sir J. G. Frazer. 2 vols. Cambridge: Harvard University Press, 1921.
"Apostolical Constitutions." *Ante-Nicene Christian Library: Translations of Writings of the Fathers Down to 325.* Vol. 17. Tr. A. Roberts and J. Donaldson. Edinburgh: Clark, 1870.
Apuleius. *The Apologia and Florida.* Tr. H. E. Butler. Oxford: Clarendon Press, 1909.
——— *The Golden Ass.* Tr. W. Adlington. Rev. ed. S. Gaselee. New York: G. P. Putnam's Sons, 1922.
Aquinas, Thomas, Saint *Summa theologiae.* Tr. Dominican Fathers. 63 vols. Cambridge: Blackfriars, 1964.
Argens, Jean-Baptiste de Boyer, Marquis d'. *Lettres juives.* The Hague: P. Paupie, 1764.
Argus Centoculi [pseud.]. *Old England, or the Broadbottom Journal,* June 2, 1750, pp. 1–2.
Aristophanes. *The Wasps, The Poet and the Women, The Frogs.* Tr. D. Barrett. Harmondsworth, England: Penguin, 1964.
Aristotle. *The "Art" of Rhetoric.* Tr. J. H. Freese. Cambridge: Harvard University Press, 1926.
——— *The Athenian Constitution, Eudemian Ethics, On Virtues and Vices.* Tr. H. Rackham. Rev. ed. Cambridge: Harvard University Press, 1967.
——— *The Nicomachean Ethics.* Tr. H. Rackham. Cambridge: Harvard University Press, 1926.
——— *The Politics of Aristotle.* Tr. P. L. P. Simpson. Chapel Hill: University of North Carolina Press, 1997.
——— *Problems.* Tr. W. S. Hett. 2 vols. Cambridge: Harvard University Press, 1936–1937.
Arnold, Edward Vernon. *Roman Stoicism.* Freeport, NY: Books for Libraries Press, 1911.
Arrian. Tr. P. A. Brunt. 2 vols. Cambridge: Harvard University Press, 1976–1983.
Asprey, Robert B. *Frederick the Great: The Magnificent Enigma.* New York: Ticknor and Fields, 1986.
Assyrian Dictionary of the Oriental Institute of Chicago. Ed. I. J. Gelb et al. Vol. 1 (Part 2). Chicago: Oriental Institute, 1956.
Athenaeus. *The Deipnosophists.* Tr. C. B. Gulick. 7 vols. Cambridge: Harvard University Press, 1927–1941.

Aubrey, John. *Brief Lives.* Ed. O. L. Dick. London: Secker and Warburg, 1950.

Augustine. *The City of God against the Pagans.* Tr. R. W. Dyson. Cambridge: Cambridge University Press, 1998.

——— *Confessions.* Tr. H. Chadwick. Oxford: Oxford University Press, 1991.

Aulus Gellius. *The Attic Nights of Aulus Gellius.* Tr. J. C. Rolfe. 3 vols. Rev. ed. Cambridge: Harvard University Press, 1946–1952.

An Authentic Relation of the Many Hardships and Sufferings of a Dutch Sailor, Who Was Put Ashore on the Uninhabited Isle of Ascension . . . 8th ed. London: George Faulkner, 1723.

Avalle, Giuseppe, ed. *Chiose anonime alla prima cantica della Divina commedia . . . Le antiche chiose anonime all'Inferno di Dante secondo il testo Marciano.* Città di Castello: S. Lapi, 1900.

The Babylonian Talmud. Ed. I. Epstein. 18 vols. London: Soncino Press, 1935–1952.

Bacon, Francis. *The Works of Francis Bacon.* Ed. J. Spedding, R. L. Ellis, and D. D. Heath. Vol. 8. London: Longman, 1869.

Bagemihl, Bruce. *Biological Exuberance: Animal Homosexuality and Natural Diversity.* New York: St. Martin's Press, 1999.

Bailey, Derrick Sherwin. *Homosexuality and the Western Christian Tradition.* London: Longmans, Green, 1955.

Baker, Sheridan. "Henry Fielding's *The Female Husband:* Fact and Fiction." *PMLA* 74.3 (1959): 213–224.

Baldwin, T. W. *William Shakspeare's "Small Latine & Lesse Greeke."* 2 vols. Urbana: University of Illinois Press, 1944.

Bale, John. *The Actes of Englysh Votaryes, Comprehendynge Their Unchast Practyses and Examples of All Ages.* London: J. Tysdale, 1560.

——— *Dramatic Writings of John Bale, Bishop of Ossory.* Ed. J. S. Farmer. London: Early English Drama Society, 1907.

——— *The Pageant of the Popes, Containing the Lyves of all the Bishops of Rome from the Beginninge of Them to the Year of Grace 1555.* Tr. J. S[tudley]. London, 1574.

Ballaster, Ros. "'The Vices of Old Rome Revived': Representations of Female Same-sex Desire in Seventeenth and Eighteenth Century England." In *Volcanoes and Pearl Divers: Essays in Lesbian Feminist Studies.* Ed. S. Raitt. Binghamton, NY: Harrington Park Press, 1995. Pp. 13–16.

[Ban Gu] Pan Ku. *The History of the Former Han Dynasty.* 3 vols. Tr. H. H. Dubs et al. Baltimore: Waverly, 1938.

Barber, Malcolm. "James of Molay, the Last Grand Master of the Order of the Temple." *Studia Monastica* 14 (1972): 91–124.

——— *The Trial of the Templars.* Cambridge: Cambridge University Press, 1978.

Barbier, Edmond-Jean-François. *Journal anecdotique d'un parisien sous Louis XV.* Ed. H. Juin. Paris: Le Livre Club du Librarie, [1963].

Barlow, Frank B. *William Rufus.* Berkeley: University of California Press, 1983.

Barnard, Nicholas. *The Penitent Death of a Woefull Sinner.* Dublin: Society of Stationers, 1641.

Barnfield, Richard. *The Complete Poems.* Ed. G. Klawitter. Selinsgrove, PA: Susquehanna University Press, 1990.
Barrett, D. S. "The Friendship of Achilles and Patroclus." *Classical Bulletin* 57 (1981): 87–92.
Barrow, John. *Travels in China.* London: T. Cadell and W. Davies, 1804.
Bartholomaeus da Saliceto. *Lectura super IX libris codicis.* Lyons: Siber [1496–1500]. (Microfilm Reprint Series. *French Books before 1601.* Lexington, KY: Erasmus Press, 1965. Roll 112.)
Barton, George A. "Hierodouli." *Encyclopaedia of Religion and Ethics.* Vol. 6. Ed. J. Hastings. New York: C. Scribner's Sons, 1959. Pp. 672–676.
Baudri de Bourgueil. *Les Oeuvres poétiques de Baudri de Bourgueil (1046–1130).* Ed. P. Abrahams. Paris: H. Champion, 1926.
Baxter, Stephen B. *William III and the Defense of European Liberty, 1650–1706.* New York: Harcourt Brace & World, 1966.
Bayle, Pierre. *Dictionnaire historique et critique.* Ed. A. J. Q. Beuchot et al. 16 vols. Paris: Desoer, 1820–1824.
Beaumanoir, Philippe de Remi, Sire de. *The Coutumes de Beauvaisis.* Tr. F. R. P. Akehurst. Philadelphia: University of Pennsylvania Press, 1992.
Beccaria, Cesare Bonesana, Marchese di. *On Crimes and Punishments.* Tr. H. Paolucci. Indianapolis: Bobbs-Merrill, 1963.
Beckford, William. *The Journal of William Beckford in Portugal and Spain, 1787–1788.* Ed. B. Alexander. New York: J. Day, 1955.
Behn, Aphra. *The Poems of Aphra Behn: A Selection.* Ed. J. Todd. New York: New York University Press, 1994.
——— *The Works of Aphra Behn.* 6 vols. Ed. M. Summers. London: W. Heinemann, 1915.
Benforado, Susan. "Anne Seymour Damer (1728–1828), Sculptor." Ph.D. Dissertation. University of New Mexico, 1986.
Bennett, Bonnie A., and David G. Wilkins. *Donatello.* Oxford: Phaedon, 1984.
Bentham, Jeremy. "Offences Against One's Self: Paederasty, Part 1," ed. L. Crompton. *JH* 3 (1978): 389–405.
——— "Jeremy Bentham's Essay on Paederasty, Part 2," ed. L. Crompton. *JH* 4 (1978): 91–107.
Bentman, Raymond. "Thomas Gray and the Poetry of 'Hopeless Love,'" *Journal of the History of Sexuality* 3 (1992): 203–222.
Bergeron, David M. *King James I and Letters of Homoerotic Desire.* Iowa City: University of Iowa Press, 1999.
——— *Royal Family, Royal Lovers: King James of England and Scotland.* Columbia: University of Missouri Press, 1991.
Bernardino of Siena, San. "Del vizio dei sodomiti," "Della sodomia," "Della dannazione de sodomiti." In *Le prediche volgari.* Ed. C. Cannarozzi. Vol. 2. Florence: Libreria editrice fiorentina, 1934. Pp. 30–36, 37–56, 57–69.
Berners, John Bourchier, Lord, tr. *The Boke of Duke Huon of Burdeux.* Ed. S. Lee. London: N. Trübner. 1882. (Early English Text Society, series 2, vol. 40.)
Bethe, Erich. "Die dorische Knabenliebe, ihre Ethik und ihre Idee." *Rheinisches Museum für Philologie* 62 (1907): 438–475.

Beurdeley, Cécile. *L'Amour bleu.* Tr. M. Taylor. New York: Rizzoli, 1978.

Beurdeley, Michel et al. *Chinese Erotic Art.* Tr. D. Imber. Rutland, VT: C. E. Tuttle, 1969.

Bieler, Ludwig, ed. *The Irish Penitentials.* Dublin: Institute for Advanced Studies, 1975. (Scriptores Latini Hiberniae, No. 5.)

Bingham, Caroline. *The Life and Times of Edward II.* London: Weidenfeld and Nicholson, 1973.

——— *The Making of a King: The Early Years of James VI and I.* London: Collins, 1968.

——— "Seventeenth-Century Attitudes towards Deviant Sex." *Journal of Interdisciplinary History* 1 (1971): 447–468.

Biographia Britannica, or The Lives of the Most Eminent Persons Who Have Flourished in Great Britain and Ireland from the Earliest Ages Down to the Present Times. Vol. 1. London: W. Innys, 1747.

Blackstone, William. *Commentaries on the Laws of England.* Book 4. Oxford: Clarendon Press, 1769.

Bleibtreu-Ehrenburg, Gisela. *Tabu Homosexualität: Die Geschichte eines Vorurteils.* Frankfurt am Main: Fischer, 1981.

Bleys, Rudi. *The Geography of Perversion: Male-to-male Sexual Behavior Outside the West and the Ethnographic Imagination, 1750–1918.* London: Cassell, 1995.

Boas, F. S. *Christopher Marlowe: A Biographical and Critical Study.* Oxford: Clarendon Press, 1960.

Boccaccio, Giovanni. *The Decameron.* Tr. M. Musa and P. Bondanella. New York: W. W. Norton, 1983.

——— *Esposizioni sopra la Comedia di Dante.* Ed. G. Padoan. [Milan]: A. Mondadori, 1965. (*Tutti le opere,* vol. 6.)

Bonnet, Marie-Jo. *Un Choix sans équivoque: Recherches historiques sur les relations amoureuses entre les femmes XVIe–XXe siècle.* Paris: Denoël, 1981.

Boon, L. J. "Those Damned Sodomites: Public Images of Sodomy in the Eighteenth Century Netherlands." In *The Pursuit of Sodomy.* Pp. 237–248.

Boswell, John. *Christianity, Social Tolerance and Homosexuality: Gay People in Western Europe from the Beginning of the Christian Era to the Fourteenth Century.* Chicago: University of Chicago Press, 1980.

——— *Same-Sex Unions in Premodern Europe.* New York: Villard Books, 1994.

Bourdaloue, Pierre. *Oeuvres complètes de Bourdaloue.* Nouv. éd. Vol. 10 ("Mystères"). Besançon: Montarsolo, 1823.

Bouteiller, Jean. *Somme rural, ou Le grand coustumier général de pratique civil et canon.* Paris: Macé, 1603.

Bowers v. Hardwick 478 *U.S. Reports* 186 (1986).

Bowra, C. M. *Greek Lyric Poetry from Alcman to Simonides.* 2nd ed. Oxford: Clarendon Press, 1961.

——— *Pindar.* Oxford: Clarendon Press, 1964.

Bowsky, William M. "The Medieval Commune and Internal Violence: Police Power and Public Safety in Siena, 1287–1355." *American Historical Review* 73 (1967): 1–17.

Boxer, C. R. *The Christian Century in Japan, 1549–1650.* Berkeley: University of California Press, 1967.

——— *South China in the Sixteenth Century, Being the Narratives of Galeote Pereira, Fr. Gaspar da Cruz, O. P., and Fr. Martin de Rada, O.E.S.A. (1550–75).* London: Hakluyt Society, 1953.

Brackman, Arnold C. *The Last Emperor.* New York: C. Scribner's Sons, 1975.

Bradford, William. *History of Plymouth Plantation 1620–47.* Ed. W. C. Ford. 2 vols. Boston: Houghton Mifflin, 1912.

Brandes, Georg. *Michelangelo: His Life, His Times, His Era.* Tr. H. Norden. New York: Ungar, 1963.

Brandon, James R., tr. *Kabuki: Five Classic Plays.* Cambridge: Harvard University Press, 1975.

Brantôme, Pierre de Bourdeille, seigneur de. *The Lives of Gallant Ladies.* Tr. A. Brown. London: Elek, 1961.

Bray, Alan. *Homosexuality in Renaissance England.* London: Gay Men's Press, 1982.

——— "Homosexuality and the Signs of Male Friendship in Elizabethan England." *History Workshop* 29 (Spring, 1990): 1–19.

Bredbeck, Gregory W. *Sodomy and Interpretation: Marlowe to Milton.* Ithaca: Cornell University Press, 1991.

Brillon, Pierre-Jacques. *Dictionnaire des arrêts, ou Jurisprudence universelle des Parlemens de France et autres tribunaux.* 6 vols. Nouv. éd. Paris: G. Cavelier, 1727.

Britton. Tr. F. M. Nichols and G. O. Sayles. 2 vols. Holmes Beach, FL: W. W. Gaunt, 1983.

Brooke, C. F. Tucker. *The Life of Marlowe and "The Tragedy of Dido, Queen of Carthage."* London: Methuen, 1930.

Brooten, Bernadette J. "Paul's Views on the Nature of Women and Female Homoeroticism." In *Immaculate and Powerful: The Female in Sacred Image and Social Reality.* Ed. C. W. Atkinson, C. H. Buchanan, and M. R. Miles. Boston: Beacon Press, 1985. Pp. 61–87.

Brooten, Bernadette J. *Love between Women: Early Christian Responses to Female Homoeroticism.* Chicago: University of Chicago Press, 1996.

Brown, Beatrice Curtis, ed. *The Letters and Diplomatic Instructions of Queen Anne.* London: Cassell, 1935.

Brunnsåker, Sture. *The Tyrant-Slayers of Kritios and Nesiotes: A Critical Study of the Sources and Restorations.* 2nd ed. Stockholm: Svenska Institutet i Athen, 1971.

Buffière, Félix. *Eros adolescent: la pédérastie dans la Grèce antique.* Paris: Les Belles Lettres, 1980.

Bullough, Vern L. *Sexual Variance in Society and History.* New York: J. Wiley & Sons, 1976.

Bullough, Vern L., and Bonnie Bullough. *Women and Prostitution: A Social History.* Buffalo: Prometheus Books, 1987.

Burnet, Gilbert. *Bishop Burnet's History of His Own Time.* New ed. London: W. Smith, 1838.

——— *A Supplement to Burnet's "History of My Own Time," Derived from His Orig-*

inal Memoirs, His Autobiography, etc. Ed. H. C. Foxcraft. Oxford: Clarendon Press, 1902.

Burton, Robert. *The Anatomy of Melancholy . . . in an All-English Text.* Ed. F. Dell and P. Jordan-Smith. New York: Farrar & Rhinehart, 1927.

Burtt, Shelley. *Virtue Transformed: Political Argument in England, 1688–1740.* Cambridge: Cambridge University Press, 1992.

Bussy, Roger de Rabutin, Conte de. *Histoire amoureuse des Gaules.* Ed. A. Adam. Paris: Garnier-Flammarion, 1967.

——— *Histoire amoureuese des Gaules.* Ed. Ch.-L. Livet. 4 vols. Paris: P. Jannet, 1858.

Byron, George Gordon Byron, Baron. *Complete Poetical Works.* 7 vols. Ed. J. J. McGann. Oxford: Clarendon Press, 1980–1993.

Cady, Joseph. "The 'Masculine Love' of the 'Princes of Sodom,' 'Practising the Art of Ganymede' at Henri III's Court: The Homosexuality of Henri III and his *Mignons* in Pierre de L'Estoile's *Mémoires-Journaux.*" In *Desire and Discipline: Sex and Sexuality in the Premodern West.* Ed. J. Murray and K. Eisenbichler. Toronto: University of Toronto Press, 1996. Pp. 124–154.

Cady, Joseph. "'Masculine Love,' Renaissance Writing, and the 'New Invention' of Homosexuality." *JH* 23 (1992): 9–40.

Calendar of the Manuscripts of the Marquis of Bath. 5 vols. Hereford: His Majesty's Stationery Office, 1904–1980.

Calendar of the State Papers Relating to Scotland and Mary, Queen of Scots, 1547–1603. Vol 6. Edinburgh: H. M. General Register House, 1910.

Callimachus and Lycophron. Tr. A. W. Mair. London: W. Heinemann, 1921.

Cameron, Keith. *Henri III: A Maligned or Malignant King? Aspects of the Satirical Iconography of Henri de Valois.* Exeter: University of Exeter, 1978.

Cantarella, Eva. *Secondo natura: la bisessualità nel mondo antico.* Rome: Riuniti, 1988.

Cao Xueqin [Tsao Hsueh-chin]. *The Story of the Stone [The Dream of the Red Chamber]* Vol. 3. Tr. D. Hawkes. Bloomington: Indiana University Press, 1981.

Capellanus, Andreas. *Andreas Capellanus on Love.* Tr. P. G. Walsh. London: Duckworth, 1982.

Carlyle, Thomas. *History of Friedrich II of Prussia, Called Frederick the Great.* 8 vols. London: Chapman and Hall, 1897–1898.

Carrasco, Rafael. *Inquisición y represión sexual en Valencia: historia de los sodomitas (1565–1785).* Barcelona: Laertes, 1985.

Cartledge, Paul. "The Politics of Spartan Pederasty." *Proceedings of the Cambridge Philological Society* 207 (1981): 17–36.

Casanova de Seingalt, Giovanni Giacomo. *Mémoires.* 3 vols. Ed. R. Abirached and E. Zorzi. Paris: Gallimard, 1958–1960.

Castle, Terry. *The Apparitional Lesbian: Female Homosexuality and Modern Culture.* New York: New York University Press, 1993.

——— "Matters Not Fit to be Mentioned: Fielding's *The Female Husband. ELH* 49 (1982): 602–622.

Cather, Willa. *The World and the Parish: Willa Cather's Articles and Reviews 1893–1902.* Ed. W. M. Curtin. 2 vols. Lincoln: University of Nebraska Press, 1970.
Catullus. *The Poetry of Catullus.* Tr. C. H. Sisson. New York: Orion Press, 1967.
Catullus, Tibullus, and Pervigilium Veneris. Tr. F. W. Cornish et al. 2nd ed. Cambridge: Harvard University Press, 1988.
Cedrenus, Georgius. *[Historiarum compendium.]* Vol. 1. Ed. I. Bekker. Bonn: E. Weber, 1838. (Corpus scriptorum historiae byzantinae 25.)
Cellini, Benvenuto. *The Life of Benvenuto Cellini.* Tr. J. A. Symonds. Ed. J. Pope-Hennessy. New York: Phaidon, 1949.
Chan, Albert. "Chinese-Philippine Relations in the Late Sixteenth Century and to 1603." *Philippine Studies* 26 (1987): 51–81.
Chastel, André. *Art et humanisme à Florence au temps de Laurent le Magnifique: Études sur la Renaissance et l'humanisme platonicien.* Paris: Presses Universitaires de France, 1959.
Chaucer, Geoffrey. *The Poetical Works of Chaucer.* Ed. F. N. Robinson. 2nd ed. Boston: Houghton Mifflin, 1957.
Chevallier, Pierre. *Henri III, roi shakespearien.* Paris: Fayard, 1985.
——— *Louis XIII, roi cornélien.* Paris: Fayard, 1979.
Chikamatsu. *Major Plays.* Tr. D. Keene. New York: Columbia University Press, 1961.
Childs, Margaret. "*Chigo Monogatari:* Love Stories or Buddhist Sermons?" *Monumenta Nipponica: Studies in Japanese Culture* 35 (1980): 127–151.
——— *Rethinking Sorrow: Revelatory Tales of Late Medieval Japan.* Ann Arbor: Center for Japanese Studies, 1991.
Childs, Margaret, tr. "The Tale of Genmu." In *Partings at Dawn.* Pp. 36–54.
Chou, Eric. *The Dragon and the Phoenix.* New York: Arbor House, 1971.
Cicero. Tr. C. Macdonald et al. 28 vols. Cambridge: Harvard University Press, 1914–1968.
Cicero. *De Oratore.* Tr. E. W. Sutton and H. Rackham. 2 vols. Cambridge: Harvard University Press, 1942.
——— *The Letters to His Friends.* Tr. W. G. Williams. 3 vols. London: W. Heinemann, 1928.
——— *Tusculan Disputations.* Tr. J. E. King. London: W. Heinemann, 1927.
Cino da Pistoia. *In codicem commentaria* [1578]. 2 vols. Turin: Botega d'Erasmo, 1964.
The Civil Law. Tr. S. P. Scott. 17 vols. in 7. Cincinnati: Central Trust Company, 1932.
Clark, Kenneth. *The Nude: A Study in Ideal Form.* New York: Pantheon, 1956.
Clarke, Aidan. "The Atherton File." *Decies* (The Old Waterford Society) 11 (1979): 45–54.
Clarke, M. L. "The Making of a Queen: The Education of Christina of Sweden." *History Today* 28 (1978): 228–235.
Clarke, W. M. "Achilles and Patroclus in Love." *Hermes* 106 (1978): 381–396.
Clement of Alexandria. *Christ the Educator [Pedagogus].* Tr. S. P. Wood. New York: Fathers of the Church, 1954

——— *The Exhortation to the Greeks, The Rich Man's Salvation, To the Newly Baptized.* Tr. G. W. Butterworth. Cambridge: Harvard University Press, 1945.

Cloots, Anacharsis. *Écrits révolutionnaires 1790–1794.* Ed. M. Duval. Paris: Éditions Champ libre, 1979.

Los códigos españoles concordados y anotados. Ed. A. de San Martín. 12 vols. 2nd ed. Madrid: Los Ministerios de Estados, 1872.

Cody, Jane M. "The *Senex Amator* in Plautus' *Casina.*" *Hermes* 104 (1976): 453–476.

Coke, Edward. *The Third Part of the Institutes of the Laws of England.* London: E. and R. Brooke, 1797.

A Collection of Tales from Uji: A Study and Translation of "Uji Shui Monogotari." Tr. D. E. Mills. Cambridge: Cambridge University Press, 1970.

Collier, Jeremy. *Essays upon Several Moral Subjects* [1698]. 3rd ed. London: G. Strahan, 1720.

Collins, Kathleen. "Pleasure's Artful Garb: Poetic Strategies of Denis Saint-Pavin (1595–1670)." *Continuum: Problems in French Literature from the Late Renaissance to the Early Enlightenment.* Vol. 3 *(Libertinage and the Art of Writing).* New York: AMS Press, 1991. Pp. 171–189.

The Columbia Anthology of Gay Literature: Readings from Western Antiquity to the Present Day. Ed. B. F. S. Fone. New York: Columbia University Press, 1998.

Columbia Encyclopedia, 5th ed. New York: Columbia University Press, 1993.

Commento alla Divina commedia d'anomino fiorentino del secolo XIV. Ed. P. Fanfani. 2 vols. Bologna: Romagnoli, 1866. (*Collezione di opere inedite e rare,* vols. 15–17.)

Compton, Linda F. *Andalusian Lyrical Poetry and Old Spanish Love Songs: The Muwashshah and Its Kharja.* New York: New York University Press, 1976. (New York University Studies in Near Eastern Civilization, 6.)

"Concilium Parisiense." *Monumenta Germaniae historica. Legum sectio III: Concilia.* Vol. 2: Part 1. Hanover: Hahn, 1906.

Condivi, Ascanio. *The Life of Michelangelo.* Tr. A. S. Wohl. Baton Rouge: Louisiana State University Press, 1976.

Constitutions and Other Select Documents Illustrative of the History of France 1789–1907. Ed. F. M. Anderson. 2nd ed. New York: Russell, 1967.

Cooper, Michael, ed. *They Came to Japan: An Anthology of European Reports on Japan, 1543–1640.* Berkeley: University of California Press, 1965.

Cormier, Raymond J. *One Heart, One Mind: The Rebirth of Virgil's Hero in Medieval French Romance.* Valencia: Artes Gráfica Soler, 1973. (University of Mississippi Romance Monographs. 3.)

Corpus iuris civilis. Vol. 2: *Codex Justinianus.* Ed. P. Krueger and T. Mommsen. Hildesheim: Weidman, 1967.

Coulton, G. G. *Five Centuries of Religion.* 5 vols. Cambridge: Cambridge University Press, 1923–1950.

Courouve, Claude. "1791 Law Reform in France." *Gay Books Bulletin* 12 (1985): 9–10.

——— *L'Affaire Lenoir-Diot.* Paris: C. Courouve, 1980.

——— *Les Gens de la manchette.* Paris: C. Courouve, 1981.

——— "Sodomy Trials in France." *Gay Books Bulletin* 1.1 (1979): 21–22.

——— *Vocabulaire de l'homosexualité masculine.* Paris: Payot, 1985.

Coward, D. A. "Attitudes to Homosexuality in Eighteenth-Century France." *Journal of European Studies* 10 (1980): 231–255.

Creighton, Mandell. *A History of the Papacy during the Period of the Reformation.* 5 vols. London: Longmans, Green, 1882–1894.

Crompton, Louis. *Byron and Greek Love: Homophobia in Nineteenth-Century England.* Berkeley: University of California Press, 1985.

——— "Gay Genocide: From Leviticus to Hitler." In *The Gay Academic.* Ed. L. Crew. Palm Springs, CA: ETC Publications, 1978. Pp. 67–91.

——— "Homosexuals and the Death Penalty in Colonial America." *JH* 1 (1976): 277–293.

——— "Jeremy Bentham's Essay on 'Paederasty': An Introduction." *JH* 3 (1978): 383–387.

——— "The Myth of Lesbian Impunity: Capital Laws from 1270 to 1791." In *Historical Perspectives on Homosexuality.* Pp. 11–25. (*JH* 6.)

Curran, Charles E. *Directions in Fundamental Moral Theology.* Notre Dame, IN: University of Notre Dame Press, 1985.

Curtius, Quintus. *Curtius Quintius: History of Alexander.* 2 vols. Tr. J. C. Rolfe. Cambridge: Harvard University Press, 1946.

Cust, Robert H. Hobart. *Giovanni Antonio Bazzi, Hitherto Usually Styled "Sodoma": The Man and the Painter 1477–1549.* London: Murray, 1906.

Cutrera, Antonino. *Cronologia dei giustiziati di Palermo 1541–1819.* Palermo: Boccone del Povero, 1917.

Dahm, Georg. *Das Strafrecht Italiens im ausgehenden Mittelalter.* Berlin: de Gruyter, 1931.

Dalla, Danilo. *"Ubi Venus mutatur": omosessualità e diritto nel mondo romano.* Milan: A. Giuffrè, 1987.

Dall'Orto, Giovanni. "Dante." *EH,* 1: 294–296.

——— "Poliziano." *EH,* 2: 1021–1022.

——— "'Socratic Love' as a Disguise for Same-Sex Love in the Italian Renaissance." In *The Pursuit of Sodomy.* Pp. 33–65.

Damian. See Peter Damian.

D'Ancona, Mirella. "The *Doni Madonna* by Michelangelo: An Iconographic Study." *Art Bulletin* 50 (1966): 43–52.

Daniel, Marc. "Arab Civilization and Male Love." Tr. W. Leyland. *Gay Sunshine* 32 (Spring 1977): 1–11, 27.

——— *Hommes du Grand Siècle: Études sur homosexualité dans les règnes de Louis XIII et Louis XIV.* Paris: Arcadie [1957].

Daniel, Walter. *The Life of Ailred of Rievaulx.* Tr. F. M. Powicke. London: Nelson, 1950.

Dante Alighieri. *The Inferno.* Tr. J. Ciardi. New York: Norton, 1970.

——— *Purgatorio.* Tr. A. Mandelbaum. Berkeley: University of California Press, 1982.

DeJean, Joan. *Fictions of Sappho, 1546–1937.* Chicago: University of Chicago Press, 1989.

Dekker, Rudolf M., and Lotte C. van de Pol. *The Tradition of Female Transvestism in Early Modern Europe.* New York: St. Martin's Press, 1989.

De la Moore, Thomas. "*Vita et Mors Edwardi II.*" In *Chronicles of the Reigns of Edward I and Edward II.* Ed. W. Stubbs. Vol. 2. London: Longman, 1883. (Rolls Series, 76.)

Delon, Michel. "The Priest, the Philosopher, and Homosexuality in Enlightenment France." *Eighteenth Century Life* 9 (1985): 122–131.

Demosthenes. *De corona and De falsa legatione.* Tr. C. A. and J. H. Vince. London: W. Heinemann, 1926.

Denniston, R. H. "Ambisexuality in Animals." In *Homosexual Behavior: A Modern Reappraisal.* Ed. J. Marmor. New York: Basic Books, 1980. Pp. 25–40.

De Tolnay, Charles. *Michelangelo.* Vol. 3: *The Medici Chapel.* Princeton: Princeton University Press, 1970.

Dewald, Jonathan. *Aristocratic Experience and the Origins of Modern Culture: France, 1570–1715.* Berkeley: University of California Press, 1993.

D'Ewes, Simonds, Sir. *The Diary of Sir Simonds D'Ewes (1622–1624).* Ed. E. Bourcier. Paris: Didier, 1974.

——— *The Journal of Sir Simonds D'Ewes from the Beginning of the Long Parliament to the Opening of the Trial of the Earl of Strafford.* Ed. W. Notestein. New Haven: Yale University Press, 1923.

Dictionary of National Biography. Ed. Sir L. Stephen and Sir S. Lee. 22 vols. London: Oxford University Press, 1885–1901.

Dictionary of the Middle Ages. Ed. J. R. Strayer. 13 vols. New York: Scribner, 1982–1989.

Dictionnaire des lettres françaises: le XVIIIe siècle. Ed. Cardinal G. Grente and F. Moreau. Paris: Fayard, 1960.

Dictionnaire du Grand Siécle. Ed. F. Bluche. Paris: Fayard, 1990.

Diderot, Denis. *Correspondance.* 16 vols. Ed. G. Roth. Paris: Éditions de Minuit, 1955–1957.

——— *The Nun.* Tr. L. Tancock. Harmondsworth, Middlesex: Penguin, 1974.

——— *Oeuvres complètes.* 15 vols. Ed. R. Lewinter. Paris: Le Club français du livre, 1969–1973.

——— *Rameau's Nephew and Other Works.* Tr. J. Barzun and R. H. Brown. New York: Doubleday, 1956.

Dio [Cassius]. *Dio's Roman History.* Tr. E. Cary. 9 vols. London: W. Heinemann, 1914–1927.

Dio Chrysostom. Tr. H. L. Crosby. 5 vols. Cambridge: Harvard University Press, 1932–1951.

Diodorus Siculus. *Library of History.* Tr. C. H. Oldfather et al. 12 vols. Cambridge: Harvard University Press, 1933–1950.

Diogenes Laertius. *Lives of Eminent Philosophers.* Tr. R. D. Hicks. 2 vols. Cambridge: Harvard University Press, 1925.

Dion, Paul E. "Did Cultic Prostitution Fall into Oblivion during the Postexilic Era? Some Evidence from Chronicles and the Septuagint." *Catholic Biblical Quarterly* 43 (1981): 41–48.

Disney, John. *A Second Essay upon the Execution of the Laws against Immorality and Prophaneness.* London: J. Downing, 1710.

Doe v. Commonwealth's Attorney for City of Richmond, 403 *Federal Supplement* 1199 (1975).

Donne, John. *Complete Poetry of John Donne.* Ed. J. T. Shawcross. New York: New York University Press, 1968.

——— *The Satires, Epigrams, and Verse Letters.* Ed. W. Milgate. Oxford: Clarendon Press, 1967.

——— *The Sermons of John Donne.* Ed. G. R. Potter and E. M. Simpson. 10 vols. Berkeley: University of California Press, 1953–1962.

Donoghue, Emma. *Passions between Women: British Lesbian Culture 1668–1801.* London: Scarlet Press, 1993.

Dover, K. J. *Greek Homosexuality.* London: Duckworth, 1978.

Drayton, Michael. *Complete Works of Michael Drayton.* Ed J. W. Hebel. 5 vols. Oxford: Blackwell, 1931–1941.

Duclos, Claude Pinot. *Mémoires secrets.* In *Oeuvres complètes.* Ed. M. Auger [1820–21]. 9 vols. Geneva: Slatkine Reprints, 1968.

Du Maurier, Daphne. *Golden Lads: A Study of Anthony Bacon, Francis, and Their Friends.* London: Gollancz, 1975.

Durant, Will, and Ariel Durant. *The Story of Civilization.* 11 vols. New York: Simon and Schuster, 1935–1975.

Dynes, Wayne R. *Homosexuality: A Research Guide.* New York: Garland, 1987.

——— *Homolexis: A Historical and Cultural Lexicon of Homosexuality.* New York: Scholarship Committee, Gay Academic Union, 1985.

Eadmer. *Eadmer's History of Recent Events in England.* Tr. G. Bosanquet. Philadelphia: Dufour, 1965.

——— *The Life of St. Anselm, Archbishop of Canterbury.* Tr. R. W. Southern. London: T. Nelson, 1962.

Eberhard, Wolfram. *Guilt and Sin in Traditional China.* Berkeley: University of California Press, 1967.

Eglinton, J. Z. *Greek Love.* New York: Oliver Layton Press, 1964.

Eissler, K. R. *Leonardo da Vinci: Psychoanalytical Notes on the Enigma.* New York: International Universities Press, 1961.

Elegy and Iambus. Tr. J. M. Edmonds. New ed. 2 vols. London: W. Heinemann, 1931.

El fuero real de España, diligentemente hecho por el noble Rey don Alonso IX [sic], glosada por Alonso Díaz de Montalvo. 2 vols. Madrid: P. Aznar, 1781.

Elyot, Thomas, Sir. *The Boke Named The Governour.* Ed. S. E. Lehmberg. London: Dent, 1962.

Encyclopaedia of Islam. New ed. Vol. 5. Ed. C. E. Bosworth et al. Leiden: Brill, 1986.

Encyclopedia of Homosexuality. Ed. W. Dynes, W. Johansson, and W. Percy. 2 vols. New York: Garland, 1990.

Encyclopédie, ou Dictionnaire raisonné des arts, des sciences, et des métiers. Ed. D. Diderot et al. 17 vols. Neuchâtel: Samuel Faulche, 1765.

Eriksson, Brigitte, tr. "A Lesbian Execution in Germany in 1721: The Trial Records." In *Historical Perspectives on Homosexuality.* Pp. 27–40.

Erskine, John. *An Institute of the Law of Scotland.* Ed. J. B. Nicolson. 2 vols. Edinburgh: Bell and Bradfute, 1871.

Estienne, Henri. *Apologie pour Hérodote: Satire de la société au XVIe siècle.* Ed. P. Ristelhuber. 2 vols. Geneva: Slatkine, 1969.

Eusebius of Caesarea. *La Préparation évangelique: Livres 12–13.* Tr. É. Des Places. Paris: Les Éditions du Cerf, 1983.

——— "Life of Constantine." *A Select Library of Nicene and Post-Nicene Fathers of the Christian Church: Second series.* Vol. 1. Tr. P. Schaff and H. Wace. New York: Christian Literature Company, 1890.

Evans, Richard J. *Rituals of Retribution: Capital Punishment in Germany, 1600–1987.* Oxford: Oxford University Press, 1996.

Eymeric, Nicolau, and Francisco Peña. *Le Manuel des inquisiteurs.* Ed. L. Sala-Molins. Paris: Mouton, 1973.

Faderman, Lillian. *Surpassing the Love of Men: Romantic Friendship and Love between Women from the Renaissance to the Present.* New York: William Morrow, 1981.

Ficino, Marsilio. *Marsilio Ficino's Commentary on Plato's Symposium.* Tr. S. R. Jayne. Columbia: University of Missouri, 1944.

Fielding, Henry. *The Female Husband and Other Writings.* Ed. C. E. Jones. Liverpool: Liverpool University Press, 1960.

Fillieule, Olivier, and Jan Willem Duyvendak. "Gay and Lesbian Activism in France: Between Integration and Community-Oriented Movements." In *The Global Emergence of Gay and Lesbian Politics.* Pp. 184–213.

Firmicus Maternus. *The Error of the Pagan Religions.* Tr. C. A. Forbes. New York: Newman Press, 1970.

Flacelière, Robert, tr. "Introduction" to Plutarch, *Dialogue sur l'amour (Eroticos).* Paris: Éditions Les Belles Lettres, 1953.

Flannery, Edward H. *The Anguish of the Jews: Twenty-Three Centuries of Anti-Semitism.* New York: Paulist Press, 1985.

Fleta. Tr. H. G. Richardson and G. O. Sayles. London: Quaritch, 1955.

Fone, Byrne. *Homophobia: A History.* New York: Henry Holt, 2000.

Forster, E. M. *Maurice: A Novel.* New York: Morton, 1971.

Foster, Jeannette H. *Sex Variant Women in Literature: A Historical and Quantitative Survey.* London: F. Muller, 1958.

Fothergill, Brian. *Beckford of Fonthill.* London: Faber, 1979.

Fraxi, Pisanus [Henry Spencer Ashbee]. *Bibliography of Prohibited Books.* 3 vols. London: J. Brussel, 1979.

Frederick the Great. *Das Palladion.* In *Oeuvres de philosophe de Sans Souci.* Vol. 1 [1750]. [Bremen]: Zeichmann, 1985. (*Forschungen und Studien für fridericianischen Zeit: Sonderband,* 1.)

Friedman, Richard Elliott. *Who Wrote the Bible?* Englewood Heights, NJ: Prentice Hall, 1987.

Friesische Rechtsquellen. Ed. Karl O. J. T., Freiherr von Richtofen. Berlin: Nicolai, 1840.

Frischauer, Paul. *Prince Eugene, 1663–1736: A Man and a Hundred Years of History.* Tr. A. Smeaton. New York: William Morrow, 1934.

Froissart, Jean. *Chroniques: Debut du premier livre, édition du manuscrit de Rome Reg. lat. 869.* Ed. G. T. Diller. Geneva: Droz, 1972.

Fry, Peter. "Homosexuality and Spirit Possession in Brazil." *JH* 1.3–4 (1985): 137–153.

Gade, Kari Ellen. "Homosexuality and Rape of Males in Old Norse Law and Literature." *Scandinavian Studies* 58 (1986): 124–141.

Garde, Noel I. *Jonathan to Gide: The Homosexual in History.* New York: Vantage Press, 1964.

The Gay and Lesbian Literary Heritage. Ed. C. J. Summers. New York: Henry Holt, 1995.

Gay Histories and Culture: An Encyclopedia. Ed. G. Haggerty. New York: Garland, 2000.

Gellius, Aulus. *The Attic Nights of Aulus Gellius.* Tr. J. C. Rolfe. 3 vols. Cambridge: Harvard University Press, 1927.

Genshin, "Genshin's *Ōjō Yōshū:* Collected Essays on Birth into Paradise." Tr. A. K. Reischauer. *Transactions of the Asiatic Society of Japan,* 2nd series, 7 (1930): 16–97.

Gibbon, Edward. *The History of the Decline and Fall of the Roman Empire.* Ed. D. Womersley. 3 vols. New York: Penguin, 1994.

Giffen, Lois Anita. *Theory of Profane Love among the Arabs: The Development of the Genre.* New York: New York University Press, 1971.

Gilbert, Thomas. "A View of the Town." In *The New Oxford Book of Eighteenth Century Verse.* Ed. R. Lonsdale. Oxford: Oxford University Press, 1984. P. 283.

Ginzberg, Louis. *The Legends of the Jews.* Tr. H. S. Szold. 7 vols. Philadelphia: Jewish Publication Society of America, 1909–1938.

The Global Emergence of Gay and Lesbian Politics: National Imprints of a Worldwide Movement. Ed. B. Adam, J. W. Duyvendak, and A. Krouwel. Philadelphia: Temple University Press, 1999.

Goldin, Hyman E. *Hebrew Criminal Law and Procedure.* New York: Twayne, 1952.

Goldsmith, Margaret. *Christina of Sweden: A Psychological Biography.* New York: Doubleday, Doran, 1935.

——— *Frederick the Great.* London: Gollancz, 1929.

Goldthwaite, Richard A. *The Building of Renaissance Florence: A Social and Economic History.* Baltimore: Johns Hopkins University Press, 1980.

Gonzáles Palencia, Angel, ed. *Noticias de Madrid 1621–1627.* Madrid: Artes Gráficas Municipales, 1942.

Goodenough, Erwin R. *The Jurisprudence of the Jewish Courts in Egypt . . . As Described by Philo Judaeus.* Amsterdam: Philo Press, 1968.

Goodich, Michael. *The Unmentionable Vice: Homosexuality in the Later Medieval Period.* Santa Barbara: ABC-Clio, 1979.

Goodrich, L. Carrington, ed. *Dictionary of Ming Biography 1368–1644.* 2 vols. New York: Columbia University Press, 1975.

Goreau, Angeline. *Reconstructing Aphra: A Social Biography of Aphra Behn.* New York: Dial Press, 1980.

Goris, J. A. "Zeden en Criminaliteit te Antwerpen in de tweede Helft van de XIVe Eeuw." *Revue belge de philologie et d'histoire* 6 (1927): 181–205.

Graillot, Henri. *Le Culte de Cybèle, mère des dieux, à Rome et dans l'Empire romain.* Paris: Fontemoing, 1912.

Gray, Thomas. *Correspondence of Thomas Gray.* Ed. P. Toynbee and L. Whibley. 3 vols. Oxford: Clarendon Press, 1935.

Gray-Fow, Michael. "Pederasty, the Scantinian Law, and the Roman Army." *Journal of Psychohistory* 13 (1986): 449–460.

The Greek Anthology. Tr. W. R. Paton. 5 vols. Cambridge: Harvard University Press, 1916–1918.

Greek Lyric. Tr. D. A. Campbell. 5 vols. Cambridge: Harvard University Press, 1982.

Greek Lyric Poetry. Tr. W. Barnstone. Bloomington: Indiana University Press, 1967.

Green, Peter. *Ancient Greece: An Illustrated History.* New York: Thames and Hudson, 1973.

Greenberg, David F. *The Social Construction of Homosexuality.* Chicago: University of Chicago Press, 1988.

Greenleaf, Richard E. *Zumárraga and the Mexican Inquisition, 1536–1543.* Washington, DC: Academy of American Franciscan History, 1961.

Gregg, Edward. *Queen Anne.* London: Routledge & Kegan Paul, 1980.

Grimm, Jacob, and Wilhelm Grimm. *Deutsches Wörterbuch.* 16 vols. Leipzig: S. Hirzel, 1854–1960.

Gubar, Susan. "Sapphistries." *Signs* 10 (1984): 43–62.

Guerra, Francisco. *The Pre-Columbian Mind: A Study into the Aberrant Nature of Sexual Drives, Drugs Affecting Behavior, and the Attitude towards Life and Death with a Survey of Psychotherapy in Pre-Columbian America.* London: Seminar Press, 1971.

Guillaume de Lorris and Jean de Meun. *The Romance of the Rose.* Tr. C. Dahlberg. Princeton: Princeton University Press, 1971.

Gunderson, Lloyd. "Quintus Curtius Rufus: On Historical Methods." In *Philip II, Alexander the Great, and the Macedonian Heritage.* Ed. W. L. Adams and E. N. Borza. Washington, DC: University Press of America, 1982. Pp. 177–196.

Halsband, Robert. *Lord Hervey: Eighteenth-Century Courtier.* New York: Oxford University Press, 1974.

Hamilton, Anthony. *Memoirs of Count Grammont.* Tr. H. Walpole. Ed. Sir W. Scott. London: Chatto and Windus, 1876.

Hamilton, Bernard. *The Medieval Inquisition.* New York: Holmes and Meier, 1981.

Hamilton, Elizabeth. *William's Mary: A Biography of Mary II.* New York: Taplinger, 1972.

Hamilton, J. S. *Piers Gaveston, Earl of Cornwall, 1307–1312: Politics and Patronage in the Reign of Edward II.* Detroit: Wayne State University Press, 1988.

Hammond, N. G. L. *A History of Greece to 322 B.C.* 2nd ed. Oxford: Clarendon Press, 1967.

[Han Fei Zi] Han Fei Tzu. *Han Fei Tzu: Basic Writings.* Tr. B. Watson. New York: Columbia University Press, 1964.

Hanan, Patrick. *The Chinese Vernacular Story.* Cambridge: Harvard University Press, 1981.

——— *The Invention of Li Yu.* Cambridge: Harvard University Press, 1988.

Hare, Thomas Blenman. *Zeami's Style: The Noh Plays of Zeami Motokiyo.* Stanford: Stanford University Press, 1986.

Harkins, Paul W. "Introduction" to John Chrysostom, *Discourses against Judaizing Christians.* Washington, DC: Catholic University of America Press, 1979. (Fathers of the Church, 86.)

Harris, John. *The Destruction of Sodom.* London: Lathum, 1628.

Harrison, Robert. *Gallic Salt: Eighteen Fabliaux Translated from the Old French.* Berkeley: University of California Press, 1974.

Hartt, Frederick. *Art: A History of Painting, Sculpture, Architecture.* 4th ed. New York: H. N. Abrams, 1993.

——— Review of *Il Carteggio di Michelangelo,* vol. 4, ed. G. Poggi. *Renaissance Quarterly* 36 (1983): 248–251.

Harvey, Paul, Sir, ed. *The Oxford Companion to Classical Literature.* Oxford: Oxford University Press, 1984.

Haskins, Charles Homer. "Robert le Bougre and the Beginnings of the Inquisition in Northern France." In *Studies in Medieval Culture.* Ed. C. H. Haskins. New York: Ungar, 1929. Pp. 193–244.

Haslip, Joan. *Marie Antoinette.* New York: Weidenfeld & Nicolson, 1988.

Hawkins, Joseph R. "Japan's Journey into Homophobia." *The Gay and Lesbian Review* 7.1 (2000): 36–38.

Hekma, Gert. "Sodomites, Platonic Lovers, Contrary Lovers: The Backgrounds of the Modern Homosexual." In *The Pursuit of Sodomy.* Pp. 433–455.

Hell upon Earth, or, the Town in an Uproar, and Satan's Harvest Home. New York: Garland, 1985.

Henderson, Susan. "Frederick the Great: A Homophile Perspective," *Gai Saber* 1.1 (Spring 1977): 46–54.

Henshaw, Richard A. *Female and Male—The Cultic Personnel: The Bible and the Rest of the Ancient Near East.* Allison Park, PA: Pickwick, 1994.

Hergemöller, Bernd-Ulrich. *Man für Mann: Biographisches Lexicon zur Geschichte von Freundesliebe und mannmännlicher Sexualität im deutschen Sprachraum.* Hamburg: MännerschwarmSkript, 1998.

Herman, Gerald. "The Sin against Nature and Its Echoes in Medieval French Literature." *Annuale Mediaevale* 17 (1976): 70–87.

Hernandez, Ludovico. *Les Procès de sodomie aux XVIe, XVIIe et XVIIIe siècles.* Paris: Bibliothèque des Curieux, 1920.

Herodotus. Tr. A. D. Godley. 4 vols. Cambridge: Harvard University Press, 1920–25.

Herrera Puga, Pedro. *Sociedad y delincuencia en el Siglo de Oro: aspectos de la vida sevillana en los siglos XVI y XVII.* Granada: Universidad de Granada, 1971.

Hesiod: Theogony, Works and Days/ Theognis: Elegies. Tr. D. Wender. Harmondsworth, Middlesex: Penguin, 1973.

Heywood, Thomas. *Gynaikeion, or Nine Bookes of Various History Concerninge Women.* London: Islip, 1624.

Hibbard, Howard. *Caravaggio.* New York: Harper and Row, 1983.
Hibbett, Howard. *The Floating World in Japanese Fiction.* New York: Oxford University Press, 1959.
Hidden from History: Reclaiming the Gay and Lesbian Past. Ed. M. Duberman, M. Vicinus, and G. Chauncey Jr. New York: New American Library, 1989.
Hindley, Clifford. "Xenophon on Male Love." *Classical Quarterly* 49.1 (1999): 74–99.
Hinsch, Bret. *Passions of the Cut Sleeve: The Male Homosexual Tradition in China.* Berkeley: University of California Press, 1990.
Hirschfeld, Magnus. *Die Homosexualität des Mannes und des Weibes* [1914]. Berlin: W. de Gruyter, 1984.
Historical Perspectives on Homosexuality. Ed. S. J. Licata and R. P. Petersen. New York: Haworth Press, 1981. (*JH* 6.)
The Historie and Life of King James the Sext. Edinburgh: [Ballantyne], 1825.
Holzman, Donald. *Poetry and Politics: The Life and Works of Juan Chi* A.D. *210–263.* Cambridge: Cambridge University Press, 1976.
Homosexuality in Modern France. Ed. J. Merrick and B. T. Ragan. New York: Oxford University Press, 1996.
Horace. *Complete Works.* Tr. C. E. Passage. New York: Ungar, 1983.
——— *The Odes of Horace.* Tr. J. Michie. New York: Orion Press, 1963.
Housman, A. E. *The Poems of A. E. Housman.* Ed. A. Burnett. Oxford: Clarendon Press, 1997.
Howell, Peter. *A Commentary on Book One of the Epigrams of Martial.* London: Athlone Press, 1980.
Howson, Gerald. *Thief-Taker General: The Rise and Fall of Jonathan Wild.* New York: St. Martin's Press, 1971.
Hrosvitha. *The Non-Dramatic Works of Hrosvitha: Text, Translation, and Commentary.* Tr. Sister M. G. Wiegand. St. Louis: St. Louis University, 1936.
Hume, David. *Commentaries on the Law of Scotland.* 2 vols. Edinburgh: Bell and Bradfute, 1844.
Hume, David. *Essays and Treatises on Various Subjects.* Boston: Mendum, 1868.
Hummel, Arthur W., ed. *Eminent Chinese of the Ch'ing Period (1644–1912).* 2 vols. Washington, DC: U.S. Government Printing Office, 1943–1944.
Huussen, Arend H., Jr. "Sodomy in the Dutch Republic during the Eighteenth Century." In *Hidden from History.* Pp. 141–149.
Hyamson, M., ed. *Mosaicarum et romanarum legum collatio.* London: Oxford University Press, 1913.
Hyginus. *The Myths of Hyginus.* Tr. Mary Grant. Lawrence: University of Kansas Press, 1960.
Ibn Hazm, Abu Muhammad. *A Book Containing the Risāla Known as The Dove's Neck-Ring about Love and Lovers.* Tr. A. R. Nykl. Paris: Paul Geuthner, 1931.
——— *The Ring of the Dove: A Treatise on the Art and Practice of Arab Love.* Tr. A. J. Arberry. London: Luzac, 1953.
Ibn Sa'id, Ali ben Mūsā, compiler. *Moorish Poetry: A Translation of "The Pennants," an Anthology Compiled in 1243 by the Andalusian Ibn Sa'id.* Tr. A. J. Arberry. Cambridge: Cambridge University Press, 1953.

Ihara Saikaku. *Comrade Loves of the Samurai.* Tr. E. P. Mathers. Rutland, VT: Charles E. Tuttle, 1972.

——— *The Great Mirror of Male Love.* Tr. P. G. Schalow. Stanford: Stanford University Press, 1990.

Isaacs, Tina Beth. "Moral Crime, Moral Reform, and the State in Early Eighteenth Century England." Ph.D. Dissertation. University of Rochester, 1979.

Ivo of Chartres. See Yves de Chartres.

James I. *Political Works of James I.* Ed. C. H. McIwain. Cambridge: Harvard University Press, 1918.

Janson, H. W. *The Sculpture of Donatello.* Princeton: Princeton University Press, 1963.

Jean de Meun. See Guillaume de Lorris.

Jeffries, John C. *Justice Lewis F. Powell, Jr.* New York: C. Scribner's Sons, 1994.

John Chrysostom, Saint. *A Comparison between a King and a Monk and Against the Opponents of the Monastic Life: Two Treastises by John Chrysostom.* Tr. D. G. Hunter. Lewiston, NY: E. Mellen, 1988.

——— "Discourse on Blessed Babylas and against the Greeks." In *Saint John Chrysostom Apologist.* Tr. M. A. Schatkin and P. W. Harkins. Washington, DC: Catholic University Press, 1983.

——— *A Select Library of the Nicene and Post-Nicene Fathers of the Christian Church.* 1st series. Vols. 11 and 13. Tr. P. Scaff. New York: C. Scribner's Sons, 1887–1894.

Jones, C. P. "Tarsos in the *Amores* Ascribed to Lucian." *Greek, Roman and Byzantine Studies* 25 (1984): 177–181.

Josephus, Flavius. *Jewish Antiquities Books XIV and XV.* Vol. 6. Tr. R. Marcus. Cambridge: Harvard University Press, 1998.

Juvenal and Persius. Tr. G. G. Ramsay. Rev. ed. Cambridge: Harvard University Press, 1940.

Karlinsky, Simon. "Russia's Gay Literature and Culture: The Impact of the October Revolution." In *Hidden from History.* Pp. 347–364.

"Karoli Magni Capitularia." *Monumenta Germaniae historica. Legum sectio II: Capitularia regum Francorum.* Ed. A. Boretius. Vol. 1: Part 1. Hanover: Hahn, 1881.

Katō Shūichi. *A History of Japanese Literature: The First Thousand Years.* Tr. D. Chibbett. New York: Kodansha International, 1979.

Kay, Richard. *Dante's Swift and Strong: Essays on Inferno XV.* Lawrence: Regents Press of Kansas, 1978.

Keene, Donald. *Travelers of a Hundred Ages.* New York: Henry Holt, 1989.

Kelly, J. N. D. *The Oxford Dictionary of Popes.* Oxford: Oxford University Press, 1986.

Ketton-Cremer, Robert Windham. *Thomas Gray: A Biography.* Cambridge: Cambridge University Press, 1955.

Kinder, A. Gordon. *Casiodoro de Reina: Spanish Reformer of the Sixteenth Century.* London: Tamesis, 1975.

Kläre, Rudolf. *Homosexualität und Strafrecht.* Hamburg: Hanseatische Verlagsanstalt, 1937.

Knowles, David Dom. *The Religious Orders in England.* Vol. 3: *The Tudor Age.* Cambridge: Cambridge University Press, 1959.

Knox, John. "Introduction" to the Acts of the Apostles and the Epistle to the Romans. *The Interpreter's Bible.* Vol. 9. New York: Abingdon, 1954.

Kodansha Encyclopedia of Japan. 9 vols. Tokyo: Kodansha, 1983.

[Koran]. *The Meaning of the Glorious Koran: An Explanatory Translation.* Tr. M. Pickthall. New York: Knopf, 1992.

Kuster, H. J., and R. J. Cormier. "Old Views and New Trends: Observations on the Problem of Homosexuality in the Middle Ages." *Studi Medievali* 25 (1984): 587–610.

Labalme, Patricia. "Sodomy and Venetian Justice in the Renaissance." *Legal History Review* 52 (1984): 217–254.

Lachèvre, Frédéric. *Le Libertinage devant le Parlement de Paris: le Procès du poète Théophile de Viau.* 2 vols. Paris: Librarie Ancienne, 1909.

Laeuchli, Samuel. *Power and Sexuality: The Emergence of Canon Law at the Synod of Elvira.* Philadelphia: Temple University Press, 1972.

Lambert, Royston. *Beloved and God: The Story of Hadrian and Antinous.* New York: Viking, 1984.

Lane, Erskine, tr. *In Praise of Boys: Moorish Poems from al-Andalus.* San Francisco: Gay Sunshine Press, 1975.

Lautmann, Rüdiger. "The Pink Triangle: The Persecution of Homosexual Males in Concentration Camps in Nazi Germany." In *Historical Perspectives on Homosexuality.* Pp. 141–160.

Lea, Henry Charles. *A History of the Inquisition of Spain.* 4 vols. New York: Macmillan, 1906–1907.

Legman, G. et al. *The Guilt of the Templars.* New York: Basic Books, 1966.

Lesbian Histories and Cultures: An Encyclopedia. Ed. B. Zimmerman. New York: Garland, 2000.

L'Estoile. Pierre. *Journal pour le règne de Henri III (1574–1589).* Ed. L.-R. Lefèvre. Paris: Gallimard, 1943.

Letters and Papers, Foreign and Domestic, of the Reign of Henry VIII. Ed. J. Gairdner. Vaduz, Liechenstein: Kraus Reprint, 1965.

Leupp, Gary P. *Male Colors: The Construction of Male Homosexuality in Tokugawa Japan.* Berkeley: University of California Press, 1995.

Lever, Maurice. *Les Bûchers de Sodome.* Paris: Fayard, 1985.

Lévi-Provençal, Evariste. *Histoire de l'Espagne musulmane jusqu'à la conquête d'Andalousie par les Almoravids.* Nouv. éd. 3 vols. Paris: G.-P. Maisonneuve, 1950.

Lewis, C. S. *English Literature in the Sixteenth Century, Excluding Drama.* Oxford: Clarendon Press, 1954.

Li Yu. *A Tower for the Summer Heat* [Six stories from the *Shih erh lou*]. Tr. P. Hanan. New York: Columbia University Press, 1992.

——— *Silent Operas [Wusheng xi].* Tr. P. Hanan. Hong Kong: Chinese University of Hong Kong, 1990.

Licht, Hans [Paul Brandt]. *Sexual Life in Ancient Greece.* Tr. J. H. Freese. London: The Abbey Library, 1932.

Liebert, Robert S. *Michelangelo: A Psychoanalytical Study of His Life and Images.* New Haven: Yale University Press, 1983.

The Life and Death of John Atherton, Lord Bishop of Waterford and Lysmore. London: n.p., 1641.

Lightbrown, Ronald. *Sandro Botticelli: Life and Work.* New York: Abbeville Press, 1989.

Lilja, Saara. *Homosexuality in Republican and Augustan Rome.* Helsinki: The Finnish Society of Sciences and Letters, 1983.

Lind, L. Robert. "The Date of Nonnus of Panopolis." *Classical Philology* 29 (1934): 69–73.

[Liu Qing] Liu I-ch'ing. *Shih-shuo hsin-yu: A New Account of Tales of the World.* Tr. R. B. Mather. Minneapolis: University of Minnesota Press, 1976.

Livy in Fourteen Volumes. Tr. B. O. Foster et al. 14 vols. Cambridge: Harvard University Press, 1919–1959.

Loader, J. A. *A Tale of Two Cities: Sodom and Gomorrah in the Old Testament, Early Jewish, and Early Christian Traditions.* Kampen, The Netherlands: J. H. Kok, 1990.

Lockyer, Roger. *Buckingham: The Life and Political Career of George Villiers, First Duke of Buckingham, 1592–1628.* London: Longman, 1981.

Lombardi, Michael. Typescript translation of Von Römer, "Der Uranismus," 131 pp.

López, Gregorio, ed. *Las siete partidas del rey Don Alfonso el Sabio* [1515]. Valencia: Benito Monfort, 1767.

Lowry, Hua-yuan Li, tr. *Chinese Love Stories from "Ch'ing-shih."* Hartford, CT: Archon, 1983.

[Lu Xun] Lu Hsun. *A Brief History of Chinese Fiction.* 3rd ed. Tr. H. and G. Yang. Peking: Foreign Languages Press, 1976.

Lucian. Tr. M. D. Macleod et al. 8 vols. Cambridge: Harvard University Press, 1913–1967.

Lucian. *The Syrian Goddess.* Tr. H. A. Strong. London: Constable, 1913.

Lucretius. *De Rerum Natura.* Tr. W. H. D. Rouse. 3rd ed. rev. Cambridge: Harvard University Press, 1975.

——— *On the Nature of the Universe.* Tr. R. E. Latham. Harmondsworth, Middlesex: Penguin, 1951.

Lyra Graeca. Tr. J. M. Edmonds. 2nd ed. 3 vols. London: W. Heinemann, 1922–1928.

Maber, R. G. *Malherbe, Théophile de Viau, and Saint-Amant: A Selection.* Durham: University of Durham, 1983.

Macaulay, Thomas Babington. *Critical and Historical Essays.* 8th ed. 3 vols. London: Longman et al., 1854.

Mackerras, Colin P. *The Rise of the Peking Opera 1770–1870: Social Aspects of the Theatre in Manchu China.* Oxford: Oxford University Press, 1972.

MacMullen, Ramsay. "Roman Attitudes to Greek Love." *Historia* 31 (1982): 484–502.

Maimonides [Abraham ben Moses ben Maimon]. *The Guide of the Perplexed.* Tr. M. Friedländer. 3 vols. London: Trübner, 1881–1885.

——— *The Code of Maimonides. Book Five: The Book of Holiness.* Tr. L. I. Rabinowitz and P. Grossman. New Haven: Yale University Press, 1965. (Yale Judaica Series, 16.)

Malalas, John. *Chronographia.* Ed. L. Dindorf. Bonn: E. Weber, 1831. (Corpus scriptorum historiae byzantinae, 32.)

Manley, Mary Delariviere. *The Novels of Mary Delariviere Manley.* Ed. P. Köster. 2 vols. Gainesville, FL: Scholars' Facsimiles & Reprints, 1971.

Marais, Mathieu. *Journal et mémoires sur la Régence et la règne de Louis XV (1715–1737).* Vol. 2. Ed. M. de Lescure. Paris: Didot, 1864.

Marat, Jean-Paul. *Plan de législation criminelle.* Paris: Rochette, 1790.

Marie de France. *The Lais of Marie de France.* Tr. R. Hanning and J. Ferrante. New York: E. P. Dutton, 1978.

Marlowe, Christopher. *Complete Works.* Vol. 3: *Edward II.* Ed. R. Rowland. Oxford: Clarendon Press, 1994.

——— *Edward the Second.* Ed. C. Forker. Manchester: Manchester University Press, 1994.

——— *The Poems.* Ed. M. Maclure. London: Methuen, 1968.

Marrou, Henri Irenée. *A History of Education in Antiquity.* Tr. G. Lamb. New York: Sheed and Ward, 1956.

Martial. *Epigrams.* Tr. D. R. Shackleton Bailey. 3 vols. Cambridge: Harvard University Press, 1993.

Martin, John Rupert. *The Farnese Gallery.* Princeton: Princeton University Press, 1965.

Mason, Haydn. *Voltaire: A Biography.* Baltimore: Johns Hopkins University Press, 1981.

Masson, Georgina. *Queen Christina.* New York: Farrar, Straus & Giroux, 1968.

Matignon, J.-J. *La Chine hermétique: Superstitions, crime et misère.* Nouv. éd. Paris: Librarie orientaliste Paul Geuthner, 1936.

Mavor, Elizabeth. *The Ladies of Llangollen: A Study in Romantic Friendship.* London: Michael Joseph, 1971.

McGuire, Brian Patrick. "Love, Friendship and Sex in the Eleventh Century: The Experience of Anselm." *Studia Theologica* 28 (1974): 111–152.

McKay, Derek. *Prince Eugene of Savoy.* London: Thames and Hudson, 1977.

McLynn, Frank. *Crime and Punishment in Eighteenth-Century England.* London: Routledge, 1989.

McMahon, Keith. *Causality and Containment in Seventeenth-Century Chinese Fiction.* Leiden: Brill, 1988.

Meijer, M. J. "Homosexual Offences in Ch'ing Law." *T'oung Pao: Revue internationale de sinologie* 71 (1985): 109–133.

Meleager. See *Greek Anthology,* Book XII.

Melville, James, Sir. *Memoirs of Sir James Melville of Halhill, 1535–1617.* Ed. A. F. Steuart. New York: Dutton, 1930.

Mémoires secrets pour servir à l'histoire de la République des Lettres en France depuis MDCCLXII jusqu'à nos jours. Ed. L. P. de Bachaumont, M. F. Pidansat de Mairobert, and Mouffle d'Angerville. Vol. 23 (bound in vol. 8 of 12). London. J. Adamson, 1777–1789.

Merrick, Jeffrey. "The Marquis de Villette and Mademoiselle de Raucourt." In *Homosexuality in Modern France.* Pp. 30–53.
Mesnil, Jacques. *Botticelli.* Paris: A. Michel, 1938.
Meylan, Edouard. "L'Évolution de la notion d'amour platonique." *Humanisme et Renaissance* 5 (1938): 418–442.
Michelangelo Buonarroti. *Complete Poems and Selected Letters.* Tr. C. Gilbert. New York: Modern Library, 1965.
——— *The Letters of Michelangelo.* Tr. E. H. Ramsden. 2 vols. Stanford: Stanford University Press, 1963.
——— *The Poetry of Michelangelo.* Tr. R. J. Clements. New York: New York University Press, 1965.
——— *The Poetry of Michelangelo.* Tr. J. Saslow. New Haven: Yale University Press, 1991.
Michelet, Jules. *Histoire de la Révolution Française.* Ed. G. Walter. 2 vols. Paris: Gallimard, 1952.
Midrash Rabbah. Ed. H. Freedman and M. Simon. 3rd ed. 10 vols. London: Soncino Press, 1983.
Miller, John. *The Life and Times of William and Mary.* London: Weidenfeld and Nicolson, 1974.
Miller, Townsend. *Henry IV of Castile, 1425–1474.* Philadelphia: Lippincott, 1972.
Minucius Felix, Marcus. *The Octavius of Marcus Minucius Felix.* Tr. G. W. Clarke. New York: Newman Press, 1974.
Mirk, John. *Instructions for Parish Priests.* Ed. G. Kristensson. Lund, Sweden: CWK Gleerup, 1974.
Mirror of Justices. Tr. W. J. Whittaker. London: Quaritch, 1895.
Mitford, Nancy. *Frederick the Great.* New York: Harper and Row, 1970.
Monk of Malmesbury. *The Life of Edward II by the So-called Monk of Malmesbury.* Tr. N. Denholm-Young. London: Nelson, 1957.
Monroe, James. T. *Hispano-Arabic Poetry: A Student Anthology.* Berkeley: University of California Press, 1974.
Montaigne, Michel Eyquem, Sieur de. *The Complete Works of Montaigne: Essays, Travel Journal, Letters.* Tr. D. M. Frame. Stanford: Stanford University Press, 1958.
Monter, William. *Frontiers of Heresy: The Spanish Inquisition from the Basque Lands to Sicily.* Cambridge: Cambridge University Press, 1990.
——— "Sodomy and Heresy in Early Modern Switzerland." In *Historical Perspectives on Homosexuality.* Pp. 41–56.
Montesquieu, Charles Louis de Secondat, Baron de la Brède de. *De l'esprit des lois.* Ed. R. Derathé. 2 vols. Paris: Garnier, 1973.
Moore, R. I. *The Formation of a Persecuting Society: Power and Deviance in Western Europe, 950–1250.* New York: Blackwell, 1987.
Moote, A. Lloyd. *Louis XIII, the Just.* Berkeley: University of California Press, 1989.
Mott, Luiz. "*Justitia et Misericordia:* A Inquisição portuguesa e a repressão ao nefando pecado de sodomia." In *Inquisição: Ensaios sobre mentalidade, heresias e arte.* Ed. A. Novinsky and M. L. Tucci Carneiro. São Paulo: Edusp, 1992. Pp. 703–738.

——— "Portuguese Pleasures: The Gay Subculture in Portugal at the Time of the Inquisition." Papers from the International Scientific Conference on Gay and Lesbian Studies: "Homosexuality: Which Homosexuality?" History: Vol. 1. Amsterdam: Free University, Dec. 15–18, 1987. Pp. 85–96.

Mueller, Janel. "Troping Utopia: Donne's Brief for Lesbianism." In *Sexuality and Gender in Early Modern Europe: Institutions, Texts, Images.* Ed. J. G. Turner. New York: Cambridge University Press, 1993. Pp. 182–207.

Müller, Karl Otfried. *The History and Antiquities of the Doric Race.* Tr. H. Tufnell. 2 vols. Oxford: Oxford University Press, 1930.

Murasaki, Shikibu. *The Tale of Genji.* Tr. E. G. Seidensticker. New York: Knopf, 1976.

Murray, Stephen O. *Homosexualities.* Chicago: University of Chicago Press, 2000.

——— "The Will Not to Know: Islamic Accommodations to Male Homosexuality." In *Islamic Homosexualities: Culture, History, and Literature.* Ed. S. O. Murray and W. Roscoe. New York: New York University Press, 1997. Pp. 15–54.

Muyart de Vouglans, Pierre-François. *Institutes au droit criminel.* Paris: Le Breton, 1757.

Nachmanides [Moses ben Nachman]. *Commentary on the Torah.* Vol. 5 (Deuteronomy). Tr. C. B. Chavel. New York: Shilo, 1976.

Nelson, Benjamin. *The Idea of Usury from Tribal Brotherhood to Universal Otherhood.* 2nd ed. Chicago: University of Chicago Press, 1969.

Nepos, Cornelius. *The Book of Cornelius Nepos on the Great Generals of Foreign Nations.* Tr. J. C. Rolfe. Cambridge: Harvard University Press, 1929.

New Encyclopedia Britannica. Vol. 12. Chicago: Encyclopedia Britannica, 1995.

New English Bible. Tr. Joint Commission on the New Translation of the Bible. 2nd. ed. Cambridge: Oxford University Press, 1970.

New Songs from a Jade Terrace: An Anthology of Early Chinese Love Poetry. Tr. A. Birrell. London: Allen and Unwin, 1982.

The New Westminster Dictionary of the Bible. Ed. S. H. Gehman. Philadelphia: Westminster Press, 1970.

Newcastle, Margaret Cavendish, Duchess of. *Plays, Never Before Printed.* London: Maxwell, 1668.

Ng, Vivien W. "Homosexuality and the State in Later Imperial China." In *Hidden from History.* Pp. 76–89, 501–502.

——— "Ideology and Sexuality: Rape Laws in Qing China." *Journal of Asian Studies* 46 (1987): 57–70.

Nonnus. *Dionysiaca.* Tr. W. H. D. Rouse et al. 3 vols. Cambridge: Harvard University Press, 1940.

Noonan, John T. *Contraception: A History of its Treatment by the Catholic Theologians and Canonists.* Cambridge: Harvard University Press, 1965.

Noordam, Dirk Japp. "Sodomites in Rural Areas of the Republic in the Early Modern Period." Papers from the International Scientific Conference on Gay and Lesbian Studies: "Homosexuality, Which Homosexuality?" History: Vol. 1. Amsterdam: Free University, Dec. 15–18, 1987. Pp. 97–109.

——— "Sodomy in the Dutch Republic, 1600–1725." In *The Pursuit of Sodomy.* Pp. 207–228.

Norton, Rictor. *Mother Clap's Molly House: The Gay Subculture in England 1700–1830.* London: GMP Publishers, 1992.

Notopoulos, James A. *The Platonism of Shelley: A Study of Platonism and the Poetic Mind.* Durham, NC: Duke University Press, 1949.

Nykl, Alois R. *Hispano-Arabic Poetry and Its Relations with the Old Provençal Troubadours.* Baltimore: [J. H. Furst], 1946.

O'Brien, John A. *The Inquisition.* New York: Macmillan, 1973.

Ogyū Sorai. *The Political Writings of Ogyū Sorai.* Tr. J. R. McEwan. Cambridge: Cambridge University Press, 1962.

The Old Testament Pseudepigrapha. Ed. J. H. Charlesworth. 2 vols. Garden City, NY: Doubleday, 1983–1985.

Orbach, William. "Homosexuality and Jewish Law." *Journal of Family Law* 14 (1975/76): 353–381.

Ordericus Vitalis. *The Ecclesiastical History of Ordericus Vitalis.* Tr. M. Chibnall. 6 vols. Oxford: Clarendon Press, 1969–1973.

Orléans, Elizabeth Charlotte, duchesse d'. *Correspondance complète de Madame, Duchesse d'Orléans, née Princesse Palatine, Mère du Régent.* Ed. M. G. Brunet. 2 vols. Paris: Charpentier, 1869.

——— *Letters from Liselotte, Elisabeth Charlotte, Princess Palatine and Duchess of Orléans, "Madame": 1652–1722.* Tr. M. Kroll. London: Gollancz, 1970.

——— *Madame Palatine: Lettres françaises.* Ed. D. van der Cruysse. Paris: Fayard, 1989.

——— *A Woman's Life at the Court of the Sun King: Letters of Liselotte von der Pfalz, Elizabeth Charlotte, Duchesse d'Orléans, 1652–1722.* Tr. E. Forster. Baltimore: Johns Hopkins University Press, 1984.

Osborne, Francis. "Some Memorialls of the Raigne of King James the First" [1658]. In *Secret History of the Court of James the First* [ed. Sir W. Scott]. 2 vols. Edinburgh: Ballantyne, 1811.

Osenbrüggen, Eduard. *Das alamannische Strafrecht im deutschen Mittelalter.* Aalen, Württemberg: Scientia, 1968.

Ovid. *Fasti.* Tr. Sir J. G. Frazer. Cambridge: Harvard University Press, 1951.

——— *The Loves, The Art of Beauty, The Remedies for Love, and The Art of Love.* Tr. R. Humphries. Bloomington: Indiana University Press, 1957.

——— *Metamorphoses.* Tr. R. Humphries. Bloomington: Indiana University Press, 1955.

——— *Tristia and Ex Ponto.* Tr. A. L. Wheeler. Cambridge: Harvard University Press, 1988.

"Ovide moralisé": Poème du commencement du quatorzième siècle. Ed. C. de Boer. 5 vols. Amsterdam: J. Müller, 1915–1938.

Oxford Dictionary of the Christian Church. 2nd. ed. F. L. Cross and E. A. Livingstone. London: Oxford University Press, 1974.

Panovsky, Erwin. *Studies in Iconology: Humanistic Themes in the Art of the Renaissance.* New York: Oxford University Press, 1939.

Partings at Dawn: An Anthology of Japanese Gay Literature. Ed. S. Miller. San Francisco: Gay Sunshine Press, 1996.

Pastor, Ludwig, Freiherr von. *The History of the Popes from the Close of the Middle Ages.* Tr. R. F. Kerr. 40 vols. London: K. Paul, Trench and Trübner, 1894–1953.

Patrologiae cursus completus. Ed. J.-P. Migne. 221 vols. Paris: J.-P. Migne et al., 1844–1866.

Patterson, Craig. "The Rage of Caliban: Eighteenth-Century Molly Houses and the Twentieth-Century Search for Sexual Identity." In *Illicit Sex: Identity Politics in Early Modern Culture.* Ed. T. di Piero and P. Gill. Athens: University of Georgia Press, 1997. Pp. 256–269.

Paulys Real-Encyclopädie der classischen Altertumswissenschaft. Vol. 16. Stuttgart: J. B. Metzler, 1924.

Pausanias. *Description of Greece.* Tr. W. H. S. Jones. 5 vols. Cambridge: Harvard University Press, 1918–1935.

Pavan, Elizabeth. "Police des moeurs, société et politique à Venise à la fin du Moyen Age." *Revue historique* 264 (1981): 241–288.

Payer, Pierre. *Sex and the Penitentials: The Development of a Sexual Code 550–1150.* Toronto: University of Toronto Press, 1984.

Payne, Robert. *Leonardo.* Garden City, NY: Doubleday 1978.

Pedretti, Carlo. *Leonardo: A Study in Chronology and Style.* Berkeley: University of California Press, 1973.

Pepys, Samuel. *The Diary of Samuel Pepys.* Vol. 4. Ed. R Latham and W. Matthews. Berkeley: University of California Press, 1971.

Pequigney, Joseph. *Such Is My Love: A Study of Shakespeare's Sonnets.* Chicago: University of Chicago Press, 1985.

Percival, Henry R., ed. *The Seven Ecumenical Councils of the Undivided Church: Their Canons and Dogmatic Decrees.* New York: C. Scribner's Sons, 1916. (A Select Library of Nicene and Post-Nicene Fathers of the Christian Church. 2nd series. Vol. 14.)

Percy, William Armstrong III. *Pederasty and Pedagogy in Archaic Greece.* Urbana: University of Illinois Press, 1996.

Perry, Mary Elizabeth. "The 'Nefarious Sin' in Early Modern Seville." In *The Pursuit of Sodomy.* Pp. 67–90.

Peter Damian. *The Book of Gomorrah: An Eleventh-Century Treatise against Clerical Homosexual Practices.* Tr. P. J. Payer. Waterloo, Ontario: Wilfred Laurier University Press, 1982.

Petronius. *The Satyricon.* Tr. W. Arrowsmith. Ann Arbor: University of Michigan Press, 1959.

Pézard, André. *Dante sous la pluie de feu (Enfer, chant XV).* Paris: J. Vrin, 1950.

Philips, Katherine. *The Collected Works of Katherine Philips "The Matchless Orinda."* Ed. P. Thomas. 3 vols. Stump Cross, Essex: Stump Cross Books, 1990.

Philo. Tr. F. H. Colson and G. H. Whitaker. 10 vols. Cambridge: Harvard University Press, 1929–1962.

Pindar. *The Odes of Pindar.* Tr. J. Sandys. Cambridge: Harvard University Press, 1915.

Pinot-Duclos, Charles. *Mémoires secrets.* In *Oeuvres complètes.* Ed. M. L-.S. Auger [1820–21]. 9 vols. Geneva: Slatkine Reprints, 1968.

Pitcairn, Robert. *Ancient Criminal Trials in Scotland.* 2 vols. Edinburgh: Maitland Club, 1833.

Plant, Richard. *The Pink Triangle: The Nazi War against Homosexuals.* New York: Henry Holt, 1986.

Plato. *The Dialogues of Plato.* Tr. B. Jowett. 4th ed. rev. Oxford: Clarendon Press, 1953.

Plautus. *Three Comedies: The Braggart Soldier, The Brothers Menaechmus, The Haunted House.* Tr. E. Segal. New York: Harper & Row, 1969.

Pliny the Elder. *Natural History.* Tr. H. Rackham et al. 10 vols. Cambridge: Harvard University Press, 1938–1963.

Plutarch. *Lives.* Tr. B. Perrin. 11 vols. Cambridge: Harvard University Press, 1914–1926.

——— *Moralia.* Tr. F. C. Babbitt et al. 15 vols. Cambridge: Harvard University Press, 1927–1969.

Poems on Affairs of State: Augustan Satirical Verse, 1660–1714. Vol. 5: 1688–1697. Ed. W. J. Cameron. New Haven: Yale University Press, 1971.

Poems on Affairs of State: Augustan Satirical Verse, 1660–1714. Vol. 7: 1704–1714. Ed. F. Ellis, New Haven: Yale University Press, 1975.

Polybius. *The Histories.* Tr. W. R. Paton. 6 vols. Cambridge: Harvard University Press, 1922–1927.

Pope, M. H. "Homosexuality." *The Interpreter's Dictionary of the Bible.* Supplementary Volume. Nashville, TN: Abingdon, 1976. Pp. 415–417.

Pope-Hennessy, John. *Cellini.* New York: Abbeville Press, 1985.

Posner, Donald. "Caravaggio's Homo-erotic Early Works." *Art Quarterly* 3 (1971): 301–324.

Prestwick, Michael. *The Three Edwards: War and State in England, 1272–1377.* London: Weidenfeld and Nicolson, 1980.

Primi Visconti, Giovanni Battista, Conte di San Maiolo. *Mémoires sur la cour de Louis XIV.* Tr. J. Lemoine. Paris: Calmann-Lévy, 1908.

Procopius. Tr. H. B. Dewing. 7 vols. Cambridge: Harvard University Press, 1914–1940.

Pseudo-Phocylides. See *The Old Testament Pseudepigraphia.*

The Pursuit of Sodomy: Male Homosexuality in Renaissancs and Enlightenment Europe. Ed. K. Gerard and G Hekma. New York: Haworth Press, 1989. (*JH* 16.)

Quintilian. *The Institutio Oratoria of Quintilian.* Tr. H. E. Butler. 4 vols. Cambridge: Harvard University Press, 1920–1922.

Radzinowicz, Leon. *A History of English Criminal Law and Its Administration from 1750.* Vol. 1: *The Movement for Reform 1750–1833.* New York: Macmillan, 1948.

Ragan, Bryant T., Jr. "The Enlightenment Confronts Homosexuality." In *Homosexuality in Modern France.* Pp. 8–29.

Rapetti, Louis Nicolas, ed. *Li Livres de jostice et de plet.* Paris: Didot frères, 1850.

Rashi [Rabbi Solomon bar Isaac]. *Pentateuch with Targum Onkelos . . . and Rashi's*

Commentary. Tr. M. Rosenbaum and A. M. Silbermann. 5 vols. in 2. London: Shapiro, Valentine, 1946.

Read, Conyers. *Mr. Secretary Walsingham and the Policy of Queen Elizabeth.* 3 vols. Oxford: Clarendon Press, 1925.

Renault, Mary. *The Nature of Alexander.* New York: Pantheon Books, 1975.

Rey, Michel. "Parisian Homosexuals Create a Lifestyle, 1700–1750: The Police Archives." *Eighteenth Century Life* 8 (1985): 179–191.

——— "Police and Sodomy in Eighteenth-Century Paris: From Sin to Disorder." In *The Pursuit of Sodomy.* Pp. 129–146.

——— "Sodomites parisiens au XVIIIème siècle." Maîtrise d'histoire. Université de Paris VIII Vincennes, 1980.

Richard, Jean. *The Latin Kingdom of Jerusalem.* Tr. J. Shirley. 2 vols. Amsterdam: North-Holland Publishing Company, 1979.

Richlin, Amy. *The Garden of Priapus: Sexuality and Aggression in Roman Humor.* New Haven: Yale University Press, 1983.

——— "Not before Homosexuality: The Materiality of the *Cinaedus* and the Roman Law against Love between Men." *Journal of the History of Sexuality* 3 (1993): 523–573.

Richter, Gisela. *The Sculpture and Sculptors of the Greeks.* 2nd ed. rev. New Haven: Yale University Press, 1950.

Robb, Nesca A. *William of Orange: A Personal Portrait.* 2 vols. London: W. Heinemann, 1962–1966.

Robinson, David M., and Edward J. Fluck. *A Study of the Greek Love-Names, Including a Discussion of Paederasty and a Prosopographia.* Baltimore: Johns Hopkins Press, 1937.

Rochester, John Wilmot, Earl of. *Collected Works of John Wilmot, Earl of Rochester.* Ed. J. Hayward. London: Nonesuch, 1926.

——— *Letters of John Wilmot, Earl of Rochester.* Ed. J. Treglown. Oxford: Blackwell, 1980.

——— *The Poems of John Wilmot, Earl of Rochester.* Ed. K. Walker. Oxford: Blackwell, 1984.

——— *Sodom, or The Quintessence of Debauchery.* Paris: Olympia, 1957.

Rocke, Michael. *Forbidden Friendships: Homosexuality and Male Culture in Renaissance Florence.* New York: Oxford University Press, 1996.

——— "Male Homosexuality and Its Regulation in Late Medieval Florence." Ph.D. Dissertation. State University of New York at Binghamton, 1989.

——— "Sodomites in Fifteenth-Century Tuscany: The Views of Bernardino of Siena." In *The Pursuit of Sodomy.* Pp. 7–31.

Rollins, Hyder, ed. *A New Variorum Edition of Shakespeare: The Sonnets.* 2 vols. Philadelphia: Lippincott, 1944.

Ross Williamson, Hugh. *George Villiers, First Duke of Buckingham: Study for a Biography.* London: Duckworth, 1940.

Roth, Norman. "The Care and Feeding of Gazelles: Medieval Arabic and Hebrew Love Poetry." In *Poetics of Love in the Middle Ages.* Ed. M. Lazar and N. J. Lacy. Fairfax, VA: George Mason University Press, 1989. Pp. 95–118.

——— "'Deal Gently with the Young Man': Love of Boys in Medieval Hebrew Poetry of Spain." *Speculum* 57 (1982): 20–51.

——— "'Fawn of My Delights': Boy-Love in Hebrew and Arabic Verse." In *Sex in the Middle Ages: A Book of Essays.* Ed. J. E. Salisbury. New York: Garland, 1991. Pp. 157–172.

Rothwell, Harry, ed. "Lanercost Chronicle," in *English Historical Documents 1189–1327.* New York: Oxford University Press, 1975. (English Historical Documents, 3.)

Rotuli Parliamentorum . . . tempore Edwardi R. III. 2 vols. London, 1767.

Rousseau, G. S. *Perilous Enlightenment: Pre- and Post-Modern Discourses, Sexual and Historical.* Manchester: Manchester University Press, 1991.

Ruan, Fang-fu, and Yung-mei Tsai. "Male Homosexuality in the Traditional Chinese Literature." *JH* 14.3/4 (1987): 21–33.

Rubini, Dennis. "Sexuality and Augustan England: Sodomy, Politics, Elite Circles and Society." In *The Pursuit of Sodomy.* Pp. 349–381.

Ruggiero, Guido. *The Boundaries of Eros: Sex Crime and Sexuality in Renaissance Venice.* New York: Oxford University Press, 1985.

——— "Sexual Criminality in the Early Renaissance: Venice 1338–58." *Journal of Social History* 8 (1975): 18–37.

Sade, Donatien Alphonse François, Marquis de. *The Complete Justine, Philosophy in the Bedroom, and Other Writings.* Tr. R. Sears and A. Wainhouse. New York: Grove, 1965.

——— *Oeuvres complètes du Marquis de Sade.* Vol. 3. Ed. A. Le Brun and J. J. Pauvert. [Paris]: Pauvert, 1986.

Saint-Simon, Louis Rouvroy, Duc de. *Mémoires.* Ed. Y. Coirault. 8 vols. Paris: Gallimard, 1983–1988.

Salvian. *The Writings of Salvian the Presbyter.* Tr. J. F. O'Sullivan. New York: CIMA, 1947. (Fathers of the Church, 4.)

*A Sapphick Epistle from Jack Cavendish to the Honourable and Most Beautiful Mrs. D****.* [London]: M. Smith, [1777?].

Sappho. *Sappho of Lesbos: Her Works Restored.* Tr. B. Saklatvala. London: Skilton, 1968.

Saslow, James M. *Ganymede in the Renaissance: Homosexuality in Art and Society.* New Haven: Yale University Press, 1986.

Satan's Harvest Home. See *Hell upon Earth.*

Scarabello, Giovanni. "Devianza sessuale ed interventi di giustizia a Venezia nella prima metà del XVI secolo." In *Tiziano e Venezia: Convegno Internazionale di Studi.* Venice: Neri Pozza, 1980. Pp. 75–84.

Schalow, Paul Gordon. "Kūkai and the Tradition of Male Love in Japanese Buddhism." In *Buddhism, Sexuality, and Gender.* Ed. J. I. Cabezón. Albany: State University of New York Press, 1992. Pp. 216–230.

——— "The Invention of a Literary Tradition of Male Love: Kitamura Kigin's *Iwatsutsuji.*" *Monumenta Nipponica* 48 (1993): 1–31.

Schama, Simon. *The Embarrassment of Riches: An Interpretation of Dutch Culture in the Golden Age.* New York: Knopf, 1987.

Schild, Maarten. "Islam." In *Sexuality and Eroticism among Males in Moslem Societies.* Ed. A. Schmitt and J. Sofer. Binghamton, NY: Harrington Park Press, 1992.

Schleiner, Winfried. "'That Matter Which Ought Not to be Heard of': Homophobic Slurs in Renaissance Cultural Politics." *JH* 26.4 (1994): 41–75.

Scott, A. C. *Mei Lan-fang: Leader of the Pear Garden.* Hong Kong: Hong Kong University Press, 1959.

The Scriptores historiae Augustae. Tr. D. Magie. 3 vols. Cambridge: Harvard University Press, 1953.

A Select Library of Nicene and Post-Nicene Fathers of the Christian Church. Ed. P. Schaff. 1st series. 14 vols. New York: Christian Literature Company, 1889–1912.

Seneca the Elder. *Controversiae.* In *Declamations.* Tr. M. Winterbottom. 2 vols. Cambridge: Harvard University Press, 1974.

Seneca. *Ad Lucilium epistulae morales.* Tr. R. M. Gummere. 3 vols. Cambridge: Harvard University Press, 1920–1925.

Senelick, Lawrence. *The Changing Room: Sex, Drag, and Theatre,* New York: Routledge, 2000.

Sergent, Bernard. *Homosexuality in Greek Myth.* Tr. A. Goldhammer. Boston: Beacon Press, 1986.

Sextus Empiricus. *Outlines of Pyrrhonism.* Tr. R. G. Bury. Cambridge: Harvard University Press, 1933.

Shapiro, H. A. "Courtship Scenes in Attic Vase-Painting." *American Journal of Archaeology* 85 (1981): 133–143.

Shaw, Christine. *Julius II: The Warrior Pope.* Oxford: Blackwell, 1993.

Shen Fu. *Chapters from a Floating Life: The Autobiography of a Chinese Artist.* Tr. S. M. Black. London: Oxford University Press, 1960.

Shively, Donald H. "*Bakufu* versus *Kabuki.*" In *Studies in the Institutional History of Early Modern Japan.* Ed. J. W. Hall and M. B. Jansen. Princeton: Princeton University Press, 1968. Pp. 231–261.

——— "Chikamatsu's Satire on the Dog Shogun." *Harvard Journal of Asiatic Studies* 18 (1955): 159–180.

——— "Tokugawa Tsunayoshi, the Genroku Shogun." In *Personality in Japanese History.* Ed. A. M. Craig and D. H. Shively. Berkeley: University of California Press, 1970. Pp. 85–126.

Sibalis, Michael David. "The Regulation of Homosexuality in Revolutionary and Napoleonic France." In *Homosexuality in Modern France.* Pp. 80–101.

Sidney, Philip, Sir. *Sir Philip Sidney's Defense of Poesy.* Ed. L. Soens. Lincoln: University of Nebraska Press, 1970.

[Sima Qian] Ssu-ma Ch'ien. *Records of the Grand Historian of China* [*Shih chi*]. Tr. B. Watson. 2 vols. New York: Renditions—Columbia University Press, 1993.

Sinistrari, Luigi Maria. *Peccatum Mutum: The Secret Sin.* Introduction by M. Summers. [Trans. of *De delictis et poenis,* title 4, chapter 11, "Sodomia," 92 paragraphs, unpaged.] [Paris]: Collection "Le Ballet des Muses," 1958.

Smith, Bruce R. *Homosexual Desire in Shakespeare's England: A Cultural Poetics.* Chicago: University of Chicago Press, 1991.

Smith, John Holland. *The Death of Classical Paganism.* New York: C. Scribner's Sons, 1976.

Smollett, Tobias. *The Adventures of Roderick Random.* Ed. P.-G. Boucé. Oxford: Oxford University Press, 1979.

Snell, Bruno. *Scenes from Greek Drama.* Berkeley: University of California Press, 1964.

The Sodomites' Shame and Doom. London: J. Dawning, 1702.

Soman, Alfred. "The Parlement of Paris and the Great Witch Hunt (1565–1640)." *Sixteenth Century Journal* 9.2 (1978): 31–44.

Sommer, Matthew. *Sex, Law, and Society in Late Imperial China.* Stanford: Stanford University Press, 2000.

Southern, R. W. *Saint Anselm: A Portrait in a Landscape.* Cambridge: Cambridge University Press, 1990.

Spence, Jonathan D. *Emperor of China: Self Portrait of K'ang-hsi.* New York: Knopf, 1974.

——— *The Memory Palace of Matteo Ricci.* New York: Viking, 1984.

Spenser, Edmund. *The Faerie Queene: Book Three.* Ed. F. M. Padelford. Baltimore: Johns Hopkins Press, 1934.

——— *Spenser's Minor Poems.* Ed. E. de Sélincourt. Oxford: Clarendon Press, 1910.

Statuta provisionesque ducales civitatis Tarvisii. Venice, 1574.

Steakley, James D. *The Homosexual Emancipation Movement in Germany.* New York: Arno, 1975.

——— "Sodomy in Enlightenment Prussia: From Execution to Suicide." In *The Pursuit of Sodomy.* Pp. 163–175.

Steel, Anthony. *Richard II.* Cambridge: Cambridge University Press, 1962.

Stehling, Thomas, tr. *Medieval Latin Poems of Male Love and Frendship.* New York: Garland, 1984.

——— "To Love a Medieval Boy." *JH* 8.3/4 (1983): 151–170.

Sternweiler, Andreas. *Die Lust der Götter: Homosexualität in der italianischen Kunst von Donatello zu Caravaggio.* Berlin: Rosa Winkel, 1993.

Stewart, Andrew F. *Art, Desire, and the Body in Ancient Greece.* Cambridge: Cambridge University Press, 1997.

Stiebel, Arlene. "Subversive Sexuality: Masking the Erotic in the Poems of Katherine Philips and Aphra Behn." In *Renaissance Discourses of Desire.* Ed. C. Summers and T.-L. Pebworth. Columbia: University of Missouri Press, 1993. Pp. 223–236.

Stockinger, Jacob. "Homosexuality and the French Enlightenment." In *Homosexuality and French Literature: Cultural Contexts/Critical Texts.*" Ed. G. Stamboulian and E. Marks. Ithaca: Cornell University Press, 1979. Pp. 161–185.

Stow, John. *The Annales of England.* London: Newberry, 1592.

Strabo. *Geography.* Tr. H. L. Jones. 8 vols. London: W. Heinemann, 1917–1933.

Suetonius. Tr. J. C. Rolfe. 2 vols. Cambridge: Harvard University Press, 1913–1914.

Sullivan, J. P. "Martial's Sexual Attitudes." *Philologus* 123 (1979): 288–302.

Swift, Jonathan. *The Prose Works of Jonathan Swift.* Vol. 5. Ed. H. Davis. Oxford: Blackwell, 1962.

Symonds, John Addington. *The Life of Michelangelo Buonarroti.* 3rd ed. 2 vols. New York: C. Scribner's Sons, 1911.

——— "A Problem in Greek Ethics." In *Sexual Inversion.* Ed. H. Ellis and J. A. Symonds [1897]. New York: Arno, 1975. Pp. 163–251.

——— *The Renassance in Italy.* Part 1: *The Age of the Despots.* New York: H. Holt, [1912].

——— *Sketches and Studies in Italy and Greece.* New ed. 3 vols. London: Smith, Elder, 1898.

Tacitus. *Dialogus, Agricola, Germania.* Tr. W. Peterson and M. Hutton. Cambridge: Harvard University Press, 1914.

Tallemant de Réaux, Gédéon. *Historiettes.* 2 vols. Ed. A. Adam. Paris: Gallimard, 1960.

——— *Portraits and Anecdotes (Historiettes).* Tr. H. Miles. London: Oxford University Press, 1965.

Taylor, Clark. "Legends, Syncretism, and Continuing Echoes of Homosexuality from Pre-Columbian and Colonial México." In *Latin American Male Homosexualities.* Ed. Stephen O. Murray. Albuquerque: New Mexico University Press. Pp. 80–99.

——— "*El Ambiente:* Male Homosexual Life in Mexico City." Ph.D. Dissertation. University of California at Berkeley, 1978.

Teasley, David. "The Charge of Sodomy as a Political Weapon in Early Modern France: The Case of Henry III in Catholic League Polemic (1585–1589)." *Maryland Historian* 18.1 (1987): 17–30.

Tertullian. *Adversus Marcionem.* Tr. E. Evans. 2 vols. Oxford: Clarendon Press, 1972.

Theocritus. *The Idylls of Theocritus: A Verse Translation.* Tr. T. Sargent. New York: Norton, 1982.

Theodoret. *History of the Church.* Tr. E. Walford. London: Bohn, 1854.

The Theodosian Code. Tr. C. Pharr. Princeton: Princeton University Press, 1952.

Theognis. See Hesiod.

Theophanes. *Chronographia.* Ed. J. Classen. Bonn: E. Weber, 1835. (Corpus scriptorum historiae byzantinae, 32.)

Thielicke, Helmut. *The Ethics of Sex.* Tr. J. W. Doberstien. New York: Harper and Row, 1964.

The Third Pink Book: A Global View of Lesbian and Gay Liberation and Oppression. Ed. A. Hendriks, R. Tielman, and E. Van der Veen. Buffalo: Prometheus Books, 1993.

Thomas, D. Winston. "*Kelebh* 'Dog': Its Origin and Some Usages of It in the Old Testament." *Vetus Testamentum* 10 (1960): 410–427.

Thomas de Burton. *Chronica Monasterii de Melsa.* Vol. 2. Ed. E. A. Bond. London: Longmans et al., 1867. (Rolls Series, 43).

Thompson, E. A. *The Goths in Spain.* Oxford: Clarendon Press, 1969.

Thrale, Hester. *Thraliana: The Diary of Hester Lynch Thrale (Later Mrs. Piozzi), 1776–1809.* Ed. K. L. Balderston. 2 vols. Oxford: Clarendon Press, 1942.

Thucydides. *History of the Peloponnesian War.* Tr. C. F. Smith. 4 vols. Cambridge: Harvard University Press, 1969.

Tibullus. *The Poems of Tibullus.* Tr. C. Carrier. Bloomington: Indiana University Press, 1968.

Tigay, Jeffrey H. *The Evolution of the Gilgamesh Epic.* Philadelphia: University of Pennsylvania Press, 1982.

Tomás y Valente, Francisco. *El derecho penal de monarquía absoluta (Siglos XVI–XVII–XVIII)* Madrid: Tacnos, 1969.

Trevisan, João S. *Perverts in Paradise.* Tr. M. Foreman. London: GMP Publishers, 1986.

Trumbach, Randolph. "The Birth of the Queen: Sodomy and the Emergence of Gender Equality in Modern Culture, 1660–1750." In *Hidden from History.* Pp. 129–140.

Twomey, Michael W. "*Cleanness,* Peter Comestor, and the *Revelationes Sancti Methodii.*" *Mediaevalia* 11 (1989): 203–217.

Valerius Maximus. *Memorable Doings and Sayings.* Tr. D. R. S. Bailey. Cambridge: Harvard University Press, 2000.

Van der Cruysse, Dirk. *Madame Palatine, princesse européenne.* Paris: Fayard, 1988.

Van der Meer, Theo. "The Persecutions of Sodomites in Eighteenth-Century Amsterdam: Changing Perceptions of Sodomy." In *The Pursuit of Sodomy.* Pp. 263–307.

——— "Sodomy and the Pursuit of a Third Sex in the Early Modern Period." In *Third Sex, Third Gender: Beyond Sexual Dimorphism in Culture and History.* Ed. G. Herdt. New York: Zone Books, 1994. Pp. 137–212, 528–541.

——— "Tribades on Trial: Female Same-Sex Offenders in Late Eighteenth-Century Amsterdam." *Journal of the History of Sexuality* 1 (1991): 424–445.

Van der Zee, Henri, and Barbara Van der Zee. *William and Mary.* New York: Knopf, 1973.

Van Gulik, Robert H. *Sexual Life in Ancient China: A Preliminary Survey of Chinese Sex and Society from ca. 1500 B.C. till 1644 A.D.* Leiden: E. J. Brill, 1961.

Van Klefffens, E. N. *Hispanic Law until the End of the Middle Ages.* Edinburgh: Edinburgh University Press, 1968.

Vasari, Giorgio. *The Lives of the Painters, Sculptors, and Architects.* Tr. A. B. Hinds. 4 vols. Rev. ed. New York: Dutton, 1963.

Verstraete, Beert C. "Slavery and the Social Dynamics of Male Homosexual Relations in Ancient Rome." *JH* 5 (1980): 227–236.

Vessey, D. W. Thomson. "Philaenis." *Revue belge de philologie et d'histoire* 54 (1976): 78–83.

Viau, Théophile de. *The Cabaret Poetry of Théophile de Viau.* Ed. C. L. Gaudiano. Paris: J.-M. Place, 1981.

Videgáin Agós, Fernando. *Crónica negra del reino de Navarra.* Pamplona: n.p., 1982.

Villani, Giovanni. *Villani's Chronicle: Selections from the First Nine Books of the "Croniche fiorentine."* Tr. R. E. Selfe. Westminster: A. Constable, 1897.

Viollet, Paul, ed. *Les Établissements de Saint Louis.* 4 vols. Paris: Renouard, 1881–1886.

Virgil. *The Aeneid.* Tr. R. Fitzgerald. New York: Random House, 1983.

Vitiello, Giovanni. "The Dragon's Whim: Ming and Qing Homoerotic Tales from

The Cut Sleeve." *T'oung Pao: Revue internationale de sinologie* 78 (1992): 341–372.
——— "Exemplary Sodomites: Male Homosexuality in Late Ming Fiction." Ph.D. Dissertation. University of California at Berkeley, 1994.
Voltaire, François Marie Arouet de. *Mémoires pour servir à la vie de M. de Voltaire écrits par lui-même.* Ed. J. Brenner. Paris: Mercure de France, 1965.
——— *Oeuvres complètes.* Ed. P. A. C. de Beaumarchais; M. J. A. N. Caritat, Marquis de Condorcet; and L. P. Decroix. 70 vols. [Kehl]: L'Imprimerie de la Société Littéraire-Typographique, 1785–1789.
——— *Oeuvres complètes de Voltaire.* Ed. L. E. D. Moland. 52 vols. Paris: Garnier Frères, 1877–1885.
——— *Complete Works of Voltaire/ Oeuvres complètes de Voltaire.* Ed. T. Besterman et al. Geneva: Institut et Musée Voltaire/ Toronto: University of Toronto Press, 1968–.
——— *Philosophical Dictionary.* Tr. P. Gay. New York: Harcourt Brace and World, 1962.
——— *Romans et contes.* Ed. F. Deloffre and J. van den Heuvel. Paris: Gallimard, 1979.
Von Römer, L. S. A. M. "Der Uranismus in den Niederlanden bis zum 19. Jahrhundert, mit besonderer Berücksichtigung der grossen Uranierverfolgung im Jahre 1730." *Jahrbuch für sexuelle Zwischenstufen* 8 (1906): 365–511.
——— "Heinrich der Dritte, König von Frankreich und Polen." *Jahrbuch für sexuelle Zwischenstufen* 4 (1902): 573–669.
Walpole, Horace. *The Yale Edition of Horace Walpole's Correspondence.* Ed. W. S. Lewis. 42 vols. New Haven: Yale University Press, 1937–1980.
Walter, Daniel. *The Life of Ailred of Rievaulx.* Tr. F. M. Powicke. London: Thomas Nelson, 1950.
Warnkönig, Leopold August. *Flandrische Staats- und Rechtsgeschichte bis zum Jahr 1305.* 3 vols. in 5. Tübingen: L. F. Fues, 1839.
Watanabe, Tsuneo, and Jun'ichi Iwata. *The Love of the Samurai: A Thousand Years of Japanese Homosexuality.* Tr. D. R. Roberts. London: GMP Publishers, 1989.
Weeks, Jeffrey. *Coming Out: Homosexual Politics in Britain from the Nineteenth Century to the Present.* London: Quartet Books, 1977.
W[eldon], A[nthony], Sir. *The Court and Character of King James* [1650]. London: G. Smeeton, 1817.
Wilhelm, James J., ed. *Gay and Lesbian Poetry: An Anthology from Sappho to Michelangelo.* New York: Garland, 1995.
Wilkinson, L. P. *Ovid Surveyed.* Cambridge: Cambridge University Press, 1962.
William of Malmesbury. *Chronicle of the Kings of England from the Earliest Period to the Reign of King Stephen.* Tr. J. A. Giles. London: Bohn, 1847.
Williams, Craig. *Roman Homosexuality: Ideologies of Masculinity in Classical Antiquity.* New York: Oxford University Press, 1999.
Williams, Gordon. *Figures of Thought in Roman Poetry.* New Haven: Yale University Press, 1980.
Williams, H. Noel. *Later Queens of the French Stage.* New York: C. Scribner's Sons, 1906.

Williams, Walter L. *The Spirit and the Flesh: Sexual Diversity in American Indian Culture.* Boston: Beacon Press, 1986.

Willson, David Harris. *King James VI and I.* New York: Oxford University Press, 1956.

Wilson, Arthur. *The History of Great Britain, Being the Life and Reign of King James the First.* London: Lownds, 1653.

Wilson, Arthur M. *Diderot.* Oxford: Oxford University Press, 1972.

Wilson, John Dover, ed. "Introduction" to William Shakespeare, *The Sonnets.* Cambridge: Cambridge University Press, 1969.

The Wisdom of Solomon. Tr. D. Winston. Garden City, NY: Doubleday, 1979.

Wunderli, Richard M. *London Church Courts and Society on the Eve of the Reformation.* Cambridge: Medieval Academy of America, 1981.

Wuxia Ameng, ed. *La manica tagliata.* [Italian translation of *Dian xiu pian—Records of the Cut Sleeve* (1911).] Tr. G. Vitiello. Palermo: Sellerio, 1990.

Xenophon. *Hellenica VI-VII and Anabasis Books I-III.* Tr. C. L. Brownson. London: W. Heinemann, 1921.

——— *Anabasis Books IV-VII, Symposium, and Apology.* Tr. C. L. Brownson and O. J. Todd. London: W. Heinemann, 1922.

——— *Scripta minora.* Tr. E. C. Marchant. London: W. Heinemann, 1925.

——— *Works.* Tr. H. G. Dakyns. Vol. 3: Part 1. London: Macmillan, 1897.

Xenophon of Ephesus. "An Ephesian Tale." In *Three Greek Romances.* Tr. M. Hadas. Indianapolis: Bobbs Merrill, 1964.

Xiaomingxiong [Ng Siu-ming]. *Zhongguo tongxingai shilu [History of Homosexuality in China].* Hong Kong: Pink Triangle Press, 1984. (Rev. ed. 1997.)

Yamauchi, Edwin M. "Cultic Prostitution: A Case Study in Cultural Diffusion." In *Orient and Occident: Essays Presented to Cyrus H. Gordon on the Occasion of His Sixty-fifth Birthday.* Ed. H. A. Hoffner, Jr. Kevelaer, Netherlands: Butzon & Bercker, 1973. Pp. 213–222.

Young, Michael B. *James I and the History of Homosexuality.* London: Macmillan, 2000.

Yves de Chartres. *Correspondance.* Tr. J. Leclerq. 2 vols. Paris: Belles Lettres, 1949. (Les Classiques de l'Histoire de France au Moyen Age, 22.)

[*Zhanguo ce*] *Chan-Kuo Ts'e [Intrigues of the Warring States].* Tr. J. I. Crump, Jr. Oxford: Clarendon Press, 1970.

Zimmermann, Johann Georg. "Defense of Frederick against Accusations of Homosexuality." In *Frederick the Great.* Ed. L. L. Snyder. Englewood Cliffs, NJ: Prentice-Hall, 1971. Pp. 132–136.

Zonaras, Joannes. *Epitomae historiarum libri XIII–XVIII.* Vol. 3. Ed. M. Pinder and T. Büttner-Wobst. Bonn: E. Weber, 1897. (Corpus scriptorum historiae byzantinae, 18.)

Zweig, Stefan. *Marie Antoinette: The Portrait of an Average Woman.* Tr. E. and C. Paul. New York: Viking, 1933.

Acknowledgments

Any history that essays to deal with a dozen cultures over a period of two and a half millennia must necessarily be dependent on the work of others. I am especially aware of what I owe to such pioneering specialists as Derrick Sherwin Bailey in biblical and early Christian studies; Félix Buffière, Kenneth Dover, and William Percy in Greek studies; Beert Verstraete and Saara Lilja for Roman history and literature; Xiaomingxiong and Bret Hinsch for China; Paul Schalow, Margaret Childs, and Gary Leupp for Japan; John Boswell and Michael Goodich for medieval Europe; William Monter and Luiz Mott for Spain and Portugal in the age of the Inquisition; Louis Godbout, Maurice Lever, Claude Courouve, and Jeffrey Merrick for seventeenth- and eighteenth-century France; L. S. A. M. von Römer, Kent Gerard, and Theo van der Meer for eighteenth-century Dutch history; and Lillian Faderman and Emma Donoghue for their work on lesbian life and literature since 1660 in England and France.

I am indebted for information gleaned from more general works by David Greenberg, Vern Bullough, Wayne Dynes, and Noel Garde, and for the support of many friends and colleagues who have encouraged me over the years: Kent Gerard, George Wolf, John Taylor, Robert Knoll, Stephen Murray, William Percy, and Craig Eckhardt, to name only a few. James Saslow has kindly responded to my enquiries about works of art and illustrations. I would in particular like to thank Susan Wallace Boehmer of Harvard University Press for her indefatigable aid in selecting and obtaining the illustrations from museums, libraries, and art collectors.

For help with translations I must acknowledge the assistance of Stanley Vandersall, Valdis Lieneiks, Ellie Thomas, Carson Simões, and especially Fan Shen who first opened to me the treasury of Chinese gay history and literature by translating Xiaomingxiong's history of China published in Hong Kong in 1984, a work I found especially useful. With regard to Chinese names, readers who are not Sinologists may well find the dual systems of romanization used in English-language texts confusing. It may therefore be useful to provide a few clues to the differences between the Wade-Giles system employed in older books and the modern Pinyin system. In Pinyin Ch'ing appears as Qing, Sung as Song, Chi as Ji, Hsiao as Xiao, Po as Bo, Ku as Gu, Chung as Zhong, Tao as Dao, Ts'ao as Cao, and so on. Pinyin "x" can very roughly be approximated by English "sh," "q" by "ch," "zh" by "j," "c" by "ts." I have tried to follow the Pinyin usage except for some quotations and for common historical names like Lao-tse and Peking. In this effort I am grateful for the generous assistance of Andrew Chen.

I have been greatly aided in tracking down rare books and documents by the staff of the Interlibrary Loan department of Love Library at the University of Nebraska at Lincoln. I am also grateful to the support I have received over the years from the UNL Department of English. Excerpts from Chapters 3 and 6 of the present work have appeared, respectively, in *History Today* and in *Islamic Homosexualities: Culture, History, and Literature,* edited by Stephen O. Murray and Will Roscoe and published by New York University Press.

Finally, I must thank my partner, Luis Diaz-Perdomo, for the patience and support that have sustained me during this long task.

ILLUSTRATION CREDITS

Frontispiece: Men Kissing. Bartolomeo Cesi (1556–1629). Galleria degli Uffizi, Florence. Art Resource, NY.

1. **Achilles binds the wounds of Patroclus.** Staatliche Museen, Berlin. © Bildarchiv Preussischer Kulturbesitz/Art Resource, NY.
2. **Zeus and Ganymede.** Archaeological Museum, Olympia. Scala/Art Resource, NY.
3. **Greek wrestlers.** Staatliche Museen, Berlin. © Bildarchiv Preussischer Kulturbesitz/Art Resource, NY.
4. **Boy kissing man.** Louvre, Paris. Réunion des Musées Nationaux/Art Resource, NY.
5. **Erastes courting an ephebe.** Gift of E. P. and Fiske Warren. © 2003 Museum of Fine Arts, Boston.
6. **Banquet scene.** Museo Archeologico Paestum, Italy. Erich Lessing/Art Resource, NY.
7. **Sappho and Alcaeus.** Staatliche Antikensammlungen und Glyptothek, Munich.
8. **Man and young athlete.** Ashmolean Museum, Oxford.
9. **Kissing competition.** Staatliche Museen, Berlin. © Bildarchiv Preussischer Kulturbesitz/Art Resource, NY.
10. **Aristogeiton and Harmodius.** Museo Archeologico Nazionale, Naples. Scala/Art Resource, NY.
11. **Epaminondas.** J. Chapman, engraving, 1807.
12. **Memorial to the Sacred Band at Chaeronea.** Photograph by Christina Gascoigne; reproduced by permission.
13. **Alexander at the Battle of Issus.** Museo Nazionale, Naples. Scala/Art Resource, NY.
14. **The Warren cup.** © Copyright The British Museum.
15. **The Warren cup, reverse.** © Copyright The British Museum.
16. **Zephyrus and Hyacinthus.** Catharine Page Perkins Fund. © 2003 Museum of Fine Arts, Boston.
17. **The Bacchantes attack Orpheus.** Scala/Art Resource, NY.
18. **Female athletes.** Piazza Armerina, Sicily. Erich Lessing/Art Resource, NY.
19. **Antinous.** Archaeological Museum, Delphi. Scala/Art Resource, NY.

20. **View of Antinoopolis, c.** 1800. From *Description d'Égypte.*
21. **Antinous as an Egyptian god.** Museo Gregoriano Egizio, Vatican Museums. Scala/Art Resource, NY.
22. **Christ and Saint John.** Staatliche Museen, Berlin. © Bildarchiv Preussischer Kulturbesitz/Art Resource, NY.
23. **Saint Paul.** Scala/Art Resource, NY.
24. **The destruction of Sodom.** Alinari/Art Resource, NY.
25. **Saint John Chrysostom.** Dumbarton Oaks, Byzantine Photograph and Fieldwork Archives, Washington, DC.
26. **Justinian.** Scala/Art Resource, NY.
27. **Charlemagne's victory over the Saracens, c.** 780. Musée Goya, Castres, France. Giraudon/Art Resource, NY.
28. **Shah Abbas I with a page.** The Metropolitan Museum of Art, New York. Purchase, Francis M. Weld Gift, 1950 (50.164). Photograph © 1977 The Metropolitan Museum of Art.
29. **Two lovers.** Louvre, Paris. Réunion des Musées Nationaux/Art Resource, NY.
30. **Templar kissing cleric.** The Pierpont Morgan Library/Art Resource, NY.
31. **Templars burned at the stake.** Bibliothèque Municipale, Besançon, France. Erich Lessing/Art Resource, NY.
32. **The death of Orpheus.** Foto Marburg/Art Resource, NY.
33. **Dante and Virgil meet the sodomites.** Musée Conde, Chantilly, France. Giraudon/Art Resource, NY.
34. **Scholars of the Northern Qi dynasty.** Denman Waldo Ross Collection. © 2003 Museum of Fine Arts, Boston.
35. **The destruction of Sodom.** *The Ink Garden of Mr. Cheng (Ch'eng shi mo yuan),* 1609.
36. **Man and boy attended by ghosts and a pipe-bearer.** Collection F. M. Bertholet, Amsterdam.
37. **Woman spying on male lovers.** Chinese Sexual Culture Museum, Shanghai.
38. **Old man received in a wealthy man's house.** Collection F. M. Bertholet, Amsterdam.
39. **A male couple with two dogs.** Collection F. M. Bertholet, Amsterdam.
40. **Man with a boy lowering a shade.** Collection F. M. Bertholet, Amsterdam.
41. **Chinese opera performers.** German, book illustration, nineteenth century.
42. **San Bernardino of Siena.** Pinacoteca Comunale, Sansepolcro, Italy. Scala/Art Resource, NY.
43. **Girolamo Savonarola.** Museo di San Marco, Florence. Scala/Art Resource, NY.
44. **The burning of Savonarola in front of the Palazzo Vecchio, Florence, May 23, 1498.** Museo di San Marco, Florence. Erich Lessing/Art Resource, NY.
45. **David.** Museo Nazionale del Bargello, Florence. Erich Lessing/Art Resource, NY.
46. **Angels.** Galleria degli Uffizi, Florence. Erich Lessing/Art Resource, NY.
47. **Saint John the Baptist.** Louvre, Paris. Réunion des Musées Nationaux/Art Resource, NY.
48. **Bacchus.** Museo Nazionale del Bargello, Florence. Scala/Art Resource, NY.

49. **Ignudo.** Vatican Palace. Scala/Art Resource, NY.
50. **The rape of Ganymede.** Fogg Art Museum, Cambridge, MA. Harvard University Art Museums, Gifts for Special Uses Fund.
51. **Saint Sebastian.** Galleria Palatina, Palazzo Pitti, Florence. Scala/Art Resource, NY.
52. **Ganymede.** Museo Nazionale del Bargello, Florence. Scala/Art Resource, NY.
53. **Narcissus.** Museo Nazionale del Bargello, Florence. Scala/Art Resource, NY.
54. **Bacchus.** Galleria degli Uffizi, Florence. Nimatallah/Art Resource, NY.
55. **Isabella of Castile and Ferdinand of Aragon.** Kunsthistorisches Museum, Gemäldegalerie, Vienna, and Patrimonio Nacional, Palacio Real, Madrid. Erich Lessing/Art Resource, NY.
56. **Auto da fe at Valladolid, May 1559.** © Copyright The British Museum.
57. **Inquisitorial torture.** Eighteenth-century prints.
58. **Auto da fe in the Plaza Mayor, Madrid, June 30, 1680.** Museo del Prado, Madrid. Art Resource, NY.
59. **Philip II.** Kunsthistorisches Museum, Gemäldegalerie, Vienna. Erich Lessing/ Art Resource, NY.
60. **Inquisitorial scene.** Louvre, Paris. Réunion des Musées Nationaux/Art Resource, NY.
61. **Balboa throws the Indians to his dogs.** The New York Public Library/Art Resource, NY.
62. **Richard Puller von Hohenberg and his servant, Anton Mätzler, burned at Zurich, September 24, 1482.** Ms. A5, p. 994. Zentralbibliothek, Zurich.
63. **"Execution for sodomitical godlessness in the city of Bruges."** Nicolas Hogenberg (1500–1539), engraving.
64. **Henry III of France.** Chateau de Versailles et de Trianon, Versailles. Réunion des Musées Nationaux/Art Resource, NY.
65. **Young noblemen carousing.** The Metropolitan Museum of Art, Rogers Fund, 1954 (54.142).
66. **Louis XIII as a youth.** Galleria Palatina, Palazzo Pitti, Florence. Nimatallah/ Art Resource, NY.
67. **Philippe, duke of Orléans, "Monsieur."** Chateau de Versailles et de Trianon, Versailles. Réunion des Musées Nationaux/Art Resource, NY.
68. **Elisabeth Charlotte, duchess of Orléans, "Madame."** Chateau de Versailles et de Trianon, Versailles. Réunion des Musées Nationaux/Art Resource, NY.
69. **Woman and her maid.** Zoan Andrea, engraving, c. 1500.
70. **Women bathing.** Jean Mignon (after Luca Penna), engraving, c. 1540.
71. **Queen Christina.** The National Swedish Art Museums, Swedish Portrait Archives, Stockholm.
72. **David and Jonathan, David and Saul (bottom); allegorical figures of "Friendship" and "Hate" (top).** Add.28182 fol. 6v. The British Library, London.
73. **James I as a youth.** The Royal Collection © 2003, Her Majesty Queen Elizabeth II.
74. **"The life and death of John Atherton."** E.167.6. The British Library.

75. **John Wilmot, Earl of Rochester, with a monkey.** National Portrait Gallery, London.
76. **Katherine Philips.** Frontispiece engraving from *Poems,* 1667.
77. **Aphra Behn.** National Portrait Gallery, London.
78. **William III.** National Galleries of Scotland, Dean Gallery, Edinburgh.
79. **A Samurai and his lover fight off their enemies.** Saikaku, *Great Mirror of Male Love (Nanshoku ōkagami),* 1687.
80. **Onnagata actor as a singing girl.** The Newark Museum/Art Resource, NY.
81. **Monks entertained by visiting actor-prostitutes.** Urushiya Ensai, *The Pickled Bud of Male Love (Nanshoku ki no me-zuke),* 1703.
82. **The entertainment district in a Japanese city.** Museé des Arts Asiatiques-Guimet, Paris. Réunion des Musées Nationaux/Art Resource, NY.
83. **Ihara Saikaku (1642-1693) in old age.** Haga Isshō, date unknown.
84. **A "woman-hater" chases away three women.** Saikaku, "Two Old Cherry Trees Still in Bloom," *Great Mirror of Male Love (Nanshoku ōkagami),* 1687.
85. **A man relaxes with a female prostitute and a handsome youth.** Nishikawa Sukenobu, print, early eighteenth century.
86. **Brothel customer with a female prostitute watch a male youth writing.** Riccar Art Museum, Tokyo.
87. **An actor-prostitute charms a client with agreeable conversation.** Victoria & Albert Museum/Art Resource, NY.
88. **Catherine Hayes, burned for the murder of her husband while two sodomites hang in the background, May 9, 1726.** 113.e.5,6. The British Library.
89. **Thomas Gray.** National Portrait Gallery, London.
90. **"Justice Triumphant."** Engraving, Amsterdam, 1730.
91. **"Timely punishment depicted as a warning to godless and damnable sinners."** Engraved broadsheet, Amsterdam, 1730.
92. **Queen Anne.** National Portrait Gallery, London.
93. **Sarah Churchill, Duchess of Marlborough.** Victoria & Albert Museum, London/Art Resource, NY.
94. **The Ladies of Llangollen.** Engraving (after Lady Leighton), early nineteenth century.
95. **Anne Damer and Mary Berry at Strawberry Hill.** Lewis Walpole Library, Yale University.
96. **Marie Antoinette, Queen of France.** Chateau de Versailles et de Trianon, Versailles. Réunion des Musées Nationaux/Art Resource, NY.
97. **The Princess Lamballe (1749–1792).** Chateau de Versailles et de Trianon, Versailles. Giraudon/Art Resource, NY.
98. **The head of Princess Lamballe paraded before the Temple where Marie Antoinette was held, September 2, 1792.** Bibliothèque National de France.
99. **The execution of Marie Antoinette, October 16, 1793.** Bibliothèque National de France.
100. **Montesquieu.** Chateau de Versailles et de Trianon, Versailles. Réunion des Musées Nationaux/Art Resource, NY.
101. **Execution of Hans Hermann von Katte, November 16, 1730; Katte, shortly before his death (inset).** AKG London.

102. **Frederick the Great and Voltaire at Sans Souci.** P. C. Baquoy, engraving (after N. A. Monsiau), date unknown.
103. **Denis Diderot.** Louvre, Paris. Réunion des Musées Nationaux/Art Resource, NY.
104. **Jeremy Bentham.** National Portrait Gallery, London.
105. **Charing Cross pillory.** August Charles Pugin and Thomas Rowlandson, illustration for R. Ackermann, *Microcosm of London*, 1808. Houghton Library, Harvard University, Cambridge, MA.

INDEX